WILLIAM SHAKESPEARE

After the Chandos Portrait in the National Portrait Gallery, London, which is attributed to Richard Burbage or John Taylor. In the catalogue of the National Portrait Gallery the following description is given:

> "The Chandos Shakespeare was the property of John Taylor, the player, by whom or by Richard Burbage it was painted. The picture was left by the former in his will to Sir William Davenant. After his death it was bought by Betterton, the actor, upon whose decease Mr. Keck of the Temple purchased it for 40 guineas, from whom it was inherited by Mr. Nicoll of Michenden House, Southgate, Middlesex, whose only daughter married James, Marquess of Caernarvon, afterwards Duke of Chandos, father to Ann Eliza, Duchess of Buckingham."
>
> The above is written on paper attached to the back of the canvas. Its authenticity, however, has been doubted in some quarters.
>
> Purchased at the Stowe Sale, September 1848, by the Earl of Ellesmere, and presented by him to the nation, March 1856.
>
> Dimensions: 22 in. by 16¾ in.

This reproduction of the portrait was made from a miniature copy on ivory by Caroline King Phillips.

OUTLINES OF
ENGLISH LITERATURE

WITH READINGS

BY

WILLIAM J. LONG

This is the wey to al good aventure. — CHAUCER

GINN AND COMPANY
BOSTON · NEW YORK · CHICAGO · LONDON
ATLANTA · DALLAS · COLUMBUS · SAN FRANCISCO

The Athenæum Press

GINN AND COMPANY · PRO-
PRIETORS · BOSTON · U.S.A.

RE

TO MY SISTER
"MILLIE"
IN GRATEFUL REMEMBRANCE OF
A LIFELONG SYMPATHY

PREFACE

The last thing we find in making a book is to
know what to put first. — Pascal

When an author has finished his history, after months or
years of happy work, there comes a dismal hour when he must
explain its purpose and apologize for its shortcomings.

The explanation in this case is very simple and goes back
to a personal experience. When the author first studied the
history of literature there was put into his hands as a textbook
a most dreary catalogue of dead authors, dead masterpieces,
dead criticisms, dead ages ; and a boy who knew chiefly that
he was alive was supposed to become interested in this literary
sepulchre or else have it said that there was something hopeless
about him. Later he learned that the great writers of England
were concerned with life alone, as the most familiar, the most
mysterious, the most fascinating thing in the world, and that
the only valuable or interesting feature of any work of literature
is its vitality.

To introduce these writers not as dead worthies but as companionable men and women, and to present their living subject
as a living thing, winsome as a smile on a human face, —
such was the author's purpose in writing this book.

The apology is harder to frame, as anyone knows who has
attempted to gather the writers of a thousand years into a
single volume that shall have the three virtues of brevity,
readableness and accuracy. That this record is brief in view
of the immensity of the subject is plainly apparent. That it
may prove pleasantly readable is a hope inspired chiefly by the
fact that it was a pleasure to write it, and that pleasure is

contagious. As for accuracy, every historian who fears God or regards man strives hard enough for that virtue ; but after all his striving, remembering the difficulty of criticism and the perversity of names and dates that tend to error as the sparks fly upward, he must still trust heaven and send forth his work with something of Chaucer's feeling when he wrote :

> O littel bookë, thou art so unconning,
> How darst thou put thy-self in prees for drede?

Which *may* mean, to one who appreciates Chaucer's wisdom and humor, that having written a little book in what seemed to him an unskilled or " unconning " way, he hesitated to give it to the world for dread of the " prees " or crowd of critics who, even in that early day, were wont to look upon each new book as a camel that must be put through the needle's eye of their tender mercies.

In the selection and arrangement of his material the author has aimed to make a usable book that may appeal to pupils and teachers alike. Because history and literature are closely related (one being the record of man's deed, the other of his thought and feeling) there is a brief historical introduction to every literary period. There is also a review of the general literary tendencies of each age, of the fashions, humors and ideals that influenced writers in forming their style or selecting their subject. Then there is a biography of every important author, written not to offer another subject for hero-worship but to present the man exactly as he was ; a review of his chief works, which is intended chiefly as a guide to the best reading ; and a critical estimate or appreciation of his writings based partly upon first-hand impressions, partly upon the assumption that an author must deal honestly with life as he finds it and that the business of criticism is, as Emerson said, " not to legislate but to raise the dead." This detailed study of the greater writers of a period is followed by an examination of some of the minor writers and their memorable

RE

works. Finally, each chapter concludes with a concise summary of the period under consideration, a list of selections for reading and a bibliography of works that will be found most useful in acquiring a larger knowledge of the subject.

In its general plan this little volume is modeled on the author's more advanced *English Literature*; but the material, the point of view, the presentation of individual writers, — all the details of the work are entirely new. Such a book is like a second journey through ample and beautiful regions filled with historic associations, a journey that one undertakes with new companions, with renewed pleasure and, it is to be hoped, with increased wisdom. It is hardly necessary to add that our subject has still its unvoiced charms, that it cannot be exhausted or even adequately presented in any number of histories. For literature deals with life; and life, with its endlessly surprising variety in unity, has happily some suggestion of infinity.

Since the prime purpose of any text of literature is to introduce men and women who have a message worth hearing, the greater part of this new edition is given to selections from the work of representative British authors, including those of the present day. These selections have been gathered together with a double motive, — to let each author speak for himself, however briefly, and to encourage the student to form his own judgment, independent of historians or critics. The result should be not only to inspire us to seek a better acquaintance with our elder writers but also to enable us to choose from among the many of our own day the few who by appealing to our particular taste or humor can best minister to our pleasure in reading.

WILLIAM J. LONG

STAMFORD, CONNECTICUT

CONTENTS

ENGLISH LITERATURE

RE   ix

Masques. Popular Comedies. Classical and English Drama. Predecessors of Shakespeare. Marlowe. Shakespeare. Elizabethan Dramatists after Shakespeare. Ben Jonson. The Prose Writers. The Fashion
of Euphuism. The Authorized Version of the Scriptures. Francis Bacon.
Summary of the Period. Selections for Reading. Bibliography.

Historical Outline. Three Typical Writers. Milton. Bunyan. Dry-
den. Puritan and Cavalier Poets. George Herbert. Butler's *Hudibras*.
The Prose Writers. Thomas Browne. Isaac Walton. Summary of the
Period. Selections for Reading. Bibliography.

History of the Period. Eighteenth-Century Classicism. The Meaning
of Classicism in Literature. Alexander Pope. Swift. Addison. Steele.
Johnson. Boswell. Burke. Historical Writing in the Eighteenth Century.
Gibbon.
The Revival of Romantic Poetry. Collins and Gray. Goldsmith.
Burns. Minor Poets of Romanticism. Cowper. Macpherson and the
Ossian Poems. Chatterton. Percy's *Reliques of Ancient English Poetry*.
William Blake.
The Early English Novel. The Old Romance and the New Novel.
Defoe. Richardson. Fielding. Influence of the Early Novelists. Sum-
mary of the Period. Selections for Reading. Bibliography.

Historical Outline. The French Revolution and English Literature.
Wordsworth. Coleridge. Southey. The Revolutionary Poets. Byron
and Shelley. Keats. The Minor Poets. Campbell, Moore, Keble,
Hood, Felicia Hemans, Leigh Hunt and Thomas Beddoes. The Fic-
tion Writers. Walter Scott. Jane Austen. The Critics and Essayists.
Charles Lamb. De Quincey. Summary of the Period. Selections for
Reading. Bibliography.

Historical Outline. The Victorian Poets. Tennyson. Browning.
Elizabeth Barrett Browning. Matthew Arnold. The Pre-Raphaelites.
Rossetti. Morris. Swinburne. Minor Poets and Songs in Many Keys.

LIST OF ILLUSTRATIONS

RE

ght that Homer was a good teacher for the nursery; we
made acquaintance with Psalm and Prophecy and Para-
with the knightly tales of Malory, with the fairy stories
Grimm or Andersen, with the poetry of Shakespeare, with
novels of Scott or Dickens,—in short, with some of the
st books that the world has ever produced. We know, there-
re, what literature is, and that it is an excellent thing which
inisters to the joy of living; but when we are asked to de-
ine the subject, we are in the position of St. Augustine, who
said of time, "If you ask me what time is, I know not; but
if you ask me not, then I know." For literature is like happiness, or love, or life itself, in that it can be understood
or appreciated but can never be exactly described. It has
certain describable qualities, however, and the best place to
discover these is our own bookcase.

Here on a shelf are a Dictionary, a History of America, a
text on Chemistry, which we read or study for information;
The Tree on a higher shelf are *As You Like It, Hiawatha,*
and the Book *Lorna Doone, The Oregon Trail,* and other works
to which we go for pleasure when the day's work is done. In
one sense all these and all other books are literature; for the
root meaning of the word is "letters," and a letter means a
character inscribed or rubbed upon a prepared surface. A series
of letters intelligently arranged forms a book, and for the root
meaning of "book" you must go to a tree; because the Latin
word for book, *liber,* means the inner layer of bark that covers
a tree bole, and "book" or "boc" is the old English name
for the beech, on whose silvery surface our ancestors carved
their first runic letters.

So also when we turn the "leaves" of a book, our mind
goes back over a long trail: through rattling printing-shop,
and peaceful monk's cell, and gloomy cave with walls covered
with picture writing, till the trail ends beside a shadowy forest,
where primitive man takes a smooth leaf and inscribes his
thought upon it by means of a pointed stick. A tree is the

OUTLINES OF
ENGLISH LITERATU

CHAPTER I

INTRODUCTION: AN ESSAY OF LITERATUR

(Not a Lesson, but an Invitation)

I sleep, yet I love to be wakened, and love to see
The fresh young faces bending over me;
And the faces of them that are old, I love them too,
For these, as well, in the days of their youth I knew.
" Song of the Well

What is Literature? In an old English book, written b
fore Columbus dreamed of a westward journey to find the East,
is the story of a traveler who set out to search the world for
wisdom. Through Palestine and India he passed, traveling by
sea or land through many seasons, till he came to a wonderful
island where he saw a man plowing in the fields. And the
wonder was, that the man was calling familiar words to his
oxen, "such wordes as men speken to bestes in his owne lond."
Startled by the sound of his mother tongue he turned back on
his course "in gret mervayle, for he knewe not how it myghte
be." But if he had passed on a little, says the old record, " he
would have founden his contree and his owne knouleche."

Facing a new study of literature our impulse is to search in
strange places for a definition; but though we compass a world
of books, we must return at last, like the worthy man of *Mandeville's Travels*, to our own knowledge. Since childhood we
have been familiar with this noble subject of literature. We
have entered into the heritage of the ancient Greeks, who

Adam of all books, and everything that the hand of man has written upon the tree or its products or its substitutes is literature. But that is too broad a definition; we must limit it by excluding what does not here concern us.

Our first exclusion is of that immense class of writings — books of science, history, philosophy, and the rest — to which **Books of** we go for information. These aim to preserve or **Knowledge** to systematize the discoveries of men; they appeal **and of Power** chiefly to the intellect, and they are known as the literature of knowledge. There remains another large class of writings, sometimes called the literature of power, consisting of poems, plays, essays, stories of every kind, to which we go treasure-hunting for happiness or counsel, for noble thoughts or fine feelings, for rest of body or exercise of spirit, — for almost everything, in fine, except information. As Chaucer said, long ago, such writings are:

> For pleasaunce high, and for noon other end.

They aim to give us pleasure; they appeal chiefly to our imagination and our emotions; they awaken in us a feeling of sympathy or admiration for whatever is beautiful in nature or society or the soul of man.

The author who would attempt books of such high purpose must be careful of both the matter and the manner of his **The Art of** writing, must give one thought to what he shall say **Literature** and another thought to how he shall say it. He selects the best or most melodious words, the finest figures, and aims to make his story or poem beautiful in itself, as a painter strives to reflect a face or a landscape in a beautiful way. Any photographer can in a few minutes reproduce a human face, but only an artist can by care and labor bring forth a beautiful portrait. So any historian can write the facts of the Battle of Gettysburg; but only a Lincoln can in noble words reveal the beauty and immortal meaning of that mighty conflict.

To all such written works, which quicken our sense of the beautiful, and which are as a Jacob's ladder on which we mount for higher views of nature or humanity, we confidently give the name "literature," meaning the art of literature in distinction from the mere craft of writing.

Such a definition, though it cuts out the greater part of human records, is still too broad for our purpose, and again **The Passing** we must limit it by a process of exclusion. For **and the Per-** to study almost any period of English letters is to **manent** discover that it produced hundreds of books which served the purpose of literature, if only for a season, by affording pleasure to readers. No sooner were they written than Time began to winnow them over and over, giving them to all the winds of opinion, one generation after another, till the hosts of ephemeral works were swept aside, and only a remnant was left in the hands of the winnower. To this remnant, books of abiding interest, on which the years have no effect save to mellow or flavor them, we give the name of great or enduring literature; and with these chiefly we deal in our present study.

To the inevitable question, What are the marks of great literature? no positive answer can be returned. As a tree is **The Quality** judged by its fruits, so is literature judged not by **of Greatness** theory but by the effect which it produces on human life; and the judgment is first personal, then general. If a book has power to awaken in you a lively sense of pleasure or a profound emotion of sympathy; if it quickens your love of beauty or truth or goodness; if it moves you to generous thought or noble action, then that book is, for you and for the time, a great book. If after ten or fifty years it still has power to quicken you, then for you at least it is a great book forever. And if it affects many other men and women as it affects you, and if it lives with power from one generation to another, gladdening the children as it gladdened the fathers, then surely it is great literature, without further qualification or need of definition. From this viewpoint the greatest poem in the world — greatest in that it abides in most human hearts as a loved and honored guest — is not a mighty *Iliad* or *Paradise Lost* or *Divine Comedy*; it is a familiar little poem of a dozen lines, beginning " The Lord is my Shepherd."

It is obvious that great literature, which appeals to all classes of men and to all times, cannot go far afield for rare subjects, or follow new inventions, or concern itself with fashions that are here to-day and gone to-morrow. Its only subjects are nature and human nature ; it deals with common experiences of joy or sorrow, pain or pleasure, that all men understand ; it cherishes the unchanging ideals of love, faith, duty, freedom, reverence, courtesy, which were old to the men who kept their flocks on the plains of Shinar, and which will be young as the morning to our children's children.

Such ideals tend to ennoble a writer, and therefore are great books characterized by lofty thought, by fine feeling and, as a rule, by a beautiful simplicity of expression. They have another quality, hard to define but easy to understand, a quality which leaves upon us the impression of eternal youth, as if they had been dipped in the fountain which Ponce de Leon sought for in vain through the New World. If a great book could speak, it would use the words of the Cobzar (poet) in his " Last Song " :

> The merry Spring, he is my brother,
> And when he comes this way
> Each year again, he always asks me:
> " Art thou not yet grown gray ? "
> But I, I keep my youth forever,
> Even as the Spring his May.

A Definition. Literature, then, if one must formulate a definition, is the written record of man's best thought and feeling, and English literature is the part of that record which belongs to the English people. In its broadest sense literature includes all writing, but as we commonly define the term it excludes works which aim at instruction, and includes only the works which aim to give pleasure, and which are artistic in that they reflect nature or human life in a way to arouse our sense of beauty. In a still narrower sense, when we study the history of literature we deal chiefly with the great, the enduring books, which may have been written in an elder or a latter day, but which have in them the magic of all time.

One may easily challenge such a definition, which, like most others, is far from faultless. It is difficult, for example, to draw the line sharply between instructive and pleasure-giving works ; for many an instructive book of history gives us pleasure, and there may be more instruction on important matters in a pleasurable poem than in a treatise on ethics. Again, there are historians who allege that English literature must include not simply the works of Britain but everything written in the English language. There are other objections ; but to straighten them all out is to be long in starting, and there is a pleasant journey ahead of us. Chaucer had literature in mind when he wrote :

> Through me men goon into that blisful place
>   Of hertës hele and dedly woundës cure ;
> Through me men goon unto the wells of grace,
>   Ther grene and lusty May shal ever endure :
> This is the wey to al good aventure.

CHAPTER II

BEGINNINGS OF ENGLISH LITERATURE

> Then the warrior, battle-tried, touched the sounding glee-wood:
> Straight awoke the harp's sweet note; straight a song uprose,
> Sooth and sad its music. Then from hero's lips there fell
> A wonder-tale, well told.
> > *Beowulf*, line 2017 (a free rendering)

In its beginnings English literature is like a river, which proceeds not from a single wellhead but from many springs, each sending forth its rivulet of sweet or bitter water. As there is a place where the river assumes a character of its own, distinct from all its tributaries, so in English literature there is a time when it becomes national rather than tribal, and English rather than Saxon or Celtic or Norman. That time was in the fifteenth century, when the poems of Chaucer and the printing press of Caxton exalted the Midland above all other dialects and established it as the literary language of England.

Before that time, if you study the records of Britain, you meet several different tribes and races of men: the native Celt, **Tributaries** the law-giving Roman, the colonizing Saxon, the **of Literature** sea-roving Dane, the feudal baron of Normandy, each with his own language and literature reflecting the traditions of his own people. Here in these old records is a strange medley of folk heroes, Arthur and Beowulf, Cnut and Brutus, Finn and Cuchulain, Roland and Robin Hood. Older than the tales of such folk-heroes are ancient riddles, charms, invocations to earth and sky:

> Hal wes thu, Folde, fira moder!
> Hail to thee, Earth, thou mother of men!

7

With these pagan spells are found the historical writings of the Venerable Bede, the devout hymns of Cædmon, Welsh legends, Irish and Scottish fairy stories, Scandinavian myths, Hebrew and Christian traditions, romances from distant Italy which had traveled far before the Italians welcomed them. All these and more, whether originating on British soil or brought in by missionaries or invaders, held each to its own course for a time, then met and mingled in the swelling stream which became English literature.

To trace all these tributaries to their obscure and lonely sources would require the labor of a lifetime. We shall here

STONEHENGE, ON SALISBURY PLAIN
Probably the ruins of a temple of the native Britons

examine only the two main branches of our early literature, to the end that we may better appreciate the vigor and variety of modern English. The first is the Anglo-Saxon, which came into England in the middle of the fifth century with the colonizing Angles, Jutes and Saxons from the shores of the North Sea and the Baltic; the second is the Norman-French, which arrived six centuries later at the time of the Norman invasion. Except in their emphasis on personal courage, there is a marked contrast between these two branches, the former being stern and somber, the latter gay and fanciful. In Anglo-Saxon poetry we meet a strong man who cherishes his own ideals of honor, in Norman-French poetry a youth eagerly interested in romantic tales gathered from all the world. One represents life as a profound mystery, the other as a happy adventure.

ANGLO–SAXON OR OLD–ENGLISH PERIOD (450–1050)

Specimens of the Language. Our English speech has changed so much in the course of centuries that it is now impossible to read our earliest records without special study; but that Anglo-Saxon is our own and not a foreign tongue may appear from the following examples. The first is a stanza from " Widsith," the chant of a wandering gleeman or minstrel; and for comparison we place beside it Andrew Lang's modern version. Nobody knows how old " Widsith " is; it may have been sung to the accompaniment of a harp that was broken fourteen hundred years ago. The second, much easier to read, is from the Anglo-Saxon Chronicle, which was prepared by King Alfred from an older record in the ninth century:

Swa scrithende	So wandering on
gesceapum hweorfath,	the world about,
Gleomen gumena	Gleemen do roam
geond grunda fela;	through many lands;
Thearfe secgath,	They say their needs,
thonc-word sprecath,	they speak their thanks,
Simle, suth oththe north	Sure, south or north
sumne gemetath,	someone to meet,
Gydda gleawne	Of songs to judge
geofam unhneawne.	and gifts not grudge.

Her Hengest and Aesc, his sunu, gefuhton wid Bryttas on thaere stowe the is gecweden Creccanford, and thaer ofslogon feower thusenda wera. And tha Bryttas tha forleton Cent-lond, and mid myclum ege flugon to Lundenbyrig.

At this time Hengist and Esk, his son, fought with the Britons at the place that is called Crayford, and there slew four thousand men. And the Britons then forsook Kentland, and with much fear fled to London town.

Beowulf. The old epic poem, called after its hero Beowulf, is more than myth or legend, more even than history; it is a picture of a life and a world that once had real existence. Of that vanished life, that world of ancient Englishmen, only a few material fragments remain : a bit of linked armor, a rusted sword with runic inscriptions, the oaken ribs of a war galley buried with the Viking who had sailed it on stormy seas, and who was entombed in it because he loved it. All these are silent witnesses ; they have no speech or language. But this old poem is a living voice, speaking with truth and sincerity of the daily habit of the fathers of modern England, of their adventures by sea or land, their stern courage and grave courtesy, their ideals of manly honor, their thoughts of life and death.

Let us hear, then, the story of *Beowulf*, picturing in our imagination the story-teller and his audience. The scene opens in a great hall, where a fire blazes on the hearth and flashes upon polished shields against the timbered walls. Down the long room stretches a table where men are feasting or passing a beaker from hand to hand, and anon crying *Hal! hal!* in answer to song or in greeting to a guest. At the head of the hall sits the chief with his chosen ealdormen. At a sign from the chief a gleeman rises and strikes a single clear note from his harp. Silence falls on the benches ; the story begins :

> Hail ! we of the Spear Danes in days of old
> Have heard the glory of warriors sung ;
> Have cheered the deeds that our chieftains wrought,
> And the brave Scyld's triumph o'er his foes.

Then because there are Scyldings present, and because brave men revere their ancestors, the gleeman tells a beautiful legend of how King Scyld came and went : how he arrived as a little child, in a war-galley that no man sailed, asleep amid jewels and weapons ; and how, when his life ended at the call of Wyrd or Fate, they placed him against the mast of a ship, with treasures heaped around him and a golden banner above his head, gave ship and cargo to the winds, and sent their chief nobly back to the deep whence he came.

So with picturesque words the gleeman thrills his hearers with a vivid picture of a Viking's sea-burial. It thrills us now, when the Vikings are no more, and when no other picture can be drawn by an eyewitness of that splendid pagan rite.

One of Scyld's descendants was King Hrothgar (Roger) who built the hall Heorot, where the king and his men used to gather nightly to feast, and to listen to the songs of scop or gleeman.[1] "There was joy of heroes," but in one night the joy was changed to mourning. Out on the lonely fens dwelt the jotun (giant or monster) Grendel, who heard the sound of men's mirth and quickly made an end of it. One night, as the thanes slept in the hall, he burst in the door and carried off thirty warriors to devour them in his lair under the sea. Another and another horrible raid followed, till Heorot was deserted and the fear of Grendel reigned among the Spear Danes. There were brave men among them, but of what use was courage when their weapons were powerless against the monster? "Their swords would not bite on his body."

The Story of Heorot

For twelve years this terror continued; then the rumor of Grendel reached the land of the Geats, where Beowulf lived at the court of his uncle, King Hygelac. No sooner did Beowulf hear of a dragon to be slain, of a friendly king "in need of a man," than he selected fourteen companions and launched his war-galley in search of adventure.

At this point the old epic becomes a remarkable portrayal of daily life. In its picturesque lines we see the galley set sail, foam flying from her prow; we catch the first sight of the southern headlands, approach land, hear the challenge of the "warder of the cliffs" and Beowulf's courteous answer. We follow the march to Heorot in war-gear, spears flashing, swords and byrnies clanking, and witness the exchange of greetings between Hrothgar and the young hero. Again is the feast spread in Heorot; once more is heard the song of glee-men, the joyous sound of warriors in comradeship. There is also a significant picture of Hrothgar's wife, "mindful of courtesies," honoring her guests by passing the mead-cup with her own hands. She is received by these stern men with profound respect.

The Sailing of Beowulf

When the feast draws to an end the fear of Grendel returns. Hrothgar warns his guests that no weapon can harm the monster, that it is death to sleep in the hall; then the Spear Danes retire, leaving Beowulf and his companions to keep watch and ward. With the careless confidence of brave men, forthwith they all fall asleep:

> Forth from the fens, from the misty moorlands,
> Grendel came gliding — God's wrath he bore —
> Came under clouds until he saw clearly,
> Glittering with gold plates, the mead-hall of men.

[1] Like Agamemnon and the Greek chieftains, every Saxon leader had his gleeman or minstrel, and had also his own poet, his scop or "shaper," whose duty it was to shape a glorious deed into more glorious verse. So did our pagan ancestors build their monuments out of songs that should live in the hearts of men when granite or earth mound had crumbled away.

> Down fell the door, though hardened with fire-bands,
> Open it sprang at the stroke of his paw.
> Swollen with rage burst in the bale-bringer,
> Flamed in his eyes a fierce light, likest fire.

Throwing himself upon the nearest sleeper Grendel crushes and swallows him; then he stretches out a paw towards Beowulf, only to find it " seized in such a grip as the fiend had never felt before." A desperate conflict begins, and a mighty uproar, — crashing of benches, shoutings of men, the " war-song " of Grendel, who is trying to break the grip of his foe. As the monster struggles toward the door, dragging the hero with him, a wide wound opens on his shoulder; the sinews snap, and with a mighty wrench Beowulf tears off the whole limb. While Grendel rushes howling across the fens, Beowulf hangs the grisly arm with its iron claws, " the whole grapple of Grendel," over the door where all may see it.

The Fight with Grendel

Once more there is joy in Heorot, songs, speeches, the liberal giving of gifts. Thinking all danger past, the Danes sleep in the hall; but at midnight comes the mother of Grendel, raging to avenge her son. Seizing the king's bravest companion she carries him away, and he is never seen again.

Here is another adventure for Beowulf. To old Hrothgar, lamenting his lost earl, the hero says simply:

> Wise chief, sorrow not. For a man it is meet
> His friend to avenge, not to mourn for his loss;
> For death comes to all, but honor endures:
> Let him win it who will, ere Wyrd to him calls,
> And fame be the fee of a warrior dead!

Following the trail of the *Brimwylf* or *Merewif* (sea-wolf or sea-woman) Beowulf and his companions pass through desolate regions to a wild cliff on the shore. There a friend offers his good sword Hrunting for the combat, and Beowulf accepts the weapon, saying:

> ic me mid Hruntinge
> Dom gewyrce, oththe mec death nimeth.
> I with Hrunting
> Honor will win, or death shall me take.

Then he plunges into the black water, is attacked on all sides by the *Grundwrygen* or bottom monsters, and as he stops to fight them is seized by the *Merewif* and dragged into a cave, a mighty " sea-hall " free from water and filled with a strange light. On its floor are vast treasures; its walls are adorned with weapons; in a corner huddles the wounded Grendel. All this Beowulf sees in a glance as he turns to fight his new foe.

The Dragon's Cave

Follows then another terrific combat, in which the brand Hrunting proves useless. Though it rings out its " clanging war-song " on the monster's scales, it will not " bite " on the charmed body. Beowulf is down, and at the point of death, when his eye lights on a huge sword forged by the jotuns of old. Struggling to his feet he seizes the weapon, whirls it around his head for a mighty blow, and the fight is won. Another blow cuts off the head of Grendel, but at the touch of the poisonous blood the steel blade melts like ice before the fire.

Leaving all the treasures, Beowulf takes only the golden hilt of the magic sword and the head of Grendel, reënters the sea and mounts up to his companions. They welcome him as one returned from the dead. They relieve him of helmet and byrnie, and swing away in a triumphal procession to Heorot. The hero towers among them, a conspicuous figure, and next to him comes the enormous head of Grendel carried on a spear-shaft by four of the stoutest thanes.

More feasting, gifts, noble speeches follow before the hero returns to his own land, laden with treasures. So ends the first part of the epic. In the second part Beowulf succeeds Hygelac as chief of the **The Firedrake** Geats, and rules them well for fifty years. Then a " firedrake," guarding an immense hoard of treasure (as in most of the old dragon stories), begins to ravage the land. Once more the aged Beowulf goes forth to champion his people; but he feels that " Wyrd is close to hand," and the fatalism which pervades all the poem is finely expressed in his speech to his companions. In his last fight he kills the dragon, winning the dragon's treasure for his people; but as he battles amid flame and smoke the fire enters his lungs, and he dies " as dies a man," paying for victory with his life. Among his last words is a command which reminds us again of the old Greeks, and of the word of Elpenor to Odysseus:

" Bid my brave men raise a barrow for me on the headland, broad, high, to be seen far out at sea; that hereafter sea-farers, driving their foamy keels through ocean's mist, may behold and say, ''T is Beowulf's mound!' "

The hero's last words and the closing scenes of the epic, including the funeral pyre, the " bale-fire " and another Viking burial to the chant of armed men riding their war steeds, are among the noblest that have come down to us from beyond the dawn of history.

Such, in brief outline, is the story of *Beowulf.* It is recorded on a fire-marked manuscript, preserved as by a miracle from the torch of the Danes, which is now one of the priceless treasures of the British Museum. The handwriting indicates that the manuscript was copied about the year 1100, but the language points to the eighth or ninth century, when the poem in its present form was probably composed on English soil.[1]

Anglo-Saxon Songs. Beside the epic of *Beowulf* a few mutilated poems have been preserved, and these are as fragments of a plate or film upon which the life of long ago left its impression. One of the oldest of these poems is "Widsith," the "wide-goer," which describes the wanderings and rewards of the ancient gleeman. It begins:

> Widsith spake, his word-hoard unlocked,
> He who farthest had fared among earth-folk and tribe-folk.

Then follows a recital of the places he had visited, and the gifts he had received for his singing. Some of the personages named are real, others mythical; and as the list covers half a world and several centuries of time, it is certain that Widsith's recital cannot be taken literally.

Two explanations offer themselves: the first, that the poem contains the work of many scops, each of whom added his **Meaning of** travels to those of his predecessor; the second, that **Widsith** Widsith, like other gleemen, was both historian and poet, a keeper of tribal legends as well as a shaper of songs, and that he was ever ready to entertain his audience with things new or old. Thus, he mentioned Hrothgar as one whom he had visited; and if a hearer called for a tale at this point, the scop would recite that part of *Beowulf* which tells of the monster Grendel. Again, he named Sigard the Volsung (the Siegfrid of the *Niebelungenlied* and of Wagner's opera), and this would recall the slaying of the dragon Fafnir, or some other

---

[1] Materials used in *Beowulf* are very old, and may have been brought to England during the Anglo-Saxon invasion. Parts of the material, such as the dragon-fights, are purely mythical. They relate to Beowa, a superman, of whom many legends were told by Scandinavian minstrels. The Grendel legend, for example, appears in the Icelandic saga of Gretti, who slays the dragon Glam. Other parts of *Beowulf* are old battle songs; and still others, relating to King Hygelac and his nephew, have some historical foundation. So little is known about the epic that one cannot safely make any positive statement as to its origin. It was written in crude, uneven lines; but a rhythmic, martial effect, as of marching men, was produced by strong accent and alliteration, and the effect was strengthened by the harp with which the gleeman always accompanied his recital.

story of the old Norse saga. So every name or place which Widsith mentioned was an invitation. When he came to a hall and "unlocked his word-hoard," he offered his hearers a variety of poems and legends from which they made their own selection. Looked at in this way, the old poem becomes an epitome of Anglo-Saxon literature.

Other fragments of the period are valuable as indicating that the Anglo-Saxons were familiar with various types of poetry.

Types of Saxon Poetry "Deor's Lament," describing the sorrows of a scop who had lost his place beside his chief, is a true lyric; that is, a poem which reflects the author's feeling rather than the deed of another man. In his grief the scop comforts himself by recalling the afflictions of various heroes, and he ends each stanza with the refrain:

> That sorrow he endured; this also may I.

Among the best of the early poems are: "The Ruined City," reflecting the feeling of one who looks on crumbling walls that were once the abode of human ambition; "The Seafarer," a chantey of the deep, which ends with an allegory comparing life to a sea voyage; "The Wanderer," which is the plaint of one who has lost home, patron, ambition, and as the easiest way out of his difficulty turns *eardstappa*, an "earth-hitter" or tramp; "The Husband's Message," which is the oldest love song in our literature; and a few ballads and battle songs, such as "The Battle of Brunanburh" (familiar to us in Tennyson's translation) and "The Fight at Finnsburgh," which was mentioned by the gleemen in *Beowulf*, and which was then probably as well known as "The Charge of the Light Brigade" is to modern Englishmen.

Another early war song, "The Battle of Maldon" or "Byrhtnoth's Death," has seldom been rivaled in savage vigor or in the expression of deathless loyalty to a chosen leader. The climax of the poem is reached when the few survivors of an uneven battle make a ring of spears about their fallen chief, shake their weapons in the face of an overwhelming horde of Danes, while Byrhtwold, "the old comrade," chants their defiance :

> The sterner shall thought be, the bolder our hearts,
> The greater the mood as lessens our might.

We know not when or by whom this stirring battle cry was written. It was copied under date of 991 in the *Anglo-Saxon Chronicle*, and is commonly called the swan song of Anglo-Saxon poetry. The lion song would be a better name for it.

Later Prose and Poetry. The works we have just considered were wholly pagan in spirit, but all reference to Thor or other gods was excluded by the monks who first wrote down the scop's poetry.

With the coming of these monks a reform swept over pagan England, and literature reflected the change in a variety of ways. For example, early Anglo-Saxon poetry was mostly warlike, for the reason that the various earldoms were in constant strife ; but now the peace of good will was preached, and moral courage, the triumph of self-control, was exalted above mere physical hardihood. In the new literature the adventures of Columb or Aidan or Brendan were quite as thrilling as any legends of Beowulf or Sigard, but the climax of the adventure was spiritual, and the emphasis was always on moral heroism.

Another result of the changed condition was that the unlettered scop, who carried his whole stock of poetry in his head, was replaced by the literary monk, who had behind him the immense culture of the Latin language, and who was interested in world history or Christian doctrine rather than in tribal fights or pagan mythology. These monks were capable men ; they understood the appeal of pagan poetry, and their motto was, "Let nothing good be wasted." So they made careful copy of the scop's best songs (else had not a shred of early poetry survived), and so the pagan's respect for womanhood, his courage, his loyalty to a chief, — all his virtues were recognized and turned to religious account in the new literature. Even the beautiful pagan scrolls, or "dragon knots," once etched on a warrior's sword, were reproduced in glowing colors in the initial letters of the monk's illuminated Gospel.

A third result of the peaceful conquest of the missionaries was that many monasteries were established in Britain, each a center of learning and of writing. So arose the famous Northumbrian School of literature, to which we owe the writings of Bede, Cædmon, Cynewulf and others associated with certain old monasteries, such as Peterborough, Jarrow, York and Whitby, all north of the river Humber.

Bede. The good work of the monks is finely exemplified in the life of the Venerable Bede, or Bæda (*cir.* 673–735), who is well called the father of English learning. As a boy he entered the Benedictine monastery at Jarrow; the temper of his manhood may be judged from a single sentence of his own record:

"While attentive to the discipline of mine order and the daily care of singing in the church, my constant delight was in learning or teaching or writing."

It is hardly too much to say that this gentle scholar was for half a century the teacher of Europe. He collected a large library of manuscripts; he was the author of some forty works, covering the whole field of human knowledge in his day; and to his school at Jarrow came hundreds of pupils from all parts of the British Isles, and hundreds more from the Continent. Of all his works the most notable is the so-called "Ecclesiastical History" (*Historia ecclesiastica gentis anglorum*) which should be named the "History of the Race of Angles." This book marks the beginning of our literature of knowledge, and to it we are largely indebted for what we know of English history from the time of Cæsar's invasion to the early part of the eighth century.

All the extant works of Bede are in Latin, but we are told by his pupil Cuthbert that he was "skilled in our English

E

songs," that he made poems and translated the Gospel of John into English. These works, which would now be of priceless value, were all destroyed by the plundering Danes.

As an example of Bede's style, we translate a typical passage from his History. The scene is the Saxon *Witenagemôt*, or council of wise men, called by King Edward (625) to consider the doctrine of Paulinus, who had been sent from Rome by Pope Gregory. The first speaker is Coifi, a priest of the old religion :

"Consider well, O king, this new doctrine which is preached to us; for I now declare, what I have learned for certain, that the old religion has no virtue in it. For none of your people has been more diligent than I in the worship of our gods; yet many receive more favors from you, and are preferred above me, and are more prosperous in their affairs. If the old gods had any discernment, they would surely favor me, since I have been most diligent in their service. It is expedient, therefore, if this new faith that is preached is any more profitable than the old, that we accept it without delay."

Whereupon Coifi, who as a priest has hitherto been obliged to ride upon an ass with wagging ears, calls loudly for a horse, a prancing horse, a stallion, and cavorts off, a crowd running at his heels, to hurl a spear into the shrine where he lately worshiped. He is a good type of the political demagogue, who clamors for progress when he wants an office, and whose spear is more likely to be hurled at the back of a friend than at the breast of an enemy.

Then a pagan chief rises to speak, and we bow to a nobler motive. His allegory of the mystery of life is like a strain of Anglo-Saxon poetry ; it moves us deeply, as it moved his hearers ten centuries ago :

"This present life of man, O king, in comparison with the time that is hidden from us, is as the flight of a sparrow through the room where you sit at supper, with companions around you and a good fire on the hearth. Outside are the storms of wintry rain and snow. The sparrow flies in at one opening, and instantly out at another : whilst he is within he is sheltered from the winter storms, but after a moment of pleasant weather he speeds from winter back to winter again, and vanishes from your sight into the darkness whence he came. Even so the life of man appears for a little time; but of what went before and of what comes after we are wholly ignorant. If this new religion can teach us anything of greater certainty, it surely deserves to be followed." [1]

Cædmon (Seventh Century). In a beautiful chapter of Bede's History we may read how Cædmon (d. 680) discovered his gift of poetry. He was, says the record, a poor unlettered servant of the Abbess Hilda, in her monastery at Whitby. At that time (and here is an interesting commentary on monastic culture) singing and poetry were so familiar that, whenever a feast was given, a harp would be brought in, and each monk or guest would in turn entertain the company with a song or poem to his own musical accompaniment. But Cædmon could not sing, and when he saw the harp coming down the table he would slip away ashamed, to perform his humble duties in the monastery:

"Now it happened once that he did this thing at a certain festivity, and went out to the stable to care for the horses, this duty being assigned him for that night. As he slept at the usual time one stood by him, saying, 'Cædmon, sing me something.' He answered, 'I cannot sing, and that is why I came hither from the feast.' But he who spake unto him said again, 'Cædmon, sing to me.' And he said, 'What shall I sing?' And that one said, 'Sing the beginning of created things.' Thereupon Cædmon began to sing verses that he had never heard before, of this import:

CÆDMON CROSS AT WHITBY ABBEY

Nu scylun hergan hefænriches ward . . .
Now shall we hallow the warden of heaven,
He the Creator, he the Allfather,
Deeds of his might and thoughts of his mind. . . ."

[1] Bede, *Historia*, Book II, chap. xiii, a free translation.

In the morning he remembered the words, and came humbly to the monks to recite the first recorded Christian hymn in our language. And a very noble hymn it is. The monks heard him in wonder, and took him to the Abbess Hilda, who gave order that Cædmon should receive instruction and enter the monastery as one of the brethren. Then the monks expounded to him the Scriptures. He in turn, reflecting on what he had heard, echoed it back to the monks "in such melodious words that his teachers became his pupils." So, says the record, the whole course of Bible history was turned into excellent poetry.

About a thousand years later, in the days of Milton, an Anglo-Saxon manuscript was discovered containing a metrical paraphrase of the books of Genesis, Exodus and Daniel, and these were supposed to be some of the poems mentioned in Bede's narrative. A study of the poems (now known as the Cædmonian Cycle) leads to the conclusion that they were probably the work of two or three writers, and it has not been determined what part Cædmon had in their composition. The nobility of style in the Genesis poem and the picturesque account of the fallen angels (which reappears in *Paradise Lost*) have won for Cædmon his designation as the Milton of the Anglo-Saxon period.[1]

Cynewulf (Eighth Century). There is a variety of poems belonging to the Cynewulf Cycle, and of some of these Cynewulf (born *cir.* 750) was certainly the author, since he wove his name into the verses in the manner of an acrostic. Of Cynewulf's life we know nothing with certainty; but from various poems which are attributed to him, and which undoubtedly reflect some personal experience, scholars have constructed the following biography, — which may or may not be true.

---

[1] A friend of Milton, calling himself Franciscus Junius, first printed the Cædmon poems in Antwerp (*cir.* 1655) during Milton's lifetime. The Puritan poet was blind at the time, and it is not certain that he ever saw or heard the poems; yet there are many parallelisms in the earlier and later works which warrant the conclusion that Milton was influenced by Cædmon's work.

In his early life Cynewulf was probably a wandering scop of the old pagan kind, delighting in wild nature, in adventure, in the clamor of fighting men. To this period belong his " Riddles " [1] and his vigorous descriptions of the sea and of battle, which show hardly a trace of Christian influence. Then came trouble to Cynewulf, perhaps in the ravages of the Danes, and some deep spiritual experience of which he writes in a way to remind us of the Puritan age :

" In the prison of the night I pondered with myself. I was stained with my own deeds, bound fast in my sins, hard smitten with sorrows, walled in by miseries."

A wondrous vision of the cross, " brightest of beacons," shone suddenly through his darkness, and led him forth into light and joy. Then he wrote his " Vision of the Rood " and probably also *Juliana* and *The Christ*. In the last period of his life, a time of great serenity, he wrote *Andreas*, a story of St. Andrew combining religious instruction with extraordinary adventure ; *Elene*, which describes the search for the cross on which Christ died, and which is a prototype of the search for the Holy Grail ; and other poems of the same general kind.[2] Aside from the value of these works as a reflection of Anglo-Saxon ideals, they are our best picture of Christianity as it appeared in England during the eighth and ninth centuries.

Alfred the Great (848–901). We shall understand the importance of Alfred's work if we remember how his country fared when he became king of the West Saxons, in 871. At that time England lay at the mercy of the Danish sea-rovers. Soon after Bede's death they fell upon Northumbria, hewed out with their swords a place of settlement, and were soon

---

[1] These riddles are ancient conundrums, in which some familiar object, such as a bow, a ship, a storm lashing the shore, the moon riding the clouds like a Viking's boat, is described in poetic language, and the last line usually calls on the hearer to name the object described. See Cook and Tinker, *Translations from Old English Poetry*.

[2] There is little agreement among scholars as to who wrote most of these poems. The only works to which Cynewulf signs his name are *The Christ, Elene, Juliana* and *Fates of the Apostles*. All others are doubtful, and our biography of Cynewulf is largely a matter of pleasant speculation.

lords of the whole north country. Being pagans ("Thor's men") they called themselves) they sacked the monasteries, burned the libraries, made a lurid end of the civilization which men like Columb and Bede had built up in North-Humberland. Then they pushed southward, and were in process of paganizing all England when they were turned back by the heroism of Alfred.

How he accomplished his task, and how from his capital at Winchester he established law and order in England, is recorded in the histories. We are dealing here with literature, and in this field Alfred is distinguished in two ways: first, by his preservation of early English poetry; and second, by his own writing, which earned for him the title of father of English prose. Finding that some fragments of poetry had escaped the fire of the Danes, he caused search to be made for old manuscripts, and had copies made of all that were legible.[1] But what gave Alfred deepest concern was that in all his kingdom there were few priests and no laymen who could read or write their own language. As he wrote sadly:

" King Alfred sends greeting to Bishop Werfrith in words of love and friendship. Let it be known to thee that it often comes to my mind what wise men and what happy times were formerly in England, . . . I remember what I saw before England had been ravaged and burned, how churches throughout the whole land were filled with treasures of books. And there was also a multitude of God's servants, but these had no knowledge of the books: they could not understand them because they were not written in their own language. It was as if the books said, ' Our fathers who once occupied these places loved wisdom, and through it they obtained wealth and left it to us. We see here their footprints, but we cannot follow them, and therefore have we lost both their wealth and their wisdom, because we would not incline our hearts to their example.' When I remember this, I marvel that good and wise men who were formerly in England, and who had learned these books, did not translate them into their own language. Then I answered myself and said, ' They never thought that their children would be so careless, or that learning would so decay.' " [2]

[1] These copies were made in Alfred's dialect (West Saxon) not in the Northumbrian dialect in which they were first written.

[2] A free version of part of Alfred's preface to his translation of Pope Gregory's *Cura Pastoralis*, which appeared in English as the Hirdeboc or Shepherd's Book.

To remedy the evil, Alfred ordered that every freeborn Englishman should learn to read and write his own language ; but before he announced the order he followed it himself. Rather late in his boyhood he had learned to spell out an English book ; now with immense difficulty he took up Latin, and translated the best works for the benefit of his people. His last notable work was the famous *Anglo-Saxon Chronicle*.

At that time it was customary in monasteries to keep a record of events which seemed to the monks of special impor-
Anglo-Saxon   tance, such as the coming of a bishop, the death of
Chronicle   a king, an eclipse of the moon, a battle with the Danes. Alfred found such a record at Winchester, rewrote it (or else caused it to be rewritten) with numerous additions from Bede's History and other sources, and so made a fairly complete chronicle of England. This was sent to other monasteries, where it was copied and enlarged, so that several different versions have come down to us. The work thus begun was continued after Alfred's death, until 1154, and is the oldest contemporary history possessed by any modern nation in its own language.

ANGLO–NORMAN OR MIDDLE–ENGLISH PERIOD
(1066–1350)

Specimens of the Language. A glance at the following selections will show how Anglo-Saxon was slowly approaching our English speech of to-day. The first is from a religious book called *Ancren Riwle* (Rule of the Anchoresses, *cir.* 1225). The second, written about a century later, is from the riming chronicle, or verse history, of Robert Manning or Robert of Brunne. In it we note the appearance of rime, a new thing in English poetry, borrowed from the French, and also a few words, such as " solace," which are of foreign origin :

"Hwoso hevide iseid to Eve, theo heo werp hire eien therone, 'A ! wend te awei ; thu worpest eien o thi death!' hwat heved heo ionswered? ' Me leove sire, ther havest wouh. Hwarof kalenges tu me? The eppel that ich loke on is forbode me to etene, and nout forto biholden.' "

"Whoso had said (or, if anyone had said) to Eve when she cast her eye
theron (i.e. on the apple) ' Ah! turn thou away; thou castest eyes on thy
death!' what would she have answered? 'My dear sir, thou art wrong.
Of what blamest thou me? The apple which I look upon is forbidden me
to eat, not to behold.'"

> Lordynges that be now here,
> If ye wille listene and lere [1]
> All the story of Inglande,
> Als Robert Mannyng wryten it fand,
> And on Inglysch has it schewed,
> Not for the lered [2] but for the lewed, [3]
> For tho that on this land wonn [4]
> That ne Latin ne Frankys conn, [5]
> For to hauf solace and gamen
> In felauschip when they sitt samen; [6]
> And it is wisdom for to wytten [7]
> The state of the land, and haf it wryten.

The Norman Conquest. For a century after the Norman conquest
native poetry disappeared from England, as a river may sink into
the earth to reappear elsewhere with added volume and new characteristics. During all this time French was the language not only of literature but of society and business; and if anyone had declared at the beginning of the twelfth century, when Norman institutions were firmly established in England, that the time was approaching

DOMESDAY BOOK

From a facsimile edition published in 1862. The volumes,
two in number, were kept in the chest here shown

when the conquerors would forget their fatherland and their mother
tongue, he would surely have been called dreamer or madman. Yet the
unexpected was precisely what happened, and the Norman conquest
is remarkable alike for what it did and for what it failed to do.

[1] learn.   [2] learned.   [3] simple or ignorant.   [4] those that dwell.
[5] That neither Latin nor French know.   [6] together.   [7] know.

It accomplished, first, the nationalization of England, uniting the petty Saxon earldoms into one powerful kingdom; and second, it brought into English life, grown sad and stern, like a man without hope, the spirit of youth, of enthusiasm, of eager adventure after the unknown, — in a word, the spirit of romance, which is but another name for that quest of some Holy Grail in which youth is forever engaged.

Norman Literature. One who reads the literature that the conquerors brought to England must be struck by the contrast between the Anglo-Saxon and the Norman-French spirit. For example, here is the death of a national hero as portrayed in *The Song of Roland*, an old French epic, which the Normans first put into polished verse:

> Li quens Rollans se jut desuz un pin,
> Envers Espaigne en ad turnet son vis,
> De plusurs choses a remembrer le prist. . . .

"Then Roland placed himself beneath a pine tree. Towards Spain he turned his face. Of many things took he remembrance: of various lands where he had made conquests; of sweet France and his kindred; of Charlemagne, his feudal lord, who had nurtured him. He could not refrain from sighs and tears; neither could he forget himself in need. He confessed his sins and besought the Lord's mercy. He raised his right glove and offered it to God; Saint Gabriel from his hand received the offering. Then upon his breast he bowed his head; he joined his hands and went to his end. God sent down his cherubim, and Saint Michael who delivers from peril. Together with Saint Gabriel they departed, bearing the Count's soul to Paradise."

We have not put Roland's ceremonious exit into rime and meter; neither do we offer any criticism of a scene in which the death of a national hero stirs no interest or emotion, not even with the help of Gabriel and the cherubim. One is reminded by contrast of Scyld, who fares forth alone in his Viking ship to meet the mystery of death; or of that last scene of human grief and grandeur in *Beowulf* where a few thanes bury their dead chief on a headland by the gray sea, riding their war steeds around the memorial mound with a chant of sorrow and victory.

The contrast is even more marked in the mass of Norman literature: in romances of the maidens that sink underground in autumn, to reappear as flowers in spring; of Alexander's journey to the bottom of the sea in a crystal barrel, to view the mermaids and monsters; of Guy of Warwick, who slew the giant Colbrant and overthrew all the

knights of Europe, just to win a smile from his Felice; of that other
hero who had offended his lady by forgetting one of the commandments of love, and who vowed to fill a barrel with his tears, and did
it. The Saxons were as serious in speech as in action, and their poetry
is a true reflection of their daily life; but the Normans, brave and re-
sourceful as they were in war and statesmanship, turned to literature
for amusement, and indulged their lively fancy in fables, satires, garrulous romances, like children reveling in the lore of elves and fairies.
As the prattle of a child was the power that awakened Silas Marner
from his stupor of despair, so this Norman element of gayety, of exuberant romanticism, was
precisely what was needed
to rouse the sterner Saxon
mind from its gloom and
lethargy.

THE NORMAN STAIR, CANTERBURY
CATHEDRAL

The New Nation. So
much, then, the Normans
accomplished: they brought
nationality into English life,
and romance into English
literature. Without essentially changing the Saxon
spirit they enlarged its
thought, aroused its hope,
gave it wider horizons.
They bound England with
their laws, covered it with
their feudal institutions,
filled it with their ideas and their language; then, as an anticlimax, they
disappeared from English history, and their institutions were modified
to suit the Saxon temperament. The race conquered in war became in
peace the conquerors. The Normans speedily forgot France, and even
warred against it. They began to speak English, dropping its cumber-
some Teutonic inflections, and adding to it the wealth of their own
fine language. They ended by adopting England as their country, and
glorifying it above all others. " There is no land in the world," writes
a poet of the thirteenth century, " where so many good kings and
saints have lived as in the isle of the English. Some were holy martyrs
who died cheerfully for God; others had strength or courage like to
that of Arthur, Edmund and Cnut."

This poet, who was a Norman monk at Westminster Abbey, wrote about the glories of England in the French language, and celebrated as the national heroes a Celt, a Saxon and a Dane.[1]

So in the space of two centuries a new nation had arisen, combining the best elements of the Anglo-Saxon and Norman-French people, with a considerable mixture of Celtic and Danish elements. Out of the union of these races and tongues came modern English life and letters.

Geoffrey and the Legends of Arthur. Geoffrey of Monmouth was a Welshman, familiar from his youth with Celtic legends; also he was a monk who knew how to write Latin; and the combination was a fortunate one, as we shall see.

Long before Geoffrey produced his celebrated History (*cir.* 1150), many stories of the Welsh hero Arthur[2] were current in Britain and on the Continent; but they were never written because of a custom of the Middle Ages which required that, before a legend could be recorded, it must have the authority of some Latin manuscript. Geoffrey undertook to supply such authority in his *Historia regum britanniae*, or History of the Kings of Britain, in which he proved Arthur's descent from Roman ancestors.[3] He quoted liberally from an ancient manuscript which, he alleged, established Arthur's lineage, but which he did not show to others. A storm instantly arose among the writers of that day, most of whom

[1] The significance of this old poem was pointed out by Jusserand, *Literary History of the English People*, Vol. I, p. 112.

[2] Who Arthur was has never been determined. There was probably a chieftain of that name who was active in opposing the Anglo-Saxon invaders of Britain, about the year 500; but Gildas, who wrote a Chronicle of Britain only half a century later, does not mention him; neither does Bede, who made study of all available records before writing his History. William of Malmesbury, a chronicler of the twelfth century, refers to " the warlike Arthur of whom the Britons tell so many extravagant fables, a man to be celebrated not in idle tales but in true history." He adds that there were two Arthurs, one a Welsh war-chief (not a king), and the other a myth or fairy creation. This, then, may be the truth of the matter, that a real Arthur, who made a deep impression on the Celtic imagination, was soon hidden in a mass of spurious legends. That Bede had heard these legends is almost certain; that he did not mention them is probably due to the fact that he considered Arthur to be wholly mythical.

[3] After the landing of the Romans in Britain a curious mingling of traditions took place, and in Geoffrey's time native Britons considered themselves as children of Brutus of Rome, and therefore as grandchildren of Æneas of Troy.

denounced Geoffrey's Latin manuscript as a myth, and his History as a shameless invention. But he had shrewdly anticipated such criticism, and issued this warning to the historians, which is solemn or humorous according to your point of view :

" I forbid William of Malmesbury and Henry of Huntingdon to speak of the kings of Britain, since they have not seen the book which Walter Archdeacon of Oxford [who was dead, of course] brought out of Brittany."

It is commonly believed that Geoffrey was an impostor, but in such matters one should be wary of passing judgment. Many records of men, cities, empires, have suddenly arisen from the tombs to put to shame the scientists who had denied their existence ; and it is possible that Geoffrey had seen one of the legion of lost manuscripts. The one thing certain is, that if he had any authority for his History he embellished the same freely from popular legends or from his own imagination, as was customary at that time.

His work made a sensation. A score of French poets seized upon his Arthurian legends and wove them into romances, **Arthurian** each adding freely to Geoffrey's narrative. The **Romances** poet Wace added the tale of the Round Table, and another poet (Walter Map, perhaps) began a cycle of stories concerning Galahad and the quest of the Holy Grail.[1]

The origin of these Arthurian romances, which reappear so often in English poetry, is forever shrouded in mystery. The point to remember is, that we owe them all to the genius of the native Celts ; that it was Geoffrey of Monmouth who first wrote them in Latin prose, and so preserved a treasure which else had been lost ; and that it was the French *trouvères*, or poets, who completed the various cycles of romances which were later collected in Malory's *Morte d'Arthur*.

Types of Middle-English Literature. It has long been customary to begin the study of English literature with Chaucer;

---

[1] The Holy Grail, or San Graal, or Sancgreal, was represented as the cup from which Christ drank with his disciples at the Last Supper. Legend said that the sacred cup had been brought to England, and Arthur's knights undertook, as the most compelling of all duties, to search until they found it.

but that does not mean that he invented any new form of poetry or prose. To examine any collection of our early literature, such as Cook's *Middle-English Reader*, is to discover that many literary types were flourishing in Chaucer's day, and that some of these had grown old-fashioned before he began to use them.

In the thirteenth century, for example, the favorite type of literature in England was the metrical romance, which was **Metrical** introduced by the French poets, and written at first **Romances** in the French language. The typical romance was a rambling story dealing with the three subjects of love, chivalry and religion; it was filled with adventures among giants, dragons, enchanted castles; and in that day romance was not romance unless liberally supplied with magic and miracle. There were hundreds of such wonder-stories, arranged loosely in three main groups : the so-called " matter of Rome " dealt with the fall of Troy in one part, and with the marvelous adventures of Alexander in the other ; the " matter of France " celebrated the heroism of Charlemagne and his Paladins ; and the " matter of Britain " wove the magic web of romance around Arthur and his knights of the Round Table.

One of the best of the metrical romances is " Sir Gawain and the Green Knight," which may be read as a measure of all the rest. If, as is commonly believed, the unknown author of " Sir Gawain " wrote also " The Pearl " (a beautiful old elegy, or poem of grief, which immortalizes a father's love for his little girl), he was the greatest poet of the early Middle-English period. Unfortunately for us, he wrote not in the king's English or speech of London (which became modern English) but in a different dialect, and his poems should be read in a present-day version ; else will the beauty of his work be lost in our effort to understand his language.

Other types of early literature are the riming chronicles or verse histories (such as Layamon's *Brut*, a famous poem, in which the Arthurian legends appear as part of English history),

stories of travel, translations, religious poems, books of devotion, miracle plays, fables, satires, ballads, hymns, lullabies,
lyrics of love and nature, — an astonishing collection for so
ancient a time, indicative at once of our changing standards of
poetry and of our unchanging human nature. For the feelings
which inspired or gave welcome to these poems, some five or
six hundred years ago, are precisely the same feelings which
warm the heart of a poet and his readers to-day. There is
nothing ancient but the spelling in this exquisite Lullaby, for
instance, which was sung on Christmas eve :

> He cam also stylle
>   Ther his moder was
> As dew in Aprylle
>   That fallyt on the gras;
> He cam also stylle
>   To his moderes bowr
> As dew in Aprylle
>   That fallyt on the flour;
> He cam also stylle
>   Ther his moder lay
> As dew in Aprylle
>   That fallyt on the spray.[1]

Or witness this other fragment from an old love song, which
reflects the feeling of one who " would fain make some mirth "
but who finds his heart sad within him :

> Now wold I fayne som myrthis make
> All oneli for my ladys sake,
>   When I hir se;
> But now I am so ferre from hir
>   Hit will nat be.
>
> Thogh I be long out of hir sight,
> I am hir man both day and night,
>   And so will be;
> Wherfor, wold God as I love hir
>   That she lovd me !

---

[1] In reading this beautiful old lullaby the *e* in "stylle" and "Aprylle" should be lightly
sounded, like *a* in " China."

When she is mery, then I am glad;
When she is sory, then am I sad,
   And causë whi:
For he livith nat that lovith hir
   So well as I.

She sayth that she hath seen hit wreten
That 'seldyn seen is soon foryeten.'
   Hit is nat so;
For in good feith, save oneli hir,
   I love no moo.

Wherfor I pray, both night and day,
That she may cast al care away,
   And leve in rest
That evermo, where'er she be,
   I love hir best;

And I to hir for to be trew,
And never chaunge her for noon new
   Unto myne ende;
And that I may in hir servise
   For evyr amend.[1]

Summary of Beginnings. The two main branches of our literature are the Anglo-Saxon and the Norman-French, both of which received some additions from Celtic, Danish and Roman sources. The Anglo-Saxon literature came to England with the invasion of Teutonic tribes, the Angles, Saxons and Jutes (*cir.* 449). The Norman-French literature appeared after the Norman conquest of England, which began with the Battle of Hastings in 1066.

The Anglo-Saxon literature is classified under two heads, pagan and Christian. The extant fragments of pagan literature include one epic or heroic poem, *Beowulf,* and several lyrics and battle songs, such as "Widsith," "Deor's Lament," "The Seafarer," "The Battle of Brunanburh" and "The Battle of Maldon." All these were written at an unknown date, and by unknown poets.

The best Christian literature of the period was written in the Northumbrian and the West-Saxon schools. The greatest names of the

---

[1] The two poems quoted above hardly belong to the Norman-French period proper, but rather to a time when the Anglo-Saxon had assimilated the French element, with its language and verse forms. They were written, probably, in the age of Chaucer, or in what is now called the Late Middle-English period.

Northumbrian school are Bede, Cædmon and Cynewulf. The most famous of the Wessex writers is Alfred the Great, who is called " the father of English prose."

The Normans were originally Northmen, or sea rovers from Scandinavia, who settled in northern France and adopted the Franco-Latin language and civilization. With their conquest of England, in the eleventh century, they brought nationality into English life, and the spirit of romance into English literature. Their stories in prose or verse were extremely fanciful, in marked contrast with the stern, somber poetry of the Anglo-Saxons.

The most notable works of the Norman-French period are: Geoffrey's *History of the Kings of Britain*, which preserved in Latin prose the native legends of King Arthur; Layamon's *Brut*, a riming chronicle or verse history in the native tongue; many metrical romances, or stories of love, chivalry, magic and religion; and various popular songs and ballads. The greatest poet of the period is the unknown author of " Sir Gawain and the Green Knight " (a metrical romance) and probably also of " The Pearl," a beautiful elegy, which is our earliest *In Memoriam*.

Selections for Reading. Without special study of Old English it is impossible to read our earliest literature. The beginner may, however, enter into the spirit of that literature by means of various modern versions, such as the following:

Beowulf. Garnett's Beowulf (Ginn and Company), a literal translation, is useful to those who study Anglo-Saxon, but is not very readable. The same may be said of Gummere's The Oldest English Epic, which follows the verse form of the original. Two of the best versions for the beginner are Child's Beowulf, in Riverside Literature Series (Houghton), and Earle's The Deeds of Beowulf (Clarendon Press).

Anglo-Saxon Poetry. The Seafarer, The Wanderer, The Husband's Message (or Love Letter), Deor's Lament, Riddles, Battle of Brunanburh, selections from The Christ, Andreas, Elene, Vision of the Rood, and The Phœnix, — all these are found in an excellent little volume, Cook and Tinker, Translations from Old English Poetry (Ginn and Company).

Anglo-Saxon Prose. Good selections in Cook and Tinker, Translations from Old English Prose (Ginn and Company). Bede's History, translated in Everyman's Library (Dutton) and in the Bohn Library (Macmillan). In the same volume of the Bohn Library is a translation of The Anglo-Saxon Chronicle. Alfred's Orosius (with stories of early exploration) translated in Pauli's Life of Alfred.

Norman-French Period. Selections in Manly, English Poetry, and English Prose (Ginn and Company); also in Morris and Skeat, Specimens of Early English (Clarendon Press). The Song of Roland in Riverside Literature Series, and in King's Classics. Selected metrical romances in Ellis Specimens of Early English Metrical Romances (Bohn Library);

also in Morley, Early English Prose Romances, and in Carisbrooke Library Series. Sir Gawain and the Green Knight, modernized by Weston, in Arthurian Romances Series. Andrew Lang, Aucassin and Nicolette (Crowell). The Pearl, translated by Jewett (Crowell), and by Weir Mitchell (Century). Selections from Layamon's Brut in Morley, English Writers, Vol. III. Geoffrey's History in Everyman's Library, and in King's Classics. The Arthurian legends in The Mabinogion (Everyman's Library); also in Sidney Lanier's The Boy's King Arthur and The Boy's Mabinogion (Scribner). A good single volume containing the best of Middle-English literature, with notes, is Cook, A Literary Middle-English Reader (Ginn and Company).

Bibliography. For extended works covering the entire field of English history and literature, and for a list of the best anthologies, school texts, etc., see the General Bibliography. The following works are of special interest in studying early English literature.

History. Allen, Anglo-Saxon Britain; Turner, History of the Anglo-Saxons; Ramsay, The Foundations of England; Freeman, Old English History; Cook, Life of Alfred; Freeman, Short History of the Norman Conquest; Jewett, Story of the Normans, in Stories of the Nations.

Literature. Brooke, History of Early English Literature; Jusserand, Literary History of the English People, Vol. I; Ten Brink, English Literature, Vol. I; Lewis, Beginnings of English Literature; Schofield, English Literature from the Norman Conquest to Chaucer; Brother Azarias, Development of Old-English Thought; Mitchell, From Celt to Tudor; Newell, King Arthur and the Round Table. A more advanced work on Arthur is Rhys, Studies in the Arthurian Legends.

Fiction and Poetry. Kingsley, Hereward the Wake; Lytton, Harold Last of the Saxon Kings; Scott, Ivanhoe; Kipling, Puck of Pook's Hill; Jane Porter, Scottish Chiefs; Shakespeare, King John; Tennyson, Becket, and The Idylls of the King; Gray, The Bard; Bates and Coman, English History Told by English Poets.

CHAPTER III

THE AGE OF CHAUCER AND THE REVIVAL OF LEARNING
(1350–1550)

> For out of oldë feldës, as men seith,
>   Cometh al this newë corn fro yeer te yere;
> And out of oldë bokës, in good feith,
>   Cometh all this newë science that men lere.
>
> Chaucer, " Parliament of Foules "

Specimens of the Language. Our first selection, from *Piers Plowman* (*cir.* 1362), is the satire of Belling the Cat. The language is that of the common people, and the verse is in the old Saxon manner, with accent and alliteration. The scene is a council of rats and mice (common people) called to consider how best to deal with the cat (court), and it satirizes the popular agitators who declaim against the government. The speaker is a rat, "a raton of renon, most renable of tonge ":

" I have y-seen segges," quod he,

  " in the cite of London
Beren beighes ful brighte
  abouten here nekkes. . . .
Were there a belle on here beighe,
  certes, as me thynketh,
Men myghte wite where thei went,
  and awei renne!
And right so," quod this raton,
  " reson me sheweth
To bugge a belle of brasse
  or of brighte sylver,
And knitten on a colere
  for owre comune profit,
And hangen it upon the cattes hals;
  than hear we mowen

" I have seen creatures " (dogs),
  quoth he,
  " in the city of London
Bearing collars full bright
  around their necks. . . .
Were there a bell on those collars,
  assuredly, in my opinion,
One might know where the dogs go,
  and run away from them !
And right so," quoth this rat,
  " reason suggests to me
To buy a bell of brass
  or of bright silver,
And tie it on a collar
  for our common profit,
And hang it on the cat's neck;
  in order that we may hear

Where he ritt or rest
    or renneth to playe." . . .
Alle this route of ratones
    to this reson thei assented;
Ac tho the belle was y-bought
    and on the beighe hanged,
Ther ne was ratoun in alle the route,
    for alle the rewme of Fraunce,
That dorst have y-bounden the belle
    aboute the cattis nekke.

Where he rides or rests
    or runneth to play." . . .
All this rout (crowd) of rats
    to this reasoning assented;
But when the bell was bought
    and hanged on the collar,
There was not a rat in the crowd
    that, for all the realm of France,
Would have dared to bind the bell
    about the cat's neck.

The second selection is from Chaucer's " Wife of Bath's Tale" (*cir.* 1375). It was written "in the French manner" with rime and meter, for the upper classes, and shows the difference between literary English and the speech of the common people :

In th' olde dayës of the Kyng Arthour,
Of which that Britons speken greet honour,
Al was this land fulfild of fayerye.
The elf-queene with hir joly companye
Dauncëd ful ofte in many a grenë mede;
This was the olde opinion, as I rede.
I speke of manye hundred yeres ago;
But now kan no man see none elvës mo.

The next two selections (written *cir.* 1450) show how rapidly the language was approaching modern English. The prose, from Malory's *Morte d' Arthur,* is the selection that Tennyson closely followed in his " Passing of Arthur." The poetry, from the ballad of " Robin Hood and the Monk," is probably a fifteenth-century version of a much older English song :

" ' Therefore,' sayd Arthur unto Syr Bedwere, ' take thou Excalybur my good swerde, and goo with it to yonder water syde, and whan thou comest there I charge the throwe my swerde in that water, and come ageyn and telle me what thou there seest.'

" ' My lord,' sayd Bedwere, ' your commaundement shal be doon, and lyghtly brynge you worde ageyn.'

" So Syr Bedwere departed; and by the waye he behelde that noble swerde, that the pomel and the hafte was al of precyous stones; and thenne he sayd to hym self, ' Yf I throwe this ryche swerde in the water, thereof shal never come good, but harme and losse.' And thenne Syr Bedwere hydde Excalybur under a tree."

In somer, when the shawes be sheyne,
    And leves be large and long,
Hit is full mery in feyr foreste
    To here the foulys song:

To se the dere draw to the dale,
    And leve the hillës hee,
And shadow hem in the levës grene,
    Under the grene-wode tre.

Historical Outline. The history of England during this period is largely a record of strife and confusion. The struggle of the House of Commons against the despotism of kings; the Hundred Years War with France, in which those whose fathers had been Celts, Danes, Saxons, Normans, were now fighting shoulder to shoulder as Englishmen all; the suffering of the common people, resulting in the Peasant Rebellion; the barbarity of the nobles, who were destroying one another in the Wars of the Roses; the beginning of commerce and manufacturing, following the lead of Holland, and the rise of a powerful middle class; the belated appearance of the Renaissance, welcomed by a few scholars but unnoticed by the masses of people, who remained in dense ignorance, — even such a brief catalogue suggests that many books must be read before we can enter into the spirit of fourteenth-century England. We shall note here only two circumstances, which may help us to understand Chaucer and the age in which he lived.

The first is that the age of Chaucer, if examined carefully, shows many striking resemblances to our own. It was, for example, an age **Modern** of warfare; and, as in our own age of hideous inventions, **Problems** military methods were all upset by the discovery that the foot soldier with his blunderbuss was more potent than the panoplied knight on horseback. While war raged abroad, there was no end of labor troubles at home, strikes, "lockouts," assaults on imported workmen (the Flemish weavers brought in by Edward III), and no end of experimental laws to remedy the evil. The Turk came into Europe, introducing the Eastern and the Balkan questions, which have ever since troubled us. Imperialism was rampant, in Edward's claim to France, for example, or in John of Gaunt's attempt to annex Castile. Even "feminism" was in the air, and its merits were shrewdly debated by Chaucer's Wife of Bath and his Clerk of Oxenford. A dozen other "modern" examples might be given, but the sum of the matter is this: that there is hardly a social or political or economic problem of the past fifty years that was not violently agitated in the latter half of the fourteenth century.[1]

A second interesting circumstance is that this medieval age produced two poets, Langland and Chaucer, who were more realistic
Realistic   even than present-day writers in their portrayal of life,
Poetry   and who together gave us such a picture of English society as no other poets have ever equaled. Langland wrote his *Piers
Plowman* in the familiar Anglo-Saxon style for the common people,
and pictured their life to the letter; while Chaucer wrote his *Canterbury Tales*, a poem shaped after Italian and French models, portraying the holiday side of the middle and upper classes. Langland drew
a terrible picture of a degraded land, desperately in need of justice,
of education, of reform in church and state; Chaucer showed a gay
company of pilgrims riding through a prosperous country which he
called his " Merrie England." Perhaps the one thing in common with
these two poets, the early types of Puritan and Cavalier, was their
attitude towards democracy. Langland preached the gospel of labor,
far more powerfully than Carlyle ever preached it, and exalted honest
work as the patent of nobility. Chaucer, writing for the court, mingled
his characters in the most democratic kind of fellowship and, though
a knight rode at the head of his procession, put into the mouth of the
Wife of Bath his definition of a gentleman:

> Loke who that is most vertuous alway,
> Privee and apert,[2] and most entendeth aye
> To do the gentle dedës that he can,
> And take him for the grettest gentilman.

Geoffrey Chaucer (*cir.* 1340–1400)

" Of Chaucer truly I know not whether to marvel more, either that he
in that misty time could see so clearly, or that we in this clear age walk so
stumblingly after him."

(Philip Sidney, *cir.* 1581)

It was the habit of Old-English chieftains to take their scops with them into battle, to the end that the scop's poem might be true to the outer world of fact as well as to the inner world of ideals. The search for " local color " is, therefore, not the

---

[1] See Kittredge, *Chaucer and his Poetry* (1915), pp. 2-5.
[2] Secretly and openly.

newest thing in fiction but the oldest thing in poetry. Chaucer, the first in time of our great English poets, was true to this old tradition. He was page, squire, soldier, statesman, diplomat, traveler; and then he was a poet, who portrayed in verse the many-colored life which he knew intimately at first hand.

For example, Chaucer had to describe a tournament, in the Knight's Tale; but instead of using his imagination, as other romancers had always done, he drew a vivid picture of one of

CHAUCER

those gorgeous pageants of decaying chivalry with which London diverted the French king, who had been brought prisoner to the city after the victory of the Black Prince at Poitiers. So with his Tabard Inn, which is a real English inn, and with his Pilgrims, who are real pilgrims; and so with every other scene or character he described. His specialty was human nature, his strong point observation, his method essentially modern. And by "modern" we mean that he portrayed the men and women of his own day so well, with such sympathy and humor and wisdom, that we recognize and welcome them as friends or neighbors, who are the same in all ages. From this viewpoint Chaucer is more modern than Tennyson or Longfellow.

Life. Chaucer's boyhood was spent in London, near Westminster, where the brilliant court of Edward was visible to the favored ones; and near the Thames, where the world's commerce, then beginning to ebb and flow with the tides, might be seen of every man. His father was a vintner, or wine merchant, who had enough influence at court

to obtain for his son a place in the house of the Princess Elizabeth.
Behold then our future poet beginning his knightly training as page
to a highborn lady. Presently he accompanied the Black Prince to the
French wars, was taken prisoner and ransomed, and on his return
entered the second stage of knighthood as esquire or personal attendant to the king. He married a maid of honor related to John of Gaunt,
the famous Duke of Lancaster, and at thirty had passed from the rank
of merchant into official and aristocratic circles.

The literary work of Chaucer is conveniently, but not accurately,
arranged in three different periods. While attached to the court, one
Periods of of his duties was to entertain the king and his visitors in
Work their leisure. French poems of love and chivalry were then
in demand, and of these Chaucer had great store; but English had
recently replaced French even at court, and King Edward and Queen
Philippa, both patrons of art and letters, encouraged Chaucer to write
in his native language. So he made translations of favorite poems into
English, and wrote others in imitation of French models. These early
works, the least interesting of all, belong to what is called the period
of French influence.

Then Chaucer, who had learned the art of silence as well as of
speech, was sent abroad on a series of diplomatic missions. In Italy
he probably met the poet Petrarch (as we infer from the Prologue to
the Clerk's Tale) and became familiar with the works of Dante and
Boccaccio. His subsequent poetry shows a decided advance in range
and originality, partly because of his own growth, no doubt, and partly
because of his better models. This second period, of about fifteen
years, is called the time of Italian influence.

In the third or English period Chaucer returned to London and was
a busy man of affairs; for at the English court, unlike those of France
and Italy, a poet was expected to earn his pension by some useful
work, literature being regarded as a recreation. He was in turn comp-
troller of customs and superintendent of public works; also he was at
times well supplied with money, and again, as the political fortunes of
his patron John of Gaunt waned, in sore need of the comforts of life.
Witness his "Complaint to His Empty Purse," the humor of which
evidently touched the king and brought Chaucer another pension.

Two poems of this period are supposed to contain autobiographical
material. In the *Legend of Good Women* he says:

> And as for me, though that my wit be lytë,
> On bokës for to rede I me delytë.

Again, in *The House of Fame* he speaks of finding his real life in books after his daily work in the customhouse is ended. Some of the "rekeninges" (itemized accounts of goods and duties) to which he refers are still preserved in Chaucer's handwriting:

> For whan thy labour doon al is,
> And hast y-maad thy rekeninges,
> In stede of reste and newë thinges
> Thou gost hoom to thy hous anoon,
> And, also domb as any stoon,
> Thou sittest at another boke
> Til fully dawsëd is thy loke,
> And livest thus as an hermytë,
> Although thine abstinence is lytë.

Such are the scanty facts concerning England's first great poet, the more elaborate biographies being made up chiefly of guesses or doubtful inferences. He died in the year 1400, and was buried in St. Benet's chapel in Westminster Abbey, a place now revered by all lovers of literature as the Poets' Corner.

On Reading Chaucer. Said Caxton, who was the first to print Chaucer's poetry, " He writeth no void words, but all his matter is full of high and quick sentence." Caxton was right, and the modern reader's first aim should be to get the sense of Chaucer rather than his pronunciation. To understand him is not so difficult as appears at first sight, for most of the words that look strange because of their spelling will reveal their meaning to the ear if spoken aloud. Thus the word "leefful" becomes "leveful" or "leaveful" or "permissible."

Next, the reader should remember that Chaucer was a master of versification, and that every stanza of his is musical. At the beginning of a poem, therefore, read a few lines aloud, emphasizing the accented syllables until the rhythm is fixed; then make every line conform to it, and every word keep step to the music. To do this it is necessary to slur certain words and run others together; also, since the mistakes of Chaucer's copyists are repeated in modern editions, it is often necessary to add a helpful word or syllable to a line, or to omit others that are plainly superfluous.

This way of reading Chaucer musically, as one would read any other poet, has three advantages: it is easy, it is pleasant, and it is far more effective than the learning of a hundred specifications laid down by the grammarians.

As for Chaucer's pronunciation, you will not get that accurately without much study, which were better spent on more important **Rules for** matters; so be content with a few rules, which aim **Reading** simply to help you enjoy the reading. As a general principle, the root vowel of a word was broadly sounded, and the rest slurred over. The characteristic sound of *a* was as in "far"; *e* was sounded like *a*, *i* like *e*, and all diphthongs as broadly as possible, — in "floures" (flowers), for example, which should be pronounced "floorës."

Another rule relates to final syllables, and these will appear more interesting if we remember that they represent the dying inflections of nouns and adjectives, which were then declined as in modern German. Final *ed* and *es* are variable, but the rhythm will always tell us whether they should be given an extra syllable or not. So also with final *e*, which is often sounded, but not if the following word begins with a vowel or with *h*. In the latter case the two words may be run together, as in reading Virgil. If a final *e* occurs at the end of a line, it may be lightly pronounced, like *a* in "China," to give added melody to the verse.

Applying these rules, and using our liberty as freely as Chaucer used his,[1] the opening lines of *The Canterbury Tales* would read something like this:

> Whan that Aprille with his shoures sote
> *Whan that Apreelë with 'is shoorës sohtë*

> The droghte of Marche hath perced to the rote,
> *The drooth of March hath paarcëd to the rohtë,*

> And bathed every veyne in swich licour,
> *And bahthëd ev'ree vyne in swech lecoor,*

> Of which vertu engendred is the flour;
> *Of whech varetu engendred is the floor;*

> Whan Zephirus eek with his swete breeth
> *Whan Zephirus aik with 'is swaite braith*

> Inspired hath in every holt and heeth
> *Inspeerëd hath in ev'ree holt and haith*

---

[1] The language was changing rapidly in Chaucer's day, and there were no printed books to fix a standard. Sometimes Chaucer's grammar and spelling are according to rule, and again as heaven pleases.

The tendre croppes, and the yonge sonne
The tendre croopës, and th' yoongë sonnë

Hath in the Ram his halfe cours y-ronne,
Hath in the Ram 'is hawfë coors ironnë,

And smale fowles maken melodye,
And smawlë foolës mahken malyodieë,

That slepen al the night with open ye
That slaipen awl the nicht with open eë

(So priketh hem nature in hir corages)
(So priketh 'eem nahtur in hir coorahgës)

Than longen folk to goon on pilgrimages.
Than longen folk to goon on peelgrimahgës.

Early Works of Chaucer. In his first period, which was dominated by French influence, Chaucer probably translated parts of the *Roman de la Rose*, a dreary allegorical poem in which love is represented as a queen-rose in a garden, surrounded by her court and ministers. In endeavoring to pluck this rose the lover learns the "commandments" and "sacraments" of love, and meets with various adventures at the hands of Virtue, Constancy, and other shadowy personages of less repute. Such allegories were the delight of the Middle Ages; now they are as dust and ashes. Other and better works of this period are *The Book of the Duchess*, an elegy written on the death of Blanche, wife of Chaucer's patron, and various minor poems, such as "Compleynte unto Pitee," the dainty love song "To Rosemunde," and "Truth" or the "Ballad of Good Counsel."

Characteristic works of the second or Italian period are *The House of Fame*, *The Legend of Good Women*, and especially *Troilus and Criseyde*. The last-named, though little known to modern readers, is one of the most remarkable narrative poems in our literature. It began as a retelling of a familiar romance; it ended in an original poem, which might easily be made into a drama or a "modern" novel.

The scene opens in Troy, during the siege of the city by the Greeks. The hero Troilus is a son of Priam, and is second only to the mighty

Story of Troilus

Hector in warlike deeds. Devoted as he is to glory, he scoffs at lovers until the moment when his eye lights on Cressida. She is a beautiful young widow, and is free to do as she pleases for the moment, her father Calchas having gone over to the Greeks to escape the doom which he sees impending on Troy. Troilus falls desperately in love with Cressida, but she does not know or care, and he is ashamed to speak his mind after scoffing so long at love. Then appears Pandarus, friend of Troilus and uncle to Cressida, who soon learns the secret and brings the young people together. After a long courtship with interminable speeches (as in the old romances) Troilus wins the lady, and all goes happily until Calchas arranges to have his daughter brought to him in exchange for a captured Trojan warrior. The lovers are separated with many tears, but Cressida comforts the despairing Troilus by promising to hoodwink her doting father and return in a few days. Calchas, however, loves his daughter too well to trust her in a city that must soon be given over to plunder, and keeps her safe in the Greek camp. There the handsome young Diomede wins her, and presently Troilus is killed in battle by Achilles.

Such is the old romance of feminine fickleness, which had been written a hundred times before Chaucer took it bodily from Boccaccio. Moreover he humored the old romantic delusion which required that a lover should fall sick in the absence of his mistress, and turn pale or swoon at the sight of her; but he added to the tale many elements not found in the old romances, such as real men and women, humor, pathos, analysis of human motives, and a sense of impending tragedy which comes not from the loss of wealth or happiness but of character. Cressida's final thought of her first lover is intensely pathetic, and a whole chapter of psychology is summed up in the line in which she promises herself to be true to Diomede at the very moment when she is false to Troilus:

> " Allas ! of me unto the worldës ende
> Shal neyther ben ywriten nor y-songë
> No good word; for these bookës wol me shende.
> O, rollëd shal I ben on many a tongë !
> Thurghout the world my bellë shal be rongë,
> And wommen moste wol haten me of allë.
> Allas, that swich a cas me sholdë fallë !

" They wol seyn, in-as-much as in me is,
I have hem doon dishonour, weylawey!
Al be I not the firste that dide amis,
What helpeth that to doon my blame awey?
But since I see ther is no betre wey,
And that too late is now for me to rewë,
To Diomede, algate, I wol be trewë."

The Canterbury Tales. The plan of gathering a company of people and letting each tell his favorite story has been used by so many poets, ancient and modern, that it is idle to seek the origin of it. Like Topsy, it wasn't born; it just grew up. Chaucer's plan, however, is more comprehensive than any other in that it includes all classes of society; it is also more original in that it does not invent heroic characters but takes such men and women as one might meet in any assembly, and shows how typical they are of humanity in all ages. As Lowell says, Chaucer made use in his *Canterbury Tales* of two things that are everywhere regarded as symbols of human life; namely, the short journey and the inn. We might add, as an indication of Chaucer's philosophy, that his inn is a comfortable one, and that the journey is made in pleasant company and in fair weather.

An outline of Chaucer's great work is as follows. On an evening in springtime the poet comes to Tabard Inn, in Southwark, and finds it filled with a merry company of men and women bent on a pilgrimage to the shrine of Thomas à Becket in Canterbury.

After supper appears the jovial host, Harry Bailey, who finds the company so attractive that he must join it on its pilgrimage. He proposes that, as they shall be long on the way, they shall furnish their own entertainment by telling stories, the best tale to be rewarded by the best of suppers when the pilgrims return from Canterbury. They assent joyfully, and on the morrow begin their journey, cheered by the Knight's Tale as they ride forth under the sunrise. The light of morning and of springtime is upon this work, which is commonly placed at the beginning of modern English literature.

As the journey proceeds we note two distinct parts to Chaucer's record. One part, made up of prologues and interludes, portrays the characters and action of the present comedy;

the other part, consisting of stories, reflects the comedies and tragedies of long ago. The one shows the perishable side of the men and women of Chaucer's day, their habits, dress, conversation; the other reveals an imperishable world of thought, feeling, ideals, in which these same men and women discover their kinship to humanity. It is possible, since some of the stories are related to each other, that Chaucer meant to arrange the *Canterbury Tales* in dramatic unity, so as to make a huge comedy of human society; but the work as it comes

PILGRIMS SETTING OUT FROM THE "TABARD"

down to us is fragmentary, and no one has discovered the order in which the fragments should be fitted together.

The Prologue is perhaps the best single fragment of the *Canterbury Tales*. In it Chaucer introduces us to the characters of his drama: to the grave Knight and the gay

The Prologue Squire, the one a model of Chivalry at its best, "a verray parfit gentil knight," the other a young man so full of life and love that "he slept namore than dooth a nightingale"; to the modest Prioress, also, with her pretty clothes, her exquisite manners, her boarding-school accomplishments:

> And Frensh she spak ful faire and fetisly,
> After the scole of Stratford attë Bowë,
> For Frensh of Paris was to hir unknowë.

In contrast to this dainty figure is the coarse Wife of Bath, as garrulous as the nurse in *Romeo and Juliet*. So one character stands to another as shade to light, as they appear in a typical novel of Dickens. The Church, the greatest factor in medieval life, is misrepresented by the hunting Monk and the begging Friar, and is well represented by the Parson, who practiced true religion before he preached it:

> But Christës lore and his apostles twelvë
> He taughte, and first he folwëd it himselvë.

Trade is represented by the Merchant, scholarship by the poor Clerk of Oxenford, the professions by the Doctor and the Man-of-law, common folk by the Yeoman, Frankelyn (farmer), Miller and many others of low degree. Prominent among the latter was the Shipman:

> Hardy he was, and wys to undertakë;
> With many a tempest hadde his berd been shakë.

From this character, whom Stevenson might have borrowed for his *Treasure Island*, we infer the barbarity that prevailed when commerce was new, when the English sailor was by turns smuggler or pirate, equally ready to sail or scuttle a ship, and to silence any tongue that might tell tales by making its wretched owner " walk the plank." Chaucer's description of the latter process is a masterpiece of piratical humor:

> If that he faught and hadde the hyer hond,
> By water he sente hem hoom to every lond.

Some thirty pilgrims appear in the famous Prologue, and as each was to tell two stories on the way to Canterbury, and two

Variety of Tales more on the return, it is probable that Chaucer contemplated a work of more than a hundred tales. Only four-and-twenty were completed, but these are enough to cover the field of light literature in that day, from the romance of love to the humorous animal fable. Between these are wonder-stories of giants and fairies, satires on the, monks, parodies on literature, and some examples of coarse horseplay for which Chaucer offers an apology, saying that he must let each pilgrim tell his tale in his own way.

A round dozen of these tales may still be read with pleasure ; but, as a suggestion of Chaucer's variety, we name only three : the Knight's romance of " Palamon and Arcite," the Nun's Priest's fable of " Chanticleer," and the Clerk's old ballad of " Patient Griselda." The last-named will be more interesting if we remember that the subject of woman's rights had been hurled at the heads of the pilgrims by the Wife of Bath, and that the Clerk told his story to illustrate his different ideal of womanhood.

The Charm of Chaucer. The first of Chaucer's qualities is that he is an excellent story-teller ; which means that he has a tale to tell, a good method of telling it, and a philosophy of life which gives us something to think about aside from the narrative. He had a profound insight of human nature, and in telling the simplest story was sure to slip in some nugget of wisdom or humor : " What wol nat be mote need be left," " For three may keep counsel if twain be away," " The lyf so short, the craft so long to lerne," " Ful wys is he that can himselven knowe,"

> The firste vertue, sone, if thou wilt lere,
> Is to restreine and kepen wel thy tonge.

There are literally hundreds of such " good things " which make Chaucer a constant delight to those who, by a very little practice, can understand him almost as easily as Shakespeare. Moreover he was a careful artist ; he knew the principles of poetry and of story-telling, and before he wrote a song or a tale he considered both his subject and his audience, repeating to himself his own rule :

> Ther nis no werkman, whatsoever he be,
> That may bothe werkë wel and hastily :
> This wol be doon at leysur, parfitly.

A second quality of Chaucer is his power of observation, a power so extraordinary that, unlike other poets, he did not need to invent scenes or characters but only to describe what he had seen and heard in this wonderful world. As he makes one of his characters say :

> For certeynly, he that me made
> To comen hider seydë me :
> I shouldë bothë hear et see
> In this place wonder thingës.

In the *Canterbury Tales* alone he employs more than a score of characters, and hardly a romantic hero among them ; rather does he delight in plain men and women, who reveal their quality not so much in their action as in their dress, manner, or tricks of speech. For Chaucer has the glance of an Indian, which passes over all obvious matters to light upon one significant detail ; and that detail furnishes the name or the adjective of the object. Sometimes his descriptions of men or nature are microscopic in their accuracy, and again in a single line he awakens the reader's imagination, — as when Pandarus (in *Troilus*), in order to make himself unobtrusive in a room where he is not wanted, picks up a manuscript and " makes a face," that is, he pretends to be absorbed in a story,

> and fand his countenance
> As for to loke upon an old romance.

A dozen striking examples might be given, but we shall note only one. In the *Book of the Duchess* the poet is in a forest, when a chase sweeps by with whoop of huntsman and clamor of hounds. After the hunt, when the woods are all still, comes a little lost dog :

> Hit com and creep to me as lowë
> Right as hit haddë me y-knowë,
> Hild down his heed and jiyned his eres,
> And leyde al smouthë doun his heres.
> I wolde han caught hit, and anoon
> Hit fleddë and was fro me goon.

Next to his power of description, Chaucer's best quality is his humor, a humor which is hard to phrase, since it runs from **Chaucer's** the keenest wit to the broadest farce, yet is always **Humor** kindly and human. A mendicant friar comes in out of the cold, glances about the snug kitchen for the best seat :

> And fro the bench he droof awey the cat.

Sometimes his humor is delicate, as in touching up the foibles of the Doctor or the Man-of-law, or in the Priest's translation of Chanticleer's evil remark about women :

> *In principio*
> *Mulier est hominis confusio.*
> Madame, the sentence of this Latin is :
> Woman is mannës joye and al his blis.

The humor broadens in the Wife of Bath, who tells how she managed several husbands by making their lives miserable ; and occasionally it grows a little grim, as when the Maunciple tells the difference between a big and a little rascal. The former does evil on a large scale, and,

> Lo ! therfor is he cleped a Capitain ;
> But for the outlawe hath but small meynee,
> And may not doon so gret an harm as he,
> Ne bring a countree to so gret mischeef,
> Men clepen him an outlawe or a theef.

A fourth quality of Chaucer is his broad tolerance, his abso-lute disinterestedness. He leaves reforms to Wyclif and Lang-**Freedom** land, and can laugh with the Shipman who turns **from Bias** smuggler, or with the worldly Monk whose " jin-gling " bridle keeps others as well as himself from hearing the chapel bell. He will not even criticize the fickle Cressida for deserting Troilus, saying that men tell tales about her, which is punishment enough for any woman. In fine, Chaucer is con-tent to picture a world in which the rain falleth alike upon the just and the unjust, and in which the latter seem to have a liberal share of the umbrellas. He enjoys it all, and describes

E

its inhabitants as they are, not as he thinks they ought to be. The reader may think that this or that character deserves to come to a bad end; but not so Chaucer, who regards them all as kindly, as impersonally as Nature herself.

So the Canterbury pilgrims are not simply fourteenth-century Englishmen; they are human types whom Chaucer met at the Tabard Inn, and whom later English writers discover on all of earth's highways. One appears unchanged in Shakespeare's drama, another in a novel of Jane Austen, a third lives over the way or down the street. From century to century they change not, save in name or dress. The poet who described or created such enduring characters stands among the few who are called universal writers.

CHAUCER'S CONTEMPORARIES AND SUCCESSORS

Someone has compared a literary period to a wood in which a few giant oaks lift head and shoulders above many other trees, all nourished by the same soil and air. If we follow this figure, Langland and Wyclif are the only growths that tower beside Chaucer, and Wyclif was a reformer who belongs to English history rather than to literature.

Langland. William Langland (*cir.* 1332–1400) is a great figure in obscurity. We are not certain even of his name, and we must search his work to discover that he was, probably, a poor lay-priest whose life was governed by two motives: a passion for the poor, which led him to plead their cause in poetry, and a longing for all knowledge:

> All the sciences under sonnë, and all the sotyle craftës,
> I wolde I knew and couthë, kyndely in mynë hertë.

His chief poem, *Piers Plowman* (*cir.* 1362), is a series of visions in which are portrayed the shams and impostures of the age and the misery of the common people. The poem is, therefore, as the heavy shadow which throws into relief the bright picture of the *Canterbury Tales*.

For example, while Chaucer portrays the Tabard Inn with its good cheer and merry company, Langland goes to another inn on the next street; there he looks with pure eyes upon sad or evil-faced men and women, drinking, gaming, quarreling, and pictures a scene of physical and moral degradation. One must look on both pictures to know what an English inn was like in the fourteenth century.

Because of its crude form and dialect *Piers Plowman* is hard to follow; but to the few who have read it and entered into Langland's vision — shared his passion for the poor, his hatred of shams, his belief in the gospel of honest work, his humor and satire and philosophy — it is one of the most powerful and original poems in English literature.[1]

Malory. Judged by its influence, the greatest prose work of the fifteenth century was the *Morte d'Arthur* of Thomas Malory (d. 1471). Of the English knight who compiled this work very little is known beyond this, that he sought to preserve in literature the spirit of medieval knighthood and religion. He tells us nothing of this purpose; but Caxton, who received the only known copy of Malory's manuscript and published it in 1485, seems to have reflected the author's spirit in these words:

" I according to my copy have set it in imprint, to the intent that noble men may see and learn the noble acts of chivalry, the gentle and virtuous deeds that some knyghts used in those days, by which they came to honour, and how they that were vicious were punished and put oft to shame and rebuke. . . . For herein may be seen noble chivalry, courtesy, humanity, hardness, love, friendship, cowardice, murder, hate, virtue and sin. Do after the good, and leave the evil, and it shall bring you to good fame and renommee."

[1] The working classes were beginning to assert themselves in this age, and to proclaim " the rights of man." Witness the followers of John Ball, and his influence over the crowd when he chanted the lines:

When Adam delved and Eve span,
Who was then the gentleman?

Langland's poem, written in the midst of the labor agitation, was the first glorification of labor to appear in English literature. Those who read it may make an interesting comparison between " Piers Plowman " and a modern labor poem, such as Hood's " Song of the Shirt " or Markham's " The Man with the Hoe."

Malory's spirit is further indicated by the fact that he passed over all extravagant tales of foreign heroes and used only the best of the Arthurian romances.[1] These had been left in a chaotic state by poets, and Malory brought order out of the chaos by omitting tedious fables and arranging his material in something like dramatic unity under three heads : the Coming of Arthur with its glorious promise, the Round Table, and the Search for the Holy Grail :

" And thenne the kynge and al estates wente home unto Camelot, and soo wente to evensonge to the grete mynster, and soo after upon that to

A STREET IN CAERLEON ON USK
The traditional home of King Arthur

souper; and every knyght sette in his owne place as they were to forehand. Thenne anone they herd crakynge and cryenge of thonder, that hem thought the place shold alle to dryve. In the myddes of this blast entred a sonne beaume more clerer by seven tymes than ever they sawe daye, and al they were alyghted of the grace of the Holy Ghoost. Then beganne every knyghte to behold other, and eyther sawe other by theire semynge fayrer than ever they sawe afore. Not for thenne there was no knyght myghte speke one word a grete whyle, and soo they loked every man on other, as

---

[1] For the origin of the Arthurian stories see p. 27. An example of the way these stories were enlarged is given by Lewis, *Beginnings of English Literature*, pp. 73-76, who records the story of Arthur's death as told, first, by Geoffrey, then by Layamon, and finally by Malory, who copied the tale from French sources. If we add Tennyson's " Passing of Arthur," we shall have the story as told from the twelfth to the nineteenth century.

they had ben domb. Thenne ther entred into the halle the Holy Graile, covered with whyte samyte, but ther was none myghte see hit, nor who bare hit. And there was al the halle fulfylled with good odoures, and every knyght had suche metes and drynkes as he best loved in this world. And when the Holy Grayle had be borne thurgh the halle, thenne the holy vessel departed sodenly, that they wyste not where hit becam. . . .

"'Now,' said Sir Gawayne, 'we have ben served this daye of what metes and drynkes we thoughte on, but one thynge begyled us; we myght not see the Holy Grayle, it was soo precyously coverd. Therfor I wil mak here avowe, that to morne, withoute lenger abydyng, I shall laboure in the quest of the Sancgreal; that I shalle hold me oute a twelve moneth and a day, or more yf nede be, and never shalle I retorne ageyne unto the courte tyl I have sene hit more openly than hit hath ben sene here.' . . . Whan they of the Table Round herde Syr Gawayne saye so, they arose up the most party and maade suche avowes as Sire Gawayne had made."

Into this holy quest sin enters like a serpent; then in quick succession tragedy, rebellion, the passing of Arthur, the penitence of guilty Launcelot and Guinevere. The figures fade away at last, as Shelley says of the figures of the Iliad, "in tenderness and inexpiable sorrow."

As the best of Malory's work is now easily accessible, we forbear further quotation. These old Arthurian legends, the common inheritance of all English-speaking people, should be known to every reader. As they appear in *Morte d'Arthur* they are notable as an example of fine old English prose, as a reflection of the enduring ideals of chivalry, and finally as a storehouse in which Spenser, Tennyson and many others have found material for some of their noblest poems.

Caxton. William Caxton (d. 1491) is famous for having brought the printing press to England, but he has other claims to literary renown. He was editor as well as printer; he translated more than a score of the books which came from his press; and, finally, it was he who did more than any other man to fix a standard of English speech.

In Caxton's day several dialects were in use, and, as we infer from one of his prefaces, he was doubtful which was most suitable for literature or most likely to become the common speech of England. His doubt was dissolved by the time he had printed the *Canterbury Tales* and the *Morte d'Arthur*. Many other works followed in the same "King's English"; his successor at the printing press, Wynkyn de Worde, continued in the same line; and when, less than sixty years after the first English book was printed, Tyndale's translation of the New Testament had found its way to every shire in England, there was no longer room for doubt that the East-Midland dialect had become the standard of the English nation. We have been speaking and writing that dialect ever since.

The story of how printing came to England, not as a literary but as a business venture, is

Story of the Printing Press

a very interesting one. Caxton was an English merchant who had established himself at Bruges, then one of the trading centers of Europe. There his business prospered, and he became governor of the *Domus Angliae*, or House of the English Guild of Merchant Adventurers. There is romance

THE ALMONRY, WESTMINSTER

Caxton's printing office. From an old print

in the very name. With moderate wealth came leisure to Caxton, and he indulged his literary taste by writing his own version of some popular romances concerning the siege of Troy, being encouraged by the English princess Margaret, Duchess of Burgundy, into whose service he had entered.

Copies of his work being in demand, Caxton consulted the professional copyists, whose beautiful work we read about in a remarkable novel called *The Cloister and the Hearth*. Then suddenly came to Bruges the rumor of Gutenberg's discovery of printing from movable types, and Caxton hastened to Germany to investigate the matter, led by the desire to get copies of his own work as cheaply as possible. The discovery fascinated him; instead of a few copies of his manuscript he brought back to Bruges a press, from which he issued his *Recuyell of the Historyes of Troy* (1474), which was probably the first book to appear in English print. Quick to see the commercial advantages of the new invention, Caxton moved his printing press to London, near Westminster Abbey, where he brought out in 1477 his *Dictes and Sayinges of the Philosophers*, the first book ever printed on English soil.[1]

From the very outset Caxton's venture was successful, and he was soon busy in supplying books that were most in demand. He has been criticized for not printing the classics and other books of the New Learning; but he evidently knew his business and his audience, and aimed to give people what they wanted, not what he thought they ought to have. Chaucer's *Canterbury Tales*, Malory's *Morte d'Arthur*, Mandeville's *Travels*, Æsop's *Fables*, parts of the *Æneid*, translations of French romances, lives of the saints (The Golden Legend), cookbooks, prayer books, books of etiquette, — the list of Caxton's eighty-odd publications becomes significant when we remember that he printed only popular books, and that the titles indicate the taste of the age which first looked upon the marvel of printing.

The First Printed Books

Popular Ballads. If it be asked, "What is a ballad?" any positive answer will lead to disputation. Originally the ballad was probably a chant to accompany a dance, and so it represents the earliest form of poetry. In theory, as various definitions indicate, it is a short poem telling a story of some exploit, usually of a valorous kind. In common practice, from Chaucer to Tennyson, the ballad is almost any kind of short poem treating of any event, grave or gay, in any descriptive or dramatic way that appeals to the poet.

[1] Another book of Caxton's, *The Game and Playe of the Chesse* (1475), was long accorded this honor, but it is fairly certain that the book on chess-playing was printed in Bruges.

For the origin of the ballad one must search far back among the social customs of primitive times. That the Anglo-Saxons were familiar with it appears from the record of Tacitus, who speaks of their *carmina* or narrative songs; but, with the exception of "The Fight at Finnsburgh" and a few other fragments, all these have disappeared.

During the Middle Ages ballads were constantly appearing among the common people,[1] but they were seldom written, and found no standing in polite literature. In the eighteenth century, however, certain men who had grown weary of the formal poetry of Pope and his school turned for relief to the old vigorous ballads of the people, and rescued them from oblivion. The one book to which, more than any other, we owe the revival of interest in balladry is *Percy's Reliques of Ancient English Poetry* (1765).

The best of our ballads date in their present form from the fifteenth or sixteenth century; but the originals were much **The Marks** older, and had been transmitted orally for years **of a Ballad** before they were recorded on manuscript. As we study them we note, as their first characteristic, that they spring from the unlettered common people, that they are by unknown authors, and that they appear in different versions because they were changed by each minstrel to suit his own taste or that of his audience.

A second characteristic is the objective quality of the ballad, which deals not with a poet's thought or feeling (such subjective emotions give rise to the lyric) but with a man or a deed. See in the ballad of "Sir Patrick Spence" (or Spens) how the unknown author goes straight to his story:

> The king sits in Dumferling towne,
> Drinking the blude-red wine:

---

[1] Thus, when Sidney says, "I never heard the old song of Percy and Douglass that I found not my heart moved more than with a trumpet," and when Shakespeare shows Autolycus at a country fair offering "songs for men and women of all sizes," both poets are referring to popular ballads. Even later, as late as the American Revolution, history was first written for the people in the form of ballads.

" O whar will I get guid sailor
    To sail this schip of mine ? ''

Up and spak an eldern knicht,
    Sat at the king's richt kne:
" Sir Patrick Spence is the best sailor
    That sails upon the se."

There is a brief pause to tell us of Sir Patrick's dismay when word comes that the king expects him to take out a ship at a time when she should be riding to anchor, then on goes the narrative :

" Mak hast, mak haste, my mirry men all,
    Our guid schip sails the morne."
" O say na sae, my master deir,
    For I feir a deadlie storme:

" Late, late yestreen I saw the new moone
    Wi the auld moone in hir arme,
And I feir, I feir, my deir master,
    That we will cum to harme."

At the end there is no wailing, no moral, no display of the poet's feeling, but just a picture :

O lang, lang may the ladies stand,
    Wi thair gold kems in their hair,
Waiting for thair ain deir lords,
    For they 'll se thame na mair.

Haf owre, haf owre to Aberdour,
    It 's fiftie fadom deip,
And thair lies guid Sir Patrick Spence,
    Wi the Scots lords at his feit.

Directness, vigor, dramatic action, an ending that appeals to the imagination, — most of the good qualities of story-telling are found in this old Scottish ballad. If we compare it with Longfellow's " Wreck of the Hesperus," we may discover that the two poets, though far apart in time and space, have followed almost identical methods.

Other good ballads, which take us out under the open sky among vigorous men, are certain parts of " The Gest of Robin

Hood," "Mary Hamilton," "The Wife of Usher's Well," "The Wee Wee Man," "Fair Helen," "Hind Horn," "Bonnie George Campbell," "Johnnie O'Cockley's Well," "Catharine Jaffray" (from which Scott borrowed his "Lochinvar"), and especially "The Nutbrown Mayde," sweetest and most artistic of all the ballads, which gives a popular and happy version of the tale that Chaucer told in his "Patient Griselda."

Summary. The period included in the Age of Chaucer and the Revival of Learning covers two centuries, from 1350 to 1550. The chief literary figure of the period, and one of the greatest of English poets, is Geoffrey Chaucer, who died in the year 1400. He was greatly influenced by French and Italian models; he wrote for the middle and upper classes; his greatest work was *The Canterbury Tales*.

Langland, another poet contemporary with Chaucer, is famous for his *Piers Plowman*, a powerful poem aiming at social reform, and vividly portraying the life of the common people. It is written in the old Saxon manner, with accent and alliteration, and is difficult to read in its original form.

After the death of Chaucer a century and a half passed before another great writer appeared in England. The time was one of general decline in literature, and the most obvious causes were: the Wars of the Roses, which destroyed many of the patrons of literature; the Reformation, which occupied the nation with religious controversy; and the Renaissance or Revival of Learning, which turned scholars to the literature of Greece and Rome rather than to English works.

In our study of the latter part of the period we reviewed: (1) the rise of the popular ballad, which was almost the only type of literature known to the common people. (2) The work of Malory, who arranged the best of the Arthurian legends in his *Morte d'Arthur*. (3) The work of Caxton, who brought the first printing press to London, and who was instrumental in establishing the East-Midland dialect as the literary language of England.

Selections for Reading. Typical selections from all authors of the period are given in Manly, English Poetry, and English Prose; Newcomer and Andrews, Twelve Centuries of English Poetry and Prose; Ward, English Poets; Morris and Skeat, Specimens of Early English.

Chaucer's Prologue, Knight's Tale, and other selections in Riverside Literature, King's Classics, and several other school series. A good single-volume edition of Chaucer's poetry is Skeat, The Student's Chaucer (Clarendon Press). A good, but expensive, modernized version is Tatlock and MacKaye, Modern Reader's Chaucer (Macmillan).

Metrical version of Piers Plowman, by Skeat, in King's Classics; modernized prose version by Kate Warren, in Treasury of English Literature (Dodge).

Selections from Malory's Morte d' Arthur in Athenæum Press Series (Ginn and Company); also in Camelot Series. An elaborate edition of Malory with introduction by Sommer and an essay by Andrew Lang (3 vols., London, 1889); another with modernized text, introduction by Rhys, illustrations by Aubrey Beardsley (London, 1893).

The best of the old ballads are published in Pocket Classics, and in Maynard's English Classics; a volume of ancient and modern English ballads in Ginn and Company's Classics for Children; Percy's Reliques, in Everyman's Library. Allingham, The Ballad Book; Hazlitt, Popular Poetry of England; Gummere, Old English Ballads; Gayley and Flaherty, Poetry of the People; Child, English and Scottish Popular Poetry (5 vols.); the last-named work, edited and abridged by Kittredge, in one volume.

Bibliography. The following works have been sifted from a much larger number dealing with the age of Chaucer and the Revival of Learning. More extended works, covering the entire field of English history and literature, are listed in the General Bibliography.

History. Snell, the Age of Chaucer; Jusserand, Wayfaring Life in the Fourteenth Century; Jenks, In the Days of Chaucer; Trevelyan, In the Age of Wyclif; Coulton, Chaucer and His England; Denton, England in the Fifteenth Century; Green, Town Life in the Fifteenth Century; Einstein, The Italian Renaissance in England; Froissart, Chronicles; Lanier, The Boy's Froissart.

Literature. Ward, Life of Chaucer (English Men of Letters Series); Kittredge, Chaucer and His Poetry (Harvard University Press); Pollard, Chaucer Primer; Lounsbury, Studies in Chaucer; Lowell's essay in My Study Windows; essay by Hazlitt, in Lectures on the English Poets; Jusserand, Piers Plowman; Roper, Life of Sir Thomas More.

Fiction and Poetry. Lytton, Last of the Barons; Yonge, Lances of Lynwood; Scott, Marmion; Shakespeare, Richard II, Henry IV, Richard III; Bates and Coman, English History Told by English Poets.

CHAPTER IV

THE ELIZABETHAN AGE (1550–1620)

This royal throne of kings, this scepter'd isle,
This earth of majesty, this seat of Mars,
This other Eden, demi-paradise,
This fortress built by Nature for herself
Against infection and the hand of war,
This happy breed of men, this little world,
This precious stone set in the silver sea, . . .
This blessed plot, this earth, this realm, this England!

Shakespeare, *King Richard II*

Historical Background. In such triumphant lines, falling from the lips of that old imperialist John of Gaunt, did Shakespeare reflect, not the rebellious spirit of the age of Richard II, but the boundless enthusiasm of his own times, when the defeat of Spain's mighty Armada had left England " in splendid isolation," unchallenged mistress of her own realm and of the encircling sea. For it was in the latter part of Elizabeth's reign that England found herself as a nation, and became conscious of her destiny as a world empire.

There is another and darker side to the political shield, but the student of literature is not concerned with it. We are to remember the patriotic enthusiasm of the age, overlooking the frequent despotism of " good Queen Bess " and entering into the spirit of national pride and power that thrilled all classes of Englishmen during her reign, if we are to understand the outburst of Elizabethan literature. Nearly two centuries of trouble and danger had passed since Chaucer died, and no national poet had appeared in England. The Renaissance came, and the Reformation, but they brought no great writers with them. During the first thirty years of Elizabeth's reign not a single important literary work was produced; then suddenly appeared the poetry of Spenser and Chapman, the prose of Hooker, Sidney and Bacon, the dramas of Marlowe, Shakespeare, Ben Jonson and a score of others, — all voicing the national feeling after the defeat of the Armada, and growing silent as soon as the enthusiasm began to wane.

Literary Characteristics. Next to the patriotic spirit of Elizabethan literature, its most notable qualities are its youthful freshness and vigor, its romantic spirit, its absorption in the theme of love, its extravagance of speech, its lively sense of the wonder of heaven and earth. The ideal beauty of Spenser's poetry, the bombast of Marlowe, the boundless zest of Shakespeare's historical plays, the romantic love celebrated in unnumbered lyrics, — all these speak of youth, of springtime, of the joy and the heroic adventure of human living.

This romantic enthusiasm of Elizabethan poetry and prose may be explained by the fact that, besides the national impulse, three other inspiring influences were at work. The first in point of time was the rediscovery of the classics of Greece and Rome, — beautiful old poems, which were as new to the Elizabethans as to Keats when he wrote his immortal sonnet, beginning:

> Much have I travell'd in the realms of gold.

The second awakening factor was the widespread interest in nature and the physical sciences, which spurred many another Elizabethan besides Bacon to "take all knowledge for his province." This new interest was generally romantic rather than scientific, was more concerned with marvels, like the philosopher's stone that would transmute all things to gold, than with the simple facts of nature. Bacon's chemical changes, which follow the "instincts" of metals, are almost on a par with those other changes described in Shakespeare's song of Ariel:

> Full fathom five thy father lies;
> Of his bones are coral made;
> Those are pearls that were his eyes:
> Nothing of him that doth fade
> But doth suffer a sea-change
> Into something rich and strange.

The third factor which stimulated the Elizabethan imagination was the discovery of the world beyond the Atlantic, a world of wealth, of beauty, of unmeasured opportunity for brave spirits, in regions long supposed to be possessed of demons, monsters, Othello's impossible

> cannibals that each other eat,
> The anthropophagi, and men whose heads
> Do grow beneath their shoulders.

When Drake returned from his voyage around the world he brought to England two things : a tale of vast regions just over **The New World** the world's rim that awaited English explorers, and a ship loaded to the hatches with gold and jewels. That the latter treasure was little better than a pirate's booty; that it was stolen from the Spaniards, who had taken it from poor savages at the price of blood and torture, — all this was not mentioned. The queen and her favorites shared the treasure with Drake's buccaneers, and the New World seemed to them a place of barbaric splendor, where the savage's wattled hut was roofed with silver, his garments beaded with all precious jewels. As a popular play of the period declares :

" Why, man, all their dripping pans are pure gold ! The prisoners they take are fettered in gold ; and as for rubies and diamonds, they goe forth on holydayes and gather 'hem by the seashore to hang on their children's coates."

Before the American settlements opened England's eyes to the stern reality of things, it was the romance of the New World that appealed most powerfully to the imagination, and that influenced Elizabethan literature to an extent which we have not yet begun to measure.

Foreign Influence. We shall understand the imitative quality of early Elizabethan poetry if we read it in the light of these facts : that in the sixteenth century England was far behind other European nations in culture ; that the Renaissance had influenced Italy and Holland for a century before it crossed the Channel ; that, at a time when every Dutch peasant read his Bible, the masses of English people remained in dense ignorance, and the majority of the official classes were like

Shakespeare's father and daughter in that they could neither read nor write. So, when the new national spirit began to express itself in literature, Englishmen turned to the more cultured nations and began to imitate them in poetry, as in dress and manners. Shakespeare gives us a hint of the matter when he makes Portia ridicule the apishness of the English. In *The Merchant of Venice* (Act I, scene 2) the maid Nerissa is speaking of various princely suitors for Portia's hand. She names them over, Frenchman, Italian, Scotsman, German; but Portia makes fun of them all. The maid tries again:

Nerissa. What say you, then, to Falconbridge, the young baron of England?
Portia. You know I say nothing to him, for he understands not me, nor I him: he hath neither Latin, French, nor Italian; and you will come into the court and swear that I have a poor pennyworth in the English. He is a proper man's picture, but, alas, who can converse with a dumb show? How oddly he is suited! I think he bought his doublet in Italy, his round hose in France, his bonnet in Germany and his behaviour every where.

When Wyatt and Surrey brought the sonnet to England, they brought also the habit of imitating the Italian poets; and this habit influenced Spenser and other Elizabethans even more than Chaucer had been influenced by Dante and Petrarch. It was the fashion at that time for Italian gentlemen to write poetry; they practiced the art as they practiced riding or fencing; and presently scores of Englishmen followed Sidney's example in taking up this phase of foreign education. It was also an Italian custom to publish the works of amateur poets in the form of anthologies, and soon there appeared in England *The Paradise of Dainty Devices*, *A Gorgeous Gallery of Gallant Inventions* and other such collections, the best of which was *England's Helicon* (1600). Still another foreign fashion was that of writing a series of sonnets to some real or imaginary mistress; and that the fashion was followed in England is evident from Spenser's *Amoretti*, Sidney's *Astrophel and Stella*, Shakespeare's *Sonnets*, and other less-famous effusions.

SPENSER AND THE LYRIC POETS

Lyrics of Love. Love was the subject of a very large part of the minor poems of the period, the monotony being relieved

MICHAEL DRAYTON

by an occasional ballad, such as Drayton's " Ballad of Agincourt" and his " Ode to the Virginian Voyage," the latter being one of the first poems inspired by the New World. Since love was still subject to literary rules, as in the metrical romances, it is not strange that most Elizabethan lyrics seem to the modern reader artificial. They deal largely with goddesses and airy shepherd folk ; they contain many references to classic characters and scenes, to Venus, Olympus and the rest ; they are nearly all characterized by extravagance of language. A single selection, "Apelles' Song" by Lyly, may serve as typical of the more fantastic love lyrics :

Cupid and my Campaspe played
At cards for kisses ; Cupid paid.
He stakes his quiver, bow and arrows,
His mother's doves and team of sparrows :
Loses them too ; then down he throws
The coral of his lip, the rose
Growing on 's cheek (but none knows how) ;
With these the crystal of his brow,
And then the dimple of his chin.
All these did my Campaspe win.
At last he set her both his eyes ;
She won, and Cupid blind did rise.
O Love, has she done this to thee ?
What shall, alas ! become of me ?

Music and Poetry. Another reason for the outburst of lyric poetry in Elizabethan times was that choral music began to be studied, and there was great demand for new songs. Then appeared a theory of the close relation between poetry and music, which was followed by the American poet Lanier more than two centuries later.[1] This interesting theory is foreshadowed in several minor works of the period ; for example, in Barnfield's sonnet " To R. L.," beginning :

> If music and sweet poetry agree,
> As they must needs, the sister and the brother,
> Then must the love be great 'twixt thee and me,
> Because thou lov'st the one, and I the other.

The stage caught up the new fashion, and hundreds of lyrics appeared in the Elizabethan drama, such as Dekker's " Content " (from the play of *Patient Grissell*), which almost sets itself to music as we read it :

> Art thou poor, yet hast thou golden slumbers?
>> O sweet content!
> Art thou rich, yet is thy mind perplexed?
>> O punishment!
> Dost laugh to see how fools are vexed
> To add to golden numbers golden numbers?
>> O sweet content, O sweet, O sweet content!
>
> *Work apace, apace, apace, apace!*
> *Honest labour bears a lovely face.*
> *Then hey noney, noney ; hey noney, noney!*
>
> Canst drink the waters of the crispéd spring?
>> O sweet content!
> Swim'st thou in wealth, yet sink'st in thine own tears?
>> O punishment!
> Then he that patiently want's burden bears
> No burden bears, but is a king, a king.
>> O sweet content, O sweet, O sweet content!

[1] Much of Lanier's verse seems more like a musical improvisation than like an ordinary poem. His theory that music and poetry are subject to the same laws is developed in his *Science of English Verse*. It is interesting to note that Lanier's ancestors were musical directors at the courts of Elizabeth and of James I.

E

So many lyric poets appeared during this period that we cannot here classify them; and it would be idle to list their names. The best place to make acquaintance with them is not in a dry history of literature, but in such a pleasant little book as Palgrave's *Golden Treasury*, where their best work is accessible to every reader.

EDMUND SPENSER (1552–1599)

Spenser was the second of the great English poets, and it is but natural to compare him with Chaucer, who was the first. In respect of time nearly two centuries separate these elder poets; in all other respects, in aims, ideals, methods, they are as far apart as two men of the same race can well be.

Life. Very little is known of Spenser; he appears in the light, then vanishes into the shadow, like his Arthur of *The Faery Queen*. We see him for a moment in the midst of rebellion in Ireland, or engaged in the scramble for preferment among the queen's favorites; he disappears, and from his obscurity comes a poem that is like the distant ringing of a chapel bell, faintly heard in the clatter of the city streets. We shall try here to understand this poet by dissolving some of the mystery that envelops him.

He was born in London, and spent his youth amid the political and religious dissensions of the times of Mary and Elizabeth. For all this turmoil Spenser had no stomach; he was a man of peace, of books, of romantic dreams. He was of noble family, but poor; his only talent was to write poetry, and as poetry would not buy much bread in those days, his pride of birth was humbled in seeking the patronage of nobles:

> Full little knowest thou, that hast not tried,
> What hell it is in suing long to bide: . . .
> To fawn, to crouch, to wait, to ride, to run,
> To spend, to give, to want, to be undone.

To the liberality of a patron he owed his education at Cambridge. It was then the heyday of Renaissance studies, and Spenser steeped himself in Greek, Latin and Italian literatures. Everything that was antique was then in favor at the universities; there was a revival of interest in Old-English poetry, which accounts largely for Spenser's use of obsolete words and his imitation of Chaucer's spelling.

After graduation he spent some time in the north of England, probably as a tutor, and had an unhappy love affair, which he celebrated in his poems to Rosalind. Then he returned to London, lived by favor in the houses of Sidney and Leicester, and through these powerful patrons was appointed secretary to Lord Grey de Wilton, the queen's deputy in Ireland.

From this time on our poet is represented as a melancholy **Spenser's Exile** "exile," but that is a poetic fiction. At that time Ireland, having refused to follow the Reformation, was engaged in a desperate struggle for civil and religious liberty. Every English army that sailed to crush this rebellion was accompanied by a swarm of parasites, each inspired by the hope of getting one of the rich estates that were confiscated from Irish owners. Spenser seems to have been one of these expectant adventurers who accompanied Lord Grey in his

EDMUND SPENSER

campaign of brutality. To the horrors of that campaign the poet was blind;[1] his sympathies were all for his patron Grey, who appears in *The Faery Queen* as Sir Artegall, "the model of true justice."

For his services Spenser was awarded the castle of Kilcolman and 3000 acres of land, which had been taken from the Earl of Desmond. In the same way Raleigh became an Irish landlord, with 40,000 acres to his credit; and so these two famous Elizabethans were thrown

[1] The barbarism of Spenser's view, a common one at that time, is reflected in his *View of the Present State of Ireland*. Honorable warfare on land or sea was unknown in Elizabeth's day. Scores of pirate ships of all nations were then openly preying on commerce. Drake, Frobisher and many other Elizabethan "heroes" were at times mere buccaneers who shared their plunder with the queen. In putting down the Irish rebellion Lords Grey and Essex used some of the same horrible methods employed by the notorious Duke of Alva in the Netherlands.

together in exile, as they termed it. Both longed to return to England, to enjoy London society and the revenues of Irish land at the same time; but unfortunately one condition of their immense grants was that they should occupy the land and keep the rightful owners from possessing it.

In Ireland Spenser began to write his masterpiece *The Faery Queen*. Raleigh, to whom the first three books were read, was so impressed **Work in** by the beauty of the work that he hurried the poet off to **Ireland** London, and gained for him the royal favor. In the poem "Colin Clout's Come Home Again" we may read Spenser's account of how the court impressed him after his sojourn in Ireland.

RALEIGH'S BIRTHPLACE, BUDLEIGH SALTERTON

Hayes, Devonshire

The publication of the first parts of *The Faery Queen* (1590) raised Spenser to the foremost place in English letters. He was made poet-laureate, and used every influence of patrons and of literary success to the end that he be allowed to remain in London; but the queen was flint-hearted, insisting that he must give up his estate or occupy it. So he returned sorrowfully to "exile," and wrote three more books of *The Faery Queen*. To his other offices was added that of sheriff of County Cork, an adventurous office for any man even in times of peace, and for a poet, in a time of turmoil, an invitation to disaster. Presently another rebellion broke out; Kilcolman castle was burned, and the poet's family barely escaped with their lives. It was said by Ben Jonson that one of Spenser's children and some parts of *The Faery Queen* perished in the fire, but the truth of the saying has not been established.

Soon after this experience, which crushed the poet's spirit, he was ordered on official business to London, and died on the journey in 1599. As he was buried beside Chaucer, in Westminster Abbey, poets were seen casting memorial verses and the pens that had written them into his tomb.

Character In character Spenser was unfitted either for the intrigues among Elizabeth's favorites or for the more desperate scenes amid which his lot was cast. Unlike his friend Raleigh, who was a man of action, Spenser was essentially a dreamer, and except in Cambridge he seems never to have felt at home. His criticism of the age as barren and hopeless, and the melancholy of the greater part of his work, indicate that for him, at least, the great Elizabethan times were " out of joint." The world, which thinks of Spenser as a great poet, has forgotten that he thought of himself as a disappointed man.

Works of Spenser. The poems of Spenser may be conveniently grouped in three classes. In the first are the pastorals of *The Shepherd's Calendar*, in which he reflects some of the poetical fashions of his age. In the second are the allegories of *The Faery Queen*, in which he pictures the state of England as a struggle between good and evil. In the third class are his occasional poems of friendship and love, such as the *Amoretti*. All his works are alike musical, and all remote from ordinary life, like the eerie music of a wind harp.

Shepherd's Calendar *The Shepherd's Calendar* (1579) is famous as the poem which announced that a successor to Chaucer had at last appeared in England. It is an amateurish work in which Spenser tried various meters ; and to analyze it is to discover two discordant elements, which we may call fashionable poetry and puritanic preaching. Let us understand these elements clearly, for apart from them the *Calendar* is a meaningless work.

It was a fashion among Italian poets to make eclogues or pastoral poems about shepherds, their dancing, piping, love-making,—everything except a shepherd's proper business. Spenser followed this artificial fashion in his *Calendar* by making twelve pastorals, one for each month of the year. These all take the form of conversations, accompanied by music and dancing, and the personages are Cuddie, Diggon, Hobbinoll, and other fantastic shepherds. According to poetic custom these should sing only of love; but in Spenser's day religious controversy was rampant, and flattery might not be overlooked by a poet who aspired to royal favor. So while the January pastoral tells of the unhappy love of Colin Clout (Spenser) for Rosalind, the springtime of April calls for a song in praise of Elizabeth:

> Lo, how finely the Graces can it foot
>   To the instrument!
> They dancen deffly and singen soote,
>   In their merriment.
> Wants not a fourth Grace to make the dance even?
> Let that room to my Lady be yeven.
>   She shall be a Grace,
>   To fill the fourth place,
> And reign with the rest in heaven.

In May the shepherds are rival pastors of the Reformation, who end their sermons with an animal fable; in summer they discourse of Puritan theology; October brings them to contemplate the trials and disappointments of a poet, and the series ends with a parable comparing life to the four seasons of the year.

The moralizing of *The Shepherd's Calendar* and the uncouth spelling which Spenser affected detract from the interest of the poem; but one who has patience to read it finds on almost every page some fine poetic line, and occasionally a good song, like the following (from the August pastoral) in which two shepherds alternately supply the lines of a roundelay:

> Sitting upon a hill so high,
>   Hey, ho, the high hill!
> The while my flock did feed thereby,
>   The while the shepherd' self did spill,

I saw the bouncing Bellibone,
    Hey, ho, Bonnibell!
Tripping over the dale alone;
    She can trip it very well.
Well deckéd in a frock of gray,
    Hey, ho, gray is greet!
And in a kirtle of green say;
    The green is for maidens meet.
A chaplet on her head she wore,
    Hey, ho, chapelet!
Of sweet violets therein was store,
    She sweeter than the violet.

The Faery Queen. Let us hear one of the stories of this celebrated poem, and after the tale is told we may discover Spenser's purpose in writing all the others.

From the court of Gloriana, Queen of Faery, the gallant Sir Guyon sets out on adventure bent, and with him is a holy Palmer, or pilgrim, to pro-

Sir Guyon
tect him from the evil that lurks by every wayside. Hardly, have the two entered the first wood when they fall into the hands of the wicked Archimago, who spends his time in devising spells or enchantments for the purpose of leading honest folk astray.

For all he did was to deceive good knights,
And draw them from pursuit of praise and fame.

Escaping from the snare, Guyon hears a lamentation, and turns aside to find a beautiful woman dying beside a dead knight. Her story is, that her man has been led astray by the Lady Acrasia, who leads many knights to her Bower of Bliss, and there makes them forget honor and knightly duty. Guyon vows to right this wrong, and proceeds on the adventure.

With the Palmer and a boatman he embarks in a skiff and crosses the Gulf of Greediness, deadly whirlpools on one side, and on the other the Magnet Mountain with wrecks of ships strewed about its foot. Sighting the fair Wandering Isles, he attempts to land, attracted here by a beautiful damsel, there by a woman in distress; but the Palmer tells him that these seeming women are evil shadows placed there to lead men astray. Next he meets the monsters of the deep, "sea-shouldering whales," "scolopendras," "grisly wassermans," "mighty monoceroses with unmeasured tails." Escaping these, he meets a greater peril in the mermaids, who sing to him alluringly:

This is port of rest from troublous toil,
The world's sweet inn from pain and wearisome turmoil.

Many other sea-dangers are passed before Guyon comes to land, where he is immediately charged by a bellowing herd of savage beasts. Only the power of the Palmer's holy staff saves the knight from annihilation.

This is the last physical danger which Guyon encounters. As he goes forward the country becomes an earthly paradise, where pleasures call to him from every side. It is his soul, not his body, which is now in peril. Here is the Palace of Pleasure, its wondrous gates carved with images representing Jason's search for the Golden Fleece. Beyond it are parks, gardens, fountains, and the beautiful Lady Excess, who squeezes grapes into a golden cup and offers it to Guyon as an invitation to linger. The scene grows ever more entrancing as he rejects the cup of Excess and pushes onward:

> Eftsoones they heard a most melodious sound
> Of all that mote delight a dainty ear,
> Such as at once might not on living ground,
> Save in this paradise, be heard elsewhere:
> Right hard it was for wight which did it hear
> To read what manner music that mote be;
> For all that pleasing is to living ear
> Was there consorted in one harmony;
> Birds, voices, instruments, winds, waters, all agree.

Amid such allurements Guyon comes at last to where beautiful Acrasia lives, with knights who forget their knighthood. From the open portal comes a melody, the voice of an unseen singer lifting up the old song of Epicurus and of Omar:

> Gather the rose of love whilst yet is time.

The following scenes in the Bower of Bliss were plainly suggested by the Palace of Circe, in the *Odyssey*; but where Homer is direct, simple, forceful, Spenser revels in luxuriant details. He charms all Guyon's senses with color, perfume, beauty, harmony; then he remembers that he is writing a moral poem, and suddenly his delighted knight turns reformer. He catches Acrasia in a net woven by the Palmer, and proceeds to smash her exquisite abode with puritanic thoroughness:

> But all those pleasaunt bowers and palace brave
> Guyon brake down with rigour pitilesse.

As they fare forth after the destruction, the herd of horrible beasts is again encountered, and lo! all these creatures are men whom Acrasia has transformed into brutal shapes. The Palmer "strooks" them all with his holy staff, and they resume their human semblance. Some are glad, others wroth at the change; and one named Grylle, who had been a hog, reviles his

rescuers for disturbing him; which gives the Palmer a final chance to
moralize:

> Let Grylle be Grylle and have his hoggish mind;
> But let us hence depart while weather serves and wind.

Such is Spenser's story of Sir Guyon, or Temperance. It is
a long story, drifting through eighty-seven stanzas, but it is
Other only a final chapter or canto of the second book of
Stories *The Faery Queen*. Preceding it are eleven other
cantos which serve as an introduction. So leisurely is Spenser
in telling a tale! One canto deals with the wiles of Archimago
and of the "false witch" Duessa; in another the varlet Bragga-
docchio steals Guyon's horse and impersonates a knight, until
he is put to shame by the fair huntress Belphœbe, who is Queen
Elizabeth in disguise. Now Elizabeth had a hawk face which
was far from comely, but behold how it appeared to a poet:

> Her face so fair, as flesh it seemëd not,
> But heavenly portrait of bright angel's hue,
> Clear as the sky, withouten blame or blot,
> Through goodly mixture of complexions due;
> And in her cheek the vermeil red did shew
> Like roses in a bed of lilies shed,
> The which ambrosial odours from them threw
> And gazers' sense with double pleasure fed,
> Able to heal the sick and to revive the dead.

There are a dozen more stanzas devoted to her voice, her
eyes, her hair, her more than mortal beauty. Other cantos of
the same book are devoted to Guyon's temptations; to his
victories over Furor and Mammon; to his rescue of the Lady
Alma, besieged by a horde of villains in her fair Castle of
Temperance. In this castle was an aged man, blind but forever doting over old records; and this gives Spenser the
inspiration for another long canto devoted to the ancient kings
of Britain. So all is fish that comes to this poet's net; but as
one who is angling for trout is vexed by the nibbling of chubs,
the reader grows weary of Spenser's story before his story
really begins.

Other books of *The Faery Queen* are so similar in character to the one just described that a canto from any one of them **The First** may be placed without change in any other. In the **Book** first book, for example, the Redcross Knight (Holiness) fares forth accompanied by the Lady Una (Religion). Straightway they meet the enchanter Archimago, who separates them by fraud and magic. The Redcross Knight, led to believe that his Una is false, comes, after many adventures, to Queen Lucifera in the House of Pride; meanwhile Una wanders alone amidst perils, and by her beauty subdues the lion and the satyrs of the wood. The rest of the book recounts their adventures with paynims, giants and monsters, with Error, Avarice, Falsehood and other allegorical figures.

It is impossible to outline such a poem, for the simple reason that it has no outlines. It is a phantasmagoria of beautiful and grotesque shapes, of romance, morality and magic. Reading it is like watching cloud masses, aloft and remote, in which the imagination pictures men, monsters, landscapes, which change as we view them without cause or consequence. Though *The Faery Queen* is overfilled with adventure, it has no action, as we ordinarily understand the term. Its continual motion is without force or direction, like the vague motions of a dream.

What, then, was Spenser's object in writing *The Faery Queen*? His professed object was to use poetry in the service **Plan of The** of morality by portraying the political and religious **Faery Queen** affairs of England as emblematic of a worldwide conflict between good and evil. According to his philosophy (which, he tells us, he borrowed from Aristotle) there were twelve chief virtues, and he planned twelve books to celebrate them.[1] In each book a knight or a lady representing a single virtue goes forth into the world to conquer evil. In all the

[1] Only six of these books are extant, treating of the Redcross Knight or Holiness, Sir Guyon or Temperance, Britomartis or Chastity, Cambel and Triamond or Friendship, Sir Artegall or Justice, and Sir Calidore or Courtesy. The rest of the allegory, if written, may have been destroyed in the fire of Kilcolman.

books Arthur, or Magnificence (the sum of all virtue), is apt to appear in any crisis; Lady Una represents religion; Archimago is another name for heresy, and Duessa for falsehood; and in order to give point to Spenser's allegory the courtiers and statesmen of the age are all flattered as glorious virtues or condemned as ugly vices.

Those who are fond of puzzles may delight in giving names and dates to these allegorical personages, in recognizing

The Allegory Elizabeth in Belphœbe or Britomart or Marcella, Sidney in the Redcross Knight, Leicester in Arthur, Raleigh in Timias, Mary Stuart in Duessa, and so on through the list of characters good or evil. The beginner will wisely ignore all such interpretation, and for two reasons: first, because Spenser's allegories are too shadowy to be taken seriously; and second, because as a chronicler of the times he is outrageously partisan and untrustworthy. In short, to search for any reality in *The Faery Queen* is to spoil the poem as a work of the imagination. "If you do not meddle with the allegory," said Hazlitt, "the allegory will not meddle with you."

Minor Poems. The minor poems of Spenser are more interesting, because more human, than the famous work which we have just considered. Prominent among these poems are the *Amoretti*, a collection of sonnets written in honor of the Irish girl Elizabeth, who became the poet's wife. They are artificial, to be sure, but no more so than other love poems of the period. In connection with a few of these sonnets may be read Spenser's four "Hymns" (in honor of Love, Beauty, Heavenly Love and Heavenly Beauty) and especially his "Epithalamion," a marriage hymn which Brooke calls, with pardonable enthusiasm, "the most glorious love song in the English language."

A Criticism of Spenser. In reading *The Faery Queen* one must note the contrast between Spenser's matter and his manner. His matter is: religion, chivalry, mythology, Italian romance, Arthurian legends, the struggles of Spain and England on the Continent, the Reformation, the turmoil of political parties, the appeal of the New World, — a summary of all stirring matters that interested his own tumultuous age. His manner is the reverse of what one might expect under the circumstances. He writes no stirring epic of victory or defeat, and never a downright word of a downright man, but a dreamy, shadowy narrative as soothing as the abode of Morpheus :

> And, more to lulle him in his slumber soft,
> A trickling stream from high rock tumbling downe,
> And ever-drizzling rain upon the loft,
> Mixt with a murmuring winde, much like the sowne
> Of swarming bees, did cast him in a swowne.
> No other noyse, nor people's troublous cryes,
> As still are wont t' annoy the wallëd towne,
> Might there be heard ; but careless Quiet lyes
> Wrapt in eternal silence far from enemyes.

Such stanzas (and they abound in every book of *The Faery Queen*) are poems in themselves ; but unfortunately they distract attention from the story, which soon loses all progression and becomes as the rocking of an idle boat on the swell of a placid sea. The invention of this melodious stanza, ever since called " Spenserian," was in itself a notable achievement which influenced all subsequent English poetry.[1]

As Spenser's faults cannot be ignored, let us be rid of them as quickly as possible. We record, then : the unreality of his

Spenser's great work ; its lack of human interest, which causes
Faults most of us to drop the poem after a single canto ;
its affected antique spelling ; its use of *fone* (foes), *dan* (master), *teene* (trouble), *swink* (labor), and of many more obsolete words ; its frequent torturing of the king's English to make a rime ; its utter lack of humor, appearing in such absurd lines as,

> Astond he stood, and up his hair did hove.

[1] The Spenserian was an improvement on the *ottava-rima*, or eight-line stanza, of the Italians. It has been used by Burns in " The Cotter's Saturday Night," by Shelley in " The Revolt of Islam," by Byron in " Childe Harold," by Keats in " The Eve of St. Agnes," and by many other poets.

Such defects are more than offset by Spenser's poetic virtues. We note, first, the moral purpose which allies him with the

Moral Ideal medieval poets in aim, but not in method. By most medieval romancers virtue was regarded as a means to an end, as in the *Morte d' Arthur*, where a knight made a vow of purity in order to obtain a sight of the Holy Grail. With Spenser virtue is not a means but an end, beautiful and desirable for its own sake ; while sin is so pictured that men avoid it because of its intrinsic ugliness. This is the moral secret of *The Faery Queen*, in which virtues are personified as noble knights or winsome women, while the vices appear in the repulsive guise of hags, monsters and "loathy beasts."

Spenser's sense of ideal beauty or, as Lanier expressed it, "the beauty of holiness and the holiness of beauty," is perhaps

Sense of Beauty his greatest poetic quality. He is the poet-painter of the Renaissance ; he fills his pages with descriptions of airy loveliness, as Italian artists covered the high ceilings of Venice with the reflected splendor of earth and heaven. Moreover, his sense of beauty found expression in such harmonious lines that one critic describes him as having set beautiful figures moving to exquisite music.

In consequence of this beauty and melody, Spenser has been the inspiration of nearly all later English singers. Milton was one of the first to call him master, and then in a long succession such diverse poets as Dryden, Burns, Wordsworth, Scott, Shelley, Keats, Byron, Tennyson and Swinburne. The poet of "Faery" has influenced all these and more so deeply that he has won the distinctive title of "the poets' poet."

THE DRAMATISTS

"Few events in our literary history are so startling as this sudden rise of the Elizabethan drama," says Green in his *History of the English People*, and his judgment is echoed by other writers who speak of the "marvelous efflorescence" of the English drama as a matter beyond explanation. Startling it may be, with its frank expression of a nation's life, the glory and the shame of it; but there is nothing sudden or inexplicable about it, as we may see by reviewing the history of playwriting in England.

The Religious Drama. In its simplicity the drama is a familiar story retold to the eye by actors who "make believe" that they are the heroes of the action. In this elemental form the play is almost as old as humanity. Indeed, it seems to be a natural impulse of children to act a story which has given them pleasure; of primitive men also, who from time immemorial have kept alive the memory of tribal heroes by representing their deeds in play or pantomime. Thus, certain parts of *Hiawatha* are survivals of dramatic myths that were once acted at the spring assembly of the Algonquin Indians. An interesting fact concerning these primitive dramas, whether in India or Greece or Persia, is that they were invariably associated with some religious belief or festival.

A later example of this is found in the Church, which at an early age began to make its holy-day services more impressive **The First** by means of Miracle plays and Mysteries.[1] At **Miracles** Christmas time, for example, the beautiful story of Bethlehem would be made more vivid by placing in a corner of the parish church an image of a babe in a manger, with shepherds and the Magi at hand, and the choir in white garments chanting the *Gloria in excelsis*. Other festivals were celebrated in a similar way until a cycle of simple dramas had been prepared, clustering around four cardinal points of Christian teaching; namely, Creation, the Fall, Redemption, and Doomsday or the Last Judgment.

At first such plays were given in the church, and were deeply religious in spirit. They made a profound impression

---

[1] In France any play representing the life of a saint was called *miracle*, and a play dealing with the life of Christ was called *mystère*. In England no such distinction was made, the name "Miracle" being given to any drama dealing with Bible history or with the lives of the saints.

in England especially, where people flocked in such numbers to see them that presently they overflowed to the churchyard, **Growth of the Miracles** and from there to the city squares or the town common. Once outside the church, they were taken up by the guilds or trades-unions, in whose hands they lost much of their religious character. Actors were trained for the stage rather than for the church, and to please the crowds elements of comedy and buffoonery were introduced,[1] until the sacred drama degenerated into a farce. Here and there, however, a true Miracle survived and kept its character unspotted even to our own day, as in the famous Passion Play at Oberammergau.

When and how these plays came to England is unknown. By the year 1300 they were extremely popular, and continued **Cycles of Plays** so until they were replaced by the Elizabethan drama. Most of the important towns of England had each its own cycle of plays[2] which were given once a year, the performance lasting from three to eight days in a prolonged festival. Every guild responsible for a play had its own stage, which was set on wheels and drawn about the town to appointed open places, where a crowd was waiting for it. When it passed on, to repeat the play to a different audience, another stage took its place. The play of " Creation " would be succeeded by the " Temptation of Adam and Eve," and so on until the whole cycle of Miracles from " Creation " to " Doomsday " had been performed. It was the play not the audience that moved, and in this trundling about of the stage van we are reminded of Thespis, the alleged founder of Greek tragedy, who went about with his cart and his play from one festival to another.

[1] In the " Shepherd's Play " or " Play of the Nativity," for example, the adoration of the Magi is interrupted by Mak, who steals a sheep and carries it to his wife. She hides the carcass in a cradle, and sings a lullaby to it while the indignant shepherds are searching the house.

[2] At present only four good cyles of Miracles are known to exist ; namely, the Chester, York, Townley (or Wakefield) and Coventry plays. The number of plays varies, from twenty-five in the Chester to forty-eight in the York cycle.

Two other dramatic types, the Morality and the Interlude, probably grew out of the religious drama. In one of the old

Moralities

Miracles we find two characters named Truth and Righteousness, who are severe in their denunciation of Adam, while Mercy and Peace plead for his life. Other virtues appear in other Miracles, then Death and the Seven Deadly Sins, until we have a play in which all the characters are personified virtues or vices. Such a play was called a Morality, and it aimed to teach right conduct, as the Miracles had at first aimed to teach right doctrine.

The Interlude was at first a crude sketch, a kind of ancient side show, introduced into the Miracle plays after the latter

Interludes

had been taken up by the guilds. A boy with a trained pig, a quarrel between husband and wife, — any farce was welcome so long as it amused the crowd or enlivened the Miracle. In time, however, the writing of Interludes became a profession; they improved rapidly in character, were separated from the Miracles, and were performed at entertainments or " revels " by trade guilds, by choir boys and by companies of strolling actors or " minstrels." At the close of such entertainments the minstrels would add a prayer for the king (an inheritance from the religious drama), and this impressive English custom still survives in the singing of " God Save the King " at the end of a public assembly.

The Secular Drama. When the Normans came to England they brought with them a love of pageants, or spectacles, that was destined to have an important influence on the drama. These pageants, representing scenes from history or mythology (such as the bout between Richard and Saladin, or the combat between St. George and the Dragon), were staged to celebrate feasts, royal weddings, treaties or any other event that seemed of special importance. From Norman times they increased steadily in favor until Elizabeth began her " progresses " through England, when every castle or town must prepare a play or pageant to entertain the royal visitor.

From simple pantomime the pageant developed into a masque; that is, a dramatic entertainment accompanied by poetry and music. Hundreds of such masques were written and acted before Shakespeare's day; the taste for them survived long after the Elizabethan drama had decayed; and a few of them, such as *The Sad Shepherd* of Ben Jonson and the *Comus* of Milton, may still be read with pleasure.

The Masque

While the nobles were thus occupied with pageants and masques, the common people were developing a crude drama in which comedy predominated. Such were the Christmas plays or "mummings," introducing the characters of Merry Andrew and Old King Cole, which began in England before the Conquest, and which survived in country places down to our own times.[1] More widespread than the mummings were crude spectacles prepared in celebration of secular holidays, — the May Day plays, for example, which represented the adventures of Robin Hood and his merry men. To these popular comedies the Church contributed liberally, though unwillingly; its holy days became holidays to the crowd, and its solemn fasts were given over to merriment, to the *festa fatuorum*, or play of fools, in which such characters as Boy Bishop, Lord of Misrule and various clowns or jesters made a scandalous caricature of things ecclesiastical. Such plays, prepared largely by clerks and choir boys, were repeatedly denounced by priest or bishop, but they increased rapidly from the twelfth to the sixteenth century.

Popular Comedy

By the latter date England seemed in danger of going spectacle-mad; and we may understand the symptoms if we remember that the play was then almost the only form of popular amusement; that it took the place of the modern newspaper, novel, political election and ball game, all combined. The trade guilds, having trained actors

Spread of the Drama

[1] In Hardy's novel *The Return of the Native* may be found a description of these mummings (from "mum," a mask) in the nineteenth century. In Scott's novel *The Abbot* we have a glimpse of other mummings, such as were given to celebrate feast days of the Church.

E

for the springtime Miracles, continued to give other plays throughout the year. The servants of a nobleman, having given a pageant to welcome the queen, went out through the country in search of money or adventure, and presented the same spectacle wherever they could find an audience. When the Renaissance came, reviving interest in the classics, Latin plays were taken up eagerly and presented in modified form by every important school or university in England. In this way our first regular comedy, *Ralph Royster Doyster* (written by Nicholas Udall, Master of Eton, and acted by his school-boys *cir.* 1552), was adapted from an old Latin comedy, the *Miles Gloriosus* of Plautus.

The awakened interest in music had also its influences on the English drama. The choir boys of a church were fre-

Boy Actors quently called upon to furnish music at a play, and from this it was but a step to furnish both the play and the music. So great was the demand to hear these boys that certain choir masters (those of St. Paul's and the Chapel Royal) obtained the right to take any poor boy with a good voice and train him, ostensibly for the service of the Church, but in reality to make a profitable actor out of him. This dangerous practice was stimulated by the fact that the feminine parts in all plays had to be taken by boys, the stage being then deemed an unfit place for a woman. And it certainly was. If a boy "took to his lines," his services were sold from one company to another, much as the popular ball player is now sold, but with this difference, that the poor boy had no voice or profit in the transaction. Some of these lads were cruelly treated ; all were in danger of moral degradation. The abuse was finally suppressed by Parliament, but not until the choir-boy players were rivals of the regular companies, in which Shakespeare and Ben Jonson played their parts.

Classical and English Drama. At the time of Shakespeare's birth two types of plays were represented in England. The classic drama, modeled upon Greek or Roman plays, was constructed according to the dramatic "unities," which Aristotle foreshadowed in his *Treatise on Poetry*. According to this authority, every play must be concerned with a " single, important and complete event"; in other words, it must have "unity of action." A second rule, relating to "unity of time," required that the events represented in a play must all occur within a single day. A third provided that the action should take place in the same locality, and this was known as the "unity of place." [1] Other rules of classic drama required that tragedy and comedy should not occur in the same play, and that battles, murders and all such violent affairs should never be represented on the stage but be announced at the proper time by a messenger.

The native plays ignored these classic unities. The public demanded chronicle plays, for example, in which the action must cover years of time, and jump from court to battlefield in following the hero. Tragedy and comedy, instead of being separated, were represented as meeting at every crossroad or entering the church door side by side. So the most solemn Miracles were scandalized by humorous Interludes, and into the most tragic of Shakespeare's scenes entered the fool and the jester. A Greek playwright might object to brutalizing scenes before a cultured audience, but the crowds who came to an Elizabethan play were of a temper to enjoy a Mohawk scalp dance. They were accustomed to violent scenes and sensations; they had witnessed the rack and gibbet in constant operation; they were familiar with the sight of human heads decorating the posts of London Bridge or carried about on the pikes of soldiers. After witnessing such horrors free of cost, they would follow their queen and pay their money to see a chained bear torn to pieces by ferocious bulldogs. Then they would go to a play, and throw stones or dead cats at the actors if their tastes were not gratified.

The Native Drama

[1] The Roman philosopher and dramatist Seneca (d. 65 A.D.) is supposed to have established this rule. The influence of Aristotle on the "unities" is a matter of dispute.

To please such crowds no stage action could possibly be too rough; hence the riotousness of the early theaters, which for safety were placed outside the city limits; hence also the blood and thunder of Shakespeare's *Andronicus* and the atrocities represented in the plays of Kyd and Marlowe.

Following such different ideals, two schools of playwrights appeared in England. One school, the University Wits, to **The Two** whom we owe our first real tragedy, *Gorboduc*,[1] aimed **Schools** to make the English drama like that of Greece and Rome. The other, or native, school aimed at a play which should represent life, or please the crowd, without regard to any rules ancient or modern. The best Elizabethan drama was a combination of classic and native elements, with the latter predominating.

Shakespeare's Predecessors. In a general way, all unknown men who for three centuries had been producing miracle plays, moralities, interludes, masques and pageants were Shakespeare's predecessors; but we refer here to a small group of playwrights who rapidly developed what is now called the Elizabethan drama. The time was the last quarter of the sixteenth century.

By that time England was as excited over the stage as a modern community over the "movies." Plays were given on every important occasion by choir boys, by noblemen's servants, by court players governed by the Master of Revels, by grammar schools and universities, by trade guilds in every shire of England. Actors were everywhere in training, and audiences gathered as to a bull-baiting whenever a new spectacle was

---

[1] This play, called also *Ferrex and Porrex*, was written by Sackville and Norton, and played in 1562, only two years before Shakespeare's birth. It related how Gorboduc divided his British kingdom between his two sons, who quarreled and threw the whole country into rebellion, — a story much like that used by Shakespeare in *King Lear*. The violent parts of this first tragedy were not represented on the stage but were announced by a messenger. At the end of each act a "chorus" summed up the situation, as in classic tragedy. *Gorboduc* differed from all earlier plays in that it was divided into acts and scenes, and was written in blank verse. It is generally regarded as the first in time of the Elizabethan dramas. A few comedies divided into acts and scenes were written before *Gorboduc*, but not in the blank verse with which we associate an Elizabethan play.

presented. Then came the awakening of the national consciousness, the sense of English pride and power after the
defeat of the Armada, and this new national spirit found expression in hundreds of chronicle plays representing the past
glories of Britain.[1]

It was at this "psychological moment," when English patriotism was aroused and London was as the heart of England,
that a group of young actors — Greene, Lyly, Peele, Dekker,
Nash, Kyd, Marlowe, and others of less degree — seized upon
the crude popular drama, enlarged it to meet the needs of the
time, and within a single generation made it such a brilliant
reflection of national thought and feeling as no other age has
thus far produced.

Marlowe. The best of these early playwrights, each of whom
contributed some element of value, was Christopher Marlowe
(1564–1593), who is sometimes called the father of the Elizabethan drama. He appeared in London sometime before 1587,
when his first drama *Tamburlaine* took the city by storm. The
prologue of this drama is at once a criticism and a promise:

> From jigging veins of rhyming mother-wits,
> And such conceits as clownage keeps in pay,
> We 'll lead you to the stately tent of war,
> Where you shall hear the Scythian Tamburlaine
> Threatening the world with high-astounding terms,
> And scourging kingdoms with his conquering sword.

The "jigging" refers to the doggerel verse of the earlier drama,
and "clownage" to the crude horseplay intended to amuse the
crowd. For the doggerel is substituted blank verse, "Marlowe's
mighty line" as it has ever since been called, since he was the
first to use it with power; and for the "clownage" he promises
a play of human interest revolving around a man whose sole
ambition is for world power, — such ambition as stirred the
English nation when it called halt to the encroachments of

---

[1] Over two hundred chronicle plays, representing almost every important character
in English history, appeared within a few years. Shakespeare wrote thirteen plays
founded on English history, and three on the history of other countries.

Spain, and announced that henceforth it must be reckoned with in the councils of the Continent. Though *Tamburlaine* is largely rant and bombast, there is something in it which fascinates us like the sight of a wild bull on a rampage; for such was Timur, the hero of the first play to which we confidently give the name Elizabethan. In the latter part of the play the action grows more intense; there is a sense of tragedy, of impending doom, in the vain attempt of the hero to oppose fate. He can conquer a world but not his own griefs; he ends his triumphant career with a pathetic admission of failure: "And Tamburlaine, the Scourge of God, must die."

The succeeding plays of Marlowe are all built on the same model; that is, they are one-man plays, and the man is dominated by a passion for power. *Doctor Faustus*, the most poetical of Marlowe's works, is a play representing a scholar who hungers for more knowledge, especially the knowledge of magic. In order to obtain it he makes a bargain with the devil, selling his soul for twenty-four years of unlimited power and pleasure.[1] *The Jew of Malta* deals with the lust for such power as wealth gives, and the hero is the money-lender Barabas, a monster of avarice and hate, who probably suggested to Shakespeare the character of Shylock in *The Merchant of Venice*. The last play written by Marlowe was *Edward II*, which dealt with a man who might have been powerful, since he was a king, but who furnished a terrible example of weakness and petty tyranny that ended miserably in a dungeon.

Marlowe's Dramas

After writing these four plays with their extraordinary promise, Marlowe, who led a wretched life, was stabbed in a tavern brawl. The splendid work which he only began (for he died under thirty years of age) was immediately taken up by the greatest of all dramatists, Shakespeare.

---

[1] The story is the same as that of Goethe's *Faust*. It was a favorite story, or rather collection of stories, of the Middle Ages, and was first printed as the *History of Johann Faust* in Frankfort, in 1587. Marlowe's play was written, probably, in the same year.

WILLIAM SHAKESPEARE (1564–1616)

" The name of Shakespeare is the greatest in all literature. No man ever came near to him in the creative power of the mind; no man ever had such strength and such variety of imagination." (Hallam) *Introd.*

" Shakespeare's mind is the horizon beyond which, at present, we do not see." (Emerson)

" I do not believe that any book or person or event in my life ever made so great an impression on me as the plays of Shakespeare. They appear to be the work of some heavenly genius." (Goethe)

Shakespeare's name has become a signal for enthusiasm. The tributes quoted above are doubtless extravagant, but they were written by men of mark in three different countries, and they serve to indicate the tremendous impression which Shakespeare has left upon the world. He wrote in his day some thirty-seven plays and a few poems; since then as many hundred volumes have been written in praise of his accomplishment. He died three centuries ago, without caring enough for his own work to print it. At the present time unnumbered critics, historians, scholars, are still explaining the mind and the art displayed in that same neglected work. Most of these eulogists begin or end their volumes with the remark that Shakespeare is so great as to be above praise or criticism. As Taine writes, before plunging into his own analysis, "Lofty words, eulogies are all used in vain; Shakespeare needs not praise but comprehension merely."

Life. It is probably because so very little is known about Shakespeare that so many bulky biographies have been written of him. Not a solitary letter of his is known to exist; not a play comes down to us as he wrote it. A few documents written by other men, and sometimes ending in a sprawling signature by Shakespeare, which looks as if made by a hand accustomed to almost any labor except that of the pen, — these are all we have to build upon. One record, in dribbling Latin, relates to the christening of " Gulielmus filius Johannes Shakspere "; a second, unreliable as a village gossip, tells an anecdote of the same person's boyhood; a third refers to Shakespeare as " one of his

Majesty's poor players"; a fourth records the burial of the poet's son Hamnet; a fifth speaks of " Willi. Shakspere, gentleman"; a sixth is a bit of wretched doggerel inscribed on the poet's tombstone; a seventh tells us that in 1622, only six years after the poet's death, the public had so little regard for his art that the council of his native Stratford bribed his old company of players to go away from the town without giving a performance.

It is from such dry and doubtful records that we must construct a biography, supplementing the meager facts by liberal use of our imagination.

In the beautiful Warwickshire village of Stratford our poet was born, probably in the month of April, in 1564. His mother, Mary
Early Days Arden, was a farmer's daughter; his father was a butcher and small tradesman, who at one time held the office of high bailiff of the village. There was a small grammar school in Stratford, and Shakespeare may have attended it for a few years. When he was about fourteen years old his father, who was often in lawsuits, was imprisoned for debt, and the boy probably left school and went to work. At eighteen he married Anne Hathaway, a peasant's daughter eight years older than himself; at twenty-three, with his father still in debt and his own family of three children to provide for, Shakespeare took the footpath that led to the world beyond his native village.[1]

From Stratford he went to London, from solitude to crowds, from beautiful rural scenes to dirty streets, from natural country people to
In London seekers after the bubble of fame or fortune. Why he went is largely a matter of speculation. That he was looking for work; that he followed a company of actors, as a boy follows a circus; that he was driven out of Stratford after poaching on the game preserves of Sir Thomas Lucy, whom he ridiculed in the plays of *Henry VI* and *Merry Wives*, — these and other theories are still debated. The most probable explanation of his departure is that the stage lured him away, as the printing press called the young Franklin from whatever else he undertook; for he seems to have headed straight for the theater, and to have found his place not by chance or calculation but by unerring instinct. England was then, as we have noted,

---

[1] Such is the prevalent opinion of Shakespeare's early days; but we are dealing here with surmises, not with established facts. There are scholars who allege that Shakespeare's poverty is a myth; that his father was prosperous to the end of his days; that he probably took the full course in Latin and Greek at the Stratford school. Almost everything connected with the poet's youth is still a matter of dispute.

in danger of going stage-mad, and Shakespeare appeared to put method into the madness.

Beginning, undoubtedly, as an actor of small parts, he soon learned the tricks of the stage and the humors of his audience. His first **Actor and Playwright** dramatic work was to revise old plays, giving them some new twist or setting to please the fickle public. Then he worked with other playwrights, with Lyly and Peele perhaps, and the horrors of his *Titus Andronicus* are sufficient evidence of his collaboration with Marlowe. Finally he walked alone, having learned his steps, and *Romeo and Juliet* and *Midsummer Night's Dream* announced that a great poet and dramatist had suddenly appeared in England.

THE LIBRARY, STRATFORD GRAMMAR SCHOOL
ATTENDED BY SHAKESPEARE

This experimental period of Shakespeare's life **Period of Gloom** in London was apparently a time of health, of joyousness, of enthusiasm which comes with the successful use of one's powers. It was followed by a period of gloom and sorrow, to which something of bitterness was added. What occasioned the change is again a matter of speculation. The first conjecture is that Shakespeare was a man to whom the low ideals of the Elizabethan stage were intolerable, and this opinion is strengthened after reading certain of Shakespeare's sonnets, which reflect a loathing for the theaters and the mannerless crowds that filled them. Another conjectural cause of his gloom was the fate of certain noblemen with whom he was apparently on terms of friendship, to whom he dedicated his poems, and from whom he received substantial gifts of money. Of these powerful friends, the Earl of Essex was beheaded for treason, Pembroke was banished, and Southampton had gone to that grave of so many high hopes, the Tower of London. Shakespeare may have shared the sorrow of these men, as once he had shared their joy, and there are critics who assume that he was personally implicated in the crazy attempt of Essex at rebellion.

Whatever the cause of his grief, Shakespeare shows in his works that he no longer looks on the world with the clear eyes of youth. The great tragedies of this period, *Lear*, *Macbeth*, *Hamlet*, *Othello* and *Cæsar*, all portray man not as a being of purpose and high destiny, but as the sport of chance, the helpless victim who cries out, as in *Henry IV*, for a sight of the Book of Fate, wherein is shown

> how chances mock,
> And changes fill the cup of alteration
> With divers liquors! O, if this were seen,
> The happiest youth, viewing his progress through,
> What perils past, what crosses to ensue,
> Would shut the book, and sit him down and die.

For such a terrible mood London offered no remedy. For a time Shakespeare seems to have gloried in the city; then he wearied of it, **Return to** grew disgusted with the stage, and finally, after some **Stratford** twenty-four years (*cir.* 1587–1611), sold his interest in the theaters, shook the dust of London from his feet, and followed his heart back to Stratford. There he adopted the ways of a country gentleman, and there peace and serenity returned to him. He wrote comparatively little after his retirement; but the few plays of this last period, such as *Cymbeline*, *Winter's Tale* and *The Tempest*, are the mellowest of all his works.

After a brief period of leisure, Shakespeare died at his prime in 1616, and was buried in the parish church of Stratford. Of his great **Shakespeare** works, now the admiration of the world, he thought so little **the Man** that he never collected or printed them. From these works many attempts are made to determine the poet's character, beliefs, philosophy, — a difficult matter, since the works portray many types of character and philosophy equally well. The testimony of a few contemporaries is more to the point, and from these we hear that our poet was " very good company," " of such civil demeanor," " of such happy industry," " of such excellent fancy and brave notions," that he won in a somewhat brutal age the characteristic title of " the gentle Shakespeare."

The Dramas of Shakespeare. In Shakespeare's day playwrights were producing various types of drama : the chronicle play, representing the glories of English history ; the domestic drama, portraying homely scenes and common people ; the court comedy (called also Lylian comedy, after the dramatist who developed it), abounding in wit and repartee for the delight of the upper classes ; the melodrama, made up of sensational elements thrown together without much plot ; the tragedy of blood, centering in one character who struggles amidst woes and

ANNE HATHAWAY'S COTTAGE

horrors ; romantic comedy and romantic tragedy, in which men and women were more or less idealized, and in which the elements of love, poetry, romance, youthful imagination and enthusiasm predominated.

It is interesting to note that Shakespeare essayed all these types — the chronicle play in *Henry IV*, the domestic drama in *Merry Wives*, the court comedy in *Love's Labor's Lost*, the melodrama in *Richard III*, the tragedy of blood in *King Lear*, romantic tragedy in *Romeo and Juliet*, romantic comedy in *As You Like It* — and that in each he showed such **a** mastery as to raise him far above all his contemporaries.

In his experimental period of work (*cir.* 1590–1595) Shakespeare began by revising old plays in conjunction with other
Early Dramas actors. *Henry VI* is supposed to be an example of such tinkering work. The first part of this play (performed by Shakespeare's company in 1592) was in all probability an older work made over by Shakespeare and some unknown dramatist. From the fact that Joan of Arc appears in the play in two entirely different characters, and is even made

THE MAIN ROOM, ANNE HATHAWAY'S COTTAGE

to do battle at Rouen several years after her death, it is almost certain that *Henry VI* in its present form was composed at different times and by different authors.

Love's Labor's Lost is an example of the poet's first independent work. In this play such characters as Holofernes the schoolmaster, Costard the clown and Adriano the fantastic Spaniard are all plainly of the "stock" variety; various rimes and meters are used experimentally; blank verse is not mastered; and some of the songs, such as "On a Day," are more or less artificial. Other plays of this early experimental period are *Two Gentlemen of Verona* and *Richard III*, the latter of which shows the influence and, possibly, the collaboration of Marlowe.

In the second period (*cir.* 1595–1600) Shakespeare constructed his plots with better skill, showed a greater mastery **Second** of blank verse, created some original characters, and **Period** especially did he give free rein to his romantic imagination. All doubt and experiment vanished in the confident enthusiasm of this period, as if Shakespeare felt within himself the coming of the sunrise in *Romeo and Juliet*:

> Night's candles are burnt out, and jocund day
> Stands tiptoe on the misty mountain tops.

Though some of his later plays are more carefully finished, in none of them are we so completely under the sway of poetry and romance as in these early works, written when Shakespeare first felt the thrill of mastery in his art.

In *Midsummer Night's Dream*, for example, the practical affairs of life seem to smother its poetic dreams; but note how the dream abides with us after the play is over. The spell of the enchanted forest is broken when the crowd invades its solitude; the witchery of moonlight fades into the light of common day; and then comes Theseus with his dogs to drive not the foxes but the fairies out of the landscape. As Chesterton points out, this masterful man, who has seen no fairies, proceeds to arrange matters in a practical way, with a wedding, a feast and a pantomime, as if these were the chief things of life. So, he thinks, the drama is ended; but after he and his noisy followers have departed to slumber, lo! enter once more Puck, Oberon, Titania and the whole train of fairies, to repeople the ancient world and dance to the music of Mendelssohn:

> Hand in hand, with fairy grace,
> While we sing, and bless this place.

So in *The Merchant of Venice* with its tragic figure of Shylock, who is hurried off the stage to make place for a final scene of love, moonlight and music ; so in every other play of this period, the poetic dream of life triumphs over its practical realities.

During the third period, of maturity of power (*cir.* 1600–1610), Shakespeare was overshadowed by some personal grief or disappointment. He wrote his " farewell to **Third Period** mirth " in *Twelfth Night*, and seems to have reflected his own perturbed state in the lines which he attributes to Achilles in *Troilus and Cressida* :

> My mind is troubled, like a fountain stirr'd,
> And I myself see not the bottom of it.

His great tragedies belong to this period, tragedies which reveal increased dramatic power in Shakespeare, but also his loss of hope, his horrible conviction that man is not a free being but a puppet blown about by every wind of fate or circumstance. In *Hamlet* great purposes wait upon a feeble will, and the strongest purpose may be either wrecked or consummated by a trifle. The whole conception of humanity in this play suggests a clock, of which, if but one small wheel is touched, all the rest are thrown into confusion. In *Macbeth* a man of courage and vaulting ambition turns coward or traitor at the appearance of a ghost, at the gibber of witches, at the whisper of conscience, at the taunts of his wife. In *King Lear* a monarch of high disposition drags himself and others down to destruction, not at the stern command of fate, but at the mere suggestion of foolishness. In *Othello* love, faith, duty, the fidelity of a brave man, the loyalty of a pure woman, — all are blasted, wrecked, dishonored by a mere breath of suspicion blown by a villain.

In his final period, of leisurely experiment (*cir.* 1610–1616), Shakespeare seems to have recovered in Stratford the cheerful-**Last** ness that he had lost in London. He did little **Dramas** work during this period, but that little is of rare charm and sweetness. He no longer portrayed human life as a comedy of errors or a tragedy of weakness but as a glowing romance, as if the mellow autumn of his own life had tinged

all the world with its own golden hues. With the exception
of *As You Like It* (written in the second period), in which
brotherhood is pictured as the end of life, and love as its un-
failing guide, it is doubtful if any of the earlier plays leaves
such a wholesome impression as *The Winter's Tale* or *The
Tempest*, which were probably the last of the poet's works.

Following is a list of Shakespeare's thirty-four plays (or thirty-seven,
counting the different parts of *Henry IV* and *Henry VI*) arranged according to the periods in which they were probably written. The dates are
approximate, not exact, and the chronological order is open to question:

FIRST PERIOD, EARLY EXPERIMENT (1590–1595). *Titus Andronicus,
Henry VI, Love's Labor's Lost, Comedy of Errors, Two Gentlemen of
Verona, Richard III, Richard II, King John.*
SECOND PERIOD, DEVELOPMENT (1595–1600). *Romeo and Juliet,
Midsummer Night's Dream, Merchant of Venice, Henry IV, Henry V,
Merry Wives of Windsor, Much Ado About Nothing, As You Like It.*
THIRD PERIOD, MATURITY AND TROUBLE (1600–1610). *Twelfth
Night, Taming of the Shrew, Julius Cæsar, Hamlet, Troilus and
Cressida, All's Well that Ends Well, Measure for Measure, Othello,
King Lear, Macbeth, Antony and Cleopatra, Timon of Athens.*
FOURTH PERIOD, LATER EXPERIMENT (1610–1616). *Coriolanus,
Pericles, Cymbeline, The Winter's Tale, The Tempest, Henry VIII*
(left unfinished, completed probably by Fletcher).

The most convenient arrangement of these plays appears in
the First Folio (1623)[1] where they are grouped in three classes
Tragedy and called tragedies, comedies and historical plays. The
Comedy tragedy is a drama in which the characters are the
victims of unhappy passions, or are involved in desperate circumstances. The style is grave and dignified, the movement
stately; the ending is disastrous to individuals, but illustrates
the triumph of a moral principle. These rules of true tragedy
are repeatedly set aside by Shakespeare, who introduces elements of buffoonery, and who contrives an ending that may
stand for the triumph of a principle but that is quite likely to

[1] This was the first edition of Shakespeare's plays. It was prepared seven years after
the poet's death by two of his fellow actors, Heminge and Condell. It contained all
the plays now attributed to Shakespeare with the exception of *Pericles*.

be the result of accident or madness. His best tragedies are *Macbeth, Romeo and Juliet, Hamlet, King Lear* and *Othello*.

Comedy is a type of drama in which the elements of fun and humor predominate. The style is gay; the action abounds in unexpected incidents; the ending brings ridicule or punishment to the villains in the plot, and satisfaction to all worthy characters. Among the best of Shakespeare's comedies, in which he is apt to introduce serious or tragic elements, are *As You Like It, Merchant of Venice, Midsummer Night's Dream, The Winter's Tale,* and *The Tempest.*

CAWDOR CASTLE, SCOTLAND, ASSOCI-
ATED WITH MACBETH

Strictly speaking there are only two dramatic types, all others, such as farce, melodrama, tragi-comedy, lyric drama, or opera, and chronicle play, being modifications of comedy or tragedy. The historical play, to which Elizabethans were devoted, aimed to present great scenes or characters from a past age, and were generally made up of both tragic and comic elements. The best of Shakespeare's historical plays are *Julius Cæsar, Henry IV, Henry V, Richard III* and *Coriolanus*.

There is no better way to feel the power of Shakespeare than to read in succession three different types of plays, such **What to Read** as the comedy of *As You Like It*, the tragedy of *Macbeth* and the historical play of *Julius Cæsar*. Another excellent trio is *The Merchant of Venice, Romeo and Juliet* and *Henry IV*; and the reading of these typical plays might well be concluded with *The Tempest*, which was probably Shakespeare's last word to his Elizabethan audience.

The Quality of Shakespeare. As the thousand details of a Gothic cathedral receive character and meaning from its towering spire, so all the works of Shakespeare are dominated by his imagination. That imagination of his was both sympathetic and creative. It was sympathetic in that it understood without conscious effort all kinds of men, from clowns to kings, and all human emotions that lie between the extremes of joy and sorrow; it was creative in that, from any given emotion or motive, it could form a human character who should be completely governed by that motive. Ambition in Macbeth, pride in Coriolanus, wit in Mercutio, broad humor in Falstaff, indecision in Hamlet, pure fancy in Ariel, brutality in Richard, a passionate love in Juliet, a merry love in Rosalind, an ideal love in Perdita, — such characters reveal Shakespeare's power to create living men and women from a single motive or emotion.²

Or take a single play, *Othello*,³ and disregarding all minor characters, fix attention on the pure devotion of Desdemona, the jealousy of Othello, the villainy of Iago. The genius that in a single hour can make us understand these contrasting characters as if we had met them in the flesh, and make our hearts ache as we enter into their joy, their anguish, their dishonor, is beyond all ordinary standards of measurement. And *Othello* must be multiplied many times before we reach the limit of Shakespeare's creative imagination. He is like the genii of the *Arabian Nights*, who produce new marvels while we wonder at the old.

Such an overpowering imagination must have created wildly, fancifully, had it not been guided by other qualities: by an observation almost as keen as that of Chaucer, and by the saving grace of humor. We need only mention the latter qualities, for if the reader will examine any great play of Shakespeare, he will surely find them in evidence: the observation keeping the characters of the poet's imagination true to the world of men and women, and the humor preventing some scene of terror or despair from overwhelming us by its terrible reality.

E

In view of these and other qualities it has become almost a fashion to speak of the "perfection" of Shakespeare's art; but

His Faults   in truth no word could be more out of place in such a connection. As Ben Jonson wrote in his *Timber*:

" I remember the players have often mentioned it as an honor to Shakespeare that in his writing, whatever he penned, he never blotted out a line. My answer hath been, ' Would he had blotted a thousand.' "

Even in his best work Shakespeare has more faults than any other poet of England. He is in turn careless, extravagant, profuse, tedious, sensational; his wit grows stale or coarse; his patriotism turns to bombast; he mars even such pathetic scenes as the burial of Ophelia by buffoonery and brawling; and all to please a public that was given to bull-baiting.

These certainly are imperfections; yet the astonishing thing is that they pass almost unnoticed in Shakespeare. He reflected his age, the evil and the good of it, just as it appeared to him; and the splendor of his representation is such that even his faults have their proper place, like shadows in a sunlit landscape.

Of Shakespeare's philosophy we may say that it reflected equally well the views of his hearers and of the hundred char-

His View of Life   acters whom he created for their pleasure. Of his personal views it is impossible to say more than this, with truth : that he seems to have been in full sympathy with the older writers whose stories he used as the sources of his drama.[1] Now these stories commonly reflected three things besides the main narrative : a problem, its solution, and the consequent moral or lesson. The problem was a form of evil; its solution depended on goodness in some form; the moral was that goodness triumphs finally and inevitably over evil.

[1] The chief sources of Shakespeare's plays are: (1) Older plays, from which he made half of his dramas, such as *Richard III*, *Hamlet*, *King John*. (2) Holinshed's *Chronicles*, from which he obtained material for his English historical plays. (3) Plutarch's *Lives*, translated by North, which furnished him material for *Cæsar*, *Coriolanus*, *Antony and Cleopatra*. (4) French, Italian and Spanish romances, in translations, from which he obtained the stories of *The Merchant of Venice*, *Othello*, *Twelfth Night* and *As You Like It*.

Many such stories were cherished by the Elizabethans, the old tale of " Gammelyn " for example (from which came *As You Like It*) ; and just as in our own day popular novels are dramatized, so three centuries ago audiences demanded to see familiar stories in vigorous action. That is why Shakespeare held to the old tales, and pleased his audience, instead of inventing new plots. But however much he changed the characters or the action of the story, he remained always true to the old moral :

> That goodness is the rule of life,
> And its glory and its triumph.

Shakespeare's women are his finest characters, and he often portrays the love of a noble woman as triumphing over the sin or weakness of men. He has little regard for abnormal or degenerate types, such as appear in the later Elizabethan drama ; he prefers vigorous men and pure women, precisely as the old story-tellers did ; and if Richard or some other villain overruns his stage for an hour, such men are finally overwhelmed by the very evil which they had planned for others. If they drag the innocent down to a common destruction, these pure characters never seem to us to perish ; they live forever in our thought as the true emblems of humanity.

It was Charles Lamb who referred to a copy of Shakespeare's plays as "this manly book." The expression is a good one, **Moral Emphasis** and epitomizes the judgment of a world which has found that, though Shakespeare introduces evil or vulgar elements into his plays, his emphasis is always upon the right man and the right action. This may seem a trite thing to say in praise of a great genius ; but when you reflect that Shakespeare is read throughout the civilized world, the simple fact that the splendor of his poetry is balanced by the rightness of his message becomes significant and impressive. It speaks not only for Shakespeare but for the moral quality of the multitudes who acknowledge his mastery. Wherever his plays are read, on land or sea, in the crowded cities of men or the far silent places of the earth, there the solitary man finds himself face to face with the unchanging ideals of his race, with honor, duty, courtesy, and the moral imperative,

> This above all: to thine own self be true,
> And it must follow, as the night the day,
> Thou canst not then be false to any man.

The Elizabethan Drama after Shakespeare

The drama began to decline during Shakespeare's lifetime. Even before his retirement to Stratford other popular drama-

FRANCIS BEAUMONT

tists appeared who catered to a vulgar taste by introducing more sensational elements into the stage spectacle. In consequence the drama degenerated so rapidly that in 1642, only twenty-six years after the master dramatist had passed away, Parliament closed the theaters as evil and degrading places. This closing is charged to the zeal of the Puritans, who were rapidly rising into power, and the charge is probably well founded. So also was the Puritan zeal. One who was compelled to read the plays of the period, to say nothing of witnessing them, must thank these stern old Roundheads for their insistence on public decency and morality. In the drama of all ages there seems to be a terrible fatality which turns the stage first to levity, then to wickedness, and which sooner or later calls for reformation.

Among those who played their parts in the rise and fall of the drama, the chief names are Jonson, Beaumont, Fletcher,

Middleton, Webster, Heywood, Dekker, Massinger, Ford and Shirley. Concerning the work of these dramatists there is wide diversity of opinion. Lamb regards them, Beaumont and Fletcher especially, as "an inferior sort of Sidneys and Shakespeares." Landor writes of them poetically :

They stood around
The throne of Shakespeare, sturdy but unclean.

Lowell finds some small things to praise in a large collection of their plays. Hazlitt regards them as "a race of giants, a common and noble brood, of whom Shakespeare was simply the tallest." Dyce, who had an extraordinary knowledge of all these dramatists, regards such praise as absurd, saying that "Shakespeare is not only immeasurably superior to the dramatists of his time, but is utterly unlike them in almost every respect."

We shall not attempt to decide where such doctors disagree. It may not be amiss, however, to record this personal opinion : that these playwrights added little to the drama and still less to literature, and that it is hardly worth while to search out their good passages amid a welter of repulsive details. If they are to be read at all, the student will find enough of their work for comparison with the Shakespearean drama in a book of selections, such as Lamb's *Specimens of English Dramatic Poetry* or Thayer's *The Best Elizabethan Plays.*

JOHN FLETCHER
From the engraving by Philip Oudinet,
published 1811

Ben Jonson (1573?–1637). The greatest figure among these dramatists was Jonson, — "O rare Ben Jonson" as his epitaph describes him, "O rough Ben Jonson" as he was known to the playwrights with whom he waged literary warfare. His first notable play, *Every Man in His Humour*, satirizing the fads or humors of London, was acted by Shakespeare's company, and Shakespeare played one of the parts. Then Jonson fell out with his fellow actors, and wrote *The Poetaster* (acted

by a rival company) to ridicule them and their work. Shakespeare was silent, but the cudgels were taken up by Marston and Dekker, the latter of whom wrote, among other and better plays, *Satiromastix*, which was played by Shakespeare's company as a counter attack on Jonson.

The value of Jonson's plays is that they give us vivid pictures of Elizabethan society, its

BEN JONSON

speech, fashions, amusements, such as no other dramatist has drawn. Shakespeare pictures men and women as they might be in any age ; but Jonson is content to picture the men and women of London as they appeared superficially in the year 1600. His chief comedies, which satirize the shams of his age, are : *Volpone, or the Fox*, a merciless exposure of greed and avarice ; *The Alchemist*, a study of quackery as it was practiced in Elizabethan days ; *Bartholomew Fair*, a riot of folly ; and *Epicæne, or the Silent Woman*, which would now be called a roaring farce. His chief tragedies are *Sejanus* and *Catiline*.

In later life Jonson was appointed poet laureate, and wrote many masques, such as the *Masque of Beauty* and the unfinished *Sad Shepherd*. These and a few lyrics, such as the "Triumph of Charis" and the song beginning, "Drink to me only with thine eyes," are the pleasantest of Jonson's works. At the end he abandoned the drama, as Shakespeare had done, and lashed it as severely as any Puritan in the ode beginning, "Come leave the loathëd stage."

THE PROSE WRITERS

Unless one have antiquarian tastes, there is little in Elizabethan prose to reward the reader. Strange to say, the most tedious part of it was written by literary men in what was supposed to be a very fine style; while the small part that still attracts us (such as Bacon's *Essays* or Hakluyt's *Voyages*) was mostly written by practical men with no thought for literary effect.

This curious result came about in the following way. In the sixteenth century poetry was old, but English prose was new; for in the two centuries that had elapsed since Mandeville wrote his *Travels*, Malory's *Morte d' Arthur* (1475) and Ascham's *Scholemaster* (1563) are about the only two books that can be said to have a prose style. Then, just as the Elizabethans were turning to literature, John Lyly appeared with his *Euphues, or the Anatomy of Wit* (1578), an alleged novel made up of rambling conversations upon love, education, fashion, — everything that came into the author's head. The style was involved, artificial, tortured; it was loaded with conceits, antitheses and decorations:

"I perceive, Camilla, that be your cloth never so bad it will take some colour, and your cause never so false it will bear some show of probability; wherein you manifest the right nature of a woman, who, having no way to win, thinketh to overcome with words. . . . Take heed, Camilla, that seeking all the wood for a straight stick you choose not at the last a crooked staff, or prescribing a good counsel to others thou thyself follow the worst, much like to Chius, who selling the best wine to others drank himself of the lees."

This "high fantastical" style, ever since called euphuistic, created a sensation. The age was given over to extravagance, The Fad of and the artificial elegance of *Euphues* seemed to Euphuism match the other fashions. Just as Elizabethan men and women began to wear grotesque ruffs about their necks as soon as they learned the art of starching from the Dutch, so now they began to decorate their writing with the conceits of Lyly.[1] Only a year after *Euphues* appeared, Spenser published *The Shepherd's Calendar*, and his prose notes show how quickly the style, like a bad habit, had taken possession of the literary world. Shakespeare ridicules the fashion in the character of Holofernes, in *Love's Labor's Lost*, yet he follows it as slavishly as the rest. He could write good prose when he would, as is shown by a part of Hamlet's speech; but as a rule he makes his characters speak as if the art of prose were like walking a tight rope, which must be done with a balancing pole and some contortions. The scholars who produced the translation of the Scriptures known as the Authorized Version could certainly write well; yet if you examine their Dedication, in which, uninfluenced by the noble sincerity of the Bible's style, they were free to follow the fashion, you may find there the two faults of Elizabethan prose; namely, the habit of servile flattery and the sham of euphuism.

Among prose writers of the period the name that appears most frequently is that of Philip Sidney (1554–1586). He wrote one of our first critical essays, *An Apologie for Poetrie* (*cir.* 1581), the spirit of which may be judged from the following:

"Nowe therein of all sciences . . . is our poet the monarch. For he dooth not only show the way but giveth so sweete a prospect into the way

---

[1] Lyly did not invent the fashion; he carried to an extreme a tendency towards artificial writing which was prevalent in England and on the Continent. As is often the case, it was the extreme of fashion that became fashionable.

as will intice any man to enter into it. Nay, he dooth, as if your journey should lie through a faire vineyard, at the first give you a cluster of grapes, that, full of that taste, you may long to passe further. He beginneth not with obscure definitions, which must blur the margent with interpretations, and load the memory with doubtful-nesse; but hee cometh to you with words set in delightfull propor-tion, either accompanied with or prepared for the well enchaunt-ing skill of musicke; and with a tale, forsooth, he cometh unto you, —with a tale which holdeth children from play and old men from the chimney corner."

SIR PHILIP SIDNEY

Sidney wrote also the pas-toral romance *Arcadia* which was famous in its day, and in which the curious reader may find an occasional good passage, such as the prayer to a heathen god, "O All-seeing Light,"—a prayer that became historic and deeply pathetic when King Charles repeated it, facing death on the scaffold. That was in 1649, more than half a century after *Arcadia* was written:

"O all-seeing Light, and eternal Life of all things, to whom nothing is either so great that it may resist or so small that it is contemned, look upon my miserie with thine eye of mercie, and let thine infinite power vouchsafe to limite out some proportion of de-liverance unto me, as to thee shall seem most convenient. Let not injurie, O Lord, triumphe over me, and let my faults by thy hands be corrected, and make not mine unjuste enemie the minister of thy justice. But yet, my God, if in thy wisdome this be the aptest chas-tisement for my inexcusable follie; if this low bondage be fittest for my over-hie desires; if the pride of my not-inough humble hearte be thus to be broken, O Lord, I yeeld unto thy will, and joyfully embrace what sorrow thou wilt have me suffer."

The finest example of the prose of the period is the King James or Authorized Version of the Bible, which appeared The King in 1611. This translation was so much influenced James Bible by the earlier work of Wyclif, Tyndale, and many others, that its style cannot properly be called Elizabethan or Jacobean; it is rather an epitome of English at its best in the two centuries between Chaucer and Shakespeare. The fifty-four scholars who prepared this translation aimed at a faithful rendering of the Book which, aside from its spiritual teaching, contains some of the noblest examples of style in the whole range of human literature : the elemental simplicity of the Books of Moses, the glowing poetry of Job and the Psalms, the sublime imagery of Isaiah, the exquisite tenderness of the Parables, the forged and tempered argument of the Epistles, the gorgeous coloring of the Apocalypse. All these elements entered in some degree into the translation of 1611, and the result was a work of such beauty, strength and simplicity that it remained a standard of English prose for more than three centuries. It has not only been a model for our best writers; it has pervaded all the minor literature of the nation, and profoundly influenced the thought and the expression of the whole English-speaking world.

FRANCIS BACON (1561–1626)

"My name and memory I leave to foreign nations, and to mine own country *after some time is passed over,*" said Bacon in his will. That reference to the future meant, not that England might learn to forget and forgive (for Bacon was not greatly troubled by his disgrace), but that she might learn to appreciate his *Instauratio Magna.* In the same document the philosopher left magnificent bequests for various purposes, but when these were claimed by the beneficiaries it was learned that the debts of the estate were three times the assets. This high-sounding will is an epitome of Bacon's life and work.

Life. Bacon belongs with Sidney and Raleigh in that group of Elizabethans who aimed to be men of affairs, politicians, reformers, explorers, rather than writers of prose or poetry. He was of noble birth, and from an early age was attached to Elizabeth's court. There he expected rapid advancement, but the queen and his uncle (Lord Burghley) were both a little suspicious of the young man who, as he said, had "taken all knowledge for his province."

Failing to advance by favor, Bacon studied law and entered Parliament, where he rose rapidly to leadership. Ben Jonson writes of him, in that not very reliable collection of opinions called *Timber*:

"There happened in my time one noble speaker who was full of gravity in his speaking. . . . No man ever spake more neatly, more pressly, more weightily, or suffered less emptiness, less idleness, in what he uttered. . . . The fear of every man that heard him was lest he should make an end."

FRANCIS BACON

When Elizabeth died, Bacon saw his way open. He offered his
His Triumph services to the royal favorite, Buckingham, and was soon in the good graces of King James. He was made Baron Verulam and Viscount St. Albans; he married a rich wife; he rose rapidly from one political honor to another, until at sixty he was Lord High Chancellor of England. So his threefold ambition for position, wealth and power was realized. It was while he held the highest state office that he published his *Novum Organum*, which established his reputation as "the first philosopher in Europe." That was in 1620, the year when a handful of Pilgrims sailed away unnoticed on one of the world's momentous voyages.

After four years of power Bacon, who had been engaged with Buckingham in selling monopolies, and in other schemes to be rich at the public expense, was brought to task by Parliament. He was accused of receiving bribes, confessed his guilt (it is said to shield the

His Disgrace king and Buckingham, who had shared the booty), was fined, imprisoned, banished from court, and forbidden to hold public office again. All these punishments except the last were remitted by King James, to whom Bacon had been a useful tool. His last few years were spent in scientific study at Gorhambury, where he lived proudly, keeping up the appearance of his former grandeur, until his death in 1626.

Such a sketch seems a cold thing, but there is little of divine fire or human warmth in Bacon to kindle one's enthusiasm. His obituary might well be the final word of his essay "Of Wisdom for a Man's Self":

"Whereas they have all their time sacrificed to themselves, they become in the end sacrifices to the inconstancy of fortune, whose wings they thought by their self-wisdom to have pinioned."

Ben Jonson had a different and, possibly, a more just opinion. In the work from which we have quoted he says:

"My conceit of his person was never increased towards him by his place or honours; but I have and do reverence him for his greatness that was only proper to himself, in that he seemed to me ever by his work one of the greatest men, and most worthy of admiration, that had been in many ages. In his adversity I ever prayed that God would give him strength; for greatness he could not want."

Works of Bacon. The *Essays* of Bacon are so highly esteemed that the critic Hallam declares it would be "derogatory to a man of the slightest claim to polite letters" to be unacquainted with them. His first venture was a tiny volume called *Essays, Religious Meditations, Places of Persuasion and Dissuasion* (1597). This was modeled upon a French work by Montaigne (*Essais*, 1580) and was considered of small consequence by the author. As time went on, and his ambitious works were overlooked in favor of his sketches, he paid more attention to the latter, revising and enlarging his work until the final edition of fifty-eight essays appeared in 1625. Then it was that Bacon wrote, "I do now publish my Essays, which of all my works have been most current; for that, as it seems, they come home to men's business and bosoms."

The spirit of these works may be judged by the essay " Of Friendship." This promises well, for near the beginning we Quality of read, "A crowd is not company, and faces are but the Essays a gallery of pictures, and talking is but a tinkling cymbal where there is no love." Excellent! As we read on, however, we find nothing of the love that beareth all things for a friend's sake. We are not even encouraged to be friendly, but rather to cultivate the friendship of other men for the following advantages: that a friend is useful in saving us from solitude; that he may increase our joy or diminish our trouble; that he gives us good counsel; that he can finish our work or take care of our children, if need be; and finally, that he can spare our modesty while trumpeting our virtues:

"How many things are there which a man cannot, with any face or comeliness, say or do himself! A man can scarce allege his own merits with modesty, much less extol them; a man cannot sometimes brook to supplicate or beg; and a number of the like. But all these things are graceful in a friend's mouth, which are blushing in a man's own."

In old Arabic manuscripts one frequently finds a record having the appearance of truth; but at the very end, in parenthesis, one reads, "This is all a lie," or "This was my thought when I was sick," or some other enlightening climax. Bacon's essay " Of Friendship " might be more in accord with the verities if it had a final note to the effect that the man who cultivates friendship in the Baconian way will never have or deserve a friend in the world.

So with many other Baconian essays: with " Love " for example, in which we are told that it is impossible for a man to love and be wise; or with " Negotiations," which informs us that, unless a man intends to use his letter to justify himself (lo! the politician), it is better to deal by speech than by writing; for a man can " disavow or expound " his speech, but his written word may be used against him.

To some men, to most men, life offers a problem to be solved by standards that are eternally right; to others life is a game, the object is to win, and the rules may be manipulated to one's own advantage. Bacon's moral philosophy was that of the gamester; his leading motive was self-interest; so when he wrote of love or friendship or any other noble sentiment he was dealing with matters of which he had no knowledge. The best he could offer was a "counsel of prudence," and many will sympathize with John Wesley, who declared that worldly prudence is a quality from which an honest man should pray God to be delivered.

Bacon's View of Life

It is only when Bacon deals with practical matters, leaving the high places of life, where he is a stranger, to write of "Discourse" or "Gardens" or "Seeming Wise" that his essays begin to strike home by their vigor and vitality. Though seldom profound or sympathetic, they are notable for their keen observation and shrewd judgment of the ambitious world in which the author himself lived. Among those that are best worth reading are "Studies," "Wisdom for a Man's Self," "Riches," "Great Place," "Atheism," and "Travel."

What to Read

The style of these essays is in refreshing contrast to most Elizabethan prose, to the sonorous periods of Hooker, to the ramblings of Sidney, to the conceits of Lyly and Shakespeare. The sentences are mostly short, clear, simple; and so much meaning is crystallized in them that they overshadow even the "Poor Richard" maxims of Franklin, the man who had a genius for packing worldly wisdom into a convenient nutshell.

Other works of Bacon are seldom read, and may be passed over lightly. We mention only, as indicative of his wide range, his *History of Henry VII*, his Utopian romance *The New Atlantis*, his *Advancement of Learning* and his *Novum Organum*. The last two works, one in English, the other in Latin, were parts of the *Instauratio Magna*, or *The Great Institution of True Philosophy*, a colossal work which Bacon did not finish, which he never even outlined very clearly.

Ambitious Works

The aim of the *Instauratio* was, first, to sweep away ancient philosophy and the classic education of the universities ; and second, to substitute a scheme of scientific study to the end of discovering and utilizing the powers of nature. It gave Bacon his reputation (in Germany especially) of a great philosopher and scientist, and it is true that his vision of vast discoveries has influenced the thought of the world ; but to read any part of his great work is to meet a mind that seems ingenious rather than philosophical, and fanciful rather than scientific. He had what his learned contemporary Peter Heylyn termed "a chymical brain," a brain that was forever busy with new theories ; and the leading theory was that some lucky man would discover a key or philosopher's stone or magic *sesame* that must straightway unlock all the secrets of nature.

Meanwhile the real scientists of his age were discovering secrets in the only sure way, of hard, self-denying work. Gilbert was studying magnetism, Harvey discovering the circulation of the blood, Kepler determining the laws that govern the planets' motions, Napier inventing logarithms, and Galileo standing in ecstasy beneath the first telescope ever pointed at the stars of heaven.

Of the work of these scientific heroes Bacon had little knowledge, and for their plodding methods he had no sympathy. He His Vast was Viscount, Lord Chancellor, "high-browed Veru-
Plans lam," and his heaven-scaling *Instauratio* which, as he said, was "for the glory of the Creator and for the relief of man's estate" must have something stupendous, Elizabethan, about it, like the victory over the Armada. In his plans there was always an impression of vastness ; his miscellaneous works were like the strange maps that geographers made when the wonders of a new world opened upon their vision. Though he never made an important discovery, his conviction that knowledge is power and that there are no metes or bounds to knowledge, his belief that the mighty forces of nature are waiting to do man's bidding, his thought of ships that navigate

the air as easily as the sea, — all this Baconian dream of mental empire inspired the scientific world for three centuries. It was as thoroughly Elizabethan in its way as the voyage of Drake or the plays of Shakespeare.

Summary. The most remarkable feature of the Elizabethan age was its patriotic enthusiasm. This enthusiasm found its best expression on the stage, in the portrayal of life in vigorous action; and dramas were produced in such number and of such quality that the whole period is sometimes called the age of the play. It was a time of poetry rather than of prose, and nearly all of the poetry is characterized by its emotional quality, by youthful freshness of feeling, by quickened imagination, and by an extravagance of language which overflows, even in Shakespeare, in a kind of glorious bombast.

Our study of the literature of the age includes: (1) The outburst of lyric poetry. (2) The life and works of Spenser, second in time of the great English poets. (3) A review of the long history of the drama, from the earliest church spectacle, through miracle, morality, interlude, pageant and masque to the Elizabethan drama. (4) The immediate forerunners of Shakespeare, of whom the most notable was Marlowe. (5) The life and work of Shakespeare. (6) Ben Jonson, the successors of Shakespeare, and the rapid decline of the drama. (7) Elizabethan prose; the appearance of euphuism; Sidney's *Apologie for Poetrie*; the Authorized Version of the Scriptures; and the life and work of Francis Bacon.

Selections for Reading. Selected lyrics in Manly, English Poetry; Newcomer, Twelve Centuries of English Poetry and Prose; Palgrave, Golden Treasury; Schilling, Elizabethan Lyrics; Ward, English Poets.

Spenser. Selected poems in Temple Classics, Cambridge Poets Series. Selections from The Faery Queen in Standard English Classics and other school editions. (See Texts, in General Bibliography.)

Early Drama. A miracle play, such as Noah, may be read in Manly, Specimens of Pre-Shakespearean Drama (Ginn and Company). Marlowe's plays in Everyman's Library; his Edward II in Holt's English Readings; his Faustus in Temple Dramatists, and in Mermaid Series.

Shakespeare. Several editions of Shakespeare's plays, such as the revised Hudson (Ginn and Company) and the Neilson (Scott) are available. Single plays, such as Julius Cæsar, Merchant of Venice, Macbeth, As You Like It, are edited for class use in Standard English Classics, Lake Classics, and various other school series. The Sonnets in Athenæum Press Series.

Ben Jonson. The Alchemist in Cambridge Poets Series; also in Thayer, Best Elizabethan Plays (Ginn and Company), which includes in one volume plays by Marlowe, Jonson, Webster, Beaumont and Fletcher.

Prose Writers. Selections from Bacon's Essays in Riverside Literature or Maynard's English Classics. The Essays complete in Everyman's Library. Selections from Hooker, Sidney and Lyly in Manly, English Prose, or Craik, English Prose. Ampler selections in Garnett, English Prose from Elizabeth to Victoria (Ginn and Company), which contains in one volume typical works of 33 prose writers from Lyly to Carlyle. Hakluyt's Voyages in Everyman's Library.

Bibliography. *History.* Creighton, The Age of Elizabeth; Winter, Shakespeare's England; Goadby, The England of Shakespeare; Harrison, Elizabethan England; Spedding, Francis Bacon and his Times; Lee, Great Englishmen of the Sixteenth Century; Payne, Voyages of Elizabethan Seamen.

Literature. Saintsbury, Short History of Elizabethan Literature; Seccombe and Allen, The Age of Shakespeare; Whipple, Literature of the Age of Elizabeth; Schilling, Elizabethan Lyrics; Lee, Elizabethan Sonnets; Sheavyn, Literary Profession in the Elizabethan Age.

Spenser. Life, by Church (English Men of Letters Series). Carpenter, Outline Guide to the Study of Spenser; Craik, Spenser and his Times. Essays, by Lowell, in Among My Books; by Dowden, in Transcripts and Studies; by Hazlitt, in Lectures on the English Poets; by Leigh Hunt, in Imagination and Fancy.

The Drama. Gayley, Plays of Our Forefathers (a study of the early drama); Evans, English Masques; Bates, The English Religious Drama; Schilling, The Elizabethan Drama; Symonds, Shakespeare's Predecessors in the English Drama; Boas, Shakespeare and his Predecessors; Collier, History of English Dramatic Poetry; Ward, English Dramatic Literature; Chambers, The Medieval Stage; Pollard, English Miracle Plays, Moralities and Interludes.

Shakespeare. Life, by Raleigh (E. M. of L.), by Lee, by Halliwell-Phillipps, by Brandes. Dowden, A Shakespeare Primer; Dowden, Shakespeare: a Critical Study of his Mind and Art; Baker, Development of Shakespeare as a Dramatist.

Other Dramatists. Lowell, Old English Dramatists; Lamb, Specimens of English Dramatic Poets; Fleay, Biographical Chronicle of the English Drama; Ingram, Christopher Marlowe.

Prose Writers. Church, Life of Bacon (E. M. of L.); Nicol, Bacon's Life and Philosophy; Macaulay, Essay on Bacon. Symonds, Life of Sidney (E. M. of L.); Bourne, Life of Sidney (Heroes of the Nations Series). Stebbing, Life of Raleigh.

Fiction and Poetry. Kingsley, Westward Ho; Black, Judith Shakespeare; Scott, Kenilworth; Schiller, Maria Stuart; Alfred Noyes, Drake; Bates and Coman, English History Told by English Poets.

CHAPTER V

THE PURITAN AGE AND THE RESTORATION (1625–1700)

> Milton, thou shouldst be living at this hour.
>   England hath need of thee: she is a fen
>   Of stagnant waters; altar, sword, and pen,
> Fireside, the heroic wealth of hall and bower,
> Have forfeited their ancient English dower
>   Of inward happiness. We are selfish men;
>   Oh! raise us up, return to us again,
> And give us manners, virtue, freedom, power.
>
> Wordsworth, " Sonnet on Milton "

Historical Outline. The period from the accession of Charles I in 1625 to the Revolution of 1688 was filled with a mighty struggle over the question whether king or Commons should be supreme in England. On this question the English people were divided into two main parties. On one side were the Royalists, or Cavaliers, who upheld the monarch with his theory of the divine right of kings; on the other were the Puritans, or Independents, who stood for the rights of the individual man and for the liberties of Parliament and people. The latter party was at first very small; it had appeared in the days of Langland and Wyclif, and had been persecuted by Elizabeth; but persecution served only to increase its numbers and determination. Though the Puritans were never a majority in England, they soon ruled the land with a firmness it had not known since the days of William the Conqueror. They were primarily men of conscience, and no institution can stand before strong men whose conscience says the institution is wrong. That is why the degenerate theaters were not reformed but abolished; that is why the theory of the divine right of kings was shattered as by a thunderbolt when King Charles was sent to the block for treason against his country.

The struggle reached a climax in the Civil War of 1642, which ended in a Puritan victory. As a result of that war, England was for a brief period a commonwealth, disciplined at home and respected abroad, through the genius and vigor and tyranny of Oliver Cromwell.

When Cromwell died (1658) there was no man in England strong enough to take his place, and two years later "Prince Charlie," who had long been an exile, was recalled to the throne as Charles II of England. He had learned nothing from his father's fate or his own experience, and proceeded by all evil ways to warrant this "Epitaph," which his favorite, Wilmot, Earl of Rochester, pinned on the door of his bedchamber:

> Here lies our Sovereign Lord the King,
>   Whose word no man relies on,
> Who never said a foolish thing,
>   Nor ever did a wise one.

The next twenty years are of such disgrace and national weakness that the historian hesitates to write about them. It was called the period of the Restoration, which meant, in effect, the restoration of all that was objectionable in monarchy. Another crisis came in the Revolution of 1688, when the country, aroused by the attempt of James II to establish another despotism in Church and state, invited Prince William of Orange (husband of the king's daughter Mary) to the English throne. That revolution meant three things: the supremacy of Parliament, the beginning of modern England, and the final triumph of the principle of political liberty for which the Puritan had fought and suffered hardship for a hundred years.

Typical Writers. Among the writers of the period three men stand out prominently, and such was the confusion of the times that in the whole range of our literature it would be difficult to find three others who differ more widely in spirit or method. Milton represents the scholarship, the culture of the Renaissance, combined with the moral earnestness of the Puritan. Bunyan, a poor tinker and lay preacher, reflects the tremendous spiritual ferment among the common people. And Dryden, the cool, calculating author who made a business of writing, regards the Renaissance and Puritanism as both things of the past. He lives in the present, aims to give readers what they like, follows the French critics of the period who advocate writing by rule, and popularizes that cold, formal, precise style which, under the assumed name of classicism, is to dominate English poetry during the following century.

JOHN MILTON (1608–1674)

Yet some there be that by due steps aspire
To lay their just hands on that golden key
That opes the palace of eternity:
To such my errand is.

In these words of the Attendant Spirit in *Comus* we seem to hear Milton speaking to his readers. To such as regard poetry as the means of an hour's pleasant recreation he brings no message; his "errand" is to those who, like Sidney, regard poetry as the handmaiden of virtue, or, like Aristotle, as the highest form of human history.

Life. Milton was born in London (1608) at a time when Shakespeare and his fellow dramatists were in their glory. He grew up in a home where the delights of poetry and music were added to the moral discipline of the Puritan. Before he was twelve years old he had formed the habit of studying far into the night; and his field included not only Greek, Latin, Hebrew and modern European literatures, but mathematics also, and science and theology and music. His parents had devoted him in infancy to noble ends, and he joyously accepted their dedication, saying, "He who would not be frustrate of his hope to write well . . . ought himself to be a true poem, that is, a composition and pattern of the best and honorablest things."

From St. Paul's school Milton went to Christ's College, Cambridge, took his master's degree, wrote a few poems in Latin, Italian and English, and formed a plan for a great epic, "a poem that **Milton at** England would not willingly let die." Then he retired to **Horton** his father's country-place at Horton, and for six years gave himself up to music, to untutored study, and to that formal pleasure in nature which is reflected in his work. Five short poems were the only literary result of this retirement, but these were the most perfect of their kind that England had thus far produced.

Milton's next step, intended like all others to cultivate his talent, took him to the Continent. For fifteen months he traveled through France and Italy, and was about to visit Greece when, hearing of the struggle between king and Parliament, he set his face towards England again. "For I thought it base," he said, "to be traveling at my ease for culture when my countrymen at home were fighting for liberty."

To find himself, or to find the service to which he could devote his great learning, seems to have been Milton's object after his return to

Home Life   London (1639). While he waited he began to educate his nephews, and enlarged this work until he had a small private school, in which he tested some of the theories that appeared later in his *Tractate on Education*. Also he married, in haste it seems, and with deplorable consequences. His wife, Mary Powell, the daughter of a Cavalier, was a pleasure-loving young woman, and after a brief experience of Puritan discipline she wearied of it and went home. She has been amply criticized for her desertion, but Milton's house must have been rather chilly for any ordinary human being to find comfort in. To him woman seemed to have been made for obedience, and man for rebellion ; his toplofty doctrine of masculine superiority found expression in a line regarding Adam and Eve, " He for God only, she for God in him,"—an old delusion, which had been seriously disturbed by the first woman.

JOHN MILTON

For a period of near twenty years Milton wrote

Period of Controversy   but little poetry, his time being occupied with controversies that were then waged even more fiercely in the press than in the field. It was after the execution of King Charles (1649), when England was stunned and all Europe aghast at the Puritans' daring, that he published his *Tenure of Kings and Magistrates*, the argument of which was, that magistrates and people are equally subject to the law, and that the divine right of kings to rule is as nothing beside the divine right of the people to defend their liberties. That argument established Milton's position as the literary champion of democracy. He was chosen Secretary of the Commonwealth, his duties being to prepare the Latin correspondence with foreign countries, and to confound all arguments of the Royalists. During the next decade Milton's pen and Cromwell's sword were the two outward bulwarks of Puritanism, and one was quite as ready and almost as potent as the other.

It was while Milton was thus occupied that he lost his eyesight, "his last sacrifice on the altar of English liberty." His famous "Son-
His   net on his Blindness" is a lament not for his lost sight
Blindness   but for his lost talent; for while serving the Common-
wealth he must abandon the dream of a great poem that he had cherished all his life:

> When I consider how my light is spent
> Ere half my days, in this dark world and wide,
> And that one talent, which is death to hide,
> Lodged with me useless, though my soul more bent
> To serve therewith my Maker, and present
> My true account, lest he returning chide;
> " Doth God exact day-labour, light denied ? "
> I fondly ask; but Patience, to prevent
> That murmur, soon replies, " God doth not need
> Either man's work or his own gifts. Who best
> Bear his mild yoke, they serve him best. His state
> Is kingly: thousands at his bidding speed,
> And post o'er land and ocean without rest;
> They also serve who only stand and wait."

With the Restoration (1660) came disaster to the blind Puritan poet, who had written too harshly against Charles I to be forgiven by Charles II. He was forced to hide; his property was confiscated; his works were burned in public by the hangman; had not his fame as a writer raised up powerful friends, he would have gone to the scaffold when Cromwell's bones were taken from the grave and hanged in impotent revenge. He was finally allowed to settle in a modest house, and to be in peace so long as he remained in obscurity. So the pen was silenced that had long been a scourge to the enemies of England.

His home life for the remainder of his years impresses us by its loneliness and grandeur. He who had delighted as a poet in the Eng-
His   lish country, and more delighted as a Puritan in the fierce
Loneliness   struggle for liberty, was now confined to a small house,
going from study to porch, and finding both in equal darkness. He who had roamed as a master through the wide fields of literature was now dependent on a chance reader. His soul also was afflicted by the

apparent loss of all that Puritanism had so hardly won, by the degradation of his country, by family troubles; for his daughters often
rebelled at the task of taking his dictation, and left him helpless.
Saddest of all, there was no love in the house, for with all his genius
Milton could not inspire affection in his own people; nor does he
ever reach the heart of his readers.

In the midst of such scenes, denied the pleasure of hope, Milton
seems to have lived largely in his memories. He took up his early
His dream of an immortal epic, lived with it seven years in
Masterpiece seclusion, and the result was *Paradise Lost*. This epic is
generally considered the finest fruit of Milton's genius, but there are
two other poems that have a more personal and human significance.

COTTAGE AT CHALFONT, ST. GILES, BUCKINGHAMSHIRE
Where Milton lived during the Plague, and where *Paradise Lost* was written

In the morning of his life he had written *Comus*, and the poem is a
reflection of a noble youth whose way lies open and smiling before
him. Almost forty years later, or just before his death in 1674, he
wrote *Samson Agonistes*, and in this tragedy of a blind giant, bound,
captive, but unconquerable, we have a picture of the agony and
moral grandeur of the poet who takes leave of life:

> I feel my genial spirits droop, . . .
> My race of glory run, and race of shame;
> And I shall shortly be with them that rest. [1]

[1] From Milton's *Samson*. For the comparison we are indebted to **Henry Reed**,
Lectures on English Literature (1863), p. 223.

The Early Poems. Milton's first notable poem, written in college days, was the " Ode on the Morning of Christ's Nativity," a chant of victory and praise such as Pindar might have written had he known the meaning of Christmas. In this boyish work one may find the dominant characteristic of all Milton's poetry ; namely, a blending of learning with piety, a devotion of all the treasures of classic culture to the service of religion.

Among the earliest of the Horton poems (so-called because they were written in the country-place of that name) are " L'Allegro " and " Il Penseroso," two of the most widely quoted works in our literature. They should be read in order to understand what people have admired for nearly three hundred years, if not for their own beauty. " L'Allegro " (from the Italian, meaning " the cheerful man ") is the poetic expression of a happy state of mind, and " Il Penseroso "[1] of a quiet, thoughtful mood that verges upon sadness, like the mood that follows good music. Both poems are largely inspired by nature, and seem to have been composed out of doors, one in the morning and the other in the evening twilight.

Comus (1634), another of the Horton poems, is to many readers the most interesting of Milton's works. In form it is The Masque of Comus a masque, that is, a dramatic poem intended to be staged to the accompaniment of music ; in execution it is the most perfect of all such poems inspired by the Elizabethan love of pageants. We may regard it, therefore, as a late echo of the Elizabethan drama, which, like many another echo, is sweeter though fainter than the original. It was performed at Ludlow Castle, before the Earl of Bridgewater, and was suggested by an accident to the Earl's children, a simple accident, in which Milton saw the possibility of "turning the common dust of opportunity to gold."

---

[1] The name is generally translated into "melancholy," but the latter term is now commonly associated with sorrow or disease. To Milton "melancholy" meant "pensiveness." In writing "Il Penseroso" he was probably influenced by a famous book, Burton's *Anatomy of Melancholy*, which appeared in 1621 and was very widely read.

The story is that of a girl who becomes separated from her brothers in a wood, and is soon lost. The magician Comus [1] appears with his band of revelers, and tries to bewitch the girl, to make her like one of his own brutish followers. She is protected by her own purity, is watched over by the Attendant Spirit, and finally rescued by her brothers. The story is somewhat like that of the old ballad of " The Children in the Wood," but it is here transformed into a kind of morality play.

In this masque may everywhere be seen the influence of Milton's predecessors and the stamp of his own independence; **Comus and** his Puritan spirit also, which must add a moral to **The Tempest** the old pagan tales. Thus, Miranda wandering about the enchanted isle (in Shakespeare's *The Tempest*) hears strange, harmonious echoes, to which Caliban gives expression :

> The isle is full of noises,
> Sounds and sweet airs, that give delight and hurt not.
> Sometimes a thousand twangling instruments
> Will hum about mine ears, and sometimes voices,
> That, if I then had waked after long sleep,
> Will make me sleep again ; and then, in dreaming,
> The clouds methought would open and show riches
> Ready to drop upon me, that when I waked
> I cried to dream again.

The bewildered girl in *Comus* also hears mysterious voices, and has glimpses of a world not her own ; but, like Sir Guyon of *The Faery Queen*, she is on moral guard against all such deceptions :

> A thousand phantasies
> Begin to throng into my memory,
> Of calling shapes, and beckoning shadows dire,
> And airy tongues that syllable men's names
> On sands and shores and desert wildernesses.
> These thoughts may startle well but not astound
> The virtuous mind, that ever walks attended
> By a strong-siding champion, Conscience.

[1] In mythology Comus, the god of revelry, was represented as the son of Dionysus (Bacchus, god of wine), and the witch Circe. In Greek poetry Comus is the leader of any gay band of satyrs or dancers. Milton's masque of *Comus* was influenced by a similar story in Peele's *Old Wives' Tale*, by Spenser's " Palace of Pleasure " in *The Faery Queen* (see p. 72), and by Homer's story of the witch Circe in the *Odyssey*.

Again, in *The Tempest* we meet " the frisky spirit" Ariel, who sings of his coming freedom from Prospero's service :

> Where the bee sucks, there suck I :
> In a cowslip's bell I lie;
> There I couch when owls do cry.
> On a bat's back I do fly
> After summer merrily :
> Merrily, merrily shall I live now
> Under the blossom that hangs on the bough.

The Attendant Spirit in *Comus* has something of Ariel's gayety, but his joy is deeper-seated; he serves not the magician Prospero

LUDLOW CASTLE

but the Almighty, and comes gladly to earth in fulfilment of the divine promise, " He shall give His angels charge over thee to keep thee in all thy ways." When his work is done he vanishes, like Ariel, but with a song which shows the difference between the Elizabethan, or Renaissance, conception of sensuous beauty (that is, beauty which appeals to the physical senses) and the Puritan's idea of moral beauty, which appeals to the soul :

> Now my task is smoothly done,
> I can fly or I can run
> Quickly to the green earth's end,
> Where the bowed welkin slow doth bend,
> And from thence can soar as soon
> To the corners of the moon.
> Mortals, that would follow me,
> Love Virtue; she alone is free :
> She can teach ye how to climb
> Higher than the sphery chime;
> Or if Virtue feeble were,
> Heaven itself would stoop to her.

Lycidas (1637), last of the Horton poems, is an elegy occasioned by the death of one who had been Milton's fellow student at Cambridge. It was an old college custom to celebrate important events by publishing a collection of Latin or English poems, and *Lycidas* may be regarded as Milton's wreath, which he offered to the memory of his classmate and to his university. The poem is beautifully fashioned, and is greatly admired for its classic form ; but it is cold as any monument, without a touch of human grief or sympathy. Probably few modern readers will care for it as they care for Tennyson's *In Memoriam*, a less perfect elegy, but one into which love enters as well as art. Other notable English elegies are the *Thyrsis* of Matthew Arnold and the *Adonais* of Shelley.

Lycidas

Milton's Left Hand. This expression was used by Milton to designate certain prose works written in the middle period of his life, at a time of turmoil and danger. These works have magnificent passages which show the power and the harmony of our English speech, but they are marred by other passages of bitter raillery and invective. The most famous of all these works is the noble plea called *Areopagitica:*[1] *a Speech for the Liberty of Unlicensed Printing* (1644).

There was a law in Milton's day forbidding the printing of any work until it had been approved by the official Licenser of Books. Such a law may have been beneficial at times, but during the seventeenth century it was another instrument of tyranny, since no Licenser would allow anything to be printed against his particular church or government. When *Areopagitica* was written the Puritans of the Long Parliament were virtually rulers of England, and Milton pleaded with his own party for the free expression of every honest opinion, for liberty in all wholesome pleasures, and for tolerance in religious matters. His stern confidence in truth, that she will not

[1] From the Areopagus or forum of Athens, the place of public appeal. This was the " Mars Hill " from which St. Paul addressed the Athenians, as recorded in the Book of Acts.

be weakened but strengthened by attack, is summarized in the famous sentence, "I cannot praise a fugitive and cloistered virtue."

Two interesting matters concerning *Areopagitica* are : first, that this eloquent plea for the freedom of printing had to be issued in defiance of law, without a license ; and second, that Milton was himself, a few years later, under Cromwell's iron government, a censor of the press.

Milton's rare sonnets seem to belong to this middle period of strife, though some of them were written earlier. Since **The Sonnets** Wyatt and Surrey had brought the Italian sonnet to England this form of verse had been employed to sing of love ; but with Milton it became a heroic utterance, a trumpet Wordsworth calls it, summoning men to virtue, to patriotism, to stern action. The most personal of these sonnets are " On Having Arrived at the Age of Twenty-three," " On his Blindness " and " To Cyriack Skinner" ; the most romantic is " To the Nightingale" ; others that are especially noteworthy are " On the Late Massacre," " On his Deceased Wife " [1] and " To Cromwell." The spirit of these sonnets, in contrast with those of Elizabethan times, is finely expressed by Landor in the lines :

> Few his words, but strong,
> And sounding through all ages and all climes;
> He caught the sonnet from the dainty hand
> Of Love, who cried to lose it, and he gave the notes
> To Glory.

Milton's Later Poetry. [2] It was in 1658, the year of Cromwell's death, when the political power of Puritanism was tottering, that Milton in his blindness began to write *Paradise Lost*. After stating his theme he begins his epic, as Virgil began the *Æneid*, in the midst of the action ; so that in reading his

---

[1] This beautiful sonnet was written to his second wife, not to Mary Powell.

[2] The three poems of Milton's later life are *Paradise Lost*, *Paradise Regained* and *Samson Agonistes*. The last-named has been referred to on page 119. *Paradise Regained* contains some noble passages, but is inferior to *Paradise Lost*, on which the poet's fame chiefly rests.

first book it is well to have in mind an outline of the whole story, which is as follows :

The scene opens in Heaven, and the time is before the creation of the world. The archangel Lucifer rebels against the Almighty, and gathers to his banner an immense company of the heavenly hosts, of **Plan of Paradise Lost** angels and flaming cherubim. A stupendous three days' battle follows between rebel and loyal legions, the issue being in doubt until the Son goes forth in his chariot of victory. Lucifer and his rebels are defeated, and are hurled over the ramparts of Heaven. Down, down through Chaos they fall " nine times the space that measures day and night," until they reach the hollow vaults of Hell.

In the second act (for *Paradise Lost* has some dramatic as well as epic construction) we follow the creation of the earth in the midst of the universe; and herein we have an echo of the old belief that the earth was the center of the solar system. Adam and Eve are formed to take in the Almighty's affection the place of the fallen angels. They live happily in Paradise, watched over by celestial guardians. Meanwhile Lucifer and his followers are plotting revenge in Hell. They first boast valiantly, and talk of mighty war; but the revenge finally degenerates into a base plan to tempt Adam and Eve and win them over to the fallen hosts.

The third act shows Lucifer, now called Satan or the Adversary, with his infernal peers in Pandemonium, plotting the ruin of the world. He makes an astounding journey through Chaos, disguises himself in various forms of bird or beast in order to watch Adam and Eve, is detected by Ithuriel and the guardian angels, and is driven away. Thereupon he haunts vast space, hiding in the shadow of the earth until his chance comes, when he creeps back into Eden by means of an underground river. Disguising himself as a serpent, he meets Eve and tempts her with the fruit of a certain " tree of knowledge," which she has been forbidden to touch. She eats the fruit and shares it with Adam; then the pair are discovered in their disobedience, and are banished from Paradise.[1]

It is evident from this outline that Milton uses material from two different sources, one an ancient legend which Cæd- **Milton's Materials** mon employed in his Paraphrase, the other the Bible narrative of Creation. Though the latter is but a small part of the epic, it is as a fixed center about which all other interests are supposed to revolve. In reading

[1] In the above outline we have arranged the events in the order in which they are supposed to have occurred. Milton tells the story in a somewhat confused way. The order of the twelve books of *Paradise Lost* is not the natural or dramatic order of the story.

Paradise Lost, therefore, with its vast scenes and colossal figures, one should keep in mind that every detail was planned by Milton to be closely related to his central theme, which is the fall of man.

In using such diverse materials Milton met with difficulties, some of which (the character of Lucifer, for example) were too great for his limited dramatic powers. In Books I and II Lucifer is a magnificent figure, the proudest in all literature, a rebel with something of celestial grandeur about him:

> " Is this the region, this the soil, the clime,"
> Said then the lost Archangel, " this the seat
> That we must change for Heaven? this mournful gloom
> For that celestial light? Be it so, since he
> Who now is sovran can dispose and bid
> What shall be right: farthest from him is best,
> Whom reason hath equalled, force hath made supreme
> Above his equals. Farewell, happy fields,
> Where joy forever dwells! Hail, horrors! hail,
> Infernal world! and thou, profoundest Hell,
> Receive thy new possessor, one who brings
> A mind not to be changed by place or time.
> The mind is its own place, and in itself
> Can make a Heaven of Hell, a Hell of Heaven.
> What matter where, if I be still the same,
> And what I should be, all but less than he
> Whom thunder hath made greater? Here at least
> We shall be free; the Almighty hath not built
> Here for his envy, will not drive us hence;
> Here we may reign secure; and in my choice
> To reign is worth ambition, though in Hell:
> Better to reign in Hell than serve in Heaven."

In other books of *Paradise Lost* the same character appears not as the heroic rebel but as the sneaking " father of lies," all his grandeur gone, creeping as a snake into Paradise or sitting in the form of an ugly toad " squat at Eve's ear," whispering petty deceits to a woman while she sleeps. It is probable that Milton meant to show here the moral results of rebellion, but there is little in his poem to explain the sudden degeneracy from Lucifer to Satan.

The reader will note, also, the strong contrast between Milton's matter and his manner. His matter is largely mythical,

Matter and Manner and the myth is not beautiful or even interesting, but childish for the most part and frequently grotesque, as when cannon are used in the battle of the angels, or when the Almighty makes plans,

> Lest unawares we lose
> This our high place, our sanctuary, our hill.

Indeed, all Milton's celestial figures, with the exception of the original Lucifer, are as banal as those of the old miracle plays ; and his Adam and Eve are dull, wooden figures that serve merely to voice the poet's theology or moral sentiments.

In contrast with this unattractive matter, Milton's manner is always and unmistakably " the grand manner." His imagination is lofty, his diction noble, and the epic of *Paradise Lost* is so filled with memorable lines, with gorgeous descriptions, with passages of unexampled majesty or harmony or eloquence, that the crude material which he injects into the Bible narrative is lost sight of in our wonder at his superb style.

The Quality of Milton. If it be asked, What is Milton's adjective? the word " sublime " rises to the lips as the best expression of his style. This word (from the Latin *sublimis*, meaning " exalted above the ordinary ") is hard to define, but may be illustrated from one's familiar experience.

You stand on a hilltop overlooking a mighty landscape on which the new snow has just fallen : the forest bending beneath its soft burden, the fields all white and still, the air scintillating with light and color, the whole world so clean and pure that it seems as if God had blotted out its imperfections and adorned it for his own pleasure. That is a sublime spectacle, and the soul of man is exalted as he looks upon it. Or here in your own village you see a woman who enters a room where a child is stricken with a deadly and contagious disease. She immolates herself for the suffering one, cares for him and saves him, then lays down her own life. That is a sublime act. Or you hear of a young patriot captured and hanged by the enemy, and as they lead him forth to death he says, " I regret that I have but one life to give to my country." That is a sublime expression, and the feeling in your heart as you hear it is one of moral sublimity.

The writer who lifts our thought and feeling above their ordinary level, who gives us an impression of outward grandeur

Sublimity

or of moral exaltation, is a sublime writer, has a sublime style; and Milton more than any other poet deserves the adjective. His scenes are immeasurable; mountain, sea and forest are but his playthings; his imagination hesitates not to paint Chaos, Heaven, Hell, the widespread Universe in which our world hangs like a pendant star and across which stretches the Milky Way:

> A broad and ample road, whose dust is gold,
> And pavement stars.

No other poet could find suitable words for such vast themes, but Milton never falters. Read the assembly of the fallen hosts before Lucifer in Book I of *Paradise Lost*, or the opening of Hellgates in Book II, or the invocation to light in Book III, or Satan's invocation to the sun in Book IV, or the morning hymn of Adam and Eve in Book V; or open *Paradise Lost* anywhere, and you shall soon find some passage which, by the grandeur of its scene or by the exalted feeling of the poet as he describes it, awakens in you the feeling of sublimity.

The harmony of Milton's verse is its second notable quality. Many of our poets use blank verse, as many other people walk,

Harmony

as if they had no sense of rhythm within them; but Milton, by reason of his long study and practice of music, seems to be always writing to melody. In consequence it is easy to read his most prolix passages, as it is easy to walk over almost any kind of ground if one but keeps step to outward or inward music. Not only is Milton's verse stately and melodious, but he is a perfect master of words, choosing them for their sound as well as for their sense, as a musician chooses different instruments to express different emotions. Note these contrasting descriptions of so simple a matter as the opening of gates:

> Heaven opened wide
> Her ever-during gates, harmonious sound,
> On golden hinges moving.

> On a sudden open fly
> With impetuous recoil and jarring sound
> Th' infernal doors, and on their hinges grate
> Harsh thunder.

In dealing with a poet of such magnificent qualities one should be wary of criticism. That Milton's poetry has little human interest, no humor, and plenty of faults may be granted. His *Paradise Lost* especially is overcrowded with mere learning or pedantry in one place and with pompous commonplaces in another. But such faults appear trivial, unworthy of mention in the presence of a poem that is as a storehouse from which the authors and statesmen of three hundred years have drawn their choicest images and expressions. It stands forever as our supreme example of sublimity and harmony, — that sublimity which reflects the human spirit standing awed and reverent before the grandeur of the universe; that harmony of expression at which every great poet aims and which Milton attained in such measure that he is called the organ-voice of England.

JOHN BUNYAN (1628–1688)

There is a striking contrast between the poet and the prose writer of the Puritan age. Milton the poet is a man of culture, familiar with the best literature of all ages; Bunyan the prose writer is a poor, self-taught laborer who reads his Bible with difficulty, stumbling over the hard passages. Milton writes for the cultivated classes, in harmonious verse adorned with classic figures; Bunyan speaks for common men in sinewy prose, and makes his meaning clear by homely illustrations drawn from daily life. Milton is a solitary and austere figure, admirable but not lovable; Bunyan is like a familiar acquaintance, ruddy-faced, clear-eyed, who wins us by his sympathy, his friendliness, his good sense and good humor. He is known as the author of one book, *The Pilgrim's Progress*, but that book has probably had more readers than any other that England has ever produced.

E

Life. During Bunyan's lifetime England was in a state of religious ferment or revival, and his experience of it is vividly portrayed in a remarkable autobiography called *Grace Abounding to the Chief of Sinners*. In reading this book we find that his life is naturally separated into two periods. His youth was a time of struggle with doubts and temptations; his later years were characterized by inward peace and tireless labor. His peace meant that he was saved, his labor that he must save others. Here, in a word, is the secret of all his works.

He was born (1628) in the village of Elstow, Bedfordshire, and was the son of a poor tinker. He was sent to school long enough to learn

JOHN BUNYAN

elementary reading and writing; then he followed the tinker's trade; but at the age of sixteen, being offended at his father's second marriage, he ran away and joined the army.

As a boy Bunyan had a vivid but morbid imagination, which led him to terrible doubts, fears, fits of despondency, hallucinations. On such a nature the emotional religious revivals of the age made a tremendous impression. He followed them for years, living in a state of torment, until he felt himself converted; whereupon he turned preacher and began to call other sinners to repentance. Such were his native power and rude eloquence that, wherever he went, the common people thronged to hear him.

After the Restoration all this was changed. Public meetings were forbidden unless authorized by bishops of the Established Church, and **In Bedford Jail** Bunyan was one of the first to be called to account. When ordered to hold no more meetings he refused to obey, saying that when the Lord called him to preach salvation he would listen only to the Lord's voice. Then he was thrown into Bedford jail. During his imprisonment he supported his family by making shoe laces, and wrote *Grace Abounding* and *The Pilgrim's Progress*.

After his release Bunyan became the most popular writer and preacher in England. He wrote a large number of works, and went cheerfully up and down the land, preaching the gospel to the poor, helping the afflicted, doing an immense amount of good. He died (1688) as the result of exposure while on an errand of mercy. His works were then known only to humble readers, and not until long years had passed did critics awaken to the fact that one of England's most powerful and original writers had passed away with the poor tinker of Elstow.

Works of Bunyan. From the pen of this uneducated preacher came nearly sixty works, great and small, the most notable of which are: *Grace Abounding* (1666), a kind of spiritual autobiography; *The Holy War* (1665), a prose allegory with a theme similar to that of Milton's epic; and *The Life and Death of Mr. Badman* (1682), a character study which was a forerunner of the English novel. These works are seldom read, and Bunyan is known to most readers as the author of *The Pilgrim's Progress* (1678). This is the famous allegory [1] in which, under guise of telling the story of a pilgrim in search of a city, Bunyan portrays the experiences of humanity in its journey from this world to the next. Here is an outline of the story:

In the City of Destruction lives a poor sinner called Christian. When he learns that the city is doomed, he is terrified and flees out of it, carrying

Story of Pilgrim's Progress

a great burden on his back. He is followed by the jeers of his neighbors, who have no fear. He seeks a safe and abiding city to dwell in, but is ignorant how to find it until Evangelist shows him the road.

As he goes on his journey Mr. Worldly Wiseman meets him and urges him to return; but he hastens on, only to plunge into the Slough of Despond. His companion Pliable is here discouraged and turns back. Christian struggles on through the mud and reaches the Wicket Gate, where Interpreter shows him the way to the Celestial City. As he passes a cross beside the path, the heavy burden which he carries (his load of sins) falls off of itself. Then with many adventures he climbs the steep hill Difficulty, where his

---

[1] Allegory is figurative writing, in which some outward object or event is described in such a way that we apply the description to humanity, to our mental or spiritual experiences. The object of allegory, as a rule, is to teach moral lessons, and in this it is like a drawn-out fable and like a parable. The two greatest allegories in our literature are Spenser's *Faery Queen* and Bunyan's *Pilgrim's Progress*.

eyes behold the Castle Beautiful. To reach this he must pass some fearful lions in the way; but he adventures on, finds that the lions are chained, is welcomed by the porter Watchful, and is entertained in the castle overnight.

Dangers thicken and difficulties multiply as he resumes his journey. His road is barred by the demon Apollyon, whom he fights to the death. The way now dips downward into the awful Valley of the Shadow. Passing through this, he enters the town of Vanity, goes to Vanity Fair, where he is abused and beaten, and where his companion Faithful is condemned to death. As he escapes from Vanity, the giant Despair seizes him and hurls him into the gloomy dungeon of Doubt. Again he escapes, struggles onward, and reaches the Delectable Mountains. There for the first time he

BUNYAN MEETINGHOUSE, SOUTHWARK

sees the Celestial City; but between him and his refuge is a river, deep and terrible, without bridge or ford. He crosses it, and the journey ends as angels come singing down the streets to welcome Christian into the city.[1]

Such an outline gives but a faint idea of Bunyan's great work, of its realistic figures, its living and speaking characters, its knowledge of humanity, its portrayal of the temptations and doubts that beset the ordinary man, its picturesque style, which of itself would make the book stand out above ten thousand ordinary stories. *Pilgrim's Progress* is still one of our best

[1] This is the story of the first part of *Pilgrim's Progress*, which was written in Bedford jail, but not published till some years later. In 1684 Bunyan published the second part of his story, describing the adventures of Christiana and her children on their journey to the Celestial City. This sequel, like most others, is of minor importance.

examples of clear, forceful, idiomatic English; and our wonder
increases when we remember that it was written by a man
ignorant of literary models. But he had read his Bible daily
until its style and imagery had taken possession of him; also
he had a vivid imagination, a sincere purpose to help his fellows, and his simple rule of rhetoric was to forget himself and
deliver his message. In one of his poems he gives us his rule of
expression, which is an excellent one for writers and speakers:

> .Thine only way,
> Before them all, is to say out thy say
> In thine own native language.

JOHN DRYDEN (1631–1700)

For fifty years Dryden lived in the city of Milton, in the
country of John Bunyan; but his works might indicate that
he inhabited a different planet. Unlike his two great contemporaries, his first object was to win favor; he sold his talent
to the highest bidder, won the leading place among second-
rate Restoration writers, and was content to reflect a generation which had neither the hearty enthusiasm of Elizabethan
times nor the moral earnestness of Puritanism.

Life. Knowledge of Dryden's life is rather meager, and as his
motives are open to question we shall state here only a few facts.
He was born of a Puritan and aristocratic family, at Aldwinkle, in
1631. After an excellent education, which included seven years at
Trinity College, Cambridge, he turned to literature as a means of
earning a livelihood, taking a worldly view of his profession and hold-
ing his pen ready to serve the winning side. Thus, he wrote his
" Heroic Stanzas," which have a hearty Puritan ring, on the death of
Cromwell; but he turned Royalist and wrote the more flattering
"Astræa Redux " to welcome Charles II back to power.

In literature Dryden proved himself a man of remarkable versatility.
Because plays were in demand, he produced many that catered to the
His evil tastes of the Restoration stage, — plays that he after-
Versatility wards condemned unsparingly. He was equally ready to
write prose or verse, songs, criticisms, political satires. In 1670 he
was made poet laureate under Charles II; his affairs prospered: he

became a literary dictator in London, holding forth nightly in Will's Coffeehouse to an admiring circle of listeners. After the Revolution of 1688 he lost his offices, and with them most of his income. In

JOHN DRYDEN

From a picture by Hudson in the Hall of
Trinity College, Cambridge

his old age, being reduced to hackwork, he wrote obituaries, epitaphs, paraphrases of the tales of Chaucer, translations of Latin poets, — anything to earn an honest living. He died in 1700, and was buried beside Chaucer in Westminster Abbey.

Such facts are not interesting; nor do they give us a true idea of the man Dryden. To understand him we should have to read his works (no easy or pleasant task) and compare his prose prefaces, in which he is at his best, with the comedies in which he is abominable. When not engaged with the degenerate stage, or with political or literary or religious controversies, he appears sane, well-balanced, good-tempered, manly; but the impression is not a lasting one. He seems to have catered to the vicious element of his own age, to have regretted the misuse of his talent, and to have recorded his own judgment in two lines from his ode "To the Memory of Mrs. Killigrew":

O gracious God, how far have we
Profaned thy heavenly grace of poesy!

Works of Dryden. The occasional poems written by Dryden may be left in the obscurity into which they fell after they had been applauded. The same may be said of his typical poem "Annus Mirabilis," which describes the wonderful events of the year 1666, a year which witnessed the taking of New Amsterdam from the Dutch and the great fire of London. Both events were celebrated in a way to contribute to the glory of King Charles and to Dryden's political fortune. Of all his poetical works, only the odes written in honor of St. Cecilia are now remembered. The second ode, "Alexander's Feast," is one of our best poems on the power of music.

Dryden's numerous plays show considerable dramatic power, and every one of them contains some memorable line or pas-

His Plays sage; but they are spoiled by the author's insincerity in trying to satisfy the depraved taste of the Restoration stage. He wrote one play, *All for Love*, to please himself, he said, and it is noticeable that this play is written in blank verse and shows the influence of Shakespeare, who was then out of fashion. If any of the plays are to be read, *All for Love* should be selected, though it is exceptional, not typical, and gives but a faint idea of Dryden's ordinary dramatic methods.

In the field of political satire Dryden was a master, and his work here is interesting as showing that unfortunate alliance

Satires between literature and politics which led many of the best English writers of the next century to sell their services to the Whigs or Tories. Dryden sided with the later party and, in a kind of allegory of the Bible story of Absalom's revolt against David, wrote "Absalom and Achitophel" to glorify the Tories and to castigate the Whigs. This powerful political satire was followed by others in the same vein, and by "MacFlecknoe," which satirized certain poets with whom Dryden was at loggerheads. As a rule, such works are for a day, having no enduring interest because they have no human kindness, but occasionally Dryden portrays a man of his own time so well that his picture applies to the vulgar politician of all ages, as in this characterization of Burnet:

> Prompt to assail and careless of defence,
> Invulnerable in his impudence,
> He dares the world, and eager of a name
> He thrusts about and justles into fame;
> So fond of loud report that, not to miss
> Of being known (his last and utmost bliss),
> He rather would be known for what he is.

These satires of Dryden were largely influential in establishing the heroic couplet,[1] which dominated the fashion of English poetry for the next century. The couplet had been used by earlier poets, Chaucer for example; but in his hands it was musical and unobtrusive, a minor part of a complete work. With Dryden, and with his contemporary Waller, the making of couplets was the main thing; in their hands the couplet became "closed," that is, it often contained a complete thought, a criticism, a nugget of common sense, a poem in itself, as in this aphorism from "MacFlecknoe":

> All human things are subject to decay,
> And when Fate summons, monarchs must obey.

In his prose works Dryden proved himself the ablest critic of his time, and the inventor of a neat, serviceable style which, **Prose Works** with flattery to ourselves, we are wont to call modern. Among his numerous critical works we note especially "An Essay of Dramatic Poesy," "Of Heroic Plays," "Discourse on Satire," and the Preface to his *Fables*. These have not the vigor or picturesqueness of Bunyan's prose, but they are written clearly, in short sentences, with the chief aim of being understood. If we compare them with the sonorous periods of Milton, or with the pretty involutions of Sidney, we shall see why Dryden is called "the father of modern prose." His sensible style appears in this criticism of Chaucer:

"He must have been a man of a most wonderful comprehensive nature, because, as it has been truly observed of him, he has taken into the compass of his *Canterbury Tales* the various manners and humours (as we now call them) of the whole English nation in his age. Not a single character has escaped him. . . . We have our fathers and great-grand-dames all before us as they were in Chaucer's days: their general characters are still remaining in mankind, and even in England, though they are called by other names than those of monks and friars and canons and lady abbesses and nuns; for mankind is ever the same, and nothing lost out of nature though everything is altered."

---

[1] The heroic couplet consists of two iambic pentameter lines that rime. By "pentameter" is meant that the line has five feet or measures; by "iambic," that each foot contains two syllables, the first short or unaccented, the second long or accented.

Secondary Writers

Puritan and Cavalier Verse. The numerous minor poets of this period are often arranged in groups, but any true classification is impossible since there was no unity among them. Each was a law unto himself, and the result was to emphasize personal oddity or eccentricity. It would seem that in writing of love, the common theme of poets, Puritan and Cavalier must alike speak the common language of the heart; but that is precisely what they did not do. With them love was no longer a passion, or even a fashion, but any fantastic conceit that might decorate a rime. Thus, Suckling habitually made love a joke:

> Why so pale and wan, fond lover,
>   Prithee why so pale?
> Will, when looking well wont move her,
>   Looking ill prevail?
> Prithee why so pale?

Crashaw turned from his religious poems to sing of love in a way to appeal to the Transcendentalists, of a later age:

> Whoe'er she be,
> That not impossible she
> That shall command my heart and me.

And Donne must search out some odd notion from natural (or unnatural) history, making love a spider that turns the wine of life into poison; or from mechanics, comparing lovers to a pair of dividers:

> If they be two, they are two so
>   As stiff twin compasses are two:
> Thy soul, the fixed foot, makes no show
>   To move, but doth if the other do.

Several of these poets, commonly grouped in a class which includes Donne, Herbert, Cowley, Crashaw, and others famous in their day, received the name of metaphysical poets, not because of their profound thought, but because of their eccentric style and queer figures of speech. Of all this group George Herbert (1593–1633) is the sanest and the sweetest. His chief work, *The Temple,* is a collection of poems celebrating the

beauty of holiness, the sacraments, the Church, the experiences of the Christian life. Some of these poems are ingenious conceits, and deserve the derisive name of "metaphysical" which Dr. Johnson flung at them; but others, such as "Virtue," "The Pulley," "Love" and "The Collar," are the expression of a beautiful and saintly soul, speaking of the deep things of God; and speaking so quietly withal that one is apt to miss the intensity that

GEORGE HERBERT

From a rare print by White, prefixed to his poems

lurks even in his calmest verses. Note in these opening and closing stanzas of "Virtue" the restraint of the one, the hidden glow of the other :

> Sweet day, so cool, so calm, so bright,
>   The bridal of the earth and sky !
> The dew shall weep thy fall to-night;
>   For thou must die.
>
> Only a sweet and virtuous soul,
>   Like seasoned timber, never gives;
> But, though the whole world turn to coal,
>   Then chiefly lives.

In contrast with the disciplined Puritan spirit of Herbert is the gayety of another group, called the Cavalier poets, among

whom are Carew, Suckling and Lovelace. They reflect clearly
the spirit of the Royalists who followed King Charles with a
Cavalier devotion worthy of a better master. Robert Herrick
Poets (1591–1674) is the best known of this group, and
his only book, *Hesperides and Noble Numbers* (1648), reflects
the two elements found in most of the minor poetry of the age;
namely, Cavalier gayety and Puritan seriousness. In the first
part of the book are some graceful verses celebrating the light
loves of the Cavaliers and the fleeting joys of country life :

> I sing of brooks, of blossoms, birds and bowers,
> Of April, May, of June and July flowers;
> I sing of Maypoles, hock-carts, wassails, wakes,
> Of bridegrooms, brides, and of their bridal cakes.

In *Noble Numbers* such poems as " Thanksgiving," " A True
Lent," " Litany," and the child's " Ode on the Birth of Our
Saviour " reflect the better side of the Cavalier, who can be
serious without pulling a long face, who goes to his devotions
cheerfully, and who retains even in his religion what Andrew
Lang calls a spirit of unregenerate happiness.

Samuel Butler (1612–1680) may also be classed with the
Cavalier poets, though in truth he stands alone in this age, a
Butler's master of doggerel rime and of ferocious satire. His
Hudibras chief work, *Hudibras*, a grotesque caricature of Puritanism, appeared in 1663, when the restored king and his
favorites were shamelessly plundering the government. The
poem (probably suggested by *Don Quixote*) relates a rambling
story of the adventures of Sir Hudibras, a sniveling Puritan
knight, and his squire Ralpho. Its doggerel style may be
inferred from the following :

> Besides, 't is known he could speak Greek
> As naturally as pigs squeak;
> That Latin was no more difficile
> Than to a blackbird 't is to whistle:
> Being rich in both, he never scanted
> His bounty unto such as wanted.

Such was the stuff that the Royalists quoted to each other as wit; and the wit was so dear to king and courtiers that they carried copies of *Hudibras* around in their pockets. The poem was enormously popular in its day, and some of its best lines are still quoted; but the selections we now meet give but a faint idea of the general scurrility of a work which amused England in the days when the Puritan's fanaticism was keenly remembered, his struggle for liberty quite forgotten.

SIR THOMAS BROWNE

Prose Writers. Of the hundreds of prose works that appeared in Puritan times very few are now known even by name. Their controversial fires are sunk to ashes; even the causes that produced or fanned them are forgotten. Meanwhile we cherish a few books that speak not of strife but of peace and charity.

Thomas Browne (1605–1682) was a physician, vastly learned in a day when he and other doctors gravely prescribed herbs or bloodsuckers for witchcraft; but he was less interested in his profession than in what was then called modern science. His most famous work is *Religio Medici* (Religion of a Physician, 1642), a beautiful book, cherished by those who know it as one of the greatest prose works in the language. His *Urn Burial* is even more remarkable for its subtle thought and condensed expression; but its charm, like that of the Silent Places, is for the few who can discover and appreciate it.

Isaac Walton (1593–1683), or Isaak, as he always wrote it, was a modest linen merchant who, in the midst of troublous times, kept his serenity of spirit by attending strictly to his own affairs, by reading good books, and by going fishing. His taste for literature is reflected with rare simplicity in his *Lives of Donne, Wotton, Hooker, George Herbert and Bishop Sanderson,* a series of biographies which are among the earliest and sweetest in our language. Their charm lies partly in their refined style, but more largely in their revelation of character; for Walton chose men of gentle spirit for his subjects, men who were like himself in cherishing the still depths of life rather than its noisy shallows, and wrote of them with the understanding of perfect sympathy. Wordsworth expressed his appreciation of the work in a noble sonnet beginning:

ISAAC WALTON

> There are no colours in the fairest sky
> So fair as these. The feather whence the pen
> Was shaped that traced the lives of these good men
> Dropped from an angel's wing.

Walton's love of fishing, and of all the lore of trout brooks and spring meadows that fishing implies, found expression in *The Complete Angler, or Contemplative Man's Recreation* (1653). This is a series of conversations in which an angler convinces his friends that fishing is not merely the sport of catching fish, but an art that men are born to, like the art of poetry. Even such a hard-hearted matter as impaling a minnow for bait becomes poetical, for this is the fashion of it: "Put your hook in at his mouth, and out at his gills, and do it as if you loved him." It is enough to say of this old work, the classic of its kind, that it deserves all the honor which the tribe of anglers have given it, and that you could hardly find a better book to fall asleep over after a day's fishing.

OLD FISHING HOUSE, ON RIVER DOVE, USED BY WALTON

No such gentle, human, lovable books were **Evelyn and Pepys** produced in Restoration times. The most famous prose works of the period are the diaries of John Evelyn and Samuel Pepys. The former was a gentleman, and his *Diary* is an interesting chronicle of matters large and small from 1641 to 1697. Pepys, though he became Secretary of the Admiralty and President of the Royal Society, was a gossip, a chatterbox, with an eye that loved to peek into closets and a tongue that ran to slander. His *Diary*, covering the period from 1660 to 1669, is a keen but malicious exposition of private and public life during the Restoration.

Summary. The literary period just studied covers the last three-quarters of the seventeenth century. Its limits are very indefinite, merging into Elizabethan romance on the one side, and into eighteenth-century formalism on the other. Historically, the period was one of bitter conflict between two main political and religious parties, the Royalists, or Cavaliers, and the Puritans. The literature of the age is extremely diverse in character, and is sadly lacking in the unity, the joyousness, the splendid enthusiasm of Elizabethan prose and poetry.

The greatest writer of the period was John Milton. He is famous in literature for his early or Horton poems, which are Elizabethan in spirit; for his controversial prose works, which reflect the strife of the age; for his epic of *Paradise Lost*, and for his tragedy of *Samson*.

Another notable Puritan, or rather Independent, writer was John Bunyan, whose works reflect the religious ferment of the seventeenth century. His chief works are *Grace Abounding*, a kind of spiritual biography, and *The Pilgrim's Progress*, an allegory of the Christian life which has been more widely read than any other English book.

The chief writer of the Restoration period was John Dryden, a professional author, who often catered to the coarser tastes of the age. There is no single work by which he is gratefully remembered. He is noted for his political satires, for his vigorous use of the heroic couplet, for his modern prose style, and for his literary criticisms.

Among the numerous minor poets of the period Robert Herrick and George Herbert are especially noteworthy. A few miscellaneous prose works are the *Religio Medici* of Thomas Browne, *The Complete Angler* of Isaac Walton, and the diaries of Pepys and Evelyn.

Selections for Reading. Minor poems of Milton, and parts of Paradise Lost, in Standard English Classics, Riverside Literature, and other school series (see Texts, in General Bibliography). Selections from Cavalier and Puritan poets in Maynard's English Classics, Golden Treasury Series, Manly's English Poetry, Century Readings, Ward's English Poets. Prose selections in Manly's English Prose, Craik's English Prose Selections, Garnett's English Prose from Elizabeth to Victoria. Pilgrim's Progress and Grace Abounding in Standard English Classics, Pocket Classics, Student's Classics. Religio Medici and Complete Angler in Temple Classics and Everyman's Library. Selections from Dryden in Manly's English Prose and Manly's English Poetry. Dryden's version of Palamon and Arcite (the Knight's Tale of Chaucer) in Standard English Classics, Riverside Literature, Lake Classics.

Bibliography. For texts and manuals dealing with the whole field of English history and literature see the General Bibliography. The following works deal chiefly with the Puritan and Restoration periods.

History. Wakeling, King and Parliament (Oxford Manuals of English History); Gardiner, The First Two Stuarts and the Puritan Revolution (Great Epochs Series); Tulloch, English Puritanism; Harrison, Oliver Cromwell; Hale, The Fall of the Stuarts; Airy, The English Restoration and Louis XIV.

Literature. Masterman, The Age of Milton; Dowden, Puritan and Anglican; Wendell, Temper of the Seventeenth Century in Literature; Gosse, Seventeenth-Century Studies; Schilling, Seventeenth-Century Lyrics (Athenæum Press Series); Isaac Walton, Lives of Donne, Wotton, Hooker, Herbert and Sanderson.

Milton. Life, by Garnett (Great Writers Series); by Pattison (English Men of Letters). Corson, Introduction to Milton; Raleigh, Milton; Stopford Brooke, Milton. Essays, by Macaulay; by Lowell, in Among My Books; by M. Arnold, in Essays in Criticism.

Bunyan. Life, by Venables (Great Writers); by Froude (E. M. of L.). Brown, John Bunyan; Woodberry's essay, in Makers of Literature.

Dryden. Life by Saintsbury (E. M. of L.). Gosse, From Shakespeare to Pope.

Thomas Browne. Life, by Gosse (E. M. of L.). Essays, by L. Stephen, in Hours in a Library; by Pater, in Appreciations.

Fiction and Poetry. Shorthouse, John Inglesant; Scott, Old Mortality, Peveril of the Peak, Woodstock; Blackmore, Lorna Doone. Milton, Sonnet on Cromwell; Scott, Rokeby; Bates and Coman, English History Told by English Poets.

CHAPTER VI

EIGHTEENTH–CENTURY LITERATURE

In words, as fashions, the same rule will hold:
Alike fantastic if too new or old.
Be not the first by whom the new are tried,
Nor yet the last to lay the old aside.

Pope, " An Essay on Criticism "

History of the Period. The most striking political feature of the times was the **rise** of constitutional and party government. The Revolution of 1688, which banished the Stuarts, had settled the king question by making Parliament supreme in England, but not all Englishmen were content with the settlement. No sooner were the people in control of the government than they divided into hostile parties: the liberal Whigs, who were determined to safeguard popular liberty, and the conservative Tories, with tender memories of kingcraft, who would leave as much authority as possible in the royal hands. On the extreme of Toryism was a third party of zealots, called the Jacobites, who aimed to bring the Stuarts back to the throne, and who for fifty years filled Britain with plots and rebellion. The literature of the age was at times dominated by the interests of these contending factions.

The two main parties were so well balanced that power shifted easily from one to the other. To overturn a Tory or a Whig cabinet only a few votes were necessary, and to influence such votes London was flooded with pamphlets. Even before the great newspapers appeared, the press had become a mighty power in England, and any writer with a talent for argument or satire was almost certain to be hired by party leaders. Addison, Steele, Defoe, Swift, — most of the great writers of the age were, on occasion, the willing servants of the Whigs or Tories. So the new politician replaced the old nobleman as a patron of letters.

Another feature of the age was the rapid development of social life. In earlier ages the typical Englishman had lived much by himself; his home was his castle, and in it he developed his intense individualism;

but in the first half of the eighteenth century some three thousand
public coffeehouses and a large number of private clubs appeared in
Social Life   London alone; and the sociability of which these clubs
were an expression was typical of all English cities. Meanwhile country life was in sore need of refinement.

The influence of this social life on literature was inevitable.
Nearly all writers frequented the coffeehouses, and matters discussed
there became subjects of literature; hence the enormous amount
of eighteenth-century writing devoted to transient affairs, to politics,
fashions, gossip. Moreover, as the club leaders set the fashion in
manners or dress, in the correct way of taking snuff or of wearing
wigs and ruffles, so the literary leaders emphasized formality or correct-
ness of style, and to write prose like Addison, or verse like Pope,
became the ambition of aspiring young authors.

There are certain books of the period (seldom studied amongst its
masterpieces) which are the best possible expression of its thought
and manners. The Letters of Lord Chesterfield, for example, especially those written to his son, are more significant, and more readable,
than anything produced by Johnson. Even better are the Memoirs of
Horace Walpole, and his gossipy Letters, of which Thackeray wrote:

" Fiddles sing all through them; wax lights, fine dresses, fine jokes, fine
plate, fine equipages glitter and sparkle; never was such a brilliant, smirking
Vanity Fair as that through which he leads us."

Two other significant features of the age were the large part played
by England in Continental wars, and the rapid expansion of the British
Spread of   empire. These Continental wars, which have ever since
Empire   influenced British policy, seem to have originated (aside
from the important matter of self-interest) in a double motive: to prevent any one nation from gaining overwhelming superiority by force
of arms, and to save the smaller " buffer " states from being absorbed
by their powerful neighbors. Thus the War of the Spanish Succession
(1711) prevented the union of the French and Spanish monarchies,
and preserved the smaller states of Holland and Germany. As
Addison then wrote, at least half truthfully:

> 'T is Britain's care to watch o'er Europe's fate,
> And hold in balance each contending state:
> To threaten bold, presumptuous kings with war,
> And answer her afflicted neighbors' prayer.[1]

1 From Addison's Address to Liberty, in his poetical " Letter to Lord Halifax."

The expansion of the empire, on the whole the most marvelous feature of English history, received a tremendous impetus in this age when India, Australia and the greater part of North America were added to the British dominions, and when Captain Cook opened the way for a belt of colonies around the whole world.

The influence of the last-named movement hardly appears in the books which we ordinarily read as typical of the age. There are other books, however, which one may well read for his own unhampered enjoyment: such expansive books as Hawkesworth's *Voyages* (1773), corresponding to Hakluyt's famous record of Elizabethan exploration, and especially the *Voyages of Captain Cook*,[1] which take us from the drawing-room chatter of politics or fashion or criticism into a world of adventure and great achievement. In such works, which make no profession of literary style, we feel the lure of the sea and of lands beyond the horizon, which is as the mighty background of English literature from Anglo-Saxon times to the present day.

It is difficult to summarize the literature of this age, or to group such antagonistic writers as Swift and Addison, Pope and Burns, Defoe and Johnson, Goldsmith and Fielding, with any fine discrimination. It is simply for convenience, therefore, that we study eighteenth-century writings in three main divisions: the reign of so-called classicism, the revival of romantic poetry, and the beginnings of the modern novel. As a whole, it is an age of prose rather than of poetry, and in this respect it differs from all preceding ages of English literature.

EIGHTEENTH-CENTURY CLASSICISM

The above title is an unfortunate one, but since it is widely used we must try to understand it as best we can. Yet when one begins to define " classicism " one is reminded of that old bore Polonius, who tells how Hamlet is affected:

> Your noble son is mad:
> Mad, call I it; for to define true madness,
> What is't but to be nothing else but mad?

[1] The first of Cook's fateful voyages appears in Hawkesworth's collection. The second was recorded by Cook himself (1777), and the third by Cook and Captain King (1784). See Synge, *Captain Cook's Voyages Around the World* (London, 1897).

In our literature the word " classic " was probably first used in connection with the writers of Greece and Rome, and any English work which showed the influence of such writers was said to have a classic style. If we seek to the root of the word, we shall find that it refers to the *classici*, that is, to the highest of the classes into which the census divided the Roman people ; hence the proper use of " classic " to designate the writings that have won first rank in any nation. As Goethe said, " Everything that is good in literature is classical."

Gradually, however, the word " classic " came to have a different meaning, a meaning now expressed by the word " formal." In the Elizabethan age, as we have seen, critics insisted that English plays should conform to the rules or " unities " of the Greek drama, and plays written according to such rules were called classic. Again, in the eighteenth century, English poets took to studying ancient authors, especially Horace, to find out how poetry should be written. Having discovered, as they thought, the rules of composition, they insisted on following such rules rather than individual genius or inspiration. It is largely because of this adherence to rules, this slavery to a fashion of the time, that so much of eighteenth-century verse seems cold and artificial, a thing made to order rather than the natural expression of human feeling. The writers themselves were well satisfied with their formality, however, and called their own the Classic or Augustan age of English letters.[1]

Classic and Pseudo-Classic *(margin note)*

ALEXANDER POPE (1688–1744)

It was in 1819 that a controversy arose over the question, Was Pope a poet ? To have asked that in 1719 would have indicated that the questioner was ignorant ; to have asked it

---

[1] Though the eighteenth century was dominated by this formal spirit, it had, like every other age, its classic and romantic movements. The work of Gray, Burns and other romantic poets will be considered later.

a half century later might have raised a doubt as to his sanity, for by that time Pope was acclaimed as a master by the great majority of poets in England and America. We judge now, looking at him in perspective and comparing him with Chaucer or Burns, that he was not a great poet but simply the kind of poet that the age demanded. He belongs to eighteenth-century London exclusively, and herein he differs from the master poets who are at home in all places and expressive of all time.

Life. Pope is an interesting but not a lovable figure. Against the petty details of his life we should place, as a background, these amazing achievements: that this poor cripple, weak of body and spiteful of mind, was the supreme literary figure of his age; that he demonstrated how an English poet could live by his pen, instead of depending on patrons; that he won greater fame and fortune than Shakespeare or Milton received from their contemporaries; that he dominated the fashion of English poetry during his lifetime, and for many years after his death.

ALEXANDER POPE

Such are the important facts of Pope's career. For the rest: he was born in London, in the year of the Revolution (1688). Soon after that date his father, having gained a modest fortune in the linen business, retired to Binfield, on the fringe of Windsor Forest. There Pope passed his boyhood, studying a little under private tutors, forming a pleasurable acquaintance with Latin and Greek poets. From fourteen to twenty, he tells us, he read for amusement; but from twenty to twenty-seven he read for " improvement and instruction." The most significant traits of these early years were his determination to be a poet and his talent for imitating any

The Writer

writer who pleased him. Dryden was his first master, from whom he
inherited the couplet ; then he imitated the French critic Boileau and
the Roman poet Horace. By the time he was twenty-four the publication of his *Essay on Criticism* and *The Rape of the Lock* had made
him the foremost poet of England. By his translation of Homer he
made a fortune, with which he bought a villa at Twickenham. There
he lived in the pale sunshine of literary success, and there he quarreled
with every writer who failed to appreciate his verses, his jealousy

TWICKENHAM PARISH CHURCH, WHERE POPE WAS BURIED

Pope lived at Twickenham for nearly thirty years

overflowing at last in *The Dunciad* (Iliad of Dunces), a witty but
venomous lampoon, in which he took revenge on all who had
angered him.

Next to his desire for glory and revenge, Pope loved to be considered a man of high character, a teacher of moral philosophy. His

The Man ethical teaching appears in his *Moral Epistles* ; his desire
for a good reputation is written large in his Letters, which
he secretly printed, and then alleged that they had been made public
against his wish. These Letters might impress us as the utterances of
a man of noble ideals, magnanimous with his friends, patient with his
enemies, until we reflect that they were published by the author for
the purpose of giving precisely that impression.

Another side of Pope's nature is revealed in this : that to some of his friends, to Swift and Bolingbroke for example, he showed gratitude, and that to his parents he was ever a dutiful son. He came perhaps as near as he could to a real rather than an artificial sentiment when he wrote of his old mother :

> Me let the tender office long engage,
> To rock the cradle of reposing age.

Works of Pope. Pope's first important work, *An Essay on Criticism* (1711), is an echo of the rules which Horace had formulated in his *Ars Poetica*, more than seventeen centuries before Pope was born. The French critic Boileau made an alleged improvement of Horace in his *L'Art Poétique*, and Pope imitated both writers with his rimed *Essay*, in which he attempted to sum up the rules by which poetry should be judged. And he did it, while still under the age of twenty-five, so brilliantly that his characterization of the critic is unmatched in our literature. A few selections will serve to show the character of the work :

> First follow nature, and your judgment frame
> By her just standard, which is still the same :
> Unerring nature, still divinely bright,
> One clear, unchanged and universal light,
> Life, force and beauty must to all impart,
> At once the source and end and test of Art.
>
> Poets, like painters, thus unskilled to trace
> The naked nature and the living grace,
> With gold and jewels cover every part,
> And hide with ornaments their want of art.
> True wit is nature to advantage dressed,
> What oft was thought, but ne'er so well expressed.
>
> Expression is the dress of thought, and still
> Appears more decent, as more suitable.

Pope's next important poem, *The Rape of the Lock* (1712), is his most original and readable work. The occasion of the poem was that a fop stole a lock of hair from a young lady, and the theft plunged two families into a quarrel which was

taken up by the fashionable set of London. Pope made a mock-heroic poem on the subject, in which he satirized the fads and
Rape of the Lock fashions of Queen Anne's age. Ordinarily Pope's fancy is of small range, and proceeds jerkily, like the flight of a woodpecker, from couplet to couplet; but here he attempts to soar like the eagle. He introduces dainty aërial creatures, gnomes, sprites, sylphs, to combat for the belles and fops in their trivial concerns; and herein we see a clever burlesque of the old epic poems, in which gods or goddesses entered into the serious affairs of mortals. The craftsmanship of the poem is above praise; it is not only a neatly pointed satire on eighteenth-century fashions but is one of the most graceful works in English verse.

An excellent supplement to *The Rape of the Lock*, which pictures the superficial elegance of the age, is *An Essay on*
Essay on Man *Man*, which reflects its philosophy. That philosophy, under the general name of Deism, had fancied to abolish the Church and all revealed religion, and had set up a new-old standard of natural faith and morals. Of this philosophy Pope had small knowledge; but he was well acquainted with the discredited Bolingbroke, his "guide, philosopher and friend," who was a fluent exponent of the new doctrine, and from Bolingbroke came the general scheme of the *Essay on Man*.

The poem appears in the form of four epistles, dealing with man's place in the universe, with his moral nature, with social and political ethics, and with the problem of happiness. These were discussed from a common-sense viewpoint, and with feet always on solid earth. As Pope declares:

> Know then thyself, presume not God to scan;
> The proper study of mankind is man. . . .
> Created half to rise, and half to fall;
> Great lord of all things, yet a prey to all;
> Sole judge of truth, in endless error hurled;
> The glory, jest and riddle of the world.

Throughout the poem these two doctrines of Deism are kept in sight: that there is a God, a Mystery, who dwells apart from the world; and that man ought to be contented, even happy, in his ignorance of matters beyond his horizon:

> All nature is but art, unknown to thee;
> All chance, direction which thou canst not see;
> All discord, harmony not understood;
> All partial evil, universal good;
> And, spite of pride, in erring reason's spite,
> One truth is clear: whatever is, is right.

The result is rubbish, so far as philosophy is concerned, but in the heap of incongruous statements which Pope brings together are a large number of quotable lines; such as:

> Honor and shame from no condition rise;
> Act well your part, there all the honor lies.

It is because of such lines, the care with which the whole poem is polished, and the occasional appearance of real beauty (such as the passage beginning, "Lo, the poor Indian") that the *Essay on Man* occupies such a high place in eighteenth-century literature.

It is hardly necessary to examine other works of Pope, since the poems already named give us the full measure of his **The Quality** strength and weakness. His talent is to formulate **of Pope** rules of poetry, to satirize fashionable society, to make brilliant epigrams in faultless couplets. His failure to move or even to interest us greatly is due to his second-hand philosophy, his inability to feel or express emotion, his artificial life apart from nature and humanity. When we read Chaucer or Shakespeare, we have the impression that they would have been at home in any age or place, since they deal with human interests that are the same yesterday, to-day and forever; but we can hardly imagine Pope feeling at ease anywhere save in his own set and in his own generation. He is the poet of one period, which set great store by formality, and in that period alone he is supreme.

JONATHAN SWIFT (1667–1745)

In the history of literature Swift occupies a large place as the most powerful of English satirists; that is, writers who search out the faults of society in order to hold them up to ridicule. To most readers, however, he is known as the author of *Gulliver's Travels*, a book which young people still read with pleasure, as they read *Robinson Crusoe* or any other story of

JONATHAN SWIFT

adventure. In the fate of that book, which was intended to scourge humanity but which has become a source of innocent entertainment, is a commentary on the colossal failure of Swift's ambition.

Life. Little need be recorded of Swift's life beyond the few facts which help us to understand his satires. He was born in Dublin, of English parents, and was so "bantered by fortune" that he was compelled to spend the greater part of his life in Ireland, a country which he detested. He was very poor, very proud; and even in youth he railed at a mocking fate which compelled him to accept aid from others. For his education he was dependent on a relative, who helped him grudgingly. After leaving Trinity College, Dublin, the only employment he could find was with another relative, Sir William Temple, a retired statesman, who hired Swift as a secretary and treated him as a servant. Galled by his position and by his feeling of superiority (for he was a man of physical and mental power, who longed to be a master of great affairs) he took orders in the Anglican Church; but the only appointment he could obtain was in a village buried, as he said, in a forsaken district of Ireland. There his bitterness overflowed in *A Tale of a Tub* and a few pamphlets of such satiric power that certain political leaders recognized Swift's value and summoned him to their assistance.

To understand his success in London one must remember the times. Politics were rampant; the city was the battleground of Whigs

Swift in London and Tories, whose best weapon was the printed pamphlet that justified one party by heaping abuse or ridicule on the other. Swift was a master of satire, and he was soon the most feared author in England. He seems to have had no fixed principles,

TRINITY COLLEGE, DUBLIN

for he was ready to join the Tories when that party came into power and to turn his literary cannon on the Whigs, whom he had recently supported. In truth, he despised both parties; his chief object was to win for himself the masterful position in Church or state for which, he believed, his talents had fitted him.

For several years Swift was the literary champion of the victorious Tories; then, when his keen eye detected signs of tottering in the party, he asked for his reward. He obtained, not the great bishopric which he expected, but an appointment as Dean of St. Patrick's

Cathedral in Dublin. Small and bitter fruit this seemed to Swift, after his years of service, but even so, it was given grudgingly.[1]

When the Tories went out of power Swift's political occupation was gone. The last thirty years of his life were spent largely in **Life in Dublin.** There in a living grave, as he regarded it, the **Ireland** scorn which he had hitherto felt for individuals or institutions widened until it included humanity. Such is the meaning of his *Gulliver's Travels.* His only pleasure during these years was to expose the gullibility of men, and a hundred good stories are current of his practical jokes, — such as his getting rid of a crowd which had gathered to watch an eclipse by sending a solemn messenger to announce that, by the Dean's orders, the eclipse was postponed till the next day. A brain disease fastened upon him gradually, and his last years were passed in a state of alternate stupor or madness from which death was a blessed deliverance.

Works of Swift. The poems of Swift, though they show undoubted power (every smallest thing he wrote bears that stamp), may be passed over with the comment of his relative Dryden, who wrote : " Cousin Swift, you will never be a poet." The criticism was right, but thereafter Swift jeered at Dryden's poetry. We may pass over also the *Battle of the Books*, the *Drapier's Letters* and a score more of satires and lampoons. Of all these minor works the *Bickerstaff Papers*, which record Swift's practical joke on the astrologers, are most amusing.[2]

[1] Swift's pride and arrogance with his official superiors worked against him. Also he had published *A Tale of a Tub*, a coarse satire against the churches, which scandalized the queen and her ministers, who could have given him preferment. Thackeray says, " I think the Bishops who advised Queen Anne not to appoint the author of the *Tale of a Tub* to a Bishopric gave perfectly good advice."

[2] Almanacs were at that time published by pretender astrologers, who read fortunes or made predictions from the stars. Against the most famous of these quacks, Partridge by name, Swift leveled his " Predictions for the year 1708, by Isaac Bickerstaff." Among the predictions of coming events was this trifle : that Partridge was doomed to die on March 29 following, about eleven o'clock at night, of a raging fever. On March 30 appeared, in the newspapers, a letter giving the details of Partridge's death, and then a pamphlet called " An Elegy of Mr. Partridge." Presently Partridge, who could not see the joke, made London laugh by his frantic attempts to prove that he was alive. Then appeared an elaborate " Vindication of Isaac Bickerstaff," which proved by the infallible stars that Partridge was dead, and that the astrologer now in his place was an impostor. This joke was copied twenty-five years later by Franklin in his *Poor Richard's Almanac.*

Swift's fame now rests largely upon his *Gulliver's Travels,* which appeared in 1726 under the title, " Travels into Several **Gulliver's** Remote Nations of the World, by Lemuel Gulliver, **Travels** first a Surgeon and then a Captain of Several Ships." In the first voyage we are taken to Lilliput, a country inhabited by human beings about six inches tall, with minds in proportion. The capers of these midgets are a satire on human society, as seen through Swift's scornful eyes. In the second voyage we go to Brobdingnag, where the people are of gigantic stature, and by contrast we are reminded of the petty " human insects " whom Gulliver represents. The third voyage, to the Island of Laputa, is a burlesque of the scientists and philosophers of Swift's day. The fourth leads to the land of the Houyhnhnms, where intelligent horses are the ruling creatures, and humanity is represented by the Yahoos, a horribly degraded race, having the forms of men and the bestial habits of monkeys.

Such is the ferocious satire on the elegant society of Queen Anne's day. Fortunately for our peace of mind we can read the book for its grim humor and adventurous action, as we read any other good story. Indeed, it surprises most readers of *Gulliver* to be told that the work was intended to wreck our faith in humanity.

In all his satires Swift's power lies in his prose style — a convincing style, clear, graphic, straightforward — and in his **Quality of** marvelous ability to make every scene, however dis- **Swift** tant or grotesque, as natural as life itself. As Emerson said, he describes his characters as if for the police. His weakness is twofold : he has a fondness for coarse or malodorous references, and he is so beclouded in his own soul that he cannot see his fellows in a true light. In one of his early works he announced the purpose of all his writing :

> My hate, whose lash just Heaven has long decreed,
> Shall on a day make Sin and Folly bleed.

That was written at twenty-six, before he took orders in the Church. As a theological student it was certainly impressed upon the young man that Heaven keeps its own prerogatives, and that sin and folly have never been effectually reformed by lashing. But Swift had a scorn of all judgment except his own. As the eyes of fishes are so arranged that they see only their prey and their enemies, so Swift had eyes only for the vices of men and for the lash that scourges them. When he wrote, therefore, he was not an observer, or even a judge ; he was a criminal lawyer prosecuting humanity on the charge of being a sham. A tendency to insanity may possibly account both for his spleen against others and for the self-tortures which made him, as Archbishop King said, " the most unhappy man on earth."

There is one oasis in the bitter desert of Swift's writings, namely, his *Journal to Stella.* While in the employ of Temple

Journal to Stella he was the daily companion of a young girl, Esther Johnson, who was an inmate of the same household. Her love for Swift was pure and constant ; wherever he went she followed and lived near him, bringing a ray of sunshine into his life, in a spirit which reminds us of the sublime expression of another woman : " For whither thou goest, I will go ; and where thou lodgest, I will lodge ; thy people shall be my people, and thy God my God." She was probably married to Swift, but his pride kept him from openly acknowledging the union. While he was at London he wrote a private journal for Esther (Stella) in which he recorded his impressions of the men and women he met, and of the political battles in which he took part. That journal, filled with strange abbreviations to which only he and Stella had the key, can hardly be called literature, but it is of profound interest. It gives us glimpses of a woman who chose to live in the shadow ; it shows the better side of Swift's nature, in contrast with his arrogance toward men and his brutal treatment of women ; and finally, it often takes us behind the scenes of a stage on which was played a mixed comedy of politics and society.

JOSEPH ADDISON (1672–1719)

In Addison we have a pleasant reflection of the new social life of England. Select almost any feature of that life, and you shall find some account of it in the papers of Addison: its party politics in his *Whig Examiner*; its "grand tour," as part of a gentleman's education, in his *Remarks on Italy*; its adventure on foreign soil in such poems as "The Campaign"; its new drama of decency in his *Cato*; its classic delusions in his *Account of the Greatest English Poets*; its frills, fashions and similar matters in his *Spectator* essays. He tried almost every type of literature, from hymns to librettos, and in each he succeeded well enough to be loudly applauded. In his own day he was accounted a master poet, but now he is remembered as a writer of prose essays.

JOSEPH ADDISON

Life. Addison's career offers an interesting contrast to that of Swift, who lived in the same age. He was the son of an English clergyman, settled in the deanery of Lichfield, and his early training left upon him the stamp of good taste and good breeding. In school he was always the model boy; in Oxford he wrote Latin verses on safe subjects, in the approved fashion; in politics he was content to "oil the machine" as he found it; in society he was shy and silent (though naturally a brilliant talker) because he feared to make some slip which might mar his prospects or the dignity of his position.

A very discreet man was Addison, and the only failure he made of discretion was when he married the Dowager Countess of Warwick, went to live in her elegant Holland House, and lived unhappily ever afterwards. The last is a mere formal expression. Addison had not depth enough to be really unhappy. From the cold comfort of the Dowager's palace he would slip off to his club or to Will's Coffeehouse. There, with a pipe and a bottle, he would loosen his eloquent tongue and proceed to make discreetly merry with a few old friends.

His characteristic quality appears in the literary work which followed his Latin verses. He began with a flattering "Address to Dryden," which pleased the old poet and brought Addison to the attention of literary celebrities. His next effort was "The Peace of Ryswick," which flattered King William's statesmen and brought the author a chance to serve the Whig party. Also it brought a pension, with a suggestion that Addison should travel abroad and learn French and diplomacy; which he did, to his great content, for the space of three years.

MAGDALEN COLLEGE, OXFORD

The death of the king brought Addison back to England. His pension stopped, and for a time he lived poorly "in a garret," as one may read in Thackeray's *Henry Esmond*. Then came news of an English victory on the Continent (Marlborough's victory at Blenheim), and the Whigs wanted to make political capital out of the event. Addison was hunted up and engaged to write a poem. He responded with

"The Campaign," which made him famous. Patriots and politicians ascribed to the poem undying glory, and their judgment was accepted by fashionable folk of London. To read it now is to meet a formal, uninspired production, containing a few stock quotations and, incidentally, a sad commentary on the union of Whiggery and poetry.

From that moment Addison's success was assured. He was given various offices of increasing importance; he entered Parliament; **His Path of Roses** he wrote a classic tragedy, *Cato*, which took London by storm (his friend Steele had carefully "packed the house" for the first performance); his essays in *The Spectator* were discussed in every fashionable club or drawing-room; he married a rich countess; he was appointed Secretary of State. The path of politics, which others find so narrow and slippery, was for Addison a broad road through pleasant gardens. Meanwhile Swift, who could not follow the Addisonian way of kindness and courtesy, was eating bitter bread and railing at humanity.

After a brief experience as Secretary of State, finding that he could not make the speeches expected of him, Addison retired on a pension. His unwavering allegiance to good form in all matters appears even in his last remark, "See how a Christian can die." That was in 1719. He had sought the easiest, pleasantest way through life, and had found it. Thackeray, who was in sympathy with such a career, summed it up in a glowing panegyric:

"A life prosperous and beautiful, a calm death; an immense fame and affection afterwards for his happy and spotless name."

Works of Addison. Addison's great reputation was won chiefly by his poetry; but with the exception of a few hymns, simple and devout, his poetical works no longer appeal to us. He was not a poet but a verse-maker. His classic tragedy *Cato*, for example (which met with such amazing success in London that it was taken over to the Continent, where it was acclaimed "a masterpiece of regularity and elegance"), has some good passages, but one who reads the context is apt to find the elegant lines running together somewhat drowsily. Nor need that reflect on our taste or intelligence. Even the cultured Greeks, as if in anticipation of classic poems, built two adjoining temples, one dedicated to the Muses and the other to Sleep.

E

The *Essays* of Addison give us the full measure of his literary talent.   In his verse, as in his political works, he seems to be speaking to strangers ; he is on guard over his dignity as a poet, as Secretary of State, as husband of a countess ; but in his *Essays* we meet the man at his ease, fluent, witty, light-hearted but not frivolous, — just as he talked to his friends in Will's Coffeehouse. The conversational quality of these *Essays* has influenced all subsequent works of the same type, — a type hard to define, but which leaves the impression of pleasant talk about a subject, as distinct from any learned discussion.

The Essays

The *Essays* cover a wide range : fashions, dress, manners, character sketches, letters of travel, ghost stories, satires on common vices, week-end sermons on moral subjects. They are never profound, but they are always pleasant, and their graceful style made such a lasting impression that, half a century later, Dr. Johnson summed up a general judgment when he said :

" Whoever wishes to attain an English style, familiar but not coarse, and elegant but not ostentatious, must give his days and nights to the volumes of Addison."

Addison and Steele. Of these two associates Richard Steele (1672–1729) had the more original mind, and his writings reveal a warm, human sympathy that is lacking in the work of his more famous contemporary. But while Addison cultivated his one talent of writing, Steele was like Defoe in that he always had some new project in his head, and some old debt urging him to put the project into immediate execution. He was in turn poet, political pamphleteer, soldier, dramatist, member of Parliament, publisher, manager of a theater, following each occupation eagerly for a brief season, then abandoning it cheerfully for another, — much like a boy picking blueberries in a good place, who moves on and on to find a better bush, eats his berries on the way, and comes home at last with an empty pail.

While holding the political office of " gazetteer " (one who had a monopoly of official news) the idea came to Steele of

The Tatler and The Spectator publishing a literary magazine. The inventive Defoe had already issued *The Review* (1704), but that had a political origin. With the first number of *The Tatler* (1709) the modern magazine made its bow to the public. This little sheet, published thrice a week and sold at a penny a copy, contained more or less politics, to be sure, but the fact

that it reflected the gossip of coffeehouses made it instantly popular. After less than two years of triumph Steele lost his official position, and *The Tatler* was discontinued. The idea remained, however, and a few months later appeared *The Spectator* (1711), a daily magazine which eschewed politics and devoted itself to essays, reviews, letters, criticisms, — in short, to " polite " literature. Addison, who had been a contributor to *The Tatler*,

SIR RICHARD STEELE

From the engraving by Freeman after original by J. Richardson

entered heartily into the new venture, which had a brief but glorious career. He became known as " Mr. Spectator," and the famous *Spectator Essays* are still commonly attributed to him, though in truth Steele furnished a large part of them.[1]

---

[1] Of the *Tatler* essays Addison contributed 42, Steele about 180, and some 36 were the work of the two authors in collaboration. Of the *Spectator* essays Addison furnished 274, Steele 236, and about 45 were the work of other writers. In some of the best essays ("Sir Roger de Coverley," for example) the two men worked together. Steele is supposed to have furnished the original ideas, the humor and overflowing kindness of such essays, while the work of polishing and perfecting the style fell to the more skillful Addison.

Because of their cultivated prose style, Steele and Addison were long regarded as models, and we are still influenced by **Addisonian** them in the direction of clearness and grace of ex-**Style** pression. How wide their influence extended may be seen in American literature. Hardly had *The Spectator* appeared when it crossed the Atlantic and began to dominate our English style on both sides of the ocean. Franklin, in Boston, studied it by night in order to imitate it in the essay which he slipped under the printing-house door next morning; and Byrd, in Virginia, reflects its influence in his charming Journal of exploration. Half a century later, the Hartford Wits were writing clever sketches that seemed like the work of a new " Spectator "; another half century, and Irving, the greatest master of English prose in his day, was still writing in the Addisonian manner, and regretting as he wrote that the leisurely style showed signs, in a bustling age, " of becoming a little old-fashioned."

Dr. Johnson and his Circle

Since Caxton established the king's English as a literary language our prose style has often followed the changing fashion of London. Thus, Lyly made it fantastic, Dryden simplified it, Addison gave it grace; and each leader set a fashion which was followed by a host of young writers. Hardly had the Addisonian style crossed the Atlantic, to be the model for American writers for a century, when London acclaimed a new prose fashion — a ponderous, grandiloquent fashion, characterized by mouth-filling words, antithetical sentences, rounded periods, sonorous commonplaces — which was eagerly adopted by orators and historians especially. The man who did more than any other to set this new oratorical fashion in motion was the same Dr. Samuel Johnson who advised young writers to study Addison as a model. And that was only one of his amusing inconsistencies.

Johnson was a man of power, who won a commanding place in English letters by his hard work and his downright sincerity. He won his name of "the great lexicographer" by his *Dictionary*, which we no longer consult, but which we remember as the first attempt at a complete English lexicon. If one asks what else he wrote, with the idea of going to the library and getting a book for pleasure, the answer must be that Johnson's voluminous works are now as dead as his dictionary. One student of literature may be interested in such a melancholy poem as "The Vanity of Human Wishes"; another will be entertained by the anecdotes or blunt criticisms of the *Lives of the Poets*; a third may be uplifted by the *Rambler Essays*, which are well called "majestically moral productions"; but we shall content ourselves here by recording Johnson's own refreshing criticism of certain ancient authors, that "it is idle to criticize what nobody reads." Perhaps the best thing he wrote was a minor work, which he did

DR. SAMUEL JOHNSON
From the portrait by Sir Joshua Reynolds

not know would ever be published. This was his manly Letter to Lord Chesterfield, a nobleman who had treated Johnson with discourtesy when the poor author was making a heroic struggle, but who offered his patronage when the Dictionary was announced as an epoch-making work. In his noble refusal of all extraneous help Johnson unconsciously voiced Literature's declaration of independence: that henceforth a book must stand or fall on its own merits, and that the day of the literary patron was gone forever.

Life. The story of Johnson's life (1709–1784) has been so well told that one is loath to attempt a summary of it. We note, therefore, a few plain facts : that he was the son of a poor bookseller ; that despite poverty and disease he obtained his classic education ; that at twenty-six he came to London, and, after an experience with patrons, rebelled against them ; that he did every kind of hackwork to earn his bread honestly, living in the very cellar of Grub Street, where he

was often cold and more often hungry ; that after nearly thirty years of labor his services to literature were rewarded by a pension, which he shared with the poor ; that he then formed the Literary Club (including Reynolds, Pitt, Gibbon, Goldsmith, Burke, and almost every other prominent man in London) and indulged nightly in his famous "conversations," which were either monologues or knockdown arguments ; and that in his old age he was regarded as the king of letters, the oracle of literary taste in England.

Such is the bare outline of Johnson's career. To his character, his rough exterior and his kind heart, his vast learning and his Tory prejudices, his piety, his melancholy, his virtues, his frailty, his "mass

DR. JOHNSON'S HOUSE (BOLT
COURT, FLEET ST.)

From the print by Charles J. Smith

of genuine manhood," only a volume could do justice. Happily that volume is at hand. It is Boswell's *Life of Johnson*, a famous book that deserves its fame.

Boswell's Johnson. Boswell was an inquisitive barrister who came from Edinburgh to London and thrust himself into the company of great men. To Johnson, then at the summit of his fame, "Bozzy" was devotion itself, following his master about by day or night, refusing to be rebuffed, jotting down notes of what he saw and heard. After Johnson's death he gathered these notes together and, after seven years of labor, produced his incomparable *Life of Johnson* (1791).

The greatness of Boswell's work may be traced to two causes. First, he had a great subject. The story of any human life is interesting, if truthfully told, and Johnson's heroic life of labor and pain and reward was passed in a capital city, among famous men, at a time which witnessed the rapid expansion of a mighty empire. Second, Boswell was as faithful as a man could be to his subject, for whom he had such admiration that even the dictator's frailties seemed more impressive than the virtues of ordinary humanity. So Boswell concealed nothing, and felt no necessity to distribute either praise or blame. He portrayed a man just as that man was, recorded the word just as the word was spoken; and facing the man we may see his enraptured audience, — at a distance, indeed, but marvelously clear, as when we look through the larger end of a field glass at a land-

JAMES BOSWELL

scape dominated by a mountain. One who reads this matchless biography will know Johnson better than he knows his own neighbor; he will gain, moreover, a better understanding of humanity, to reflect which clearly and truthfully is the prime object of all good literature.

Edmund Burke (1729–1797). This brilliant Irishman came up to London as a young man of twenty-one. Within a few years — such was his character, his education, his genius — he had won a reputation among old statesmen as a political philosopher. Then he entered Parliament, where for twenty years the House listened with growing amazement to his rhythmic periods, and he was acclaimed the most eloquent of orators.

Among Burke's numerous works those on America, India and France are deservedly the most famous. Of his orations on American subjects a student of literature or history may profitably read " On Taxation " (1774) and " On Conciliation "

EDMUND BURKE

From the print by John Jones, after Romney

(1775), in which Burke presents the Whig argument in favor of a liberal colonial policy. The Tory view of the same question was bluntly presented by Johnson in his essay "Taxation No Tyranny"; while like a reverberation from America, powerful enough to carry across the Atlantic, came Thomas Paine's "Common Sense," which was a ringing plea for colonial independence.

Of Burke's works pertaining to India " The Nabob of Arcot's Debts " (1785) and the " Impeachment of Warren Hastings " (1786) are interesting to those who can enjoy a long flight of sustained eloquence. Here again Burke presents the liberal, the humane view of what was then largely a political question ; but in his *Reflections on the French Revolution* (1790) he goes over to the Tories, thunders against the revolutionists or their English sympathizers, and exalts the undying glories of the British constitution. The *Reflections* is the most brilliant of all Burke's works, and is admired for its superb rhetorical style.

To examine any of these works is to discover the author's characteristic method : first, his framework or argument is carefully constructed so as to appeal to reason ; then this framework is buried out of sight and memory by a mass of description, digression, emotional appeal, allusions, illustrative matter from the author's wide reading or from his prolific imagination. Note this passage from the *French Revolution* :

Burke's Method

" It is now sixteen or seventeen years since I saw the Queen of France, then the Dauphiness, at Versailles ; and surely never lighted on this orb, which she hardly seemed to touch, a more delightful vision. I saw her just above the horizon, decorating and cheering the elevated sphere she had just begun to move in, glittering like the morning star, full of life and splendor and joy. Oh, what a revolution ! And what a heart must I have to contemplate without emotion that elevation and that fall ! Little did I dream, when she added titles of veneration to those of distant, enthusiastic, respectful love, that she should ever be obliged to carry the sharp antidote against disgrace concealed in that bosom ; little did I dream that I should have lived to see such disasters fallen upon her in a nation of gallant men, in a nation of men of honour and of cavaliers. I thought ten thousand swords must have leaped from their scabbards to avenge even a look that threatened her with insult. But the age of chivalry is gone. That of sophisters, economists and calculators has succeeded ; and the glory of Europe is extinguished for ever. Never, never more shall we behold that generous loyalty to rank and sex, that proud submission, that dignified obedience, that subordination of the heart, which kept alive, even in servitude itself, the spirit of an exalted freedom. The unbought grace of life, the cheap defence of nations, the nurse of manly sentiment and heroic enterprise is gone ! It is gone, that sensibility of principle, that chastity of honour, which felt a stain like a wound, which inspired courage whilst it mitigated ferocity, which ennobled whatever it touched, and under which vice itself lost half its evil by losing all its grossness."

That is finely expressed, but it has no bearing on the political matter in question ; namely, whether the sympathy of England should be extended to the French revolutionists in their struggle for liberty. This irrelevancy of Burke suggests our first criticism : that he is always eloquent, and usually right ; but he is seldom convincing, and his eloquence is a hindrance rather than a help to his main purpose. So we are not surprised to hear that his eloquent speech on Conciliation emptied the benches; or that after his supreme effort in the impeachment of Hastings — an effort so tremendously dramatic that spectators sobbed, screamed, were carried out in fits — the object of all this invective was acquitted by his judges. Reading the works now, they seem to us praiseworthy not for their sustained eloquence, which is wearisome, but for the brilliancy of certain detached passages which catch the eye like sparkling raindrops after a drenching shower. It was the splendor of such passages, their vivid imagery and harmonious rhythm, which led Matthew Arnold to assert that Burke was the greatest master of prose style in our literature. Anybody can make such an assertion; nobody can prove or disprove it.

The Historians. Perhaps it was the rapid expansion of the empire in the latter part of the eighteenth century which aroused such interest in historical subjects that works of history were then more eagerly welcomed than poetry or fiction. Gibbon says in his *Memoirs* that in his day "history was the most popular species of composition." It was also the best rewarded; for while Johnson, the most renowned author of his time, wrote a romance (*Rasselas*) hoping to sell it for enough to pay for his mother's funeral, Robertson easily disposed of his *History of the Emperor Charles V* for £4500; and there were others who were even better paid for popular histories, the very titles of which are now forgotten.

Of all the historical works of the age, and their name was legion, only one survives with something of its original vitality, standing the double test of time and scholarship.
Gibbon
This is *The Decline and Fall of the Roman Empire* (1776), a work which remained famous for a century, and which still has its admiring readers. It was written by Edward Gibbon (1737–1794), who belonged to the Literary Club that gathered about Johnson, and who cultivated his style, he tells us, first by adopting the dictator's rounded periods, and then practicing them "till they moved to flutes and hautboys."

The scope of Gibbon's work is enormous. It begins with the Emperor Trajan (A.D. 98) and carries us through the convulsions of a dying civilization, the descent of the Barbarians on Rome, the spread of Christianity, the Crusades, the rise of Mohammedanism, — through all the confused history of thirteen centuries, ending with the capture of Constantinople by the Turks, in 1453. The mind that could grasp such vast and chaotic materials, arrange them in orderly sequence and present them as in a gorgeous panorama, moves us to wonder. To be sure, there are many things to criticize in Gibbon's masterpiece, — the author's love of mere pageants; his materialism; his inability to understand religious movements, or even religious motives; his lifeless figures, which move as if by mechanical springs, — but one who reads the *Decline and Fall* may be too much impressed by the evidences of scholarship, of vast labor, of

EDWARD GIBBON

From an enamel by H. Bone, R.A.; after
Sir Joshua Reynolds

genius even, to linger over faults. It is a "monumental" work, most interesting to those who admire monuments; and its style is the perfection of that oratorical, Johnsonese style which was popular in England in 1776, and which, half a century later, found its best American mouthpiece in Daniel Webster. The influence of Gibbon may still be seen in the orators and historians who, lacking the charm of simplicity, clothe even their platitudes in high-sounding phrases.

THE REVIVAL OF ROMANTIC POETRY

Every age has had its romantic poets — that is, poets who sing the dreams and ideals of life, and whose songs seem to be written naturally, spontaneously, as from a full heart [1] — but in the eighteenth century they were completely overshadowed by formal versifiers who made poetry by rule. At that time the imaginative verse which had delighted an earlier age was regarded much as we now regard an old beaver hat; Shakespeare and Milton were neglected, Spenser was but a name, Chaucer was clean forgotten. If a poet aspired to fame, he imitated the couplets of Dryden or Pope, who, as Cowper said,

THOMAS GRAY

From a portrait by Benjamin Wilson, in the possession of John Murray

> Made poetry a mere mechanic art,
> And every warbler has his tune by heart.

Among those who made vigorous protest against the precise and dreary formalism of the age were Collins and Gray, whose names are commonly associated in poetry, as are the names of Addison and Steele in prose. They had the same tastes, the same gentle melancholy, the same freedom from the bondage of literary fashion. Of the two, William Collins (1721–1759) was perhaps the more gifted poet. His exquisite "Ode to Evening" is without a rival in its own field, and his brief elegy beginning,

[1] For specific examples of formal and romantic poetry see the comparison between Addison and Wordsworth on pages 206–207.

"How sleep the brave," is a worthy commemoration of a soldier's death and a nation's gratitude. It has, says Andrew Lang, the magic of an elder day and of all time.

Thomas Gray (1716–1771) is more widely known than his fellow poet, largely because of one fortunate poem which "returned to men's bosoms" as if sure of its place and welcome. This is the "Elegy Written in a Country Churchyard" (1750), which has been translated into all civilized tongues, and which is known, loved, quoted wherever English is spoken.

To criticize this favorite of a million readers seems almost **Gray's Elegy** ruthless, as if one were pulling a flower to pieces for the sake of giving it a botanical name. A pleasanter task is to explain, if one can, the immense popularity of the "Elegy." The theme is of profound interest to every man who reveres the last resting place of his parents,

STOKE POGES CHURCHYARD, SHOWING PART OF THE CHURCH AND GRAY'S TOMB

to the nation which cherishes every monument of its founders, and even to primitive peoples, like the Indians, who refuse to leave the place where their fathers are buried, and who make the grave a symbol of patriotism. With this great theme our poet is in perfect sympathy. His attitude is simple and reverent; he treads softly, as if on holy ground. The natural setting or atmosphere of his poem, the peace of evening falling on the old churchyard at Stoke Poges, the curfew bell, the cessation of daily toil, the hush which falls upon the twilight landscape like a summons to prayer, — all this is exactly as it should be. Finally, Gray's craftsmanship, his choice of words, his simple figures, his careful fitting of every line to its place and context, is as near perfection as human skill could make it.

Other poems of Gray, which make his little book precious, are the four odes : " To Spring," " On a Distant Prospect of Eton College," " The Progress of Poesy " and " The Bard," the last named being a description of the dramatic end of an old Welsh minstrel, who chants a wild prophecy as he goes to his death. These romantic odes, together with certain translations which Gray made from Norse mythology, mark the end of " classic " domination in English poetry.

OLIVER GOLDSMITH (1728–1774)

Most versatile of eighteenth-century writers was " poor Noll," a most improvident kind of man in all worldly ways, but so skillful with his pen that Johnson wrote a sincere epitaph to the effect that Goldsmith attempted every form of literature, and adorned everything which he attempted. The form of his verse suggests the formal school, and his polished couplets rival those of Pope ; but there the resemblance ceases. In his tenderness and humor, in his homely subjects and the warm human sympathy with which he describes them, Goldsmith belongs to the new romantic school of poetry.

Life. The life of Goldsmith has inspired many pens ; but the subject, far from being exhausted, is still awaiting the right biographer. The poet's youthful escapades in the Irish country, his classical education at Trinity College, Dublin, and his vagabond studies among gypsies and peddlers, his childish attempts at various professions, his wanderings over Europe, his shifts and makeshifts to earn a living in London, his tilts with Johnson at the Literary Club, his love of gorgeous raiment, his indiscriminate charity, his poverty, his simplicity, his success in the art of writing and his total failure in the art of living, — such kaleidoscopic elements make a brief biography impossible. The character of the man appears in a single incident.

Landing one day on the Continent with a flute, a spare shirt and a guinea as his sole outward possessions, the guinea went for a feast and a game of cards at the nearest inn, and the shirt to the first beggar that asked for it. There remained only the flute, and with that Goldsmith fared forth confidently, like the gleeman of old with his harp, delighted at seeing the world, utterly forgetful of the fact that he had crossed the Channel in search of a medical education.

That aimless, happy-go-lucky journey was typical of Goldsmith's whole life of forty-odd years. Those who knew him loved but despaired of him. When he passed away (1774) Johnson summed up the feeling of the English literary world in the sentence, " He was a very great man; let not his frailties be remembered."

OLIVER GOLDSMITH
After the portrait by Sir Joshua Reynolds

Goldsmith's Prose and Verse. Among the forgotten works of Goldsmith we note with interest several that he wrote for children: a fanciful *History of England*, an entertaining but most unreliable *Animated Nature*, and probably also the tale of " Little Goody Twoshoes." These were written (as were all his other works) to satisfy the demands of his landlady, or to pay an old debt, or to buy a new cloak, — a plum-colored velvet cloak, wherewith to appear at the opera or to dazzle the Literary Club. From among his works we select four, as illustrative of Goldsmith's versatility.

The Citizen of the World, a series of letters from an alleged Chinese visitor, invites comparison with the essays of Addison or Steele. All three writers are satirical, all have a high moral purpose, all are masters of a graceful style; but where the "Spectator" touches the surface of life, Goldsmith often goes deeper and probes the very spirit of the eighteenth century. Here is a paragraph from the first letter, in which the alleged visitor, who has heard much of the wealth and culture of London, sets down his first impressions:

THE "CHESHIRE CHEESE," LONDON, SHOWING DR. JOHNSON'S FAVORITE SEAT

The tavern, which still stands, was the favorite haunt of both Johnson and Goldsmith

"From these circumstances in their buildings, and from the dismal looks of the inhabitants, I am induced to conclude that the nation is actually poor; and that, like the Persians, they make a splendid figure everywhere but at home. The proverb of Xixofou is, that a man's riches may be seen in his eyes: if we judge of the English by this rule, there is not a poorer nation under the sun."

The Deserted Village (1770) is the best remembered of Goldsmith's poems, or perhaps one should say "verses" in

The Deserted Village   deference to critics like Matthew Arnold who classify the work with Pope's *Essay on Man*, as a rimed dissertation rather than a true poem.

To compare the two works just mentioned is to discover how far Goldsmith is from his formal model. In Pope's "Essay" we find common sense, moral maxims and some alleged philosophy, but no emotion, no romance, no men or women. The

"Village," on the other hand, is romantic even in desolation; it awakens our interest, our sympathy; and it gives us two characters, the Parson and the Schoolmaster, who live in our memories with the best of Chaucer's creations. Moreover, it makes the commonplace life of man ideal and beautiful, and so appeals to readers of widely different tastes or nationalities. Of the many ambitious poems written in the eighteenth century, the two most widely read (aside from the songs of Burns) are Goldsmith's "Village," which portrays the life of simple country people, and Gray's "Elegy," which laments their death.

CANONBURY TOWER (LONDON)

Goldsmith lived here when he wrote the "Vicar of Wakefield"

Goldsmith's one novel, *The Vicar of Wakefield*

Vicar of Wakefield (1766), has been well called "the Prince Charming" of our early works of fiction. This work has a threefold distinction: its style alone is enough to make it pleasant reading; as a story it retains much of its original charm, after a century and a half of proving; by its moral purity it offered the best kind of rebuke to the vulgar tendency of the early English novel, and influenced subsequent fiction in the direction of cleanness and decency.

The story is that of a certain vicar, or clergyman, Dr. Primrose and his family, who pass through heavy trials and misfortunes. These might crush or embitter an ordinary man, but they only serve to make the Vicar's love for his children, his trust in God, his tenderness for humanity, shine out more clearly, like stars after a tempest. Mingled with these affecting

E

trials are many droll situations which probably reflect something of the author's personal escapades; for Goldsmith was the son of a clergyman, and brought himself and his father into his tale. As a novel, that is, a reflection of human life in the form of a story, it contains many weaknesses; but despite its faults of moralizing and sentimentality, the impression which the story leaves is one of "sweetness and light." Swinburne says that, of all novels he had seen rise and fall in three generations, *The Vicar of Wakefield* alone had retained the same high level in the opinion of its readers.

Another notable work is Goldsmith's comedy *She Stoops to Conquer.* The date of that comedy (1773) recalls the fact that, **She Stoops** though it has been played for nearly a century and **to Conquer** a half, during which a thousand popular plays have been forgotten, it is still a prime favorite on the amateur stage. Perhaps the only other comedies of which the same can be said with approximate truth are *The Rivals* (1775) and *The School for Scandal* (1777) of Richard Brinsley Sheridan.

The plot of *She Stoops to Conquer* is said to have been suggested by one of Goldsmith's queer adventures. He arrived one day at a village, riding a borrowed nag, and with the air of a lordly traveler asked a stranger to direct him "to the best house in the place." The stranger misunderstood, or else was a rare wag, for he showed the way to the abode of a wealthy gentleman. There Goldsmith made himself at home, ordered the servants about, invited his host to share a bottle of wine, — in short, made a great fool of himself. Evidently the host was also a wag, for he let the joke run on till the victim was ready to ride away.[1]

From some such crazy escapade Goldsmith made his comedy of manners, a lively, rollicking comedy of topsy-turvy scenes, all hinging upon the incident of mistaking a private house for a public inn. We have called *She Stoops to Conquer* a comedy

---

[1] There is some doubt as to the source of Goldsmith's plot. It may have been suggested by an earlier French comedy by Marivaux.

of eighteenth-century manners, but our continued interest in
its absurdities would seem to indicate that it is a comedy of
human nature in all ages.

ROBERT BURNS (1759–1796)

Burns is everywhere acclaimed the poet of Scotland, and for
two good reasons : because he reflects better than any other
the emotions of the Scottish
people, and because his book
is a summary of the best verse
of his native land. Practically all his songs, such as
"Bonnie Doon" and "Auld
Lang Syne," are late echoes
of much older verses ; his
more ambitious poems borrow
their ideas, their satire or
sentiment, their form even,
from Ferguson, Allan Ram-
say and other poets, all of
whom aimed (as Scott aimed
in "Lochinvar") to preserve
the work of unnamed min-
strels whose lines had been
repeated in Highlands or
Lowlands for two centuries.
Burns may be regarded,

ROBERT BURNS
After Alexander Nasmyth

therefore, as a treasury of all that is best in Scottish song.
His genius was to take this old material, dear to the heart of
the native, and give it final expression.

Life. The life of Burns is one to discourage a biographer who does
not relish the alternative of either concealing the facts or apologizing
for his subject. We shall record here only a few personal matters
which may help us to understand Burns's poetry.

Perhaps the most potent influence in his life was that which came from his labor in the field. He was born in a clay biggin, or cottage, in the parish of Alloway, near the little town of Ayr:

> Auld Ayr, wham ne'er a town surpasses
> For honest men and bonnie lasses.

His father was a poor crofter, a hard-working, God-fearing man of the Covenanter type, who labored unceasingly to earn a living from the soil of a rented farm. The children went barefoot in all seasons; almost from the time they could walk they were expected to labor; and

"ELLISLAND"

The hundred-acre farm near Dumfries, where Burns worked as a farmer. The happiest days of his life were spent here, 1787–1791

at thirteen Bobbie was doing a man's work at the plow or the reaping. The toil was severe; the reward, at best, was to escape dire poverty or disgraceful debt; but there was yet a nobility in the life which is finely reflected in "The Cotter's Saturday Night," a poem which ranks with Whittier's "Snow Bound" among the best that labor has ever inspired.

As a farmer's boy Burns worked in the open, in close contact with nature, and the result is evident in all his verse. Sunshine or storm, **The Element of Nature** bird song or winter wind, the flowers, the stars, the dew of the morning,—open Burns where you will, and you are face to face with these elemental realities. Sometimes his reflection of nature is exquisitely tender, as in "To a Mouse" or "To a

Mountain Daisy"; but for the most part he regards nature not sentimentally, like Gray, or religiously, like Wordsworth and Bryant, but in a breezy, companionable way which suggests the song of "Under the Greenwood Tree" in *As You Like It*.

Another influence in Burns's life came from his elementary education. There were no ancient classics studied in the school which he **His** attended, — fortunately, perhaps, for his best work is free **Education** from the outworn classical allusions which decorate the bulk of eighteenth-century verse. In the evening he listened to tales from Scottish history, which stirred him deeply and made him live in a present world rather than in the misty region of Greek mythology. One result of this education was the downright honesty of Burns's poems. Here is no echo from a vanished world of gods and goddesses, but the voice of a man, living, working, feeling joy or sorrow in the presence of everyday nature and humanity.

For another formative influence Burns was indebted to Betty Davidson, a relative and an inmate of the household, who carried such a stock of old wives' tales as would scare any child into fits on a dark night. Hear Burns speak of her:

"She had, I suppose, the largest collection in the country of tales and songs concerning devils, ghosts, fairies, brownies, witches, warlocks, spunkies, kelpies, elf-candles, dead-lights, wraiths, apparitions, cantrips, giants, enchanted towers, dragons, and other trumpery. This cultivated the latent seeds of poetry, but had so strong an effect upon my imagination that to this hour, in my nocturnal rambles, I sometimes keep a sharp look-out in suspicious places."

Reflections of these grotesque superstitions appear in such poems as the "Address to the Deil" and "Tam o' Shanter." The latter is commonly named as one of the few original works of Burns, but it is probably a retelling of some old witch-tale of Betty Davidson.

The evil influence in Burns's life may be only suggested. It leads first to the tavern, to roistering and dissipation, to entanglements in **Evil** vulgar love affairs; then swiftly to the loss of a splendid **Elements** poetic gift, to hopeless debts, to degrading poverty, to an untimely death. Burns had his chance, if ever poet had it, after the publication of his first book (the famous Kilmarnock edition of 1786) when he was called in triumph to Edinburgh. There he sold another edition of his poems for a sum that seemed fabulous to a poor crofter; whereupon he bought a farm and married his Jean Armour. He was acclaimed throughout the length and breadth of his native land; his poems were read by the wise and by the ignorant; he was the poet of Scotland, and the nation, proud of its gifted son, stood ready to honor and follow him. But the old habits were too strong, and Burns took the downhill road. To this element of dissipation we owe his occasional bitterness, railing and coarseness, which make an expurgated edition of his poems essential to one who would enjoy the reading.

There is another element, often emphasized for its alleged influence on Burns's poetry. During his lifetime the political world

THE VILLAGE OF TARBOLTON, NEAR WHICH BURNS LIVED WHEN ABOUT
NINETEEN YEARS OLD

was shaken by the American and French revolutions; democracy was in the air, and the watchwords "Liberty, Equality, Fraternity" inspired many a song besides the *Marseillaise* and many a document besides the Declaration of Independence. That Burns was aware of this political commotion is true, but he was not much influenced by it. He was at home only in his own Scottish field, and even there his interests were limited, — not to be compared with those of Walter Scott, for example. When the Bastille was stormed, and the world stood aghast, Burns was too much engrossed in personal matters to be greatly moved by distant affairs in France. Not to the Revolution, therefore, but to his Scottish blood do we owe the thrilling "Scots Wha Hae," one of the world's best battle songs; not to the new spirit of democracy abroad but to the old Covenanter spirit at home do we owe "A Man's a Man for a' That" with its assertion of elemental manhood.

The Songs of Burns. From such an analysis of Burns's life one may forecast his subject and his method. Living intensely in a small field, he must discover that there are just two poetic subjects of abiding interest. These are Nature and Humanity, and of these Burns must write from first-hand knowledge, simply, straightforwardly, and with sincerity. Moreover, as Burns lives in an intense way, reading himself rather than books, he must discover that the ordinary man is more swayed by strong feeling than by logical reasons. He will write, therefore, of the common emotions that lie between the extremes of laughter and tears, and his appeal will be to the heart rather than to the head of his reader.

This emotional power of Burns, his masterful touch upon human heartstrings, is the first of his poetic qualities; and he

AULD ALLOWAY KIRK

Made famous by the poem of "Tam o' Shanter"

has others which fairly force themselves upon the attention. For example, many of his lyrics ("Auld Lang Syne," "Banks o' Doon," "Flow Gently, Sweet Afton," "O, Wert Thou in the Cauld Blast") have been repeatedly set to music; and the reason is that they were written to music, that in such poems Burns was refashioning some old material to the tune of a Scottish song. There is a singing quality in his poetry which not only makes it pleasant reading but which is apt to set the words tripping to melody. For a specific example take this stanza from "Of a' the Airts," a lyric which one can hardly read without making a tune to match it:

> I see her in the dewy flow'rs,
> I see her sweet and fair;
> I hear her in the tunefu' birds,
> I hear her charm the air:
> There 's not a bonie flow'r that springs
> By fountain, shaw or green,
> There 's not a bonie bird that sings,
> But minds me o' my Jean.

Sympathy is another marked characteristic of Burns, a wide, all-embracing sympathy that knows no limit save for hypocrites, at whom he pointed his keenest satire. His feeling for nature is reflected in " To a Mouse " and " To a Daisy "; his comradeship with noble men appears in " The Cotter's Saturday Night," with riotous and bibulous men in " The Jolly Beggars," with smugglers and their ilk in " The Deil 's Awa' with the Exciseman," [1] with patriots in " Bannockburn," with men who mourn in " To Mary in Heaven," and with all lovers in a score of famous lyrics. Side by side with Burns's sympathy (for Smiles live next door to Tears) appears his keen sense of humor, a humor that is sometimes rollicking, as in " Contented wi' Little," and again too broad for decency. For the most part, however, Burns contents himself with dry, quiet sarcasm delivered with an air of great seriousness:

> Ah, gentle dames, it gars me greet
> To think how mony counsels sweet,
> How mony lengthened sage advices
> The husband frae the wife despises!

Why Burns is Read. Such qualities, appearing on almost every page of Burns's little book of poetry, show how widely he differs from the formal school of Pope and Dryden. They labor to compose poetry, while Burns gives the impression of singing, as naturally as a child sings from a full heart. Again, most eighteenth-century poets wrote for the favored few, but

---

[1] Burns was himself an exciseman; that is, a collector of taxes on alcoholic liquors. He wrote this song while watching a smuggler's craft, and waiting in the storm for officers to come and make an arrest.

Burns wrote for all his neighbors. His first book was bought by farmers, plowboys, milkmaids, — by every Lowlander who could scrape together three shillings to buy a treasure. Then scholars got hold of it, taking it from humble hands, and Burns was called to Edinburgh to prepare a larger edition of his songs. For a half-century Scotland kept him to herself;[1] then his work went wide in the world, to be read again by plain men and women, by sailors on the sea, by soldiers round the camp-fire, by farmers, mechanics, tradesmen, who in their new homes in Australia or America warmed themselves at the divine fire which was kindled, long ago, in the little clay biggin at Allo-way.

If one should ask, Why this world-wide wel-

The Genius of Burns

come to Burns, the while Pope remains a mark for liter-ary criticism? the answer is that Burns has a most extraordinary power of touching the hearts of common men. He is one of the most democratic

BURNS'S MAUSOLEUM

of poets; he takes for his subject a simple experience — a family gathering at eventide, a fair, a merrymaking, a joy, a grief, the finding of a flower, the love of a lad for a lass — and with rare simplicity reflects the emotion that such an experience awakens. Seen through the poet's eyes, this simple emotion becomes radiant and lovely, a thing not of earth but

---

[1] Up to 1850 Burns was rarely mentioned in treatises on English literature. One reason for his late recognition was that the Lowland vocabulary employed in most of his poems was only half intelligible to the ordinary English reader.

of heaven. That is the genius of Burns, to ennoble human feeling, to reveal some hidden beauty in a commonplace experience. The luminous world of fine thought and fine emotion which we associate with the name of poetry he opened not to scholars alone but to all humble folk who toil and endure. As a shoemaker critic once said, "Burns confirms my former suspicion that the world was made for me as well as for Cæsar."

MINOR POETS OF ROMANTICISM

There were other poets who aided in the romantic revival, and among them William Cowper (1731–1800) is one of the most notable. His most ambitious works, such as *The Task* and the translation of Homer into blank verse, have fallen into neglect, and he is known to modern readers chiefly by a few familiar hymns and by the ballad of "John Gilpin."

WILLIAM COWPER

From the rare engraving by W. Blake (1802). After the painting by T. Lawrence, R.A. (1793)

Less gifted but more popular than Cowper was James Macpherson (1736–1796), who made a sensation that spread rapidly over Europe and America with his *Fingal* (1762) and other works of the same kind, — wildly heroic poems which, he alleged, were translations from Celtic manuscripts written by an ancient bard named Ossian. Another and better literary forgery appeared in a series of ballads called *The Rowley Papers*, dealing with medieval themes. These were written by "the marvelous boy"

Thomas Chatterton (1752–1770), who professed to have found the poems in a chest of old manuscripts. The success of these forgeries, especially of the " Ossian " poems, is an indication of the awakened interest in medieval poetry and legend which characterized the whole romantic movement.

In this connection, Thomas Percy (1729–1811) did a notable work when he published, after years of research, his *Reliques of Ancient English Poetry* (1765). This was a collection of old ballads, which profoundly influenced Walter Scott, and which established a foundation for all later works of balladry.

Another interesting figure in the romantic revival is William Blake (1757–1827), a strange, mystic child, a veritable John o' Dreams, whom some call madman because of his huge, chaotic, unintelligible poems, but whom others regard as the supreme poetical genius of the eighteenth century. His only readable works are the boyish *Poetical Sketches* (1783) and two later volumes called *Songs of Innocence* and *Songs of Experience* (1794). Even these contain much to make us question Blake's sanity ; but they contain also a few lyrics that might have been written by an elf rather than a man, — beautiful, elusive lyrics that haunt us like a strain of gypsy music, a memory of child- hood, a bird song in the night :

> Can the eagle see what is in the pit,
>   Or wilt thou go ask the mole?
> Can wisdom be put in a silver rod,
>   Or love in a golden bowl?

In the witchery of these lyrics eighteenth-century poetry appears commonplace ; but they attracted no attention, even " Holy Thursday," the sweetest song of poor children ever written, passing unnoticed. That did not trouble Blake, however, who cared nothing for rewards. He was a childlike soul, well content

> To see the world in a grain of sand,
>   And a heaven in a wild flower ;
> Hold infinity in the palm of your hand,
>   And eternity in an hour.

THE EARLY ENGLISH NOVEL

An important literary event of the eighteenth century was the appearance of the modern novel. This invention, generally credited to the English, differs radically from the old romance, which was known to all civilized peoples. Walter Scott made the following distinction between the two types of fiction : the romance is a story in which our interest centers in marvelous incidents, brought to pass by extraordinary or superhuman characters ; the novel is a story which is more natural, more in harmony with our experience of life. Such a definition, though faulty, is valuable in that it points to the element of imagination as the distinguishing mark between the romance and the true novel.

Take, for example, the romances of Arthur or Sindbad or the Green Knight. Here are heroes of more than human endurance, ladies of surpassing loveliness, giants, dragons, enchanters, marvelous adventures in the land of imagination. Such fanciful stories, valuable as a reflection of the ideals of different races, reached their highest point in the Middle Ages, when they were used to convey the ideals of chivalry and knightly duty. They grew more fantastic as they ran to seed, till in the Elizabethan age they had degenerated into picaresque stories (from *pícaro*, "a rogue ") which recounted the adventures not of a noble knight but of some scoundrel or outcast. They were finally laughed out of literature in numerous burlesques, of which the most famous is *Don Quixote* (1605). In the humor of this story, in the hero's fighting windmills and meeting so many adventures that he had no time to breathe, we have an excellent criticism not of chivalry, as is sometimes alleged, but of extravagant popular romances on the subject.[1]

The Romance

---

[1] *Don Quixote* is commonly named as a type of extravagant humor, but from another viewpoint it is a sad book, intensely sad. For it recounts the experience of a man who had a knightly heart and who believed the world to be governed by knightly ideals, but who went forth to find a world filled with vulgarity and villainy.

Compare now these old romances with *Ivanhoe* or *Robinson Crusoe* or *Lorna Doone* or *A Tale of Two Cities*. In each of
The Novel the last-named novels one may find three elements : a story, a study, and an exercise of the creative imagination. A modern work of fiction must still have a good story, if anybody is to read it ; must contain also a study or observation of humanity, not of superhuman heroes but of men and women who work or play or worship in close relationship to their fellows. Finally, the story and the study must be fused by the imagination, which selects or creates various scenes, characters, incidents, and which orders or arranges its materials so as to make a harmonious work that appeals to our sense of truth and beauty ; in other words, a work of art.

Such is the real novel, a well-told story in tune with human experience, holding true to life, exercising fancy but keeping it under control, arousing thought as well as feeling, and appealing to our intellect as well as to our imagination.[1]

Defoe (1661–1731). Among the forerunners of the modern novel is Daniel Foe, author of *Robinson Crusoe*, who began to call himself " Defoe " after he attained fame. He produced an amazing variety of wares : newspapers, magazines, ghost stories, biographies, journals, memoirs, satires, picaresque romances, essays on religion, reform, trade, projects, — in all more than two hundred works. These were written in a picturesque style and with such a wealth of detail that, though barefaced inventions

---

[1] This convenient division of prose fiction into romances and novels is open to challenge. Some critics use the name " novel " for any work of prose fiction. They divide novels into two classes, stories (or short stories) and romances. The story relates simple or detached incidents ; the romance deals with life in complex relations, dominated by strong emotions, especially by the emotion of love.

Other critics arrange prose fiction in the following classes : novels of adventure (Robinson Crusoe, The Last of the Mohicans), historical novels (Ivanhoe, The Spy), romantic novels (Lorna Doone, The Heart of Midlothian), novels of manners (Cranford, Pride and Prejudice), novels of personality (Silas Marner, The Scarlet Letter), novels of purpose (Oliver Twist, Uncle Tom's Cabin).

Still another classification arranges fiction under two heads, romance and realism. In the romance, which portrays unusual incidents or characters, we see the ideal, the poetic side of humanity ; in the realistic novel, dealing with ordinary men and women, the prosaic element of life is emphasized.

for the most part, they passed for veracious chronicles. One critic, thinking of the vividly realistic *Journal of the Plague Year* and *Memoirs of a Cavalier,* says that " Defoe wrote history, but invented the facts " ; another declares that " the one little art of which Defoe was past master was the art of forging a story and imposing it on the world as truth." The long list of his works ends with a *History of the Devil,* in 1726.

DANIEL DEFOE

Foe's career was an extraordinary one. By nature and training he seems to have preferred devious ways to straight, and to have concealed his chief motive whether he appeared as reformer or politician, tradesman or writer, police-spy or friend of outcasts. His education, which he picked up from men and circumstance, was more varied than any university could have given him. Perhaps the chief factor in this practical education was his ability to turn every experience to profitable account. As a journalist he invented the modern magazine (his *Review* appeared in 1704, five years before Steele's *Tatler*) ; also he projected the interview, the editorial, the " scoop," and other features which still figure in our newspapers. As a hired pamphleteer, writing satires against Whigs or Tories, he learned so many political secrets that when one party fell he was the best possible man to be employed by the other. While sitting in the stocks (in punishment for writing a satirical pamphlet that set Tories and Churchmen by the ears) he made such a hit with his doggerel verses against the authorities that crowds came to the pillory to cheer him and to buy his poem. While in durance vile, in the old Newgate Prison, he mingled freely with all sorts of criminals (there were no separate cells in those days), won their secrets, and used them to advantage in his picaresque romances. He learned also so much of the shady side of London life that no sooner was he released than he was employed as a secret-service agent, or spy, by the government which had jailed him.

It is as difficult to find the real Foe amidst such devious trails as to determine where a caribou is from the maze of footprints which he leaves behind him. He seems to have been untiring in his effort to secure better treatment of outcast folk; he speaks of himself, with apparent sincerity, as having received his message from the Divine Spirit; but the impression which he made upon the upper classes was reflected by Swift, who called him "a grave, dogmatical rogue." For many years he was a popular hero, trusted not only by the poor but by the criminal classes (ordinarily keen judges of honesty in other men), until his secret connection with the gov-

CUPOLA HOUSE
Defoe's residence at Bury

ernment became known. Then suspicion fell upon him; his popularity was destroyed and he fled from London. The last few years of his life were spent in hiding from real or imaginary enemies.

Defoe was approaching his sixtieth year when he wrote *Robinson Crusoe* (1719), a story which has been read through-
Robinson Crusoe out the civilized world, and which, after two centuries of life, is still young and vigorous. The first charm of the book is in its moving adventures, which are surprising enough to carry us through the moralizing passages.

These also have their value; for who ever read them without asking, What would I have done or thought or felt under such circumstances? The work of society is now so comfortably divided that one seldom dreams of being his own mechanic, farmer, hunter, herdsman, cook and tailor, as Crusoe was. Thinking of his experience we are brought face to face with our dependence on others, with our debt to the countless, unnamed men whose labor made civilization possible. We understand also the pioneers, who in the far, lonely places of the earth have won a home and country from the wilderness.

When the adventures are duly appreciated we discover another charm of *Robinson Crusoe*, namely, its intense reality. Defoe had that experience of many projects, and that vivid imagination, which enabled him to put himself in the place of his hero,[1] to anticipate his needs, his feelings, his labors and triumph. That Crusoe was heroic none will deny; yet his heroism was of a different kind from that which we meet in the old romances. Here was no knight "without fear and without reproach," but a plain man with his strength and weakness. He despaired like other men; but instead of giving way to despair he drew up a list of his blessings and afflictions, "like debtor and creditor," found a reasonable balance in his favor, and straightway conquered himself, — which is the first task of all real heroes. Again, he had horrible fears; he beat his breast, cried out as one in mortal terror; then "I thought that would do little good, so I began to make a raft." So he overcame his fears, as he overcame the difficulties of the place, by setting himself to do alone what a whole race of men had done before him. *Robinson Crusoe* is therefore history as well as fiction; its subject is not Alexander Selkirk but Homo Sapiens; its lesson is the everlasting triumph of will and work.

[1] The basis of *Robinson Crusoe* was the experience of an English sailor, Alexander Selkirk, or Selcraig, who was marooned on the lonely island of Juan Fernandez, off the coast of Chile. There he lived in solitude for the space of five years before he was rescued. When Selkirk returned to England (1709) an account of his adventures appeared in the public press.

Richardson. One morning in 1740 the readers of London found a new work for sale in the bookshops. It was made up of alleged letters from a girl to her parents, a sentimental girl who opened her heart freely, explaining its hopes, fears, griefs, temptations, and especially its moral sensibilities. Such a work of fiction was unique at that time. Delighted readers waited for another and yet another volume of the same story, till more than a year had passed and *Pamela, or Virtue Rewarded* reached its happy ending.

The book made a sensation in England; it was speedily translated, and repeated its triumph on the other side of the Channel. Comparatively few people could read it now without being bored, but it is famous in the history of literature as the first English novel; that is, a story of a human life under stress of emotion, told by one who understood the tastes of his own age, and who strove to keep his work true to human nature in all ages.

The First Novel

The author of *Pamela*, Samuel Richardson (1689–1761), was a very proper person, well satisfied with himself, who conducted a modest business as printer and bookseller. For years he had practiced writing, and had often been employed by sentimental young women who came to him for model love letters. Hence the extraordinary knowledge of feminine feelings which Richardson displayed; hence also the epistolary form in which his novels were written. His aim in all his work was to teach morality and correct deportment. His strength was in his power to analyze and portray emotions. His weakness lay in his vanity, which led him to shun masculine society and to foregather at tea tables with women who flattered him.

Led by the success of *Pamela*, which portrayed the feelings of a servant girl, the author began another series of letters which ended in the eight-volume novel *Clarissa, or The History of a Young Lady* (1748). The story appeared in installments, which were awaited with feverish impatience till the agony drew to an end, and the heroine died amid the sobs of

E

ten thousand readers. Yet the story had power, and the central figure of Clarissa was impressive in its pathos and tragedy. The novel would still be readable if it were stripped of the stilted conversations and sentimental gush in which Richardson delighted; but that would leave precious little of the story.

Fielding. In vigorous contrast with the prim and priggish Richardson is Henry Fielding (1707–1754), a big, jovial, reckless man, full of animal spirits, who was ready to mitigate any man's troubles or forget his own by means of a punch bowl or a venison potpie. He was noble born, but seems to have been thrown on the world to shift for himself. After an excellent education he studied law, and was for some years a police magistrate, in which position he increased his large knowledge of the seamy side of life. He had a pen for vigorous writing, and after squandering two modest fortunes (his own and his wife's) he proceeded to earn his living by writing buffooneries for the stage. Then appeared Richardson's *Pamela, or Virtue Rewarded*, and in ridiculing its sentimental heroine Fielding found his vocation as a novelist.

He began *Joseph Andrews* (1742) as a joke, by taking for his hero an alleged brother of Pamela, who was also virtuous
Burlesque of but whose reward was to be kicked out of doors.
Richardson Then the story took to the open road, among the inns and highways of an age when traveling in rural England was almost as adventurous as campaigning in Flanders. In the joy of his story Fielding soon forgot his burlesque of Richardson, and attempted what he called a realistic novel; that is, a story of real life. The morality and decorum which Richardson exalted appeared to Fielding as hypocrisy; so he devoted himself to a portrayal of men and manners as he found them.

Undoubtedly there were plenty of good men and manners at that time, but Fielding had a vagabond taste that delighted in rough scenes, and of these also eighteenth-century England could furnish an abundance. Hence his *Joseph Andrews* is a picture not of English society, as is often alleged, but only of the least significant part of society. The same is true of *Tom Jones* (1749), which is the author's most vigorous work, and of *Amelia* (1751), in which, though he portrays one good woman, he repeats many of the questionable incidents of his earlier works.

There is power in all these novels, the power of keen observation, of rough humor, of downright sincerity; but unhappily the power often runs to waste in long speeches to the reader, in descriptions of brutal or degrading scenes, and in a wholly unnecessary coarseness of expression.

Influence of the Early Novels. The idea of the modern novel seems to have been developed by several English authors, each of whom, like pioneers in a new country, left his stamp on subsequent works in the same field. Richardson's governing motive may be summed up in the word "sensibility," which means "delicacy of feeling," and which was a fashion, almost a fetish, in eighteenth-century society. Because it was deemed essential to display proper or decorous feeling on all occasions, Richardson's heroines were always analyzing their emotions; they talked like a book of etiquette; they indulged in tears, fainting, transports of joy, paroxysms of grief, apparently striving to make themselves as unlike a real woman as possible. It is astonishing how far and wide this fad of sensibility spread through the literary world, and how many gushing heroines of English and American fiction during the next seventy-five years were modeled on Pamela or Clarissa.

In view of this artificial fashion, the influence of Fielding was like the rush of crisp air into a hot house. His aim was realistic, that is, to portray real people in their accustomed ways. Unfortunately his aim was spoiled by the idea that to be realistic one must go to the gutter for material. And then appeared Goldsmith, too much influenced by the fad of sensibility, but aiming to depict human life as governed by high ideals, and helping to cleanse the English novel from brutality and indecency.

There were other early novelists, a host of them, but in Richardson, Fielding and Goldsmith we have enough. Richard-
Threefold Influence son emphasized the analysis of human feeling or motive, and that of itself was excellent; but his exaggerated sentimentality set a bad fashion which our novelists were almost a century in overcoming. Fielding laid stress on realism, and that his influence was effective is shown in the work of his disciple Thackeray, who could be realistic without being coarse. And Goldsmith made all subsequent novelists his debtors by exalting that purity of domestic life to which every home worthy of the name forever strives or aspires.

If it be asked, What novels of the early type ought one to read? the answer is simple. Unless you want to curdle your blood by a tale of mystery and horror (in which case Mrs. Radcliffe's *Mysteries of Udolpho* will serve the purpose) there are only two that young readers will find satisfactory: the realistic *Robinson Crusoe* by Defoe, and the romantic *Vicar of Wakefield* by Goldsmith.

Summary. What we call eighteenth-century literature appeared between two great political upheavals, the English Revolution of 1688 and the French Revolution of 1789. Some of the chief characteristics of that literature — such as the emphasis on form, the union of poetry with politics, the prevalence of satire, the interest in historical subjects — have been accounted for, in part at least, in our summary of the history of the period.

The writings of the century are here arranged in three main divisions: the reign of formalism (miscalled classicism), the revival of romantic poetry, and the development of the modern novel. Our study of the so-called classic period includes: (1) The meaning of classicism in literature. (2) The life and works of Pope, the leading poet of the age; of Swift, a master of satire; of Addison and Steele, the graceful essayists who originated the modern literary magazine. (3) The work of Dr. Johnson and his school; in which we have included, for convenience, Edmund Burke, most eloquent of English orators, and Gibbon the historian, famous for his *Decline and Fall of the Roman Empire*.

Our review of the romantic writers of the age covers: (1) The work of Collins and Gray, whose imaginative poems are in refreshing contrast to the formalism of Pope and his school. (2) The life and works of Goldsmith, poet, playwright, novelist; and of Burns, the greatest of Scottish song writers. (3) A glance at other poets, such as Cowper and Blake, who aided in the romantic revival. (4) The renewed interest in ballads and legends, which showed itself in Percy's *Reliques of Ancient English Poetry*, and in two famous forgeries, the *Ossian* poems of Macpherson and *The Rowley Papers* of the boy Chatterton.

Our study of the novel includes : (1) The meaning of the modern novel, as distinct from the ancient romance. (2) A study of Defoe, author of *Robinson Crusoe*, who was a forerunner of the modern realistic novelist. (3) The works of Richardson and of Fielding, contrasting types of eighteenth-century story-tellers. (4) The influence of Richardson's sentimentality, of Fielding's realism, and of Goldsmith's moral purity on subsequent English fiction.

Selections for Reading. Typical selections are given in Manly, English Poetry and English Prose, Century Readings, and other miscellaneous collections. Important works of major writers are published in inexpensive editions for school use, a few of which are named below.

Pope's poems, selected, in Standard English Classics, Pocket Classics, Riverside Literature, and other series. (See Texts, in General Bibliography.)

Selections from Swift's works, in Athenæum Press, Holt's English Readings, Clarendon Press. Gulliver's Travels, in Standard English Classics, in Ginn and Company's Classics for Children, in Carisbrooke Library, in Temple Classics.

Selections from Addison and Steele, in Athenæum Press, Golden Treasury, Maynard's English Classics. Sir Roger de Coverley Papers, in Standard English Classics, Riverside Literature, Academy Classics.

Chesterfield's Letters to his son, selected, in Ginn and Company's Classics for Children, and in Maynard's English Classics.

Boswell's Life of Johnson, in Clarendon Press, Temple Classics, Everyman's Library.

Burke's Speeches, selected, in Standard English Classics, Pocket Classics, English Readings.

Selections from Gray, in Athenæum Press, Canterbury Poets, Riverside Literature.

Goldsmith's Deserted Village and Vicar of Wakefield, in Standard English Classics, King's Classics ; She Stoops to Conquer, in Pocket Classics, Belles Lettres Series, Cassell's National Library.

Sheridan's The Rivals, in Athenæum Press, Camelot Series, Riverside Literature, Everyman's Library.

Poems of Burns, selected, in Standard English Classics, Riverside Literature, Silver Classics.

Defoe's Robinson Crusoe, school edition by Ginn and Company ; the same in Everyman's Library, Pocket Classics.

Bibliography. For extensive manuals and texts see the General Bibliography. The following works deal chiefly with the eighteenth century.

History. Morris, Age of Queen Anne and the Early Hanoverians (Epochs of Modern History Series); Sydney, England and the English in the Eighteenth Century; Susan Hale, Men and Manners in the Eighteenth Century; Ashton, Social Life in the Reign of Queen Anne; Thackeray, The Four Georges.

Literature. L. Stephen, English Literature in the Eighteenth Century; Perry, English Literature in the Eighteenth Century; Seccombe, The Age of Johnson; Dennis, The Age of Pope; Gosse, History of English Literature in the Eighteenth Century; Whitwell, Some Eighteenth-Century Men of Letters; Phelps, Beginnings of the English Romantic Movement; Beers, English Romanticism in the Eighteenth Century; Thackeray, English Humorists.

Pope. Life, by Courthope; by L. Stephen (English Men of Letters Series). Essays, by Thackeray, in English Humorists; by L. Stephen, in Hours in a Library; by Lowell, in My Study Windows.

Swift. Life, by Forster; by L. Stephen (E. M. of L.). Essays, by Thackeray, in English Humorists; by Dobson, in Eighteenth Century Vignettes.

Addison and Steele. Life of Addison, by Courthope (E. M. of L.). Life of Steele, by Dobson. Essays by Macaulay, by Thackeray, by Dobson.

Johnson. Life, by Boswell (for personal details); by L. Stephen (E. M. of L.). Hill, Dr. Johnson : his Friends and his Critics. Essays by Macaulay, by Thackeray, by L. Stephen.

Burke. Life, by Morley (E. M. of L.), by Prior. Macknight, Life and Times of Burke.

Gibbon. Life, by Morrison (E. M. of L.). Essays, by Birrell, in Collected Essays; by L. Stephen, in Studies of a Biographer; by Harrison, in Ruskin and Other Literary Estimates; by Sainte-Beuve, in English Portraits.

Gray. Life, by Gosse. Essays by Lowell, M. Arnold, L. Stephen, Dobson.

Goldsmith. Life, by Washington Irving, by Dobson (Great Writers Series), by Black (E. M. of L.), by Forster. Essays, by Macaulay; by Thackeray, in English Humorists; by Dobson, in Miscellanies.

Burns. Life, by Shairp (E. M. of L.), by Blackie (Great Writers). Carlyle's Essay on Burns, in Standard English Classics and other school editions. Essays, by Stevenson, in Familiar Studies of Men and Books; by Hazlitt, in Lectures on the English Poets; by Henley, in Introduction to the Cambridge Edition of Burns.

The Novel. Raleigh, The English Novel; Cross, Development of the English Novel; Perry, A Study of Prose Fiction; Symonds, Introduction to the Study of English Fiction; Dawson, Makers of English Fiction.

Defoe. Life, by Minto (E. M. of L.), by William Lee. Essay by L. Stephen, in Hours in a Library.

Richardson. Life, by Thomson, by Dobson. Essays, by L. Stephen, in Hours in a Library; by Dobson, in Eighteenth Century Vignettes.

Fielding. Life, by Dobson (E. M. of L.). Lawrence, Life and Times of Fielding. Essays by Lowell, L. Stephen, Dobson; Thackeray, in English Humorists; G. B. Smith, in Poets and Novelists.

Fiction. Thackeray, Henry Esmond, and The Virginians; Scott, Guy Mannering, Rob Roy, Heart of Midlothian, Redgauntlet; Reade, Peg Woffington.

CHAPTER VII

THE EARLY NINETEENTH CENTURY

Two voices are there; one is of the sea,
One of the mountains; each a mighty voice:
In both from age to age thou didst rejoice,
They were thy chosen music, Liberty!

Wordsworth, " Sonnet to Switzerland "

The many changes recorded in the political and literary history of nineteenth-century England may be grouped under two heads : the progress of democracy in government, and the triumph of romanticism in literature. By democracy we mean the assumption by common men of the responsibilities of government, with a consequent enlargement of human liberty. Romanticism, as we use the term here, means simply that literature, like politics, has become liberalized ; that it is concerned with the common life of men, and that the delights of literature, like the powers of government, are no longer the possession of the few but of the many.

Historical Outline. To study either democracy or romanticism, the Whig party or the poetry of Wordsworth, is to discover how greatly England was influenced by matters that appeared beyond her borders. The famous Reform Bill (1832) which established manhood suffrage, the emancipation of the slaves in all British colonies, the hard-won freedom of the press, the plan of popular education, — these and numberless other reforms of the age may be regarded as part of a general movement, as the attempt to fulfill in England a promise made to the world by two events which occurred earlier and on foreign soil. These two events, which profoundly influenced English politics and literature, were the Declaration of Independence and the French Revolution.

In the Declaration we read, "We hold these truths to be self-evident: that all men are created equal; that they are endowed by their Creator with certain unalienable rights; that among these are life, liberty and the pursuit of happiness." Glorious words! But they were not new; they were old and familiar when Jefferson wrote them. The American Revolution, which led up to the Declaration, is especially significant in this: that it began as a struggle not for new privileges but for old rights. So the constructive character of that Revolution, which ended with a democracy and a noble constitution, was due largely to the fact that brave men stood ready to defend the old freedom, the old manhood, the old charters, "the good old cause" for which other brave men had lived or died through a thousand years.

Two Revolutions

A little later, and influenced by the American triumph, came another uprising of a different kind. In France the unalienable rights of man had been forgotten during ages of tyranny and class privilege; so the French Revolution, shouting its watchwords of Liberty, Equality, Fraternity, had no conception of that liberty and equality which were as ancient as the hills. Leaders and followers of the Revolution were clamoring for new privileges, new rights, new morals, new creeds. They acclaimed an "Age of Reason" as a modern and marvelous discovery; they dreamed not simply of a new society, but of a new man. A multitude of clubs or parties, some political, some literary or educational, some with a pretense of philosophy, sprang up as if by magic, all believing that they must soon enter the Kingdom of Heaven, but nearly all forgetful of the fact that to enter the Kingdom one must accept the old conditions, and pay the same old price. Partly because of this strange conception of liberty, as a new thing to be established by fiat, the terrible struggle in France ended in the ignoble military despotism of Napoleon.

These two revolutions, one establishing and the other clamoring for the dignity of manhood, created a mighty stir throughout the civilized world. Following the French Revolution, most European nations were thrown into political ferment, and the object of all their agitation, rebellion, upheaval, was to obtain a greater measure of democracy by overturning every form of class or caste government. Thrones seemed to be tottering, and in terror of their houses Continental sovereigns entered into their Holy Alliance (1815) with the unholy object of joining forces to crush democracy wherever it appeared.

Effect of the Revolutions

The Revolution and Literature. The young writers of liberty-loving England felt the stir, the *sursum* of the age. Wordsworth, most sedate of men, saw in the French Revolution a glorious prophecy, and wrote with unwonted enthusiasm:

> Bliss was it in that dawn to be alive,
> But to be young was very Heaven.

Coleridge and Southey formed their grand scheme of a Pantisocracy, a government of perfect equality, on the banks of the Susquehanna. Scott (always a Tory, and therefore distrustful of change) reflected the democratic enthusiasm in a score of romances, the chief point of which was this : that almost every character was at heart a king, and spake in right kingly fashion. Byron won his popularity largely because he was an uncompromising rebel, and appealed to young rebels who were proclaiming the necessity of a new human society. And Shelley, after himself rebelling at almost every social law of his day, wrote his *Prometheus Unbound,* which is a vague but beautiful vision of humanity redeemed in some magical way from all oppression and sorrow.

All these and other writers of the age give the impression, as we read them now, that they were gloriously expectant of a new day of liberty that was about to dawn on the world. Their romantic enthusiasm, so different from the cold formality of the age preceding, is a reflection, like a rosy sunset-glow, of the stirring scenes of revolution through which the world had just passed.

WILLIAM WORDSWORTH (1770–1850)

There is but one way to know Wordsworth, and that way leads to his nature poems. Though he lived in a revolutionary age, his life was singularly uneventful. His letters are terribly prosaic ; and his *Excursion,* in which he attempted an autobiography, has so many dull lines that few have patience to read it. Though he asserted, finely, that there is but one great society on earth, "the noble living and the noble dead," he held no communion with the great minds of the past or of the present. He lived in his own solitary world, and his only real companion was nature. To know nature at first hand, and to reflect human thought or feeling in nature's pure presence, — this was his chief object. His field, therefore, is a small one, but in that field he is the greatest master that England has thus far produced.

Life. Wordsworth is as inseparably connected with the English Lake District as Burns with the Low-lands or Scott with the Border. A large part of the formative period of his life was spent out of doors amid beautiful scenery, where he felt the abound-ing life of nature streaming upon him in the sunshine, or booming in his ears with the steady roar of the March winds. He felt also (what sensitive spirits still feel) a living presence that met him in the loneli-est wood, or spoke to him in the flowers, or preceded him over the wind-swept

WILLIAM WORDSWORTH

hills. He was one of those favored mortals who are surest of the Unseen. From school he would hurry away to his skating or bird-nesting or aimless roaming, and every new day afield was to him "One of those heavenly days that cannot die."

From the Lake Region he went to Cambridge, but found little in college life to attract or hold him. Then, stirred by the promise of the Revolution, he went to France, where his help was eagerly sought by rival parties; for in that day every traveler from America or England, whether an astute Jefferson or a lamblike Wordsworth, was supposed

to be, by virtue of his country, a master politician. Wordsworth threw himself rather blindly into the Revolution, joined the Girondists
Wordsworth (the ruling faction in 1792) and might have gone to the
and the guillotine with the leaders of that party had not his
Revolution friends brought him home by the simple expedient of cutting off his supply of money. Thus ended ingloriously the only adventure that ever quickened his placid life.

For a time Wordsworth mourned over the failure of his plans; but his grief turned to bitterness when the Revolution passed over into the Reign of Terror and ended in the despotism of Napoleon. His country was now at war with France, and he followed his country, giving mild support to Burke and the Tory party. After a few uncertain years, during which he debated his calling in life, he resolved on two things: to be a poet, and to bring back to English poetry the romantic spirit and the naturalness of expression which had been displaced by the formal elegance of the age of Pope and Johnson.

WORDSWORTH'S DESK IN HAWKSHEAD
SCHOOL

For that resolution we are indebted partly to Coleridge, who had been attracted by some of Wordsworth's early poems, and who encouraged him to write more. From the association of these two men came the famous *Lyrical Ballads* (1798), a book which marks the beginning of a new era in English poetry.

To Wordsworth's sister Dorothy we are even more indebted. It was she who soothed Wordsworth's disappointment, reminded him of the world of nature in which alone he was at home, and quietly showed him where his power lay. As he says, in *The Prelude*:

> She whispered still that brightness would return;
> She, in the midst of all, preserved me still
> A poet, made me seek beneath that name,
> And that alone, my office upon earth.

The latter half of Wordsworth's life was passed in the Lake Region, at Grasmere and Rydal Mount for the most part, the continuity being **Personal** broken by walking trips in Britain or on the Continent. **Traits** A very quiet, uneventful life it was, but it revealed two qualities which are of interest to Wordsworth's readers. The first was his devotion to his art; the second was his granite steadfastness. His work was at first neglected, while the poems of Scott, Byron and Tennyson in succession attained immense popularity. The critics were nearly all against him, misunderstanding his best work and ridiculing the rest. The ground of their opposition was, that his theory of the utmost simplicity in poetry was wrong; their ridicule was made easier by the fact that Wordsworth produced as much bad work as good. Moreover, he took himself very seriously, had no humor, and, as visitors like Emerson found to their disappointment, was interested chiefly in himself and his own work. For was he not engaged in the greatest of all projects, an immense poem (*The Recluse*) which should reflect the universe in the life of one man, and that man William Wordsworth? Such self-satisfaction invited attack; even Lamb, the gentlest of critics, could hardly refrain from poking fun at it:

" Wordsworth, the great poet, is coming to town; he is to have apartments in the Mansion House. He says he does not see much difficulty in writing like Shakespeare, if he had a mind to try it. It is clear that nothing is wanting but the mind."

Slowly but surely Wordsworth won recognition, not simply in being made Laureate, but in having his ideal of poetry vindicated. Poets in England and America began to follow him; the critics **His Triumph** were silenced, if not convinced. While the popularity of Scott and Byron waned, the readers of Wordsworth increased steadily, finding him a poet not of the hour but of all time. " If a single man plant himself indomitably on his instincts, and there abide," says Emerson, " the huge world will come around to him." If the reading world has not yet come around to Wordsworth, that is perhaps not the poet's fault.

Wordsworth : his Theme and Theory. The theory which Wordsworth and Coleridge formulated was simply this : that poetry is the spontaneous overflow of powerful human feeling.

Its only subjects are nature and human nature; its only object is to reflect the emotions awakened by our contemplation of the world or of humanity; its language must be as direct and simple as possible, such language as rises unbidden to the lips whenever the heart is touched. Though some of the world's best poets have taken a different view, Wordsworth maintained steadily that poetry must deal with common subjects in the plainest language; that it must not attempt to describe, in elegant phrases, what a poet is supposed to feel about art or some other subject selected for its poetic possibilities.

In the last contention Wordsworth was aiming at the formal school of poetry, and we may better understand him by a com-

Natural vs. Formal Poetry parison. Read, for example, his exquisite " Early Spring" ("I heard a thousand blended notes"). Here in twenty-four lines are more naturalness, more real feeling finely expressed, than you can find in the poems of Dryden, Johnson and Addison combined. Or take the best part of " The Campaign," which made Addison's fortune, and which was acclaimed the finest thing ever written:

> So when an angel by divine command
> With rising tempests shakes a guilty land,
> (Such as of late o'er pale Britannia past)
> Calm and serene he drives the furious blast;
> And, pleased th' Almighty's orders to perform,
> Rides in the whirlwind and directs the storm.

To know how artificial that famous simile is, read a few lines from Wordsworth's " On the Sea-Shore," which lingers in our mind like a strain of Handel's music:

> It is a beauteous evening, calm and free,
>   The holy time is quiet as a Nun
>   Breathless with adoration; the broad sun
> Is sinking down in its tranquillity;
> The gentleness of heaven broods o'er the Sea:
>   Listen! the mighty Being is awake,
>   And doth with his eternal motion make
> A sound like thunder — everlastingly.

If such comparisons interest the student, let him read Addison's " Letter to Lord Halifax," with its Apostrophe to Liberty, which was considered sublime in its day :

> O Liberty, thou goddess heavenly bright,
> Profuse of bliss, and pregnant with delight !
> Eternal pleasures in thy presence reign,
> And smiling Plenty leads thy wanton train ;
> Eased of her load, Subjection grows more light,
> And Poverty looks cheerful in thy sight ;
> Thou mak'st the gloomy face of nature gay,
> Giv'st beauty to the sun, and pleasure to the day.

Place beside that the first four lines of Wordsworth's sonnet " To Switzerland " (quoted at the head of this chapter), or a stanza from his " Ode to Duty " :

> Stern Lawgiver ! yet thou dost wear
>   The Godhead's most benignant grace ;
> Nor know we anything so fair
>   As is the smile upon thy face :
> Flowers laugh before thee on their beds,
> And fragrance in thy footing treads ;
>   Thou dost preserve the stars from wrong,
>   And the most ancient heavens, through thee,
>   are fresh and strong.

To follow such a comparison is to understand Wordsworth by sympathy ; it is to understand also the difference between poetry and formal verse.

The Poems of Wordsworth. As the reading of literature is the main thing, the only word of criticism which remains is to direct the beginner ; and direction is especially necessary in dealing with Wordsworth, who wrote voluminously, and who lacked both the critical judgment and the sense of humor to tell him what parts of his work were inferior or ridiculous :

> There 's something in a flying horse,
> There 's something in a huge balloon !

To be sure ; springs in the one, gas in the other ; but if there were anything more poetic in horse or balloon, Wordsworth

did not discover it. There is something also in a cuckoo clock,
or even in

> A household tub, one such as those
> Which women use to wash their clothes.

Such banalities are to be found in the work of a poet who could
produce the exquisite sonnet " On Westminster Bridge," the
finely simple " I Wandered Lonely as a Cloud," the stirring
" Ode to Duty," the tenderly reflective " Tintern Abbey," and
the magnificent " Intimations of Immortality," which Emerson
(who was not a very safe judge) called " the high-water mark
of poetry in the nineteenth century." These five poems may
serve as the first measure of Wordsworth's genius.

A few of Wordsworth's best nature poems are: " Early
Spring," " Three Years She Grew," " The Fountain," " My
Heart Leaps Up," " The Tables Turned," " To a
Cuckoo," " To a Skylark " (the second poem, beginning, " Ethereal minstrel ") and " Yarrow Revisited." The
spirit of all his nature poems is reflected in " Tintern Abbey,"
which gives us two complementary views of nature, corresponding to Wordsworth's earlier and later experience. The
first is that of the boy, roaming foot-loose over the face of
nature, finding, as Coleridge said, " Rhythm in all thought,
and joyance everywhere." The second is that of the man who
returns to the scenes of his boyhood, finds them as beautiful as
ever, but pervaded now by a spiritual quality, — " something
which defies analysis, undefined and ineffable, which must be
felt and perceived by the soul."

Poems of Nature

It was this spiritual view of nature, as a reflection of the
Divine, which profoundly influenced Bryant, Emerson and
other American writers. The essence of Wordsworth's teaching,
in his nature poems, appears in the last two lines of his " Skylark," a bird that soars the more gladly to heaven because he
must soon return with joy to his own nest:

> Type of the wise, who soar but never roam:
> True to the kindred points of heaven and home.

Of the poems more closely associated with human life, a few of the best are : "Michael," "The Solitary Reaper," "The **Poems of** Leech Gatherers," "Margaret" (in *The Excursion*), **Humble Life** "Brougham Castle," "The Happy Warrior," "Peel Castle in a Storm," "Three Years She Grew," "She Dwelt among the Untrodden Ways" and "She was a Phantom of Delight." In such poems we note two significant character- istics : that Wordsworth does not seek extraordinary characters, but is content to show the hidden beauty in the lives of plain men and women ; and that his heroes and heroines dwell, as he said, where "labor still preserves his rosy face." They are natural men and women, and are therefore simple and strong ; the quiet light in their faces is reflected from the face of the fields. In his emphasis on natural simplicity, virtue, beauty, Wordsworth has again been, as he desired, a teacher of multi- tudes. His moral teaching may be summed up in three lines from *The Excursion* :

> The primal duties shine aloft like stars ;
> The charities that soothe and heal and bless
> Are scattered at the feet of man like flowers.

In the number and fine quality of his sonnets Wordsworth has no superior in English poetry. Simplicity, strength, deep thought, fine feeling, careful workmanship, — these **The Sonnets** qualities are present in measure more abundant than can be found elsewhere in the poet's work :

> Bees that soar for bloom,
> High as the highest peak of Furness-fells,
> Will murmur by the hour in foxglove bells.

These three lines from the sonnet, "Nuns fret not at their Con- vent's Narrow Room," explain why Wordsworth, who was often diffuse, found joy in compressing his whole poem into fourteen lines. A few other sonnets which can be heartily recommended are : "Westminster Bridge," "The Seashore," "The World," "Venetian Republic," "To Sleep," "Toussaint L'Ouverture,"

E

"Afterthoughts," "To Milton" (sometimes called "London, 1802") and the farewell to Scott when he sailed in search of health, beginning, "A trouble not of clouds or weeping rain."

Not until one has learned to appreciate Wordsworth at his best will it be safe to attempt *The Prelude, or the Growth of a Poet's Mind.* Most people grow weary of this poem, which is too long; but a few read it with pleasure for its portrayal of Wordsworth's education at the hand of Nature, or for occasional good lines which lure us on like miners in search of gold. *The Prelude*, though written at thirty-five, was not published till after Wordsworth's death, and for this reason : he had planned an immense poem, dealing with Nature, Man and Society, which he called *The Recluse*, and which he likened to a Gothic cathedral. His *Prelude* was the "ante-chapel" of this work ; his miscellaneous odes, sonnets and narrative poems were to be as so many "cells and oratories";

ST. OSWALD'S CHURCH, GRASMERE

Wordsworth's body was buried in the churchyard
See *The Excursion*, Book V

other parts of the structure were *The Home at Grasmere* and *The Excursion*, which he may have intended as transepts, or as chapels.

This great work was left unfinished, and one may say of it, as of Spenser's *Faery Queen*, that it is better so. Like other poets of venerable years Wordsworth wrote many verses that were better left in the inkpot ; and it is a pity, in dealing with so beautiful and necessary a thing as poetry, that one should ever reach the point of saying, sadly but truthfully, " Enough is too much."

COLERIDGE AND SOUTHEY

The story of these two men is a commentary on the uncertainties of literary fortune. Both won greater reward and reputation than fell to the lot of Wordsworth ; but while the fame of the latter poet mounts steadily with the years, the former have become, as it were, footnotes to the great contemporary with whom they were associated, under the name of "Lake Poets," for half a glorious century.

Samuel Taylor Coleridge (1772–1834). The tragedy *Remorse,* which Coleridge wrote, is as nothing compared with the tragedy of his own life. He was a man of superb natural gifts, of vast literary culture, to whose genius the writers of that age — Wordsworth, Hazlitt, Lamb, De Quincey,

SAMUEL TAYLOR COLERIDGE

Shelley, Landor, Southey — nearly all bear witness. He might well have been a great poet, or critic, or philosopher, or teacher; but he lacked the will power to direct his gifts to any definite end. His irresolution became pitiful weakness when he began to indulge in the drug habit, which soon made a slave of him. Thereafter he impressed all who met him with a sense of loss and inexpressible sorrow.

Coleridge began to read at three years of age ; at five he had gone through the Bible and the Arabian Nights ; at thirty he was perhaps the most widely read man of his generation in the fields of literature and philosophy. He was a student in a famous charity school in London when he met Charles Lamb, who records his memories of the boy and the place in his charming essay of "Christ's Hospital." At college he was one of a band of enthusiasts inspired by the French Revolution, and with Southey he formed a plan to establish in America a world-reforming Pantisocracy, or communistic settlement, where all should be brothers and equals, and where a little manual work was to be tempered by much play, poetry and culture. Europeans had queer ideas of America in those days. This beautiful plan failed, because the reformers did not have money enough to cross the ocean and stake out their Paradise.

Life of Coleridge

THE COLERIDGE COTTAGE, NETHER STOWEY, IN SOMERSETSHIRE

The next important association of Coleridge was with Wordsworth and his sister Dorothy, in Somerset, where the three friends planned and published the *Lyrical Ballads* of 1798. In this work Wordsworth attempted to portray the charm of common things, and Coleridge to give reality to a world of dreams and fantasies. Witness the two most original poems in the book, "Tintern Abbey" and "The Ancient Mariner."

During the latter part of his life Coleridge won fame by his lectures on English poetry and German philosophy, and still greater fame by his conversations, — brilliant, heaven-scaling monologues, which brought together a company of young enthusiasts. And presently these disciples of Coleridge were spreading abroad a new idealistic philosophy, which crossed the ocean, was welcomed by Emerson and a host of young writers or reformers, and appeared in American literature as Transcendentalism.

Others who heard the conversations were impressed in a somewhat different way. Keats met Coleridge on the road, one day, and listened dumbfounded to an ecstatic discourse on poetry, nightingales, the origin of sensation, dreams (four kinds), consciousness, creeds, ghost stories, — " he broached a thousand matters " while the poets were walking a space of two miles.

Stories of Coleridge

Walter Scott, meeting Coleridge at a dinner, listened with his head in a whirl to a monologue on fairies, the classics, ancient mysteries, visions, ecstasies, the psychology of poetry, the poetry of metaphysics. " Zounds ! " says Scott, " I was never so bethumped with words."

Charles Lamb, hurrying to his work, encountered Coleridge and was drawn aside to a quiet garden. There the poet took Lamb by a button of his coat, closed his eyes, and began to discourse, his right hand waving to the rhythm of the flowing words. No sooner was Coleridge well started than Lamb slyly took out his penknife, cut off the button, and escaped unobserved. Some hours later, as he passed the garden on his return, Lamb heard a voice speaking most musically; he turned aside in wonder, and there stood Coleridge, his eyes closed, his left hand holding the button, his right hand waving, " still talking like an angel."

Such are the stories, true or apocryphal, of Coleridge's conversations. Their bewildering quality appears, somewhat dimmed, in his prose works, which have been finely compared with the flight of an eagle on set wings, sweeping in wide circles, balancing, soaring, mounting on the winds. But we must note this difference : that the eagle keeps his keen eye on the distant earth, and always knows just where he is; while Coleridge sees only the wonders of Cloudland, and appears to be hopelessly lost.

The chief prose works of Coleridge are his *Biographia Literaria* (a brilliant patchwork of poetry and metaphysics), *Aids to Reflection, Letters and Table Talk* (the most readable of his works), and *Lectures and Notes on Shakespeare*. These all contain fine gold, but the treasure is for those doughty miners the critics rather than for readers who go to literature for recreation. Among the best of his miscellaneous poems (and Coleridge at his best has few superiors) are " Youth and Age," " Love Poems," " Hymn before Sunrise," " Ode to the Departing Year," and the pathetic " Ode to Dejection," which is a reflection of the poet's saddened but ever hopeful life.

His Prose and Poetry

Two other poems, highly recommended by most critics, are the fragments "Kubla Khan" and "Christabel"; but in dealing with these the reader may do well to form his own judgment. Both fragments contain beautiful lines, but as a whole they are wandering, disjointed, inconsequent, — mere sketches, they seem, of some weird dream of mystery or terror which Coleridge is trying in vain to remember.

The most popular of Coleridge's works is his imperishable "Rime of the Ancient Mariner," a wildly improbable poem of **The Ancient** icebound or tropic seas, of thirst-killed sailors, of **Mariner** a phantom ship sailed by a crew of ghosts, — all portrayed in the vivid, picturesque style of the old ballad. When the "Mariner" first appeared it was dismissed as a cock-and-bull story; yet somehow readers went back to it, again and again, as if fascinated. It was passed on to the next generation; and still we read it, and pass it on. For this grotesque tale differs from all others of its kind in that its lines have been quoted for over a hundred years as a reflection of some profound human experience. That is the genius of the work: it takes the most fantastic illusions and makes them appear as real as any sober journey recorded in a sailor's log book.[1]

At the present time our enjoyment of the "Mariner" is somewhat hampered by the critical commentaries which have fastened upon the poem, like barnacles on an old ship. It has been studied as a type of the romantic ballad, as a moral lesson, as a tract against cruelty to animals, as a model of college English. But that is no way to abuse a poet's fancy! To appreciate the "Mariner" as the author intended, one should carry it off to the hammock or orchard; there to have freedom of soul to enjoy a well-spun yarn, a gorgeous flight of imagination, a poem which illustrates Coleridge's definition of poetry

---

[1] In connection with the "Ancient Mariner" one should read the legends of "The Flying Dutchman" and "The Wandering Jew." Poe's story "A Manuscript Found in a Bottle" is based on these legends and on Coleridge's poem.

as "the bloom and the fragrance of all human knowledge, thoughts, emotions, language." It broadens one's sympathy, as well as one's horizon, to accompany this ancient sailor through scenes of terror and desolation :

> O Wedding-Guest! this soul hath been
> Alone on a wide, wide sea:
> So lonely 't was, that God himself
> Scarce seemëd there to be.

In the midst of such scenes come blessed memories of a real world, of the beauty of unappreciated things, such as the "sweet jargoning" of birds :

> And now 't was like all instruments,
> Now like a lonely flute;
> And now it is an angel's song,
> That makes the heavens be mute.

> It ceased; yet still the sails made on
> A pleasant noise till noon,
> A noise like of a hidden brook
> In the leafy month of June,
> That to the sleeping woods all night
> Singeth a quiet tune.

Whoever is not satisfied with that for its own sake, without moral or analysis, has missed the chief interest of all good poetry.

Robert Southey. In contrast with the irresolution of Coleridge is the steadfastness of Southey (1774–1843), a man of strong character, of enormous industry. For fifty years he worked steadily, day and half the night, turning out lyrics, ballads, epics, histories, biographies, translations, reviews, — an immense amount of stuff, filling endless volumes. Kind nature made up for Southey's small talent by giving him a great opinion of it, and he believed firmly that his work was as immortal as the *Iliad*.

With the exception of a few short poems, such as the " Battle of Blenheim," " Lodore," " The Inchcape Rock " and

"Father William" (parodied in the nonsense of *Alice in Wonderland*), the mass of Southey's work is already forgotten. Deserving of mention, however, are his *Peninsular War* and his *Life of Nelson*, both written in a straightforward style, portraying patriotism without the usual sham, and a first-class fighting man without brag or bluster. Curious readers may also be attracted by the epics of Southey (such as *Madoc*, the story of a Welsh prince who anticipated Columbus), which contain plenty of the marvelous adventures that give interest to the romances of Jules Verne and the yarns of Rider Haggard.

ROBERT SOUTHEY

It was Southey's habit to work by the clock, turning out chapters as another man might dig potatoes. One day, as he plodded along, a fairy must have whispered in his ear; for he suddenly produced a little story, a gem, a treasure of a story, and hid it away in a jungle of chapters in a book called *The Doctor*. Somebody soon discovered the treasure; indeed, one might as well try to conceal a lighted candle as to hide a good story; and now it is the most famous work to be found in Southey's hundred volumes of prose and verse. Few professors could give you any information concerning *The Doctor*, but almost any child will tell you all about "The Three Bears." The happy fate of this little nursery tale might indicate that the final judges of literature are not always or often the learned critics.

The Revolutionary Poets

The above title is often applied to Byron and Shelley, and for two reasons: because they were themselves rebellious of heart, and because they voiced the rebellion of numerous other young enthusiasts who, disappointed by the failure of the French Revolution to bring in the promised age of happiness, were ready to cry out against the existing humdrum order of society. Both poets were sadly lacking in mental or moral balance; and finding no chance in England to wage heroic warfare against political tyranny, as the French had done, they proceeded in rather headlong fashion to an attack on well-established customs in society, and especially did they strike out wildly against " the monster Public Opinion." Because the " monster " was stronger than they were, and more nearly right, their rebellion ended in tragedy.

GRETA HALL (IN THE LAKE REGION)
Where Southey lived, 1803-1839

Life of Byron. In the life of George Gordon, Lord Byron (1788-1824), is so much that calls for apology or silence that one is glad to review his career in briefest outline.

Of his family, noble in name but in nothing else, the least said the better. He was born in London, but spent his childhood in Aberdeen, under the alternate care or negligence of his erratic mother. At ten he fell heir to a title, to the family seat of Newstead Abbey, and to estates yielding an income of some £1400 per year, — a large income for a poet, but as nothing to a lord accustomed to make ducks and drakes of his money. In school and college his conduct was rather wild, and his taste fantastic. For example, he kept a bull-dog and a bear in his rooms, and read romances instead of books recommended by the faculty. He tells us that he detested poetry; yet he wrote numerous poems which show plainly that he not only read but copied some of the poets.[1]

At twenty-one Byron entered the House of Lords, and almost immediately thereafter set sail for Lisbon and the Levant. On his

A Literary Lion return he published the first two cantos of *Childe Harold's Pilgrimage*, which made him famous. Though he affected to despise his triumph, he followed it up shrewdly by publishing *The Giaour*, *The Corsair* and *Lara*, in which the same mys-

LORD BYRON

After the portrait by T. Phillips

terious hero of his first work reappears, under different disguises, amid romantic surroundings. The vigor of these poems attracted many readers, and when it was whispered about that the author was recounting his own adventures, Byron became the center of literary interest. At home he was a social lion; abroad he was acclaimed the greatest of British poets. But his life tended more and more to shock the English sense of decency; and when his wife (whom he had married for her money) abruptly left him, public opinion made its power felt. Byron's popularity waned; his vanity was wounded; he left his country, vowing never to return. Also he railed against what he called British hypocrisy.

In Geneva he first met Shelley, admired him, was greatly helped by him, and then grossly abused his hospitality. After a scandalous career in Italy he went to help the Greeks in their fight for independence, but died of fever before he reached the battle line.

[1] These poems (revised and published as *Hours of Idleness*) were savagely criticized in the *Edinburgh Review*. Byron answered with his satiric *English Bards and Scotch Reviewers*, which ridiculed not only his Scottish critics but also Wordsworth, Scott, — in fact, most of the English poets, with the exception of Pope, whom he praised as the only poet ancient or modern who was not a barbarian.

The Poetry of Byron. There is one little song of Byron which serves well as the measure of his poetic talent. It is found in *Don Juan,* and it begins as follows:

> 'T is sweet to hear
>   At midnight on the blue and moonlit deep
> The song and oar of Adria's gondolier,
>   By distance mellow'd, o'er the waters sweep;
> 'T is sweet to see the evening star appear;
>   'T is sweet to listen, as the night-winds creep
> From leaf to leaf; 't is sweet to view on high
> The rainbow, based on ocean, span the sky.
>
> 'T is sweet to hear the watch-dog's honest bark
>   Bay deep-mouthed welcome as we draw near home;
> 'T is sweet to know there is an eye will mark
>   Our coming, and look brighter when we come;
> 'T is sweet to be awaken'd by the lark,
>   Or lulled by falling waters; sweet the hum
> Of bees, the voice of girls, the song of birds,
> The lisp of children, and their earliest words.

That is not great poetry, and may not be compared with a son-net of Wordsworth; but it is good, honest sentiment expressed in such a melodious way that we like to read it, and feel better after the reading. In the next stanza, however, Byron grows commonplace and ends with:

> Sweet is revenge, especially to women,
> Pillage to soldiers, prize-money to seamen.

And that is bad sentiment and worse rime, without any resemblance to poetry. The remaining stanzas are mere drivel, unworthy of the poet's talent or of the reader's patience.

It is so with a large part of Byron's work; it often begins well, and usually has some vivid description of nature, or some gallant passage in swinging verse, which stirs us like martial music; then the poem falls to earth like a stone, and presently appears some wretched pun or jest or scurrility. Our present remedy lies in a book of selections, in which we can enjoy the poetry without being unpleasantly reminded of the author's besetting sins of flippancy and bad taste.

Of the longer poems of Byron, which took all Europe by storm, only three or four are memorable. *Manfred* (1817) is

Manfred a dramatic poem, in which the author's pride, his theatric posing, his talent for rhythmic expression, are all seen at their worst or best. The mysterious hero of the poem lives in a gloomy castle under the high Alps, but he is seldom found under roof. Instead he wanders amidst storms and glaciers, holding communion with powers of darkness, forever voicing his rebellion, his boundless pride, his bottomless remorse. Nobody knows what the rebellion and the remorse are all about. Some readers may tire of the shadowy hero's egoism,

NEWSTEAD ABBEY AND BYRON OAK

but few will fail to be impressed by the vigor of the verse, or by the splendid reflection of picturesque scenes. And here and there is a lyric that seems to set itself to music :

> Mont Blanc is the monarch of mountains ;
> They crowned him long ago
> On a throne of rocks, in a robe of clouds,
> With a diadem of snow.

Cain (1821) is another dramatic poem, reflecting the rebellion of another hero, or rather the same hero, who appears this time as the elder son of Adam. After murdering his brother, the hero takes guidance of Lucifer and explores hell ; where, instead of repentance, he finds occasion to hate almost everything that is dear to God or man. The drama is a kind of gloomy parody of Milton's *Paradise Lost*, as *Manfred* is a parody of Goethe's *Faust*. Both dramas are interesting, aside from their poetic passages, as examples of the so-called Titan literature, to which we shall presently refer in our study of Shelley's *Prometheus*.

The most readable work of Byron is *Childe Harold's Pilgrimage*, a

Childe Harold brilliant narrative poem, which reflects the impressions of another misanthropic hero in presence of the romantic scenery of the Continent. It was the publication of the first two cantos of this poem, in 1812, that made Byron the leading figure in English poetry; and these cantos are still widely read as a kind of poetic guidebook. To many readers, however, the third and fourth cantos are more

THE CASTLE OF CHILLON

sincere and more pleasurable. The most memorable parts of *Childe Harold* are the " Farewell " in the first canto, " Waterloo " in the third, and " Lake Leman," " Venice," " Rome," " The Coliseum," " The Dying Gladiator " and " The Ocean " in the fourth. When one has read these magnificent passages he has the best of which Byron was capable. We have called *Childe Harold* the most readable of Byron's works, but those who like a story will probably be more interested in *Mazeppa* and *The Prisoner of Chillon*.

One significant quality of these long poems is that they are intensely personal, voicing one man's remorse or rebellion, and perpetually repeating his "Vanity of vanities, all is vanity!" They are concerned with the same hero (who is Byron under **The Byronic** various disguises) and they picture him as a proud, **Hero** mysterious stranger, carelessly generous, fiendishly wicked, profoundly melancholy, irresistibly fascinating to women. Byron is credited with the invention of this hero, ever since called Byronic; but in truth the melodramatic outcast was a popular character in fiction long before Byron adopted him, gave him a new dress and called him Manfred or Don Juan. A score of romances (such as Mrs. Radcliffe's *The Italian* in England, and Charles Brockden Brown's *Wieland* in America) had used the same hero to add horror to a grotesque tale; Scott modified him somewhat, as the Templar in *Ivanhoe*, for example; and Byron made him more real by giving him the revolutionary spirit, by employing him to voice the rebellion against social customs which many young enthusiasts felt so strongly in the early part of the nineteenth century.

The vigor of this stage hero, his rebellious spirit, his picturesque adventures, the gaudy tinsel (mistaken for gold) in **Two Views** which he was dressed, — all this made a tremendous **of Byron** impression in that romantic age. Goethe called Byron "the prince of modern poetry, the most talented and impressive figure which the literary world has ever produced"; and this unbalanced judgment was shared by other critics on the Continent, where Byron is still regarded as one of the greatest of English poets.

Swinburne, on the other hand, can hardly find words strong enough to express his contempt for the "blare and brassiness" of Byron; but that also is an exaggeration. Though Byron is no longer a popular hero, and though his work is more rhetorical than poetical, we may still gladly acknowledge the swinging rhythm, the martial dash and vigor of his best verse. Also, remembering the Revolution, we may understand the dazzling impression which he made upon the poets of his day. When the news came from Greece that his meteoric career was ended, the young Tennyson wept passionately and went out to carve on a stone, "Byron is dead," as if poetry had perished with him. Even the coldly critical Matthew Arnold was deeply moved to write:

> When Byron's eyes were closed in death
> We bowed our head, and held our breath.
> He taught us little, but our soul
> Had *felt* him like the thunder roll.

Life of Shelley. The career of Percy Bysshe Shelley (1792-1822) is, in comparison with that of Byron, as a will-o'-the-wisp to a meteor. Byron was of the earth earthy; he fed upon coarse food, shady adventures, scandal, the limelight; but Shelley

> Seemed nourished upon starbeams, and the stuff
> Of rainbows and the tempest and the foam.

He was a delicate child, shy, sensitive, elflike, who wandered through the woods near his home, in Sussex, on the lookout for sprites and hobgoblins. His reading was of the wildest kind; and when he began the study of chemistry he was forever putting together things that made horrible smells or explosions, in expectation that the genii of the *Arabian Nights* would rise from the smoke of his test tube.

At Eton the boy promptly rebelled against the brutal fagging system, then tolerated in all English schools. He was presently in hot
A Young water, and the name "Mad Shelley," which the boys gave
Rebel him, followed him through life. He had been in the university (Oxford) hardly two years when his head was turned by some book of shallow philosophy, and he printed a rattle-brained tract called "The Necessity of Atheism." This got him into such trouble with the Dons that he was expelled for insubordination.

Forthwith Shelley published more tracts of a more rebellious kind. His sister Helen put them into the hands of her girl friend, Harriet
The Wind Westbrook, who showed her belief in revolutionary the-
and the ories by running away from school and parental discipline
Whirlwind and coming to Shelley for "protection." These two social rebels, both in the green-apple stage (their combined age was thirty-five), were presently married; not that either of them believed in marriage, but because they were compelled by "Anarch Custom."

After some two years of a wandering, will-o'-the-wisp life, Shelley and his wife were estranged and separated. The young poet then met a certain William Godwin, known at that time as a novelist and revo lutionary philosopher, and showed his appreciation of Godwin's radi- cal teaching by running away with his daughter Mary, aged seventeen. The first wife, tired of liberalism, drowned herself, and Shelley was plunged into remorse at the tragedy. The right to care for his children was denied him, as an improper person, and he was practically driven out of England by force of that public opinion which he had so frequently outraged or defied.

Life is a good teacher, though stern in its reckoning, and in Italy life taught Shelley that the rights and beliefs of other men were no less sacred than his own. He was a strange combination of hot head and kind heart, the one filled with wild social theories, the other with compassion for humanity. He was immensely generous with his friends, and tender to the point of tears at the thought of suffering men, — not real men, such as he met in the streets (even the beggars in Italy are cheerful), but idealized men, with mysterious sorrows, whom he met in the clouds. While in England his weak head had its foolish way, and his early poems, such as

PERCY BYSSHE SHELLEY

Queen Mab, are violent declamations. In Italy his heart had its day, and his later poems, such as *Adonais* and *Prometheus Unbound*, are rhapsodies ennobled by Shelley's love of beauty and by his unquench- able hope that a bright day of justice must soon dawn upon the world. He was drowned (1822) while sailing his boat off the Italian coast, before he had reached the age of thirty years.

The Poetry of Shelley. In the longer poems of Shelley there are two prominent elements, and two others less con- spicuous but more important. The first element is revolt. The poet was violently opposed to the existing order of society, and lost no opportunity to express his hatred of Tyranny, which was Shelley's name for what sober men called law and order. Feeding his spirit of revolution were numerous anarchistic theories, called the new philosophy, which had this curious quality : that they hotly denied the old faith, law, morality, as other men formulated such matters, and fervently believed any quack who appeared with a new nostrum warranted to cure all social disorders.

The second obvious element in Shelley's poetry is his love of beauty, not the common beauty of nature or humanity which Wordsworth celebrated, but a strange "supernal" beauty with no earthly quality or reality. His best lines leave a vague impression of something beautiful and lovely, but we know not what it is.

Less conspicuous in Shelley's poems are the sense of personal loss or grief which pervades them, and the exquisite melody of certain words which he used for their emotional effect rather than to convey any definite meaning. Like Byron he sang chiefly of his own feelings, his rage or despair, his sorrow or loneliness. He reflected his idea of the origin and motive of lyric poesy in the lines :

> Most wretched men
> Are cradled into poetry by wrong;
> They learn in suffering what they teach in song, —

an idea which Poe adopted in its entirety, and which Heine expressed in a sentimental lyric, telling how from his great grief he made his little songs :

> Aus meinen groszen Schmerzen
> Mach' ich die kleinen Lieder.

Hardly another English poet uses words so musically as Shelley (witness "The Cloud" and "The Skylark"), and here again his idea of verbal melody was carried to an extreme by Poe, in whose poetry words are used not so much to express ideas as to awaken vague emotions.

E

All the above-named qualities appear in *Alastor* (the Spirit of Solitude), which is less interesting as a poem than as a study of Shelley. In this poem we may skip the revolt, which is of no consequence, and follow the poet in his search for a supernally lovely maiden who shall satisfy his love for ideal beauty. To find her he goes, not among human habitations, but to gloomy forests, dizzy cliffs, raging torrents, tempest-blown seashore, — to every place where a maiden in her senses would not be. Such places, terrible or picturesque, are but symbols of the poet's soul in its suffering and loneliness. He does not find his maiden (and herein we read the poet's first confession that he has failed in life, that the world is too strong for him) ; but he sees the setting moon, and somehow that pale comforter brings him peace with death.

Alastor

In *Prometheus Unbound* Shelley uses the old myth of the Titan who rebelled against the tyranny of the gods, and who was punished by being chained to a rock.[1] In this poem Prometheus (man) is represented as being tortured by Jove (law or custom) until he is released by Demogorgon (progress or necessity) ; whereupon he marries Asia (love or goodness), and stars and moon break out into a happy song of redemption.

Prometheus

Obviously there is no reality or human interest in such a fantasy. The only pleasurable parts of the poem are its detached passages of great melody or beauty ; and the chief value of the work is as a modern example of Titan literature. Many poets have at various times represented mankind in the person of a Titan, that is, a man written large, colossal in his courage or power or suffering : Æschylus in *Prometheus*, Marlowe in *Tamburlaine*, Milton in Lucifer, of *Paradise Lost*, Goethe in *Faust*, Byron in *Manfred*, Shelley in *Prometheus*

---

[1] The original tragedy of *Prometheus Bound* was written by Æschylus, a famous old Greek dramatist. The same poet wrote also *Prometheus Unbound*, but the latter drama has been lost. Shelley borrowed the idea of his poem from this lost drama.

Unbound. The Greek Titan is resigned, uncomplaining, know-ing himself to be a victim of Fate, which may not be opposed ; Marlowe's Titan is bombastic and violent; Milton's is ambitious, proud, revengeful ; Goethe's is cultured and philosophical ; Byron's is gloomy, rebellious, theatrical. So all these poets portray each his own bent of mind, and something also of the temper of the age, in the character of his Titan. The signifi-cance of Shelley's poem is in this : that his Titan is patient and hopeful, trusting in the spirit of Love to redeem mankind from all evil. Herein Shelley is far removed from the caviling temper of his fellow rebel Byron. He celebrates a golden age not of the past but of the future, when the dream of justice inspired by the French Revolution shall have become a glorious reality.

These longer poems of Shelley are read by the few ; they are too vague, with too little meaning or message, for ordinary **His Best** readers who like to understand as well as to enjoy **Poems** poetry. To such readers the only interesting works of Shelley are a few shorter poems : " The Cloud," " To a Skylark," " Ode to the West Wind," " Indian Serenade," " A Lament," " When the Lamp is Lighted " and some parts of *Adonais* (a beautiful elegy in memory of Keats), such as the passage beginning, " Go thou to Rome." For splendor of imagination and for melody of expression these poems have few peers and no superiors in English literature. To read them is to discover that Shelley was at times so sensitive, so respon-sive to every harmony of nature, that he seemed like the poet of *Alastor,*

> A fragile lute, on whose harmonious strings
> The breath of Heaven did wander.

The breath of heaven is constant, but lutes and strings are variable matters of human arrangement. When Shelley's lute was tuned to nature it brought forth aërial melody ; when he strained its strings to voice some social rebellion or anarchistic theory it produced wild discord.

John Keats (1795–1821)

A thing of beauty is a joy forever:
Its loveliness increases; it will never
Pass into nothingness, but still will keep
A bower quiet for us, and a sleep
Full of sweet dreams and health and quiet breathing.

The above lines, from *Endymion,* reflect the ideal of the young singer whom we rank with the best poets of the nineteenth century. Unlike other romanticists of that day, he seems to have lived for poetry alone and to have loved it for its own sake, as we love the first spring flowers. His work was shamefully treated by reviewers; it was neglected by the public; but still he wrote, trying to make each line perfect, in the spirit of those medieval workmen who put their hearts into a carving that would rest on some lofty spire far above the eyes of men. To reverence beauty wherever he found it, and then in gratitude to produce a new work of beauty which should live forever, — that was Keats's only aim. It is the more wonderful in view of his humble origin, his painful experience, his tragic end.

Life. Only twenty-five years of life, which included seven years of uncongenial tasks, and three of writing, and three of wandering in search of health, — that sums up the story of Keats. He was born in London; he was the son of a hostler; his home was over the stable; his playground was the dirty street. The family prospered, moved to a better locality, and the children were sent to a good school. Then the parents died, and at fifteen Keats was bound out to a surgeon and apothecary. For four years he worked as an apprentice, and for three years more in a hospital; then, for his heart was never in the work, he laid aside his surgeon's kit, resolving never to touch it again.

Since childhood he had been a reader, a dreamer, but not till a volume of Spenser's *Faery Queen* was put into his hands did he turn with intense eagerness to poetry. The influence of that volume is seen in the somewhat monotonous sweetness of his early work. Next he explored the classics (he had read Virgil in the original, but he

knew no Greek), and the joy he found in Chapman's translation of Homer is reflected in a noble sonnet. From that time on he was
Two Poetic influenced by two ideals which he found in Greek and
Ideals medieval literature, the one with its emphasis on form, the other with its rich and varied coloring.

During the next three years Keats published three small volumes, his entire life's work. These were brutally criticized by literary magazines; they met with ridicule at the hands of Byron, with indifference on the part of Scott and Wordsworth. The pathetic legend that the poet's life was shortened by this abuse is still repeated, but there is little truth in it. Keats held manfully to his course, having more weighty things than criticism to think about. He was conscious that his time was short; he was in love with his Fannie Brawne, but separated from her by illness and poverty; and, like the American poet Lanier, he faced death across the table as he wrote. To throw off the consumption which had fastened upon him he tried to live in the open, making walking trips in the Lake Region; but he met with rough fare

JOHN KEATS

and returned from each trip weaker than before. He turned at last to Italy, dreading the voyage and what lay beyond. Night fell as the ship put to sea; the evening star shone clear through the storm clouds, and Keats sent his farewell to life and love and poetry in the sonnet beginning:

> Bright star, would I were steadfast as thou art.

He died soon after his arrival in Rome, in 1821. Shelley, who had hailed Keats as a genius, and who had sent a generous invitation to come and share his home, commemorated the poet's death and the world's loss in *Adonais*, which ranks with Milton's *Lycidas*, Tennyson's *In Memoriam* and Emerson's *Threnody* among the great elegiac poems of our literature.

The Work of Keats. The first small volume of Keats (*Poems*, 1817) seems now like an experiment. The part of that experiment which we cherish above all others is the sonnet "On Chapman's Homer," which should be read entire for its note of joy and for its fine expression of the influence of classic poetry. The second volume, *Endymion*, may be regarded as a promise. There is little reality in the rambling poem which gives title to the volume (the story of a shepherd beloved of a moon-goddess), but the bold imagery of the work, its Spenserian melody, its passages of rare beauty, — all these speak of a true poet who has not yet quite found himself or his subject. A third volume, *Lamia, Isabella, The Eve of St. Agnes and Other Poems* (1820), is in every sense a fulfillment, for it contains a large proportion of excellent poetry, fresh, vital, melodious, which improves with years, and which carries on its face the stamp of permanency.

The contents of this little volume may be arranged, not very accurately, in three classes. In the first are certain His Best Poems   poems that by their perfection of form show the Greek or classic spirit. Best known of these poems are the fragment "Hyperion," with its Milton-like nobility of style, and "Lamia," which is the story of an enchantress whom love transforms into a beautiful woman, but who quickly vanishes because of her lover's too great curiosity, — a parable, perhaps, of the futility of science and philosophy, as Keats regarded them.

Of the poems of the second class, which reflect old medieval legends, "The Pot of Basil," "The Eve of St. Agnes" and "La Belle Dame sans Merci" are praised by poets and critics alike. "St. Agnes," which reflects a vague longing rather than a story, is the best known; but "La Belle Dame" may appeal to some readers as the most moving of Keats's poems.

The essence of all old metrical romances is preserved in a few lines, which have an added personal interest from the fact that they may reveal something of the poet's sad love story.

In the third class are a few sonnets and miscellaneous poems, all permeated by the sense of beauty, showing in every line the genius of Keats and his exquisite workmanship. The sonnets "On the Sea," "When I have Fears," "On the Grasshopper and Cricket" and "To Sleep"; the fragment beginning "In a drear-nighted December"; the marvelous odes "On a Grecian Urn," "To a Nightingale" and "To Autumn," in which he combines the simplicity of the old classics with the romance and magic of medieval writers, — there are no works in English of a similar kind that make stronger appeal to our ideal of poetry and of verbal melody. Into the three stanzas of "Autumn," for example, Keats has compressed the vague feelings of beauty, of melancholy, of immortal aspiration, which come to sensitive souls in the "season of mists and mellow fruitfulness." It may be compared, or rather contrasted, with another poem on the same subject which voices the despair in the heart of the French poet Verlaine, who hears "the sobbing of the violins of autumn":

> Les sanglots longs
> Des violons
>   De l'automne
> Blessent mon cœur
> D'une langueur
>   Monotone.

Keats : an Essay of Criticism. Beyond recommending a few of his poems for their beauty, there is really so little to be said of Keats that critics are at their wit's end to express their appreciation. So we read of Keats's "pure æstheticism," his "copious perfection," his "idyllic visualization," his "haunting poignancy of feeling," his "subtle felicities of diction," his "tone color," and more to the same effect. Such criticisms are doubtless well meant, but they are harder to follow than

Keats's "Endymion"; and that is no short or easy road of poesy. Perhaps by trying more familiar ways we may better understand Keats, why he appeals so strongly to poets, and why he is so seldom read by other people.

The first characteristic of the man was his love for every beautiful thing he saw or heard. Sometimes the object which **The Sense** fascinated him was the widespread sea or a solitary **of Beauty** star; sometimes it was the work of man, the product of his heart and brain attuned, such as a passage from Homer, a legend of the Middle Ages, a vase of pure lines amid the rubbish of a museum, like a bird call or the scent of violets in a city street. Whatever the object that aroused his sense of beauty, he turned aside to stay with it a while, as on the byways of Europe you will sometimes see a man lay down his burden and bare his head before a shrine that beckons him to pray. With this reverence for beauty Keats had other and rarer qualities: the power to express what he felt, the imagination which gave him beautiful figures, and the taste which enabled him to choose the finest words, the most melodious phrases, wherewith to reflect his thought or mood or emotion.

Such was the power of Keats, to be simple and reverent in the presence of beauty, and to give his feeling poetic or imaginative expression. In respect of such power he probably had no peer in English literature. His limitations were twofold: he looked too exclusively on the physical side of beauty, and he lived too far removed from the common, wholesome life of men.

To illustrate our criticism: that man whom we saw by the wayside shrine acknowledged the presence of some spiritual **Sense** beauty and truth, the beauty of holiness, the ineffable **and Soul** loveliness of God. So the man who trains a child, or gives thanks for a friend, or remembers his mother, is always at heart a lover of beauty, — the moral beauty of character, of comradeship, of self-sacrifice. But the poetry of Keats deals largely with outward matters, with form, color,

melody, odors, with what is called " sensuous " beauty because
it delights our human senses. Such beauty is good, but it is
not supreme. Moreover, the artist who would appeal widely
to men must by sympathy understand their whole life, their
mirth as well as their sorrow, their days of labor, their hours
of play, their moments of worship. But Keats, living apart
with his ideal of beauty, like a hermit in his cell, was able to
understand and to voice only one of the profound interests of
humanity. For this reason, and because of the deep note of
sadness which sounds through all his work like the monotone
of the sea, his exquisite poems have never had any general
appreciation. Like Spenser, who was his first master, he is a
poet's poet.

MINOR POETS OF ROMANTICISM

In the early nineteenth century the Literary Annuals appeared, took root and flourished mightily in England and
America. These annuals (such a vigorous crop should have
been called hardy annuals) were collections of contemporary
prose or verse that appeared once a year under such sentimental
names as " Friendship's Offering," " The Token " and " The
Garland." That they were sold in large numbers on both sides
of the Atlantic speaks of the growing popular interest in literature. Moreover, they served an excellent purpose at a time
when books and libraries were less accessible than they are
now. They satisfied the need of ordinary readers for poetry
and romance ; they often made known to the world a talented
author, who found in public approval that sweet encouragement
which critics denied him ; they made it unlikely that henceforth
" some mute, inglorious Milton " should remain either mute
or inglorious ; and they not only preserved the best work
of minor poets but, what is much better, they gave it a
wide reading.

Thanks to such collections, from which every newspaper
filled its Poet's Corner, good poems which else might have

hid their little light under a bushel — Campbell's "Hohen-linden," Mrs. Hemans' "Landing of the Pilgrim Fathers," Hunt's "Abou ben Adhem," Hood's "The Song of the Shirt," and many others — are now as widely known as are the best works of Wordsworth or Byron.

We can name only a few poets of the age, leaving the reader to form acquaintance with their songs in an anthology. Especially worthy of remembrance are: Thomas Campbell,

who greatly influenced the American poets Halleck and Drake; Thomas Moore, whose *Irish Melodies* have an attractive singing quality; James Hogg (The Ettrick Shepherd); John Keble, author of *The Christian Year*; Thomas Hood; Felicia Hemans; and Leigh Hunt, whose encouragement of Keats is as memorable as his "Abou ben Adhem" or "The Glove and the Lions." There are other poets of equal rank with those we have ventured to name, and their melodious quality is such that a modern critic has spoken of them, in terms com-

LEIGH HUNT

monly applied to the Elizabethans, as "a nest of singing birds"; which would be an excellent figure if we could forget the fact that birds in a nest never sing. Their work is perhaps less imaginative (and certainly less fantastic) than that of Elizabethan singers, but it comes nearer to present life and reality.

One of the least known of these minor poets, Thomas Beddoes, was gifted in a way to remind us of the strange genius of Blake. He wrote not much, his life being too broken and disappointed; but running through his scanty verse is a thread of the pure gold of poetry. In a single stanza of his "Dream Pedlary" he has reflected the spirit of the whole romantic movement :

> If there were dreams to sell,
>   What would you buy?
> Some cost a passing bell,
>   Some a light sigh
> That shakes from Life's fresh crown
> Only a rose-leaf down.
> If there were dreams to sell,
> Merry and sad to tell,
> And the crier rang the bell,
>   What would you buy?

THE WORK OF WALTER SCOTT (1771–1832)

To read Scott is to read Scotland. Of no other modern author can it so freely be said that he gave to literature a whole country, its scenery, its people, its history and traditions, its ideals of faith and courage and loyalty.

That is a large achievement, but that is not all. It was Scott, more than any other author, who brought poetry and romance home to ordinary readers ; and with romance came pleasure, wholesome and refreshing as a drink from a living spring. When he began to write, the novel was in a sad state, — sentimental, sensational, fantastic, devoted to what Charles Lamb described as wildly improbable events and to characters that belong neither to this world nor to any other conceivable one. When his work was done, the novel had been raised to its present position as the most powerful literary influence that bears upon the human mind. Among novelists, therefore, Scott deserves his title of "the first of the modern race of giants."

Life. To his family, descendants of the old Borderers, Scott owed that intensely patriotic quality which glows in all his work. He is said to have borne strong resemblance to his grandfather, "Old Bardie Scott," an unbending clansman who vowed never to cut his beard till a Stuart prince came back to the throne. The clansmen were now citizens of the Empire, but their loyalty to hereditary chiefs is reflected in Scott's reverence for everything pertaining to rank or royalty.

He was born (1771) in Edinburgh, but his early associations were all of the open country. Some illness had left him lame of foot, and **First Impressions** with the hope of a cure he was sent to relatives at Sandy Knowe. There in the heart of the Border he spent his days on the hills with the shepherds, listening to Scottish legends. At bedtime his grandmother told him tales of the clans; and when he could read for himself he learned by heart Percy's *Reliques of Ancient Poetry*. So the scenes which he loved because of their wild beauty became sacred because of their historical association. Even in that early day his heart had framed the sentiment which found expression in his *Lay of the Last Minstrel*:

> Breathes there the man with soul so dead,
> Who never to himself hath said:
> This is my own, my native land?

At school, and at college at Edinburgh, the boy's heart was never in his books, unless perchance they contained something of the tradi- **Work and Play** tion of Scotland. After college he worked in his father's law office, became an advocate, and for twenty years followed the law. His vacations were spent "making raids," as he said, into the Highlands, adding to his enormous store of old tales and ballads. A companion on one of these trips gives us a picture of the man:

"Eh me, sic an endless fund o' humour and drollery as he had wi' him! Never ten yards but we were either laughing or roaring and singing. Whenever we stopped, how brawlie he suited himsel' to everybody! He aye did as the lave did; never made himsel' the great man, or took ony airs in the company."

This boyish delight in roaming, in new scenes, in new people met frankly under the open sky, is characteristic of Scott's poems and novels, which never move freely until they are out of doors. The vigor of these works may be partially accounted for by the fact that Scott was a hard worker and a hearty player, — a capital combination.

He was past thirty when he began to write.[1] By that time he had been appointed Clerk of Sessions, and also Sheriff of Selkirkshire

---

[1] This refers to original composition. In 1796 Scott published some translations of German romantic ballads, and in 1802 his *Minstrelsy of the Scottish Border*. The latter was a collection of old ballads, to some of which Scott gave a more modern form.

(he took that hangman's job, and kept it even after he had won fame, just for the money there was in it) ; and these offices, together with
His Poems his wife's dowry, provided a comfortable income. When his first poem, *The Lay of the Last Minstrel* (1805), met with immense success he gladly gave up the law, and wrote *Marmion* (1808) and *The Lady of the Lake* (1810). These increased his good fortune; but his later poems were of inferior quality, and met with a cool reception. Meanwhile Byron had appeared to dazzle the reading public. Scott recognized the greater poetic genius of the author of *Childe Harold*, and sought another field where he was safe from all rivals.

Rummaging in a cabinet one day after some fish-
First ing tackle, he
Romances found a manu-
script long neglected and forgotten. Instead of going fishing Scott read his manuscript, was fascinated by it, and presently began to write in headlong fashion. In three weeks he added sixty-five chapters to his old romance, and published it as *Waverley* (1814) without signing his name. Then he went away on another " raid "

WALTER SCOTT

to the Highlands. When he returned, at the end of the summer, he learned that his book had made a tremendous sensation, and that Fame, hat in hand, had been waiting at his door for some weeks.

In the next ten years Scott won his name of " the Wizard of the North," for it seemed that only magic could produce stories of such quality in such numbers : *Guy Mannering, Rob Roy, Old Mortality, Redgauntlet, Heart of Midlothian,* portraying the deathless romance of Scotland; and *Ivanhoe, Kenilworth, The Talisman* and other novels which changed dull history to a drama of fascinating characters. Not only England but the Continent hailed this magnificent work with delight. Money and fame poured in upon the author. Fortune appeared for once " with both hands full." Then the crash came.

To understand the calamity one must remember that Scott regarded literature not as an art but as a profitable business; that he aimed to be not a great writer but a lord of high degree. He had been made a baronet, and was childishly proud of the title; his work and his vast earnings were devoted to the dream of a feudal house which should endure through the centuries and look back to Sir Walter as its noble founder. While living modestly on his income at Ashestiel he had used the earnings of his poems to buy a rough farm at Clarty Hole, on the Tweed, and had changed its unromantic name to Abbotsford.

ABBOTSFORD

More land was rapidly added and "improved" to make a lordly estate; then came the building of a castle, where Scott entertained lavishly, as lavishly as any laird or chieftain of the olden time, offering to all visitors " the honors of Scotland."

Enormous sums were spent on this bubble, and still more money was needed. To increase his income Scott went into secret partnership with his publishers, indulged in speculative ventures, ran the firm upon the shoals, drew large sums in advance of his earnings. Suddenly came a business panic; the publishing firm failed miserably; and at fifty-five Scott, having too much honest pride to take advantage of the bankruptcy laws, found himself facing a debt of more than a hundred thousand pounds.

His last years were spent in an heroic struggle to retrieve his lost fortunes. He wrote more novels, but without much zest or inspiration ;
His Last Years he undertook other works, such as the voluminous *Life of Napoleon*, for which he was hardly fitted, but which brought him money in large measure. In four years he had repaid the greater part of his debt, but mind and body were breaking under the strain. When the end came, in 1832, he had literally worked himself to death. The murmur of the Tweed over its shallows, music that he had loved since childhood, was the last earthly sound of which he was conscious. The house of Abbotsford, for which he had planned and toiled, went into strange hands, and the noble family which he had hoped to found died out within a few years. Only his work remains, and that endures the wear of time and the tooth of criticism.

The Poems of Scott. Three good poems of Scott are *Marmion*, *The Lay of the Last Minstrel* and *The Lady of the Lake* ; three others, not so good, are *Rokeby*, *Vision of Don Roderick* and *Lord of the Isles*. Among these *The Lady of the Lake* is such a favorite that, if one were to question the tourists who annually visit the Trossachs, a surprisingly large number of them would probably confess that they were led not so much by love of natural beauty as by desire to visit " Fair Ellen's Isle" and other scenes which Scott has immortalized in verse.

We may as well admit frankly that even the best of these poems is not first-class ; that it shows careless workmanship, and is lacking in the finer elements of beauty and imagination. But Scott did not aim to create a work of beauty ; his purpose was to tell a good story, and in that he succeeded. His *Lady of the Lake*, for example, has at least two virtues : it holds the reader's attention ; and it fulfills the first law of poetry, which is to give pleasure.

Another charm of the poems, for young readers especially, is that they are simple, vigorous, easily understood. Their
Quality of the Poems rapid action and flying verse show hardly a trace of conscious effort. Reading them is like sweeping downstream with a good current, no labor required save for steering, and attention free for what awaits us around the next

bend. When the bend is passed, Scott has always something new and interesting: charming scenery, heroic adventure, picturesque incidents (such as the flight of the Fiery Cross to summon the clans), interesting fragments of folklore, and occasionally a ballad like " Lochinvar," or a song like " Bonnie Dundee," which stays with us as a happy memory long after the poem is forgotten.

A secondary reason for the success of these poems was that they satisfied a fashion, very popular in Scott's day, which we have not yet outgrown. That fashion was to attribute chivalrous virtues to outlaws and other merry men, who in their own day and generation were imprisoned or hanged, and who deserved their fate. Robin Hood's gang, for example, or the Raiders of the Border, were in fact a tough lot of thieves and cutthroats ; but when they appeared in romantic literature they must of course appeal to ladies ; so Scott made them fine, dashing, manly fellows, sacrificing to the fashion of the hour the truth of history and humanity. As Andrew Lang says :

" In their own days the Border Riders were regarded as public nuisances by statesmen, who attempted to educate them by means of the gibbet. But now they were the delight of fine ladies, contending who should be most extravagant in encomium. A blessing on such fine ladies, who know what is good when they see it ! " [1]

Scott's Novels. To appreciate the value of Scott's work one should read some of the novels that were fashionable in his day, — silly, sentimental novels, portraying the "sensibilities" of imaginary ladies.[2] That Scott was influenced by this inane fashion appears plainly in some of his characters, his fine ladies especially, who pose and sentimentalize till we are mortally weary of them ; but this influence passed when he discovered his real power, which was to portray men and women

---

[1] Quoted in Nicoll and Seccombe, *A History of English Literature*, Vol. III, p. 957.

[2] In America, Cooper's first romance, *Precaution* (1820), was of this artificial type. After Scott's outdoor romances appeared, Cooper discovered his talent, and wrote *The Spy* and the Leather-Stocking tales. Maria Edgeworth and Jane Austen began to improve or naturalize the English novel before Scott attempted it.

in vigorous action. *Waverley, Rob Roy, Ivanhoe, Redgauntlet,* — such stories of brave adventure were like the winds of the North, bringing to novel-readers the tang of the sea and the earth and the heather. They braced their readers for life, made them feel their kinship with nature and humanity. Incidentally, they announced that two new types of fiction, the outdoor romance and the historical novel, had appeared with power to influence the work of Cooper, Thackeray, Dickens and a host of minor novelists.

The most convenient way of dealing with Scott's works is to arrange them in three groups. In the first are the novels of Scotland: *Waverley*, dealing with the loyalty of the clans to the Pretender; *Old Mortality*, with the faith and struggles of the Covenanters; *Redgauntlet*, with the plots of the Jacobites; *The Abbot* and *The Monastery*, with the traditions concerning Mary Queen of Scots; *Guy Mannering, The Antiquary* and *The Heart of Midlothian*, with private life and humble Scottish characters.

Groups of Stories

THE GREAT WINDOW (MELROSE ABBEY)

In the second group are the novels which reveal the romance of English history: *Ivanhoe*, dealing with Saxon and Norman in the stormy days when Richard Lionheart returned to his kingdom; *Kenilworth*, with the intrigues of Elizabeth's Court; *The Fortunes of Nigel*, with London life in the days of Charles First; *Woodstock*, with Cromwell's iron age; *Peveril of the Peak*, with the conflict between Puritan and Cavalier during the Restoration period.

In the third group are the novels which take us to foreign lands: *Quentin Durward*, showing us the French court as dominated by the cunning of Louis Eleventh, and *The Talisman*, dealing with the Third Crusade.

In the above list we have named not all but only the best of Scott's novels. They differ superficially, in scenes or incidents; they are all alike in motive, which is to tell a tale of adventure that shall be true to human nature, no matter what liberties it may take with the facts of history.

E

In all these novels the faults are almost as numerous as the virtues; but while the faults appear small, having little influ-

Quality of
the Novels

ence on the final result, the virtues are big, manly, wholesome, — such virtues as only the greatest writers of fiction possess. Probably all Scott's faults spring from one fundamental weakness: he never had a high ideal of his own art. He wrote to make money, and was inclined to regard his day's labor as "so much scribbling." Hence his style is frequently slovenly, lacking vigor and concentration; his characters talk too much, apparently to fill space; he caters to the romantic fashion (and at the same time indulges his Tory prejudice) by enlarging on the somewhat imaginary virtues of knights, nobles, feudal or royal institutions, and so presents a one-sided view of history.

On the other hand, Scott strove to be true to the great movements of history, and to the moral forces which, in the end, prevail in all human activity. His sympathies were broad; he mingled in comradeship with all classes of society, saw the best in each; and from his observation and sympathy came an enormous number of characters, high or low, good or bad, grave or ridiculous, but nearly all natural and human, because drawn from life and experience.

Another of Scott's literary virtues is his love of wild nature, which led him to depict many grand or gloomy scenes, partly

Scene and
Incident

for their own sake, but largely because they formed a fitting background for human action. Thus, *The Talisman* opens with a pen picture of a solitary Crusader moving across a sun-scorched desert towards a distant island of green. Every line in that description points to action, to the rush of a horseman from the oasis, to the fierce trial of arms before the enemies speak truce and drink together from the same spring. Many another of Scott's descriptions of wild nature is followed by some gallant adventure, which we enjoy the more because we imagine that adventures ought to occur (though they seldom do) amid romantic surroundings.

What to Read. At least one novel in each group should be read; but if it be asked, Which one? the answer is as much a matter of taste as of judgment. Of the novels dealing with Scottish life, *Waverley*, which was Scott's first attempt, is still an excellent measure of his story-telling genius; but there is more adventurous interest in *Old Mortality* or *Rob Roy*; and in *The Heart of Midlothian* (regarded by many as the finest of Scott's works) one feels closer to nature and human nature, and especially to the heart of Scotland. *Ivanhoe* is perhaps the best of the romances of English history; and of stories dealing with adventure in strange lands, *The Talisman* will probably appeal strongest to young readers, and *Quentin Durward* to their elders. To these may be added *The Antiquary*, which is a good story, and which has an element of personal interest in that it gives us glimpses of Scott him-

SCOTT'S TOMB IN DRYBURGH ABBEY

self, surrounded by old armor, old legends, old costumes, — mute testimonies to the dreams and deeds of yesterday's men and women.

Such novels should be read once for the story, as Scott intended; and then, if one should grow weary of modern-problem novels, they may be read again for their wholesome, bracing atmosphere, for their tenderness and wisdom, for their wide horizons, for their joy of climbing to heights where we look out upon a glorious Present, and a yet more glorious Past that is not dead but living.

OTHER FICTION WRITERS

Of the work of Walter Scott we have already spoken. When such a genius appears, dominating his age, we think of him as a great inventor, and so he was; but like most other inventors his trail had been blazed, his way prepared by others who had gone before him. His first romance, *Waverley*, shows the influence of earlier historical romances, such as Jane Porter's

Thaddeus of Warsaw and *Scottish Chiefs*; in his later work he acknowledged his indebtedness to Maria Edgeworth, whose *Castle Rackrent* had aroused enthusiasm at the beginning of the nineteenth century. In brief, the romantic movement greatly encouraged fiction writing, and Scott did excellently what many others were doing well.

Two things are noticeable as we review the fiction of this period: the first, that nearly all the successful writers were women;[1] the second, that of these writers only one, the

MRS. HANNAH MORE

most neglected by her own generation, holds a secure place in the hearts of present-day readers. If it be asked why Jane Austen's works endure while others are forgotten, the answer is that almost any trained writer can produce a modern romance, but it takes a genius to write a novel.[2]

---

[1] The list includes: Fanny Burney, Ann Radcliffe, Jane Porter, Maria Edgeworth, Susan Ferrier, Sydney Owenson (Lady Morgan), Mary Brunton, Hannah More, Mary Russell Mitford, — all of whom were famous in their day, and each of whom produced at least one " best seller."

[2] The difference between the modern romance and the novel is evident in the works of Scott and Miss Austen. Scott takes an unusual subject; he calls up kings, nobles,

Jane Austen.   The rare genius of Miss Austen (1775–1817) was as a forest flower during her lifetime. While Fanny Burney, Jane Porter and Maria Edgeworth were widely acclaimed, this little woman remained almost unknown, following no school of fiction, writing for her own pleasure, and destroying whatever did not satisfy her own sense of fitness.   If she had any theory of fiction, it was simply this : to use no incident but such as had occurred before her eyes, to describe no scene that was not familiar, and to portray only such characters as she knew intimately, their speech, dress, manner, and the motives that governed their action.   If unconsciously she followed any rule of expression, it was that of Cowper, who said that to touch and retouch is the secret of almost all good writing..   To her theory and rule she added personal charm, intelligence, wit, genius of a high order.   Neglected by her own generation, she has now an ever-widening circle of readers, and is ranked by critics among the five or six greatest writers of English fiction.

Jane Austen's life was short and extremely placid.   She was born (1775) in a little Hampshire village ; she spent her entire life in one country parish or another, varying the scene by an occasional summer at the watering-place of Bath, which was not very exciting.   Her father was an easy-going clergyman who read Pope, avoided politics, and left preaching to his curate.   She was one of a large family of children, who were brought up to regard elegance of manner as a cardinal virtue, and vulgarity of any kind as the epitome of the seven deadly sins.   Her two brothers entered the navy ; hence the flutter in her books whenever a naval officer comes on a furlough to his native village.   She spent her life in homely, pleasant duties, and did her writing while the chatter of family life went on around her.   Her only characters were visitors who came to the rectory, or who gathered around the tea-table in a neighbor's

Her Life

chieftains, clansmen, robber barons,— a host of picturesque characters ; he uses his imagination freely, and makes a story for the story's sake.   Miss Austen takes an ordinary country village, observes its people as through a microscope, and portrays them to the life.   She is not interested in making a thrilling story, but in showing us men and women as they are ; and our interest is held by the verity of her portrayal.   (For a different distinction between romance and novel, see p. 188.)

house. They were absolutely unconscious of the keen scrutiny to which they were subjected; no one whispered to them, "A chiel's amang ye, takin' notes"; and so they had no suspicion that they were being transferred into books.

The first three of Miss Austen's novels were written at Steventon, among her innocent subjects, but her precious manuscripts went begging in vain for a publisher.[1] The last three, reflecting as in a glass the manners of another parish, were written at Chawton, near Winchester. Then the good work suddenly began to flag. The same disease that, a little later, was to call halt to Keats's poetry of beauty now made an end of Miss Austen's portrayal of everyday life. When she died (1817) she was only forty-two years old, and her heart was still that of a young girl. A stained-glass window in beautiful old Winchester Cathedral speaks eloquently of her life and work.

If we must recommend one of Miss Austen's novels, perhaps *Pride and Prejudice* is the most typical; but there is very little to justify this choice when the alternative is *Northanger Abbey*, or *Emma*, or *Sense and Sensibility*, or *Persuasion*, or *Mansfield Park*. All are good; the most definite stricture that one can safely make is that *Mansfield Park* is not so good as the others. Four of the novels are confined to country parishes; but in *Northanger Abbey* and *Persuasion* the horizon is broadened to include a watering place, whither genteel folk went "to take the air."

Novels and Characters

The characters of all these novels are: first, the members of five or six families, with their relatives, who try to escape individual boredom by gregariousness; and second, more of the same kind assembled at a local fair or sociable. Here you meet a dull country squire or two, a feeble-minded baronet, a curate laboriously upholding the burden of his dignity, a doctor trying to hide his emptiness of mind by looking occupied, an uncomfortable male person in tow of his wife, maiden aunts, fond mammas with their awkward daughters, chatterboxes, poor

---

[1] *Northanger Abbey, Pride and Prejudice* and *Sense and Sensibility* were written between 1796 and 1799, when Jane Austen had just passed her twenty-first year. Her first novel was bought by a publisher who neglected to print it. The second could not be sold till after the third was published, in 1811.

relations, spoiled children, — a characteristic gathering. All these, except the spoiled children, talk with perfect propriety about the weather. If in the course of a long day anything witty is said, it is an accident, a phenomenon; conversation halts, and everybody looks at the speaker as if he must have had "a rush of brains to the head."

Such is Jane Austen's little field, an eddy of life revolving endlessly around small parish interests. Her subjects are not **Her Small** even the whole parish, but only "the quality," whom **Field** the favored ones may meet at Mrs. B's afternoon at home. They read proper novels, knit wristlets, discuss fevers and their remedies, raise their eyebrows at gossip, connive at matrimony, and take tea. The workers of the world enter not here; neither do men of ideas, nor social rebels, nor the wicked, nor the happily unworthy poor; and the parish is blessed in having no reformers.

In this barren field, hopeless to romancers like Scott, there never was such another explorer as Jane Austen. Her demure observation is marvelously keen; sometimes it is mischievous, or even a bit malicious, but always sparkling with wit or running over with good humor. Almost alone in that romantic age she had no story to tell, and needed none. She had never met any heroes or heroines. Plots, adventures, villains, persecuted innocence, skeletons in closets, — all the ordinary machinery of fiction seemed to her absurd and unnecessary. She was content to portray the life that she knew best, and found it so interesting that, a century later, we share her enthusiasm. And that is the genius of Miss Austen, to interest us not by a romantic story but by the truth of her observation and by the fidelity of her portrayal of human nature, especially of feminine nature.

There is one more thing to note in connection with Miss Austen's work; namely, her wholesome influence on the English novel. In *Northanger Abbey* and in *Sense and Sensibility* she satirizes the popular romances of the period, with their

Byronic heroes, melodramatic horrors and perpetual harping on some pale heroine's sensibilities. Her satire is perhaps the

Influence on English Fiction best that has been written on the subject, so delicate, so flashing, so keen, that a critic compares it to the exploit of Saladin (in *The Talisman*) who could not with his sword hack through an iron mace, as Richard did, but who accomplished the more difficult feat of slicing a gossamer veil as it floated in the air.

Such satire was not lost; yet it was Miss Austen's example rather than her precept which put to shame the sentimental romances of her day, and which influenced subsequent English fiction in the direction of truth and naturalness. Young people still prefer romance and adventure as portrayed by Scott and his followers, and that is as it should be; but an increasingly large number of mature readers (especially those who are interested in human nature) find a greater charm in the novel of characters and manners, as exemplified by Jane Austen.

THE CRITICS AND ESSAYISTS

From the seventeenth to the nineteenth century (or from Shakespeare to Wordsworth) England was preparing a great literature ; and then appeared writers whose business or pleasure it was to appreciate that literature, to point out its virtues or its defects, to explain by what principle this or that work was permanent, and to share their enjoyment of good prose and poetry with others, — in a word, the critics.

In the list of such writers, who give us literature at second hand, the names of Leigh Hunt, William Hazlitt, Walter Savage Landor, Charles Lamb and Thomas De Quincey are written large. The two last-named are selected for special study, not because of their superior critical ability (for Hazlitt was probably a better critic than either), but because of a few essays in which these men left us an appreciation of life, as they saw it for themselves at first hand.

Charles Lamb (1775–1834). There is a little book called *Essays of Elia* which stands out from all other prose works of the age. If we examine this book to discover the source of its charm, we find it pervaded by a winsome "human" quality which makes us want to know the man who wrote it. In this respect Charles Lamb differs from certain of his contemporaries. Wordsworth was too solitary, Coleridge and De Quincey too unbalanced, Shelley too visionary and Keats too aloof to awaken a feeling of personal allegiance ; but the essays of Lamb reveal two qualities which, like fine gold, are current among readers of all ages. These are sympathy and humor. By the one we enter understandingly into life, while the other keeps us from taking life too tragically.

CHARLES LAMB
From the engraving by S. Aslent Edwards

His Life Lamb was born (1775) in the midst of London, and never felt at home anywhere else. London is a world in itself, and of all its corners there were only three that Lamb found comfortable. The first was the modest little home where he lived with his gifted sister Mary, reading with her through the long evenings, or tenderly caring for her during a period of insanity ; the second was the commercial house where he toiled as a clerk ; the third was the busy street which lay between home and work, — a street forever ebbing and flowing with a great tide of human life that affected Lamb profoundly, mysteriously, as Wordsworth was affected by the hills or the sea.

The boy's education began at Christ's Hospital, where he met Coleridge and entered with him into a lifelong friendship. At fifteen he left school to help support his family; and for the next thirty-three years he was a clerk, first in the South Sea House, then in the East India Company. Rather late in life he began to write, his prime object being to earn a little extra money, which he sadly needed. Then the Company, influenced partly by his faithful service and partly by his growing reputation, retired him on a pension. Most eagerly, like a boy out of school, he welcomed his release, intending to do great things with his pen; but curiously enough he wrote less, and less excellently, than before. His decline began with his hour of liberty. For a time, in order that his invalid sister might have quiet,

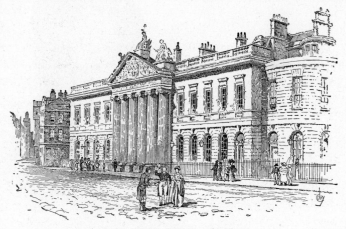

EAST INDIA HOUSE, LONDON

Where Charles Lamb worked for many years. From an engraving by M. Tombleson, after a drawing made by Thomas H. Shepherd in 1829

he lived outside the city, at Islington and Enfield; but he missed the work, the street, the crowd, and especially did he miss his old habits. He had no feeling for nature, nor for any art except that which he found in old books. "I hate the country," he wrote; and the cause of his dislike was that, not knowing what to do with himself, he grew weary of a day that was "all day long."

The earlier works of Lamb (some poems, a romance and a drama) are of little interest except to critics. The first book that brought him any considerable recognition was the *Tales from Shakespeare*. This was a summary of the stories used by Shakespeare in his plays, and was largely the work of Mary Lamb, who had a talent for writing children's books. The charm of the *Tales* lies in the fact that the Lambs were so familiar with old literature that they reproduced the stories in a style which might have done credit to a writer in the days of Elizabeth. The book is still widely read, and is as good as any other if one wants that kind of book. But the chief thing in *Macbeth* or *The Tempest* is the poetry, not the tale or the plot; and even if one wants only the story, why not get it from Shakespeare himself? Another and better book by Lamb of the same general kind is *Specimens of English Dramatic Poets Contemporary with Shakespeare.* In this book he saves us a deal of unprofitable reading by gathering together the best of the Elizabethan dramas, to which he adds some admirable notes of criticism or interpretation.

MARY LAMB
After the portrait by F. S. Cary

Most memorable of Lamb's works are the essays which he contributed for many years to the London magazines, and **Essays of Elia** which he collected under the titles *Essays of Elia* (1823) and *Last Essays of Elia* (1830).[1] To the question, Which of these essays should be read? the answer given must depend largely upon personal taste. They are all

[1] The name "Elia" (pronounced ē'-li-ä) was a pseudonym, taken from an old Italian clerk (Ellia) in the South Sea House. When "Elia" appears in the *Essays* he is Charles Lamb himself; "Cousin Bridget" is sister Mary, and "James Elia" is a brother. The last-named was a selfish kind of person, who seems to have lived for himself, letting Charles take all the care of the family.

good ; they all contain both a reflection and a criticism of life, as Lamb viewed it by light of his personal experience. A good way to read the essays, therefore, is to consider them as somewhat autobiographical, and to use them for making acquaintance with the author at various periods of his life.

For example, "My Relations" and "Mackery End" acquaint us with Lamb's family and descent; "Old Benchers of the Inner Temple" with his early surroundings; "Witches and Other Night-fears" with his sensitive childhood; "Recollections of Christ's Hospital" and "Christ's Hospital Five-and-thirty Years Ago" with his school days and comradeship with Coleridge; "The South Sea House" with his daily work; "Old China" with his home life; "The Superannuated Man" with his feelings when he was retired on a pension; and finally, "Character of the Late Elia," in which Lamb whimsically writes his own obituary.

If these call for too much reading at first, then one may select three or four typical essays : "Dream Children," notable for its exquisite pathos; "Dissertation on Roast Pig," famous for its peculiar humor; and "Praise of Chimney Sweepers," of which it is enough to say that it is just like Charles Lamb. To these one other should be added, "Imperfect Sympathies," or "A Chapter on Ears," or "Mrs. Battle's Opinions on Whist," in order to appreciate how pleasantly Lamb could write on small matters of no consequence. Still another good way of reading (which need not be emphasized, since everybody favors it) is to open the *Essays* here or there till we find something that interests us, — a method which allows every reader the explorer's joy of discovery.

To read such essays is to understand the spell they have cast on successive generations of readers. They are, first of all, very personal; they begin, as a rule, with some pleasant trifle that interests the author; then, almost before we are aware, they broaden into an essay of life itself, an essay illuminated by the steady light of Lamb's sympathy or by the flashes of his whimsical humor. Next, we note in the *Essays* their air of literary culture, which is due to Lamb's wide reading, and to the excellent taste with which he selected his old authors, — Sidney, Brown, Burton, Fuller, Walton and Jeremy Taylor. Often it was the quaintness of these authors, their conceits or oddities, that charmed him. These oddities reappear in his own style to such an extent that even when he speaks a large truth, as he often does, he is apt to give the impression of being a little hare-brained. Yet if you examine his queer idea or his merry jest, you may find that it contains more cardinal virtue than many a sober moral treatise.

On the whole *Elia* is the quintessence of modern essay-writing from Addison to Stevenson. There are probably no better works of the same kind in our literature. Some critics aver that there are none others so good.

THE LAMB BUILDING, INNER TEMPLE, LONDON

Thomas De Quincey (1785–1859). It used to be said in a college classroom that what De Quincey wrote was seldom important and always doubtful, but that we ought to read him for his style; which means, as you might say, that caviar is a stomach-upsetting food, but we ought to eat a little of it because it comes in a pretty box.

To this criticism, which reflects a prevalent opinion, we may take some exceptions. For example, what De Quincey has to say of Style, though it were written in style-defying German, is of value to everyone who would teach that impossible subject.

What he says or implies in " Levana " (the goddess who performed "the earliest office of ennobling kindness " for a new-born child, lifting him from the ground, where he was first laid, and presenting his forehead to the stars of heaven) has potency to awaken two of the great faculties of humanity, the power to think and the power to imagine. Again, many people are fascinated by dreams, those mysterious fantasies which carry us away on swift wings to meet strange experiences; and what De Quincey has to say of dreams, though doubtful as a dream itself, has never been rivaled. To a few mature minds, therefore, De Quincey is interesting entirely apart from his dazzling style and inimitable rhetoric.

THOMAS DE QUINCEY
From an engraving by C. H. Jeens

To do justice to De Quincey's erratic, storm-tossed life; to record his precocious youth, his marvelous achievements in school or college, his wanderings amid lonely mountains or more lonely city streets, his drug habits with their gorgeous dreams and terrible depressions, his timidity, his courtesy, his soul-solitude, his uncanny genius,—all that is impossible in a brief summary. Let it suffice, then, to record: that he resembled his friend Coleridge, both in his character and in his vast learning; that he studied in profound seclusion for twenty years; then for forty years more, during which time his brain was more or less beclouded by opium, he poured out a flood of magazine articles, which he collected later in fourteen chaotic volumes. These deal with an astonishing variety of subjects, and cover almost every phase of mental activity from portraying a nightmare to building a philosophical system. If he had any dominating interest in his strange life, it was the study of literature.

The historian can but name a few characteristic works of De Quincey, without recommending any of them to readers.

Typical Works To those interested in De Quincey's personality his *Confessions of an English Opium-Eater* will be illuminating. This book astonished Londoners in 1821, and may well astonish a Bushman in the year 2000. It records his wandering life, and the alternate transport or suffering which resulted from his drug habits. This may be followed by his *Suspiria de Profundis* (Sighs from the Depths), which describes, as well as such a thing could be done, the phantoms born of opium dreams. There are too many of the latter, and the reader may well be satisfied with the wonderful "Dream Fugue" in *The English Mail Coach*.

DOVE COTTAGE, GRASMERE

Here both Wordsworth and De Quincey resided

As an illustration of De Quincey's review of history, one should try *Joan of Arc* or *The Revolt of the Tartars*, which are not historical studies but romantic dreams inspired by reading history. In the critical field, "The Knocking at the Gate in *Macbeth*," "Wordsworth's Poetry" and the "Essay on Style" are immensely suggestive. As an example of ingenious humor "Murder Considered as One of the Fine Arts" is often recommended; but it has this serious fault, that it is not humorous. For a concrete example of De Quincey's matter and manner there is nothing better than "Levana or Our Ladies of Sorrow" (from the *Suspiria*), with its *mater lachrymarum* Our Lady of Tears, *mater suspiriorum* Our Lady of Sighs, and that strange phantom, forbidding and terrible, *mater tenebrarum* Our Lady of Darkness.

The style of all these works is indescribable. One may exhaust the whole list of adjectives — chanting, rhythmic, **De Quincey's** cadenced, harmonious, impassioned — that have **Style** been applied to it, and yet leave much to say. Therefore we note only these prosaic elements : that the style reflects De Quincey's powers of logical analysis and of brilliant imagination ; that it is pervaded by a tremendous mental excitement, though one does not know what the stir is all about ; and that the impression produced by this nervous, impassioned style is usually spoiled by digressions, by hair-splitting, and by something elusive, intangible, to which we can give no name, but which blurs the author's vision as a drifting fog obscures a familiar landscape.

Notwithstanding such strictures, De Quincey's style is still, as when it first appeared, a thing to marvel at, revealing as it does the grace, the harmony, the wide range and the minute precision of our English speech.

Summary. The early nineteenth century is notable for the rapid progress of democracy in English government, and for the triumph of romanticism in English literature. The most influential factor of the age was the French Revolution, with its watchwords of Liberty, Equality, Fraternity. English writers felt the stir of the times, and were inspired by the dream of a new human society ruled by justice and love. In their writing they revolted from the formal standards of the age of Pope, followed their own genius rather than set rules, and wrote with feeling and imagination of the two great subjects of nature and humanity. Such was the contrast in politics and literature with the preceding century that the whole period is sometimes called the age of revolution.

Our study of the literature of the period includes : (1) The poets Wordsworth and Coleridge, who did not so much originate as give direction to the romantic revival. (2) Byron and Shelley, often called revolutionary poets. (3) The poet Keats, whose works are famous for their sense of beauty and for their almost perfect workmanship. (4) A review of the minor poets of romanticism, Campbell, Moore, Hood, Beddoes, Hunt, and Felicia Hemans. (5) The life and works of Walter Scott, romantic poet and novelist. (6) A glance at the fiction writers of the period, and a study of the works of Jane Austen. (7) The critics and essayists, of whom we selected these two as the most typical : Charles Lamb, famous for his *Essays of Elia* ;

and De Quincey, notable for his brilliant style, his analysis of dreams, and his endeavor to make a science of literary criticism.

Selections for Reading. For general reference such anthologies as Manly's English Poetry and English Prose are useful. The works of major authors are available in various school editions, prepared especially for class use. A few of these handy editions are named below; others are listed in the General Bibliography.

Best poems of Wordsworth and of Coleridge in Athenæum Press Series. Briefer selections from Wordsworth in Golden Treasury, Cassell's National Library, Maynard's English Classics. Coleridge's Ancient Mariner in Standard English Classics, Pocket Classics. Selections from Coleridge and Campbell in one volume of Riverside Literature.

Scott's Lady of the Lake and Ivanhoe in Standard English Classics; Marmion and The Talisman in Pocket Classics; Lay of the Last Minstrel and Quentin Durward in Lake English Classics; the same and other works of Scott in various other school editions.

Selected poems of Byron in Standard English Classics, English Readings. Best poems of Shelley in Athenæum Press; briefer selections in Belles Lettres, Golden Treasury, English Classics.

Selections from Keats in Athenæum Press, Muses Library, Riverside Literature.

Lamb's Essays of Elia in Lake English Classics; selected essays in Standard English Classics, Temple Classics, Camelot Series. Tales from Shakespeare in Ginn and Company's Classics for Children.

Selections from De Quincey, a representative collection, in Athenæum Press; English Mail Coach and Joan of Arc in Standard English Classics, English Readings; Confessions of an Opium Eater in Temple Classics, Everyman's Library; Revolt of the Tartars in Lake Classics, Silver Classics.

Jane Austen's Pride and Prejudice in Pocket Classics; the same and other novels in Everyman's Library.

Bibliography. Extended works in English history and literature are listed in the General Bibliography. The following works are valuable in a study of the early nineteenth century and the romantic movement.

History. Morris, Age of Queen Anne and the Early Hanoverians; McCarthy, The Epoch of Reform (Epochs of Modern History Series); Cheyne, Industrial and Social History of England; Hassall, Making of the British Empire; Trevelyan, Early Life of Charles James Fox.

Literature. Saintsbury, History of Nineteenth Century Literature; Beers, English Romanticism in the Nineteenth Century; Symons, The Romantic Movement in English Poetry; Dowden, French Revolution and

E

English Literature; Hancock, French Revolution and The English Poets; Masson, Wordsworth, Shelley, Keats and Other Essays; De Quincey, Literary Reminiscences.

Wordsworth. Life, by Myers (English Men of Letters Series), by Raleigh. Herford, The Age of Wordsworth; Rannie, Wordsworth and his Circle; Sneath, Wordsworth, Poet of Nature and Poet of Man. Essays, by Lowell, in Among My Books; by M. Arnold, in Essays in Criticism; by Pater, in Appreciations; by L. Stephen, in Hours in a Library; by Hutton, in Literary Essays; by Bagehot, in Literary Studies.

Coleridge. Life, by Traill (E. M. of L.), by Hall Caine (Great Writers Series). Brandl, Coleridge and the English Romantic Movement. Essays, by Woodberry, in Makers of Literature; by Shairp, in Studies in Poetry and Philosophy; by Forster, in Great Teachers; by Dowden, in New Studies.

Scott. Life, by Hutton (E. M. of L.), by Lockhart (5 vols.), by Yonge (Great Writers), by Saintsbury, by Hudson, by Andrew Lang. Jack, Essay on the Novel as Illustrated by Scott and Miss Austen. Essays, by Stevenson, in Memories and Portraits; by Swinburne, in Studies in Prose and Poetry; by Hazlitt, in The Spirit of the Age; by Saintsbury, in Essays in English Literature.

Byron. Life, by Noel (Great Writers), by Nicol (E. M. of L.). Hunt, Lord Byron and his Contemporaries. Essays by Macaulay, M. Arnold, Hazlitt, Swinburne.

Shelley. Life, by Symonds (E. M. of L.), by Shairp, by Dowden, by W. M. Rossetti. Salt, A Shelley Primer. Essays by Dowden, Woodberry, M. Arnold, Bagehot, Forster, Hutton, L. Stephen.

Keats. Life, by Colvin (E. M. of L.), by Rossetti, by Hancock. H. C. Shelley, Keats and his Circle; Masson, Wordsworth and Other Essays. Essays by De Quincey, Lowell, M. Arnold, Swinburne.

Charles Lamb. Life, by Ainger (E. M. of L.), by Lucas. Fitzgerald, Charles Lamb; Talfourd, Memoirs of Charles Lamb. Essays by Woodberry, Pater, De Quincey.

De Quincey. Life, by Masson (E. M. of L.), by Page. Hogg, De Quincey and his Friends; Findlay, Personal Recollections of De Quincey. Essays by Saintsbury, Masson, L. Stephen.

Jane Austen. Life, by Malden, by Goldwin Smith, by Adams. Austen-Leigh, Memoir of Jane Austen; Mitton, Jane Austen and her Times; Hill, Jane Austen, her Home and her Friends; Jack, Essay on the Novel as Illustrated by Scott and Miss Austen. Essay by Howells, in Heroines of Fiction.

CHAPTER VIII

THE VICTORIAN AGE (1837-1901)

> The current sweeps the Old World,
> The current sweeps the New;
> The wind will blow, the dawn will glow,
> Ere thou hast sailed them through.
>
> Kingsley, " A Myth "

Historical Outline. Amid the many changes which make the reign of Victoria the most progressive in English history, one may discover three tendencies which have profoundly affected our present life and literature. The first is political and democratic; it may be said to have begun with the Reform Bill of 1832 ; it is still in progress, and its evident end is to deliver the government of England into the hands of the common people. In earlier ages we witnessed a government which laid stress on royalty and class privilege, the spirit of which was clarioned by Shakespeare in the lines:

> Not all the water in the rough rude sea
> Can wash the balm from an anointed king.

In the Victorian or modern age the divine right of kings is as obsolete as a suit of armor; the privileges of royalty and nobility are either curbed or abolished, and ordinary men by their representatives in the House of Commons are the real rulers of England.

With a change in government comes a corresponding change in literature. In former ages literature was almost as exclusive as politics; it was largely in the hands of the few; it was supported by princely patrons; it reflected the taste of the upper classes. Now the masses of men begin to be educated, begin to think for themselves, and a host of periodicals appear in answer to their demand for reading matter. Poets, novelists, essayists, historians, — all serious writers feel the inspiration of a great audience, and their works have a thousand readers where formerly they had but one. In a word, English government, society and literature have all become more democratic. This is the most significant feature of modern history.

The second tendency may be summed up in the word " scientific."
At the basis of this tendency is man's desire to know the truth, if
possible the whole truth of life ; and it sets no limits to
the exploring spirit, whether in the heavens above or the
earth beneath or the waters under the earth. From star-
dust in infinite space (which we hope to measure) to fossils on the
bed of an ocean which is no longer unfathomed, nothing is too great
or too small to attract man, to fascinate him, to influence his thought,
his life, his literature. Darwin's *Origin of Species* (1859), which laid
the foundation for a general theory of evolution, is one of the most
famous books of the age, and of the world. Associated with Darwin
were Wallace, Lyell, Huxley, Tyndall and many others, whose essays
are, in their own way, quite as significant as the poems of Tennyson
or the novels of Dickens.

The Scientific Spirit

It would be quite as erroneous to allege that modern science began
with these men as to assume that it began with the Chinese or with
Roger Bacon ; the most that can be said truthfully is, that the scientific spirit which they reflected began to dominate our thought, to
influence even our poetry and fiction, even as the voyages of Drake
and Magellan furnished a mighty and mysterious background for the
play of human life on the Elizabethan stage. The Elizabethans looked
upon an enlarging visible world, and the wonder of it is reflected in
their prose and poetry ; the Victorians overran that world almost
from pole to pole, then turned their attention to an unexplored world
of invisible forces, and their best literature thrills again with the
grandeur of the universe in which men live.

A third tendency of the Victorian age in England is expressed by
the word " imperialism." In earlier ages the work of planting English colonies had been well done ; in the Victorian age
the scattered colonies increased mightily in wealth and
power, and were closely federated into a world-wide Empire of people
speaking the same noble speech, following the same high ideals of
justice and liberty.

Imperialism

The literature of the period reflects the wide horizons of the
Empire. Among historical writers, Parkman the American was one
of the first and best to reflect the imperial spirit. In such works as
A Half-Century of Conflict and *Montcalm and Wolfe* he portrayed the
conflict not of one nation against another but rather of two antagonistic types of civilization : the military and feudal system of France
against the democratic institutions of the Anglo-Saxons. Among the

explorers, Mungo Park had anticipated the Victorians in his *Travels in the Interior of Africa* (1799), a wonderful book which set England to dreaming great dreams; but not until the heroic Livingstone's *Missionary Travels and Research in South Africa, The Zambesi and its Tributaries* and *Last Journals*[1] appeared was the veil lifted from the Dark Continent. Beside such works should be placed numerous stirring journals of exploration in Canada, in India, in Australia, in tropical or frozen seas, — wherever in the round world the colonizing genius of England saw opportunity to extend the boundaries and institutions of the Empire. Macaulay's *Warren Hastings*, Edwin Arnold's *Indian Idylls*, Kipling's *Soldiers Three*, — a few such works must be read if we are to appreciate the imperial spirit of modern English history and literature.

I. POETS OF THE VICTORIAN AGE

ALFRED TENNYSON (1809–1892)

Though the Victorian age is notable for the quality and variety of its prose works, its dominant figure for years was the poet Tennyson. He alone, of all that brilliant group of Victorian writers, seemed to speak not for himself but for his age and nation; and the nation, grown weary of Byronic rebellion, and finding its joy or sorrow expressed with almost faultless taste by one whose life was noble, gave to Tennyson a whole-souled allegiance such as few poets have ever won. In 1850 he was made Laureate to succeed Wordsworth, receiving, as he said,

> This laurel, greener from the brow
> Of him that uttered nothing base;

and from that time on he steadily adhered to his purpose, which was to know his people and to be their spokesman. Of all the poets who have been called to the Laureateship, he is probably the only one of whom it can truthfully be said that he understood his high office and was worthy of it.

[1] In connection with Livingstone's works, Stanley's *How I Found Livingstone* (1872) should also be read. Livingstone died in Africa in 1873, and his *Journals* were edited by another hand. For a summary of his work and its continuation see *Livingstone and the Exploration of Central Africa* (London, 1897).

Life. When we attempt a biography of a person we assume unconsciously that he was a public man; but that is precisely what Tennyson refused to be. He lived a retired life of thoughtfulness, of communion with nature, of friendships too sacred for the world's gaze, a life blameless in conduct, unswerving in its loyalty to noble ideals. From boyhood to old age he wrote poetry, and in that poetry alone, not in biography or letters or essays of criticism, do we ever touch the real man.

Tennyson was the son of a cultured clergyman, and was born in the rectory of Somersby, Lincolnshire, in 1809, the same year that

TENNYSON'S BIRTHPLACE, SOMERSBY RECTORY, LINCOLNSHIRE

saw the birth of Lincoln and Darwin. Like Milton he devoted himself to poetry at an early age; in his resolve he was strengthened by his mother; and from it he never departed. The influences of his early life, the quiet beauty of the English landscape, the surge and mystery of the surrounding sea, the emphasis on domestic virtues, the pride and love of an Englishman for his country and his country's history, — these are everywhere reflected in the poet's work.

His education was largely a matter of reading under his father's direction. He had a short experience of the grammar school at Louth, which he hated forever after. He entered Cambridge, and formed a circle of rare friends ("apostles" they called themselves) who afterwards became famous; but he left college without taking a degree, probably because he was too poor to continue his course. Not till 1850 did he earn enough by his work to establish a home of his own. Then he leased a house at Farringford, Isle of Wight, which we have ever since associated with Tennyson's name. But his real place is the Heart of England.

His first book (a boyish piece of work, undertaken with his brother Charles) appeared under the title *Poems by Two Brothers* (1827). In 1830, and again in 1832, he published a small volume

A Poet and His Critics containing such poems as "The Palace of Art," "The Lotos-Eaters," "The Lady of Shalott" and "The Miller's Daughter"; but the critics of the age, overlooking the poet's youth and its promise, treated the volumes unmercifully. Tennyson, always sensitive to criticism, was sensible enough to see that the critics had ground for their opinions, if not for their harshness; and for ten long years, while he labored to perfect his art, his name did not again appear in print.

There was another reason for his silence. In 1833 his dearest friend, Arthur Hallam, died suddenly in Vienna, and it was years before Tennyson began to recover from the blow. His first expression of grief is seen in the lyric beginning, "Break, break, break," which contains the memorable stanza:

> And the stately ships go on
> To their haven under the hill;
> But O for the touch of a vanished hand,
> And the sound of a voice that is still!

Then he began that series of elegies for his friend which appeared, seventeen years later, as *In Memoriam*.

Influenced by his friends, Tennyson broke his long silence with a volume containing "Morte d'Arthur," "Locksley Hall," "Sir Galahad," "Lady Clare" and a few more poems which have

He Wins and Holds His Place never lost their power over readers; but it must have commanded attention had it contained only "Ulysses," that magnificent appeal to manhood, reflecting the indomitable spirit of all those restless explorers who dared unknown lands or seas to make wide the foundations of imperial England. It was a wonderful volume, and almost its first effect was to raise the hidden Tennyson to the foremost place in English letters.

Whatever he wrote thereafter was sure of a wide reading. Critics, workingmen, scientists, reformers, theologians, — all recognized the power of the poet to give melodious expression to their thought or feeling. Yet he remained averse to everything that savored of popularity, devoting himself as in earlier days to poetry alone. As a critic writes, " Tennyson never forgot that the poet's work was to convince the world of love and beauty ; that he was born to do that work, and do it worthily."

There are two poems which are especially significant in view of this steadfast purpose. The first is " Merlin and the Gleam," which reflects Tennyson's lifelong devotion to his art ; the other is " Crossing the Bar," which was his farewell and hail to life when the end came in 1892.

Works of Tennyson. There is a wide variety in Tennyson's work : legend, romance, battle song, nature, classic and medieval heroes, problems of society, questions of science, the answer of faith, — almost everything that could interest an alert Victorian mind found some expression in his poetry. It ranges in subject from a thrush song to a religious philosophy, in form from the simplest love lyric to the labored historical drama.

Of the shorter poems of Tennyson there are a few which should be known to every student: first, because they are typical
Typical Short Poems of the man who stands for modern English poetry ; and second, because one is constantly meeting references to these poems in books or magazines or even newspapers. Among such representative poems are : " The Lotos-Eaters," a dream picture characterized by a beauty and verbal melody that recall Spenser's work ; " Locksley Hall " and " Locksley Hall Sixty Years After," the one a romance throbbing with youth and hope, the other representing the same hero grown old, despondent and a little carping, but still holding fast to his ideals ; " Sir Galahad," a medieval romance of purity ; " Ulysses," an epitome of exploration in all ages ; " The Revenge," a stirring war song ; " Rizpah," a dramatic portrayal of a mother's grief for a wayward son ; " Romney's Remorse,"

a character study of Tennyson's later years ; and a few shorter poems, such as "The Higher Pantheism," "Flower in the Crannied Wall," "Wages" and "The Making of Man," which reflect the poet's mood before the problems of science and of faith.

To these should be added a few typical patriotic pieces, which show Tennyson speaking as Poet Laureate for his country: "Ode on the Death of Wellington," "Charge of the Light Brigade," "Defense of Lucknow," "Hands all Round," and the imperial appeal of "Britons, Hold Your Own" or, as it is tamely called, "Opening of the Indian and Colonial Exposition." The beginner may also be reminded of certain famous little melodies, such as the "Bugle Song," "Sweet and Low," "Tears," "The Brook," "Far, Far, Away" and "Crossing the Bar," which are

ALFRED TENNYSON

among the most perfect that England has produced. And, as showing Tennyson's extraordinary power of youthful feeling, at least one lyric of his old age should be read, such as "The Throstle" (a song that will appeal especially to all bird lovers), beginning :

> "Summer is coming, summer is coming,
>   I know it, I know it, I know it ;
> Light again, leaf again, life again, love again " —
>   Yes, my wild little poet !

Here Tennyson is so merged in his subject as to produce the impression that the lyric must have been written not by an aged poet but by the bird himself. Reading the poem one seems to hear the brown thrasher on a twig of the wild-apple tree, pouring his heart out over the thicket which his mate has just chosen for a nesting place.

Of the longer works of Tennyson the most notable is the *Idylls of the King*, a series of twelve poems retelling part of the story of Arthur and his knights. Tennyson seems to have worked at this poem in haphazard fashion, writing the end first, then a fragment here or there, at intervals during half a century. Finally he welded his material into its present form, making it a kind of allegory of human life, in which man's animal nature fights with his spiritual aspirations. As Tennyson wrote, in his "Finale" to Queen Victoria:

Idylls of
the King

> Accept this old, imperfect tale,
> New-old, and shadowing Sense at war with Soul.

The beginner will do well to forget the allegory and read the poem for its sustained beauty of expression and for its reflection of the modern ideal of honor. For, though Malory and Tennyson tell the same story, there is this significant difference between the *Morte d'Arthur* and the *Idylls of the King*: one is thoroughly medieval, and the other almost as thoroughly modern. Malory in simple prose makes his story the expression of chivalry in the Middle Ages; his heroes are true to their own time and place. Tennyson in melodious blank verse changes his material freely so as to make it a reflection of a nineteenth-century gentleman disguised in a suit of armor and some old knightly raiment.

One may add that some readers cleave to Tennyson, while others greatly prefer Malory. There is little or no comparison between the two, and selections from both should be read, if only to understand how this old romance of Arthur has appealed to writers of different times. In making a selection from the *Idylls* (the length of the poem is rather forbidding) it is well to begin with the twelfth book, "The Passing of Arthur," which was first to be written, and which reflects the noble spirit of the entire work.

In *The Princess: a Medley* the poet attempts the difficult task of combining an old romantic story with a modern social problem ; and he does not succeed very well in harmonizing his incongruous materials.

The story is, briefly, of a princess who in youth is betrothed to a prince. When she reaches what is called the age of discretion (doubtless because that age is so frequently marked by indiscretions) she rebels

The Princess

against the idea of marriage, and founds a college, herself the principal, devoted to the higher education of women. The prince, a gallant blade, and a few of his followers disguise themselves as girls and enter the school. When an unruly masculine tongue betrays him he is cast out with maledictions on his head. His father comes with an army, and makes war against the father of the princess. The prince joins blithely in the fight, is sore wounded, and is carried to the woman's college as to a hospital. The princess nurses him, listens to his love tale, and the story ends in the good old-fashioned way.

There are many beautiful passages in *The Princess,* and had Tennyson been content to tell the romantic story his work would have had some pleasant suggestion of Shakespeare's *As You Like It*; but the social problem spoils the work, as a moralizing intruder spoils a bit of innocent fun. Tennyson is either too serious or not serious enough ; he does not know the answer to his own problem, and is not quite sincere in dealing with it or in coming to his lame and impotent conclusion. Few readers now attempt the three thousand lines of *The Princess,* but content themselves with a few lyrics, such as "Ask Me No More," "O Swallow Flying South," "Tears," "Bugle Song" and "Sweet and Low," which are familiar songs in many households that remember not whence they came.[1]

[1] The above criticism of *The Princess* applies, in some measure, to Tennyson's *Maud: a Monodrama,* a story of passionate love and loss and sorrow. Tennyson wrote also several dramatic works, such as *Harold, Becket* and *Queen Mary,* in which he attempted to fill some of the gaps in Shakespeare's list of chronicle plays.

More consistent than *The Princess* is a group of poems reflecting the life and ideals of simple people, to which Tennyson gave the general name of *English Idyls*. The
longest and in some respects the best of these is
" Enoch Arden," a romance which was once very popular, but
which is now in danger of being shelved because the modern
reader prefers his romance in prose form. Certain of the
famous poems which we have already named are classed
among these English idyls ; but more typical of Tennyson's

English Idyls

SUMMERHOUSE AT FARRINGFORD
Here Tennyson wrote "Enoch Arden"

purpose in writing them are
" Dora," " The Gardener's
Daughter " and "Aylmer's
Field," in which he turns
from ancient heroes to sing
the romance of present-day
life.

Among mature readers,
who have met the sorrows
of life or pondered its problems, the most admired
of Tennyson's work is
In Memoriam (1850), an
elegy inspired by the death
of Arthur Hallam. As a
memorial poem it invites

comparison with others, with Milton's " Lycidas," or Shelley's
" Adonais," or Gray's " Elegy in a Country Churchyard."
Without going deeply into the comparison we may note this
difference : that Tennyson's work is more personal and sympathetic than any of the others. Milton had only a slight
acquaintance with his human subject (Edward King) and wrote
his poem as a memorial for the college rather than for the
man ; Shelley had never met Keats, whose early death he
commemorates ; Gray voiced an impersonal melancholy in the
presence of the unknown dead ; but Tennyson had lost his

dearest friend, and wrote to solace his own grief and to keep alive a beautiful memory. Then, as he wrote, came the thought of other men and women mourning their dead; his view broadened with his sympathy, and he wrote other lyrics in the same strain to reflect the doubt or fear of humanity and its deathless faith even in the shadow of death.

It is this combination of personal and universal elements which makes *In Memoriam* remarkable. The only other elegy to which we may liken it is Emerson's "Threnody," written after the death of his little boy. But where Tennyson offers an elaborate wreath and a polished monument, Emerson is content with a rugged block of granite and a spray of nature's evergreen.

In Memoriam occupied Tennyson at intervals for many years, and though he attempted to give it unity before its publication in 1850, it is

Plan of the Poem

still rather fragmentary. Moreover, it is too long; for the poet never lived who could write a hundred and thirty-one lyrics upon the same subject, in the same manner, without growing monotonous.

There are three more or less distinct parts of the work,[1] corresponding to three successive Christmas seasons. The first part (extending to poem 30) is concerned with grief and doubt; the second (to poem 78) exhibits a calm, serious questioning of the problem of faith; the third introduces a great hope amid tender memories or regrets, and ends (poem 106) with that splendid outlook on a new year and a new life, "Ring Out Wild Bells." This was followed by a few more lyrics of mounting faith, inspired by the thought that divine love rules the world and that our human love is immortal and cannot die. The work ends, rather incongruously, with a marriage hymn for Tennyson's sister.

The spirit of *In Memoriam* is well reflected in the "Proem" or introductory hymn, "Strong Son of God, Immortal Love"; its message is epitomized in the last three lines:

> One God, one law, one element,
> And one far-off divine event
> To which the whole creation moves.

The Quality of Tennyson. The charm of Tennyson is two-fold. As the voice of the Victorian Age, reflecting its thought

---

[1] Tennyson divided *In Memoriam* into nine sections. Various attempts have recently been made to organize the poem and to make a philosophy of it, but these are ingenious rather than convincing.

or feeling or culture, its intellectual quest, its moral endeavor, its passion for social justice, he represents to us the spirit of modern poetry; that is, poetry which comes close to our own life, to the aims, hopes, endeavors of the men and women of to-day. With this modern quality Tennyson has the secret of all old poetry, which is to be eternally young. He looked out upon a world from which the first wonder of creation had not vanished, where the sunrise was still "a glorious birth," and where love, truth, beauty, all inspiring realities, were still waiting with divine patience to reveal themselves to human eyes.

There are other charms in Tennyson : his romantic spirit, his love of nature, his sense of verbal melody, his almost perfect workmanship; but these the reader must find and appreciate for himself. The sum of our criticism is that Tennyson is a poet to have handy on the table for the pleasure of an idle hour. He is also (and this is a better test) an excellent poet to put in your pocket when you go on a journey. So shall you be sure of traveling in good company.

Robert Browning (1812–1889)

In their lifelong devotion to a single purpose the two chief poets of the Victorian Age are much alike; in most other respects they are men of contrasts. Tennyson looked like a poet, Browning like a business man. Tennyson was a solitary singer, never in better company than when alone; Browning was a city man, who must have the excitement of society. Tennyson's field was the nation, its traditions, heroes, problems, ideals; but Browning seldom went beyond the individual man, and his purpose was to play Columbus to some obscure human soul. Tennyson was at times rather narrowly British; Browning was a cosmopolitan who dealt broadly with humanity. Tennyson was the poet of youth, and will always be read by the young in heart; Browning was the philosopher, the psychologist, the poet of mature years and of a few cultivated readers.

Life. Browning portrays so many different human types as to make us marvel, but we may partly understand his wide range of character-studies by remembering he was an Englishman with some Celtic and German ancestors, and with a trace of Creole (Spanish-Negro) blood. He was born and grew up at Camberwell, a suburb of London, and the early home of Ruskin. His father was a Bank-of-England clerk, a prosperous man and fond of books, who encouraged his boy to read and to let education follow the lead of fancy. Before Browning was twenty years old, father and son had a serious talk which ended in a kind of bargain: the boy was to live a life of culture, and the father was to take care of all financial matters, —an arrangement which suited them both very well.

ROBERT BROWNING

Since boyhood Browning had been writing romantic verses, influenced first by Byron, then by Shelley, then by Keats. His first published works, *Pauline* and *Paracelsus*, were what he called soul-studies, the one of a visionary, "a star-treader" (its hero was Shelley), the other of a medieval astrologer somewhat like Faust. These two works, if one had the patience of a puzzle-worker to read them, would be found typical of all the longer poems that Browning produced in his sixty years of writing.

These early works were not read, were not even criticized; and it was not till 1846 that Browning became famous, not because of his books but because he eloped with Elizabeth Barrett, who was then the most popular poet in England.[1] The two went to Florence,

---

[1] The fame of Miss Barrett in mid-century was above that of Tennyson or Browning. She had been for a long time an invalid. Her father, a tyrannical kind of person, insisted on her keeping her room, and expected her to die properly there. He had no personal objection to Browning, but flouted the idea of his famous daughter marrying with anybody.

discovered that they were "made for each other," and in mutual helpfulness did their best work. They lived at "Casa Guidi," a house made famous by the fact that Browning's *Men and Women* and Mrs. Browning's *Sonnets from the Portuguese* were written there.

This happy period of work was broken by Mrs. Browning's death in 1861. Browning returned to England with his son, and to forget

The Browning Cult   his loss he labored with unusual care on *The Ring and the Book* (1868), his bulkiest work. The rest of his life was spent largely in London and in Venice. Fame came to him tardily, and with some unfortunate results. He became known as a poet to

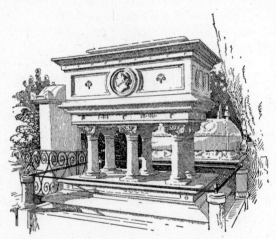

be likened unto Shakespeare, but more analytical, calling for a superior intelligence on the part of his readers; and presently a multitude of Browning clubs sprang up in England and America. Delighted with his popularity among the elect, Browning seems to have cultivated his talent for obscurity; or it may be that his natural eccen-

MRS. BROWNING'S TOMB IN THE PROTESTANT CEMETERY AT FLORENCE

tricity of style increased with age, as did Wordsworth's prosiness. Whatever the cause, his work grew steadily worse until a succession of grammar-defying volumes threatened to separate all but a few devotees from their love of Browning. He died in Venice in 1889. On the day of his death appeared in London his last book, *Asolando*. The "Epilogue" to that volume is a splendid finale to a robust life:

> One who never turned his back but marched breast forward,
> Never doubted clouds would break,
> Never dreamed, though right were worsted, wrong would triumph,
> Held we fall to rise, are baffled to fight better,
> Sleep to wake.

Tennyson's "Crossing the Bar" is a beautiful swan song; but Browning's last poem is a bugle call, and it sounds not "taps" but the "reveille."

Browning's Dramatic Quality. Nearly all the works of Browning are dramatic in spirit, and are commonly dramatic also in form. Sometimes he writes a drama for the stage, such as *A Blot in the 'Scutcheon, Colombe's Birthday* and *In a Balcony,* — dramas without much action, but packed with thought in a way that would have delighted the Schoolmen. More often his work takes the form of a dramatic monologue, such as "My Last Duchess" and "The Bishop Orders his Tomb," in which one person speaks and, like Peter, his speech bewrayeth him; for he reveals very plainly the kind of man he is. Occasionally Browning tries to sing like another poet, but even here his dramatic instinct is strong. He takes some crisis, some unexpected meeting or parting of the ways of life, and proceeds to show the hero's character by the way he faces the situation, or talks about it. So when he attempts even a love song, such as "The Last Ride Together," or a ballad, such as "The Pied Piper," he regards his subject from an unusual viewpoint and produces what he calls a dramatic lyric.

There are at least two ways in which Browning's work differs from that of other dramatists. When a trained playwright

Action vs. produces a drama his rule is, "Action, more action,
Thought and still more action." Moreover, he stands aside in order to permit his characters to reveal their quality by their own speech or action. For example, Shakespeare's plays are filled with movement, and he never tells you what he thinks of Portia or Rosalind or Macbeth, or what ought to become of them. He does not need to tell. But Browning often halts his story to inform you how this or that situation should be met, or what must come out of it. His theory is that it is not action but thought which determines human character; for a man may be doing what appears to be a brave or generous deed, yet be craven or selfish at heart; or he may be engaged in some

E

apparently sinful proceeding in obedience to a motive that we would acclaim as noble if the whole truth were known. "It is the soul and its thoughts that make the man," says Browning; "little else is worthy of study." So he calls most of his works soul-studies. If we label them now dramas, or dramatic mono-logues, or dramatic lyrics (the three classifications of his works), we are to remember that Browning is the one dramatist who deals with thoughts or motives rather than with action.

THE PALAZZO REZZONICO, BROWNING'S HOME
IN VENICE

What to Read. One should begin with the simplest of Browning's works, and preferably with those in which he shows some regard for verbal melody. As romantic love is his favorite theme, it is perhaps well to begin with a few of the love lyrics: "My Star," "By the Fireside," "Evelyn Hope," and espe-cially "The Last Ride Together." To these may be added some of the songs that brighten the obscurity of his longer pieces, such as "I Send my Heart," "Oh Love — No Love" and "There's a Woman Like a Dewdrop." Next in order are the ballads, "The Pied Piper," "Hervé Riel" and "How they Brought the Good News"; and then a few miscellaneous short poems, such as "Home Thoughts from Abroad," "Prospice," "The Boy and the Angel" and "Up at a Villa — Down in the City."

The above poems are named not because they are particularly fine examples of their kind, but by way of introduction to Dramatic a poet who is rather hard to read. When these are Monologues known, and are found not so obscure as we feared, then will be the time to attempt some of Browning's dramatic monologues. Of these there is a large variety, portraying many different types of character, but we shall name only a few. "Andrea del Sarto" is a study of the great Italian painter, "the perfect painter," whose love for a pretty but shallow woman was as a millstone about his neck. "My Last Duchess" is a powerfully drawn outline of a vain and selfish nobleman. "Abt Vogler" is a study of the soul of a musician. "Rabbi ben Ezra," one of the most typical of Browning's works, is the word of an old man who faces death, as he had faced life, with magnificent courage. "An Epistle" relates the strange experience of Karshish, an Arab physician, as recorded in a letter to his master Abib. Karshish meets Lazarus (him who was raised from the dead) and, regarding him as a patient, describes his symptoms, — such symptoms as a man might have who must live on earth after having looked on heaven. The physician's half-scoffing words show how his habitual skepticism is shaken by a glimpse of the unseen world. He concludes, but his doubt is stronger than his conclusion, that Lazarus must be a madman :

> "And thou must love me who have died for thee."
> The madman saith He said so : it is strange!

Another poem belonging to the same group (published under the general title of *Men and Women*) is "Saul," which finely Saul illustrates the method that makes Browning different from other poets. He would select some familiar event, the brief record of which is preserved in history, and say, "Here we see merely the deed, the outward act or circumstance of life : now let us get acquainted with these men or women by showing that they thought and felt precisely as we do under similar conditions." In "Saul" he reproduces the scene recorded in the sixteenth chapter of the first Book of Samuel, where the king is "troubled by an evil spirit" and the young David comes to play the harp before him. Saul is represented as the disillusioned, the despairing man who has lost all interest in life, and David as the embodiment of youthful enthusiasm. The poem is a remarkable portrayal of the ancient scene and characters ; but it is something greater than that ; it is a splendid song of the fullness and joy of a brave, forward-looking life inspired by noble ideals. It is also one of the best answers ever given to the question, Is life worth living? The length of the poem, however, and its many difficult or digressive passages are apt to repel the beginner unless he have the advantage of an abridged version.

Of the longer works of Browning, only *Pippa Passes* can be recommended with any confidence that it will give pleasure **Pippa** to the reader. Other works, such as *The Ring and* **Passes** *the Book*,[1] are doubtless more famous ; but reading them is like solving a puzzle : a few enjoy the matter, and therefore count it pleasure, but to the majority it is a task to be undertaken as mental discipline.

Pippa is the story of a working girl, a silk weaver of Asolo, who has a precious holiday and goes forth to enjoy it, wishing she could share her happiness with others, especially with the great people of her town. But the great live in another world, she thinks, a world far removed from that of the poor little working girl ; so she puts the wish out of her head, and goes on her way singing :

---

[1] *The Ring and the Book* is remarkable for other things than its inordinate length. In it Browning tells how he found an old book containing the record of a murder trial in Rome, — a horrible story of a certain Count Guido, who in a jealous rage killed his beautiful young wife. That is the only story element of the poem, and it is told, with many irritating digressions, at the beginning. The rest of the work is devoted to "soul studies," the subjects being nine different characters who rehearse the same story, each for his own justification. Thus, Guido gives his view of the matter, and Pompilia the wife gives hers. "Half Rome," siding with Guido, is personified to tell one tale, and then "The Other Half" has its say. Final judgment rests with the Pope, an impressive figure, who upholds the decision of the civil judges. Altogether it is a remarkable piece of work ; but it would have been more remarkable, better in every way, if fifteen thousand of its twenty thousand lines had been left in the inkpot.

The year's at the spring,
And day's at the morn;
Morning's at seven;
The hillside 's dew-pearled;
The lark 's on the wing;
The snail 's on the thorn:
God's in his heaven —
All 's right with the world!

It happens that her songs come, in succession, to the ears of the four greatest people in Asolo at moments when they are facing a terrible crisis, when a straw may turn them one way or the other, to do evil or to do good. In each case the song and the pure heart of the singer turn the scale in the right direction; but Pippa knows nothing of her influence. She enjoys her holiday and goes to bed still happy, still singing, quite ignorant of the wonder she has accomplished.

PIAZZA OF SAN LORENZO, FLORENCE
Where Browning bought the book in which he found the story of "The Ring and the Book"

A mere story-teller would have brought Pippa and the rescued ones together, making an affecting scene with rewards, in the romantic manner; but Browning is content to depict a bit of ordinary human life, which is daily filled with deeds worthy to be written in a book of gold, but of which only the Recording Angel takes any notice.

A Criticism of Browning. Comparatively few people appreciate the force, the daring, the vitality of Browning, and those who know him best are least inclined to formulate a favorable criticism. They know too well the faults of their hero, his whims, crotchets, digressions, garrulity; his disjointed ideas, like rich plums in a poor pudding; his ejaculatory style, as of a man of second thoughts; his wing-bound fancy, which hops around his subject like a grasshopper instead of soaring steadily over it like an eagle. Many of his lines are rather gritty:

> Irks care the crop-full bird? Frets doubt the maw-crammed beast?

and half his blank verse is neither prose nor poetry:

> What, you, Sir, come too? (Just the man I'd meet.)
> Be ruled by me and have a care o' the crowd:
> This way, while fresh folk go and get their gaze:
> I 'll tell you like a book and save your shins.
> Fie, what a roaring day we 've had! Whose fault?
> Lorenzo in Lucina, — here 's a church!

Instead of criticism, therefore, his admirers offer this word of advice: Try to like Browning; in other words, try to understand him. He is not "easy"; he is not to be read for relaxation after dinner, but in the morning and in a straight-backed chair, with eyes clear and intellect at attention. If you so read him, you must soon discover that he has something of courage and cheer which no other poet can give you in such full measure. If you read nothing else, try at least "Rabbi ben Ezra," and after the reading reflect that the optimism of this poem colors everything that the author wrote. For Browning differs from all other poets in this: that they have their moods of doubt or despondency, but he has no weary days or melancholy hours. They sing at times in the twilight, but Browning is the herald of the sunrise. Always and everywhere he represents "the will to live," to live bravely, confidently here; then forward still with cheerful hearts to immortality:

> Grow old along with me!
> The best is yet to be,
> The last of life, for which the first was made:
> Our times are in his hand
> Who saith, "A whole I planned,
> Youth shows but half: trust God: see all, nor be afraid!"

Other Victorian Poets

Elizabeth Barrett Browning (1806–1861). Among the lesser poets of the age the most famous was Elizabeth Barrett, who eloped in romantic fashion with Browning in 1846. Her early volumes, written while she was an invalid, seem now a little feverish, but a few of her poems of childhood, such as "Hector" and "Little Ellie," have still their admirers. Later she became interested in social problems, and reflected the passion of the age for reform in such poems as "The Cry of the Children," a protest against child labor which once vied in interest with Hood's famous "Song of the Shirt." Also she wrote *Aurora Leigh*, a popular novel in verse, having for its subject a hero who was a social reformer. Then Miss Barrett married Robert

ELIZABETH BARRETT BROWNING

Browning after a rather emotional and sentimental courtship, as reflected in certain extravagant pages of the Browning *Letters*.

In her new-found happiness she produced her most enduring work, the *Sonnets from the Portuguese* (1850). This is a

Sonnets   collection of love songs, so personal and intimate that the author thought perhaps to disguise them by calling them "From the Portuguese." In reality their source was no further distant than her own heart, and their hero was seen across the breakfast table every morning. They reflect Mrs. Browning's love for her husband, and those who read them should read also Browning's answer in "One Word More." Some of the sonnets ("I Thought How Once" and "How Do I Love Thee," for example) are very fine, and deserve their high place among love poems ; but others, being too intimate, raise a question of taste in showing one's heart throbs to the public. Some readers may question whether many of the *Sonnets* and most of the *Letters* had not better been left exclusively to those for whom they were intended.

Matthew Arnold (1822–1888). The work of this poet (a son of Dr. Arnold of Rugby, made famous by *Tom Brown's Schooldays*) is in strong contrast to that of the Brownings, to the robust optimism of the one and to the emotionalism of the other. He was a man of two distinct moods : in his poetry he reflected the doubt or despair of those whose faith had been shaken by the alleged discoveries of science ; in prose he became almost light-hearted as he bantered middle-class Englishmen for their old-fogy prejudices, or tried to awaken them to the joys of culture. In both moods he was coldly intellectual, appealing to the head rather than to the heart of his readers ; and it is still a question whether his poetry or his criticism will be longest remembered.

Arnold is called the poet of Oxford, as Holmes is of Harvard, and those who know the beautiful old college town will best The Poet of appreciate certain verses in which he reflects the Oxford quiet loveliness of a scene that has impressed so many students, century after century. To general readers one may safely recommend Arnold's elegies written in memory of the poet Clough, such as "Thyrsis" and "The Scholar Gypsy" ; certain poems reflecting the religious doubts of the age, such as "Dover Beach," "Morality" and "The Future" ; the love lyrics entitled "Switzerland"; and a few miscellaneous poems, such as "Resignation," "The Forsaken Merman," "The Last Word," and "Geist's Grave."

To these some critics would add the long narrative poem "Sohrab and Rustum," which is one of the models set before students of "college English." The reasons for the choice are not quite obvious; for the story, which is taken from the Persian *Shah Namah*, or Book of Kings, is rather coldly told, and the blank verse is far from melodious.

In reading these poems of Arnold his own motives should be borne in mind. He tried to write on classic lines, repressing the emotions, holding to a severe, unimpassioned style; and he proceeded on the assumption that poetry is "a criticism of life." It is not quite clear what he meant by his definition, but he was certainly on the wrong trail. Poetry is the natural language of man in moments of strong or deep feeling; it is the expression of life, of life at high tide or low tide; when it turns to criticism it loses its chief charm, as a flower loses its beauty and fragrance in the hands of a botanist. Some poets, however (Lucretius among the ancients, Pope among the moderns, for example), have taken a different view of the matter.

MATTHEW ARNOLD

Arnold's chief prose works were written, curiously enough, after he was appointed professor of poetry at Oxford. There **The Literary** he proceeded, in a sincere but somewhat toplofty **Critic** way, to enlighten the British public on the subject of culture. For years he was a kind of dictator of literary taste, and he is still known as a master of criticism; but to examine his prose is to discover that it is notable for its even style and occasional good expressions, such as "sweetness and light," rather than for its illuminating ideas.

For example, in *Literature and Dogma* and other books in which Arnold attempted to solve the problems of the age, he was apt to make large theories from a small knowledge of his subject. So in his *Study of Celtic Literature* (an interesting book, by the way) he wrote with surprising confidence for one who had no first-hand acquaintance with his material, and led his readers pleasantly astray in the flowery fields of Celtic poetry. Moreover, he had one favorite method of criticism, which was to take the bad lines of one poet and compare them with the good lines of another, — a method which would make Shakespeare a sorry figure if he happened to be on the wrong side of the comparison.

In brief, Arnold is always a stimulating and at times a provoking critic; he stirs our thought, disturbs our pet prejudices, **What to** challenges our opposition; but he is not a very reli-**Read** able guide in any field. What one should read of his prose depends largely on one's personal taste. The essay *On Translating Homer* is perhaps his most famous work, but few readers are really interested in the question of hexameters. *Culture and Anarchy* is his best plea for a combination of the moral and intellectual or, as he calls them, the Hebrew and Greek elements in our human education. Among the best of the shorter works are " Emerson " in *Discourses in America*, and " Wordsworth," " Byron " and " The Study of Poetry " in *Essays in Criticism*.

The Pre-Raphaelites. In the middle of the nineteenth century, or in 1848 to be specific, a number of English poets and painters banded themselves together as a Pre-Raphaelite Brotherhood.[1] They aimed to make all art more simple, sincere, religious, and to restore "the sense of wonder, reverence and awe " which, they believed, had been lost since medieval times. Their sincerity was unquestioned; their influence, though small,

---

[1] The name was used earlier by some German artists, who worked together in Rome with the purpose of restoring art to the medieval simplicity and purity which, as was alleged, it possessed before the time of the Italian painter Raphael. The most famous artists of the English brotherhood were John Everett Millais and William Holman Hunt.

was almost wholly good ; but unfortunately they were, as Morris said, like men born out of due season. They lived too much apart from their own age and from the great stream of common life out of which superior art proceeds. For there was never a great book or a great picture that was not in the best sense representative, that did not draw its greatness from the common ideals of the age in which it was produced.

THE MANOR HOUSE OF WILLIAM MORRIS

The first poet among the Pre-Raphaelites was Dante Gabriel Rossetti (1828–1882), the son of an exiled Italian writer. Like others of the group he was both painter and poet,
Rossetti   and seemed to be always trying to put into his verse the rich coloring which belonged on canvas. Perhaps the most romantic episode of his life was, that upon the death of his wife (the beautiful model, Lizzie Siddal, who appears in Millais' picture " Ophelia ") he buried his poetry with her. After some years his friends persuaded him that his poems belonged to the living, and he exhumed and published them (*Poems*, 1870). His most notable volume, *Ballads and Sonnets*, appeared eleven years later. The ballads are nearly all weird, uncanny, but with

something in them of the witchery of Coleridge's "Ancient Mariner." The sonnets under the general title of "The House of Life" are devoted to the poet's lost love, and rank with Mrs. Browning's *From the Portuguese.*

William Morris (1834–1896) has been called by his admirers the most Homeric of English poets. The phrase was probably applied to him because of his *Sigurd the Volsung,* in which he uses the material of an old Icelandic saga. There is a captivating vigor and swing in this poem, but it lacks the poetic imagination of an earlier work, *The Defence of Guenevere,* in which Morris retells in a new way some of the fading medieval romances. His best-known work in poetry[1] is *The Earthly Paradise,* a collection of twenty-four stories strung together on a plan somewhat resembling that of the *Canterbury Tales.* A band of mariners are cast away on an island inhabited by a superior race of men, and to while away the time the seamen and their hosts exchange stories. Some of these are from classic sources, others from Norse legends or hero tales. The stories are gracefully told, in very good verse ; but in reading them one has the impression that something essential is lacking, some touch, it may be, of present life and reality. For the island is but

WILLIAM MORRIS
From a photograph by Walker and Cockerell

---

[1] Some readers will be more interested in Morris's prose romances, *The House of the Wolfings, The Roots of the Mountains* and *The Story of the Glittering Plain.*

another Cloudland, and the characters are shadowy creatures having souls but no bodies; or else, as some may find, having the appearance of bodies and no souls whatever. Indeed, in reading the greater part of Pre-Raphaelite literature, one is reminded of Morris's estimate of himself, in the Prelude to *The Earthly Paradise*:

> Dreamer of dreams, born out of my due time,
> Why should I strive to set the crooked straight?
> Let it suffice me that my murmuring rhyme
> Beats with light wing against the ivory gate,
> Telling a tale not too importunate
> To those who in the sleepy region stay,
> Lulled by the singer of an empty day.

Algernon Charles Swinburne (1837–1909). This voluminous writer, born in the year of Victoria's accession, is yet so close to our own day that it is difficult to think of him as part of an age that is gone. As a poet he was a master of verbal melody, and had such a command of verse forms that he won his title of "inventor of harmonies." As a critic he showed a wide knowledge of English and French literature, a discriminating taste, and an enthusiasm which bubbled over in eulogy of those whom he liked, and which emptied vials of wrath upon Byron, Carlyle and others who fell under his displeasure. His criticisms are written in an extravagant, almost a torrential, style; at times his prose falls into a chanting rhythm so attractive in itself as to make us overlook the fact that the praise and censure which he dispenses with prodigal liberality are too personal to be quite trustworthy.

We are still too near Swinburne to judge him accurately, and his place in the long history of English poetry is yet to be determined. We note here only two character-

His Poetry istics, which may or may not be evident to other readers. In the first place, with his marvelous command of meter and melody, Swinburne has a fatal fluency of speech which tends to bury his thought in a mass of jingling verbiage. As we read we seem to hear the question, "What readest thou,

Hamlet ? " and again the Dane makes answer, " Words, words, words." Again, like the Pre-Raphaelites with whom he was at one time associated, Swinburne lived too much apart from the tide of common life. He wrote for the chosen few, and in the mass of his verse one must search long for a passage of which one may say, This goes home to the hearts of men, and abides there in the treasure-house of all good poetry.

Among the longer works of Swinburne his masterpiece is the lyrical drama *Atalanta in Calydon.* If one would merely sample the flavor of the poet, such minor works as " Itylus " and the fine sea pieces, " Off Shore," " By the North Sea " and "A Forsaken Garden " may be recommended. Nor should we overlook what, to many, is Swinburne's best quality ; namely, his love of children, as reflected in such poems as " The Salt of the Earth " and " A Child's Laughter." Among the best of his prose works are his *William Blake, Essays and Studies, Miscellanies* and *Studies in Prose and Verse.*

Songs in Many Keys. In calling attention to the above-named poets, we have merely indicated a few who seem to be chief ; but the judgment is a personal one, and subject to challenge. The American critic Stedman, in his *Victorian Anthology*, recognizes two hundred and fifty singers ; of these eighty are represented by five or more poems ; and of the eighty a few are given higher places than those we have selected as typical. There are many readers who prefer the *Goblin Market* of Christina Rossetti to anything produced by her gifted brother, who place Jean Ingelow above Elizabeth Barrett, who find more pleasure in Edwin Arnold's *Light of Asia* than in all the poems of Matthew Arnold, and who cannot be interested in even the best of Pre-Raphaelite verse because of its unreality. Many men, many minds ! Time has not yet recorded its verdict on the Victorians, and until there is some settled criticism which shall express the judgment of several generations of men, the best plan for the beginner is to make acquaintance with all the minor poets in an anthology or book of selections. It may even be a mistake to call any of these poets minor ; for he who has written one song that lives in the hearts of men has produced a work more enduring than the pyramids.

II. THE VICTORIAN NOVELISTS

CHARLES DICKENS (1812–1870)

Among the Victorian novelists were two men who were frequent rivals in the race for fame and fortune. Thackeray, well born and well bred, with artistic tastes and literary culture, looked doubtfully at the bustling life around him, found his inspiration in a past age, and tried to uphold the best traditions of English literature. Dickens, with little education and less interest in literary culture, looked with joy upon the struggle for democracy, and with an observation that was almost microscopic saw all its picturesque details of speech and character and incident.

CHARLES DICKENS

He was the eye of the mighty Victorian age, as Tennyson was its ear, and Browning its psychologist, and Carlyle its chronic grumbler.

Life. In the childhood of Dickens one may see a forecast of his entire career. His father, a good-natured but shiftless man (caricatured as Mr. Micawber in *David Copperfield*), was a clerk in the Navy Pay Office, at Portsmouth. There Dickens was born in 1812. The father's salary was £80 per year, enough at that time to warrant living in middle-class comfort rather than in the poverty of the lower classes, with whom Dickens is commonly associated. The mother was a sentimental woman, whom Dickens, with questionable taste, has caricatured as Mrs. Micawber and again as Mrs. Nickleby. Both parents were somewhat neglectful of their children, and uncommonly fond of creature comforts, especially of good dinners and a bowl of punch. Though there is nothing in such a family to explain Dickens's character, there is much to throw light on the characters that appear in his novels.

The boy himself was far from robust. Having no taste for sports, he amused himself by reading romances or by listening to his nurse's **The Stage** tales, — beautiful tales, he thought, which "almost scared him into fits." His elfish fancy in childhood is probably reflected in Pip, of *Great Expectations*. He had a strong dramatic instinct to act a story, or sing a song, or imitate a neighbor's speech, and the father used to amuse his friends by putting little Charles on a chair and encouraging him to mimicry, — a dangerous proceeding, though it happened to turn out well in the case of Dickens.

This stagey tendency increased as the boy grew older. He had a passion for private theatricals, and when he wrote a good story was not satisfied till he had read it in public. When *Pickwick* appeared (1837) the young man, till then an unknown reporter, was brought before an immense audience which included a large part of England and America. Thereafter he was never satisfied unless he was in the public eye ; his career was a succession of theatrical incidents, of big successes, big lecture tours, big audiences, — always the footlights, till he lay at last between the pale wax tapers. But we are far ahead of our story.

When Dickens was nine years old his family moved to London. There the father fell into debt, and by the brutal laws of the period **The London** was thrown into prison. The boy went to work in the **Streets** cellar of a blacking factory, and there began that intimate acquaintance with lowly characters which he used later to such advantage. He has described his bitter experience so often (in *David Copperfield* for instance) that the biographer may well pass over it. We note only this significant fact : that wherever Dickens went he had an instinct for exploration like that of a farm dog, which will not rest in a place till he has first examined all the neighborhood, putting his nose into every likely or unlikely spot that may shelter friend or enemy. So Dickens used his spare hours in roaming the byways of London by night; so he gained his marvelous knowledge of that foreign land called The Street, with its flitting life of gamins and nondescripts, through which we pass daily as through an unknown country.

A small inheritance brought the father from prison; the family was again united, and for two years the boy attended the academy **The Scramble** which he has held up to the laughter and scorn of two **for Place** continents. There the genius of Dickens seemed suddenly to awaken. He studied little, being given to pranks and theatricals; but he discovered within him an immense ambition, an imperious will

GADSHILL PLACE, NEAR ROCHESTER
The last residence of Dickens

to win a place and a name in the great world, and a hopeful temper that must carry him over or under all obstacles.

No sooner was his discovery made than he left school and entered a law office, where he picked up enough knowledge to make court practices forever ridiculous, in *Bleak House* and other stories. He studied shorthand and quickly mastered it; then undertook to report Parliamentary speeches (a good training in oratory) and presently began a prosperous career as a reporter. This had two advantages; it developed his natural taste for odd people and picturesque incidents, and it brought him close to the great reading public. To please that

E

public, to humor its whims and prejudices, its love for fun and tears and sentimentality, was thereafter the ruling motive in Dickens's life.

His first literary success came with some short stories contributed to the magazines, which appeared in book form as *Sketches by Boz* (1835). A publisher marked these sketches, engaged Dickens to write the text or letterpress for some comic pictures, and the result was *Pickwick*, which took England and America by storm. Then followed *Oliver Twist, Nicholas Nickleby, Old Curiosity Shop,* — a flood of works that made readers rub their eyes, wondering if such a fountain of laughter and tears were inexhaustible.

Literary Ventures

There is little else to record except this : that from the time of his first triumph Dickens held his place as the most popular writer in English. With his novels he was not satisfied, but wrote a history of England, and edited various popular magazines, such as *Household Words*. Also he gave public readings, reveling in the applause, the lionizing, which greeted him wherever he went. He earned much money ; he bought the place " Gadshill," near Rochester, which he had coveted since childhood ; but he was a free spender, and his great income was less than his fancied need. To increase his revenue he " toured " the States in a series of readings from his own works, and capitalized his experience in *American Notes* and parts of *Martin Chuzzlewit.*

A question of taste must arise even now in connection with these works. Dickens had gone to a foreign country for just two things, money and applause ; he received both in full measure ; then he bit the friendly hand which had given him what he wanted.[1] Thackeray, who followed him to America, had a finer sense of the laws of hospitality and good breeding.

In 1844 Dickens resolved to make both ends meet, and carried out his resolve with promptness and precision. To decrease expenses he went to the Continent, and lived there, hungry for the footlights,

---

[1] The chief source of Dickens's irritation was the money loss resulting from the " pirating " of his stories. There was no international copyright in those days ; the works of any popular writer were freely appropriated by foreign publishers. This custom was wrong, undoubtedly, but it had been in use for centuries. Scott's novels had been pirated in the same way ; and until Cooper got to windward of the pirates (by arranging for foreign copyrights) his work was stolen freely in England and on the Continent. But Dickens saw only his own grievance, and even at public dinners was apt to make his hosts uncomfortable by proclaiming his rights or denouncing their moral standards. Moreover, he had a vast conceit of himself, and, like most visitors of a week, thought he knew America like a book. It was as if he looked once at the welter cast ashore by mighty Lake Superior in a storm, and said, " What a dirty sea ! "

till a series of stories ending with *Dombey and Son* put his finances on a secure basis. Then he returned to London, wrote more novels, **The Price of** and saved a fortune for his descendants, who promptly **Popularity** spent it. Evidently it was a family trait. More and more he lived on his nerves, grew imperious, exacting, till he separated from his wife and made wreck of domestic happiness. The self-esteem of which he made comedy in his novels was for him a tragedy. Also he resumed the public read-ings, with their false glory and nervous wear and tear, which finally brought him to the grave.

He died, worn out by his own exertions, in 1870. He had steadily refused titles and decorations, but a grate-ful nation laid his body to rest in the Poets' Corner at Westminster Abbey. It is doubtful whether he would have accepted this honor, which was forced upon him, for he had declared proudly that by his works alone he would live in the memory of his countrymen.

DICKENS'S BIRTHPLACE, LANDPORT, PORTSEA

Works of Dickens. In the early stories of Dick-ens is a promise of all the rest. His first work was called *Sketches by Boz*, and " Boz " was invented by some little girl (was it in *The Vicar of Wakefield?*) who could not say " Moses " ; also it was a pet name for a small brother of Dickens. There was, therefore, something childlike in this first title, and childhood was to enter very largely into the novelist's work. He could hardly finish a story without bring-ing a child into it ; not an ordinary child, to make us smile, but a wistful or pathetic child whose sorrows, since we cannot help them, are apt to make our hearts ache.

Dickens is charged with exaggerating the woes of his children, and the charge is true; but he had a very human reason The Pathetic for his method. In the first place, the pathetic Element quality of his children is due to this simple fact, that they bear the burden and the care of age. And burdens which men or women accept for themselves without complaint seem all wrong, and are wrong, when laid upon a child's innocent shoulders. Again, Dickens sought to show us our error in thinking, as most grown-ups do, that childish troubles are of small account. So they are, to us; but to the child they are desperately real. Later in life we learn that troubles are not permanent, and so give them their proper place; but in childhood a trouble is the whole world; and a very hopeless world it is while it lasts. Dickens knew and loved children, as he knew the public whom he made to cry with his Little Nell and Tiny Tim; and he had discovered that tears are the key to many a heart at which reason knocks in vain.

The second work, *Pickwick*, written in a harum-scarum way, is even more typical of Dickens in its spirit of fun and laugh-Pickwickian ter. He had been engaged, as we have noted, to Humor furnish a text for some comic drawings, thus reversing the usual order of illustration. The pictures were intended to poke fun at a club of sportsmen; and Dickens, who knew nothing of sport, bravely set out with Mr. Winkle on his rook-shooting. Then, while the story was appearing in monthly numbers, the illustrator committed suicide; Dickens was left with Mr. Pickwick on his hands, and that innocent old gentleman promptly ran away with the author. Not being in the least adventurous, Mr. Pickwick was precisely the person for whom adventures were lying in wait; but with his chivalrous heart within him, and Sam Weller on guard outside, he was not to be trifled with by cabman or constable. So these two took to the open road, and to the inns where punch, good

cheer and the unexpected were awaiting them. Never was
such another book! It is not a novel; it is a medley of fun
and drollery resulting from high animal spirits.

In his next novel, *Oliver Twist*, the author makes a new
departure by using the motive of horror. One of his heroes is
The Motive an unfortunate child, but when our sympathies for
of Horror   the little fellow are stretched to the point of tears,
Dickens turns over a page and relieves us by Pickwickian
laughter. Also he has his usual medley of picturesque characters and incidents, but the shadow of Fagin is over them all.
One cannot go into any house in the book, and lock the door
and draw the shades, without feeling that somewhere in the
outer darkness this horrible creature is prowling. The horror
which Fagin inspires is never morbid; for Dickens with his
healthy spirit could not err in this direction. It is a boyish,
melodramatic horror, such as immature minds seek in "movies,"
dime novels, secret societies, detective stories and "thrillers"
at the circus.

In the fourth work, *Nicholas Nickleby*, Dickens shows that
he is nearing the limit of his invention so far as plot is concerned. In this novel he seems to rest a bit by writing an old-
fashioned romance, with its hero and villain and moral ending.
But if you study this or any subsequent work of Dickens, you
are apt to find the four elements already noted; namely, an
unfortunate child, humorous interludes, a grotesque or horrible
creature who serves as a foil to virtue or innocence, and a medley of characters good or bad that might be transferred without
change to any other story. The most interesting thing about
Dickens's men and women is that they are human enough to
make themselves at home anywhere.

What to Read. Whether one wants to study the method of
Dickens or to enjoy his works, there is hardly a better plan for
the beginner than to read in succession *Pickwick, Oliver Twist*
and *Nicholas Nickleby*, which are as the seed plot out of which
grow all his stories. For the rest, the reader must follow his own

fancy. If one must choose a single work, perhaps *Copperfield* is the most typical. "Of all my books," said Dickens, "I like this the best; like many parents I have my favorite child, and his name is David Copperfield." Some of the heroines of this book are rather stagey, but the Peggotys, Betsy Trotwood, Mrs. Gummidge, the Micawbers, — all these are unrivaled.

YARD OF REINDEER INN, DANBURY
The scene of the races, in *Old Curiosity Shop*

"There is no writing against such power," said Thackeray, who was himself writing *Pendennis* while Dickens was at work on his masterpiece.

Opinion is divided on the matter of *A Tale of Two Cities.* Some critics regard it as the finest of Dickens's work, reveal-**Tale of Two Cities** ing as it does his powers of description and of character-drawing without his usual exaggeration. Other critics, who regard the exaggeration of Dickens as his most characteristic quality, see in *Two Cities* only an evidence of his weakening power. It has perhaps this advantage over other works of the author, that of them we remember only the extraordinary scenes or characters, while the entire story of *Two Cities* remains with us as a finished and impressive thing. But there is also this disadvantage, that the story ends and is done with, while *Pickwick* goes on forever. We may lose sight of the heroes, but we have the conviction, as Chesterton says, that they are still on the road of adventure, that Mr. Pickwick is somewhere drinking punch or making a speech, and that Sam Weller may step out from behind the next stable and ask with a droll wink what we are up to now.

It is hardly necessary to add that our reading of Dickens must not end until we are familiar with some of his Yuletide stories, in which he gladly followed the lead of Washington Irving. The best of all his short stories is *A Christmas Carol*, which one must read but not criticize. At best it is a farce, but a glorious, care-lifting, heart-warming farce. Would there were more of the same kind!

A Criticism of Dickens. The first quality of Dickens is his extravagant humor. This was due to the fact that he was alive, so thoroughly, consciously alive that his vitality overflowed like a spring. Here, in a word, is the secret of that bubbling spirit of prodigality which occasions the criticism that Dickens produced not characters but caricatures.

The criticism is true; but it proclaims the strength of the novelist rather than his weakness. Indeed, it is in the very His Ex-   exaggeration of Dickens that his astonishing crea-aggeration   tive power is most clearly manifest. There is something primal, stupendous, in his grotesque characters which reminds us of the uncouth monsters that nature created in her sportive moods. Some readers, meeting with Bunsby, are reminded of a walrus; and who ever saw a walrus without thinking of the creature as nature's Bunsby? So with Quilp, Toots, Squeers, Pumblechook; so with giraffes, baboons, dodoes, dromedaries, — all are freaks from the æsthetic viewpoint, but think of the overflowing energy implied in creating them!

The same sense of prodigality characterized Dickens even in his sober moods, when he portrayed hundreds of human characters, and not a dead or dull person among them. To be sure they are all exaggerated; they weep too copiously, eat or drink too intemperately, laugh too uproariously for normal men; but to criticize their superabundant vitality is to criticize Beowulf or Ulysses or Hiawatha; nay, it is to criticize life itself, which at high tide is wont to overflow in heroics or absurdity. The exuberance of Pickwick, Micawber, Pecksniff,

THE GATEHOUSE AT ROCHESTER, NEAR DICKENS'S HOME

Sairey Gamp, Sam Weller and a host of others is perhaps the most normal thing about them; it is as the rattling of a safety valve, which speaks not of stagnant water but of a full head of steam. For Dickens deals with life, and you can exaggerate life as much as you please, since there is no end to either its wisdom or foolishness. Nothing but a question can be added to the silent simplicity of death.

Aside from his purpose of portraying life as he saw it, in all its strange complexity, Dickens had a twofold object in **His Motive** writing. He was a radical democrat, and he aimed **and Method** to show the immense hopefulness and compassion of Democracy on its upward way to liberty. He was also a reformer, with a profound respect for the poor, but no respect whatever for ancient laws or institutions that stood in the way of justice. The influence of his novels in establishing better schools, prisons, workhouses, is beyond measure; but we are not so much interested in his reforms as in his method, which was unique. He aimed to make men understand the oppressed, and to make a laughing stock of the oppressors; and he succeeded as no other had ever done in making literature a power in the land. Thus, the man or the law that stands defiantly against public opinion is beaten the moment you make that man or that law look like a joke; and Dickens made a huge joke of the parish beadle (as Mr. Bumble) and of many another meddlesome British institution. Moreover, he was master of this paradox: that to cure misery you must meet it with a merry heart, — this is on the principle that what the poor need is not charity but comradeship. By showing that humble folk might be as poor as the Cratchits and yet have the medicine of mirth, the divine gift of laughter, he made men rejoice with the poor even while they relieved the poverty.

As for the shortcomings of Dickens, they are so apparent that he who runs may read. We may say of him, as of Shakespeare, that his taste is questionable, that he is too **His Faults** fond of a mere show, that his style is often melodramatic, that there is hardly a fault in the whole critical category of which he is not habitually guilty. But we may say of him also that he is never petty or mean or morbid or unclean; and he could not be dull if he tried. His faults, if you analyze them, spring from precisely the same source as his virtues; that is, from his abundant vitality, from his excess of life and animal spirits. So we pardon, nay, we rejoice over him as over a boy who must throw a handspring or raise a *whillilew* when he breaks loose from school. For Dickens, when he started his triumphal progress with *Pickwick*, had a glorious sense of taking his cue from life and of breaking loose from literary traditions. In comparison with Ruskin or Thackeray he is not a good writer, but something more — a splendidly great writer. If you would limit or define his greatness, try first to marshal his array of characters, characters so vital and human that we can hardly think of them as fictitious or imaginary creatures; then remember the millions of men and women to whom he has given pure and lasting pleasure.

WILLIAM MAKEPEACE THACKERAY (1811–1863)

In fiction Thackeray stands to Dickens as Hamilton to Jefferson in the field of politics. The radical difference between the novelists is exemplified in their attitude toward the public. Thackeray, who lived among the privileged classes, spoke of "this great stupid public," and thought that the only way to get

WILLIAM MAKEPEACE THACKERAY
From a drawing by Samuel Laurence

a hearing from the common people was to "take them by the ears." He was a true Hamiltonian. Dickens had an immense sympathy for the common people, a profound respect for their elemental virtues ; and in writing for them he was, as it were, the Jefferson, the triumphant democrat of English letters. Thackeray was intellectual ; he looked at men with critical eyes, and was a realist and a pessimist. Dickens was emotional ; he looked at men with kindled imagination, judged them by the dreams they cherished in their hearts, and was a romanticist and an optimist. Both men were humorists ; but where Thackeray was delicately satirical, causing us a momentary smile, Dickens was broadly comic or farcical, winning us by hearty laughter.

Life. To one who has been trained, like Dickens, in the school of hardship it seems the most natural thing in the world to pass over into a state of affluence. It is another matter to fare sumptuously every day till luxurious habits are formed, and then be cast suddenly on one's own resources, face to face with the unexpected monster of bread and butter. This was Thackeray's experience, and it colored all his work.

A second important matter is that Thackeray had a great tenderness for children, a longing for home and homely comforts; but as a child he was sent far from his home in India, and was thrown among young barbarians in various schools, one of which, the "Charterhouse," was called the "Slaughterhouse" in the boy's letters to his mother. "There are three hundred and seventy boys in this school," he wrote; "I wish there were only three hundred and sixty-nine!" He married for love, and with great joy began housekeeping; then a terrible accident happened, his wife was taken to an insane asylum, and for the rest of his life Thackeray was a wanderer amid the empty splendors of clubs and hotels.

These two experiences did not break Thackeray, but they bowed him. They help to explain the languor, the melancholy, the gentle pessimism, as if life had no more sunrises, of which we are vaguely conscious in reading *The Virginians* or *The Newcomes*.

Thackeray was born (1811) in Calcutta, of a family of English "nabobs" who had accumulated wealth and influence as factors or civil officers. At the death of his father, who was a judge in Bengal, the child was sent to England to be educated. **Early Years** Here is a significant incident of the journey:

" Our ship touched at an island, where my black servant took me a walk over rocks and hills till we passed a garden, where we saw a man walking. ' That is Bonaparte,' said the black; ' he eats three sheep every day, and all the children he can lay hands on.' "

Napoleon was then safely imprisoned at St. Helena; but his shadow, as of a terrible ogre, was still dark over Europe.

Thackeray's education, at the Charterhouse School and at Cambridge, was neither a happy nor a profitable experience, as we judge from his unflattering picture of English school life in *Pendennis*. He had a strongly artistic bent, and after leaving college studied art in Germany and France. Presently he lost his fortune by gambling and bad investments, and was confronted by the necessity of earning his living. He tried the law, but gave it up because, as he said, it had no soul. He tried illustrating, having a small talent for comic drawings, and sought various civil appointments in vain. As a last resource he turned to the magazines, wrote satires, sketches of travel, burlesques of popular novelists, and, fighting all the time against his habit of idleness, slowly but surely won his way.

His first notable work, *Vanity Fair* (1847), won a few readers; and the critics' judgment that it was " a book written by a gentleman for gentlemen " was the foundation of Thackeray's repu-

Literary Labor   tation as a writer for the upper classes. Other notable novels followed, *Henry Esmond, Pendennis, The New-comes, The Virginians*, and two series of literary and historical essays called *English Humorists* and *The Four Georges*. The latter were delivered as lectures in a successful tour of England and America. Needless to say, Thackeray hated lecturing and publicity; he was driven to his " dollar-hunting " by necessity.

In 1860 his fame was firmly established, and he won his first financial success by taking charge of the *Cornhill Magazine*, which prospered greatly in his hands. He did not long enjoy his new-found comfort, for he died in 1863. His early sketches had been satirical in spirit, his first novels largely so; but his last novels and his Cornhill essays were written in a different spirit, — not kinder, for Thackeray's heart was always right, but broader, wiser, more patient of human nature, and more hopeful.

In view of these later works some critics declare that Thackeray's best novel was never written. His stories were produced not joyously but laboriously, to earn his living; and when leisure came at last, then came death also, and the work was over.

Works of Thackeray. It would be flying in the face of all the critics to suggest that the beginner might do well to postpone the famous novels of Thackeray, and to meet the author at his best, or cheerfulest, in such forgotten works as the *Book of Ballads* and *The Rose and the Ring*. The latter is a kind of fairy story, with a poor little good princess, a rich little bad princess, a witch of a godmother, and such villainous characters as Hedzoff and Gruffanuff. It was written for some children whom Thackeray loved, and is almost the only book of his which leaves the impression that the author found any real pleasure in writing it.

If one must begin with a novel, then *Henry Esmond* (1852) is the book. This is an historical novel; the scene is laid in the eighteenth century, during the reign of Queen Anne; and it differs from most other historical novels in this important **Henry** respect: the author knows his ground thoroughly, **Esmond** is familiar not only with political events but with the thoughts, ideals, books, even the literary style of the age which he describes. The hero of the novel, Colonel Esmond, is represented as telling his own story; he speaks as a gentleman spoke in those days, telling us about the politicians, soldiers, ladies and literary men of his time, with frank exposure of their manners or morals. As a realistic portrayal of an age gone by, not only of its thoughts but of the very language in which those thoughts were expressed, *Esmond* is the most remarkable novel of its kind in our language. It is a prodigy of realism, and it is written in a charming prose style.

One must add frankly that *Esmond* is not an inspiring work, that the atmosphere is gloomy, and the plot a disappointment. The hero, after ten years of devotion to a woman, ends his romance by happily marrying with her mother. Any reader could have told him that this is what he ought to have done, or tried to do, in the beginning; but Thackeray's heroes will never take the reader's good advice. In this respect they are quite human.

The two social satires of Thackeray are *Vanity Fair* (1847) and *The History of Arthur Pendennis* (1849). The former **Vanity Fair** takes its title from that fair described in *Pilgrim's Progress*, where all sorts of cheats are exposed for sale; and Thackeray makes his novel a moralizing exposition of the shams of society. The slight action of the story revolves about two unlovely heroines, the unprincipled Becky Sharp and the spineless Amelia. We call them both unlovely, though Thackeray tries hard to make us admire his tearful Amelia and to detest his more interesting Becky. Meeting these two contrasting characters is a variety of fools and snobs, mostly well-drawn, all carefully analyzed to show the weakness or villainy that is in them.

One interesting but unnoticed thing about these minor characters is that they all have their life-size prototypes in the
novels of Dickens. Thackeray's characters, as he explains in
his preface, are "mere puppets," who must move when he
pulls the strings. Dickens does not have to explain that his
characters are men and women who do very much as they
please. That is, perhaps, the chief difference between the
two novelists.

Pendennis is a more readable novel than *Vanity Fair* in this
respect, that its interest centers in one character rather than in
a variety of knaves or fools. Thackeray takes a
youthful hero, follows him through school and later
life, and shows the steady degeneration of a man who is governed not by vicious but by selfish impulses. From beginning
to end *Pendennis* is a penetrating ethical study (like George
Eliot's *Romola*), and the story is often interrupted while we
listen to the author's moralizing. To some readers this is an
offense; to others it is a pleasure, since it makes them better
acquainted with the mind and heart of Thackeray, the gentlest
of Victorian moralists.

Pendennis

The last notable works of Thackeray are like afterthoughts.
The Virginians continues the story of Colonel Esmond, and
The Newcomes recounts the later fortunes of Arthur
Pendennis. *The Virginians* has two or three splendid scenes, and some critics regard *The Newcomes* as the finest expression of the author's genius; but both works, which
appeared in the leisurely form of monthly instalments, are too
languid in action for sustained interest. We grow acquainted
with certain characters, and are heartily glad when they make
their exit; perhaps someone else will come, some adventurer
from the road or the inn, to relieve the dullness. The door
opens, and in comes the bore again to take another leave.
That is realism, undoubtedly; and Laura Pendennis is as realistic as the mumps, which one may catch a second time. The
atmosphere of both novels — indeed, of all Thackeray's greater

After-
thoughts

works, with the exception of *English Humorists* and *The Four Georges* — is rather depressing. One gets the impression that life among "the quality" is a dreary experience, hardly worth the effort of living.

Thackeray : a Criticism. It is significant that Thackeray's first work appeared in a college leaflet called "The Snob," and that it showed a talent for satire. In his earlier stories he plainly followed his natural bent, for his *Vanity Fair, Barry*

CHARTERHOUSE SCHOOL

After a rare engraving by J. Rogers from the drawing made by Thomas H. Shepherd at the time Thackeray was a student there

Lyndon (a story of a scoundrelly adventurer) and several minor works are all satires on the general snobbery of society. This tendency of the author reached a climax in 1848, when he wrote *The Book of Snobs*. It is still an entertaining book, witty, and with a kind of merciless fairness about its cruel passages ; yet some readers will remember what the author himself said later, that he was something of a snob himself to write such a book. The chief trouble with the half of his work is that he was so obsessed with the idea of snobbery that he did injustice to humanity, or rather to his countrymen; for Thackeray

was very English, and interest in his characters depends largely
on familiarity with the life he describes. His pictures of English
servants, for instance, are wonderfully deft, though one might
wish that he had drawn them with a more sympathetic pencil.

In the later part of his life the essential kindness of the
man came to the surface, but still was he hampered by his expe-
The Personal rience and his philosophy. His experience was that
Element   life is too big to be grasped, too mysterious to be
understood; therefore he faced life doubtfully, with a mixture
of timidity and respect, as in *Henry Esmond*. His philosophy
was that every person is at heart an egoist, is selfish in spite
of himself; therefore is every man or woman unhappy, because
selfishness is the eternal enemy of happiness. This is the lesson written large in *Pendennis*. He lived in the small world of
his own class, while the great world of Dickens — the world of
the common people, with their sympathy, their eternal hopefulness, their enjoyment of whatever good they find in life —
passed unnoticed outside his club windows. He conceived it to
be the business of a novelist to view the world with his own
eyes, to describe it as he saw it; and it was not his fault that
his world was a small one. Fate was answerable for that. So
far as he went, Thackeray did his work admirably, portraying
the few virtues and the many shams of his set with candor
and sincerity. Though he used satire freely (and satire is a
two-edged weapon), his object was never malicious or vindic-
tive but corrective; he aimed to win or drive men to virtue
by exposing the native ugliness of vice.

The result of his effort may be summed up as follows:
Thackeray is a novelist for the few who can enjoy his accurate
but petty views of society, and his cultivated prose style. He
is not very cheerful; he does not seek the blue flower that
grows in every field, or the gold that is at every rainbow's end,
or the romance that hides in every human heart whether of
rich or poor. Therefore are the young not conspicuous among
his followers.

Mary Ann Evans, "George Eliot" (1819–1880)

More than other Victorian story-tellers George Eliot regarded her work with great seriousness as a means of public instruction. Her purpose was to show that human life is effective only as it follows its sense of duty, and that society is as much in need of the moral law as of daily bread. Other novelists moralized more or less, Thackeray especially; but George Eliot made the teaching of morality her chief business.

Life. In the work as in the face of George Eliot there is a certain masculine quality which is apt to mislead one who reads *Adam Bede* or studies a portrait of the author. Even those who knew her well, and who tried to express the charm of her personality, seem to have overlooked the fact that they were describing a woman. For example, a friend wrote:

" Everything in her aspect and presence was in keeping with the bent of her soul. The deeply lined face, the too marked and massive features, were united with an air of delicate refinement, which in one way was the more impressive, because it seemed to proceed so entirely from within. Nay, the inward beauty would sometimes quite transform the outward harshness; there would be moments when the thin hands that entwined themselves in their eagerness, the earnest figure that bowed forward to speak and hear, the deep gaze moving from one face to another with a grave appeal, — all these seemed the transparent symbols that showed the presence of a wise, benignant soul."

That is very good, but somehow it is not feminine. So the impression has gone forth that George Eliot was a " strong-minded " woman;
A Clinging Vine but that is far from the truth. One might emphasize her affectionate nature, her timidity, her lack of confidence in her own judgment; but the essence of the matter is this, that so dependent was she on masculine support that she was always idealizing some man, and looking up to him as a superior being. In short, she was one of " the clinging kind." Though some may regard this as traditional nonsense, it was nevertheless the most characteristic quality of the woman with whom we are dealing.

Mary Ann Evans, or Marian as she was called, was born (1819) and spent her childhood in Shakespeare's county of Warwickshire. Her father (whose portrait she has faintly drawn in the characters

E

of Adam Bede and Caleb Garth) was a strong, quiet man, a farmer and land agent, who made a companion of his daughter rather than **Her Girlhood** of his son, the two being described more or less faithfully in the characters of Maggie and Tom Tulliver in *The Mill on the Floss*. At twelve years of age she was sent to a boarding school; at fifteen her mother died, and she was brought home to manage her father's house. The rest of her education — which included music and a reading knowledge of German, Italian and Greek — was obtained by solitary study at intervals of rest from domestic work. That the intervals were neither long nor frequent may be inferred from the fact that her work included not only her father's accounts and the thousand duties of housekeeping but also the managing of a poultry yard, the making of butter, and other farm or dairy matters which at that time were left wholly to women.

GEORGE ELIOT

From a portrait painted in Rome by
M. d'Albert Durade, and now in Geneva

The first marked change in her life came at the age of twenty-two, when the household removed to Coventry, and Miss Evans was there brought in contact with the family of a wealthy ribbon-maker named Bray. He was a man of some culture, and the atmosphere of his house, with its numerous guests, was decidedly skeptical. To Miss Evans, brought up in a home ruled by early Methodist ideals of piety, the change was a little startling. Soon she was listening to glib evolutionary theories that settled everything from an earthworm to a cosmos; next she was eagerly reading such unbaked works as Bray's *Philosophy of Necessity* and the essays of certain young scientists who, without knowledge of either philosophy or religion, were cocksure of their ability to provide "modern" substitutes for both at an hour's notice.

Miss Evans went over rather impulsively to the crude skepticism of her friends; then, finding no soul or comfort in their theories, she invented for herself a creed of duty and morality, without however tracing either to its origin. She was naturally a religious woman, and there is no evidence that she found her new creed very satisfactory. Indeed, her melancholy and the gloom of her novels are both traceable to the loss of her early religious ideals.

A trip abroad (1849) was followed by some editorial work on *The Westminster Review*, then the organ of the freethinkers. This in turn **Her Union with Lewes** led to her association with Herbert Spencer, John Stuart Mill and other liberals, and to her union with George Henry Lewes in 1854. Of that union little need be said except this: though it lacked the law and the sacrament, it seems to have been in other respects a fair covenant which was honestly kept by both parties.[1]

Encouraged by Lewes she began to write fiction. Her first attempt, "Amos Barton," was an excellent short story, and in 1859 she produced her first novel, *Adam Bede*, being then about forty years old. The great success of this work had the unusual effect of discouraging the author. She despaired of her ability, and began to agonize, as she said, over her work; but her material was not yet exhausted, and in *The Mill on the Floss* and *Silas Marner* she repeated her triumph.

The rest of her life seems a matter of growth or of atrophy, according to your point of view. She grew more scientific, as she fan- **On a Pedestal** cied, but she lost the freshness and inspiration of her earlier novels. The reason seems to be that her head was turned by her fame as a moralist and exponent of culture; so she forgot that she "was born to please," and attempted something else for which she had no particular ability: an historical novel in *Romola*, a drama in *The Spanish Gypsy*, a theory of social reform in *Felix Holt*, a study of the Hebrew race in *Daniel Deronda*, a book of elephantine gambols in *The Opinions of Theophrastus Such*. More and more she "agonized" over these works, and though each of them contained some scene or passage of rare power, it was evident even to her admirers that the pleasing novelist of the earlier days had been sacrificed to the moral philosopher.

[1] Lewes was separated from his first wife, from whom he was unable to obtain a legal divorce. This was the only obstacle to a regular marriage, and after facing the obstacle for a time the couple decided to ignore it. The moral element in George Eliot's works is due largely, no doubt, to her own moral sense; but it was greatly influenced by the fact that, in her union with Lewes, she had placed herself in a false position and was morally on the defensive against society.

The death of Lewes (1878) made an end, as she believed, of
all earthly happiness. For twenty-four years he had been husband,
She Renews friend and literary adviser, encouraging her talent, shield-
Her Youth ing her from every hostile criticism. Left suddenly alone
in the world, she felt like an abandoned child; her writing stopped,
and her letters echoed the old gleeman's song, "All is gone, both life
and light." Then she surprised everybody by marrying an American
banker, many years her junior, who had been an intimate friend of
the Lewes household. Once more she found the world "intensely
interesting," for at sixty she was the same clinging vine, the same
hero-worshiper, as at sixteen. The marriage occurred in 1880, and
her death the same year. An elaborate biography, interesting but too
fulsome, was written by her husband, John Walter Cross.

Works. George Eliot's first works in fiction were the
magazine stories which she published later as *Scenes of Cleri-
cal Life* (1858). These were produced comparatively late in
life, and they indicate both originality and maturity, as if the
author had a message of her own, and had pondered it well
before writing it. That message, as reflected in "Amos Barton"
and "Janet's Repentance," may be summarized in four cardinal principles : that duty is the supreme law of life ; that the
humblest life is as interesting as the most exalted, since
both are subject to the same law; that our daily choices have
deep moral significance, since they all react on character and
their total result is either happiness or misery ; and that there
is no possible escape from the reward or punishment that is
due to one's individual action.

Such is the message of the author's first work. In its stern
insistence on the moral quality of life and of every human
action, it distinguishes George Eliot from all other fiction
writers of the period.

In her first three novels she repeats the same message with
more detail, and with a gleam of humor here and there to light
up the gloomy places. *Adam Bede* (1859) has been called a
story of early Methodism, but in reality it is a story of moral
principles which work their inevitable ends among simple

country people. The same may be said of *The Mill on the Floss* (1860) and of *Silas Marner* (1861). The former is as **Her Best Novels** interesting to readers of George Eliot as *Copperfield* is to readers of Dickens, because much of it is a reflection of a personal experience; but the latter work, having more unity, more story interest and more cheerfulness, is a better novel with which to begin our acquaintance with the author.

The scene of all these novels is laid in the country; the characters are true to life, and move naturally in an almost perfect setting. One secret of their success is that they deal with people whom the author knew well, and with scenes in which she was as much at home as Dickens was in the London streets. Each of the novels, notwithstanding its faulty or melancholy conclusion, leaves an impression

GRIFF HOUSE, GEORGE ELIOT'S EARLY HOME IN WARWICKSHIRE

so powerful that we gladly, and perhaps uncritically, place it among the great literary works of the Victorian era.

Of the later novels one cannot speak so confidently. They move some critics to enthusiasm, and put others to sleep. **Later Works** Thus, *Daniel Deronda* has some excellent passages, and Gwendolen is perhaps the best-drawn of all George Eliot's characters; but for many readers the novel is spoiled by scientific jargon, by essay writing on the Jews and other matters of which the author knew little or nothing at first hand. In *Middlemarch* she returned to the scenes with which she was familiar and produced a novel which some critics rank very high, while others point to its superfluous essays and its proneness to moralizing instead of telling a story.

Romola is another labored novel, a study of Italy during the Renaissance, and a profound ethical lesson. If you can read this work without criticizing its Italian views, you may find in the characters of Tito and Romola, one selfish and the other generous, the best example of George Eliot's moral method, which is to show the cumulative effect on character of everyday choices or actions. You will find also a good story, one of the best that the author told. But if you read *Romola* as an historical novel, with some knowledge of Italy and the Renaissance, you may decide that George Eliot — though she slaved at this novel until, as she said, it made an old woman of her — did not understand the people or the country which she tried to describe. She portrayed life not as she had seen and known and loved it, but as she found it reflected at second hand in the works of other writers.

Romola

The Quality of George Eliot. Of the moral quality of George Eliot we have already said enough. To our summary of her method this should be added, that she tried to make each of her characters not individual but typical. In other words, if Tito came finally to grief, and Adam arrived at a state of gloomy satisfaction (there is no real happiness in George Eliot's world), it was not because Tito and Adam lived in different times or circumstances, but because both were subject to the same eternal laws. Each must have gone to his own place whether he lived in wealth or poverty, in Florence or England, in the fifteenth or the nineteenth century. The moral law is universal and unchanging; it has no favorites, and makes no exceptions. It is more like the old Greek conception of Nemesis, or the Anglo-Saxon conception of Wyrd, or Fate, than anything else you will find in modern fiction.

In this last respect George Eliot again differs radically from her contemporaries. In her gloomy view of life as an unanswerable puzzle she is like Thackeray; but where Thackeray offers a cultured resignation, a gentlemanly making the best of a bad case, George Eliot advocates self-sacrifice for the good of others. In her portrayal of weak or sinful characters she is quite as compassionate as Dickens, and more thoughtfully **Fate and** charitable ; for where Dickens sometimes makes **Self-sacrifice** light of misery, and relieves it by the easy expedient of good dinners and all-around comfort for saints and sinners, George Eliot remembers the broken moral law and the suffering of the innocent for the guilty. Behind every one of her characters that does wrong follows an avenging fate, waiting the moment to exact the full penalty ; and before every character that does right hovers a vision of sacrifice and redemption.

Her real philosophy, therefore, was quite different from that which her scientific friends formulated for her, and was not modern but ancient as the hills. On the one hand, she never quite freed herself from the old pagan conception of Nemesis, or Fate ; on the other, her early Methodist training entered deep into her soul and made her mindful of the Cross that forever towers above humanity.

Other Victorian Novelists

We have followed literary custom rather than individual judgment in studying Dickens, Thackeray and George Eliot as the typical Victorian novelists. On Dickens, as the most original genius of the age, most people are agreed ; but the rank of the other two is open to question. There are critics besides Swinburne who regard Charlotte Brontë as a greater genius than George Eliot ; and many uncritical readers find more pleasure or profit in the Barchester novels of Anthony Trollope than in anything written by Thackeray. It may even be that the three or four leading novels of the age were none of them written by the novelists in question ; but it is still essential to know their works if only for these reasons : that they greatly influenced other story-tellers of the period, and that they furnish us a standard by which to judge all modern fiction.

To treat the many Victorian novelists adequately would in itself require a volume. We shall note here only a few leading figures, naming in each case a novel or two which may serve as an invitation to a better acquaintance with their authors.

The Brontë sisters, Charlotte and Emily, made a tremendous sensation in England when, from their retirement, they sent out certain works of such passionate intensity that readers who had long been familiar with novels were startled into renewed attention. Reading these works now we recognize the genius of the writers, but we recognize also a morbid, unwholesome quality, which is a reflection not of English life but of the personal and unhappy temperament of two girls who looked on life first as a gorgeous romance and then as a gloomy tragedy.

CHARLOTTE BRONTË

Charlotte Brontë (1816–1855) was perhaps the more gifted of the two sisters, and her best-known works are *Jane Eyre* and *Villette*. The date of the latter novel (1853) was made noteworthy by the masterpiece of another woman novelist, Mrs. Elizabeth Gaskell (1810–1865), who was the exact opposite of the Brontë sisters, — serene, well-balanced, and with a fund of delicious humor. All these qualities and more appeared in *Cranford* (1853), a series of sketches of country life (first contributed to Dickens's *Household Words*) which together form one of the most charming stories produced during the Victorian era. The same author wrote a few other novels and an admirable *Life of Charlotte Brontë*.

Charles Reade (1814–1884) was a follower of Dickens in his earlier novels, such as *Peg Woffington*; but he made one **Charles** notable departure when he wrote *The Cloister and* **Reade** *the Hearth* (1861). This is a story of student life and vagabond life in Europe, in the stirring times that followed the invention of printing. The action moves rapidly; many different characters appear; the scene shifts from Holland across Europe to Italy, and back again; adventures of a startling kind meet the hero at every stage of his foot journey. It is a stirring tale, remarkably well told; so much will every uncritical reader gladly acknowledge. Moreover, there are critics who, after studying *The Cloister and the Hearth*, rank it with the best historical novels in all literature.

Anthony Trollope (1815–1882) began as a follower of Thackeray, but **Trollope** in the immense range of his characters and incidents he soon outstripped

MRS. ELIZABETH GASKELL
From the portrait by George Richmond, R.A.

his master. Perhaps his best work is *Barchester Towers* (1857), one of a series of novels which picture with marvelous fidelity the life of a cathedral town in England.

Another novelist who followed Thackeray, and then changed his allegiance to Dickens, was Bulwer Lytton (1803–1873). He was essentially an imitator, a follower of the market, and before Thackeray and Dickens were famous he had followed almost every important English novelist from Mrs. Radcliffe to Walter Scott. Two of his historical novels, *Rienzi* and

The Last Days of Pompeii, may be mildly recommended. The rest are of the popular and somewhat trashy kind; critics jeer at them, and the public buys them in large numbers.

One of the most charming books of the Victorian age was produced by Richard Blackmore (1825–1900). He wrote several novels, some of them of excellent quality, but they were all overshadowed by his beautiful old romance of *Lorna Doone* (1869). It is hard to over-praise such a story, wholesome and sweet as a breath from the moors, and the critic's praise will be unnecessary if the reader only opens the book. It should be read, with *Cranford*, if one reads nothing else of Victorian fiction.

RICHARD DODDRIDGE BLACKMORE

Two other notable romances of a vanished age came from the hand of Charles Kingsley (1819–1875). He produced many works in poetry and prose, but his fame now rests upon *Hypatia*, *Westward Ho!* and a few stories for children. *Hypatia* (1853) is an interesting novel dealing with the conflict of pagan and Christian ideals in the early centuries. *Westward Ho!* (1855) is a stirring narrative of seafaring and adventure in the days of Elizabeth. It has been described as a "stunning" boys' book, and it would prove an absorbing story for any reader who likes adventure were it not marred by one serious fault. The author's personal beliefs and his desire to glorify certain Elizabethan adventurers lead him to pronounce judgment of a somewhat wholesale kind. He treats one religious party of the period to a golden halo, and the other to a lash of scorpions; and this is apt to alienate many readers who else would gladly follow Sir Amyas Leigh on his gallant ventures in the New World or on the Spanish Main. Kingsley had a rare talent for writing for children (his heart never grew old), and his *Heroes* and *Water Babies* are still widely read as bedtime stories.

Of the later Victorian novelists, chief among them being Meredith, Hardy and Stevenson, little may be said here, as they are much too near us to judge of their true place in the long perspective of English literature. Meredith, with the analytical temper and the disconnected style of Browning, is for mature readers, not for young people. Hardy has decided power, but is too hopelessly pessimistic for anybody's comfort,— except in his earlier works, which have a romantic

ROBERT LOUIS STEVENSON
From a photograph

charm that brightens the obscurity of his later philosophy.

In Robert Louis Stevenson (1850–1894) we have the spirit of romance personified. His novels, such as *Kidnapped* and *David Balfour*, are stories of adventure written in a very attractive style; but he is more widely known, among young people at least, by his charming *Child's Garden of Verses* and his *Treasure Island* (1883). This last is a kind of dime-novel of pirates and buried treasure. If one is to read

Stevenson

stories of that kind, there is no better place to begin than with this masterpiece of Stevenson. Other works by the same versatile author are the novels, *Master of Ballantrae*, *Weir of Hermiston* and *Dr. Jekyll and Mr. Hyde* ; various collections of essays, such as *Virginibus Puerisque* and *Familiar Studies of Men and Books* ; and some rather thin sketches of journeying called *An Inland Voyage* and *Travels with a Donkey*.

The cheery spirit of Stevenson, who bravely fought a losing battle with disease, is evident in everything he wrote ; and it was the author's spirit, quite as much as his romantic tales or fine prose style, that won for him a large and enthusiastic following. Of all the later Victorians he seems, at the present time, to have the widest circle of cultivated readers and to exercise the strongest influence on our writers of fiction.

III. VICTORIAN ESSAYISTS AND HISTORIANS

There is rich reading in Victorian essays, which reflect not only the practical affairs of the age but also the ideals that inspire every great movement whether in history or literature. For example, the intense religious interests of the period, the growth of the Nonconformists or Independents, the Oxford movement, which aimed to define the historic position of the English Church, the chill of doubt and the glow of renewed faith in face of the apparent conflict between the old religion and the new science, — all these were brilliantly reflected by excellent writers, among whom Martineau, Newman and Maurice stand out prominently. The deep thought, the serene spirit and the fine style of these men are unsurpassed in Victorian prose.

Somewhat apart from their age stood a remarkable group of historians — Hallam, Freeman, Green, Gardiner, Symonds and others no less praiseworthy — who changed the whole conception of history from a record of political or military events to a profound study of human society in all its activities. In another typical group were the critics, Pater, Bagehot, Hutton, Leslie

Stephen, who have given deeper meaning and enlarged pleasure to the study of literature. In a fourth group were the scientists — Darwin, Wallace, Lyell, Mivart, Tyndall, Mill, Spencer, Huxley, and their followers — some of whom aimed not simply to increase our knowledge but to use the essay, as others used the novel, to portray some new scene in the old comedy of human life. Darwin was a great and, therefore, a modest man; but some of his disciples were sadly lacking in humor. Spencer and Mill especially wrote with colossal self-confidence, as if the world no longer wore its veil of mystery. They remind us, curiously, that while poetry endures forever, nothing on earth is more subject to change and error than so-called scientific truth.

It is impossible in a small volume to do justice to so many writers, reflecting nature or humanity from various angles, and **Typical Writers** sometimes insisting that a particular angle was the only one from which a true view could be obtained. Some rigorous selection is necessary; and we name here for special study Macaulay, Carlyle, Ruskin, who are commonly regarded as the typical Victorian essayists. This selection does not mean, however, that some other group might not be quite as representative of their age and nation. Our chosen authors stand not for Victorian thought but only for certain interesting phases thereof. Macaulay, the busy man of affairs, voiced the pride of his generation in British traditions. Carlyle lived aloof, grumbling at democracy, denouncing its shams, calling it to repentance. Ruskin, a child of fortune, was absorbed in art till the burden of the world oppressed him; whereupon he gave his money to the cause of social reform and went himself among the poor to share with them whatever wealth of spirit he possessed. These three men, utterly unlike in character, were as one in their endeavor to make modern literature a power wherewith to uplift humanity. They illustrate, better even than poets or novelists, the characteristic moral earnestness of the Victorian era.

Thomas Babington Macaulay (1800–1859)

To many readers the life of Macaulay is more interesting than any of his books. For the details of that brilliantly successful life, which fairly won and richly deserved its success, the student is referred to Trevelyan's fine biography. We record here only such personal matters as may help to explain the exuberant spirit of Macaulay's literary work.

THOMAS BABINGTON MACAULAY

Life. One notes first of all the man's inheritance. The Norse element predominated in him, for the name Macaulay (son of Aulay) is a late form of the Scandinavian *Olafson*. His mother was a brilliant woman of Quaker descent; his father, at one time governor of the Sierra Leone Colony in Africa, was a business man who gained a fortune in trade, and who spent the whole of it in helping to free the slaves. In consequence, when Macaulay left college he faced the immediate problem of supporting himself and his family, a hard matter, which he handled not only with his customary success but also with characteristic enthusiasm.

Next we note Macaulay's personal endowment, his gift of rapid reading, his marvelous memory which suggests Coleridge and Cotton Mather. He read everything from Plato to the trashiest novel, and after reading a book could recall practically the whole of it after a lapse of twenty years. To this photographic memory we are indebted for the wealth of quotation, allusion and anecdote which brightens almost every page of his writings.

After a brilliant career at college Macaulay began the study of law. At twenty-five he jumped into prominence by a magazine essay on Milton, and after that his progress was uninterrupted. He was repeatedly elected to Parliament; he was appointed legal adviser **His Brilliant** to the Supreme Council of India, in which position he **Career** acquired the knowledge that appears in his essays on Clive and Hastings; he became Secretary for War, and was elevated to the peerage as Baron Macaulay of Rothley. It was said of him at that time that he was "the only man whom England ever made a lord for the power of his pen."

The last thing we note, because it was to Macaulay of least moment, is his literary work. With the exception of the *History of* **His** *England* his writing was done at spare moments, as a **Recreation** relaxation from what he considered more important labors. In this respect, of writing for pleasure in the midst of practical affairs, he resembles the Elizabethan rather than the Victorian authors.

While at work on his masterpiece Macaulay suddenly faltered, worn out by too much work. He died on Christmas Day (1859) and was buried in the place which he liked best to visit, the Poets' Corner of Westminster Abbey. From the day on which he attracted notice by his Milton essay he had never once lost his hold on the attention of England. Gladstone summed up the matter in oratorical fashion when he said, "Full-orbed Macaulay was seen above the horizon; and full-orbed, after thirty-five years of constantly emitted splendor, he sank below it." But Macaulay's final comment, "Well, I have had a happy life," is more suggestive of the man and his work.

Works of Macaulay. Macaulay's poems, which he regarded as of no consequence, are practically all in the ballad style. Among them are various narratives from French or English history, such as "The Battle of Ivry" and "The Armada," and a few others which made a popular little book when they were published as *Lays of Ancient Rome* (1842). The prime favorite not only of the *Lays* but of all Macaulay's works is "Horatius Cocles," or "Horatius at the Bridge." Those who read its stirring lines should know that Macaulay intended it not as a modern ballad but as an example of ancient methods of teaching history. According to Niebuhr the early history of Rome was written in the form of popular ballads; and

Macaulay attempted to reproduce a few of these historical documents in the heroic style that roused a Roman audience of long ago to pride and love of country.

The essays of Macaulay appeared in the magazines of that day ; but though official England acclaimed their brilliancy and **The Essays** flooded their author with invitations to dine, nobody seemed to think of them as food for ordinary readers till a Philadelphia publisher collected a few of them into a book, which sold in America like a good novel. That was in 1841, and not till two years had passed did a London publisher gain courage to issue the *Critical and Historical Essays*, a book which vindicated the taste of readers of that day by becoming immensely popular.

The charm of such a book is evident in the very first essay, on Milton. Here is no critic, airing his rules cr making his dry talk palatable by a few quotations ; here is a live man pleading for another man whom he considers one of the greatest figures in history. Macaulay may be mistaken, possibly, but he is going to make you doff your hat to a hero before he is done ; so he speaks eloquently not only of Milton but of the classics on which Milton fed, of the ideals and struggles of his age, of the Commonwealth and the Restoration, — of everything which may catch your attention and then focus it on one Titanic figure battling like Samson among the Philistines. It may be that your sympathies are with the Philistines rather than with Samson ; but presently you stop objecting and are carried along by the author's eloquence as by a torrent. His style is the combined style of novelist and public speaker, the one striving to make his characters real, the other bound to make his subject interesting.

That is Macaulay's way in all his essays. They are seldom wholly right in their judgments ; they are so often one-sided that the author declared in later life he would burn them all if he could ; but they are all splendid, all worth reading, not simply for their matter but for their style and for the wealth of allusion with which Macaulay makes his subject vital and interesting. Among the best of the literary essays are those on Bunyan, Addison, Bacon, Johnson, Goldsmith and Byron ; among the historical essays one may sample Macaulay's variety in Lord Clive, Frederick the Great, Machiavelli and Mirabeau. Careful readers may note a difference between these literary and historical essays. Those on Bunyan, Johnson and Goldsmith, for example (written originally for the *Encyclopædia Britannica*), are more finished and more careful of statement than others in which the author talks freely, sharing without measure or restraint "the heaped-up treasures of his memory."

Macaulay began to write his *History of England* with the declaration that he would cover the century and a half follow-

History of   ing the accession of James II (1685), and that he
England   would make his story as interesting as any novel.

Only the latter promise was fulfilled. His five volumes, the labor of more than a decade, cover only sixteen years of English history ; but these are pictured with such minuteness and such splendor that we can hardly imagine anyone brave enough to attempt to finish the record in a single lifetime.

Of this masterpiece of Macaulay we may confidently say three things : that for many years it was the most popular historical work in our language ; that by its brilliant style and absorbing interest it deserved its popularity, as literature if not as history ; and that, though it contains its share of error and more than its share of Whig partisanship, it has probably as few serious faults as any other history which attempts to cover the immense field of the political, social and intellectual life of a nation. Read, for example, one of the introductory chapters (the third is excellent) which draws such a picture of England in the days of the Stuarts as no other historian has ever attempted. When you have finished that chapter, with its wealth of picturesque detail, you may be content to read Macaulay simply for the pleasure he gives you, and go to some other historian for accurate information.

H

Thomas Carlyle (1795–1881)

There is little harmony of opinion concerning Carlyle, criticism of the man being divided between praise and disparagement. If you are to read only one of his works, it is perhaps advisable to avoid all biographies at first and to let the *Essay on Burns* or *Heroes and Hero Worship* make its own impression. But if you intend to read more widely, some knowledge of Carlyle's personal history is essential in order to furnish the grain of salt with which most of his opinions must be taken.

THOMAS CARLYLE

From engraving by Sartain from a daguerrotype

Life. In the village of Ecclefechan Carlyle was born in 1795, the year before Burns's death. His father was a stone-mason, an honest man of caustic tongue; his mother, judged by her son's account, was one of nature's noblewomen. The love of his mother and a proud respect for his father were the two sentiments in Carlyle that went with him unchanged through a troubled and oft-complaining life.

Of his tearful school days in Annandale and of his wretched years at Edinburgh University we have glimpses in *Sartor Resartus*. In **His Wrestlings** the chapters of the same book entitled "The Everlasting Nay" and "The Everlasting Yea" is a picture of the conflict between doubt and faith in the stormy years when Carlyle was finding himself. He taught school, and hated it; he abandoned the ministry, for which his parents had intended him; he resolved on a literary life, and did hack work to earn his bread. All the while he wrestled with his gloomy temper or with the petty demons of dyspepsia, which he was wont to magnify into giant doubts and despairs.

In 1826 he married Jane Welsh, and went to live in a house she had inherited at Craigenputtock, or Hill of the Hawks. There on a lonely moorland farm he spent six or seven years, writing books which few cared to read; and there Emerson appeared one day (" He came **Carlyle and** and went like an angel," said the Carlyles) with the heart- **Emerson** ening news that the neglected writings were winning a great audience in America. The letters of Carlyle and Emerson, as edited by Charles Eliot Norton, are among the pleasantest results of Carlyle's whole career.

Carlyle's wife was a brilliant but nervous woman with literary gifts of her own. She had always received attention; she expected and **Mrs.** probably deserved admiration; but so did Carlyle, who **Carlyle** expected also to be made the center of all solicitude when he called heaven and earth to witness against democracy, crowing roosters, weak tea and other grievous afflictions. After her death (in London, 1866) he was plunged into deepest grief. In his *Reminiscences* and *Letters* he fairly deifies his wife, calling her his queen, his star, his light and joy of life, and portrays a companionship as of two mortals in a Paradise without a serpent. All that is doubtless as it should be, in a romance; but the unfortunate publication of Mrs. Carlyle's letters and journals introduced a jarring note of reality. A jungle of contro- versial writings has since grown up around the domestic relations of the Carlyles, — impertinent, deplorable writings, which serve no purpose but to make us cry, " Enough, let them rest in peace! " Both had sharp tongues, and probably both were often sorry.

From the moors the Carlyles went to London and settled for the remainder of their lives in a house in Cheyne Row, in the suburb of Chelsea. There Carlyle slowly won recognition, his success being founded on his *French Revolution*. Invitations began to pour in upon him; great men visited and praised him, and his fame spread as **Work in** " the sage of Chelsea." Then followed his *Cromwell* and **London** *Frederick the Great*, the latter completed after years of complaining labor which made wreck of home happiness. And then came a period of unusual irritation, to which we owe, in part at least, Carlyle's railings against progress and his deplorable criticism of England's great men and women, — poor little Browning, animalcular De Quincey, rabbit-brained Newman, sawdustish Mill, chattering

George Eliot, ghastly-shrieky Shelley, once-enough Lamb, stinted-scanty Wordsworth, poor thin fool Darwin and his book (*The Origin of Species*, of which Carlyle confessed he never read a page) which was wonderful as an example of the stupidity of mankind.

Such criticisms were reserved for Carlyle's private memoirs. The world knew him only by his books, and revered him as a great and good man. He died in 1881, and of the thousand notices which appeared in English or American periodicals of that year there is hardly one that does not overflow with praise.

CARLYLE'S HOUSE, CHEYNE ROW, CHELSEA, LONDON

In the home at Chelsea were numerous letters and journals which Carlyle committed to his friend Froude the historian. The publication of these private papers raised a storm of protest. Admirers of Carlyle, shocked at the revelation of another side to their hero, denounced Froude for his disloyalty and malice; whereupon the literary world divided into two camps, the Jane Carlyleists and the Thomas Carlyleists, as they are still called. That Froude showed poor taste is evident; but we must acquit him of all malice. Private papers had been given him with the charge to publish them if he saw fit; and from them he attempted to draw not a flattering but a truthful portrait of Carlyle, who had always preached the doctrine that a man must speak truth as he sees it. Nor will Carlyle suffer in the long run from being deprived of a halo which he never deserved. Already the crustiness of the man begins to grow dim in the distance; it is his rugged earnestness that will be longest remembered.

Works of Carlyle. The beginner will do well to make acquaintance with Carlyle in some of the minor essays, which

are less original but more pleasing than his labored works.
Among the best essays are those on Goethe (who was Carlyle's
first master), Signs of the Times, Novalis, and especially Scott
and Burns. With Scott he was not in sympathy, and though
he tried as a Scotsman to be "loyal to kith and clan," a strong
touch of prejudice mars his work. With Burns he succeeded
better, and his picture of the plowboy genius in misfortune is
one of the best we have on the subject. This *Essay on Burns*
is also notable as the best example of Carlyle's early style,
before he compounded the strange mixture which appeared in
his later books.

The most readable of Carlyle's longer works is *Heroes and
Hero Worship* (1840), which deals with certain leaders in the
Heroes fields of religion, poetry, war and politics. It is
and Hero an interesting study to compare this work with the
Worship *Representative Men* of Emerson. The latter looks
upon the world as governed by ideals, which belong not to individuals but to humanity. When some man appears in whom
the common ideal is written large, other men follow him because they see in him a truth which they revere in their own
souls. So the leader is always in the highest sense a representative of his race. But Carlyle will have nothing of such
democracy; to him common men are stupid or helpless and
must be governed from without. Occasionally, when humanity
is in the Slough of Despond, appears a hero, a superman, and
proceeds by his own force to drag or drive his subjects to a
higher level. When the hero dies, humanity must halt and
pray heaven to send another master.

It is evident before one has read much of *Heroes* that Carlyle is at heart a force-worshiper. To him history means the
biography of a few heroes, and heroism is a matter of power,
not of physical or moral courage. The hero may have the
rugged courage of a Cromwell, or he may be an easy-living
poet like Shakespeare, or a ruthless despot like Napoleon, or
an epitome of all meanness like Rousseau; but if he shows

superior force of any kind, that is the hall-mark of his heroism, and before such an one humanity should bow down. Of
real history, therefore, you will learn nothing from *Heroes*;
neither will you get any trustworthy information concerning
Odin, Mahomet and the rest of Carlyle's oddly consorted characters. One does not read the book for facts but for a new view
of old matters. With hero-worshipers especially it ranks very
high among the thought-provoking books of the past century.

Of the historical works[1] of Carlyle the most famous is
The French Revolution (1837). On this work Carlyle spent
The French   much heart-breaking labor, and the story of the first
Revolution   volume shows that the author, who made himself
miserable over petty matters, could be patient in face of a real
misfortune.[2] Moreover, it furnishes a striking example of Carlyle's method, which was not historical in the modern sense,
but essentially pictorial or dramatic. He selected a few dramatic scenes, such as the storming of the Bastille, and painted
them in flaming colors. Also he was strong in drawing portraits, and his portrayal of Robespierre, Danton and other
actors in the terrible drama is astonishingly vigorous, though
seldom accurate. His chief purpose in drawing all these pictures and portraits was to prove that order can never come out
of chaos save by the iron grip of a governing hand. Hence,
if you want to learn the real history of the French Revolution,
you must seek elsewhere; but if you want an impression of it,
an impression that burns its way into the mind, you will hardly
find the equal of Carlyle's book in any language.

Of Carlyle's miscellaneous works one must speak with some
hesitation. As an expression of what some call his prophetic

---

[1] These include *Oliver Cromwell's Letters and Speeches* (1850) and *History of Frederick the Great* (1858).

[2] The manuscript of the first volume was submitted to Carlyle's friend Mill (him
of the "sawdustish" mind) for criticism. Mill lent it to a lady, who lost it. When he
appeared "white as a ghost" to confess his carelessness, the Carlyles did their best to
make light of it. Yet it was a terrible blow to them; for aside from the wearisome labor
of doing the work over again, they were counting on the sale of the book to pay for their
daily bread.

mood, and others his ranting, one who has patience might try
Shooting Niagara or the *Latter Day Pamphlets*. A reflection of
his doctrine of honest work as the cure for social ills is found in
Past and Present; and for a summary of his philosophy there
is nothing quite so good as his early *Sartor Resartus* (1834).
The last-named work is called philosophy only by courtesy.
The title means "the tailor retailored," or "the patcher re-
Sartor patched," and the book professed to be "a complete
Resartus philosophy of clothes." Since everything wears
clothes of some kind (the soul wears a body, and the body
garments; earth puts forth grass, and the firmament stars;
ideas clothe themselves in words; society puts on fashions and
habits), it can be seen that Carlyle felt free to bring in any subject he pleased; and so he did. Moreover, in order to have
liberty of style, he represented himself to be the editor not the
author of *Sartor*. The alleged author was a German professor,
Diogenes Teufelsdroeckh, an odd stick, half genius, half madman, whose chaotic notes Carlyle professed to arrange with a
running commentary of his own.

In consequence of this overlabored plan *Sartor* has no plan
at all. It is a jumble of thoughts, notions, attacks on shams,
scraps of German philosophy, — everything that Carlyle wrote
about during his seven-years sojourn on his moorland farm.
The only valuable things in *Sartor* are a few autobiographical
chapters, such as "The Everlasting Yea," and certain passages
dealing with night, the stars, the yearnings of humanity, the
splendors of earth and heaven. Note this picture of Teufelsdroeckh standing alone at the North Cape, "looking like a
little belfry":

" Silence as of death, for Midnight, even in the Arctic latitudes, has its
character: nothing but the granite cliffs ruddy-tinged, the peaceable gurgle
of that slow-heaving Polar Ocean, over which in the utmost North the
great Sun hangs low and lazy, as if he too were slumbering. Yet is his
cloud-couch wrought of crimson and cloth-of-gold; yet does his light stream
over the mirror of waters, like a tremulous fire-pillar shooting downwards
to the abyss, and hide itself under my feet. In such moments Solitude also

is invaluable; for who would speak, or be looked on, when behind him lies all Europe and Africa, fast asleep, except the watchmen; and before him the silent Immensity and Palace of the Eternal, whereof our Sun is but a porch-lamp?"

The book has several such passages, written in a psalmodic style, appealing to elemental feeling, to our sense of wonder or reverence before the mystery of life and death. It is a pity that we have no edition of *Sartor* which does justice to its golden nuggets by the simple expedient of sifting out the mass of rubbish in which the gold is hidden. The central doctrines of the book are the suppression of self, or selfishness, and the value of honest work in contrast with the evil of mammon-worship.

A Criticism of Carlyle. Except in his literary essays Carlyle's " rumfustianish growlery of style," as he called it, is so uneven that no description will apply to it. In moments of emotion he uses a chanting prose that is like primitive poetry. Sometimes he forgets Thomas Carlyle, keeps his eye on his subject, and describes it in vivid, picturesque words; then, when he has nothing to say, he thinks of himself and tries to hold you by his manner, by his ranting or dogmatism. In one mood he is a poet, in another a painter, in a third a stump speaker. In all moods he must have your ear, but he succeeds better in getting than in holding it. It has been said that his prose is on a level with Browning's verse, but a better comparison may be drawn between Carlyle and Walt Whitman. Of each of these writers the best that can be said is that his style was his own, that it served his purpose, and that it is not to be imitated.

In formulating any summary of Carlyle the critic must remember that he is dealing with a man of two sides, one His Two prejudiced, dogmatic, jealous of rivals, the other Sides roughly sincere. On either side Carlyle is a man of contradictions. For an odious dead despot like Frederick, who happens to please him, he turns criticism into eulogy;

and for a living poet like Wordsworth he tempers praise by spiteful criticism.[1] He writes a score of letters to show that his grief is too deep for words. He is voluble on "the infinite virtue of silence." He proclaims to-day that he "will write no word on any subject till he has studied it to the bottom," and to-morrow will pronounce judgment on America or science or some other matter of which he knows nothing. In all this Carlyle sees no inconsistency; he is sincere in either rôle, of prophet or stump speaker, and even thinks that humor is one of his prime qualities.

Another matter to remember is Carlyle's constant motive rather than his constant mistakes. He had the gloomy conviction that he was ordained to cry out against the shams of society; and as most modern things appeared to him as shams, he had to be very busy. Moreover,

ARCH HOME, ECCLEFECHAN
The birthplace of Carlyle

he had an eye like a hawk for the small failings of men, especially of living men, but was almost blind to their large virtues. This hawklike vision, which ignores all large matters in a swoop on some petty object, accounts for two things: for the marvelous detail of Carlyle's portraits, and for his merciless criticism of the faults of society in general, and of the Victorian age in particular.

Such a writer invites both applause and opposition, and in Carlyle's case the one is as hearty as the other. The only

---

[1] Carlyle's praise of Wordsworth's "fine, wholesome rusticity" is often quoted, but only in part. If you read the whole passage (in *Reminiscences*) you will find the effect of Carlyle's praise wholly spoiled by a heartless dissection of a poet, with whom, as Carlyle confessed, he had very slight acquaintance.

point on which critics are fairly well agreed is that his rugged independence of mind and his picturesque style appealed powerfully to a small circle of readers in England and to a large circle in America. It is doubtful whether any other essayist, with the possible exception of the serene and hopeful Emerson, had a more stimulating influence on the thought of the latter half of the nineteenth century.

JOHN RUSKIN (1819–1900)

The prose of Ruskin is a treasure house. Nature portrayed as everyman's Holy Land; descriptions of mountain or landscape, and more beautiful descriptions of leaf or lichen or the glint of light on a breaking wave; appreciations of literature, and finer appreciations of life itself; startling views of art, and more revolutionary views of that frightful waste of human life and labor which we call political economy, — all these and many more impressions of nature, art and human society are eloquently recorded in the ten thousand pages which are the work of Ruskin's hand.

If you would know the secret that binds all his work together, it may be expressed in two words, sensitiveness and sincerity. From childhood Ruskin was extremely sensitive to both beauty and ugliness. The beauty of the world and of all noble things that ever were accomplished in the world affected him like music; but he shrank, as if from a blow, from all sordidness and evil, from the mammon-worship of trade, from the cloud of smoke that hung over a factory district as if trying to shield from the eye of heaven so much needless poverty and aimless toil below. So Ruskin was a man halting between two opinions : the artist in him was forever troubled by the reformer seeking to make the crooked places of life straight and its rough places plain. He made as many mistakes as another man ; in his pages you may light upon error or vagary ; but you will find nothing to make you doubt his entire sincerity, his desire to speak truth, his passion for helping his fellow men.

Life. The early training of Ruskin may explain both the strength and the weakness of his work. His father was a wealthy wine merchant, his mother a devout woman with puritanic ideas of duty. Both parents were of Scottish and, as Ruskin boasted, of plebeian descent. They had but one child, and in training him they used a strange mixture of severity and coddling, of wisdom and nonsense.

The young Ruskin was kept apart from other boys and from the sports which breed a modesty of one's own opinion; his time, work and lonely play were minutely regulated; the slightest infringement of rules brought the stern discipline of rod or reproof. On the other hand he was given the best pictures and the best books; he was taken on luxurious journeys through England and the Continent; he was furnished with tutors for any study to which he turned his mind. When he went up to Oxford, at seventeen, he knew many things which are Greek to the ordinary boy, but was ignorant of almost everything that a boy knows, and that a man finds useful in dealing with the world.

JOHN RUSKIN

From a photograph by Elliott and Fry

There were several results of this early discipline. One

Training and its Results was Ruskin's devotion to art, which came from his familiarity with pictures and galleries; another was his minute study of natural objects, which were to him in place of toys; a third was his habit of "speaking his mind" on every subject; a fourth was his rhythmic prose style, which came largely from his daily habit of memorizing the Bible. Still another result of his lonely magnificence, in which he was deprived of boys' society, was that his affection went out on a flood tide of romance to the first attractive girl he met. So he loved, and was laughed at, and was desperately unhappy. Then he married, not the woman of his choice, but one whom his parents picked out for him. The tastes of the couple were hopelessly different; the end was estrangement, with humiliation and sorrow for Ruskin.

At twenty-four he produced his first important work, *Modern Painters* (1843), which he began as a defense of the neglected artist **Twenty** Turner. This controversial book led Ruskin to a deeper **Years of Art** study of his subject, which resulted in four more volumes on modern painting. Before these were completed he had " fairly created a new literature of art" by his *Seven Lamps of Architecture* and *Stones of Venice.* He was appointed professor of fine arts at Oxford; he gave several series of lectures which appeared later as *Lectures on Architecture and Painting, Michael Angelo and Tintoret, Val d'Arno* and *The Art of England.*

By this time he was renowned as an art critic; but his theories were strongly opposed and he was continually in hot water. In his zeal to defend Turner or Millais or Burne-Jones he was rather slashing in his criticism of other artists. The libel suit brought against him by Whistler, whom he described as a coxcomb who flung a pot of paint in the face of the public, is still talked about in England. The jury (fancy a jury wrestling with a question of art!) found Ruskin guilty, and decided that he should pay for the artist's damaged reputation the sum of one farthing. Whistler ever afterwards wore the coin on his watch chain.

It was about the year 1860 that Ruskin came under the influence of Carlyle, and then began the effort at social reform which made **Ruskin the** wreck of fame and hope and peace of mind. Carlyle had **Reformer** merely preached of manual work; but Ruskin, wholehearted in whatever he did, went out to mend roads and do other useful tasks to show his belief in the doctrine. Carlyle railed against the industrial system of England; but Ruskin devoted his fortune to remedying its evils. He established model tenements; he founded libraries and centers of recreation for workingmen; he took women and children out of factories and set them to spinning or weaving in their own homes; he founded St. George's Guild, a well-housed community which combined work with education, and which shared profits fairly among the workers.

England at first rubbed its eyes at these reforms, then shrugged its shoulders as at a harmless kind of madman. But Ruskin had the temper of a crusader; his sword was out against what was even then called " vested interests," and presently his theories aroused a tempest of opposition. Thackeray, who as editor of the *Cornhill Magazine* had gladly published Ruskin's first economic essays, was forced by the clamor of readers to discontinue the series.[1] To this reform period belong *Unto This Last* and other books dealing with political economy, and also *Sesame and Lilies, Crown of Wild Olive* and *Ethics of the Dust*, which were written chiefly for young people.

For twenty years this crusade continued; then, worn out and misunderstood by both capitalists and workingmen, Ruskin retired (1879) **End of the** to a small estate called " Brantwood " in the Lake District. **Crusade** His fortune had been spent in his attempt to improve labor conditions, and he lived now upon the modest income from his books. Before he died, in 1900, his friend Charles Eliot Norton persuaded him to write the story of his early life in *Praeterita*. The title is strange, but the book itself is, with one exception, the most interesting of Ruskin's works.

Works of Ruskin. The works of Ruskin fall naturally into three classes, which are called criticisms of art, industry and life, but which are, in fact, profound studies of the origin and meaning of art on the one hand, and of the infinite value of human life on the other.

The most popular of his art criticisms are *St. Mark's Rest* and *Mornings in Florence*, which are widely used as guidebooks, and which may be postponed until the happy time when, in Venice or Florence, one may read them to best advantage. Meanwhile, in *Seven Lamps of Architecture* or *Stones of Venice* or the first two volumes of *Modern Painters*, one may grow acquainted with Ruskin's theory of art.

His fundamental principle was summarized by Pope in the line, " All nature is but art unknown to thee." That nature is **His Theory** the artist's source of inspiration, that art at its best **of Art** can but copy some natural beauty, and that the copy should be preceded by careful and loving study of the original, — this was the sum of his early teaching. Next, Ruskin looked

[1] While these essays were appearing, there was published (1864) a textbook of English literature. It spoke well of Ruskin's books of art, but added, " Of late he has lost his way and has written things — papers in the *Cornhill* chiefly — which are not likely to add to his fame as a writer or to his character as a man of common sense " (Collier, *History of English Literature*, p. 512).

within the soul of the artist and announced that true art has a spiritual motive, that it springs from the noblest ideals of life, that the moral value of any people may be read in the pictures or buildings which they produced. A third principle was that the best works of art, reflecting as they do the ideals of a community, should belong to the people, not to a few collectors ; and a fourth exalted the usefulness of art in increasing not only the pleasure but the power of life. So Ruskin urged that art be taught in all schools and workshops, and that every man be encouraged to put the stamp of beauty as well as of utility upon the work of his hands ; so also he formulated a plan to abolish factories, and by a system of hand labor to give every worker the chance and the joy of self-expression.

In his theory of economics Ruskin was even more revolutionary. He wrote several works on the subject, but the sum of his teaching may be found in *Unto This Last* ; and **Theory of Economics** the sum is that political economy is merely commercial economy ; that it aims to increase trade and wealth at the expense of men and morals. " There is no wealth but life," announced Ruskin, " life including all its power of love, of joy and of admiration." And with minute exactness he outlined a plan for making the nation wealthy, not by more factories and ships, but by increasing the health and happiness of human beings.

Three quarters of a century earlier Thomas Jefferson, in America, had pleaded for the same ideal of national wealth, and had characterized the race of the nations for commercial supremacy as a contagion of insanity. Jefferson was called a demagogue, Ruskin a madman ; but both men were profoundly right in estimating the wealth of a nation by its store of happiness for home consumption rather than by its store of goods for export. They were misunderstood because they were too far in advance of their age to speak its trade language. They belong not to the past or present, but to the future.

If but one work of Ruskin is to be read, let it be *Sesame and Lilies* (1865), which is one of the books that no intelligent reader can afford to neglect. The first chapter, "Of Kings' Treasuries," is a noble essay on the subject of reading. The **For Young Readers** second, "Of Queens' Gardens," is a study of woman's life and education, a study which may appear old-fashioned now, but which has so much of truth and beauty that it must again, like Colonial furniture, become our best fashion. These two essays [1] contain Ruskin's best thought on books and womanly character, and also an outline of his teaching on nature, art and society. If we read *Sesame and Lilies* in connection with two other little books, *Crown of Wild Olive*, which treats of work, trade and war, and *Ethics of the Dust*, which deals with housekeeping, we shall have the best that Ruskin produced for his younger disciples.

The Quality of Ruskin. To the sensitiveness and sincerity of Ruskin we have already called attention. There is a third quality which appears frequently, and which we call pedagogical insistence, because the author seems to labor under the impression that he must drive something into one's head.

This insistent note is apt to offend readers until they learn of Ruskin's motive and experience. He lived in a commercial age, an age that seemed to him blind to the beauty of the world; and the purpose of his whole life was, as he said, to help those who, having eyes, see not. His aim was high, his effort heroic; but for all his pains he was called a visionary, a man with a dream book. Yet he was always exact and specific. He would say, "Go to a certain spot at a certain hour, look in a certain direction, and such and such beauties shall ye see." And people would go, and wag their heads, and declare that no such prospect as Ruskin described was visible to mortal eyes.[2]

[1] A third essay, "The Mystery of Life," was added to *Sesame and Lilies*. It is a sad, despairing monologue, and the book might be better without it.

[2] For example, Ruskin gave in *Fors Clavigera* a description of a beautiful view from a bridge over the Ettrick, in Scotland. Some people have sought that view in vain, and a recent critic insists that it is invisible (Andrew Lang, *History of English Literature*, p. 592). In Venice or Florence you may still meet travelers with one of Ruskin's books in hand, peering about for the beauty which he says is apparent from such and such a spot and which every traveler ought to see.

Naturally Ruskin, with his dogmatic temper, grew impatient of such blindness; hence the increasing note of insistence, of scolding even, to which critics have called attention. But we can forgive much in a writer who, with marvelously clear vision, sought only to point out the beauty of nature and the moral dignity of humanity.

The beauty of Ruskin's style, its musical rhythm or cadence, its wealth of figure and allusion, its brilliant coloring, like a **Ruskin's** landscape of his favorite artist Turner, — all this is **Style** a source of pleasure to the reader, entirely aside from the subject matter. Read, for example, the description of St. Mark's Cathedral in *Stones of Venice*, or the reflected glories of nature in *Præterita*, or the contrast between Salisbury tower and Giotto's campanile in *Seven Lamps of Architecture*, and see there descriptive eloquence at its best. That this superb eloquence was devoted not to personal or party ends, but to winning men to the love of beauty and truth and right living, is the secret of Ruskin's high place in English letters and of his enduring influence on English life.

Summary. The age of Victoria (1837–1901) approaches our own so closely that it is still difficult to form an accurate judgment of its history or literature. In a review of the history of the age we noted three factors, democracy, science, imperialism, which have profoundly influenced English letters from 1850 to the present time.

Our study of Victorian literature includes (1) The life and works of the two greater poets of the age, Tennyson and Browning. (2) The work of Elizabeth Barrett, Matthew Arnold, Rossetti, Morris and Swinburne, who were selected from the two hundred representative poets of the period. (3) The life and the chief works of the major novelists, Dickens, Thackeray and George Eliot. (4) A review of some other novelists of the age, the Brontë Sisters, Mrs. Gaskell, Anthony Trollope, Blackmore, Kingsley, Meredith, Hardy and Stevenson. (5) The typical essayists and historians, Macaulay, Carlyle, Ruskin, with a review of other typical groups of writers in the fields of religion, history and science.

Selections for Reading. Typical selections from all authors named in the text are found in Manly, English Poetry, English Prose; Pancoast, Standard English Poems, Standard English Prose; and several other collections, which are especially useful in a study of the minor writers. The works of the major authors may be read to much better advantage in various inexpensive editions prepared for school use. Only a few such editions are named below for each author, but a fairly complete list is given under Texts in the General Bibliography.

Tennyson's selected minor poems, Idylls of the King, The Princess and In Memoriam, in Standard English Classics, Riverside Literature, Pocket Classics, Silver Classics. A good volume containing the best of Tennyson's poems in Athenæum Press Series.

Browning and Mrs. Browning, selected poems in Standard English Classics, Lake Classics, English Readings, Belles Lettres Series.

Matthew Arnold, selected poems in Golden Treasury Series, Maynard's English Classics; Sohrab and Rustum in Standard English Classics; prose selections in English Readings, Academy Classics.

Dickens, Tale of Two Cities, David Copperfield, Christmas Carol in Standard English Classics, Lake Classics; other novels in Everyman's Library.

Thackeray, Henry Esmond in Standard English Classics, Pocket Classics; English Humorists in Lake Classics, English Readings; other works in Everyman's Library.

George Eliot, Silas Marner, in Standard English Classics, Riverside Literature; Mill on the Floss and other novels in Everyman's Library.

Blackmore's Lorna Doone and Mrs. Gaskell's Cranford in Standard English Classics. Reade's Cloister and the Hearth, Kingsley's Westward Ho and Hypatia in Everyman's Library.

Macaulay, selected essays in Standard English Classics, Riverside Literature, Lake Classics.

Carlyle, Essay on Burns in Standard English Classics, Academy Classics; Heroes and Hero Worship in Athenæum Press, Pocket Classics; French Revolution in Everyman's Library.

Ruskin, Sesame and Lilies and selected essays and letters in Standard English Classics; selections from Ruskin's art books in Riverside Literature; other works in Everyman's Library.

Bibliography. The works named below are selected from a large list dealing with the Victorian age chiefly. For more extended works see the General Bibliography.

History. McCarthy, History of Our Own Times and The Epoch of Reform. Oman, England in the Nineteenth Century; Lee, Queen Victoria; Bryce, Studies in Contemporary Biography.

Literature. Saintsbury, History of Nineteenth Century Literature; Harrison, Studies in Early Victorian Literature; Mrs. Oliphant, Literary History of England in the Nineteenth Century; Walker, The Age of Tennyson; Morley, Literature of the Age of Victoria: Stedman, Victorian Poets; Brownell, Victorian Prose Masters.

E

Tennyson. Life, by Lyall (English Men of Letters Series), by Horton; Alfred Lord Tennyson, a Memoir by his Son. Napier, Homes and Haunts of Tennyson; Andrew Lang, Alfred Tennyson; Dixon, A Tennyson Primer; Sneath, The Mind of Tennyson; Van Dyke, The Poetry of Tennyson. Essays by Harrison, in Tennyson, Ruskin, Mill and Other Literary Estimates; by Stedman, in Victorian Poets; by Hutton, in Literary Essays; by Dowden, in Studies in Literature; by Forster, in Great Teachers; by Gates, in Studies and Appreciations.

Browning. Life, by Sharp (Great Writers Series), by Chesterton (E. M. of L.). Alexander, Introduction to Browning (Ginn and Company); Corson, Introduction to the Study of Browning; Phelps, Browning: How to Know Him; Symonds, Introduction to the Study of Browning; Brooke, Poetry of Robert Browning; Harrington, Browning Studies. Essays by Stedman, Dowden, Hutton, Forster.

Dickens. Life, by Forster, by Ward (E. M. of L.), by Marzials. Gissing, Charles Dickens; Chesterton, Charles Dickens; Kitton, Novels of Dickens. Essays by Harrison, Bagehot; A. Lang, in Gadshill edition of Dickens's works.

Thackeray. Life, by Merivale and Marzials, by Trollope (E. M. of L.). Crowe, Homes and Haunts of Thackeray. Essays, by Brownell, in English Prose Masters; by Lilly, in Four English Humorists; by Harrison, in Studies in Early Victorian Literature; by Scudder, in Social Ideals in English Letters.

George Eliot. Life, by L. Stephen (E. M. of L.), by O. Browning, by Cross. Cooke, George Eliot: a Critical Study of her Life and Writings. Essays by Brownell, Harrison, Dowden, Hutton.

Macaulay. Life, by Trevelyan, by Morrison (E. M. of L.). Essays by L. Stephen, Bagehot, Saintsbury, Harrison, M. Arnold.

Carlyle. Life, by Garnett, by Nichol (E. M. of L.), by Froude. Carlyle's Letters and Reminiscences, edited by Norton. Craig, The Making of Carlyle. Essays by Lowell, Brownell, Hutton, Harrison.

Ruskin. Life, by Harrison (E. M. of L.), by Collingwood. Ruskin's Præterita (autobiography). Mather, Ruskin, his Life and Teaching; Cooke, Studies in Ruskin; Waldstein, The Work of John Ruskin; W. M. Rossetti, Ruskin, Rossetti and Pre-Raphaelitism. Essays by Brownell, Saintsbury, Forster, Harrison.

CHAPTER IX

AN ESSAY OF RECENT LITERATURE

What of the faith and fire within us,
Men who march away . . .
To hazards whence no tears can win us,
What of the faith and fire within us,
Men who march away?

Hardy, " The Song of the Soldier "

Before the World War wrought its change on the spirits of men, fusing the will and feeling of millions into one superb national impulse, life seemed very complex in England, and literature was busily reflecting its complexity rather than its unity, its surface eddies or cross-currents rather than its deep underflow. A host of writers held up each some problem or interest or field of the far-flung empire, and their collective work now makes upon the reader an impression of hopeless confusion. At the outset of our study, therefore, let these three matters be clearly understood :

First, this essay is not in any sense a " history " of recent literature, since no man can possibly write the history of his own times. The best we can do is to select a few representative writers, to the exclusion of many who may prove of equal or greater power. The general plan is to examine the work of one important author in some detail (this to suggest a study method) and to view the others broadly in convenient groups.

Second, the standard of selection is not the opinion of any critic, but rather a consensus of readers' opinions whenever such can be found. If you object that a selection based on fickle popularity can have little value, the answer is that until Time has its way with books popularity and personal taste are the only means we have of judging them.

Of taste and its vagaries *non disputandum*, but of popularity something may still be said — enough, at least, to distinguish the false from the true. There are many so-called popular books which are superficial or clever or funny or sentimental or sensational, each appealing to its own class of readers, and with such books, which come and go like summer hats, we have here no concern. But there is another kind of popularity in literature that goes back to the root-word "people," which means men and women, old and young, wise and ignorant. To be popular in the true sense, therefore, a writer must show some elemental human quality that appeals to folk generally, and that not only diverts them for a moment but makes them think and remember and approve or disapprove.

Popularity

Such popularity indicates power of some kind. It may be the power of truth or falsehood, of a genius or a dancing dervish ; but the writer who holds the attention of many different people is not common ; he should be looked at twice. If he is "merely popular," his book will be forgotten on the appearance of another, as *Trilby* was forgotten ; but if he wins the next generation and the next, he is on the Road of Few Travelers which leads to Parnassus. Kipling serves us well as an illustration : some critics call him a great writer, others a showman in letters ; but all agree on his immense and fairly won popularity.

The third matter to be emphasized is that no essay of recent literature can be authoritative, and that at every point the reader, no less than the writer, is free to follow his own judgment. The essayist, examining by light of his personal taste a few works which are popular in the best sense, must try to be temperate with what he likes and fair with what he heartily dislikes ; but if he wholly succeeded in the latter aim, he would be more or less than human. The reader, on the other hand, will remember that Time is the only critic who can surely tell which authors have the quality of greatness. Meanwhile the best means of anticipating Time's verdict in the future is to be acquainted with what Time has approved in the past. In other words, the more you know of old books the more likely are you to estimate the new aright.

This does not mean that new books are critically to be regarded as of small consequence ; for many of them are excellent, well worthy of study, and because they reflect our own life and thought and speech they come to us with a familiar appeal that the books of a distant age can never quite equal. Each generation likes its own books best. Therein is perhaps the danger, that the lively present interest of recent literature may blind us to its serious defects ; hence the need of a standard of value, which only the old and tried books can give us.

RUDYARD KIPLING

For more than thirty years, or ever since he came from India with his *Plain Tales*, Kipling has been the most famous writer of the English-speaking world. Yet he cares naught for fame, apparently, and affects to despise or to patronize the country that gives him the truest homage and the greater part of his readers, to say nothing of his daily bread. What is there in the author or his message to account for this phenomenon of popularity ? One cannot explain Kipling, or any other man for that matter, but a glance at his career and method may help us understand his audience.

His life began in Bombay, in 1865. As a child he was sent to England, where he received such mingled scraps of education and barbarism as are commonly furnished by an

His Career   English school for boys. (This is judging the matter as Tennyson and twenty other English writers have judged it. If any evidence is needed, Kipling furnishes it in *Stalky and Co.*) At sixteen or thereabouts he went back to India, where he " ate the bread of discontent " as reporter for a small newspaper. He wrote some " local " poems and stories, which attracted the attention of newspaper readers ; he published them in a little book, and suddenly found himself on the way to fame and fortune. Then he traveled widely about the English-speaking world, and everywhere on land or sea he had the reporter's eye for the odd, the new, the picturesque incident which would be certain to "hit" his readers. He was a journalist by instinct, and even now, after thirty years of book-making, the newspaper man shows in his slang, his "pep," his up-to-the-minute theme, his air of lofty superiority, as if indeed all things were known to him. But he is much more than a journalist; he is a very clever craftsman in words, and few can match him in power of presenting a vivid picture to the eye or creating an effect of fear or wonder in the mind. Thus by his choice of fresh subjects he wins an audience, and by his good writing he holds it.

Two other matters, of style and philosophy, should be noted in explanation of Kipling's popularity. His verse goes blithely, **His Readers** as if to the drums; his prose is always vigorous, picturesque, and manly when he does not deliberately seek an effect by sheer brutality. His philosophy of life (or such as appears in his writing) is very simple: he believes in work, and this with heroism constitutes his creed. Moreover, he is very exclusive in his notion of work, which makes it easy to agree with him. Soldier, sailor, explorer, governor of a colony, inventor of strange machines, — such only are workers; while thinkers, teachers, congressmen, and all who must get up at the whistle are weaklings, oafs, or such "flanneled fools" as are held up to scorn in "The Islanders." By a curious whim of fate most of these useful persons are wishing they could chuck their unromantic jobs and go off exploring or governing a colony; therefore do they read Kipling, finding him a kindred spirit and a voice of their souls' desire.

Kipling's Verse. As a type of popular verse consider well "The Feet of the Young Men." It appeared many years ago, celebrating a vague youth heading off into a vague wilderness because the "red gods" were calling him; and wherever he went many fell in behind him, as if he were the pied piper. Now his name is legion; those who write for the sporting magazines, or go big-game hunting or tenting in the wilds or bass-fishing in the creek, are all devotees of the red gods. We do not know exactly who these divinities are, or how they differ from the green gods, which are more abundant, or from the pink gods, which are more feminine. In other words, Kipling's affectation of a compelling "something lost beyond the ranges" was poetic humbug; but it was a very catchy humbug and we all caught it—yes, and are glad of the catching.

Perhaps the lilt of Kipling's verse is what chiefly recommends it. There is martial rhythm in his lines which makes them pleasant to the ear, aside from their subject or meaning. Thus, you cannot read "The Bell Buoy" without feeling the heave of the unquiet sea, or "Danny Deever" without mentally hearing the dead march that attends a soldier's burial.

Aside from this attractive rhythm, it is often difficult to name anything of value in Kipling's songs, most of which

Typical
Poems

bear the same relation to poetry that popular "ragtime" bears to music. Of the early *Departmental Ditties* little need be said, except perhaps this: the author might better have put them in the fire than in his collected works. *Barrack-Room Ballads* is better in spots, but the "Mandalay" spots are far between. "The Ballad of East and West" (which is not of the barracks) is a stirring tale and the best of its kind. Other good lines are found scattered through the prose works and in "occasional" poems such as "The Flag of England," "The Truce of the Bear" (read this in connection with the story of "The Man Who Was"), the famous "Recessional," and "For All We Have and Are" written at the outbreak of the Great War and giving the word "Hun" its new meaning. Such poems, with their vigorous expression of national feeling, explain why many regard Kipling as the real poet laureate of England, no matter who may be appointed to that high office.

Prose Works. Reading the exquisite "Without Benefit of Clergy" in comparison with the ruffianly *Stalky and Co.* or the stale and unprofitable *A Diversity of Creatures,* one may agree with critics who say that Kipling's early prose was his best. That is a matter of opinion, however, and the reader may be more interested in following the successive stages of Kipling's work. He began with stories of Anglo-Indian life, such as appear in *Plain Tales from the Hills* and *Soldiers Three.* Then in England, apparently in answer to those who said he was not artist enough to reflect life in a novel, he wrote *The Light that Failed.* Next came a round-the-world stage, reflected in several volumes of short stories, such as *Many Inventions,* and another of absorption in engines and technical terms. These stages overlap, and betweenwhiles appeared *Kim,* a panorama of Indian scenes, *Captains Courageous,* a boys' story of the fishing fleet, and that delight of all children young or old, *The Jungle Book.*

To the Anglo-Indian stories "The Man Who Was" or "The Tomb of his Ancestors" will serve well as an intro- **Typical** duction; while "The Incarnation of Krishna Mul- **Stories** vaney" will surely make you want to know more of *Soldiers Three.* Mulvaney is considered the best of Kipling's characters; but he is a "stage Irishman" nevertheless, and Ortheris is more true to life. One of the finest of his tales of native life is "The Miracle of Purun Bhagat," in the second *Jungle Book.* "The Ship that Found Herself" and "007" are favorites among the mechanical stories; those who know how boiler plates talk will like them, but other readers will more enjoy "The Bridge Builders," which is a better tale.

Kipling is at his best when he writes a dream-story that has happily no pretense of reality. "The Brushwood Boy," a beautiful piece of imaginative writing, seems to have more admirers than any other of his short-stories. *Kim* is not so much a novel as a kind of mirage of that mysterious land which we call India. There are those who regard *Kim* as a picture drawn from life by one who knows; but you may fill your head with delusions if you view it in that light. Kipling got his knowledge of natives, as of wolves and other beasts, chiefly from his imagination, and *Kim* and *The Jungle Book* are both in the same class of excellent fiction.

The animal stories suggest a curious grouping of Kipling's characters into the less real, the more real, and the wholly

The Jungle Book real, — curious because reality is found where you least expect it. When his men or women talk we are skeptical, thinking them too clever to be natural; his machines talk a little more humanly; but not till his animals talk do we recognize our own kind. So we look askance at Mulvaney or Mrs. Hauksbee or Cottar, finding one stagy, another artificial, a third illusory; but we welcome Mowgli and grumbling old Baloo as fellow travelers on life's highway. Such characters, original and fascinating, are here to stay. Remembering them gratefully, most young critics from seven to seventy acclaim *The Jungle Book*, the Mowgli stories especially, as the most enduring of Kipling's works.

Some Modern Novelists

Facing the fact that the novel now dwarfs all other forms of literature, the student will ask, Why this flood of fiction? The answer is, People want it; which is precisely the answer an Elizabethan would have given to explain his flood of drama. In 1600 very few Englishmen could read; for amusement they demanded plays, and many besides Shakespeare were ready to serve them at a price. In 1900, when everybody reads, people want stories, and a plethora of novelists is the result. In this, as in every other age, the prevailing type of literature is determined not by writers but by readers.

The Realists. To avoid endless debate let us agree, if we can, on this working definition : the realist is bound to portray life as he sees men live it; while the maker of romance is free to picture life as men dream or desire it to be, or strive to make it, the larger freedom being what chiefly distinguishes the romantic from the realistic novel. Both deal with life, one seeing it with the eye, the other with eye and imagination. There are faults in that definition, but no more than in any other you may formulate.

Herbert G. Wells, an honest novelist who takes his art very seriously, is the most conspicuous of contemporary realists.

Wells   "We are going to write about the whole of life," he announces. "We are going to deal with political questions and religious questions and social questions, until a thousand pretenses and ten thousand impostures shrivel in the cold clear air of our elucidations."

Questions of such import, with eleven thousand complications to bedevil them, might make even Solomon hold his tongue; but they give Wells his mission and his instrument. His mission is to reform; his instrument the novel, that shall go forth like a knight of old to destroy evil. One must admire his courage, and his robust 'faith in the written word. He sees more shams than ever Carlyle counted; society, religion, business, — everywhere is muddle (his favorite word), and at each new muddle he hurls a book. That, and not mere story-telling, is the prime meaning of his twenty or thirty novels, beginning with pseudo-scientific tales modeled on Jules Verne or More's *Utopia* and halting for the moment with *Joan and Peter*, which professes to picture England in the stress of the Great War but is really a tirade against modern education.

Like other reformers Wells has his strong and his weak points; he is strong on sociology and science, which he exalts to a god, but rather weak on souls and human nature. Thus, in *Marriage* he takes his hero and heroine off to Labrador, there to live in a hut and prove how beautifully simple life can be; which shows that he has great delusions about Labrador. One who has lived on that bleak coast knows that life there is rather more complex than in a fashionable hotel, and decidedly less comfortable. Simplicity is not learned of science or cultivated by a fish diet; it is a soul quality which shines with the same clear light in every corner of the earth. And complexity is not the result of town life or capitalism or any other modernity; it is due solely to cross-purposes, and there may be as much of it between two persons in a hut as among five millions in London city.

In sum, most of the deeper meanings of life, its faith, its courage, its laughter, its invincible hope, seem largely to have escaped this realist's observation. He is so bent on reforming the evil of society that he misses nearly all the good in it. As a type of his early wonder-stories *The War of the Worlds* will serve as well as another; of his later fiction *Tono-Bungay* or *The New Machiavelli* will show the author's zeal for knocking the humbug out of business or politics. He is a good writer, vigorous and sincere, but in his work one is very apt to lose sight of the story-teller in the reformer. An exception is found in *The Wheels of Chance*, a pleasant story written before Wells turned knight-errant with a trenchant pen for a weapon.

Joseph Conrad (English for Teodor Jozef Konrad Korzeniofski) is unlike any other recent novelist, which may account for his smaller circle of readers. We shall better

Conrad

appreciate the peculiar quality of his work if we view it in the light of his personal history. He is Polish by birth; his life began in the Ukraine, where his cultured father and mother were done to death by Russian officials. At nineteen, after his education at the hands of a French tutor, he learned English, followed a wandering heart to sea, and for twenty years went up and down the world in sailing ships. In all that time he never met one of his countrymen (the Poles are not a seafaring folk), and the solitude of exile and the vast solitude of the waters entered deep into his impressionable Slavic nature.

Somewhere Conrad speaks feelingly of "the loneliness that surrounds every human soul from the cradle to the grave," and in that word he unconsciously revealed himself and what he must write. Solitude, the mystery of fate, and the melancholy that attends one who sees life as solitude and mystery, — such is the theme of his novels. So far he is like Hawthorne; he suggests the American novelist in this also, that to him the events of any man's life are measured by their moral effect on the man's character.

The scene of his story is always in keeping with his somber and fateful theme. Occasionally he locates on the African or American coast, but more often on some lonely South Sea island, where every sailor who makes port is a stranger to every other and where the undertone of the sea is never stilled. He writes well, surprisingly so when you remember that English is not his native speech, and always with restrained power. His characters seem half real for the moment, like other strangers, but soon fade as if one had been following a daydream. Presently their very names are forgotten; only an impression remains, as of mystery made visible. To read *Chance* or *Victory* is to know this writer, for all his work is in the same vein. *Nostromo* is perhaps his best novel, and *Typhoon* is especially notable for its word-pictures of the changing but ever-changeless sea.

John Galsworthy is a reformer, like Wells, but approaches his victim in satiric rather than in hammer-and-tongs fashion.

Galsworthy He is master of a good style, quiet, assured, unconscious, and there is a finely dramatic quality in his work which shows in the dialogue and in the arrangement of chapters, each being finished like a scene from a drama. In his typical story two orders of society appear in contrast: an aristocratic class, dull, self-satisfied, opposed to change; and a lower class of radicals, brainy and restless, who are bent on reforming things. Among his best works are *The Man of Property*, *The Patrician*, and *The Country House*. In his latest novels he falls sadly away, and tells an unpleasant story that serves no artistic or useful end.

Excepting only Conrad, the realists deal largely with the "muddle" of family life, and if one believed their report the English must be in a parlous state. Such
Butler
atrocious parents and rebellious children make one wonder whether no nice homes are left in England, — such lovely homes as one has entered and must ever gratefully remember. And if they still exist, why in the name of Columbus do not the realists discover them? Our amazement is increased in reading Samuel Butler (not the author of *Hudibras*, but a later Butler of growing fame), who regards the family as a modern Juggernaut and cries out for a law that shall divorce all children from their unworthy parents.

Here again some personal experience — some parental restraint or Sunday compulsion which bred a hatred of family and church — seems to color all the author's work. It is said that he rejoiced when his father died, leaving him money and unrestrained liberty, the two only things which he considered essential to human welfare. His chief work, *The Way of All Flesh*, carries a tale through three generations, each proving anew the necessity of divorcing children from their elders. It is a powerful work, artistically the best realistic novel that has lately appeared, with a saturnine humor and an air of disinterested fairness that make it both readable and plausible. Butler thought much but published very little, and, as his *Note-Books* indicate, was the most careful craftsman among recent novelists; but again one must ask, Did he find no worthy mothers and no happy children in all England that he should turn devil's advocate in his portrayal of family life?

Two other realists, Eden Phillpotts and Arnold Bennett, are somewhat alike in that both are swamped by their "materials";
Phillpotts
they fill endless pages with mere things rather than human action, assuming that if they minutely describe a woman's dress, her house, her furniture, and all her relatives to the third and fourth generation, they have somehow created a real character. Phillpotts has produced a staggering

number of novels dealing with all matters of possible interest in the South of England. *Widecombe Fair* (in which a village appears as a character) is his brightest work. *The Thief of Virtue* and *The Three Brothers* are considered his best novels.

Arnold Bennett finds his "material" in the alleged Five Towns of a pottery district. His American readers, and they

Bennett are many, are in two groups : one finds a novel very clever, or possibly good, and recommends Bennett to a friend ; the friend goes to the library, takes out a different novel, finds frothy conceits without human interest or literary virtue, and wonders why anyone should waste an hour over such truck. This curious difference, which involves more than personal taste, may possibly be explained by the novelist's way of work. He began, as journalist for a woman's periodical, to write trashy fiction for the frank purpose of making money. When he failed of his purpose, his seven or eight novels finding few readers in England and no recognition in America, he gave time and thought and some conscience to *The Old Wives' Tale*, making a novel to please himself, it is said. A multitude of American readers greeted this book, as it deserved ; whereupon the author followed his market while the following was good, hastily writing more novels and republishing his early trash in America as "new editions" of date subsequent to that of *The Old Wives' Tale* (1908), giving readers here the impression that they were new works. So the matter is explained by Professor Phelps. To judge it fairly you must remember that modern literature has its commercial side (the only side that appeals to some publishers of fiction) and that many authors now write to make a living.

The Old Wives' Tale, relating the tragic life-story of two sisters, is Bennett's best novel, and it makes one wish he had written fewer books with more sincerity. A second choice is the humorous *Denry the Audacious* (published in England as *The Card*, 1911), and with any third, such as *Helen of the High Hand*, you approach the trashy borderland.

An older and more earnest novelist is Mrs. Humphry Ward, famous ever since her *Robert Elsmere* was trumpeted by Gladstone and read by almost everybody else. One who now yawns over that quasi-religious story must wonder at the literary commotion which it occasioned. Yet remember its day and generation. Appearing at a time when religion was supposed to be shaken by the discoveries of science, it appealed to that multitude of readers who are interested in any serious treatment of a religious question. And Mrs. Ward is always serious; well informed also, and up to date. She is an intellectual by inheritance, belonging to the Arnold family renowned in English life and letters.

Mrs. Ward

Her later novels, *Marcella, The Marriage of William Ashe, Lady Rose's Daughter* and the rest, are all alike, — conscientious, well written, of high purpose, but without genius or humor or even a frivolous feminine touch to give them charm. She deals exclusively with the "best" society, introducing you to brilliant statesmen, modest geniuses, beautiful and clever young women, and other desirables whom you expect to meet, and don't, when you pass the portal of society. That is perhaps the secret of Mrs. Ward's popularity : she takes you into the "upper circles" and flatters your delusion that they are any more brainy or happy than your own. Her best and least popular novel is *David Grieve*, in the vein of *Robert Elsmere* but showing more ability to draw a human character humanly ; that is, without putting him on intellectual stilts.

The Modern Romance. After reading a score of reformatory novels with their overwrought problems and woolly socialistic theories, one wearies for a good story and asks, Are there in recent fiction no pleasant books of life or love or nonsense "for happy folk in housen"? Yes, plenty. Locke has one to keep you mentally smiling, and De Morgan one to evoke smiles and tears at the same time — a rare experience, almost forgotten since Dickens used to compound his stories of pathos and irrepressible humor.

William J. Locke is an architect, officer of some ponderous Royal British Institute, who writes for relaxation. His philoso-

Locke phy is that every person past the wonderland of childhood has two natures, one of everyday habit, the other of primitive stuff which runs to dreams, emotions, new sensations. Work satisfies the former man, literature the latter; therefore does Locke work by day and write novels by night — a happy fashion, which Raleigh and other Elizabethans cherished. *Septimus* is his brightest work of fancy, and *The Beloved Vagabond* is by many considered his masterpiece. The latter, a readable story dealing with the adventures of a foot-loose fiddler, is bohemian and rather pagan in spirit. After reading it one may want to know the author's deeper view of life, which appears in *The Three Wise Men*.

William Frend De Morgan was first an artist, then a designer and maker of pottery, and not till he was past sixty did he

De Morgan begin to write fiction. His first novel, *Joseph Vance*, appeared in 1906 and took two countries by storm. Almost everyone who read the story thought of Dickens; but De Morgan is always himself, not an echo of somebody else; he only suggests Dickens in his hearty love of life and in his literary method, which is to plunge into the middle of a story trusting heaven and human nature to bring him to a good end. Also he commonly begins with unpromising characters of the slums, and tells a tale of "the spark in the clod" turning to pure flame and burning away all dross. His two best novels are *Alice-for-Short* and *Joseph Vance*, one dealing with a girl, the other with a boy, both of the street but on their upward way to womanhood or manhood. They are rarely good novels, but haphazard and not everywhere easy to read.

James M. Barrie was the most popular of recent romancers till he wrote *Peter Pan*, which made him the most popular of

Barrie playwrights. He began in *A Window in Thrums* and *Auld Licht Idylls* to portray the life of a Scottish village, — a drear life at best, with here and there a glint of

humor or pathos or sentiment to light up its dullness. Soon
his emotionalism ran away with him; his readers liked it, and
he harped on it more, and more artificially, till honest human
sentiment degenerated into sentimentality, as in *The Little
Minister*. Then it was that Stevenson wrote to a friend,
"There's genius in Barrie, but there's a journalist at his
elbow — there's the risk."

Thereafter Barrie showed the journalist by playing on his
readers' feelings, and there is a negative quality in his work, a
lack of candor or proper manliness, which is hard to define but
harder still to escape. His *Margaret Ogilvy* may or may not
be an exception; it is a semi-biography of his mother and is
all sentiment, rare and delicate, which you read with pleasure
until you begin to question an author's taste in selling a
mother's confidence to the public. His *Sentimental Tommy*,
the story of a detestable boy, is considered his masterpiece;
but many readers find the teary Tommy a sentimental bore.
As if to emphasize the moral of this book Barrie followed it
with *Tommy and Grizel*, in which the selfish hero came to a
bad end. As a little girl said, "First he wrote a story, and
then he wrote a squeal to it." Like every other sequel to a
masterpiece, *Tommy and Grizel* is a disappointment; which
makes one wonder why authors continue to write them. Barrie
is at his best in charming plays, such as *Peter Pan*, or in
frolicsome adventure-stories such as *The Little White Bird*,
in which he makes no attempt to draw character but gives free
rein to his elfish fancy.

There are scores more of realistic and romantic novels, altogether too many to be summarized. For those who like adventure there is Rider Haggard, with his *King Solomon's Mines*
and a dozen other gloriously impossible romances of Africa;
readers of detective stories will find just what they like in the
Sherlock Holmes series of Arthur Conan Doyle; and because
everybody likes a good dog everybody will want to read the
best of dog stories in Ollivant's *Bob, Son of Battle*. Hudson's

E

Green Mansions and other tales of the tropical forest; Anthony Hope, May Sinclair, Mary Willcocks (before she went wrong on woman's rights), Quiller-Couch, Maurice Hewlett, W. B. Maxwell, Leonard Merrick, — these are a few names which serve as signboards to the pleasant or rocky roads of recent fiction.

THE POETS

By some whim of human psychology, or it may be of human love, most of us regard poetry as a mother regards her grown-up boy: he may be exploring Alaska or fighting in France, but always in her thought he remains a child who must be mothered from the cold and the rain. Even so does poetry, old and rugged as the hills, reappear in our memory as a frail, tender, youthful thing unfit for the rough and busy ways of men. So we expect the language of poetry to be that of the nursery or the moonlight or the lover's plea, while prose is reserved for greater or sterner matters.

Now, though a few singers have died young, the world's poets are mostly strong men; they write of things natural or things human in the simplest way, and their verse is more concise and more powerful than any prose. Poetry is the elemental speech of humanity in moments of noble thought or deep feeling, and because it contains nothing artificial or superfluous it is easily memorized. Therefore did the earliest historians write only ballads of brave deeds; and even in this prosaic age, if you think a strong thought or a wise thought and want it to be remembered, you must give it poetic expression.

This little homily is based upon the work of recent English poets. There are many of them, more than in any other age; they deal with the big things or the deep things of life, and deal with them honestly, in man-fashion. The one quality which they have in common is their sincerity, their purpose to keep poetry near to common men, where it originated and where it ever belongs.

Poetry of Everyday Life. John Masefield, most rugged of recent poets, is a veritable saga-man who would have been at home in the viking ship of Eric the Red, but who appears now in a tame or conventional age to sing the seamy side of civilization. As a boy he ran away to sea, and knocked about the rough fringes of earth for many seasons. One night, it is said, he found a copy of Chaucer, sat up with it till the stars paled, and went forth in the morning knowing what his calling was. Of all great poets Chaucer is perhaps the most sensible, the most human, the most "modern," and Masefield is his disciple. If you read the simple opening of the Nun's Priest's story of Chanticleer (in the *Canterbury Tales*) and the powerfully compressed beginning of Masefield's *Widow in the Bye Street*, you will see the master honored in his pupil.

Practically all Masefield's narrative poems deal with common men or women, as his lyrics deal with the ordinary things of sea or land. Chaucer was great enough to include all types of humanity in his sympathy, but Masefield knows no gallant knights or dainty Madame Eglentynes; his range is narrowed to working folk; he has no romantic heroes but only such half-failures as you meet any day at the dock or in the street:

> The sailor, the stoker of steamers, the man with a clout,
> The chanteyman bent at the halliards, putting a tune to the shout,
> The drowsy man at the wheel and the tired lookout, . . .
> Of these shall my song be fashioned, my story be told.

Of the longer narratives *Dauber*, recounting the experience of a poor artist who shipped before the mast and was done **Masefield's** to death by heartless seamen, is commonly recom- **Poems** mended by critics. It has some memorable lines of the ship and the ocean in storm or calm; but the tale is too harsh and the sailors too horribly brutal to be interesting. Two better narratives are *The Widow in the Bye Street* and *The Everlasting Mercy*. These are the author's favorites, and by them he would be judged as a poet; but avoid them if you are looking for merely pleasant reading. They are mostly scenes of human poverty or degradation, powerfully drawn against a background of nature. The lyrics are too many for brief review. They abound in strong or beautiful lines; but they clearly indicate that Masefield writes too much and too rapidly for the best results. Among the volumes that one may profitably dip into are *Good Friday*, *Philip the King*, and *Salt-Water Ballads and Lyrics*.

Very different from Masefield is Alfred Noyes, a poet of cheerful mood who lives and works on the sunny side of the road. He is one of the most melodious of present-day singers, using a great variety of verse forms very skillfully, and though he rarely produces anything of striking power or beauty his verse is always musical and good to read. As an indication of his wide variety of pleasant subjects we need quote only his titles : *The Forest of Wild Thyme*, with its Alice-in-Wonderland spirit; *Forty Singing Seamen*, with some excellent lyrics; *The Barrel Organ*, a rollicking song of the street, into which blows a breath of spring to make men glad; *Drake*, an epic of the Elizabethan seaman; *Sherwood*, a dramatic poem of the days of Robin Hood, with a rare fool or jester called Shadow-of-a-Leaf; and several others as different as *The Flower of Old Japan* and *Tales of the Mermaid Tavern*.

Noyes

The Symbolists. We give this poor name to a group of poets, late followers of Spenser and Rossetti, who represent life or beauty by a road or flower or some other symbol, which is like a flag in that it speaks more than words. Coventry Patmore seems to have been the leader of this group. His simplest work, *The Angel in the House*, a placid narrative of life and love, was once widely read. It is still a good test, not of the poet but of the reader, who may quickly learn from it whether or not Patmore is to be followed into other fields. But if you care not much for *The Angel*, be not discouraged; try another poet. There is as much latitude of taste in poetry as in food or romance.

Thompson

Francis Thompson is in spirit a follower of those Puritan symbolists whom Dr. Johnson called the metaphysical poets, because he did not like or understand them. He wrote many fine religious poems which have a double suggestion of the rugged power of Donne and the heavenly grace of George Herbert. "The Hound of Heaven" is not his best but only his most famous poem; and this also is a test of the reader's taste. The symbolism is a little unfortunate, the "hound" being the divine love which follows a man wherever he may wander, as the Spirit followed the Psalmist in one of the most beautiful poems in any language, beginning, "O Lord, thou hast searched me and known me." The symbol of the brute may be less distasteful if you remember the noble dogs of St. Bernard, which go forth in the winter storm to find and save the perishing.

Phillips

Stephen Phillips is the most widely known of recent symbolists. He had the same passionate love of beauty that animated Keats, and like Keats he died young, apparently at the beginning of a great career. In his first little volume, *Poems* (1897), turn to "Marpessa," one of his finest works, and read the lines of Idas to the maid:

> Thou meanest what the sea has striven to say
> So long, and yearnéd up the cliffs to tell;
> Thou art what all the winds have uttered not,
> What the still night suggesteth to the heart. . . .
> Thy face remembered is from other worlds,
> It has been died for, though I know not when,
> It has been sung of, though I know not where.

If such symbolic lines appeal to your sense of beauty, there are plenty more like them, both in the early volume and in *New Poems* (1907). Phillips soon turned to drama and wrote *Herod* and *Paolo and Francesca* for the stage; but these, though they met with favor not often accorded a poet's play in recent times, are more notable for their poetic lines than for their dramatic or "acting" quality.

The Celtic Revival. Of late years certain poets and dramatists of Irish birth or sympathy have been calling attention to the old Erin of song and romance. Their work is supposed to be a renaissance of Celtic literature, and occasionally is; but more often it is a modern version of that ideal beauty which Spenser located in the Land of Faery, and which now finds a local habitation and a name in Ireland.

William Butler Yeats is the leading poet of this busy group, who have already established a national theater in Dublin, and

Yeats

who are even trying to revive the ancient Irish language. In his poetry and drama he thinks of himself as a reviver of old symbols, and writes in prose a theory of his art; but—"a rose by any other name would smell as sweet." He is first and last a lover of beauty, which knows no age, no death, no revival, being forever young as the morning; and so long as he writes of beauty his English readers care little for his theory. There is a rare purity and simplicity in his work, which bespeak a child's heart; so he can write of one whom he loves, and before whom he would spread a cloth of gold or stars, as Raleigh spread his cloak before the Queen:

> But I, being poor, have only my dreams;
> I have spread my dreams under your feet.

Yeats's poetic titles, *The Wind among the Reeds, In the Seven Woods, Shadowy Waters, The Land of Heart's Desire* (the last two being dramas), are as inviting as an open door. Enter freely into any of his little volumes, for there is no best where all is simple and good. But if you must have direction, skip at first *The Wanderings of Oisin* and other revivals of long-dead heroes, and begin with a collection of ballads and lyrics.

Other glimpses of the Celtic "renaissance" may be had in the plays of Lady Gregory and John Millington Synge (try his *Riders to the Sea*), in the poems of Padraic Colum and George W. Russell, and in the happy short stories of Seumas Mac Manus collected in *Through the Turf Smoke.*

Books of Many Kinds

In contrast with the Victorian age the present is extraordinarily interested in plays of every kind. Aside from professional playwrights, who are many and well rewarded, most of the poets and novelists we have just met have turned their hand to drama, and no sooner does a novel appeal to the public than the author or somebody else quickly makes it over for the stage.

To summarize these plays in a chapter of literature is inadvisable for various reasons : they are hopelessly abundant ; with
Plays rare exceptions they are ephemeral in character ; and finally, their essential dramatic quality demands that one who would criticize them must view them on the stage, not in the cold pages of a book. They need actors, light, scenery, — all the illusion of the theater, if they are to be fairly judged. To take them out of their proper setting is to examine a diamond in the dusk. Arthur Wing Pinero is an excellent illustration ; he has made some forty plays, light or serious, and seldom a poor work among them ; but they are not read ; their very names are forgotten save by a few old theatergoers and a few young playwrights who study them as models ; so why should we coldly consider them as literature ?

In a different and purely literary class are the essays ; but here again we are bewildered by the number of writers who
Essays reflect every interest of modern life, its business, politics, religion and science no less than its fun and nonsense, in a flood of magazine articles that for force and brilliancy have rarely been surpassed. From the multitude we select only three as typical ; but the student will remember that this particular selection is wholly a matter of personal taste, and that happily tastes differ.

Of works dealing with literature and criticism *A Bookman's Letters* by W. Robertson Nicoll (who appears as " Claudius Clear " in *The British Weekly*) is one of the pleasantest. It

is a book of wide range and wide sympathy, dealing gener-
ously with modern literature, — a wise, helpful, kindly book,
kind to the author under discussion and, above all, kind to the
reader. In the ethical and religious fields there are few essays
to compare with those of J. Brierley (the modest "J. B." of
the periodicals), which are collected in *Ourselves and the Universe* and three or four similar volumes characterized by deep
thought, lucid expression and a very wide range of literary
allusion. And for a criticism of literature and life there arc
the numerous books of Chesterton ("G. K. C.," not Cecil
Chesterton), a bluff, fat, hearty man of Falstaffian wit and
logic. He is a master of paradox, of topsy-turvy observation;
and he has a genius for presenting any old subject under the
sun, or any new fad or fashion, in a way nobody ever happened
to think of before. Moreover, under his most extravagant
whim or paradox there is always thought and life, a downright
hatred of sham and a genuine love of humanity.

Books of the War. Three things of literary interest have
already emerged from the World War. The first is the marvelous spirit of England. Masefield voiced it for us, simply
and manfully, in one of his addresses to an American audience
("St. George and the Dragon," in *The War and the Future*,
1918). Never before, not even in the days of Elizabeth, were
Englishmen so brave, so strong, so united; and with England
went heart and soul the mighty English-speaking world. This
glorious national spirit, fusing men to unity of thought and feeling, must again have a tremendous influence on English literature. The coming days shall see it; the flood of books has
already begun, and in them, unless all signs fail, shall be something of fire and faith that no English books ever had before.

The second phenomenon is the return of old writers with a
new song or tale on their lips, and the appearance of new poets
Writers   in whom the fierce light of war has revealed a hid-
Old and New den talent. A few popular authors have used the
war unworthily, in a catchpenny spirit; but they are exceptions,

and we shall not name them. The aged Thomas Hardy comes out of his twilight brooding with his "Song of the Soldier," which has all the vigor of his vanished youth; and Wells forgets his everlasting reform to show, in *Mr. Britling Sees It Through,* a cross section of English life as the war discovers it. (Too bad he was not content with that, but must at the end tinker up a reformed god to supplant his helpless science!) William Watson the poet, who as a lover of peace used to be recommended to us as an antidote to Kipling's jingoism, comes out bravely with *The Man Who Saw* in the old martial spirit of his forebears. Masefield leaves his poetry to haunt the trenches; in vivid prose he writes *Gallipoli* and *The Old Front Line,* one dealing with the Dardanelles expedition, the other with the Battle of the Somme, each a splendid story of heroism splendidly told.

Besides these familiar writers (we have mentioned but a few of those who reflect the national feeling) a number of unlooked-for poets appeared in both England and America, in Canada and Australia also, and poetry resumed its old function of speaking more urgently and more truly than is possible in prose. The general quality of their work is surprisingly good, as you may judge from any one of a dozen volumes of war songs; and the strange thing is, that of scores of names attached to this poetry rarely is there one that was before known to the literary world.

The third phenomenon is the change that has mysteriously come over writers in their attitude toward the strife of arms. Poetry of the War From Beowulf to Tennyson practically all English poets sang the glory and heroism and panoply of war in the trump-and-drum style of "The Charge of the Light Brigade" and "The Helmet of Navarre." But now, though we have witnessed such heroism as was never sung or dreamed, and this not in plumed knights but in neighborly men, our poets are strangely mute to the glory of conflict; when they write of war they pass over its martial splendor to show you a soldier's heart with its tender memories. So for one old-style poem of "How the Guard Came Through" there are hundreds, like Lieutenant Asquith's "The Volunteer," which say nothing whatever of fighting, though they leave you with deeper respect for human courage and almost a reverence for the men of your own breed. Masefield's "August, 1914" is typical of another strange kind of war poem; it draws a picture of quiet English fields, leaving your imagination to see or hear the stark horror of the trenches, the flash and boom of guns and the glare of burning homes across the Channel.

In all these poets, young or old, two noble qualities appear : a deathless loyalty to an ideal England and a deep love of peace as the only normal condition of human life. Both qualities appear, with a promise that was never fulfilled, in the work of Rupert Brooke, for example, a young poet who went out as a soldier on the Dardanelles expedition. He died there, in the Ægean, and they made his grave in Skyros that Achilles knew. Ere he gave a life for his country he bravely wrote, as our Nathan Hale spoke, his own immortal epitaph :

> If I should die, think only this of me :
>   That there's some corner of a foreign field
> That is forever England. There shall be
>   In that rich earth a richer dust concealed,
> A dust whom England bore, shaped, made aware,
>   Gave once her flowers to love, her ways to roam,
> A body of England's, breathing English air,
>   Washed by the rivers, blest by suns of home.
>
> And think : this heart, all evil shed away,
>   A pulse in the eternal mind, no less,
>   Gives somewhere back the thoughts by England given,
> Her sights and sounds, dreams happy as her day,
>   And laughter learnt of friends, and gentleness
> In hearts at peace, under an English heaven.[1]

[1] Reprinted from *Collected Poems of Rupert Brooke* by permission of the literary executor and of the publishers, Sidgwick and Jackson, Ltd., and Dodd, Mead & Company, Inc. Copyright, 1915, by Dodd, Mead & Company, Inc.

Bibliography. There are near a hundred books dealing with recent literature, but not one to tell you what you want to know; that is, for each important author such events of his life as may color his work, his chief books in order, his philosophy or world view, his motive in writing, and then a word of criticism or appreciation. The books available are mostly collections of magazine articles; the selection of authors is consequently haphazard, many of the most important being omitted; and they are almost wholly critical, giving you not the author or his work but the critic's reaction on the author. Among the best of these reactions are:

Phelps, Advance of the English Novel (Dodd), and Essays on Modern Novelists (Macmillan); Cooper, Some English Story Tellers (Holt); Follett, Some Modern Novelists (Holt); Freeman, The Moderns (Crowell). Phelps, Advance of English Poetry in the Twentieth Century (Dodd). Chandler, Aspects of Modern Drama (Macmillan); Phelps, Twentieth Century Theatre (Macmillan); Andrews, The Drama of To-day (Lippincott); Howe, Dramatic Portraits (Kennerley); Clark, British and American Drama of To-day (Holt).

A book which attempts to continue the history of English prose and verse from the Victorian Age to the present day is Cunliffe, English Literature during the Last Half-Century (Macmillan, 1919).

In addition to the above collective studies there are numerous presentations of Kipling, Barrie, Chesterton, Yeats, Synge and other recent writers and dramatists, each in a single volume.

GENERAL BIBLIOGRAPHY

Books dealing with individual authors and with special periods of English literature are listed in the various chapter endings of this history. Following are some of the best works for general reference, for extended study and for supplementary reading.

History. A brief, trustworthy textbook of history, such as Cheyney's Short History of England (Ginn and Company) or Gardiner's Student's History (Longmans), should always be at hand in studying English literature. More detailed works are Traill, Social England, 6 vols. (Putnam); Bright, History of England, 5 vols. (Longmans); Green, History of the English People, 4 vols. (Harper); Green, Short History of the English People, revised edition, 1 vol. (American Book Co.); latest revision of Green's Short History, with appendix of recent events to 1900, in Everyman's Library (Putnam); Kendall, Source Book of English History (Macmillan); Colby, Selections from the Sources of English History (Longmans); Lingard, History of England, to 1688, 10 vols. (a standard Catholic history). Mitchell, English Lands, Letters and Kings, 5 vols. (Scribner), a series of pleasant essays of history and literature.

Literary History. Cambridge History of English Literature, to be completed in 14 vols. (Putnam), by different authors, not always in harmony; Channels of English Literature (Dutton) treats of epic, drama, history, essay, novel and other types, each in a separate volume; Jusserand, Literary History of the English People, to 1650, 2 vols. (Putnam), a fascinating record; Ten Brink, English Literature, to 1550, 3 vols. (Holt), good material, clumsy style; Taine, English Literature, 2 vols. (Holt), brilliant but not trustworthy; Handbooks of English Literature, 9 vols. (Macmillan); Garnett and Gosse, Illustrated History of English Literature, 4 bulky volumes (Macmillan), good for pictures; Nicoll and Seccombe, History of English Literature, from Chaucer to end of Victorian era, 3 vols. (Dodd); Morley, English Writers, to 1650, 11 vols. (Cassell); Chambers, Cyclopedia of English Literature, 3 vols. (Lippincott).

Biography. Dictionary of National Biography, 63 vols. (Macmillan). English Men of Letters, a volume to each author (Macmillan);

briefer series of the same kind are Great Writers (Scribner), Beacon Biographies (Houghton), Westminster Biographies (Small). Allibone, Dictionary of Authors, 5 vols. (Lippincott). Hinchman and Gummere, Lives of Great English Writers (Houghton), offers thirty-eight biographies in a single volume.

Literary Types. Courthope, History of English Poetry, 4 vols. (Macmillan); Gummere, Handbook of Poetics (Ginn and Company); Stedman, Nature and Elements of Poetry (Houghton); Saintsbury, History of English Prosody (Macmillan); Alden, Specimens of English Verse (Holt).

Steenstrup, The Mediæval Popular Ballad, translated from the Danish by Edward Cox (Ginn and Company); Gummere, The Popular Ballad (Houghton).

Ward, History of Dramatic Literature, to 1714, 3 vols. (Macmillan); Caffin, Appreciation of the Drama (Baker).

Raleigh, The English Novel (Scribner); Hamilton, Materials and Methods of Fiction (Baker); Cross, Development of the English Novel (Macmillan); Perry, Study of Prose Fiction (Houghton).

Saintsbury, History of Criticism, 3 vols. (Dodd); Gayley and Scott, Introduction to Methods and Materials of Literary Criticism (Ginn and Company); Winchester, Principles of Criticism (Macmillan); Worsfold, Principles of Criticism (Longmans); Moulton, Library of Literary Criticism, 8 vols. (Malkan).

Essays of Literature. Bagehot, Literary Studies; Hazlitt, Lectures on the English poets; Lowell, Literary Essays; Mackail, Springs of Helicon (English poets from Chaucer to Milton); Minto, Characteristics of English Poets (Chaucer to Elizabethan dramatists); Matthew Arnold, Essays in Criticism; Leslie Stephen, Hours in a Library; Stevenson, Familiar Studies of Men and Books; Birrell, Obiter Dicta; Hales, Folia Litteraria; Walter Pater, Appreciations; Woodberry, Makers of Literature; Dowden, Studies in Literature and Transcripts and Studies; Gates, Studies in Appreciation; Harrison, The Choice of Books; Bates, Talks on the Study of Literature.

Collections of Poetry and Prose. Manly, English Poetry, English Prose, 2 vols., containing selections from all important English authors (Ginn and Company); Newcomer and Andrews, Twelve Centuries of English Poetry and Prose (Scott); Century Readings in English Literature (Century Co.); Pancoast, Standard English Poetry, Standard English Prose, 2 vols. (Holt); Leading English Poets from Chaucer to Browning (Houghton); Oxford Book of English Verse,

Oxford Treasury of English Literature, 3 vols. (Clarendon Press); Ward, English Poets, 4 vols., and Craik, English Prose Selections, 5 vols. (Macmillan); Morley, Library of English Literature, 5 vols. (Cassell).

Language. Lounsbury, History of the English Language (Holt); Emerson, Brief History of the English Language (Macmillan); Welsh, Development of English Language and Literature (Scott); Bradley, Making of English (Macmillan); Greenough and Kittredge, Words and their Ways in English Speech (Macmillan); Anderson, Study of English Words (American Book Co.).

Miscellaneous. Classic Myths in English Literature (Ginn and Company); Ryland, Chronological Outlines of English Literature, names and dates only (Macmillan); Raleigh, Style (Longmans); Brewer, Reader's Handbook (Lippincott); Hutton, Literary Landmarks of London (Harper); Boynton, London in English Literature (University of Chicago Press); Dalbiac, Dictionary of English Quotations (Macmillan); Bartlett, Familiar Quotations (Little); Walsh, International Encyclopedia of Quotations (Winston).

School Texts.[1] Standard English Classics and Athenæum Press Series (Ginn and Company); Riverside Literature (Houghton); Pocket Classics, Golden Treasury Series (Macmillan); Lake Classics (Scott); Silver Classics (Silver); Longmans' English Classics (Longmans); English Readings (Holt); Maynard's English Classics (Merrill); Caxton Classics (Scribner); Belles Lettres Series (Heath); King's Classics (Luce); Canterbury Classics (Rand); Academy Classics (Allyn); Cambridge Literature (Sanborn); Student's Series (Sibley); Camelot Series (Simmons); Carisbrooke Library (Routledge); World's Classics (Clarendon Press); Lakeside Classics (Ainsworth); Standard Literature (University Publishing Company); Eclectic English Classics (American Book Co.); Cassell's National Library (Cassell); Everyman's Library (Dutton); Morley's Universal Library (Routledge); Bohn Library (Macmillan); Little Masterpieces (Doubleday); Handy Volume Classics (Crowell); Arthurian Romances (Nutt); New Mediæval Library (Duffield); Arber's English Reprints (Macmillan); Mermaid Dramatists (Scribner); Temple Dramatists (Macmillan); Home and School Library, a series of texts prepared for young readers (Ginn and Company).

---

[1] The chief works of English and American literature are now widely published in inexpensive editions prepared especially for classroom use. Descriptive catalogues of these handy little editions are issued by the various educational publishers.

READINGS IN ENGLISH
LITERATURE

CONTENTS

THE PURITAN AGE AND THE RESTORATION

CONTENTS

THE VICTORIAN AGE

BEGINNINGS OF ENGLISH LITERATURE

THE TALE OF BEOWULF[1]

[Beowulf and the Dragon]

Greeted he then each one of men,
The brave helmet-bearers, for the last time,
His own dear comrades: "I would not the sword bear,
Weapon 'gainst worm,[2] if I knew how
Upon this monster I might otherwise   5
My boast maintain, as once upon Grendel.
But I there expect hot battle-fire,
Breath and poison: therefore I have on me
Shield and burnie.[3] I will not the hill's guard,
The foe, flee from even part of one foot,   10
But at wall it shall be as for us Weird[4] provides,
Each man's Creator: I am in mind brave,
So that 'gainst the war-flier[2] from boast I refrain.
Await ye on mountain, clad in your burnies,
Heroes in armor, which one may better,   15
After the contest, from wounds escape
Of both of us. That is not your work,
Nor the might of a man but of me alone,
That he 'gainst the monster his strength should try,
Heroic deeds do. I shall with might   20
The gold obtain, or war shall take off,
Terrible life-bale,[5] your own sovereign."
Arose then by the rock the warrior fierce

[1] Reprinted from Garnett: *Beowulf*, Ginn and Company, publishers.
[2] dragon.   [3] coat of mail.   [4] Fate.   [5] evil, calamity.

I

Brave under his helmet, his battle-sark[1] bore
'Neath the stone-cliffs, to the strength trusted
Of one man alone; such is no coward's work.
He saw then by the wall (he who very many,
5   In man's virtues good, of contests survived,
Struggles of battle, when warriors contended)
A stony arch stand, a stream out thence
Break from the mountain; the burn's[2] flood was
With battle-fire hot; might not near the hoard
10   One without burning any while then
Endure the deep for the flame of the dragon.
Let then from his breast, since he was enraged,
The Wedergeats' prince his words go forth,
The strong-hearted stormed: his voice came in,
15   In battle clear-sounding, 'neath the hoar stone.
Strife was stirred up; the hoard-keeper knew
The voice of a man: there was not more time
Friendship to seek. First there came forth
The breath of the monster out of the rock,
20   Hot battle-sweat; the earth resounded.
The man 'neath the mountain his shield upraised
'Gainst the terrible demon, the lord of the Geats:
Then was the ring-bowed[3] eager in heart
The contest to seek. The sword ere brandished
25   The good war-king, the ancient relic
Sharp in its edges: to each one was
Of those bent on bale dread from the other.
The strong-minded stood against the steep rock,
The prince of friends, when the worm bent
30   Quickly together: he in armor awaited.
Went he then burning advancing in curves,
To his fate hasting; the shield well protected
In life and in body a lesser while
The mighty chief than his wish sought,

[1] garment, armor.   [2] brook's.
[3] the dragon, with back curved into the shape of a bow.

If he that time, on the first day,
Was to control, as Weird did not permit him
Triumph in battle. His hand he uplifted,
The prince of the Geats, the fearful foe struck
With the mighty relic, so that the edge softened   5
Brown on the bone, bit less strongly
Than the folk-king need of it had,
Oppressed with the fight. Then was the hill's keeper,
After the battle-blow, fierce in his mood,
Threw with death-fire; far and wide spread   10
The flame of the battle. Of triumphs he boasted not,
The gold-friend of the Geats: the war-bill[1] failed
Naked in fight, as it should not,
Excellent weapon. That was no easy task,
So that the mighty kinsman of Ecgtheow   15
The plain of this earth was to forsake,
Must at the worm's will take up his abode
Elsewhere than here; so shall every man
His fleeting life leave. It was not then long
That the fierce ones again each other met.   20
The hoard-keeper raged, his breast swelled with breath:
A second time he suffered distress
Surrounded by fire, who before ruled his folk.
Not at all in a band did his companions,
Children of nobles, him stand around   25
With warlike virtues, but they to wood went,
Protected their lives. In one of them welled
His mind with sorrows; friendship may never
Be at all put aside by one who thinks well.

·   ·   ·   ·   ·   ·   ·   ·

He might not then refrain, his hand seized the shield,   30
The yellow wood, he drew his old sword:

·   ·   ·   ·   ·   ·   ·   ·

Went he then through the flame, his war-helmet bore
For help to his lord, spoke a few words:

[1] sword.

"Beowulf dear! do thou all well,
As thou in thy youth long ago said'st,
That thou would'st not let for thyself living
Honor e'er cease; now shalt thou, strong in deeds,
5 Firm-minded prince, with all thy might
Thy life protect; I shall assist thee."
After these words the angry worm came,
The terrible demon, a second time
With fire-waves shining to seek his foes,
10 The hostile men. With flame-billows burned
The shield to the rim: the burnie might not
To the young spear-warrior assistance afford.
But the young hero 'neath the shield of his kinsman
With courage went, when his own was
15 Destroyed by flames.

   .   .   .   .

Then I heard say in the folk-king's need
The earl displayed unceasing bravery,
Strength and valor, as was natural to him:
He cared not for his head, but the hand burned
20 Of the brave man, where he helped with his strength,
So that the fell demon he struck somewhat lower,
The hero in armor, that the sword sank in,
Shining and gold-plated, that the fire began
After to lessen. Then still the king
25 His senses possessed, struck with his war-knife,
Cutting and battle-sharp, which he bore on his burnie:
The Weders' defence cut the serpent in two.
The foe they felled, force drove out life,
And they him then both had destroyed,
30 Kindred princes: such should a man be,
A thane[1] in need. That was to the prince
The last of his victories by his own deeds,
Of work in the world. . . .

   .   .   .   .

[1] military follower, warrior.

[Of the Burial of Beowulf]

For him then prepared the folk of the Geats
A funeral-pyre on the earth firm,
Hung with helmets, with shields of war,
With burnies bright, as he had begged.
Laid they then in the midst the mighty prince, 5
The mourning warriors their lord beloved.
'Gan they then on the mountain the greatest of pyres
The warriors to kindle: the wood-smoke arose
From the burning pile black, the crackling flame
Mingled with mourning (the wind-roar was still), 10
Until it had broken the house of bone,
Hot in the breast. Sad in their minds
With sorrow they mourned their dear lord's death;
Also a sad song uttered the spouse,
Pained in her breast, grieved in her heart, 15
Mournful she frequently fettered her mind,
So that for her husband's most grievous blows
She wept, the grim fate of his bloody death,
. . . terror of fire
. . . heaven swallowed the smoke. 20
Wrought they there then the folk of the Weders
A mound on the steep, which high was and broad,
For the sea-goers to see from afar,
And they built up within ten days,
The warlike one's beacon; the brightest of flames 25
They girt with a wall, as it most worthily
Very wise men might there devise.
They in the mound placed rings and bright jewels,
All such precious things as before in the hoard
Brave-minded men had taken away. 30
They let the earth hold the treasure of earls,
Gold in the ground, where it still lives
As useless to men as it before was.
Then 'round the mound the battle-brave rode,

Children of nobles (they were twelve in all),
Their sorrow would tell, grieve for their king,
Their mourning utter, and about the man speak;
His earlship they praised, and his noble deeds
5 They extolled to the courtiers, as it is right
That one his dear lord in word should praise,
With soul him love, when he shall forth
From his own body be severed by death.
So then lamented the folk of the Geats
10 The fall of their lord, the hearth-companions,
Said that he was a mighty king,
Mildest to men and most tender-hearted,
To his folk most kind and fondest of praise.

THE SEAFARER[1]

Part I

I can sing of myself a true song, of my voyages telling,
15 How oft through laborious days, through the wearisome
hours
I have suffered; have borne tribulations; explored in my ship,
Mid the terrible rolling of waves, habitations of sorrow.
Benumbed by the cold, oft the comfortless night-watch hath
held me
At the prow of my craft as it tossed about under the cliffs.
20 My feet were imprisoned with frost, were fettered with ice-
chains,
Yet hotly were wailing the querulous sighs round my heart;
And hunger within me, sea-wearied, made havoc of courage.
This he, whose lot happily chances on land, doth not know;
Nor how I on the ice-cold sea passed the winter in exile,
25 In wretchedness, robbed of my kinsmen, with icicles hung.
The hail flew in showers about me; and there I heard only

---

[1] Reprinted from Cook and Tinker, *Translations from Old English Poetry*, Ginn and Company, publishers.

The roar of the sea, ice-cold waves, and the song of the swan;
For pastime the gannets'[1] cry served me; the kittiwakes'[1]
    chatter
For laughter of men; and for mead-drink[2] the call of the
    sea mews.[1]
When storms on the rocky cliffs beat, then the terns, icy-
    feathered,
Made answer; full oft the sea-eagle forebodingly screamed,   5
The eagle with pinions wave-wet. There none of my kinsmen
Might gladden my desolate soul; of this little he knows
Who possesses the pleasures of life, who has felt in the city
Some hardship, some trifling adversity, proud and wine-
    flushed.
    How weary I oft had to tarry upon the sea-way!   10
The shadows of night became darker, it snowed from the
    north;
The world was enchained by the frost; hail fell upon earth;
'Twas the coldest of grain. Yet the thoughts of my heart
    now are throbbing
To test the high streams, the salt waves in tumultuous play.
Desire in my heart ever urges my spirit to wander   15
To seek out the home of the stranger in lands afar off.
    There is no one that dwells upon earth, so exalted in mind,
So large in his bounty, nor yet of such vigorous youth,
Nor so daring in deeds, nor to whom his liege lord is so kind,
But that he has always a longing, a sea-faring passion   20
For what the Lord God shall bestow, be it honor or death.
No heart for the harp has he, nor for acceptance of treasure,
No pleasure has he in a wife, no delight in the world,
Nor in aught save the roll of the billows; but always a
    longing,
A yearning uneasiness, hastens him on to the sea.   25
    The woodlands are captured by blossoms, the hamlets
    grow fair,

---

[1] Sea birds. The last two are gulls.
[2] a fermented drink made from honey.

Broad meadows are beautiful, earth again bursts into life,
And all stir the heart of the wanderer eager to journey,
So he meditates going afar on the pathway of tides.
The cuckoo, moreover, gives warning with sorrowful note,
5 Summer's harbinger[1] sings, and forebodes to the heart bitter
    sorrow.
The nobleman comprehends not, the luxurious man,
What some must endure, who travel the farthest in exile.
    Now my spirit uneasily turns in the heart's narrow
    chamber,
Now wanders forth over the tide, o'er the home of the whale,
10 To the ends of the earth—and comes back to me. Eager and
    greedy,
The lone wanderer screams, and resistlessly drives my soul
    onward,
Over the whale-path, over the tracts of the sea.

CÆDMONIAN CYCLE[2]

GENESIS

THE BEGINNING OF CREATION

But after as before was peace in Heaven,
Fair rule of love; dear unto all the Lord
15   Of lords, the King of hosts, to all His own,
And glories of the good who possessed joy
In heaven the almighty Father still increased.
Then peace was among dwellers in the sky,
Blaming and lawless malice were gone out,
20   And angels feared no more, since plotting foes
Who cast off heaven were bereft of light.
Their glory-seats behind them in God's realm,

---

[1] forerunner.
[2] Reprinted from Cook and Tinker, *Translations from Old English Poetry*, Ginn and Company, publishers.

Enlarged with gifts, stood happy, bright with bloom,
But ownerless since the cursed spirits went
Wretched to exile within bars of hell.

Then thought within His mind the Lord of hosts
How He again might fix within His rule   5
The great creation, thrones of heavenly light
High in the heavens for a better band,
Since the proud scathers[1] had relinquished them.
The holy God, therefore, in His great might
Willed that there should be set beneath heaven's span   10
Earth, firmament,[2] wide waves, created world,
Replacing foes cast headlong from their home.
Here yet was naught save darkness of the cave,
The broad abyss, whereon the steadfast King
Looked with His eyes and saw that space of gloom,   15
Saw the dark cloud lower in lasting night,
Was deep and dim, vain, useless, strange to God,
Black under heaven, wan, waste, till through His word
The King of glory had created life.

Here first the eternal Father, guard of all,   20
Of heaven and earth, raised up the firmament,
The almighty Lord set firm by His strong power
This roomy land; grass greened not yet the plain,
Ocean far spread hid the wan ways in gloom.
Then was the Spirit gloriously bright   25
Of heaven's Keeper borne over the deep
Swiftly. The Life-giver, the angel's Lord,
Over the ample ground bade come forth light.
Quickly the high King's bidding was obeyed,
Over the waste there shone light's holy ray.   30
Then parted He, Lord of triumphant might,
Shadow from shining, darkness from the light.
Light, by the word of God, was first named day.

[1] those who did scathe or damage.
[2] sky, heavens.

CYNEWULF CYCLE[1]

RIDDLE: THE STORM-SPIRIT IN THE SEA

The billows crash above me while I move,
No man knows whither, searching out the earth
In the vast caverns of the sea. Then stirs
The ocean, and impels the watery mass
5 To burst in foam. Fiercely the whale-mere[2] rises
And shouts aloud and groans in mighty pain,
While sounds the tramp of floods along the shore.
Against precipitous cliffs incessantly
Rocks, sand, and heaving waves and weeds are hurled.
10 Yet toiling, robed with the strength of many waters,
I stir the soil of ocean's ample grounds,
Nor can I 'scape the whelming tide, till he
That is my guide allows. O man of wisdom,
Tell who may wrest me from the encircling grasp
15 Of water, when the streams again are stilled,
And waves that covered me beat harmony.

ANDREAS

A Storm at Sea

Then was the ocean stirred
And deeply troubled, then the horn-fish played,
Shot through the raging deep; the sea-gull gray,
20 Greedy for slaughter, flew in circling flight.
The candle of the sky grew straightway dark,
The winds waxed strong, the waves whirled, and the surge
Leapt high, the ropes creaked, dripping with the waves;
The Terror of the waters rose, and stood
25 Above them with the might of multitudes.

[1] Reprinted from Cook and Tinker, *Translations from Old English Poetry*, Ginn and Company, publishers.   [2] sea.

The thanes were sore afraid; not one of them
Dared hope that he should ever reach the land,
Of those who by the sea had sought a ship
With Andrew, for as yet they did not know
Who pointed out the course for that sea-bark.   5

ELENE

The Battle

Trumpets resounded before the troop.
The raven was watching and waiting joyfully,
The dewy-winged eagle saw from the distance,
And the wolf from his haunt in the desolate wood
Howled at the terror of death and hate.   10
Arrows rained on them as they rushed together;
Shields were broken, javelins shattered,
And the sword that swayed with the swinging arm
Came crashing down on the death-doomed foe.
They pressed on resolutely, pushing with effort,   15
Thrusting with swords and swinging battle-axes,
And ever their banner was borne forward
With shouts of triumph that were loud and shrill,
As the heathen fell joyless on that field.
Hastily the host of Huns fled away   20
When the Roman king, the fighter unconquerable,
The fierce leader, lifted the cross.
Wide was the ruin that was wrought on the heathen.
Some perished there in that place of death,
Some fled half alive to rocky fastnesses,   25
And won their way back to Danube's banks;
And some found death in the depths of the lake-stream:
But the proud victors chased the vanquished
From the day's dawning till night came down,
And with ash-darts and arrows (fierce battle-adders)   30
They destroyed the hateful host of the enemy.

ANGLO-SAXON CHRONICLE[1]

[William the Conqueror]

A.D. 1087. . . . He died in Normandy the day after the Nativity of St. Mary,[2] and was buried in Caen, at St. Stephen's monastery, which he had built and richly endowed. Oh, how false and untrustworthy is the good of this world! He who had been a powerful king and the lord of many lands, possessed not then, of all his land, more than the space of seven feet; and he that aforetime had been adorned with gold and with gems lay covered with mold. . . .

If any one would know what manner of man he was, what honor he had, or of how many lands he was lord, I will write of him as I have known him, I who have looked upon him, and at one time lived in his family. This King William, of whom I speak, was a very wise and powerful man, and more honored and mighty than any of his predecessors. He was mild to the good men who loved God, but severe beyond measure toward those who withstood his will. He erected a noble monastery on the very spot where God granted him to conquer England, establishing monks in it, and making it rich. In his days the great monastery at Canterbury was built, and many others besides throughout all England. Moreover, this land was filled with monks, who lived their life after the rule of St. Benedict. . . . Great state did he hold: thrice every year did he wear his crown when he was in England: at Easter he wore it at Winchester, at Pentecost at Westminster, and at Christmas at Gloucester. And at these times all the powerful men of all England were with him—archbishops and bishops, abbots and earls, thanes and knights. Moreover, he was a very stern and severe man, so that no one durst do anything against his will. He kept earls in bonds who acted contrary to his wishes. He deposed bishops from their sees, and abbots from their monasteries,

[1] Reprinted from Cook and Tinker, *Translations from Old English Prose*, Ginn and Company, publishers.   [2] September 9.

he cast thanes into prison, and finally spared not his own
brother Odo, who was a very powerful bishop in Normandy,
with his see at Bayeux, and highest of all men, the king alone
excepted. In England he had an earldom; and when the king
was absent in Normandy, he was the first in this land; but him 5
he put in prison. . . . He ruled over England, and so closely
examined into it, by reason of his astuteness, that there was
not a single hide of land in the country whose ownership he
did not know, and its value, and afterward enter in his register. . . . Truly men had much hardship in his time, and very 10
many had distress. He had castles built, and afflicted the poor.
The king was very harsh, and took from his subjects many
a mark of gold, and many a hundred pounds of silver; and
this he took of his people rightfully or very wrongfully, and
for little need. He fell into avarice, and greediness he loved 15
above everything. He established a great deer-preserve, and
passed laws that whosoever should slay hart or hind should be
blinded. As he forbade the slaying of harts, so also of bears;
the stags he loved as if he had been their father; and he de-
creed that the hares should go free. The rich grumbled, and 20
the poor murmured, but he was so stout that he recked not of
all their ill will. They must bend themselves wholly to his will,
if they would have life, or land, or goods, or even his peace.

SIR GAWAIN AND THE GREEN KNIGHT[1]

FYTTE THE FIRST

XI

Long was there looking, that lord to behold,
For each man had marvel what might be the meaning   25
That a horseman and a horse might such a hue catch.
As grow-green as the grass and greener yet seemed they,
Than green enamel on gold glowing brighter.

[1] Reprinted from J. M. Manly, *English Prose and Poetry*, Ginn and
Company, publishers.

All studied that stood there, and stalked to him nearer,
With all the wonder in the world what wiles he was planning;
For many sights had they seen, but such a sight never;
So for phantom and faërie the folk there did deem it.
5 Therefore to answer was fearful many a fine fellow,
And all were stunned by his speech and stone-still sat they,
In a sheer silence through the hall splendid;
As if they had slipped into sleep, so slacked they their talking,
    That day;
10   Not all for fear, I trow,
        But some in courteous way,
        Let him to whom all bow
        The stranger first assay.

XVI

"Would you, most gracious lord," quoth Gawain to the king,[1]
15 "But bid me leave this bench and bide by you there,
So that I without rudeness might rise from this table,
And that to my liege lady there were lacking no courtesy,
I would come to your counsel, before your court splendid;
For methinks it is unseemly, as sage men weigh things,
20 When such an asking is honoured so high in your hall—
Though you yourself be eager for all undertakings—
While about you on bench sit so many bold ones,
Than whom under heaven, I think none hardier are of temper,
Nor better bodies in battle when banners are lifted.
25 I am the weakest, I wot,[2] and of wit feeblest,
And least the loss of my life, if no lie shall be spoken;
But forasmuch as you are my uncle I am only of merit—
No desert but your blood I in my body reckon—
And since this affair is so foolish that you it befits not,
30 And I have sued for it first, let my suit be granted!
And if my conduct is not comely, let all this court judge me
    To blame."

    [1] Arthur.   [2] know.

Nobles 'gan whispering;
Their verdict was the same,
To exempt the crownèd king
And give Gawain the game.

XVII

Then kindly the king commanded him to rise;   5
And he came forward quickly and curtsied duly,
Kneels down before the king and catches the weapon;
And he releases it lovingly and lifts up his hand
And gives him God's blessing and gladly bids him
That his heart and his hand should both be hardy.   10
"Take care, cousin," said the king, "that thou carve him
     once,
And if thou touchest him tidily, truly I trow
That thou canst endure any dint[1] that he will deal thee."
Gawain goes to the green man, with gisarme[2] in hand;
And he boldly abides him, abashed was he never.   15
Then calls to Sir Gawain the champion in green:
"Let us canvass our compact ere we carry this further.
First, knight, I must know what thy name is;
That tell thou me truly that I may trust to it."
"In good faith," quoth the good knight, "Gawain men call
     me,   20
Who shall bid[3] thee this buffet, whate'er befalls after,
And at this time twelve month take from thee another,
With what weapon so thou wilt, and from no wight else
                    Alive."
              That other answers again,   25
              "Sir Gawain, so may I thrive
              As I am wondrous fain[4]
              'Tis thou this dint shalt drive."

---

[1] blow, stroke.   [3] offer.
[2] a long-handled weapon, a poleax.   [4] eager.

XVIII

"By God," quoth the Green Knight, "Sir Gawain, I like it
That I shall have from thy hand what I here sought for;
And thou hast rightly rehearsed, as reason was truly,
Clearly all the covenant that of the king I asked,
5 Save that thou must assure me, sir, by thy honour,
That thou wilt seek me thyself in what spot soever
Thou thinkst to find me, in faith, and fetch thee such wages
As thou dealest me to-day before these doughty[1] nobles."
"In what climes shall I seek thee? In what country is thy
    dwelling?
10 Of thy habitation have I ne'er heard, by Him that wrought
    me;
Nor know I thee, knight, thy court, nor thy name;
But direct me to thy dwelling and disclose how men call
    thee,
And I shall strive with my strength to steer my steps
    thither;
And that I swear thee surely and by my sacred honour."
15 "That is enough at New Year; no more is needful,"
Quoth the grim man in green to Gawain the courteous;
"If I tell thee truly, when I the tap have taken
And thou hast smoothly smitten me, if smartly I teach thee
Of my house and my home and how men call me,
20 Then mayst thou enquire my country and hold our covenant.
And if I spend then no speech, thou shalt speed the better,
For thou mayst stop in this stead[2] and step no further,
                    But stay.
                Take now thy grim tool duly;
25   Let's see thee hack away!"
                "Yea, sir," quoth Gawain, "truly";
                His axe he strokes in play.

---

[1] valiant, brave.   [2] place.

THE PEARL[1]

[Extracts]

A radiant pearl for royal array
Clean to enclose in gold so clear;
Out of the Orient, I boldly say,
Found have I never her precious peer,
So pure, so perfect at each assay,   5
So small, so smooth that blissful sphere;
Wherever I judged of jewels gay,
I set her apart as the prize most dear.
    Alas! in an arbor I lost her here,
    Slipping through grass to earth, I wot;   10
    I pine, cut off from the loving cheer
    Of my own pearl without a spot.

There where I lost it, since have I long
Waited and wished for return of the weal[2]
That whilom[3] made me forget my wrong   15
And brought me comfort, my spirit to heal,
That now is oppressed with passions strong
Till all my senses whirl and reel.
Yet methought was never so sweet a song
As the quiet hour to me let steal;   20
    Many strange fancies did it reveal—
    To think that her fairness earth should clot!
    O grave, the rarest of gems thou dost seal,
    My own dear pearl without a spot.
     . . . .

More wonder my judgment stole away;   25
I saw beyond that river fair
A crystal cliff as clear as day,
Its royal rays gleamed through the air;

---

[1] Reprinted from J. M. Manly, *English Prose and Poetry*, Ginn and Company, publishers.   [2] happiness.   [3] formerly.

At its foot there sat a child full gay,
A mannerly maiden, debonair,[1]
All argent[2] white was her array;
I knew her well, I had seen her ere.[3]

5   As glistening gold, refined and rare,
So sheen[4] she shone upon the shore;
Long while I looked upon her there;
The longer, I knew her more and more.

The more I questioned her fair face
10   And came to know her figure bright,
Such joy shed over me its grace
That scarce before I had known delight;
Desire to address her grew apace,
But abashment filled my heart with fright;
15   Seeing her in so strange a place
Full well my heart astonish might.
        Then lifts she up her forehead white,
Her visage fairer than e'er before;
Bewildered my heart was at the sight
20   And ever the longer, the more and more.

     .   .   .   .

Delight me drove in eye and ear;
My earthly mind was maddened nigh.
When I saw my darling, I would be near,
Beyond the water that she stood by:
25   "Nothing," methought, "can harm me here,
Deal me a blow and low make lie;
To wade the stream have I no fear,
Or to swim the deeps, though I should die."
        But from that purpose withheld was I;
30   As unto the stream I started still,
        Clean from that plan I was turned awry;
It was not at my Prince's will.

---

[1] kindly, gracious.   [3] before.
[2] silvery.   [4] beautiful.

It pleased him not I should pass quite,
O'er marvellous meres,[1] so mad arrayed;
Though in my rush I had strength and might,
Yet hastily therein I was stayed;
For as I strove to the bank aright,   5
My haste me of my dream betrayed;
Then waked I in that arbor bright,
My head upon that mound was laid
    Where my own pearl to ground had strayed.
    I roused me, with many a fear a-thrill,   10
    And sighing to myself I said:
    "Now all be at that Prince's will."

LAYAMON[2]

THE BRUT

[Extracts]

Arthur went to Cornwall,
The host with him was countless;
Modred heard the tidings   15
And took his way against him
With host no man could number.
Many there were death-doomed!
By the river Tamar
The troops came together;   20
The place was christened Camelford;
Forever-more shall last that word!
And at Camelford was assembled
Sixty thousand
And thousands many more too;   25
Modred was their leader.

[1] seas.
[2] Reprinted from J. M. Manly, *English Prose and Poetry*, Ginn and Company, publishers.

Then thitherward went riding
Arthur the royal
With army unnumbered,
Doomed though they all were.
5   By the river Tamar
The troops came together;
Raised their royal standards;
Rushed there together;
Long swords locked they,
10 Laying blows on helmets;
Sparks they struck out,
Spears did rattle;
Shields were a-shaking,
Shafts were a-breaking.
15 There fought all together
Folk beyond counting.
Tamar was a flood
With measureless blood.
Of men in the fight there
20 Nobody might there
Distinguish any warrior,
Nor who did better, who did worse,
So was that conflict mingled;
For each struck adown right,
25 Were he yeoman,[1] or were he knight.
There was Modred stricken,
And life in him did sicken.
. . . in that conflict.
There fell in that battle
30 All of the brave ones,
Arthur's own henchmen,
The high and the lowly,
And all the Britons
Of Arthur's board too,

---

[1] a common man, a free-born man.

And all his fosterlings
Of foreign nations many,
And Arthur sorely wounded
With broad blade of war-spear.
Fifteen times was he   5
Fiendishly wounded;
Even into the smallest
Two gloves might one have thrust.
   Then were there in that battle
Left among the living   10
Of two hundred thousand soldiers
Who lay there slaughtered
But Arthur the king only
And two of his warriors.
Arthur was wounded   15
Wondrous severely.
   To him came a child[1] then
Who was of his kindred;
He was Cador's first-born,
Who Earl was of Cornwall.   20
Constantine his name was;
He was to the king dear.
Arthur looked upon him,
As he lay on the ground there,
And these words spake he   25
With heart full of sorrow:
"Constantine, welcome art thou!
Thou wert Cador's first-born!
To thee do I commit here
The care of my kingdom;   30
And guard well my Britons
Ever whilst thou livest;
And keep thou all the customs
That loved were in my life-time,

---

[1] A youth of noble family. Cf. Childe Harold, p. 161.

And all the customs splendid
That Uther's reign attended.
And I will fare to Avalon
To the fairest of all maidens,
5   Where Queen Argantè tarries,
Most beautiful of fairies;
And she shall every wound
Make both whole and sound,
All whole shall she make me
10   With health-giving potions.
And come shall I hereafter
Back to my kingdom
And abide with my Britons
With bliss forever."
15   E'en as he was speaking
There came from sea speeding
A very small boat gliding
Before the waves a-riding;
And women twain within it
20   Wondrously attired.
And they raised up Arthur anon,
And aboard rapidly bore him,
And adown softly they set him,
And forth went they sailing.
25   Then was fulfilled there
What Merlin said aforetime,
That infinite grieving
Should be at Arthur's leaving.
Britons believe ever
30   That still he is living
And fostered in Avalon[1]
With the fairest of all fairies;
And ever hope the Britons
For Arthur's coming hither.

[1] (ăv′à lŏn) the Island of the Blessed, the paradise of Celtic mythology; cf. p. 249 and note on **233 33.**

Was never the man born
Of mother on lucky morn
Who can of the true tale
Of Arthur tell us further.
But once there was a wizard,   5
Merlin they called him,
With words he predicted—
His sayings were truthful—
That an Arthur should one day
Come England to succour.   10

THE AGE OF CHAUCER AND THE
REVIVAL OF LEARNING

GEOFFREY CHAUCER

CANTERBURY TALES

Extracts from the Prologue[1]

A Knyght ther was and that a worthy man,
That fro the tyme that he first bigan
To riden out, he lovede chivalrie,
Trouthe and honour, fredom and curteisie.
Ful worthy was he in his lordes werre,[2]
And thereto[3] hadde he riden, no man ferre,[4]
As wel in Cristendom as in hethenesse,
And ever honoured for his worthynesse.
At Alisaundre he was whan it was wonne;
Ful ofte tyme he hadde the bord bigonne[5]
Aboven alle nacions in Pruce.[6]
In Lettow[7] hadde he reysed[8] and in Ruce,[9]
No Cristen man so ofte of his degree.
In Gernade[10] at the seege eek[11] hadde he be
Of Algezir, and riden in Belmarye.[12]
At Lyeys was he, and at Satalye,
Whan they were wonne; and in the Grete See[13]
At many a noble armee hadde he be.

5

10

15

---

[1] Reprinted from J. M. Manly, *English Prose and Poetry*, Ginn and Company, publishers. [2] war. [3] moreover, besides. [4] farther. [5] begun the board, sat at the head of the table. [6] Prussia. [7] Lithuania. [8] traveled, raided. [9] Russia. [10] Granada. [11] also. [12] Moorish kingdom in northern Africa. [13] Mediterranean.

At mortal batailles hadde he been fiftene,
And foughten for oure feith at Tramyssene
In lystes thries,[1] and ay slayn his foo.
This ilke[2] worthy knyght hadde been also
Somtyme with the lord of Palatye[3]   5
Agayn[4] another hethen in Turkye;
And evermoore he hadde a sovereyn prys.[5]
And though that he were worthy, he was wys,
And of his port[6] as meeke as is a mayde.
He never yet no vileynye[7] ne sayde   10
In al his lyf unto no maner wight.[8]
He was a verray, parfit, gentil knyght.
   But for to tellen yow of his array,
His hors were goode, but he was nat gay;
Of fustian[9] he wered a gypon[10]   15
Al bismotered[11] with his habergeon[12];
For he was late y-come from his viage,[13]
And wente for to doon his pilgrymage.
   With hym ther was his sone, a yong Squier,
A lovyere[14] and a lusty bacheler,[15]   20
With lokkes crulle,[16] as they were leyd in presse.
Of twenty yeer of age he was, I gesse.
Of his stature he was of evene lengthe,[17]
And wonderly delyvere[18] and greet of strengthe;
And he hadde been somtyme in chyvachye,[19]   25
In Flaundres, in Artoys and Pycardye,
And born hym weel, as of so litel space,
In hope to stonden in his lady[20] grace.
Embrouded[21] was he, as it were a meede[22]

---

[1] thrice.   [2] same.   [3] a domain in Asia Minor held by Christians under the Turks.   [4] against.   [5] high esteem, renown.   [6] bearing. [7] coarseness, discourteous language.   [8] any sort of person.   [9] coarse cloth.   [10] shirt, short coat, tunic.   [11] stained.   [12] (hăb'ẽr jŭn) coat of mail.   [13] voyage, journey.   [14] lover.   [15] aspirant to knighthood. [16] curly.   [17] fair, or moderate, height.   [18] deliver, active.   [19] cavalry expedition, raid.   [20] lady's.   [21] embroidered.   [22] meadow.

Al ful of fresshe floures whyte and reede;
Syngynge he was or floytynge[1] al the day;
He was as fressh as is the monthe of May.
Short was his gowne, with sleves longe and wyde;
5 Wel coude he sitte on hors, and faire ryde;
He coude songes make and wel endite,[2]
Juste[3] and eek daunce and weel purtreye[4] and write.
So hoote he lovede that by nyghtertale[5]
He sleep namoore than dooth a nyghtyngale.
10 Curteis he was, lowely and servysable,
And carf[6] biforn his fader at the table.
   A Yeman[7] hadde he, and servants namo[8]
At that tyme, for hym liste ride soo;
And he was clad in cote and hood of grene;
15 A sheef of pocok[9] arwes bright and kene
Under his belt he bar ful thriftily—
Wel coude he dresse[10] his takel[11] yemanly;
His arwes drouped noght with fetheres lowe—
And in his hand he bar a myghty bowe.
20 A not-heed[12] hadde he with a broun visage.
Of woodecraft wel coude he al the usage.
Upon his arm he bar a gay bracer,[13]
And by his syde a swerd and a bokeler,[14]
And on that oother syde a gay daggere
25 Harneised wel and sharpe as point of spere;
A Cristofre[15] on his brest of silver sheene;
An horn he bar, the bawdryk[16] was of grene.
A forster[17] was he soothly, as I gesse.

---

[1] fluting, whistling.   [2] compose.   [3] engage in combat on horseback with lances.   [4] portray, draw.   [5] night-time.   [6] carved.   [7] yeoman, a retainer of lower rank than a squire.   [8] no more.   [9] bundle of twenty-four peacock arrows.   [10] put in order, make ready for use. [11] tackle, weapons.   [12] cropped head, that is, with close-cut hair.   [13] arm guard.   [14] buckler, small shield.   [15] an image of St. Christopher. [16] baldric, cord or belt, worn over one shoulder and under the opposite arm to support the horn.   [17] forester.

A Monk ther was, a fair for the maistrie,[1]
An outridere that lovede venerie,[2]
A manly man, to been an abbot able.
Ful many a deyntee[3] hors hadde he in stable,
And whan he rood, men myghte his brydel heere 5
Gynglen in a whistlynge wynd as cleere
And eek as loude as dooth the chapel-belle
Ther-as this lord was kepere of the celle.[4]
The reule of Seint Maure or of Seint Beneit,
By-cause that it was old and som-del streit[5]— 10
This ilke monk leet olde thynges pace[6]
And heeld after the newe world the space.
He yaf[7] nat of that text a pulled[8] hen
That seith that hunters beth nat hooly men,
Ne that a monk when he is recchelees[9] 15
Is likned til a fissh that is waterlees;
This is to seyn, a monk out of his cloystre.
But thilke text heeld he nat worth an oystre;
And I seyde his opinioun was good;
What sholde he studie and make hym-selven wood,[10] 20
Upon a book in cloystre alwey to poure,
Or swynken[11] with his handes and laboure
As Austyn bit?[12] How shal the world be served?
Lat Austyn have his swynk to him reserved.
Therfore he was a pricasour[13] aright; 25
Grehoundes he hadde, as swift as fowel in flight:
Of prikyng[14] and of huntyng for the hare
Was al his lust,[15] for no cost wolde he spare.
I seigh[16] his sleves purfiled[17] at the hond
With grys,[18] and that the fyneste of a lond; 30

---

[1] an exceedingly fine one. [2] hunting. [3] dainty, fine. [4] head of the branch monastery. [5] somewhat strict. [6] pass on, go. [7] gave, cared. [8] plucked, thin, skinny. [9] reckless, vagrant, negligent of duty. [10] mad, crazy. [11] toil, labor. [12] bids. [13] a hard rider. [14] tracking (the hare). [15] desire, pleasure. [16] saw. [17] purfled, edged. [18] a costly gray fur.

And for to festne his hood under his chyn
He hadde of gold y-wroght a curious pyn;
A love-knotte in the gretter ende ther was.
His heed was balled, that shoon as any glas,
5   And eek his face as it hadde been enoynt.
He was a lord ful fat and in good poynt;[1]
Hise eyen stepe[2] and rollynge in his heed,
That stemed[3] as a forneys of a leed;[4]
His bootes souple, his hors in greet estaat.
10   Now certeinly he was a fair prelaat.
He was nat pale, as a forpyned goost;[5]
A fat swan loved he best of any roost.
His palfrey[6] was as broun as is a berye.
A Marchant was ther with a forked berd,
15   In mottelee,[7] and hye on horse he sat;
Upon his heed a Flaundrish bever hat,
His botes clasped faire and fetisly.[8]
His resons[9] spak he ful solempnely,[10]
Souning[11] alway thencrees[12] of his winning.
20   He wolde the see were kept for anything[13]
Betwixe Middelburgh and Orewelle.
Wel coude he in eschaunge[14] sheeldes[15] selle.
This worthy man ful well his wit bisette[16];
Ther wiste no wight[17] that he was in dette,
25   So estatly[18] was he of governaunce[19]
With his bargaynes and with his chevisaunce.[20]
For sothe he was a worthy man withalle,
But sooth to seyn,[21] I noot[22] how men him calle.

---

[1] in good condition.   [2] prominent, large, also bright.   [3] glowed, flamed.   [4] fire under a cauldron.   [5] ghost of one tortured to death.
[6] saddle horse.   [7] cloth of a mixed color, gray.   [8] neatly.   [9] opinions, remarks.   [10] pompously.   [11] sounding, proclaiming.   [12] the increase.   [13] guarded at any cost.   [14] exchange.   [15] écus, French coins having a shield on one side.   [16] employed.   [17] nobody knew.   [18] stately, impressive.   [19] behavior.   [20] expedients, borrowing.   [21] to tell the truth.   [22] I don't know.

A Clerk[1] ther was of Oxenford also
That unto logyk hadde longe y-go.
As leene was his hors as is a rake,
And he was not right fat, I undertake,
But looked holwe[2] and ther-to sobrely.   5
Ful thredbare was his overeste courtepy,[3]
For he hadde geten hym yet no benefice,[4]
Ne was so worldly for to have office;
For hym was levere[5] have at his beddes heed
Twenty bookes clad in blak or reed   10
Of Aristotle and his philosophie
Than robes riche, or fithele,[6] or gay sautrie.[7]
But al be[8] that he was a philosophre,
Yet hadde he but litel gold in cofre;
But al that he myghte of his freendes hente[9]   15
On bookes and his lernynge he it spente,
And bisily gan for the soules preye
Of hem that gaf hym wher-with to scoleye.[10]
Of studie took he moost cure[11] and moost heede;
Noght o word spak he moore than was neede,   20
And that was seyd in forme and reverence,
And short and quyk and ful of hy sentence.[12]
Sownynge in[13] moral vertu was his speche,
And gladly wolde he lerne and gladly teche.

[1] scholar.   [2] hollow.   [3] short overcoat of coarse material.   [4] living,
position in the church.   [5] he had rather.   [6] fiddle.   [7] psaltery, a
stringed instrument.   [8] although.   [9] get.   [10] go to school, study.
[11] care.   [12] significance, meaning.   [13] tending to, full of.

THE NUN'S PRIEST'S TALE

[Introduction]

A povre widwe[1] somdel stope[2] in age,
Was whilom[3] dwelling in a narwe[4] cotage,
Biside a grove, stonding in a dale.
This widwe, of which I telle yow my tale,
5   Syn thilke[5] day that she was last a wyf,
In pacience ladde a ful simple lyf,
For litel was hir catel[6] and hir rente.[7]
By Housbondry[8] of such as God hir sente,
She fond[9] hirself, and eek hir doughtres two.
10   Three large sowes had she, and namo,[10]
Three kyn[11] and eek a sheep that highte[12] Malle.
Ful sooty was hir bour and eek hir halle,
In which she eet ful many a slender meel;
Of poynaunt[13] sauce hir needed never a deel.[14]
15   No deyntee morsel passed thrugh hir throte;
Hir diete was accordant to hir cote.
Repleccioun ne made hir never sik;
Attempre[15] diete was al hir phisik,
And exercise, and hertes suffisaunce.[16]
20   The goute lette[17] hir nothing[18] for to daunce,
N'apoplexie shente[19] nat hir heed;
No wyn ne drank she, neither whit ne reed;
Hir bord was served most with whit and blak,
Milk and broun breed, in which she fond no lak,
25   Seynd[20] bacoun and somtime an ey[21] or tweye,[22]
For she was as it were a maner[23] deye.[24]

---

[1] poor widow.   [2] somewhat stooped.   [3] once.   [4] narrow, small.
[5] that same.   [6] property (chattels).   [7] income.   [8] economy.   [9] found,
provided for.   [10] no more.   [11] cows.   [12] was called.   [13] poignant,
sharp, pungent.   [14] deal, portion.   [15] temperate.   [16] sufficiency, contentment.   [17] prevented, hindered.   [18] not at all.   [19] injured.
[20] singed, broiled.   [21] egg.   [22] two.   [23] sort of.   [24] dairy-
woman.

WILLIAM LANGLAND

PIERS PLOWMAN[1]

[Extracts from the Prologue]

In a summer season   when soft was the sunshine,
I got me into a garment   that grew on a sheep's back;
In habit like a hermit   unholy in living,
I went wide in this world   wonders to seek out.
But on a May morning,   on Malvern hillside,   5
I met with a marvel,   of magic I thought it.
  I was weary, forwandered,[2]   and went to refresh me
Under a broad bank   by the side of a brooklet.
And as I lay and leaned there   and looked on the waters,
I slumbered in a sleeping,   the sound was so soothing.   10
  Then came to my mind's eye   a marvellous vision,
That I was in a wilderness,   where wist[3] I never;
And as I looked into the east   and up where the sun was,
I saw a tower on a toft[4]   trimly constructed;
A deep dale[5] beneath   a dungeon within it,   15
With deep ditch and dark   and dreadful to look on.
A fair field full of folk   found I between them,
Of all manner of men,   the mean and the mighty,
Working and wandering   as the world asketh.
  Some put hand to the plow,   played very seldom,   20
In setting and sowing   sweated they hardly,
And won what these wasters   with gluttony devour.
  And some pranked[6] them   in pride,   appareled them
    accordingly,
In quaint guise of clothing   came they disfigured.
  To prayers and to penance   put themselves many,   25
All for love of our Lord   lived they most strictly,

---

[1] Reprinted from J. M. Manly, *English Prose and Poetry*, Ginn and Company, publishers.   [2] worn out with wandering.   [3] knew.   [4] knoll, hill.   [5] valley.   [6] dressed in a showy manner.

In hope of having heaven's bliss after;
As nuns and as hermits that in their cells hold them,
Covet not careering about through the country,
With no lustful luxuries their living to pamper.
5   And some took to trade, to thrive by the better,
As to our sight it seemeth that such men prosper.
   And some, merriments to make, with minstrels' cunning,
And get gold with their glee,[1] guiltless, methinketh;
But jesters and jugglers, Judas'[2] children,
10 Forged them wild fantasies as fools pretended,
Yet have wit at their will to work, were they willing.
What Paul preacheth of them prove here I dare not:
Qui loquitur turpiloquium[3] he is Lucifer's[4] henchman.
   Bidders and beggars fast about bustled,
15 Till their bags and their bellies were brimful and bulging;
Faking for their food, and fighting at the alehouse,
In gluttony, God wot,[5] go they to slumber,
And rise up with ribaldry,[6] these robber rascals;
Sleep and sloth too pursue them forever.
20   Pilgrims and palmers[7] pledged them together
To seek St. James's and saints' shrines at Rome too;
Went they forth on their way with many wise stories,
And had leave to be liars all their lives after.

  . . . .

Parsons and parish priests complain to their bishops
25 That their parish hath been poor since the pestilence season,
To have a license and leave in London to linger,
To sing there for simony,[8] for sweet is silver.
   There hovered a hundred in hoods of silk stuff;
It seemed they were sergeants[9] to serve in the law courts,
30 To plead for pennies and pounds for verdicts,
Not for love of our Lord unloose their lips ever.

---

[1] music, singing. [2] the disciple who betrayed Christ. [3] who talks scandal. [4] Satan's. [5] knows. [6] coarseness, vulgarity. [7] wandering monks, carrying palm branches to show that they had visited the Holy Land. [8] for hire, traffic in that which is sacred. [9] counselors, lawyers.

Thou couldst better measure the mist   on Malvern hillsides
Than get a mum[1] of their mouths   till money were showed
   them.
  I saw there bishops bold   and bachelors of divinity
Become clerks of account   and king's own servants.
Archdeacons and deans,   whose duty binds them   5
To preach to the people   and poor men to care for,
Have lighted out to London,   by leave of their bishops,
To be clerks of the King's Bench,   the country to injure.
  Barons and burgesses[2]   and bondmen also
I saw in that assembly,   as I shall show later ;   10
Bakers, butchers,   and brewers many ;
Woolen-weavers   and weavers of linen ;
Tailors, tanners,   and tuckers[3] likewise ;
Masons, miners,   and many other craftsmen ;
Dikers[4] and diggers   that do their deeds badly,   15
And drive forth the long day   with "*Dieu save Dame
   Emme !*"[5]
Cooks and their cookboys   crying, "Hot pies ! hot !
Good geese and piglets !   Go we dine, go we !"
Tavern-keepers told them   a tale of traffic,
With wine of Alsace   and wine of Gascon,   20
Of the Rhine and the Rochelle,   the roast to digest well.
  All this saw I sleeping,   and seven times more.

[1] sound, syllable.   [2] representatives in Parliament.   [3] fullers of cloth.
[4] ditchers.   [5] a popular song.

SIR THOMAS MALORY

LE MORTE DARTHUR[1]

[How Arthur was chosen King]

Then stood the realm in great jeopardy long while, for
every lord that was mighty of men made him strong, and
many weened[2] to have been king. Then Merlin went to the
Archbishop of Canterbury, and counselled him for to send for
5 all the lords of the realm, and all the gentlemen of arms, that
they should to London come by Christmas, upon pain of cursing; and for this cause, that Jesus, that was born on that
night, that he would of his great mercy show some miracle,
as he was come to be king of mankind, for to show some
10 miracle who should be rightways king of this realm. So the
Archbishop, by the advice of Merlin, sent for all the lords
and gentlemen of arms that they should come by Christmas
even unto London. And many of them made them clean of
their life, that their prayer might be the more acceptable
15 unto God. So in the greatest church of London (whether it
were Paul's or not the French book maketh no mention) all
the estates were long or day in the church for to pray. And
when matins and the first mass was done, there was seen in
the churchyard, against[3] the high altar, a great stone four
20 square, like unto a marble stone, and in midst thereof was
like an anvil of steel a foot on high, and therein stuck a fair
sword naked by the point, and letters there were written in
gold about the sword that said thus:—Whoso pulleth out this
sword of this stone and anvil, is rightwise king born of all
25 England. Then the people marvelled, and told it to the Archbishop. I command, said the Archbishop, that ye keep you
within your church, and pray unto God still; that no man

---

[1] Reprinted from Hopkins and Hughes, *The English Novel before the
Nineteenth Century*, Ginn and Company, publishers.   [2] thought,
expected.   [3] over against, facing.

touch the sword till the high mass be all done. So when all
masses were done all the lords went to behold the stone and
the sword. And when they saw the scripture,[1] some essayed,[2]
such as would have been king. But none might stir the
sword nor move it. He is not here, said the Archbishop, that 5
shall achieve the sword, but doubt not God will make him
known. But this is my counsel, said the Archbishop, that we
let purvey[3] ten knights, men of good fame, and they to keep this
sword. So it was ordained, and then there was made a cry,
that every man should essay that would, for to win the sword. 10
And upon New Year's Day the barons let make a jousts[4] and
a tournament,[5] that all knights that would joust or tourney
there might play, and all this was ordained for to keep the
lords and the commons together, for the Archbishop trusted
that God would make him known that should win the sword. 15
So upon New Year's Day, when the service was done, the
barons rode unto the field, some to joust and some to tourney,
and so it happened that Sir Ector, that had great livelihood[6]
about London, rode unto the jousts, and with him rode
Sir Kay his son, and young Arthur that was his nourished[7] 20
brother; and Sir Kay was made knight at All Hallowmass[8]
afore. So as they rode to the joustsward, Sir Kay had lost
his sword, for he had left it at his father's lodging, and so he
prayed young Arthur for to ride for his sword. I will well,
said Arthur, and rode fast after the sword, and when he came 25
home, the lady and all were out to see the jousting. Then
was Arthur wroth, and said to himself, I will ride to the
churchyard, and take the sword with me that sticketh in the
stone, for my brother Sir Kay shall not be without a sword
this day. So when he came to the churchyard, Sir Arthur alit 30
and tied his horse to the stile, and so he went to the tent, and
found no knights there, for they were at jousting; and so he
handled the sword by the handles, and lightly and fiercely

---

[1] inscription.   [2] tried.   [3] have provided.   [4] a combat between
two knights on horseback with lances.   [5] a jousting contest between two
groups of knights.   [6] estates.   [7] foster.   [8] November 1.

pulled it out of the stone, and took his horse and rode his way until he came to his brother Sir Kay, and delivered him the sword. And as soon as Sir Kay saw the sword, he wist well it was the sword of the stone, and so he rode to his father
5 Sir Ector, and said: Sir, lo here is the sword of the stone, wherefore I must be king of this land. When Sir Ector beheld the sword, he returned again and came to the church, and there they alit all three, and went into the church. And anon he made Sir Kay to swear upon a book how he came to that
10 sword. Sir, said Sir Kay, by my brother Arthur, for he brought it to me. How gat ye this sword? said Sir Ector to Arthur. Sir, I will tell you. When I came home for my brother's sword, I found nobody at home to deliver me his sword, and so I thought my brother Sir Kay should not be
15 swordless, and so I came hither eagerly and pulled it out of the stone without any pain. Found ye any knights about this sword? said Sir Ector. Nay, said Arthur. Now, said Sir Ector to Arthur, I understand ye must be king of this land. Wherefore I, said Arthur, and for what cause? Sir,
20 said Ector, for God will have it so, for there should never man have drawn out this sword, but he that shall be rightways king of this land. Now let me see whether ye can put the sword there as it was, and pull it out again. That is no mastery, said Arthur, and so he put it in the
25 stone, therewithal Sir Ector essayed to pull out the sword and failed.

.   .   .   .

And at the feast of Pentecost all manner of men essayed to pull at the sword that would essay, but none might prevail but Arthur, and pulled it out afore all the lords and commons
30 that were there; wherefore all the commons cried at once, We will have Arthur unto our king, we will put him no more in delay, for we all see that it is God's will that he shall be our king, and who that holdeth against it, we will slay him. And therewith they all kneeled at once, both rich and poor,

and cried Arthur mercy because they had delayed him so
long, and Arthur forgave them, and took the sword between
both his hands, and offered it upon the altar where the Archbishop was, and so was he made knight of the best man that
was there. And so anon[1] was the coronation made. And 5
there was he sworn unto his lords and the commons for to be
a true king, to stand with true justice from thenceforth the
days of this life. Also then he made all lords that held of the
crown to come in, and to do service as they ought to do. And
many complaints were made unto Sir Arthur of great wrongs 10
that were done since the death of King Uther, of many lands
that were bereaved[2] lords, knights, ladies, and gentlemen.
Wherefore King Arthur made the lands to be given again
unto them that owned them.

When this was done, that the king had stablished all the 15
countries about London, then he let make Sir Kay seneschal
of England; and Sir Baudwin of Britain was made constable;
and Sir Ulfius was made chamberlain; and Sir Brastias was
made warden to wait upon the north from Trent forwards,
for it was that time the most part the king's enemies. But 20
within few years after, Arthur won all the north, Scotland,
and all that were under their obeissance.[3] Also Wales, a part
of it held against Arthur, but he overcame them all, as he did
the remnant, through the noble prowess of himself and his
knights of the Round Table. 25

[1] at once.
[2] taken away from.
[3] dominion, power.

WILLIAM CAXTON

PROLOGUE TO VIRGIL'S ÆNEID

[Extract]

And fain would I satisfy every man, and so to do took an
old book, and read therein, and certainly the English was so
rude and broad, that I could not well understand it. And
also my Lord Abbot of Westminster did so show to me lately
5 certain evidences[1] written in old English, for to reduce it into
our English now used; and certainly it was written in such
wise that it was more like to Dutch than English; I could not
reduce ne bring it to be understood. And certainly our language now used varieth far from that which was used and
10 spoken when I was born. For we Englishmen be born under
the domination of the moon, which is never steadfast but ever
wavering, waxing one season and waneth and decreaseth another season. And that common English that is spoken in
one shire varieth from another, insomuch that in my days
15 happened that certain merchants were in a ship in Thames
for to have sailed over the sea into Zeeland,[2] and for lack of
wind they tarried at the Foreland,[3] and went to land for to
refresh them. And one of them, named Sheffield, a mercer,[4]
came into a house and asked for meat,[5] and especially he
20 asked after eggs; and the goodwife answered that she could
speak no French, and the merchant was angry, for he also
could speak no French, but would have had eggs; and she understood him not. And then at last another said, that he would
have "eyren." Then the goodwife said that she understood
25 him well. Lo, what should a man in these days now write,
eggs or eyren? Certainly it is hard to please every man because of diversity and change of language, for in these days

---

[1] legal documents.   [2] a province in the southern part of the Netherlands.   [3] the promontory at the mouth of the Thames.   [4] dealer in
silk and woolen cloth.   [5] food.

every man that is in any reputation in his country will utter
his communication and matters in such manners and terms
that few men shall understand them. And some honest and
great clerks[1] have been with me and desired me to write the
most curious terms that I could find; and thus between plain, 5
rude, and curious I stand abashed. But in my judgment the
common terms that be daily used be lighter to be understood
than the old and ancient English. And forasmuch as this
present book is not for a rude uplandish man to labour therein
ne[2] read[3] it, but only for a clerk and a noble gentleman that 10
feeleth and understandeth in feats of arms, in love, and in
noble chivalry, therefore in a mean between both I have reduced and translated this said book into our English, not
over-rude ne curious, but in such terms as shall be understood, by God's grace, according to my copy.   15

THE NUTBROWN MAYDE[4]

[Abridged]

"It stondeth so, a dede is do[5] wherefore moche harme shal
    growe.
My desteny is for to dey a shamful dethe, I trowe,
Or ellis to flee; the ton[6] must bee, none other wey I knowe
But to withdrawe as an outlaw and take me to my bowe.
Wherfore adew, my owne hert trewe, none other red[7] I can; 20
For I muste to the grenewode goo, alone, a banysshed man."

"Now syth[8] that ye have shewed to me the secret of your
    mynde,
I shalbe playne to you agayne, lyke as ye shal me fynde;

---

[1] Scholars. In the Dark Ages only the clergy could read and write.
[2] nor.   [3] study.   [4] Reprinted from J. M. Manly, *English Prose and
Poetry*, Ginn and Company, publishers.   [5] a deed has been done.   [6] one.
[7] I know no other way (plan).   [8] since.

Syth it is so that ye wyll goo, I wol not leve behynde,[1]
Shal ne'er be sayd the Nutbrown Mayde was to her love
    unkind.
Make you redy, for soo am I, all though it were anoon[2];
For in my mynde of all mankynde I love but you alone."

5 "I councel yow, remembre how it is noo maydens lawe
Nothing to dought, but to renne out to wod with an outlawe;
For ye must there in your hands bere a bowe redy to drawe,
And as a theef thus must ye lyve ever in drede and awe,
By whiche to yow gret harme myght grow; yet had I lever
    than[3]
10 That I had too the grenewode goo,[4] alone, a banysshed man."

"I thinke not nay, but as ye saye, it is noo maydens lore;
But love may make me for your sake, as ye have said before,
To com on fote, to hunte and shote to get us mete and store;
For soo that I your company may have, I aske noo more;
15 From whiche to parte, it makith myn herte as colde as ony
    ston;
For in my mynde of all mankynde I love but you alone."

"For an outlawe this is the lawe, that men hym take and
    binde,
Wythout pytee hanged to bee, and waver wyth the wynde.
Yf I had neede, as God forbede, what rescous[5] coude ye finde?
20 For sothe I trowe,[6] you and your bowe shul drawe for fere
    behynde;
And noo merveyle, for lytel avayle were in your councel than;
Wherfore I too the woode wyl goo, alone, a banysshed man."

"Ful wel knowe ye that wymen bee ful febyl for to fyght;
Noo womanhed is it indeede to bee bolde as a knight;

---

[1] I will not stay behind.
[2] anon, at once.
[3] I had rather then.

[4] I had gone to the greenwood.
[5] rescue, aid.
[6] indeed I believe.

Yet in suche fere yf that ye were, amonge enemys day and
    nyght,
I wolde wythstonde, with bowe in hande, to greve them as I
    myght,
And you to save, as wymen have from deth [ful] many one;
For in my mynde of all mankynde I love but you alone."

"Yet take good hede, for ever I drede that ye coude not
    sustein   5
The thorney wayes, the depe valeis, the snowe, the frost, the
    reyn,
The colde, the hete; for, drye or wete, we must lodge on
    the playn,
And, us above, noon other rove[1] but a brake, bussh, or
    twayne;
Whiche sone shulde greve you, I believe, and ye wolde gladly
    than
That I had too the grenewode goo, alone, a banysshed man." 10

"Syth I have here ben partynere with you of joy and blysse,
I muste also parte of your woo endure, as reason is;
Yet am I sure of oo plesure,[2] and shortly it is this,
That where ye bee, me semeth, perdè,[3] I coude not fare
    amysse.
Wythout more speche, I you beseche that we were sooи
    agone;   15
For in my mynde of all mankynde I love but you alone."

"Yef ye goo thedyr, ye must consider, whan ye have lust[4]
    to dyne,
Ther shal no mete be fore to gete, nor drinke, bere, ale, ne
    wine,

---

[1] roof.   [3] certainly (Old French, par Dé, by God).
[2] one pleasure.   [4] desire, wish.

Ne shetis clene to lye betwene, made of thred and twyne,
Noon other house but levys and bowes, to kever your hed
    and myn.
Loo! myn herte swete, this ylle dyet shuld make you pale
    and wan;
Wherfore I to the wood wyl goo, alone, a banysshed man."

5 "Amonge the wylde dere suche an archier as men say that
    ye bee
Ne may not fayle of good vitayle,[1] where is so grete plente;
And watir cleere of the ryvere shalbe ful swete to me,
Wyth whiche in hele[2] I shal right wele endure, as ye shal
    see;
And, er we goo, a bed or twoo I can provide anoon;
10 For in my mynde of all mankynde I love but you alone."

"Loo! yet before ye must doo more, yf ye wyl goo with me,—
As cutte your here[3] up by your ere, your kirtel[4] by the knee,
Wyth bowe in hande, for to withstonde your enmys, yf nede
    be,
And this same nyght before daylyght to woodward wyl I flee;
15 And if ye wyl all this fulfylle, doo it shortely as ye can;
Ellis wil I to the grenewode goo, alone, a banysshed man."

"I shal, as now, do more for you than longeth to womanhede,
To short my here, a bowe to bere to shote in time of nede.
O my swete moder, before all other, for you have I most
    drede;
20 But now adiew! I must ensue,[5] wher fortune doth me leede:
All this make ye; now lete us flee, the day cummeth fast
    upon;
For in my mynde of all mankynde I love but you alone."

---

[1] victual (now usually in the plural and colloquial), food.   [2] health.
[3] hair.   [4] skirt.   [5] follow.

"Myn owne dere love, I see the prove that ye be kynde and
    trewe;
Of mayde and wyfe, in all my lyf, the best that ever I knewe!
Be mery and glad, be no more sad, the case is chaungèd newe;
For it were ruthe[1] that for your trouth you shuld have cause
    to rewe.
Be not dismayed, whatsoever I sayd, to you whan I began,   5
I wyl not too the grenewode goo, I am noo banysshed man."

"Theis tidingis be more glad to me than to be made a quene,
Yf I were sure they shuld endure; but it is often seen,
When men wyl breke promyse, they speke the wordis on the
    splene.[2]
Ye shape some wyle, me to begyle, and stele fro me, I wene.   10
Then were the case wurs than it was, and I more woo-begone;
For in my mynde of al mankynde I love but you alone."

"Ye shal not nede further to drede, I wyl not disparage[3]
You, God defende,[4] sith you descende of so grete a lynage.
Now understonde, to Westmerlande, whiche is my herytage, 15
I wyl you bringe, and wyth a rynge, be wey of maryage,
I wyl you take, and lady make, as shortly as I can;
Thus have ye wone an erles son, and not a banysshed man."

[1] cause for regret.   [3] degrade.
[2] impulsively, capriciously.   [4] God forbid.

THE ELIZABETHAN AGE

MICHAEL DRAYTON

BALLAD OF AGINCOURT

Fair stood the wind for France,
When we our sails advance;
Nor now to prove our chance
   Longer will tarry;
5   But putting to the main,
At Caux, the mouth of Seine,
With all his martial train
   Landed King Harry.

And taking many a fort,
10   Furnished in warlike sort,
Marcheth towards Agincourt
   In happy hour;
Skirmishing, day by day,
With those that stopped his way,
15   Where the French general lay
   With all his power.

Which, in his height of pride,
King Henry to deride,
His ransom to provide,
20   To the King sending;
Which he neglects the while,
As from a nation vile,
Yet, with an angry smile,
   Their fall portending.

And turning to his men,
Quoth our brave Henry then:
"Though they to one be ten
   Be not amazèd!
Yet have we well begun: 5
Battles so bravely won
Have ever to the sun
   By Fame been raisèd!

"And for myself," quoth he,
"This my full rest shall be: 10
England ne'er mourn for me,
   Nor more esteem me!
Victor I will remain,
Or on this earth lie slain;
Never shall She sustain   15
   Loss to redeem me!

"Poitiers and Cressy tell,
When most their pride did swell,
Under our swords they fell.
   No less our skill is,   20
Than when our Grandsire great,
Claiming the regal seat,
By many a warlike feat
   Lopped the French lilies."

The Duke of York so dread   25
The eager vanward led;
With the main, Henry sped
   Amongst his henchmen:
Exeter had the rear,
A braver man not there!   30
O Lord, how hot they were
   On the false Frenchmen!

They now to fight are gone;
Armour on armour shone;
Drum now to drum did groan:
　　To hear, was wonder;
5　That, with the cries they make,
The very earth did shake;
Trumpet to trumpet spake;
　　Thunder to thunder.

Well it thine age became,
10　O noble Erpingham,
Which didst the signal aim
　　To our hid forces!
When, from a meadow by,
Like a storm suddenly,
15　The English archery　　′
　　Stuck the French horses.

With Spanish yew so strong;
Arrows a cloth-yard long,
That like to serpent stung,
20　　Piercing the weather.
None from his fellow starts;
But, playing manly parts,
And like true English hearts,
　　Stuck close together.

25　When down their bows they threw,
And forth their bilboes[1] drew,
And on the French they flew:
　　Not one was tardy.
Arms were from shoulders sent,[2]
30　Scalps to the teeth were rent,
Down the French peasants went:
　　Our men were hardy.

[1] swords.　　　　　　[2] cut, torn.

This while our noble King,
His broad sword brandishing,
Down the French host did ding,[1]
   As to o'erwhelm it.
And many a deep wound lent;   5
His arms with blood besprent,
And many a cruel dent
   Bruisèd his helmet.

Gloucester, that duke so good,
Next of the royal blood,   10
For famous England stood
   With his brave brother.
Clarence, in steel so bright,
Though but a maiden knight,
Yet in that furious fight   15
   Scarce such another!

Warwick in blood did wade;
Oxford, the foe invade,
And cruel slaughter made,
   Still as they ran up.   20
Suffolk his axe did ply;
Beaumont and Willoughby
Bare them right doughtily;
   Ferrers, and Fanhope.

Upon Saint Crispin's Day   25
Fought was this noble fray;
Which Fame did not delay
   To England to carry.
O when shall English men
With such acts fill a pen?[2]   30
Or England breed again
   Such a King Harry?

---

[1] thrash, beat.   [2] give a subject for a poem.

EDMUND SPENSER

THE FAERY QUEEN

Book I, Canto I

[The Hermit]

At length they chaunst to meet upon the way
   An aged Sire, in long blacke weedes[1] yclad,
   His feete all bare, his beard all hoarie gray,
   And by his belt his booke he hanging had:
5   Sober he seemde, and very sagely sad,
   And to the ground his eyes were lowly bent,
   Simple in shew, and voide of malice bad;
   And all the way he prayèd as he went,
And often knockt his brest, as one that did repent.

10 He faire the knight saluted, louting[2] low,
   Who faire him quited,[3] as that courteous was;
   And after askèd him, if he did know
   Of straunge adventures, which abroad did pas.
   "Ah! my dear sonne," (quoth he) "how should, alas!
15 Silly old man, that lives in hidden cell,
   Bidding[4] his beades all day for his trespas,
   Tydings of warre and worldly trouble tell?
With holy father sits[5] not with such thinges to mell.[6]

   "But if of daunger, which hereby doth dwell,
20 And homebredd evil ye desire to heare,
   Of a straunge man I can you tidings tell,
   That wasteth all this countrie, farre and neare."
   "Of such," (saide he,) "I chiefly doe inquere,
   And shall you well rewarde to shew the place

[1] clothing.
[2] bowing.
[3] requited, answered.
[4] telling.
[5] suits, befits.
[6] meddle.

In which that wicked wight his dayes doth weare;
For to all knighthood it is foule disgrace,
That such a cursèd creature lives so long a space."

"Far hence" (quoth he) "in wastfull wildernesse
  His dwelling is, by which no living wight   5
  May ever passe, but thorough[1] great distresse."
  "Now," (saide the Ladie,) "draweth toward night,
  And well I wote, that of your later fight
  Ye all forwearied be; for what so strong,
  But, wanting rest, will also want of might?   10
  The Sunne, that measures heaven all day long,
At night doth baite[2] his steedes the Ocean waves emong.

"Then with the Sunne take, Sir, your timely rest,
  And with new day new worke at once begin:
  Untroubled night, they say, gives counsell best."   15
  "Right well, Sir knight, ye have advisèd bin."
  Quoth then that aged man: "the way to win
  Is wisely to advise[3]; now day is spent:
  Therefore with me ye may take up your In
  For this same night." The knight was well content;   20
So with that godly father to his home they went.

A litle lowly Hermitage it was,
  Downe in a dale, hard by a forests side,
  Far from resort of people that did pas
  In traveill to and froe: a litle wyde[4]   25
  There was an holy chappell edifyde,[5]
  Wherein the Hermite dewly wont[6] to say
  His holy thinges each morne and even-tyde;
  Thereby a christall streame did gently play,
Which from a sacred fountaine wellèd forth alway.   30

[1] through.
[2] feed.
[3] consider.

[4] wide, aside, at one side.
[5] built.
[6] used.

Arrivèd there, the litle house they fill,
Ne looke for entertainement where none was;
Rest is their feast, and all thinges at their will.
The noblest mind the best contentment has.
5   With faire discourse the evening so they pas;
For that olde man of pleasing wordes had store,
And well could file his tongue as smooth as glas:
He told of Saintes and Popes, and evermore
He strowd an Ave-Mary after and before.

AMORETTI[1]

Sonnet LXXV

10   One day I wrote her name upon the strand;
But came the waves and washèd it away:
Agayne I wrote it with a second hand;
And came the tyde, and made my paynes his pray.
"Vayne man," sayd she, "that doest in vayne assay[2]
15   A mortall thing so to immortalize;
For I myselve shall lyke to this decay,
And eek my name bee wypèd out lykewize."
"Not so" (quod[3] I); "let baser things devize
To dy in dust, but you shall live by fame:
20   My verse your vertues rare shall eternize,
And in the heavens wryte your glorious name;
Where, when as death shall all the world subdew,
Our love shall live, and later life renew."

SONG FROM *EPITHALAMION*[4]

Wake now, my love, awake! for it is time;
25   The rosy morn long since left Tithon's bed,
All ready to her silver coach to climb;

[1] love songs.
[2] essay, try.
[3] quoth, said.
[4] a poem in honor of a marriage.

And Phœbus[1] 'gins to show his glorious head.
Hark, how the cheerful birds do chant their lays
And carol of love's praise.
The merry lark her matins sings aloft;
The thrush replies; the mavis[2] descant[3] plays;   5
The ouzel[4] shrills; the ruddock[5] warbles soft;
So goodly all agree, with sweet concent,[6]
To this day's merriment.
Ah! my dear love, why do ye sleep thus long
When meeter were that ye should now awake,   10
T' await the coming of your joyous make,[7]
And hearken to the birds' love-learnèd song,
The dewy leaves among!
For they of joy and pleasance to you sing,
That all the woods them answer, and their echo ring.   15

SIR PHILIP SIDNEY

MY TRUE-LOVE HATH MY HEART

My true-love hath my heart, and I have his,
By just exchange one for the other given:
I hold his dear, and mine he cannot miss;
There never was a better bargain driven:
    My true-love hath my heart, and I have his.   20

His heart in me keeps him and me in one,
My heart in him his thoughts and senses guides:
He loves my heart, for once it was his own,
I cherish his because in me it bides:
    My true-love hath my heart, and I have his.   25

[1] the sun.   [2] song thrush.   [3] a variation of the main melody, the early form of counterpoint.   [4] blackbird.   [5] robin.   [6] harmony.   [7] mate.

ASTROPHEL AND STELLA

XXXIX

Come, Sleep! O Sleep, the certain knot of peace,
The baiting-place[1] of wit, the balm of woe,
The poor man's wealth, the prisoner's release,
Th' indifferent judge between the high and low;
5   With shield of proof[2] shield me from out the prease[3]
Of those fierce darts Despair at me doth throw:
O make in me those civil wars to cease;
I will good tribute pay, if thou do so.
Take thou of me smooth pillows, sweetest bed,
10   A chamber deaf of noise and blind of light,
A rosy garland and a weary head:
And if these things, as being thine in right,
Move not thy heavy grace, thou shalt in me,
Livelier then else-where, Stella's image see.

PERCY'S RELIQUES OF ENGLISH POETRY

THE GREAT ADVENTURER

15   Over the mountains
And over the waves,
Under the fountains
And under the graves;
Under floods that are deepest,
20   Which Neptune obey;
Over rocks that are steepest
Love will find out the way.

Where there is no place
For the glow-worm to lie;

---

[1] feeding place, place of refreshment.   [2] of fine quality, impenetrable.
[3] press, throng.

Where there is no space
For receipt of a fly;
Where the midge dares not venture
Lest herself fast she lay;
If love come, he will enter   5
And soon find out his way.

You may esteem him
A child for his might;
Or you may deem him
A coward from his flight;   10
But if she whom love doth honor
Be conceal'd from the day,
Set a thousand guards upon her,
Love will find out the way.

Some think to lose him   15
By having him confined;
And some do suppose him,
Poor thing, to be blind;
But if ne'er so close ye wall him,
Do the best that you may,   20
Blind love, if so ye call him,
Will find out his way.

You may train the eagle
To stoop to your fist;
Or you may inveigle   25
The phœnix[1] of the east;
The lioness, ye may move her
To give o'er her prey;
But you'll ne'er stop a lover:
He will find out his way.   30

---

[1] a legendary bird, which lived for five hundred years, then was consumed by fire, and rose with renewed youth from its ashes.

ROBERT GREENE

SONG FROM *FAREWELL TO FOLLY*

Sweet are the thoughts that savour of content;
   The quiet mind is richer than a crown;
Sweet are the nights in careless slumber spent;
   The poor estate scorns fortune's angry frown:
5   Such sweet content, such minds, such sleep, such bliss,
Beggars enjoy, when princes oft do miss.

The homely house that harbours quiet rest;
   The cottage that affords no pride nor care;
The mean that 'grees with country music best;
10   The sweet consort of mirth and music's fare;
Obscurèd life sets down a type of bliss:
A mind content both crown and kingdom is.

PHILOMELA'S ODE

Sitting by a river's side,
Where a silent stream did glide,
15   Muse I did of many things
That the mind in quiet brings.
I 'gan think how some men deem
Gold their god; and some esteem
Honour is the chief content
20   That to man in life is lent.
And some others do contend,
Quiet none like to a friend.
Others hold there is no wealth
Comparèd to a perfect health.
25   Some man's mind in quiet stands,
When he is lord of many lands.
But I did sigh, and said all this
Was but a shade of perfect bliss;

And in my thoughts I did approve,
Nought so sweet as is true love.
Love 'twixt lovers passeth these,
When mouth kisseth and heart 'gres,
With folded arms and lips meeting,   5
Each soul another sweetly greeting;
For by the breath the soul fleeteth,
And soul with soul in kissing meeteth.
If love be so sweet a thing,
That such happy bliss doth bring,   10
Happy is love's sugared thrall,
But unhappy maidens all,
Who esteem your virgin blisses
Sweeter than a wife's sweet kisses.
No such quiet to the mind   15
As true Love with kisses kind;
But if a kiss prove unchaste,
Then is true love quite disgraced.
Though love be sweet, learn this of me,
No sweet love but honesty.   20

THOMAS DEKKER

SONG OF THE CYCLOPS

Brave iron, brave hammer, from your sound
The art of music has her ground;
On the anvil thou keep'st time,
Thy knick-a-knock is a smith's best chime.
  Yet thwick-a-thwack, thwick, thwack-a-thwack, thwack, 25
  Make our brawny sinews crack:
  Then pit-a-pat, pat, pit-a-pat, pat,
  Till thickest bars be beaten flat.

We shoe the horses of the sun,
Harness the dragons of the moon;   30

Forge Cupid's quiver, bow, and arrows,
And our dame's coach that's drawn with sparrows.
   Till thwick-a-thwack, etc.

Jove's roaring cannons and his rammers
5   We beat out with our Lemnian[1] hammers;
Mars his[2] gauntlet, helm, and spear,
And Gorgon shield are all made here.
   Till thwick-a-thwack, etc.

The grate which, shut, the day outbars,
10   Those golden studs which nail the stars,
The globe's case and the axle-tree,
Who can hammer these but we?
   Till thwick-a-thwack, etc.

A warming-pan to heat earth's bed,
15   Lying i' th' frozen zone half-dead;
Hob-nails to serve the man i' th' moon,
And sparrowbills[3] to clout Pan's shoon,
   Whose work but ours?
   Till thwick-a-thwack, etc.

20   Venus' kettles, pots, and pans
We make, or else she brawls and bans;
Tongs, shovels, andirons have their places,
Else she scratches all our faces.
   Till thwick-a-thwack, thwick, thwack-a-thwack, thwack,
25   Make our brawny sinews crack:
Then pit-a-pat, pat, pit-a-pat, pat,
Till thickest bars be beaten flat.

[1] belonging to Vulcan.
[2] Mars's.
[3] small nails used by shoemakers.

CHRISTOPHER MARLOWE

THE PASSIONATE SHEPHERD TO HIS LOVE

Come live with me and be my love,
And we will all the pleasures prove,
That valleys, groves, hills, and fields,
Woods, or steepy mountains yields.

And we will sit upon the rocks,   5
Seeing the shepherds feed their flocks,
By shallow rivers, to whose falls
Melodious birds sing madrigals.[1]

And I will make thee beds of roses,
And a thousand fragrant posies,   10
A cap of flowers and a kirtle
Embroider'd all with leaves of myrtle:

A gown made of the finest wool,
Which from our pretty lambs we pull;
Fair lined slippers for the cold,   15
With buckles of the purest gold;

A belt of straw and ivy buds,
With coral clasps and amber studs;
And if these pleasures may thee move,
Come live with me and be my love.   20

The shepherd swains shall dance and sing
For thy delights each May morning;
If these delights thy mind may move,
Then live with me and be my love.

[1] love songs.

TAMBURLAINE THE GREAT

Part I, Act V, Scene II

[Tamburlaine Boasts of his Victory over the Soldan of Egypt]

 Tamb. 'Twas I, my lord, that got the victory,
And therefore grieve not at your overthrow,
Since I shall render all into your hands,
And add more strength to your dominions
5 Than ever yet confirmed the Egyptian crown.
The God of war[1] resigns his room[2] to me,
Meaning to make me general of the world:
Jove, viewing me in arms, looks pale and wan,
Fearing my power should pull him from his throne.
10 Where'er I come the Fatal Sisters[3] sweat,
And grisly Death, by running to and fro,
To do their ceaseless homage to my sword;
And here in Afric, where it seldom rains,
Since I arrived with my triumphant host,
15 Have swelling clouds, drawn from wide gasping wounds,
Been oft resolved in bloody purple showers,
A meteor that might terrify the earth,
And make it quake at every drop it drinks.
Millions of souls sit on the banks of Styx[4]
20 Waiting the back-return of Charon's boat;
Hell and Elysian[5] swarm with ghosts of men,
That I have sent from sundry foughten fields,
To spread my fame through hell and up to heaven.
And see, my lord, a sight of strange import,
25 Emperors and Kings lie breathless at my feet:
The Turk and his great Empress, as it seems,
Left to themselves while we were at the fight,
Have desperately despatched their slavish lives:

---

 [1] Mars. [2] gives up his place. [3] the three Fates. [4] the river of the lower world, across which Charon ferried the souls of the dead. [5] Elysium, heaven.

With them Arabia,[1] too, hath left his life:
All sights of power to grace my victory;
And such are objects fit for Tamburlaine;
Wherein, as in a mirror, may be seen
His honour, that consists in shedding blood,   5
When men presume to manage arms with him.

WILLIAM SHAKESPEARE

SONNETS

XXIX

When, in disgrace with fortune and men's eyes,
I all alone beweep my outcast state
And trouble deaf heaven with my bootless cries
And look upon myself and curse my fate,   10
Wishing me like to one more rich in hope,
Featured like him, like him with friends possess'd,
Desiring this man's art and that man's scope,
With what I most enjoy contented least;
Yet in these thoughts myself almost despising,   15
Haply I think on thee, and then my state,
Like to the lark at break of day arising
From sullen earth, sings hymns at heaven's gate;
    For thy sweet love remember'd such wealth brings
    That then I scorn to change my state with kings. 20

CXVI

Let me not to the marriage of true minds
Admit impediments. Love is not love
Which alters when it alteration finds,
Or bends with the remover to remove:
O, no! it is an ever-fixèd mark   25

[1] the king of Arabia.

That looks on tempests and is never shaken;
It is the star to every wandering bark,
Whose worth's[1] unknown, although his height be taken.
Love's not Time's fool, though rosy lips and cheeks
5 Within his bending sickle's compass come;
Love alters not with his brief hours and weeks,
But bears it out even to the edge of doom.
　　If this be error and upon me proved,
　　I never writ, nor no man ever loved.

SONGS FROM THE PLAYS

From LOVE'S LABOUR'S LOST

10　　When icicles hang by the wall,
　　　　And Dick the shepherd blows his nail,
　　And Tom bears logs into the hall,
　　　　And milk comes frozen home in pail,
　　When blood is nipped and ways be foul,
15　　Then nightly sings the staring owl,
　　　　Tu-whit, tu-who! a merry note,
　　While greasy Joan doth keel[2] the pot.

　　When all aloud the wind doth blow,
　　　　And coughing drowns the parson's saw,
20　　And birds sit brooding in the snow,
　　　　And Marian's nose looks red and raw,
　　When roasted crabs hiss in the bowl,
　　Then nightly sings the staring owl,
　　　　Tu-whit, tu-who! a merry note,
25　　While greasy Joan doth keel the pot.

[1] from the point of view of astrology, occult influence.
[2] stir, cool.

FROM *TWELFTH NIGHT*

O Mistress mine, where are you roaming?
O, stay and hear; your true love's coming,
　That can sing both high and low:
Trip no further, pretty sweeting,
Journeys end in lovers meeting,   5
　Every wise man's son doth know.

What is love? 'tis not hereafter;
Present mirth hath present laughter;
　What's to come is still unsure:
In delay there lies no plenty;   10
Then come kiss me, sweet and twenty,[1]
　Youth's a stuff will not endure.

FROM *AS YOU LIKE IT*

　Under the greenwood tree
　Who loves to lie with me,
　And turn his merry note   15
　Unto the sweet bird's throat,
Come hither! come hither! come hither!
　　Here shall he see
　　No enemy
But winter and rough weather.   20

　Who doth ambition shun
　And loves to live i' the sun,
　Seeking the food he eats
　And pleased with what he gets,
Come hither! come hither! come hither!   25
　　Here shall he see
　　No enemy
But winter and rough weather.

[1] often and often.

From *As You Like It*

Blow, blow, thou winter wind,
Thou art not so unkind
   As man's ingratitude;
Thy tooth is not so keen,
Because thou art not seen,
   Although thy breath be rude.
Heigh ho! sing, heigh ho! unto the green holly:
Most friendship is feigning, most loving mere folly:
   Then, heigh ho, the holly!
   This life is most jolly.

Freeze, freeze, thou bitter sky,
That dost not bite so nigh
   As benefits forgot:
Though thou the waters warp,
Thy sting is not so sharp
   As friend remembered not.
Heigh ho! sing, heigh ho! etc.

From *Cymbeline*

Fear no more the heat o' th' sun,
   Nor the furious winter's rages;
Thou thy worldly task hast done,
   Home art gone, and ta'en thy wages:
Golden lads and girls all must,
As chimney-sweepers, come to dust.

Fear no more the frown o' th' great;
   Thou art past the tyrant's stroke;
Care no more to clothe and eat;
   To thee the reed is as the oak:
The Sceptre, Learning, Physic,[1] must
All follow this, and come to dust.

[1] science.

Fear no more the lightning-flash,
    Nor th' all-dreaded thunder-stone[1];
Fear not slander, censure rash;
    Thou hast finished joy and moan:
All lovers young, all lovers must   5
Consign[2] to thee, and come to dust.

No exorciser[3] harm thee!
    Nor no witchcraft charm thee!
Ghost unlaid forbear thee!
    Nothing ill come near thee!   10
Quiet consummation have;
And renownèd be thy grave!

KING HENRY THE FIFTH

HENRY'S SPEECH BEFORE HARFLEUR

Once more unto the breach, dear friends, once more;
Or close the wall up with our English dead!
In peace there's nothing so becomes a man   15
As modest stillness and humility:
But, when the blast of war blows in our ears,
Then imitate the action of the tiger;
Stiffen the sinews, summon up the blood,
Disguise fair nature with hard-favour'd rage: 20
Then lend the eye a terrible aspect;
Let it pry through the portage[4] of the head
Like the brass cannon; let the brow o'erwhelm it
As fearfully as doth a galled[5] rock
O'erhang and jutty[6] his confounded base,   25
Swill'd with the wild and wasteful ocean.
Now set the teeth, and stretch the nostril wide;
Hold hard the breath, and bend up every spirit

[1] thunderbolt.
[2] give over, surrender.
[3] one who conjures up evil spirits.
[4] portholes.
[5] rubbed, worn by the sea.
[6] jut, project over.

To his full height! On, on, you noblest English,
Whose blood is fet[1] from fathers of war-proof!
Fathers that, like so many Alexanders,
Have in these parts from morn till even fought,
5   And sheath'd their swords for lack of argument:
Dishonour not your mothers; now attest
That those whom you call'd fathers did beget you!
Be copy now to men of grosser blood,
And teach them how to war! And you, good yeomen,[2]
10   Whose limbs were made in England, show us here
The mettle of your pasture;[3] let us swear
That you are worth your breeding: which I doubt not;
For there is none of you so mean and base,
That hath not noble lustre in your eyes.
15   I see you stand like greyhounds in the slips,[4]
Straining upon the start. The game's afoot:
Follow your spirit; and upon this charge
Cry 'God for Harry! England and Saint George!'

JOHN FLETCHER

SONG TO BACCHUS[5]

God Lyæus,[6] ever young,
20   Ever honoured, ever sung;
Stained with blood of lusty grapes,
In a thousand lusty shapes,
Dance upon the mazer's[7] brim,
In the crimson liquor swim;
25   From thy plenteous hand divine
Let a river run with wine;
God of youth, let this day here
Enter neither care nor fear!

---

[1] fetched.   [2] freeborn men, freeholders.   [3] quality of your training.
[4] leashes.   [5] The god of wine. Cf. Gayley, *Classic Myths*, p. 44.
[6] (lī ē'ŭs) deliverer from care.   [7] a large drinking bowl.

FRANCIS BEAUMONT

LETTER TO BEN JONSON

[Extracts]

The sun (which doth the greatest comfort bring
To absent friends, because the selfsame thing
They know they see, however absent) is
Here our best haymaker! Forgive me this;
It is our country's style! In this warm shine   5
I lie and dream of your full Mermaid Wine!

   .   .   .   .

Methinks the little wit I had is lost
Since I saw you! For wit is like a rest[1]
Held up[2] at tennis, which men do the best
With the best gamesters. What things have we seen   10
Done at the Mermaid! heard words that have been
So nimble and so full of subtle flame,
As if that every one from whence they came
Had meant to put his whole wit in a jest
And had resolved to live a fool the rest   15
Of his dull life! Then, when there hath been thrown
Wit able enough to justify the town
For three days past! Wit, that might warrant be
For the whole city to talk foolishly
Till that were cancelled! And, when we were gone,   20
We left an air behind us, which alone
Was able to make the two next companies
Right witty! though but downright fools, more wise!

   .   .   .   .

Only strong Destiny, which all controls,
I hope hath left a better fate in store   25
For me, thy friend, than to live ever poor,
Banished unto this home! Fate, once again,
Bring me to thee, who canst make smooth and plain

[1] rally, volley.   [2] maintained, kept up.

The way of knowledge for me; and then I,
Who have no good but in thy company,
Protest it will my greatest comfort be
To acknowledge all I have to flow from thee!
5   Ben, when these scenes are perfect, we'll taste wine!
I'll drink thy Muse's health! thou shalt quaff mine!

BEN JONSON

PROLOGUE TO *THE SAD SHEPHERD*

[*Enter the Prologue.*[1]]
He that hath feasted you these forty years,
And fitted fables for your finer ears,
Although at first he scarce could hit the bore;
10   Yet you, with patience harkening more and more,
At length have grown up to him, and made known
The working of his pen is now your own:
He prays you would vouchsafe, for your own sake,
To hear him this once more, but sit awake.
15   And though he now present you with such wool
As from mere English flocks his muse can pull,
He hopes when it is made up into cloth,
Not the most curious head here will be loth
To wear a hood of it, it being a fleece,
20   To match or those of Sicily or Greece.
His scene is Sherwood, and his play a Tale,
Of Robin Hood's inviting from the vale
Of Belvoir, all the shepherds to a feast:
Where, by the casual absence of one guest,
25   The mirth is troubled much, and in one man
As much of sadness shown as passion can:
The sad young shepherd, whom we here present,
Like his woes figure, dark and discontent,
[*The sad Shepherd passeth silently over the stage.*]

[1] The speaker who delivers the prologue.

For his lost love, who in the Trent is said
To have miscarried[1]; 'las! what knows the head
Of a calm river, whom the feet have drown'd?—
Hear what his sorrows are; and if they wound
Your gentle breasts, so that the end crown all,   5
Which in the scope of one day's chance may fall;
Old Trent will send you more such tales as these,
And shall grow young again as one doth please.

[Exit, but instantly reënters.]

But here's an heresy of late let fall,
That mirth by no means fits a pastoral[2];   10
Such say so, who can make none, he presumes:
Else there's no scene more properly assumes
The sock.[3] For whence can sport in kind arise,
But from the rural routs[4] and families?
Safe on this ground then, we not fear to-day,   15
To tempt your laughter by our rustic play:
Wherein if we distaste, or be cried down,
We think we therefore shall not leave the town;
Nor that the fore-wits[5] that would draw the rest
Unto their liking, always like the best.   20
The wise and knowing critic will not say,
This worst, or better is, before he weigh
Wher[6] every piece be perfect in the kind:
And then, though in themselves he difference find,
Yet if the place require it where they stood,   25
The equal fitting makes them equal good.
You shall have love and hate, and jealousy,
As well as mirth, and rage, and melancholy:
Or whatsoever else may either move,
Or stir affections, and your likings prove.   30

---

[1] perished.   [2] A poem or drama concerned with the life of shepherds
or with rural life in general.   [3] There's no subject more suitable for
comedy. In ancient Greece and Rome actors in comedy wore socks, while
those in tragedy wore buskins.   [4] parties.   [5] leaders.   [6] whether.

But that no style for pastoral should go
Current, but what is stamp'd with Ah! and O!
Who judgeth so, may singularly err;
As if all poesie had one character
5   In which what were not written, were not right;
Or that the man who made such one poor flight,
In his whole life, had with his wingèd skill
Advanced him upmost on the muses' hill.
When he like poet yet remains, as those
10   Are painters who can only make a rose.
From such your wits redeem you, or your chance,
Lest to a greater height you do advance
Of folly, to contemn[1] those that are known
Artificers,[2] and trust such as are none!

SIMPLEX MUNDITIIS[3]

From *The Silent Woman*

15   Still to be neat, still to be drest,
As you were going to a feast;
Still to be powdered, still perfumed:
Lady, it is to be presumed,
Though art's hid causes are not found,
20   All is not sweet, all is not sound.

Give me a look, give me a face,
That makes simplicity a grace;
Robes loosely flowing, hair as free:
Such sweet neglect more taketh me
25   Than all the adulteries[4] of art;
They strike mine eyes, but not my heart.

---

[1] despise.
[2] skilled workmen.
[3] in unadorned neatness, elegant simplicity.
[4] adulterations.

SONG TO CELIA

Drink to me only with thine eyes,
   And I will pledge with mine;
Or leave a kiss but in the cup,
   And I'll not look for wine.
The thirst that from the soul doth rise   5
   Doth ask a drink divine;
But might I of Jove's nectar sup,
   I would not change for thine.

I sent thee late a rosy wreath,
   Not so much honouring thee   10
As giving it a hope, that there
   It could not wither'd be.
But thou thereon didst only breathe,
   And sent'st it back to me;
Since when it grows, and smells, I swear,   15
   Not of itself, but thee.

THE TRIUMPH OF CHARIS[1]

See the chariot at hand here of Love,
   Wherein my Lady rideth!
Each that draws is a swan or a dove,
   And well the car Love guideth.   20
As she goes, all hearts do duty
         Unto her beauty;
And enamour'd, do wish, so they might
         But enjoy such a sight,
That they still were to run by her side,   25
Through swords, through seas, whither she would ride.

Do but look on her eyes, they do light
   All that Love's world compriseth!

[1] In the Iliad the wife of Vulcan, the personification of beauty and grace.

Do but look on her hair, it is bright
   As Love's star when it riseth!
Do but mark, her forehead's smoother
      Than words that soothe her;
5   And from her arched brows, such a grace
       Sheds itself through the face
As alone there triumphs to the life
All the gain, all the good, of the elements' strife.

Have you seen but a bright lily grow,
10   Before rude hands have touched it?
Have you marked but the fall of the snow,
   Before the soil hath smutched it?
Have you felt the wool of the beaver?
      Or swan's down ever?
15   Or have smelt o' the bud of the briar?
      Or the nard[1] in the fire?
Or have tasted the bag of the bee?
Oh so white! Oh so soft! Oh so sweet is she!

THE NOBLE NATURE

   It is not growing like a tree
20   In bulk, doth make Man better be;
Or standing long an oak, three hundred year,
To fall a log at last, dry, bald, and sere:
    A lily of a day
    Is fairer far in May,
25   Although it fall and die that night—
   It was the plant and flower of Light.
In small proportions we just beauties see;
And in short measures life may perfect be.

[1] a fragrant ointment.

FRANCIS BACON

ESSAYS

OF TRAVEL

Travel in the younger sort is a part of education; in the elder a part of experience. He that travelleth into a country, before he hath some entrance into the language, goeth to school, and not to travel. That young men travel under some tutor or grave servant, I allow well; so that he be such a one 5 that hath the language, and hath been in the country before; whereby he may be able to tell them what things are worthy to be seen in the country where they go, what acquaintances they are to seek, what exercises or discipline the place yieldeth; for else young men shall go hooded, and look 10 abroad little. It is a strange thing that in sea voyages, where there is nothing to be seen but sky and sea, men should make diaries; but in land travel, wherein so much is to be observed, for the most part they omit it; as if chance were fitter to be registered than observation. Let diaries, therefore, be brought 15 in use. The things to be seen and observed are the courts of princes, especially when they give audience to ambassadors; the courts of justice while they sit and hear causes; and so of consistories ecclesiastic; the churches and monasteries, with the monuments which are therein extant; the walls and 20 fortifications of cities and towns; and so the havens and harbours, antiquities and ruins, libraries, colleges, disputations, and lectures where any are, shipping and navies; houses and gardens of state and pleasure near great cities; armories, arsenals, magazines, exchanges, burses,[1] warehouses, exercises 25 of horsemanship, fencing, training of soldiers, and the like; comedies, such whereunto the better sort of persons do resort; treasuries of jewels and robes; cabinets and rareties;

[1] bourses, exchanges (the stock exchange of Paris is known as the Bourse).

and to conclude, whatsoever is memorable in the places where
they go; after all which the tutors or servants ought to make
diligent inquiry. As for triumphs, masks,[1] feasts, weddings,
funerals, capital executions, and such shows, men need not to
be put in mind of them; yet are they not to be neglected. If
you will have a young man to put his travel into a little
room,[2] and in a short time to gather much, this you must do:
first, as was said, he must have some entrance into the language before he goeth. Then he must have such a servant or
tutor as knoweth the country, as was likewise said. Let him
carry with him also some card or book describing the country where he travelleth, which will be a good key to his
inquiry. Let him keep also a diary. Let him not stay long
in one city or town, more or less as the place deserveth,
but not long; nay, when he stayeth in one city or town,
let him change his lodging from one end and part of the
town to another, which is a great adamant[3] of acquaintance. Let him sequester himself from the company of his
countrymen, and diet[4] in such places where there is good
company of the nation where he travelleth. Let him, upon
his removes from one place to another, procure recom-
mendation to some person of quality residing in the place
whither he removeth, that he may use his favour in those
things he desireth to see or know: thus he may abridge his
travel with much profit. As for the acquaintance which is to
be sought in travel, that which is most of all profitable is
acquaintance with the secretaries and employed men of ambassadors; for so in travelling in one country he shall suck
the experience of many. Let him also see and visit eminent
persons in all kinds which are of great name abroad, that he
may be able to tell how the life agreeth with the fame. For
quarrels, they are with care and discretion to be avoided;
they are commonly for mistresses, healths, place, and words.

---

[1] a form of drama popular in the sixteenth and seventeenth centuries,
in which the actors wore masks and represented allegorical or mythical
characters.   [2] space.   [3] magnet.   [4] eat, take meals.

And let a man beware how he keepeth company with choleric[1]
and quarrelsome persons; for they will engage him into their
own quarrels. When a traveller returneth home, let him not
leave the countries where he hath travelled altogether behind
him; but maintain a correspondence by letters with those of 5
his acquaintance which are of most worth. And let his travel
appear rather in his discourse, than in his apparel or gesture;
and in his discourse let him be rather advised in his answers,
than forward to tell stories: and let it appear that he doth
not change his country manners for those of foreign parts; 10
but only prick in[2] some flowers of that he hath learned
abroad into the customs of his country.

OF STUDIES

  Studies serve for delight, for ornament, and for ability.
Their chief use for delight is in privateness and retiring; for
ornament, is in discourse; and for ability, is in the judgment 15
and disposition of business; for expert men can execute, and
perhaps judge of particulars, one by one; but the general
counsels, and the plots and marshalling of affairs, come best
from those that are learned. To spend too much time in
studies, is sloth; to use them too much for ornament, is affec- 20
tation; to make judgment wholly by their rules, is the
humour of a scholar;[3] they perfect nature, and are perfected
by experience: for natural abilities are like natural plants,
that need pruning by study; and studies themselves do give
forth directions too much at large, except they be bounded in 25
by experience. Crafty men contemn studies, simple men admire them, and wise men use them, for they teach not their
own use; but that is a wisdom without them, and above
them, won by observation. Read not to contradict and con-
fute, nor to believe and take for granted, nor to find talk and 30

[1] hot-tempered.
[2] embroider.
[3] peculiar weakness of the academic temperament.

discourse, but to weigh and consider. Some books are to be tasted, others to be swallowed, and some few to be chewed and digested; that is, some books are to be read only in parts; others to be read, but not curiously[1]; and some few to be read
5 wholly, and with diligence and attention. Some books also may be read by deputy, and extracts made of them by others; but that would be only in the less important arguments, and the meaner sort of books; else distilled books are, like common distilled waters, flashy things. Reading maketh a full
10 man, conference a ready man, and writing an exact man: and, therefore, if a man write little, he had need have a great memory; if he confer little, he had need have a present wit; and if he read little, he had need have much cunning, to seem to know that he doth not. Histories make men wise; poets
15 witty; the mathematics subtle; natural philosophy deep; moral, grave; logic and rhetoric, able to contend. "Abeunt studia in mores"[2]—nay, there is no stond[3] nor impediment in the wit, but may be wrought out by fit studies, like as diseases of the body may have appropriate exercises—bowling
20 is good for the stone and reins, shooting for the lungs and breast, gentle walking for the stomach, riding for the head, and the like; so, if a man's wits be wandering, let him study the mathematics, for in demonstrations, if his wit be called away never so little, he must begin again; if his wit be not
25 apt to distinguish or find differences, let him study the schoolmen,[4] for they are "cymini sectores"[5]; if he be not apt to beat over matters, and to call upon one thing to prove and illustrate another, let him study the lawyers' cases—so every defect of the mind may have a special receipt.[6]

[1] carefully.
[2] studies pass into character.
[3] stand, difficulty, obstruction.
[4] Christian philosophers of the Middle Ages.
[5] splitters of cumin seed, hair-splitters.
[6] prescription.

THE PURITAN AGE AND THE RESTORATION

JOHN MILTON

ON HIS HAVING ARRIVED AT THE AGE OF TWENTY-THREE

How soon hath Time, the subtle thief of youth,
  Stolen on his wing my three and twentieth year!
  My hasting days fly on with full career,
  But my late spring no bud or blossom shew'th.
Perhaps my semblance[1] might deceive the truth   5
  That I to manhood am arrived so near;
  And inward ripeness doth much less appear,
  That some more timely-happy spirits endu'th.
Yet be it less or more, or soon or slow,
  It shall be still in strictest measure even   10
  To that same lot, however mean or high,
Toward which Time leads me, and the will of Heaven;
  All is, if I have grace to use it so,
  As ever in my great Task-Master's eye.

TO THE NIGHTINGALE

O Nightingale, that on yon bloomy spray   15
  Warblest at eve, when all the woods are still,
  Thou with fresh hope the lover's heart dost fill,
  While the jolly hours lead on propitious May.

[1] appearance.

Thy liquid notes that close the eye of day,
    First heard before the shallow cuckoo's bill,
    Portend success in love;[1] oh, if Jove's will
    Have linked that amorous power to thy soft lay,
5   Now timely sing, ere the rude bird of hate
    Foretell my hopeless doom in some grove nigh;
    As thou from year to year hast sung too late
For my relief, yet hadst no reason why:
    Whether the Muse, or Love, call thee his mate,
10 Both them I serve, and of their train am I.

EXTRACTS FROM *AREOPAGITICA*[2]

A Speech for the Liberty of Unlicensed Printing

To the Parliament of England

I deny not but that it is of greatest concernment in the church and commonwealth, to have a vigilant eye how books demean themselves as well as men; and thereafter to confine, imprison, and do sharpest justice on them as malefactors:
15 for books are not absolutely dead things, but do contain a potency of life in them to be as active as that soul was whose progeny they are; nay, they do preserve as in a vial the purest efficacy and extraction of that living intellect that bred them. I know they are as lively, and as vigorously productive, as
20 those fabulous dragon's teeth;[3] and being sown up and down, may chance to spring up armed men. And yet on the other hand, unless wariness be used, as good almost kill a man as kill a good book; who kills a man kills a reasonable creature, God's image; but he who destroys a good book, kills reason
25 itself, kills the image of God as it were in the eye. Many a

---

[1] There was a superstition that he who heard the nightingale sing before the cuckoo would love successfully before the year was over.

[2] from the high court of Athens, held on the Areopagus (Mars' Hill), which condemned Protagoras to be banished and his books to be burned.

[3] which Cadmus sowed; cf. Gayley, *Classic Myths*, pp. 87–90.

man lives a burden to the earth; but a good book is the precious life-blood of a master spirit, imbalmed and treasured up on purpose to a life beyond life. 'Tis true, no age can restore a life, whereof perhaps there is no great loss; and revolutions of ages do not oft recover the loss of a rejected truth, 5 for the want of which whole nations fare the worse. We should be wary therefore what persecution we raise against the living labours of public men, how we spill[1] the seasoned life of man preserved and stored up in books; since we see a kind of homicide may be thus committed, sometimes a mar- 10 tyrdom, and if it extend to the whole impression, a kind of massacre, whereof the execution ends not in the slaying of an elemental life, but strikes at that ethereal and fifth essence, the breath of reason itself, slays an immortality rather than a life. But lest I should be condemned of introducing license, 15 while I oppose licensing, I refuse not the pains to be so much historical as will serve to show what hath been done by ancient and famous commonwealths against this disorder, till the very time that this project of licensing crept out of the *inquisition*, was catched up by our prelates, and hath caught 20 some of our presbyters.

. . . .

Methinks I see in my mind a noble and puissant nation rousing herself like a strong man after sleep, and shaking her invincible locks. Methinks I see her as an eagle muing[2] her mighty youth, and kindling her undazzled eyes at the full 25 midday beam, purging and unscaling her long abused sight at the fountain itself of heavenly radiance, while the whole noise of timorous and flocking birds, with those also that love the twilight, flutter about, amazed at what she means, and in their envious gabble would prognosticate a year of 30 sects and schisms.

What should ye do then, should ye suppress all this flowery crop of knowledge and new light sprung up and yet springing daily in this city, should ye set an oligarchy of twenty in-

---

[1] destroy.   [2] renewing by molting.

grossers[1] over it, to bring a famine upon our minds again, when we shall know nothing but what is measured to us by their bushel? Believe it, Lords and Commons, they who counsel ye to such a suppressing do as good as bid ye suppress
5 yourselves; and I will soon show how. If it be desired to know the immediate cause of all this free writing and free speaking, there cannot be assigned a truer than your own mild and free and humane government; it is the liberty, Lords and Commons, which your own valorous and happy
10 counsels have purchased us, liberty which is the nurse of all great wits[2]; this is that which hath rarefied and enlightened our spirits like the influence of heaven; this is that which hath enfranchised, enlarged and lifted up our apprehensions degrees above themselves. Ye cannot make us now less capa-
15 ble, less knowing, less eagerly pursuing of the truth, unless ye first make yourselves, that made us so, less the lovers, less the founders of our true liberty. We can grow ignorant again, brutish, formal, and slavish, as ye found us; but you then must first become that which ye cannot be, oppressive, arbi-
20 trary, and tyrannous, as they were from whom ye have freed us. That our hearts are now more capacious, our thoughts more erected to the search and expectation of greatest and exactest things, is the issue of your own virtue propagated in us; ye cannot suppress that unless ye reinforce an abrogated
25 and merciless law, that fathers may despatch at will their own children. And who shall then stick closest to ye, and excite others? Not he who takes up arms for coat and conduct and his four nobles[3] of Danegelt.[4] Although I dispraise not the defence of just immunities, yet love my peace
30 better, if that were all. Give me the liberty to know, to utter, and to argue freely according to conscience, above all liberties.

. . . .

---

[1] monopolists, those who corner necessary commodities.   [2] minds.
[3] gold coins, first issued in the reign of Edward III with a value of about $5.96.   [4] a tax originally levied to buy off marauding Danes.

And though all the winds of doctrine were let loose to play
upon the earth, so Truth be in the field, we do injuriously by
licensing and prohibiting to misdoubt her strength. Let her
and Falsehood grapple; who ever knew Truth put to the
worse in a free and open encounter? Her confuting is the 5
best and surest suppressing. . . . For who knows not that
Truth is strong next to the Almighty? She needs no policies,
no stratagems, nor licensings to make her victorious; those
are the shifts and the defences that Error uses against her
power.   10

PARADISE LOST

Book IV

[Satan's Invocation to the Sun]

"O thou, that, with surpassing glory crowned,
Look'st from thy sole dominion like the god
Of this new world—at whose sight all the stars
Hide their diminished heads—to thee I call,
But with no friendly voice, and add thy name,   15
O Sun, to tell thee how I hate thy beams,
That bring to my remembrance from what state
I fell, how glorious once above thy sphere,
Till pride and worse ambition threw me down,
Warring in Heaven against Heaven's matchless King!   20
Ah, wherefore? He deserved no such return
From me, whom he created what I was
In that bright eminence, and with his good
Upbraided none; nor was his service hard.
What could be less than to afford him praise,   25
The easiest recompense, and pay him thanks,
How due! Yet all his good proved ill in me,
And wrought but malice. Lifted up so high,
I sdained[1] subjection, and thought one step higher
Would set me highest, and in a moment quit   30
The debt immense of endless gratitude,

[1] disdained.

So burdensome still paying, still to owe;
Forgetful what from him I still received;
And understood not that a grateful mind
By owing owes not, but still pays, at once
5   Indebted and discharged—what burden then?
Oh, had his powerful destiny ordained
Me some inferior angel, I had stood
Then happy; no unbounded hope had raised
Ambition. Yet why not? Some other power
10   As great might have aspired, and me, though mean,
Drawn to his part. But other powers as great
Fell not, but stand unshaken, from within
Or from without, to all temptations armed!
Hadst thou[1] the same free will and power to stand?
15   Thou hadst. Whom hast thou then, or what, to accuse,
But Heaven's free love dealt equally to all?
Be then his love accursed, since, love or hate,
To me alike, it deals eternal woe.
Nay, cursed be thou; since against his thy will
20   Chose freely what it now so justly rues.
Me miserable! which way shall I fly
Infinite wrath and infinite despair?
Which way I fly is Hell; myself am Hell;
And in the lowest deep a lower deep
25   Still threatening to devour me opens wide,
To which the Hell I suffer seems a Heaven.
Oh, then at last relent! Is there no place
Left for repentance, none for pardon left?
None left but by submission; and that word
30   Disdain forbids me, and my dread of shame
Among the spirits beneath, whom I seduced
With other promises and other vaunts
Than to submit, boasting I could subdue
The Omnipotent. Ay me! they little know
35   How dearly I abide that boast so vain,

[1] Satan here addresses himself.

Under what torments inwardly I groan,
While they adore me on the throne of Hell.
With diadem and sceptre high advanced,
The lower still I fall, only supreme
In misery; such joy ambition finds! 5
But say I could repent, and could obtain
By act of grace my former state; how soon
Would height recall high thoughts, how soon unsay
What feigned submission swore! Ease would recant
Vows made in pain, as violent as void 10
(For never can true reconcilement grow
Where wounds of deadly hate have pierced so deep);
Which would but lead me to a worse relapse
And heavier fall: so should I purchase dear
Short intermission, bought with double smart. 15
This knows my Punisher; therefore as far
From granting he, as I from begging, peace.
All hope excluded thus, behold instead
Of us outcast, exiled, his new delight,
Mankind, created, and for him this world! 20
So farewell hope, and with hope, farewell fear,
Farewell remorse! All good to me is lost;
Evil, be thou my good: by thee at least
Divided empire with Heaven's King I hold,
By thee, and more than half perhaps will reign; 25
As man ere long, and this new world, shall know."

JOHN BUNYAN

THE PILGRIM'S PROGRESS

[The Hill Difficulty and the Castle Beautiful]

I beheld then, that they all went on till they came to the
foot of the hill Difficulty, at the bottom of which there was a
spring. There were also in the same place two other ways
besides that which came straight from the gate: one turned 30

to the left hand, and the other to the right, at the bottom of the hill; but the narrow way lay right up the hill, and the name of the going up the side of the hill is called Difficulty. Christian now went to the spring, and drank thereof to re-
5 fresh himself, and then began to go up the hill.

The other two also came to the foot of the hill. But when they saw that the hill was steep and high, and that there were two other ways to go; and supposing also that these two ways might meet again with that up which Christian went,
10 on the other side of the hill; therefore they were resolved to go in those ways. Now the name of one of those ways was Danger, and the name of the other Destruction. So the one took the way which is called Danger, which led him into a great wood; and the other took directly up the
15 way to Destruction, which led him into a wide field, full of dark mountains, where he stumbled and fell, and rose no more.

I looked then after Christian, to see him go up the hill, where I perceived he fell from running to going, and from
20 going to clambering upon his hands and his knees, because of the steepness of the place. Now about midway to the top of the hill was a pleasant arbor, made by the Lord of the hill for the refreshment of weary travellers. Thither, therefore, Christian got, where also he sat down to rest him: then he pulled
25 his roll out of his bosom, and read therein to his comfort; he also now began afresh to take a review of the coat or garment that was given to him as he stood by the cross. Thus pleasing himself awhile, he at last fell into a slumber, and thence into a fast sleep, which detained him in that place until it
30 was almost night; and in his sleep his roll fell out of his hand. Now, as he was sleeping, there came one unto him, and awaked him, saying, "Go to the ant, thou sluggard; consider her ways, and be wise." And with that, Christian suddenly started up, and sped him on his way, and went apace till he
35 came to the top of the hill.

Now when he was got up to the top of the hill, there came

two men running hard; the name of the one was Timorous, and of the other Mistrust: to whom Christian said, Sirs, what's the matter? you run the wrong way. Timorous answered, that they were going to the city of Zion, and had got up that difficult place: but, said he, the farther we go, the 5 more danger we meet with; wherefore we turned, and are going back again.

Yes, said Mistrust, for just before us lie a couple of lions in the way, whether sleeping or waking we know not; and we could not think, if we came within reach, but they would 10 presently pull us in pieces.

CHR. Then said Christian, You make me afraid; but whither shall I fly to be safe? If I go back to my own country, I shall certainly perish there; if I can get to the celestial city, I am sure to be in safety there: I must venture. To go 15 back is nothing but death: to go forward is fear of death and life everlasting beyond it: I will yet go forward. So Mistrust and Timorous ran down the hill, and Christian went on his way. But thinking again of what he had heard from the men, he felt in his bosom for his roll, that he might read therein 20 and be comforted; but he felt, and found it not. Then was Christian in great distress, and knew not what to do; for he wanted that which used to relieve him, and that which should have been his pass into the celestial city. Here, therefore, he began to be much perplexed, and knew not what to do. At 25 last he bethought himself that he had slept in the arbor that is on the side of the hill; and falling down upon his knees, he asked God's forgiveness for that foolish act, and then went back to look for his roll. But all the way he went back, who can sufficiently set forth the sorrow of Christian's heart? 30 Sometimes he sighed, sometimes he wept, and oftentimes he chid himself for being so foolish as to fall asleep in that place, which was erected only for a little refreshment from his weariness. Thus, therefore, he went back, carefully looking on this side and on that, all the way as he went, if happily he 35 might find his roll, that had been his comfort so many times

on his journey. He went thus till he came again within sight
of the arbor, where he sat and slept; but that sight renewed
his sorrow the more, by bringing again, even afresh, his evil
of sleeping unto his mind. Thus, therefore, he now went on,
5 bewailing his sinful sleep, saying, Oh, wretched man that I
am, that I should sleep in the daytime! that I should sleep in
the midst of difficulty! that I should so indulge the flesh as
to use that rest for ease to my flesh which the Lord of the hill
hath erected only for the relief of the spirits of pilgrims!
10 How many steps have I taken in vain! Thus it happened to
Israel; for their sin they were sent back again by the way of
the Red Sea; and I am made to tread those steps with sorrow, which I might have trod with delight, had it not been
for this sinful sleep. How far might I have been on my way
15 by this time! I am made to tread those steps thrice over,
which I needed not to have trod but once: yea, now also I
am like to be benighted, for the day is almost spent. Oh,
that I had not slept!

Now by this time he was come to the arbor again, where
20 for a while he sat down and wept; but at last (as Providence
would have it), looking sorrowfully down under the seat,
there he espied his roll, the which he with trembling and
haste catched up, and put it into his bosom. But who can
tell how joyful this man was when he had gotten his roll
25 again? For this roll was the assurance of his life, and acceptance at the desired haven. Therefore he laid it up in his
bosom, gave thanks to God for directing his eye to the place
where it lay, and with joy and tears betook himself again to
his journey. But oh, how nimbly did he go up the rest of
30 the hill! Yet before he got up, the sun went down upon
Christian; and this made him again recall the vanity of his
sleeping to his remembrance; and thus he again began to con-
dole with himself: Oh, thou sinful sleep! how for thy sake
am I like to be benighted in my journey! I must walk with-
35 out the sun, darkness must cover the path of my feet, and I
must hear the noise of the doleful creatures, because of my

sinful sleep! Now also he remembered the story that Mistrust and Timorous told him of, how they were frightened with the sight of the lions. Then said Christian to himself again, These beasts range in the night for their prey, and if they should meet with me in the dark, how should I shift 5 them? how should I escape being by them torn in pieces? Thus he went on his way. But while he was bewailing his unhappy misconduct, he lifted up his eyes, and behold, there was a very stately palace before him, the name of which was Beautiful, and it stood by the highway-side.   10

So I saw in my dream that he made haste, and went forward, that if possible he might get lodging there. Now before he had gone far, he entered into a very narrow passage, which was about a furlong[1] off the Porter's lodge;[2] and looking very narrowly before him as he went, he espied two lions in the 15 way. Now, thought he, I see the dangers that Mistrust and Timorous were driven back by. (The lions were chained, but he saw not the chains.) Then he was afraid, and thought also himself to go back after them; for he thought nothing but death was before him. But the Porter at the lodge, whose 20 name is Watchful, perceiving that Christian made a halt, as if he would go back, cried unto him, saying, Is thy strength so small? Fear not the lions, for they are chained, and are placed there for trial of faith where it is, and for discovery of those that have none: keep in the midst of the path, and no 25 hurt shall come unto thee.

Then I saw that he went on, trembling for fear of the lions, but taking good heed to the directions of the Porter; he heard them roar, but they did him no harm. Then he clapped his hands, and went on till he came and stood before the gate 30 where the Porter was. Then said Christian to the Porter, Sir, what house is this? and may I lodge here to-night? The Porter answered, This house was built by the Lord of the hill, and he built it for the relief and security of

[1] an eighth of a mile, originally the length of a furrow in a square, ten-acre field.   [2] gate-keeper's cottage.

pilgrims. The Porter also asked whence he was and whither he was going.

CHR. I am come from the city of Destruction, and am going to Mount Zion: but because the sun is now set, I desire,
5 if I may, to lodge here to-night.

PORT. What is your name?

CHR. My name is now Christian, but my name at the first was Graceless.

PORT. But how does it happen that you come so late?
10 The sun is set.

CHR. I had been here sooner, but that, wretched man that I am, I slept in the arbor that stands on the hillside! Nay, I had, notwithstanding that, been here much sooner, but that in my sleep I lost my roll, and came without it to the brow
15 of the hill; and then feeling for it, and not finding it, I was forced with sorrow of heart to go back to the place where I slept my sleep, where I found it; and now I am come.

PORT. Well, I will call out one of the maidens of this place, who will, if she likes your talk, bring you in to the rest of the
20 family, according to the rules of the house. So Watchful the Porter rang a bell, at the sound of which came out of the door of the house a grave and beautiful damsel, named Discretion, and asked why she was called.

The Porter answered, This man is on a journey from the
25 city of Destruction to Mount Zion; but being weary and benighted, he asked me if he might lodge here to-night: so I told him I would call for thee, who, after discourse had with him, mayest do as seemeth thee good, even according to the law of the house.

30 Then she asked him whence he was, and whither he was going; and he told her. She asked him, also, how he got into the way; and he told her. Then she asked him what he had seen and met with in the way, and he told her. And at last she asked his name. So he said, It is Christian; and I have
35 so much the more a desire to lodge here to-night, because, by what I perceive, this place was built by the Lord of the hill

for the relief and security of pilgrims. So she smiled, but the water stood in her eyes; and, after a little pause, she said, I will call forth two or three more of the family. So she ran to the door, and called out Prudence, Piety, and Charity, who, after a little more discourse with him, had him into the family; and many of them meeting him at the threshold of the house, said, Come in, thou blessed of the Lord: this house was built by the Lord of the hill on purpose to entertain such pilgrims in. Then he bowed his head, and followed them into the house. So when he was come in and sat down, they gave him something to drink, and consented together that, until supper was ready, some of them should have some particular discourse with Christian, for the best improvement of time; and they appointed Piety, Prudence, and Charity to discourse with him.

Now I saw in my dream, that thus they sat talking together until supper was ready. So when they had made ready, they sat down to meat. Now the table was furnished with nice things, and with excellent wine, and all their talk at the table was about the Lord of the hill, about what he had done, and wherefore he did what he did, and why he had builded that house; and by what they said, I perceived that he had been a great warrior, and had fought with and slain him that had the power of death; but not without great danger to himself, which made me love him the more.

Thus they discoursed together till late at night; and after they had committed themselves to their Lord for protection, they betook themselves to rest. The pilgrim they laid in a large upper chamber, whose window opened towards the sunrising. The name of the chamber was Peace, where he slept till break of day, and then he awoke and sang.

JOHN DRYDEN

ALEXANDER'S FEAST; OR, THE POWER OF MUSIC

A SONG IN HONOUR OF ST. CECILIA'S[1] DAY: 1697

'Twas at the royal feast[2] for Persia won
    By Philip's warlike son[3]:
    Aloft in awful state
    The godlike hero sate
5   On his imperial throne;
His valiant peers were placed around;
Their brows with roses and with myrtles bound:
(So should desert in arms be crowned.)
The lovely Thais,[4] by his side,
10 Sate like a blooming Eastern bride,
In flower of youth and beauty's pride.
    Happy, happy, happy pair!
      None but the brave,
      None but the brave,
15   None but the brave deserves the fair.

    Timotheus,[5] placed on high
    Amid the tuneful quire,
With flying fingers touched the lyre:
The trembling notes ascend the sky,
20   And heavenly joys inspire.
The song began from Jove,
Who left his blissful seats above,

[1] Patron saint of music and musicians. She was supposed to have invented the organ. Her day is November 22.

[2] held in the royal city of Persepolis, to celebrate the victory of Macedonians and Greeks over the Persians.

[3] Alexander the Great.

[4] a Greek woman who accompanied Alexander on the campaign against Persia.

[5] a Bœotian musician.

(Such is the power of mighty love.)
A dragon's fiery form belied the god:
Sublime on radiant spires he rode,
When he to fair Olympia[1] pressed:
And while he sought her snowy breast,   5
Then round her slender waist he curled,
And stamped an image of himself, a sovereign of the world.
The listening crowd admire the lofty sound,
A present deity, they shout around;
A present deity, the vaulted roofs rebound: 10
    With ravished ears
    The monarch hears,
    Assumes the god,
    Affects to nod,
And seems to shake the spheres.   15

The praise of Bacchus then the sweet musician sung,
Of Bacchus ever fair, and ever young.
    The jolly god in triumph comes;
    Sound the trumpets, beat the drums;
    Flushed with a purple grace   20
    He shows his honest face:
Now give the hautboys[2] breath; he comes, he comes.
Bacchus, ever fair and young,
    Drinking joys did first ordain;
Bacchus' blessings are a treasure,   25
Drinking is the soldier's pleasure;
    Rich the treasure,
    Sweet the pleasure,
Sweet is pleasure after pain.

Soothed with the sound the king grew vain;   30
    Fought all his battles o'er again;
And thrice he routed all his foes, and thrice he slew the slain.

[1] Alexander's mother. Her name was Olympias. Probably Dryden omitted the *s* for the sake of euphony.
[2] (hō'boi) a musical instrument.

The master saw the madness rise,
His glowing cheeks, his ardent eyes;
And while he heaven and earth defied,
Changed his hand, and checked his pride.
5   He chose a mournful muse,
         Soft pity to infuse;
He sung Darius great and good,
    By too severe a fate,
Fallen, fallen, fallen, fallen,
10   Fallen from his high estate,
    And weltering in his blood;
Deserted at his utmost need
By those his former bounty fed;
On the bare earth exposed he lies,
15   With not a friend to close his eyes.
With downcast looks the joyless victor sate,
    Revolving in his altered soul
      The various turns of chance below;
    And, now and then, a sigh he stole,
20   And tears began to flow.

The mighty master smiled to see
That love was in the next degree;
'Twas but a kindred-sound to move,
For pity melts the mind to love.
25   Softly sweet, in Lydian[1] measures,
      Soon he soothed his soul to pleasures.
War, he sung, is toil and trouble;
Honour but an empty bubble;
    Never ending, still beginning,
30   Fighting still, and still destroying:
    If the world be worth thy winning,
Think, O think it worth enjoying:
    Lovely Thais sits beside thee,
    Take the good the gods provide thee.

[1] from Lydia, a country of Asia Minor, noted for its wealth and luxury.

The many rend the skies with loud applause;
So Love was crowned, but Music won the cause.
    The prince, unable to conceal his pain,
        Gazed on the fair
        Who caused his care,   5
    And sighed and looked, sighed and looked,
    Sighed and looked, and sighed again;
At length, with love and wine at once oppressed,
The vanquished victor sunk upon her breast.

    Now strike the golden lyre again;   10
    A louder yet, and yet a louder strain.
    Break his bands of sleep asunder,
    And rouse him, like a rattling peal of thunder.
        Hark, hark, the horrid sound
          Has raised up his head;   15
        As awaked from the dead,
        And, amazed, he stares around.
    Revenge, revenge! Timotheus cries,
        See the Furies arise;
        See the snakes that they rear,   20
        How they hiss in their hair,
    And the sparkles that flash from their eyes!
        Behold a ghastly band,
        Each a torch in his hand!
Those are Grecian ghosts, that in battle were slain,   25
        And unburied remain
        Inglorious on the plain:
        Give the vengeance due
        To the valiant crew.
    Behold how they toss their torches on high,   30
        How they point to the Persian abodes,
    And glittering temples of their hostile gods.
The princes applaud with a furious joy;
And the king seized a flambeau[1] with zeal to destroy;

        [1] torch.

Thais led the way,
To light him to his prey,
And, like another Helen, fired another Troy.

Thus long ago,
5   Ere heaving bellows learned to blow,
While organs yet were mute,
Timotheus, to his breathing flute
And sounding lyre,
Could swell the soul to rage, or kindle soft desire.
10   At last divine Cecilia came,
Inventress of the vocal frame;
The sweet enthusiast, from her sacred store,
Enlarged the former narrow bounds,
And added length to solemn sounds,
15   With Nature's mother-wit, and arts unknown before.
Let old Timotheus yield the prize,
Or both divide the crown:
He raised a mortal to the skies;
She drew an angel down.

PREFACE TO THE *FABLES*

[Chaucer and Ovid]

20   . . . With Ovid[1] ended the golden age of the Roman
tongue; from Chaucer the purity of the English tongue began. . . . Both of them built on the inventions of other
men; yet since Chaucer had something of his own, as "The
Wife of Bath's Tale," "The Cock and the Fox," which I have
25 translated, and some others, I may justly give our country-
man the precedence in that part; since I can remember
nothing of Ovid which was wholly his. Both of them understood the manners, under which name I comprehend the pas-

---

[1] Roman poet (43 B.C.–A.D. 17).

sions, and, in a larger sense, the descriptions of persons,
and their very habits. For an example, I see Baucis and
Philemon[1] as perfectly before me, as if some ancient painter
had drawn them; and all the pilgrims in the "Canterbury
Tales," their humours, their features, and the very dress, as 5
distinctly as if I had supped with them at the Tabard in
Southwark. Yet even there too the figures in Chaucer are
much more lively, and set in a better light; which though I
have not time to prove, yet I appeal to the reader, and am
sure he will clear me from partiality. The thoughts and 10
words remain to be considered in the comparison of the two
poets; and I have saved my self one half of that labour, by
owning that Ovid lived when the Roman tongue was in its
meridian, Chaucer in the dawning of our language; therefore
that part of the comparison stands not on an equal foot, any 15
more than the diction of Ennius[2] and Ovid, or of Chaucer
and our present English. The words are given up as a post
not to be defended in our poet, because he wanted[3] the
modern art of fortifying. The thoughts remain to be considered, and they are to be measured only by their propriety; 20
that is, as they flow more or less naturally from the persons
described, on such and such occasions. The vulgar[4] judges,
which are nine parts in ten of all nations, who call conceits[5]
and jingles wit, who see Ovid full of them, and Chaucer altogether without them, will think me little less than mad for 25
preferring the Englishman to the Roman: yet, with their
leave, I must presume to say, that the things they admire are
only glittering trifles, and so far from being witty, that in a
serious poem they are nauseous, because they are unnatural.
Would any man who is ready to die for love describe his 30
passion like Narcissus?[6] Would he think of *inopem me copia*

---

[1] an old peasant couple who entertained the gods unawares; cf. Gayley,
Classic Myths, pp. 77–80.   [2] Roman poet (239–169 B.C.).   [3] lacked.
[4] ordinary, of the common people, unlearned.   [5] fanciful notions, artificial or witty turns of expression.   [6] a beautiful youth who fell in love
with his own reflection; cf. Gayley, *Classic Myths*, p. 189.

fecit,[1] and a dozen more of such expressions, poured on the neck of one another, and signifying all the same thing? If this were wit, was this a time to be witty, when the poor wretch was in the agony of death? This is just John Little-
5 wit in "Bartholomew Fair,"[2] who had a conceit (as he tells you) left him in his misery; a miserable conceit. On these occasions the poet should endeavour to raise pity; but instead of this, Ovid is tickling you to laugh. Virgil never made use of such machines; when he was moving you to
10 commiserate the death of Dido, he would not destroy what he was building. Chaucer makes Arcite[3] violent in his love, and unjust in the pursuit of it: yet when he came to die, he made him think more reasonably; he repents not of his love, for that had altered his character; but acknowledges the in-
15 justice of his proceedings, and resigns Emilia to Palamon.[3] What would Ovid have done on this occasion? He would certainly have made Arcite witty on his deathbed. He had complained he was farther off from possession, by being so near, and a thousand such boyisms, which Chaucer rejected
20 as below the dignity of the subject. They who think otherwise would, by the same reason, prefer Lucan[4] and Ovid to Homer and Virgil, and Martial[5] to all four of them. As for the turn of words, in which Ovid particularly excels all poets, they are sometimes a fault, and sometimes a beauty,
25 as they are used properly or improperly; but in strong passions always to be shunned, because passions are serious, and will admit no playing. . . . It remains that I say somewhat of Chaucer in particular.

In the first place, as he is the father of English poetry, so
30 I hold him in the same degree of veneration as the Grecians held Homer, or the Romans Virgil. He is a perpetual fountain of good sense, learned in all sciences, and therefore speaks

---

[1] abundance made me poor.   [2] comedy by Ben Jonson.   [3] (är'sīt) a character in Chaucer's "Knight's Tale." Arcite and his friend Palamon (păl'a mŏn) contended for the love of Emilia.   [4] Roman poet (A.D. 39–65). [5] Latin poet (about A.D. 40–102).

properly on all subjects. As he knew what to say, so he knows also when to leave off, a continence which is practised by few writers, and scarcely by any of the ancients, excepting Virgil and Horace. One of our late great poets is sunk in his reputation because he could never forego any conceit which 5 came in his way, but swept, like a drag-net, great and small. There was plenty enough, but the dishes were ill sorted, whole pyramids of sweetmeats for boys and women, but little of solid meat for men. All this proceeded not from any want of knowledge, but of judgment. Neither did he want that in 10 discerning the beauties and faults of other poets, but only indulged himself in the luxury of writing, and perhaps knew it was a fault, but hoped the reader would not find it. . . .

Chaucer followed nature everywhere; but was never so bold to go beyond her: and there is a great difference of be- 15 ing *poeta*[1] and *nimis*[2] *poeta*, if we believe Catullus,[3] as much as betwixt a modest behaviour and affectation. The verse of Chaucer, I confess, is not harmonious to us; but is like the eloquence of one whom Tacitus[4] commends, it was *auribus istius temporis accommodata*.[5] They who lived with him, 20 and some time after him, thought it musical; and it continues so even in our judgment, if compared with the numbers of Lydgate and Gower, his contemporaries: there is the rude sweetness of a Scotch tune in it, which is natural and pleasing, though not perfect. . . . We can only say that he lived 25 in the infancy of our poetry, and that nothing is brought to perfection at the first. We must be children before we grow men. . . .

[1] a maker, a poet.
[2] too much, excessively.
[3] Roman poet (87–54 B.C.).
[4] Roman historian (A.D. 55–117).
[5] suited to the ears of that period.

GEORGE HERBERT

THE PULLEY

When God at first made man,
Having a glass of blessing standing by;
Let us (said he) pour on him all we can:
Let the world's riches which dispersed lie
5   Contract into a span.[1]

So strength first made a way;
Then beauty flow'd, then wisdom, honour, pleasure;
When almost all was out, God made a stay,
Perceiving that alone, of all his treasure,
10   Rest in the bottom lay.

For if I should (said he)
Bestow this jewel also on my creature,
He would adore my gifts instead of me,
And rest in Nature, not the God of Nature;
15   So both should losers be.

Yet let him keep the rest,
But keep them with repining restlessness:
Let him be rich and weary, that at least,
If goodness lead him not, yet weariness
20   May toss him to my breast.

LOVE

Love bade me welcome; yet my soul drew back,
    Guilty of dust and sin.
But quick-eyed Love, observing me grow slack
    From my first entrance in,
25 Drew nearer to me, sweetly questioning,
    If I lacked anything.

[1] the distance from the end of the thumb to the end of the little finger,
9 in., hence a limited space or a brief portion of time.

"A guest," I answered, "worthy to be here:"
    Love said, "You shall be he."
"I, the unkind, ungrateful? Ah, my dear,
    I cannot look on Thee!"
Love took my hand and smiling did reply,   5
    "Who made the eyes but I?"

"Truth, Lord; but I have marred them: let my shame
    Go where it doth deserve."
"And know you not," says Love, "who bore the blame?"
    "My dear, then I will serve."   10
"You must sit down," says Love, "and taste my meat."
    So I did sit and eat.

ROBERT HERRICK

DELIGHT IN DISORDER

A sweet disorder in the dress
Kindles in clothes a wantonness[1];
A lawn about the shoulders thrown   15
Into a fine distraction;
An erring lace, which here and there
Enthrals the crimson stomacher[2];
A cuff neglectful, and thereby
Ribbons to flow confusedly;   20
A winning wave, deserving note,
In the tempestuous petticoat;
A careless shoestring, in whose tie
I see a wild civility;—
Do more beseem[3] me, than when art   25
Is too precise in every part.

[1] luxuriousness, playfulness.
[2] an ornamental garment for the front of the upper part of the body.
[3] are more seemly, fitting.

TO THE VIRGINS, TO MAKE MUCH OF TIME

Gather ye rosebuds while ye may,
   Old Time is still a-flying;
And this same flower that smiles to-day,
   To-morrow will be dying.

5   The glorious lamp of heaven, the sun,
   The higher he's a-getting,
The sooner will his race be run,
   And nearer he's to setting.

That age is best which is the first,
10   When youth and blood are warmer;
But being spent, the worse and worst
   Times still succeed the former.

Then be not coy, but use your time,
   And while ye may, go marry;
15 For, having lost but once your prime,
   You may forever tarry.

TO KEEP A TRUE LENT

Is this a fast, to keep
   The larder lean,
     And clean
20 From fat of veals and sheep?

Is it to quit the dish
   Of flesh, yet still
     To fill
The platter high with fish?

Is it to fast an hour,
        Or ragg'd to go,
        Or show
A downcast look, and sour?

No; 'tis a fast, to dole   5
        Thy sheaf of wheat
        And meat
Unto the hungry soul.

It is to fast from strife,
        From old debate,   10
        And hate;
To circumcise[1] thy life.

To show a heart grief-rent;
        To starve thy sin,
        Not bin;   15
And that's to keep thy Lent.

RICHARD LOVELACE

TO LUCASTA, ON GOING TO THE WARS

Tell me not, Sweet, I am unkind
    That from the nunnery
Of thy chaste breast and quiet mind,
    To war and arms I fly.   20

True, a new mistress now I chase,
    The first foe in the field;
And with a stronger faith embrace
    A sword, a horse, a shield.

[1] purify.

Yet this inconstancy is such
  As thou too shalt adore;
I could not love thee, Dear, so much,
  Loved I not Honour more.

TO ALTHEA FROM PRISON

5   When Love with unconfinèd wings
         Hovers within my gates,
       And my divine Althea brings
         To whisper at the grates;
       When I lie tangled in her hair
10   And fetter'd to her eye,
       The birds that wanton in the air
         Know no such liberty.

       When flowing cups run swiftly round
         With no allaying Thames,
15   Our careless heads with roses bound,
         Our hearts with loyal flames;
       When thirsty grief in wine we steep,
         When healths and draughts go free—
       Fishes that tipple in the deep
20   Know no such liberty.

       When, like committed linnets, I
         With shriller throat shall sing
       The sweetness, mercy, majesty
         And glories of my King;
25   When I shall voice aloud how good
         He is, how great should be,
       Enlargèd winds, that curl the flood,
         Know no such liberty.

       Stone walls do not a prison make,
30   Nor iron bars a cage;

Minds innocent and quiet take
That for an hermitage;
If I have freedom in my love
And in my soul am free,
Angels alone, that soar above,   5
Enjoy such liberty.

SIR THOMAS BROWNE

RELIGIO MEDICI[1]

Part the Second

Sect. III.—But, to return from philosophy to charity, I
hold not so narrow a conceit of this virtue as to conceive that
to give alms is only to be charitable, or think a piece of
liberality can comprehend the total of charity. Divinity[2] 10
hath wisely divided the act thereof into many branches, and
hath taught us in this narrow way many paths unto goodness; as many ways as we may do good, so many ways we
may be charitable. There are infirmities not only of body,
but of soul and fortunes, which do require the merciful hand 15
of our abilities. I cannot contemn a man for ignorance, but
behold him with as much pity as I do Lazarus.[3] It is no
greater charity to clothe his body than apparel the nakedness
of his soul. It is an honourable object to see the reasons of
other men wear our liveries, and their borrowed understand- 20
ings do homage to the bounty of ours. It is the cheapest way
of beneficence, and, like the natural charity of the sun,
illuminates another without obscuring itself. To be reserved
and caitiff[4] in this part of goodness is the sordidest piece of
covetousness, and more contemptible than the pecuniary 25
avarice. To this (as calling myself a scholar) I am obliged

[1] a physician's religion.   [2] theology.   [3] the personification of poverty, from the beggar of that name in the parable of the rich man and
Lazarus, Luke xvi.   [4] wicked, mean, cowardly.

by the duty of my condition. I make not therefore my head
a grave, but a treasury of knowledge. I intend no monopoly,
but a community in learning. I study not for my own sake
only, but for theirs that study not for themselves. I envy no
5 man that knows more than myself, but pity them that know
less. I instruct no man as an exercise of my knowledge, or
with an intent rather to nourish and keep it alive in mine own
head than beget and propagate it in his. And, in the midst of
all my endeavours, there is but one thought that dejects me,
10 that my acquired parts[1] must perish with myself, nor can
be legacied among my honoured friends. I cannot fall out
with or contemn a man for an errour, or conceive why a difference in opinion should divide an affection; for controversies, disputes, and argumentations, both in philosophy and
15 in divinity, if they meet with discreet and peaceable natures,
do not infringe the laws of charity. In all disputes, so much
as there is of passion, so much there is of nothing to the purpose; for then reason, like a bad hound, spends upon a false
scent, and forsakes the question first started. . . .

ISAAC WALTON

THE COMPLETE ANGLER

Chapter V

[Extract]

20   PISCATOR.[2] My honest Scholar, it is now past five of the
clock, we will fish till nine, and then go to breakfast. Go you
to yonder sycamore-tree, and hide your bottle of drink under
the hollow root of it: for about that time, and in that place,
we will make a brave breakfast with a piece of powdered[3]
25 beef, and a radish or two that I have in my fish-bag; we shall,
I warrant you, make a good, honest, wholesome, hungry

---

[1] capabilities, talents.   [2] (pēs cä′tor) fisherman.   [3] spiced, salted,
or corned.

breakfast, and I will then give you direction for the making and using of your flies: and in the meantime there is your rod and line; and my advice is, that you fish as you see me do, and let's try which can catch the first fish.

VENATOR.[1] I thank you, Master; I will observe and prac- 5
tice your directions, as far as I am able.

PISCATOR. Look you, Scholar, you see I have hold of a good fish: I now see it is a trout; I pray put that net under him, and touch not my line, for if you do, then we break all.
Well done, Scholar; I thank you. 10

Now for another. Trust me I have another bite: come, Scholar, come lay down your rod, and help me to land this as you did the other. So, now we shall be sure to have a good dish of fish for supper.

VENATOR. I am glad of that; but I have no fortune; sure, 15
Master, yours is a better rod, and better tackling.

PISCATOR. Nay, then, take mine, and I will fish with yours.
Look you, Scholar, I have another; come, do as you did before. And now I have a bite at another. Oh me! he has broke all; there's half a line and a good hook lost. 20

VENATOR. Ay, and a good trout too.

PISCATOR. Nay, the trout is not lost; for pray take notice, no man can lose what he never had.

VENATOR. Master, I can neither catch with the first nor second angle[2]; I have no fortune. 25

PISCATOR. Look you, Scholar, I have yet another: and now having caught three brace of trouts, I will tell you a short tale as we walk towards our breakfast: A scholar, a preacher I should say, that was to preach to procure the approbation of a parish, that he might be their lecturer, had 30
got from his fellow-pupil the copy of a sermon that was first preached with great commendation by him that composed it; and though the borrower of it preached it word for word as it was at first, yet it was utterly disliked as it was preached by the second to his congregation: which the sermon-borrower 35

---

[1] (wā nä'tor) hunter. [2] fishhook.

complained of to the lender of it, and was thus answered: "I lent you indeed my fiddle, but not my fiddle-stick; for you are to know that every one cannot make music with my words, which are fitted for my own mouth." And so, my
5 Scholar, you are to know that, as the ill pronunciation or ill accenting of words in a sermon spoils it, so the ill carriage of your line, or not fishing even to a foot in a right place, makes you lose your labour: and you are to know, that though you have my fiddle, that is, my very rod and tackling with which
10 you see I catch fish, yet you have not my fiddle-stick; that is, you yet have not skill to know how to carry your hand and line, nor how to guide it to a right place: and this must be taught you,—for you are to remember I told you angling is an art,—either by practice, or a long observation, or both.
15 But take this for a rule, when you fish for a trout with a worm, let your line have so much, and no more lead than will fit the stream in which you fish; that is to say, more in a great troublesome stream than in a smaller that is quieter; as near as may be, so much as will sink the bait to the bot-
20 tom, and keep it still in motion, and not more.

But now let's say grace and fall to breakfast: what say you, Scholar, to the providence of an old angler? Does not this meat taste well? and was not this place well chosen to eat it? for this sycamore-tree will shade us from the sun's
25 heat.

EIGHTEENTH–CENTURY LITERATURE

ALEXANDER POPE

ESSAY ON MAN

[Extract]

Lo, the poor Indian! whose untutor'd mind
Sees God in clouds, or hears him in the wind;
His soul, proud science never taught to stray
Far as the solar walk,[1] or milky way;
Yet simple nature to his hope has given,   5
Behind the cloud-topped hill, an humbler Heaven;
Some safer world, in depths of woods embraced,
Some happier island in the watery waste,
Where slaves once more their native land behold,
No fiends torment, no Christians thirst for gold.   10
To be, contents his natural desire,
He asks no angel's wing, no seraph's fire;
But thinks, admitted to that equal sky,
His faithful dog shall bear him company.

THE RAPE OF THE LOCK

Canto III

Close by those meads, for ever crowned with flowers, 15
Where Thames with pride surveys his rising towers,
There stands a structure of majestic frame,[1]

[1] the sun's path through the sky.
[2] Hampton Court, a royal palace on the Thames River near London.
William of Orange laid out extensive gardens in the Dutch fashion there.

105

Which from the neighbouring Hampton takes its name
Here Britain's statesmen oft the fall foredoom
Of foreign tyrants, and of nymphs at home;
Here thou, great Anna![1] whom three realms obey,
5   Dost sometimes counsel take—and sometimes tea.[2]
    Hither the heroes and the nymphs[3] resort,
To taste awhile the pleasures of a court;
In various talk th' instructive hours they passed,
Who gave the ball, or paid the visit last;
10 One speaks the glory of the British Queen,
And one describes a charming Indian screen;
A third interprets motions, looks, and eyes;
At every word a reputation dies.
Snuff, or the fan, supplies each pause of chat,
15 With singing, laughing, ogling, and all that.
    Meanwhile, declining from the noon of day,
The sun obliquely shoots his burning ray:
The hungry judges soon the sentence sign,
And wretches hang that jurymen may dine;
20 The merchant from th' Exchange returns in peace,
And the long labours of the toilet cease.
Belinda[4] now, whom thirst of fame invites,
Burns to encounter two adventurous knights,
At ombre[5] singly to decide their doom;
25 And swells her breast with conquests yet to come.
Straight the three bands[6] prepare in arms to join,

[1] Queen Anne of England, Scotland, and Ireland, 1702–1714.

[2] pronounced *tā* till about 1750.

[3] the group of young people who, in Canto II, set out on a boating party on the Thames.

[4] The heroine of the poem, in real life Miss Arabella Fermor. The "rash youth" who cut off a lock of her hair and precipitated a quarrel in London society was Lord Petre.

[5] a Spanish game of cards, popular in the seventeenth and eighteenth centuries, played by three persons.

[6] Pope represents Belinda as under the protection of mythical inhabitants of the air, called sylphs, which once had been women. Of these Ariel was Belinda's special guardian.

Each band the number of the sacred nine.[1]
Soon as she spreads her hand, the aërial guard
Descend, and sit on each important card:
First Ariel perched upon a Matadore,[2]
Then each according to the rank they bore; 5
For sylphs, yet mindful of their ancient race,
Are, as when women, wondrous fond of place.

Behold, four kings, in majesty revered,
With hoary whiskers and a forky beard;
And four fair queens whose hands sustain a flower, 10
The expressive emblem of their softer power;
Four knaves in garbs succinct,[3] a trusty band,
Caps on their heads, and halberts[4] in their hand;
And party-coloured[5] troops, a shining train,
Draw forth to combat on the velvet plain. 15

The skilful nymph reviews her force with care;
Let spades be trumps![6] she said, and trumps they were.

Now move to war her sable Matadores,
In show like leaders of the swarthy Moors.
Spadillio first, unconquerable lord! 20
Led off two captive trumps, and swept the board.
As many more Manillio forced to yield,
And march'd a victor from the verdant field.
Him Basto follow'd, but his fate more hard
Gain'd but one trump and one plebeian card. 25
With his broad sabre next, a chief in years,
The hoary majesty of spades appears,
Puts forth one manly leg, to sight reveal'd,
The rest, his many-colour'd robe conceal'd.

[1] The Muses. See Gayley, *Classic Myths*, p. 37. Each player in ombre received nine cards. [2] Killer, one of the three most important cards in ombre. In order of importance the matadores were: Spadillio, the ace of spades; Manillio, which varied with the trump, in this case the two of spades; Basto, the ace of clubs. [3] girded, tucked up. [4] long-handled, pointed weapons. [5] variegated. [6] By naming the trump Belinda became the "ombre" (from the Spanish *Yo soy el hombre*, "I am the man"), and played against the other two.

The rebel knave, who dares his prince engage,
Proves the just victim of his royal rage.
Even mighty Pam,[1] that kings and queens o'erthrew,
And mow'd down armies in the fights of Loo,
5   Sad chance of war! now destitute of aid,
Falls undistinguish'd by the victor spade!
    Thus far both armies to Belinda yield.
Now to the baron fate inclines the field;
His warlike Amazon[2] her host invades,
10   The imperial consort of the crown of spades.
The club's black tyrant[3] first her victim died,
Spite of his haughty mien and barbarous pride.
What boots[4] the regal circle on his head,
His giant limbs, in state unwieldy spread;
15   That long behind he trails his pompous robe,
And, of all monarchs, only grasps the globe?
    The baron now his diamonds pours apace;
The embroider'd king who shows but half his face,
And his refulgent queen, with powers combined,
20   Of broken troops an easy conquest find.
Clubs, diamonds, hearts, in wild disorder seen,
With throngs promiscuous strew the level green.
Thus when dispersed a routed army runs,
Of Asia's troops, and Afric's sable sons,
25   With like confusion different nations fly,
Of various habit, and of various dye,
The pierced battalions disunited fall,
In heaps on heaps; one fate o'erwhelms them all.
    The knave of diamonds tries his wily arts,
30   And wins (oh shameful chance!) the queen of hearts.
At this, the blood the virgin's cheek forsook,
A livid paleness spreads o'er all her look;

---

[1] the knave of clubs in Loo, a game played for stakes with three or five cards dealt to each player. [2] queen of spades. [3] king of clubs. [4] avails.

She sees, and trembles at the approaching ill,
Just in the jaws of ruin, and codille.[1]
And now (as oft in some distemper'd state)
On one nice trick depends the general fate.
An ace of hearts steps forth; the king, unseen,   5
Lurked in her hand, and mourn'd his captive queen:
He springs to vengeance with an eager pace,
And falls like thunder on the prostrate ace.
The nymph exulting fills with shouts the sky;
The walls, the woods, and long canals[2] reply.   10

   Oh, thoughtless mortals! ever blind to fate,
Too soon dejected, and too soon elate.
Sudden these honours shall be snatch'd away,
And cursed for ever this victorious day.

   For lo! the board with cups and spoons is crowned, 15
The berries[3] crackle, and the mill turns round;
On shining altars of Japan[4] they raise
The silver lamp; the fiery spirits blaze:
From silver spouts the grateful liquors glide,
While China's earth[5] receives the smoking tide: 20
At once they gratify their scent and taste,
And frequent cups prolong the rich repast.
Straight hover round the fair her airy band;
Some, as she sipp'd, the fuming liquor fann'd,
Some o'er her lap their careful plumes display'd,   25
Trembling, and conscious of the rich brocade.
Coffee (which makes the politician wise,
And see through all things with his half-shut eyes)
Sent up in vapours to the baron's brain
New stratagems, the radiant Lock to gain.   30
Ah cease, rash youth! desist ere 'tis too late,
Fear the just gods, and think of Scylla's fate!

---

[1] the term used when the opponents took more tricks than the "ombre."
[2] of the Dutch gardens.   [3] coffee.   [4] lacquered, or japanned, tables.
[5] cups of Chinese porcelain.

Changed to a bird, and sent to flit in air,
She dearly pays for Nisus'[1] injured hair!
But when to mischief mortals bend their will,
How soon they find fit instruments of ill!
5   Just then Clarissa[2] drew, with tempting grace,
A two-edged weapon from her shining case:
So ladies in romance assist their knight,
Present the spear and arm him for the fight.
He takes the gift with reverence, and extends
10   The little engine on his fingers' ends;
This just behind Belinda's neck he spread,
As o'er the fragrant steams she bends her head.
Swift to the Lock a thousand sprites repair,
A thousand wings, by turns, blow back the hair;
15   And thrice they twitch'd the diamond in her ear;
Thrice she look'd back, and thrice the foe drew near.
Just in that instant anxious Ariel sought
The close recesses of the virgin's thought:
As on the nosegay in her breast reclined,
20   He watch'd the ideas rising in her mind,
Sudden he view'd, in spite of all her art,
An earthly lover lurking at her heart.
Amazed, confused, he found his power expired,
Resign'd to fate, and with a sigh retired.
25   The peer now spreads the glittering forfex[3] wide,
To inclose the Lock; now joins it, to divide.
Even then, before the fatal engine closed,
A wretched sylph too fondly interposed;

[1] In Greek mythology, Nisus, king of Megara, had a lock of purple hair on which his life and fortune depended. His daughter, Scylla, cut off this lock and sent it to Minos II of Crete, her lover and her father's enemy. Minos, in horror of her treachery, after conquering Nisus, dragged Scylla through the sea at the rudder of his ship. Ultimately Scylla was transformed into a bird, continually preyed upon by her father in the form of an eagle.

[2] So far as is known, Pope had no one particularly in mind.

[3] scissors.

Fate urged the shears, and cut the sylph in twain,
(But airy substance soon unites again;)
The meeting points the sacred hair dissever
From the fair head, for ever, and for ever!
Then flash'd the living lightning from her eyes,   5
And screams of horror rend the affrighted skies;
Not louder shrieks to pitying Heaven are cast,
When husbands, or when lapdogs, breathe their last;
Or when rich China vessels, fallen from high,
In glittering dust and painted fragments lie!   10
Let wreaths of triumph now my temples twine,
(The victor cried,) the glorious prize is mine!
While fish in streams, or birds delight in air,
Or in a coach-and-six the British fair,
As long as Atalantis[1] shall be read,   15
Or the small pillow grace a lady's bed,
While visits shall be paid on solemn days,
When numerous wax-lights in bright order blaze,
While nymphs take treats, or assignations give,
So long my honour, name, and praise, shall live!   20
What time would spare, from steel receives its date,
And monuments, like men, submit to fate!
Steel could the labour of the gods[2] destroy,
And strike to dust the imperial towers of Troy;
Steel could the works of mortal pride confound,   25
And hew triumphal arches to the ground.
What wonder then, fair nymph! thy hairs should feel
The conquering force of unresisted steel?

[1] *The New Atalantis*, by Mrs. Manley, published in 1709, was a popular
book of scandalous gossip about prominent persons of the time.
[2] the walls of Troy, built by Neptune and Apollo.

JONATHAN SWIFT

GULLIVER'S TRAVELS

A Voyage to Lilliput

[Extract from Chapter II]

When I found myself on my feet, I looked about me, and must confess I never beheld a more entertaining prospect. The country around appeared like a continued garden, and the enclosed fields, which were generally forty foot square,
5 resembled so many beds of flowers. These fields were intermingled with woods of half a stang,[1] and the tallest trees, as I could judge, appeared to be seven foot high. I viewed the town on my left hand, which looked like the painted scene of a city in a theatre.

10 The Emperor was already descended from the tower and advancing on horseback towards me, which had like to have cost him dear; for the beast, though very well trained, yet wholly unused to such a sight, which appeared as if a mountain moved before him, reared up on his hinder feet: but
15 that prince, who is an excellent horseman, kept his seat, till his attendants ran in, and held the bridle, while his Majesty had time to dismount. While he alighted, he surveyed me round with great admiration, but kept beyond the length of my chain. He ordered his cooks and butlers, who were al-
20 ready prepared, to give me victuals and drink, which they pushed forward in a sort of vehicle upon wheels, till I could reach them. I took these vehicles, and soon emptied them all; twenty of them were filled with meat, and ten with liquor; each of the former afforded me two or three good
25 mouthfuls, and I emptied the liquor of ten vessels, which was contained in earthen vials, into one vehicle, drinking it off at a draught; and so I did with the rest. The Empress and young Princes of the blood of both sexes, attended by many

---

[1] a Swedish measure, equal to 9.74 ft.

ladies, sat at some distance in their chairs; but upon the accident that happened to the Emperor's horse, they alighted, and came near his person, which I am now going to describe. He is taller by almost the breadth of my nail than any of his court, which alone is enough to strike an awe into the beholders. His features are strong and masculine, with an Austrian lip and arched nose, his complexion olive, his countenance erect, his body and limbs well proportioned, all his motions graceful, and his deportment majestic. He was then past his prime, being twenty-eight years and three quarters old, of which he had reigned about seven, in great felicity, and generally victorious. For the better convenience of beholding him, I lay on my side, so that my face was parallel to his, and he stood but three yards off: however, I have had him since many times in my hand, and therefore cannot be deceived in the description. His dress was very plain and simple, and the fashion of it between the Asiatic and the European: but he had on his head a light helmet of gold, adorned with jewels, and a plume on the crest. He held his sword drawn in his hand, to defend himself, if I should happen to break loose; it was almost three inches long, the hilt and scabbard were gold enriched with diamonds. His voice was shrill, but very clear and articulate, and I could distinctly hear it when I stood up. The ladies and courtiers were all most magnificently clad, so that the spot they stood upon seemed to resemble a skirt spread on the ground, embroidered with figures of gold and silver. His Imperial Majesty spoke often to me, and I returned answers, but neither of us could understand a syllable. There were several of his priests and lawyers present (as I conjectured by their habits) who were commanded to address themselves to me, and I spoke to them in as many languages as I had the least smattering of, which were High and Low Dutch,[1] Latin, French, Spanish, Italian, and Lingua Franca,[2] but all to no purpose. After about two hours the court retired, and I was

---

[1] German.   [2] a hybrid, commercial language.

left with a strong guard, to prevent the impertinence, and
probably the malice of the rabble, who were very impatient
to crowd about me as near as they durst, and some of them
had the impudence to shoot their arrows at me as I sat on the
5 ground by the door of my house, whereof one very narrowly
missed my left eye. But the colonel ordered six of the ring-
leaders to be seized, and thought no punishment so proper as
to deliver them bound into my hands, which some of the soldiers accordingly did, pushing them forwards with the butt-
10 ends of their pikes into my reach; I took them all in my right
hand, put five of them into my coat pocket, and as to the
sixth, I made a countenance as if I would eat him alive. The
poor man squalled terribly, and the colonel and his officers
were in much pain, especially when they saw me take out my
15 penknife: but I soon put them out of fear; for, looking
mildly, and immediately cutting the strings he was bound
with, I set him gently on the ground, and away he ran; I
treated the rest in the same manner, taking them one by one
out of my pocket, and I observed both the soldiers and peo-
20 ple were highly obliged at this mark of my clemency, which
was represented very much to my advantage at court.

JOSEPH ADDISON

SIR ROGER DE COVERLEY PAPERS

A Village Witch

Saturday, July 14, 1711

Ipsi sibi somnia fingunt.[1]
                          Virg.

There are some opinions in which a man should stand neu-
ter,[2] without engaging his assent to one side or the other.
25 Such a hovering faith as this, which refuses to settle upon
any determination, is absolutely necessary to a mind that is

---

[1] Their visions are of their own imagining, Virgil, Eclogues VIII, 108.
[2] neutral.

careful to avoid errors and prepossessions. When the arguments press equally on both sides, in matters that are indifferent to us, the safest method is to give up ourselves to neither.

It is with this temper of mind that I consider the subject of witchcraft. When I hear the relations[1] that are made from all parts of the world,—not only from Norway and Lapland, from the East and West Indies, but from every particular nation in Europe,—I cannot forbear thinking that there is such an intercourse and commerce with evil spirits as that which we express by the name of witchcraft. But when I consider that the ignorant and credulous parts of the world abound most in these relations, and that the persons among us who are supposed to engage in such an infernal commerce are people of a weak understanding and a crazed imagination, and at the same time reflect upon the many impostures and delusions of this nature that have been detected in all ages, I endeavor to suspend my belief till I hear more certain accounts than any which have yet come to my knowledge. In short, when I consider the question whether there are such persons in the world as those we call witches, my mind is divided between the two opposite opinions; or rather, to speak my thoughts freely, I believe in general that there is, and has been, such a thing as witchcraft; but at the same time can give no credit to any particular instance of it.

I am engaged in this speculation by some occurrences that I met with yesterday, which I shall give my reader an account of at large. As I was walking with my friend Sir Roger by the side of one of his woods, an old woman applied herself to me for my charity. Her dress and figure put me in mind of the following description in Otway:

> "In a close lane as I pursued my journey,
> I spied a wrinkled hag, with age grown double,
> Picking dry sticks, and mumbling to herself.
> Her eyes with scalding rheum were gall'd and red;

[1] accounts, stories.

> Cold palsy shook her head; her hands seem'd wither'd;
> And on her crooked shoulders had she wrapp'd
> The tatter'd remnants of an old striped hanging,
> Which served to keep her carcase from the cold:
> 5   So there was nothing of a piece about her.
> Her lower weeds were all o'er coarsely patch'd
> With diff'rent color'd rags—black, red, white, yellow—
> And seem'd to speak variety of wretchedness."

As I was musing on this description and comparing it with
10 the object before me, the knight told me that this very old
woman had the reputation of a witch all over the country,
that her lips were observed to be always in motion, and that
there was not a switch about her house which her neighbors
did not believe had carried her several hundreds of miles. If
15 she chanced to stumble, they always found sticks or straws
that lay in the figure of a cross before her. If she made any
mistake at church, and cried "Amen" in a wrong place, they
never failed to conclude that she was saying her prayer back-
wards. There was not a maid in the parish that would take
20 a pin of her, though she would offer a bag of money with it.
She goes by the name of Moll White, and has made the country ring with several imaginary exploits which are palmed
upon her. If the dairy maid does not make her butter come
so soon as she should have it, Moll White is at the bottom of
25 the churn. If a horse sweats in the stable, Moll White has
been upon his back. If a hare makes an unexpected escape
from the hounds, the huntsman curses Moll White. "Nay,"
says Sir Roger, "I have known the master of the pack, upon
such an occasion, send one of his servants to see if Moll
30 White had been out that morning."

This account raised my curiosity so far that I begged my
friend Sir Roger to go with me into her hovel, which stood in
a solitary corner under the side of the wood. Upon our first
entering, Sir Roger winked to me, and pointed at something
35 that stood behind the door, which, upon looking that way, I
found to be an old broomstaff. At the same time, he whis-

pered me in the ear to take notice of a tabby cat that sat in
the chimney-corner, which, as the old knight told me, lay
under as bad a report as Moll White herself; for besides that
Moll is said often to accompany her in the same shape, the
cat is reported to have spoken twice or thrice in her life, and 5
to have played several pranks above the capacity of an ordinary cat.

I was secretly concerned to see human nature in so much
wretchedness and disgrace, but at the same time could not
forbear smiling to hear Sir Roger, who is a little puzzled 10
about the old woman, advising her, as a justice of peace, to
avoid all communication with the devil, and never to hurt
any of her neighbors' cattle. We concluded our visit with a
bounty, which was very acceptable.

In our return home, Sir Roger told me that old Moll had 15
been often brought before him for making children spit pins,
and giving maids the nightmare; and that the country people would be tossing her into a pond and trying experiments
with her every day, if it was not for him and his chaplain.

I have since found, upon inquiry, that Sir Roger was sev- 20
eral times staggered with the reports that had been brought
him concerning this old woman, and would frequently have
bound her over to the county sessions[1] had not his chaplain
with much ado persuaded him to the contrary.

I have been the more particular in this account because I 25
hear there is scarce a village in England that has not a Moll
White in it. When an old woman begins to dote,[2] and grow
chargeable to a parish, she is generally turned into a witch,
and fills the whole country with extravagant fancies, imaginary distempers, and terrifying dreams. In the mean time the 30
poor wretch that is the innocent occasion of so many evils begins to be frighted at herself, and sometimes confesses secret
commerce[3] and familiarities that her imagination forms in a

---

[1] put her under bonds to appear at the county court, of which sessions
were held quarterly.   [2] to be weak-minded, especially through old age.
[3] with the powers of evil.

delirious old age. This frequently cuts off charity from the greatest objects of compassion, and inspires people with a malevolence towards those poor, decrepit parts of our species in whom human nature is defaced by infirmity and dotage.

RICHARD STEELE

SIR ROGER DE COVERLEY PAPERS

TO LONDON BY STAGE-COACH

Wednesday, August 1, 1711

5   Qui aut tempus quid postulet non videt, aut plura loquitur, aut se osten-
tat, aut eorum quibuscum est rationem non habet, is ineptus esse dicitur.[1]
TULL.

Having notified to my good friend Sir Roger that I should set out for London the next day, his horses were ready at the appointed hour in the evening; and attended by one of his 10 grooms, I arrived at the county town at twilight, in order to be ready for the stage-coach the day following. As soon as we arrived at the inn, the servant who waited upon me inquired of the chamberlain,[2] in my hearing, what company he had for the coach. The fellow answered, "Mrs.[3] Betty Arable, 15 the great fortune, and the widow, her mother; a recruiting officer,—who took a place because they were to go; young Squire Quickset, her cousin,—that her mother wished her to be married to; Ephraim, the Quaker, her guardian; and a gentleman that had studied himself dumb from Sir Roger de 20 Coverley's." I observed, by what he said of myself that, according to his office, he dealt much in intelligence; and doubted not but there was some foundation for his reports of

[1] He who does not see what the occasion demands, or talks too much, or shows off, or lacks consideration for those with whom he is,—such a one is called impertinent. Cicero, De Oratione, ii, 4.
[2] the servant who had charge of the inn bedrooms.
[3] formerly applied to a woman whether married or unmarried.

the rest of the company, as well as for the whimsical account
he gave of me.

The next morning at daybreak we were all called; and I,
who know my own natural shyness, and endeavor to be as
little liable to be disputed with as possible, dressed imme- 5
diately, that I might make no one wait. The first preparation for our setting out was, that the captain's half-pike was
placed near the coachman, and a drum behind the coach. In
the meantime the drummer, the captain's equipage,[1] was
very loud that none of the captain's things should be placed 10
so as to be spoiled; upon which his cloak bag was fixed
in the seat of the coach; and the captain himself, according to a frequent though invidious[2] behavior of military
men, ordered his man to look sharp that none but one of the
ladies should have the place he had taken fronting to the 15
coach-box.

We were in some little time fixed in our seats, and sat with
that dislike which people not too good-natured usually conceive of each other at first sight. The coach jumbled us in-
sensibly into some sort of familiarity, and we had not moved 20
above two miles when the widow asked the captain what success he had in his recruiting. The officer, with a frankness he
believed very graceful, told her that indeed he had but very
little luck, and had suffered much by desertion, therefore
should be glad to end his warfare in the service of her or her 25
fair daughter. "In a word," continued he, "I am a soldier,
and to be plain is my character; you see me, madam, young,
sound, and impudent; take me yourself, widow, or give me
to her; I will be wholly at your disposal. I am a soldier of
fortune, ha!" This was followed by a vain laugh of his own, 30
and a deep silence of all the rest of the company. I had nothing left for it but to fall fast asleep, which I did with all
speed. "Come," said he, "resolve upon it, we will make a
wedding at the next town: we will wake this pleasant companion who has fallen asleep, to be the brideman,[3] and,"— 35

---

[1] retinue.   [2] disagreeable.   [3] groomsman, best man.

giving the Quaker a clap on the knee,—he concluded, "this sly saint, who, I'll warrant, understands what's what as well as you or I, widow, shall give the bride as father."

The Quaker, who happened to be a man of smartness, an-
5 swered, "Friend, I take it in good part that thou hast given me the authority of a father over this comely and virtuous child; and I must assure thee that if I have the giving her, I shall not bestow her on thee. Thy mirth, friend, savoreth of folly; thou art a person of a light mind; thy drum is a type
10 of thee,—it soundeth because it is empty. Verily, it is not from thy fullness, but thy emptiness, that thou hast spoken this day. Friend, friend, we have hired this coach in partner-ship with thee, to carry us to the great city; we cannot go any other way. This worthy mother must hear thee if thou wilt
15 needs utter thy follies; we cannot help it, friend, I say; if thou wilt, we must hear thee: but, if thou wert a man of understanding, thou wouldst not take advantage of thy courageous countenance to abash us children of peace. Thou art, thou sayest, a soldier; give quarter to us, who cannot re-
20 sist thee. Why didst thou fleer[1] at our friend, who feigned himself asleep? He said nothing, but how dost thou know what he containeth? If thou speakest improper things in the hearing of this virtuous young virgin, consider it is an out-rage against a distressed person that cannot get from thee:
25 to speak indiscreetly what we are obliged to hear, by being hasped up with thee in this public vehicle, is in some degree assaulting on the high road."

Here Ephraim paused, and the captain, with an happy and uncommon impudence,—which can be convicted and support
30 itself at the same time,—cries, "Faith, friend, I thank thee; I should have been a little impertinent if thou hadst not rep-rimanded me. Come, thou art, I see, a smoky[2] old fellow, and I'll be very orderly the ensuing part of the journey. I was going to give myself airs; but, ladies, I beg pardon."
35 The captain was so little out of humor, and our company

---

[1] laugh at, make fun of.   [2] suspicious.

was so far from being soured by this little ruffle, that Ephraim and he took a particular delight in being agreeable to each other for the future, and assumed their different provinces in the conduct of the company. Our reckonings, apartments, and accommodation fell under Ephraim; and the captain looked to all disputes on the road,—as the good behavior of our coachman, and the right we had of taking place as going to London of all vehicles coming from thence.

The occurrences we met with were ordinary, and very little happened which could entertain by the relation of them; but when I considered the company we were in, I took it for no small good fortune that the whole journey was not spent in impertinences, which to one part of us might be an entertainment, to the other a suffering.

What, therefore, Ephraim said when we were almost arrived at London, had to me an air not only of good understanding, but good breeding. Upon the young lady's expressing her satisfaction in the journey, and declaring how delightful it had been to her, Ephraim declared himself as follows: "There is no ordinary part of human life which expresseth so much a good mind, and a right inward man, as his behavior upon meeting with strangers, especially such as may seem the most unsuitable companions to him: such a man, when he falleth in the way with persons of simplicity and innocence, however knowing he may be in the ways of men, will not vaunt himself thereof; but will the rather hide his superiority to them, that he may not be painful unto them. My good friend," continued he, turning to the officer, "thee and I are to part by and by, and peradventure we may never meet again; but be advised by a plain man; modes and apparel are but trifles to the real man, therefore do not think such a man as thyself terrible for thy garb, nor such a one as me contemptible for mine. When two such as thee and I meet, with affections as we ought to have towards each other, thou shouldst rejoice to see my peaceable demeanor, and I should be glad to see thy strength and ability to protect me in it." T.

JAMES BOSWELL

THE LIFE OF SAMUEL JOHNSON, LL.D.

[Extracts from Chapter XIII (1763)]

He talked very contemptuously of Churchill's poetry, observing, that "it had a temporary currency, only from its au-
dacity of abuse, and being filled with living names, and that
it would sink into oblivion." I ventured to hint that he was
5 not quite a fair judge, as Churchill had attacked him violently. Johnson: "Nay, Sir, I am a very fair judge. He did
not attack me violently till he found I did not like his poetry; and his attack on me shall not prevent me from con-
tinuing to say what I think of him, from an apprehension
10 that it may be ascribed to resentment. No, Sir, I called the
fellow a blockhead at first, and I will call him a blockhead
still. However, I will acknowledge that I have a better
opinion of him now than I once had; for he has shown more
fertility than I expected. To be sure, he is a tree that cannot
15 produce good fruit: he only bears crabs. But, Sir, a tree
that produces a great many crabs, is better than a tree which
produces only a few."

.   .   .   .

On Wednesday, July 6, he was engaged to sup with me at
my lodgings in Downing-street, Westminster. But on the
20 preceding night my landlord having behaved very rudely to
me and some company who were with me, I had resolved not
to remain another night in his house. I was exceedingly uneasy at the awkward appearance I supposed I should make
to Johnson and the other gentlemen whom I had invited, not
25 being able to receive them at home, and being obliged to
order supper at the Mitre. I went to Johnson in the morning,
and talked of it as of a serious distress. He laughed, and
said, "Consider, Sir, how insignificant this will appear a
twelvemonth hence." Were this consideration to be applied
30 to most of the little vexatious incidents of life, by which our

quiet is too often disturbed, it would prevent many painful sensations. I have tried it frequently with good effect. "There is nothing," continued he, "in this mighty misfortune; nay, we shall be better at the Mitre." I told him that I had been at Sir John Fielding's office,[1] complaining of my landlord, and had been informed that though I had taken my lodgings for a year, I might, upon proof of his bad behaviour, quit them when I pleased, without being under an obligation to pay rent for any longer time than while I possessed them. The fertility of Johnson's mind could show itself even upon so small a matter as this. "Why, Sir," said he, "I suppose this must be the law, since you have been told so in Bow-street.[1] But if your landlord could hold you to your bargain, and the lodgings should be yours for a year, you may certainly use them as you think fit. So, Sir, you may quarter two life-guardsmen[2] upon him; or you may send the greatest scoundrel you can find into your apartments; or you may say that you want to make some experiments in natural philosophy,[3] and may burn a large quantity of asafœtida in his house."

. . . .

Goldsmith,[4] as usual, endeavoured with too much eagerness to *shine* and disputed very warmly with Johnson against the well-known maxim of the British constitution, "the king can do no wrong;" affirming, that "what was morally false could not be politically true; and as the king might, in the exercise of his regal power, command and cause the doing of what was wrong, it certainly might be said, in sense and in reason, that he could do wrong." Johnson: "Sir, you are to consider that in our constitution, according to its true principles, the king is the head, he is supreme; he is above everything, and there is no power by which he can be tried. Therefore, it is, Sir, that we hold the king can do no wrong; that whatever may

---

[1] police headquarters.   [2] soldiers of the regiments which form the bodyguard of the sovereign.   [3] natural science, here chemistry.   [4] Oliver Goldsmith, one of Boswell's guests at this party at the Mitre Tavern.

happen to be wrong in government may not be above our reach by being ascribed to majesty. Redress is always to be had against oppression by punishing the immediate agents. The king, though he should command, cannot force a judge to condemn a man unjustly; therefore it is the judge whom we prosecute and punish. Political institutions are formed upon the consideration of what will most frequently tend to the good of the whole, although now and then exceptions may occur. Thus it is better in general that a nation should have a supreme legislative power, although it may at times be abused. And then, Sir, there is this consideration, that *if the abuse be enormous, nature will rise up, and claiming her original rights, overturn a corrupt political system.*" I mark this animated sentence with peculiar pleasure, as a noble instance of that truly dignified spirit of freedom which ever glowed in his heart, though he was charged with slavish tenets by superficial observers, because he was at all times indignant against that false patriotism, that pretended love of freedom, that unruly restlessness which is inconsistent with the stable authority of any good government.

. . . .

Feeling myself now quite at ease as his companion, though I had all possible reverence for him, I expressed a regret that I could not be so easy with my father, though he was not much older than Johnson, and certainly, however respectable, had not more learning and greater abilities to depress me. I asked him the reason of this. Johnson: "Why, Sir, I am a man of the world. I live in the world, and I take, in some degree, the colour of the world as it moves along. Your father is a judge in a remote part of the island, and all his notions are taken from the old world. Besides, Sir, there must always be a struggle between a father and son, while one aims at power and the other at independence." I said, I was afraid my father would force me to be a lawyer. Johnson: "Sir, you need not be afraid of his forcing you to be a laborious practising lawyer; that is not in his power. For, as the prov-

erb says, 'One man may lead a horse to the water, but twenty
cannot make him drink.' He may be displeased that you
are not what he wishes you to be; but that displeasure will
not go far. If he insists only on your having as much law
as is necessary for a man of property, and then endeavours to 5
get you into parliament, he is quite in the right."

He enlarged very convincingly upon the excellence of
rhyme over blank verse in English poetry. I mentioned to
him that Dr. Adam Smith,[1] in his lectures upon composition,
when I studied under him in the College of Glasgow, had 10
maintained the same opinion strenuously, and I repeated
some of his arguments. Johnson: "Sir, I was once in company with Smith, and we did not take to each other; but had
I known that he loved rhyme as much as you tell me he does,
I should have hugged him."   15

WILLIAM COLLINS

ODE

Written in the Beginning of the Year 1746

How sleep the brave who sink to rest
By all their country's wishes blest!
When Spring, with dewy fingers cold,
Returns to deck their hallow'd mold,
She there shall dress a sweeter sod   20
Than Fancy's feet have ever trod.

By fairy hands their knell is rung,
By forms unseen their dirge is sung;
There Honour comes, a pilgrim grey,
To bless the turf that wraps their clay;   25
And Freedom shall awhile repair,
To dwell a weeping hermit there!

[1] the economist, author of *The Wealth of Nations*.

THOMAS GRAY

ELEGY

Written in a Country Churchyard

The Curfew tolls the knell of parting day,
　　The lowing herd wind slowly o'er the lea,
The plowman homeward plods his weary way,
　　And leaves the world to darkness and to me.

5　Now fades the glimmering landscape on the sight,
　　And all the air a solemn stillness holds,
Save where the beetle wheels his droning flight,
　　And drowsy tinklings lull the distant folds;

Save that from yonder ivy-mantled tow'r
10　　The moping owl does to the moon complain
Of such, as wand'ring near her secret bow'r,
　　Molest her ancient solitary reign.

Beneath those rugged elms, that yew-tree's shade,
　　Where heaves the turf in many a mould'ring heap,
15　Each in his narrow cell for ever laid,
　　The rude Forefathers of the hamlet sleep.

The breezy call of incense-breathing Morn,
　　The swallow twitt'ring from the straw-built shed,
The cock's shrill clarion, or the echoing horn,
20　　No more shall rouse them from their lowly bed.

For them no more the blazing hearth shall burn,
　　Or busy housewife ply her evening care:
No children run to lisp their sire's return,
　　Or climb his knees the envied kiss to share.

25　Oft did the harvest to their sickle yield,
　　Their furrow oft the stubborn glebe has broke;

How jocund did they drive their team afield!
　How bow'd the woods beneath their sturdy stroke!

Let not Ambition mock their useful toil,
　Their homely joys, and destiny obscure;
Nor Grandeur hear with a disdainful smile,　　　　5
　The short and simple annals of the poor.

The boast of heraldry, the pomp of pow'r,
　And all that beauty, all that wealth e'er gave,
Awaits alike th' inevitable hour.[1]
　The paths of glory lead but to the grave.　　　　10

Nor you, ye Proud, impute to These the fault,
　If Mem'ry o'er their Tomb no Trophies raise,
Where thro' the long-drawn aisle and fretted vault
　The pealing anthem swells the note of praise.

Can storied urn or animated bust　　　　15
　Back to its mansion call the fleeting breath?
Can Honour's voice provoke[2] the silent dust,
　Or Flatt'ry sooth the dull cold ear of Death?

Perhaps in this neglected spot is laid
　Some heart once pregnant with celestial fire;　　20
Hands, that the rod of empire might have sway'd,
　Or wak'd to extasy the living lyre.

But Knowledge to their eyes her ample page
　Rich with the spoils of time did ne'er unroll;
Chill Penury repress'd their noble rage,　　　　25
　And froze the genial current of the soul.

Full many a gem of purest ray serene,
　The dark unfathom'd caves of ocean bear:
Full many a flower is born to blush unseen,
　And waste its sweetness on the desert air.　　　　30

　　[1] *subject.*　　　　　[2] call forth, call into action.

Some village-Hampden, that with dauntless breast
    The little Tyrant of his fields withstood;
Some mute inglorious Milton here may rest,
    Some Cromwell guiltless of his country's blood.

5   Th' applause of list'ning senates to command,
    The threats of pain and ruin to despise,
To scatter plenty o'er a smiling land,
    And read their hist'ry in a nation's eyes,

Their lot forbade: nor circumscrib'd alone
10   Their growing virtues, but their crimes confin'd;
Forbade to wade through slaughter to a throne,
    And shut the gates of mercy on mankind,

The struggling pangs of conscious truth to hide,
    To quench the blushes of ingenuous shame,
15   Or heap the shrine of Luxury and Pride
    With incense kindled at the Muse's flame.

Far from the madding crowd's ignoble strife,
    Their sober wishes never learn'd to stray;
Along the cool sequester'd vale of life
20   They kept the noiseless tenor of their way.

Yet ev'n these bones from insult to protect,
    Some frail memorial still erected nigh,
With uncouth rhymes and shapeless sculpture deck'd,
    Implores the passing tribute of a sigh.

25   Their name, their years, spelt by th' unletter'd Muse,
    The place of fame and elegy supply:
And many a holy text around she strews,
    That teach the rustic moralist to die.

For who to dumb Forgetfulness a prey,
30   This pleasing anxious being e'er resign'd,

Left the warm precincts of the cheerful day,
　　Nor cast one longing ling'ring look behind?

On some fond breast the parting soul relies,
　　Some pious drops the closing eye requires;
Ev'n from the tomb the voice of Nature cries,　　5
　　Ev'n in our Ashes live their wonted Fires.

For thee, who mindful of th' unhonour'd Dead
　　Dost in these lines their artless tale relate;
If chance,[1] by lonely contemplation led,
　　Some kindred Spirit shall inquire thy fate,　　10

Haply some hoary-headed Swain may say,
　　"Oft have we seen him at the peep of dawn
Brushing with hasty steps the dews away,
　　To meet the sun upon the upland lawn.

"There at the foot of yonder nodding beech　　15
　　That wreathes its old fantastic roots so high,
His listless length at noontide would he stretch,
　　And pore upon the brook that babbles by.

"Hard by yon wood, now smiling as in scorn,
　　Mutt'ring his wayward fancies he would rove,　　20
Now drooping, woeful wan, like one forlorn,
　　Or craz'd with care, or cross'd in hopeless love.

"One morn I miss'd him on the custom'd hill,
　　Along the heath and near his fav'rite tree,
Another came; nor yet beside the rill,　　25
　　Nor up the lawn, nor at the wood was he;

"The next, with dirges due in sad array
　　Slow thro' the church-way path we saw him borne.
Approach and read (for thou can'st read) the lay,
　　Grav'd on the stone beneath yon aged thorn."　　30

[1] perchance, by chance.

THE EPITAPH

Here rests his head upon the lap of Earth
A Youth to Fortune and to Fame unknown.
Fair Science frown'd not on his humble birth,
And Melancholy mark'd him for her own.

5   *Large was his bounty, and his soul sincere,*
Heav'n did a recompense as largely send:
He gave to Mis'ry all he had, a tear,
He gain'd from Heav'n ('twas all he wish'd) a friend.

No farther seek his merits to disclose,
10   *Or draw his frailties from their dread abode,*
(There they alike in trembling hope repose)
The bosom of his Father and his God.

OLIVER GOLDSMITH

THE DESERTED VILLAGE

[The Schoolmaster]

Beside yon straggling fence that skirts the way,
With blossomed furze unprofitably gay,
15   There, in his noisy mansion, skill'd to rule,
The village master taught his little school.
A man severe he was, and stern to view;
I knew him well, and every truant knew;
Well had the boding tremblers learned to trace
20   The day's disasters in his morning face;
Full well they laughed with counterfeited glee
At all his jokes, for many a joke had he;
Full well the busy whisper circling round
Conveyed the dismal tidings when he frowned.
25   Yet he was kind, or, if severe in aught,
The love he bore to learning was in fault;

The village all declared how much he knew:
'Twas certain he could write, and cipher too;
Lands he could measure, terms and tides presage,
And even the story ran that he could gauge;
In arguing, too, the parson owned his skill,   5
For, even tho' vanquished, he could argue still;
While words of learned length and thundering sound
Amazed the gazing rustics ranged around;
And still they gazed, and still the wonder grew,
That one small head could carry all he knew.   10

THE CITIZEN OF THE WORLD

LETTER IV

The English seem as silent as the Japanese, yet vainer than
the inhabitants of Siam. Upon my arrival I attributed that
reserve to modesty which I now find has its origin in pride.
Condescend to address them first, and you are sure of their
acquaintance; stoop to flattery, and you conciliate their   15
friendship and esteem. They bear hunger, cold, fatigue, and
all the miseries of life without shrinking; danger only calls
forth their fortitude; they even exult in calamity: but contempt is what they cannot bear. An Englishman fears contempt more than death; he often flies to death as a refuge   20
from its pressure; and dies when he fancies the world has
ceased to esteem him.

Pride seems the source not only of their national vices, but
of their national virtues also. An Englishman is taught to
love his king as his friend, but to acknowledge no other mas- 25
ter than the laws which himself has contributed to enact. He
despises those nations who, that one may be free, are all
content to be slaves; who first lift a tyrant into terror, and
then shrink under his power as if delegated from heaven.
Liberty is echoed in all their assemblies; and thousands might 30
be found ready to offer up their lives for the sound, though

perhaps not one of all the number understands its meaning. The lowest mechanic, however, looks upon it as his duty to be a watchful guardian of his country's freedom, and often uses a language that might seem haughty, even in the mouth of
5 the great emperor who traces his ancestry to the moon.

A few days ago, passing by one of their prisons, I could not avoid stopping, in order to listen to a dialogue which I thought might afford me some entertainment. The conversation was carried on between a debtor through the grate of his
10 prison, a porter, who had stopped to rest his burden, and a soldier at the window. The subject was upon a threatened invasion from France, and each seemed extremely anxious to rescue his country from the impending danger. "For my part," cries the prisoner, "the greatest of my apprehensions
15 is for our freedom; if the French should conquer, what would become of English liberty? My dear friends, liberty is the Englishman's prerogative; we must preserve that at the expense of our lives, of that the French shall never deprive us. It is not to be expected that men who are slaves themselves
20 would preserve our freedom should they happen to conquer." "Ay, slaves," cries the porter, "they are all slaves, fit only to carry burdens every one of them. Before I would stoop to slavery, may this be my poison (and he held the goblet in his hand) may this be my poison—but I would sooner list for a
25 soldier."

The soldier taking the goblet from his friend, with much awe, fervently cried out, "It is not so much our liberties, as our religion, that would suffer by such a change: Ay, our religion, my lads. May the Devil sink me into flames, (such
30 was the solemnity of his adjuration) if the French should come over, but our religion would be utterly undone." So saying, instead of a libation,[1] he applied the goblet to his lips, and confirmed his sentiments with a ceremony of the most persevering devotion.

[1] a drink offering, wine or other liquid poured on the ground in honor of a god.

In short, every man here pretends to be a politician; even the fair sex are sometimes found to mix the severity of national altercation with the blandishments of love, and often become conquerors by more weapons of destruction than their eyes. 5

This universal passion for politics is gratified by daily gazettes, as with us in China. But as in ours the emperor endeavours to instruct his people, in theirs the people endeavour to instruct the administration. You must not, however, imagine that they who compile these papers have any 10 actual knowledge of the politics or the government of a state; they only collect their materials from the oracle of some coffee-house, which oracle has himself gathered them the night before from a beau at a gaming-table, who has pillaged his knowledge from a great man's porter, who has had his in- 15 formation from the great man's gentleman,[1] who has invented the whole story for his own amusement the night preceding.

The English in general seem fonder of gaining the esteem than the love of those they converse with: this gives a for- 20 mality to their amusements; their gayest conversations have something too wise for innocent relaxation; though in company you are seldom disgusted with the absurdity of a fool, you are seldom lifted into rapture by those strokes of vivacity which give instant, though not permanent, pleasure. 25

What they want, however, in gaiety they make up in politeness. You smile at hearing me praise the English for their politeness; you who have heard very different accounts from the missionaries at Pekin, who have seen such a different behaviour in their merchants and seamen at home. But I must 30 still repeat it, the English seem more polite than any of their neighbours: their great art in this respect lies in endeavouring, while they oblige, to lessen the force of the favour. Other countries are fond of obliging a stranger; but seem desirous that he should be sensible of the obligation. The English 35

[1] valet, servant to a man of rank.

confer their kindness with an appearance of indifference, and give away benefits with an air as if they despised them.

Walking a few days ago between an English and a Frenchman in the suburbs of the city, we were overtaken by a heavy
5 shower of rain. I was unprepared; but they had each large coats which defended them from what seemed to me a perfect inundation. The Englishman seeing me shrink from the weather, accosted me thus: "Psha, man; what dost shrink at? here, take this coat; I don't want it; I find it no way
10 useful to me; I had as lief be without it." The Frenchman began to show his politeness in turn. "My dear friend," cries he, "why won't you oblige me by making use of my coat? You see how well it defends me from the rain; I should not choose to part with it to others, but to such a friend as you,
15 I could even part with my skin to do him service."

From such minute instances as these, most reverend Fum Hoam, I am sensible your sagacity will collect instruction. The volume of nature is the book of knowledge; and he becomes most wise who makes the most judicious selection.
20 Farewell.

ROBERT BURNS

THE COTTER'S SATURDAY NIGHT

[Abridged]

November chill blaws loud wi' angry sugh,
　　The short'ning winter day is near a close;
The miry beasts retreating frae the pleugh,
　　The black'ning trains o' craws to their repose;
25　　The toil-worn Cotter[1] frae his labour goes,—
　　This night his weekly moil[2] is at an end,—
　　Collects his spades, his mattocks, and his hoes,

---

[1] cottager, peasant, tenant of a small farm.　　[2] drudgery, hard work.

Hoping the morn in ease and rest to spend,
And weary, o'er the moor,[1] his course does hameward bend.

At length his lonely cot appears in view,
  Beneath the shelter of an agèd tree ;
Th' expectant wee-things, toddlin, stacher[2] through   5
  To meet their dad, wi' flichterin[3] noise an' glee.
His wee bit ingle,[4] blinkin bonilie,
His clean hearth-stane, his thrifty wifie's smile,
  The lisping infant prattling on his knee,
Does a' his weary kiaugh[5] and care beguile,   10
An' makes him quite forget his labour an' his toil.

Belyve,[6] the elder bairns[7] come drappin in,
  At service out amang the farmers roun' ;
Some ca the pleugh,[8] some herd, some tentie[9] rin
  A cannie[10] errand to a neibor toun.[11]   15
  Their eldest hope, their Jenny, woman-grown,
In youthfu' bloom, love sparkling in her ee,
  Comes hame, perhaps to shew a braw[12] new gown,
Or deposite her sair-won penny-fee,
To help her parents dear, if they in hardship be.   20

With joy unfeign'd brothers and sisters meet,
  An' each for other's weelfare kindly spiers[13] :
The social hours, swift-wing'd, unnotic'd fleet ;
  Each tells the uncos[14] that he sees or hears.
  The parents, partial, eye their hopeful years ;   25
Anticipation forward points the view ;
  The mother, wi' her needle an' her sheers,
Gars[15] auld claes look amaist as weel's the new ;
The father mixes a' wi' admonition due.

---

[1] waste land.   [2] stagger.   [3] fluttering.   [4] fireplace.   [5] anxiety.
[6] by and by, presently.   [7] children.   [8] drive the plow.   [9] careful.
[10] canny, prudent, thrifty.   [11] farm.   [12] fine, handsome.   [13] asks.
[14] uncommon things, news.   [15] makes.

Their master's an' their mistress's command
    The younkers a' are warnèd to obey;
An' mind their labours wi' an eydent[1] hand,
    An' ne'er, tho' out o' sight, to jauk[2] or play:
5   "An' O! be sure to fear the Lord alway,
    An' mind your duty, duly, morn an' night!
    Lest in temptation's path ye gang astray,
    Implore His counsel and assisting might:
They never sought in vain that sought the Lord aright!"

10   But hark! a rap comes gently to the door.
    Jenny, wha kens the meaning o' the same,
Tells how a neibor lad cam o'er the moor,
    To do some errands, and convoy her hame.
    The wily mother sees the conscious flame
15   Sparkle in Jenny's ee, and flush her cheek;
    Wi' heart-struck, anxious care, inquires his name,
    While Jenny hafflins[3] is afraid to speak;
Weel pleas'd the mother hears it's nae wild worthless rake.

    Wi' kindly welcome Jenny brings him ben,[4]
20   A strappin youth; he takes the mother's eye;
Blythe Jenny sees the visit's no ill taen;
    The father cracks[5] of horses, pleughs, and kye.[6]
    The youngster's artless heart o'erflows wi' joy,
    But, blate[7] and laithfu',[8] scarce can weel behave;
25   The mother wi' a woman's wiles can spy
    What maks the youth sae bashfu' an' sae grave,
Weel pleas'd to think her bairn's respected like the lave.[9]

.   .   .   .

But now the supper crowns their simple board,
    The halesome parritch,[10] chief of Scotia's food;

---

[1] diligent.   [2] dally, trifle.   [3] half, partly.   [4] Into the parlor. The
entrance of a Scottish cottage was at the kitchen end; one went through
the but, or kitchen, to the ben, or parlor. Cf. p. 384.   [5] talks.   [6] cows.
[7] bashful.   [8] shy.   [9] rest.   [10] porridge.

The sowpe[1] their only hawkie[2] does afford,
 That yont the hallan[3] snugly chows her cud.
The dame brings forth, in complimental mood,
 To grace the lad, her weel-hain'd kebbuck[4] fell,[5]
An' aft[6] he's prest, an' aft he ca's it guid;   5
The frugal wifie, garrulous, will tell,
How 'twas a towmond[7] auld, sin' lint was i' the bell.[8]

The cheerfu' supper done, wi' serious face,
 They round the ingle form a circle wide;
The sire turns o'er with patriarchal grace   10
 The big ha'-bible,[9] ance his father's pride;
His bonnet rev'rently is laid aside,
 His lyart haffets[10] wearing thin and bare;
Those strains that once did sweet in Zion glide,
 He wales[11] a portion with judicious care;   15
And, "Let us worship God," he says with solemn air.

 . . . .

Then kneeling down to Heaven's Eternal King,
 The saint, the father, and the husband prays:
Hope "springs exulting on triumphant wing,"
 That thus they all shall meet in future days: 20
 There ever bask in uncreated rays,
No more to sigh or shed the bitter tear,
 Together hymning their Creator's praise,
In such society, yet still more dear,
While circling Time moves round in an eternal sphere. 25

 . . . .

Then homeward all take off their sev'ral way;
 The youngling cottagers retire to rest;
The parent-pair their secret homage pay,
 And proffer up to Heav'n the warm request,

---

[1] sup, liquid, milk. [2] cow, especially a white-faced cow. [3] beyond
the partition. [4] well-saved cheese. [5] strong. [6] often. [7] twelvemonth. [8] since flax was in bloom. [9] hall Bible. [10] grey side-
locks. [11] chooses.

That He, who stills the raven's clam'rous nest
And decks the lily fair in flow'ry pride,
   Would, in the way His wisdom sees the best,
   For them and for their little ones provide;
5   But chiefly, in their hearts with grace divine preside.

From scenes like these old Scotia's grandeur springs,
That makes her lov'd at home, rever'd abroad:
Princes and lords are but the breath of kings,
   "An honest man's the noblest work of God":
10   And certes, in fair Virtue's heavenly road,
The cottage leaves the palace far behind:
   What is a lordling's pomp? a cumbrous load,
Disguising oft the wretch of human kind,
Studied in arts of hell, in wickedness refin'd!

15   O Scotia! my dear, my native soil!
   For whom my warmest wish to Heaven is sent!
Long may thy hardy sons of rustic toil
   Be blest with health, and peace, and sweet content!
   And, oh! may Heaven their simple lives prevent
20   From luxury's contagion, weak and vile!
   Then, howe'er crowns and coronets be rent,
A virtuous populace may rise the while,
And stand a wall of fire around their much-lov'd isle.

O Thou! who pour'd the patriotic tide
25   That stream'd thro' Wallace's¹ undaunted heart,
Who dar'd to nobly stem tyrannic pride,
   Or nobly die, the second glorious part,—
   (The patriot's God peculiarly thou art,
His friend, inspirer, guardian, and reward!)
30   O never, never Scotia's realm desert,
   But still the patriot, and the patriot-bard,
In bright succession raise, her ornament and guard!

¹ William Wallace, the Scottish national hero, who in 1297 roused the Scots to resistance after their defeat by Edward I of England.

TO A MOUSE

On Turning up Her Nest with the Plough,
November, 1785

Wee, sleekit, cowrin, tim'rous beastie,
Oh, what a panic's in thy breastie!
Thou need na start awa sae hasty
    Wi' bickerin brattle![1]
I wad be laith[2] to rin an' chase thee   5
    Wi' murd'rin pattle![3]

I'm truly sorry man's dominion
Has broken nature's social union,
An' justifies that ill opinion
    Which makes thee startle   10
At me, thy poor earth-born companion,
    An' fellow-mortal!

I doubt na, whyles,[4] but thou may thieve:
What then? poor beastie, thou maun live!
A daimen icker in a thrave[5]   15
    'S a sma' request;
I'll get a blessin wi' the lave,
    An' never miss't!

Thy wee bit housie, too, in ruin!
Its silly wa's[6] the win's are strewin!   20
An' naething, now, to big[7] a new ane,
    O' foggage[8] green!
An' bleak December's winds ensuin
    Baith snell[9] an' keen!

Thou saw the fields laid bare and waste,   25
An' weary winter comin fast,

[1] hurrying scamper.   [2] loath, unwilling.   [3] paddle, long-handled, narrow spade.   [4] sometimes.   [5] an occasional ear of grain in twenty-four sheaves.   [6] poor, frail walls.   [7] build.   [8] decaying grass.   [9] biting.

An' cozie here beneath the blast
    Thou thought to dwell,
Till crash! the cruel coulter past
    Out thro' thy cell.

5   That wee bit heap o' leaves an' stibble
Has cost thee mony a weary nibble!
Now thou's turn'd out for a' thy trouble,
    But[1] house or hald,
To thole[2] the winter's sleety dribble
10   An' cranreuch[3] cauld!

But, Mousie, thou art no thy lane[4]
In proving foresight may be vain:
The best laid schemes o' mice an' men
    Gang aft a-gley,[5]
15   An' lea'e us nought but grief an' pain
    For promis'd joy.

Still thou art blest, compar'd wi' me!
The present only toucheth thee:
But, och! I backward cast my ee[6]
20   On prospects drear!
An' forward, tho' I canna see,
    I guess an' fear!

A MAN'S A MAN FOR A' THAT

Is there, for honest poverty,
    That hings his head, an' a' that?
25   The coward slave, we pass him by,
    We dare be poor for a' that!
      For a' that, an' a' that,
        Our toils obscure, an' a' that;
    The rank is but the guinea's stamp;
30   The man's the gowd[7] for a' that.

[1] without.   [2] endure.   [3] (krān'rŭk) hoar-frost.   [4] alone.
[5] askew, amiss.   [6] eye.   [7] gold.

What tho' on hamely fare we dine,
　　Wear hodden-gray,[1] an' a' that;
Gie fools their silks, and knaves their wine,
　　A man's a man for a' that.
　　　　For a' that, an' a' that, 5
　　　　　　Their tinsel show, an' a' that;
　　　　The honest man, tho' e'er sae poor,
　　　　　　Is king o' men for a' that.

Ye see yon birkie,[2] ca'd a lord,
　　Wha struts, an' stares, an' a' that; 10
Tho' hundreds worship at his word,
　　He's but a coof[3] for a' that:
　　　　For a' that, an' a' that,
　　　　　　His riband, star, an' a' that,
　　　　The man o' independent mind, 15
　　　　　　He looks and laughs at a' that.

A prince can mak a belted knight,
　　A marquis, duke, an' a' that;
But an honest man's aboon his might,[4]
　　Guid faith he mauna fa'[5] that! 20
　　　　For a' that, an' a' that,
　　　　　　Their dignities, an' a' that,
　　　　The pith o' sense, an' pride o' worth,
　　　　　　Are higher rank than a' that.

Then let us pray that come it may, 25
　　As come it will for a' that,
That sense and worth, o'er a' the earth,
　　Shall bear the gree,[6] an' a' that.
　　　　For a' that, an' a' that,
　　　　　　It's coming yet, for a' that, 30
　　　　That man to man, the warld o'er,
　　　　　　Shall brothers be for a' that.

[1] coarse gray woolen.　　[2] fellow.　　[3] blockhead, fool.　　[4] above,
beyond his power.　　[5] cannot accomplish.　　[6] carry off the prize.

AE FOND KISS

Ae[1] fond kiss, and then we sever;
Ae fareweel, and then for ever!
Deep in heart-wrung tears I'll pledge thee,
Warring sighs and groans I'll wage thee.
5 Who shall say that Fortune grieves him,
While the star of hope she leaves him?
Me, nae cheerfu' twinkle lights me;
Dark despair around benights me.

I'll ne'er blame my partial fancy,
10 Naething could resist my Nancy;
But to see her was to love her;
Love but her, and love for ever.
Had we never lov'd sae kindly,
Had we never lov'd sae blindly,
15 Never met—or never parted—
We had ne'er been broken-hearted.

Fare thee weel, thou first and fairest!
Fare thee weel, thou best and dearest!
Thine be ilka[2] joy and treasure,
20 Peace, enjoyment, love, and pleasure!
Ae fond kiss, and then we sever;
Ae fareweel, alas, for ever!
Deep in heart-wrung tears I'll pledge thee,
Warring sighs and groans I'll wage thee!

O, WERT THOU IN THE CAULD BLAST

25 O, wert thou in the cauld blast,
    On yonder lea, on yonder lea,[3]
My plaidie to the angry airt,[4]
    I'd shelter thee, I'd shelter thee.

[1] one.
[2] every.
[3] pasture *or* grassland.
[4] direction, quarter.

Or did misfortune's bitter storms
   Around thee blaw, around thee blaw,
Thy beild[1] should be my bosom,
   To share it a', to share it a'.

Or were I in the wildest waste,   5
   Sae black and bare, sae black and bare,
The desert were a paradise,
   If thou wert there, if thou wert there.
Or were I monarch o' the globe,
   Wi' thee to reign, wi' thee to reign,   10
The brightest jewel in my crown
   Wad be my queen, wad be my queen.

BANNOCKBURN

Scots, wha hae wi' Wallace bled,
Scots, wham Bruce has aften led,
Welcome to your gory bed,   15
   Or to victory!
Now's the day, and now's the hour;
See the front o' battle lour;
See approach proud Edward's power—
   Chains and slavery!   20

Wha will be a traitor knave?
Wha can fill a coward's grave?
Wha sae base as be a slave?
   Let him turn and flee!
Wha for Scotland's king and law   25
Freedom's sword will strongly draw,
Freeman stand or Freeman fa',
   Let him follow me!

[1](bēld) shelter.

By oppression's woes and pains
By your sons in servile chains!
We will drain our dearest veins,
   But they shall be free!
5   Lay the proud usurpers low!
Tyrants fall in every foe!
Liberty's in every blow!—
   Let us do or die!

CONTENTED WI' LITTLE

Contented wi' little and cantie[1] wi' mair,
10   Whene'er I forgather wi' Sorrow and Care,
I gie them a skelp,[2] as they're creepin alang,
Wi' a cog[3] o' guid swats[4] and an auld Scottish sang.

I whyles claw the elbow o' troublesome Thought;
But Man is a soger,[5] and Life is a faught.[6]
15   My mirth and guid humour are coin in my pouch,
And my Freedom's my lairdship nae monarch daur touch.

A towmond[7] o' trouble, should that be my fa',[8]
A night o' guid fellowship sowthers[9] it a':
When at the blythe end o' our journey at last,
20   Wha the Deil ever thinks o' the road he has past?

Blind chance, let her snapper[10] and stoyte[11] on her way,
Be't to me, be't frae me, e'en let the jade gae!
Come Ease or come Travail,[12] come Pleasure or Pain,
My warst word is:—"Welcome, and welcome again!"

[1] cheerful, merry.	[7] twelvemonth.
[2] slap.	[8] lot.
[3] wooden drinking-vessel.	[9] solders, mends.
[4] ale.	[10] stumble.
[5] soldier.	[11] stagger.
[6] fight.	[12] toil.

DANIEL DEFOE

JOURNAL OF THE PLAGUE YEAR[1]

WRITTEN BY A CITIZEN WHO CONTINUED ALL THE WHILE
IN LONDON

[Extracts]

I lived without Aldgate, about midway between Aldgate
Church and Whitechapel Bars, on the left hand or north side
of the street; and as the distemper had not reached to that
side of the city, our neighbourhood continued very easy. But
at the other end of the town their consternation was very 5
great; and the richer sort of people, especially the nobility
and gentry from the west part of the city, thronged out of
town with their families and servants in an unusual manner;
and this was more particularly seen in Whitechapel; that is
to say, the Broad Street where I lived; indeed, nothing was 10
to be seen but waggons and carts, with goods, women, servants, children, &c.; coaches filled with people of the better
sort, and horsemen attending them, and all hurrying away;
then empty waggons and carts appeared, and spare horses
with servants, who, it was apparent, were returning or sent 15
from the countries to fetch more people; besides innumerable
numbers of men on horseback, some alone, others with servants, and, generally speaking, all loaded with baggage and
fitted out for travelling, as any one might perceive by their
appearance.   20

This was a very terrible and melancholy thing to see, and
as it was a sight which I could not but look on from morning
to night, for indeed there was nothing else of moment to be
seen, it filled me with very serious thoughts of the misery
that was coming upon the city, and the unhappy condition 25
of those that would be left in it.

This hurry of the people was such for some weeks that

[1] 1665.

there was no getting at the Lord Mayor's door without exceeding difficulty; there was such pressing and crowding there to get passes and certificates of health for such as travelled abroad, for without these there was no being admitted to pass through the towns upon the road, or to lodge in any inn. Now, as there had none died in the city for all this time, my Lord Mayor gave certificates of health without any difficulty to all those who lived in the ninety-seven parishes, and to those within the liberties[1] too for a while.

.   .   .   .

It must not be forgot here that the city and suburbs were prodigiously full of people at the time of this visitation, I mean at the time that it began; for though I have lived to see a further increase, and mighty throngs of people settling in London more than ever, yet we had always a notion that the numbers of people which, the wars being over, the armies disbanded, and the royal family and the monarchy being restored,[2] had flocked to London to settle in business, or to depend upon and attend the Court for rewards of services, preferments, and the like, was such that the town was computed to have in it above a hundred thousand people more than ever it held before; nay, some took upon them to say it had twice as many, because all the ruined families of the royal party flocked hither. All the old soldiers set up trades here, and abundance of families settled here. Again, the Court brought with them a great flux of pride and new fashions. All people were grown gay and luxurious, and the joy of the Restoration had brought a vast many families to London.

.   .   .   .

It was under this John Hayward's care, and within his bounds, that the story of the piper, with which people have made themselves so merry, happened, and he assured me that it was true. It is said that it was a blind piper; but, as

---

[1] districts outside the City but subject to its jurisdiction, suburbs.
[2] in 1660.

John told me, the fellow was not blind, but an ignorant, weak, poor man, and usually walked his rounds about ten o'clock at night and went piping along from door to door, and the people usually took him in at public-houses where they knew him, and would give him drink and victuals, and sometimes 5 farthings; and he in return would pipe and sing and talk simply, which diverted the people; and thus he lived. It was but a very bad time for this diversion while things were as I have told, yet the poor fellow went about as usual, but was almost starved; and when anybody asked how he did he 10 would answer, the dead cart had not taken him yet, but that they had promised to call for him next week.

It happened one night that this poor fellow, whether somebody had given him too much drink or no—John Hayward said he had not drink in his house, but that they had given 15 him a little more victuals than ordinary at a public-house in Coleman Street—and the poor fellow, having not usually had a bellyful for perhaps not a good while, was laid all along upon the top of a bulk or stall, and fast asleep, at a door in the street near London Wall, towards Cripplegate, and that 20 upon the same bulk or stall the people of some house, in the alley of which the house was a corner, hearing a bell, which they always rang before the cart came, had laid a body really dead of the plague just by him, thinking, too, that this poor fellow had been a dead body, as the other was, and laid there 25 by some of the neighbours.

Accordingly, when John Hayward with his bell and the cart came along, finding two dead bodies lie upon the stall, they took them up with the instrument they used and threw them into the cart, and all this while the piper slept soundly. 30

From hence they passed along and took in other dead bodies, till, as honest John Hayward told me, they almost buried him alive in the cart; yet all this while he slept soundly. At length the cart came to the place where the bodies were to be thrown into the ground, which, as I do 35 remember, was at Mount Mill; and as the cart usually

stopped some time before they were ready to shoot out the
melancholy load they had in it, as soon as the cart stopped
the fellow awaked and struggled a little to get his head out
from among the dead bodies, when, raising himself up in the
5 cart, he called out, "Hey! where am I?" This frighted the
fellow that attended about the work; but after some pause
John Hayward, recovering himself, said, "Lord, bless us!
There's somebody in the cart not quite dead!" So another
called to him and said, "Who are you?" The fellow an-
10 swered, "I am the poor piper. Where am I?" "Where are
you?" says Hayward. "Why, you are in the dead cart, and
we are going to bury you." "But I an't dead though, am I?"
says the piper, which made them laugh a little, though, as
John said, they were heartily frighted at first; so they helped
15 the poor fellow down, and he went about his business.

I know the story goes he set up his pipes in the cart and
frighted the bearers and others so that they ran away; but
John Hayward did not tell the story so, nor say anything of
his piping at all; but that he was a poor piper, and that he
20 was carried away as above I am fully satisfied of the truth of.
. . . .

As this puts me upon mentioning my walking the streets
and fields, I cannot omit taking notice what a desolate place
the city was at that time. The great street I lived in, which
is known to be one of the broadest of all the streets of Lon-
25 don, I mean of the suburbs as well as the liberties, all the
side where the butchers lived, especially without the bars,
was more like a green field than a paved street, and the people
generally went in the middle with the horses and carts. It is
true that the farthest end towards Whitechapel Church was
30 not all paved, but even the part that was paved was full of
grass also; but this need not seem strange, since the great
streets within the city, such as Leadenhall Street, Bishopsgate Street, Cornhill, and even the Exchange itself, had grass
growing in them in several places; neither cart or coach were
35 seen in the streets from morning to evening, except some

country carts to bring roots and beans, or peas, hay, and
straw to the market, and those but very few compared to
what was usual. As for coaches, they were scarce used but
to carry sick people to the pest-house, and to other hospitals,
and some few to carry physicians to such places as they 5
thought fit to venture to visit; for really coaches were dangerous things, and people did not care to venture into them,
because they did not know who might have been carried in
them last, and sick, infected people were, as I have said, ordinarily carried in them to the pest-houses, and sometimes 10
people expired in them as they went along.

THE EARLY NINETEENTH CENTURY

WILLIAM WORDSWORTH

LINES WRITTEN IN EARLY SPRING

I heard a thousand blended notes,
While in a grove I sate reclined,
In that sweet mood when pleasant thoughts
Bring sad thoughts to the mind.

5   To her fair works did Nature link
The human soul that through me ran;
And much it grieved my heart to think
What man has made of man.

Through primrose tufts, in that green bower,
10   The periwinkle[1] trailed its wreaths;
And 'tis my faith that every flower
Enjoys the air it breathes.

The birds around me hopped and played,
Their thoughts I cannot measure:—
15   But the least motion which they made,
It seemed a thrill of pleasure.

The budding twigs spread out their fan,
To catch the breezy air;
And I must think, do all I can,
20   That there was pleasure there.

[1] A trailing plant with evergreen leaves and blue or white flowers, commonly called myrtle in the United States.

If this belief from heaven be sent,
If such be Nature's holy plan,
Have I not reason to lament
What man has made of man?

TO A SKY-LARK

WRITTEN AT RYDAL MOUNT

Ethereal minstrel! pilgrim of the sky!   5
Dost thou despise the earth where cares abound?
Or, while the wings aspire, are heart and eye
Both with thy nest upon the dewy ground?
Thy nest which thou canst drop into at will,
Those quivering wings composed, that music still!   10

Leave to the nightingale her shady wood;
A privacy of glorious light is thine;
Whence thou dost pour upon the world a flood
Of harmony, with instinct more divine;
Type of the wise who soar, but never roam;   15
True to the kindred points of Heaven and Home!

I WANDERED LONELY AS A CLOUD

I wandered lonely as a cloud
That floats on high o'er vales and hills,
When all at once I saw a crowd,
A host, of golden daffodils;   20
Beside the lake, beneath the trees,
Fluttering and dancing in the breeze.

Continuous as the stars that shine
And twinkle on the milky way,
They stretched in never-ending line   25
Along the margin of a bay:
Ten thousand saw I at a glance,
Tossing their heads in sprightly dance.

The waves beside them danced; but they
Out-did the sparkling waves in glee:
A poet could not but be gay,
In such a jocund company:
I gazed—and gazed—but little thought
What wealth the show to me had brought:

For oft, when on my couch I lie
In vacant or in pensive mood,
They flash upon that inward eye
Which is the bliss of solitude;
And then my heart with pleasure fills,
And dances with the daffodils.

INTIMATIONS OF IMMORTALITY

V

Our birth is but a sleep and a forgetting:
The Soul that rises with us, our life's Star,
  Hath had elsewhere its setting,
   And cometh from afar:
  Not in entire forgetfulness,
  And not in utter nakedness,
But trailing clouds of glory do we come
  From God, who is our home:
Heaven lies about us in our infancy!
Shades of the prison-house begin to close
  Upon the growing Boy,
But He beholds the light, and whence it flows
  He sees it in his joy;
The Youth, who daily farther from the east
  Must travel, still is Nature's Priest,
  And by the vision splendid
  Is on his way attended;
At length the Man perceives it die away,
And fade into the light of common day.

THE SOLITARY REAPER

Behold her, single in the field,
Yon solitary Highland Lass!
Reaping and singing by herself;
Stop here, or gently pass!
Alone she cuts and binds the grain,   5
And sings a melancholy strain;
O listen! for the vale profound
Is overflowing with the sound.

No nightingale did ever chant
More welcome notes to weary bands   10
Of travellers in some shady haunt,
Among Arabian sands:
A voice so thrilling ne'er was heard
In spring-time from the cuckoo-bird,
Breaking the silence of the seas   15
Among the farthest Hebrides.

Will no one tell me what she sings?
Perhaps the plaintive numbers flow
For old, unhappy, far-off things,
And battles long ago;   20
Or is it some more humble lay,
Familiar matter of to-day?
Some natural sorrow, loss, or pain,
That has been, and may be again?

Whate'er the theme, the maiden sang   25
As if her song could have no ending;
I saw her singing at her work,
And o'er the sickle bending;—
I listened, motionless and still;
And, as I mounted up the hill,   30
The music in my heart I bore,
Long after it was heard no more.

SHE WAS A PHANTOM OF DELIGHT

She was a phantom[1] of delight
When first she gleamed upon my sight;
A lovely apparition, sent
To be a moment's ornament;
5   Her eyes as stars of twilight fair;
Like twilight's, too, her dusky hair;
But all things else about her drawn
From May-time and the cheerful dawn;
A dancing shape, an image gay,
10   To haunt, to startle, and way-lay.

I saw her upon nearer view,
A spirit, yet a woman too!
Her household motions light and free,
And steps of virgin-liberty;
15   A countenance in which did meet
Sweet records, promises as sweet;
A creature not too bright or good
For human nature's daily food;
For transient sorrows, simple wiles,
20   Praise, blame, love, kisses, tears, and smiles.

And now I see with eye serene
The very pulse of the machine;
A being breathing thoughtful breath,
A traveller between life and death;
25   The reason firm, the temperate will,
Endurance, foresight, strength, and skill;
A perfect woman, nobly planned,
To warn, to comfort, and command;
And yet a spirit still, and bright
30   With something of angelic light.

[1] vision.

NUNS FRET NOT AT THEIR CONVENT'S NARROW ROOM

Nuns fret not at their convent's narrow room;
And hermits are contented with their cells;
And students with their pensive citadels;
Maids at the wheel, the weaver at his loom,
Sit blithe and happy; bees that soar for bloom,   5
High as the highest Peak of Furness-fells,
Will murmur by the hour in foxglove bells:
In truth the prison, unto which we doom
Ourselves, no prison is: and hence for me,
In sundry moods, 'twas pastime to be bound   10
Within the Sonnet's scanty plot of ground;
Pleased if some Souls (for such there needs must be)
Who have felt the weight of too much liberty,
Should find brief solace there, as I have found.

COMPOSED UPON WESTMINSTER BRIDGE,
SEPTEMBER 3, 1802

Earth has not anything to show more fair: 15
Dull would he be of soul who could pass by
A sight so touching in its majesty:
This City now doth, like a garment, wear
The beauty of the morning; silent, bare,
Ships, towers, domes, theatres, and temples lie   20
Open unto the fields, and to the sky;
All bright and glittering in the smokeless air.
Never did sun more beautifully steep
In his first splendor, valley, rock, or hill;
Ne'er saw I, never felt, a calm so deep!   25
The river glideth at his own sweet will:
Dear God! the very houses seem asleep;
And all that mighty heart is lying still!

ON THE EXTINCTION OF THE VENETIAN REPUBLIC

Once did She hold the gorgeous east in fee;
And was the safeguard of the west: the worth
Of Venice did not fall below her birth,
Venice, the eldest Child of Liberty.
5 She was a maiden City, bright and free;
No guile seduced, no force could violate;
And, when she took unto herself a Mate,
She must espouse the everlasting Sea.
And what if she had seen those glories fade,
10 Those titles vanish, and that strength decay;
Yet shall some tribute of regret be paid
When her long life hath reached its final day:
Men are we, and must grieve when even the Shade
Of that which once was great, is passed away.

SAMUEL TAYLOR COLERIDGE

HYMN

Before Sun-Rise, in the Vale of Chamouni[1]

Besides the rivers Arve and Arveiron, which have their sources in
the foot of Mont Blanc, five conspicuous torrents rush down its sides;
and within a few paces of the Glaciers, the Gentiana Major grows in
immense numbers with its 'flowers of loveliest blue.'

15 Hast thou a charm to stay the morning-star
In his steep course? So long he seems to pause
On thy bald awful head, O sovran Blanc!
The Arve and Arveiron at thy base
Rave ceaselessly; but thou, most awful Form!
20 Risest from forth thy silent sea of pines,
How silently! Around thee and above

---

[1] (shä mōō nē′) more commonly Chamonix, in France, north of Mont
Blanc.

Deep is the air and dark, substantial, black,
An ebon mass: methinks thou piercest it,
As with a wedge!   But when I look again,
It is thine own calm home, thy crystal shrine,
Thy habitation from eternity!   5
O dread and silent Mount!   I gazed upon thee,
Till thou, still present to the bodily sense,
Didst vanish from my thought: entranced in prayer
I worshipped the Invisible alone.

    Yet, like some sweet beguiling melody,   10
So sweet, we know not we are listening to it,
Thou, the meanwhile, wast blending with my thought,
Yea, with my life and life's own secret joy:
Till the dilating Soul, enrapt, transfused,
Into the mighty vision passing—there,   15
As in her natural form, swelled vast to Heaven!

    Awake, my soul! not only passive praise
Thou owest! not alone these swelling tears,
Mute thanks and secret ecstasy!   Awake,
Voice of sweet song!   Awake, my heart, awake!   20
Green vales and icy cliffs, all join my Hymn.

    Thou first and chief, sole sovran of the Vale!
O struggling with the darkness all the night,
And visited all night by troops of stars,
Or when they climb the sky or when they sink: 25
Companion of the morning-star at dawn,
Thyself Earth's rosy star, and of the dawn
Co-herald: wake, O wake, and utter praise!
Who sank thy sunless pillars deep in Earth?
Who filled thy countenance with rosy light?   30
Who made thee parent of perpetual streams?

    And you, ye five wild torrents fiercely glad!
Who called you forth from night and utter death,

From dark and icy caverns called you forth,
Down those precipitous, black, jagged rocks,
For ever shattered and the same for ever?
Who gave you your invulnerable life,
Your strength, your speed, your fury, and your joy,
Unceasing thunder and eternal foam?
And who commanded (and the silence came),
Here let the billows stiffen, and have rest?

Ye ice-falls! ye that from the mountain's brow
Adown enormous ravines slope amain—
Torrents, methinks, that heard a mighty voice,
And stopped at once amid their maddest plunge!
Motionless torrents! silent cataracts!
Who made you glorious as the gates of Heaven
Beneath the keen full moon? Who bade the sun
Clothe you with rainbows? Who, with living flowers
Of loveliest blue, spread garlands at your feet?—
God! let the torrents, like a shout of nations,
Answer! and let the ice-plains echo, God!
God! sing ye meadow-streams with gladsome voice!
Ye pine-groves, with your soft and soul-like sounds!
And they too have a voice, yon piles of snow,
And in their perilous fall shall thunder, God!

Ye living flowers that skirt the eternal frost!
Ye wild goats sporting round the eagle's nest!
Ye eagles, play-mates of the mountain-storm!
Ye lightnings, the dread arrows of the clouds!
Ye signs and wonders of the element!
Utter forth God, and fill the hills with praise!

Thou too, hoar Mount! with thy sky-pointing peaks,
Oft from whose feet the avalanche, unheard,
Shoots downward, glittering through the pure serene
Into the depth of clouds that veil thy breast—

Thou too again, stupendous Mountain! thou
That as I raise my head, awhile bowed low
In adoration, upward from thy base
Slow-travelling with dim eyes suffused with tears,
Solemnly seemest, like a vapory cloud,   5
To rise before me—Rise, O ever rise,
Rise like a cloud of incense, from the Earth!
Thou kingly Spirit throned among the hills,
Thou dread ambassador from Earth to Heaven,
Great hierarch! tell thou the silent sky,   10
And tell the stars, and tell yon rising sun,
Earth, with her thousand voices, praises God.

KUBLA KHAN: OR, A VISION IN A DREAM

A Fragment

In Xanadu did Kubla Khan
A stately pleasure-dome decree:
Where Alph, the sacred river, ran   15
Through caverns measureless to man
Down to a sunless sea.

So twice five miles of fertile ground
With walls and towers were girdled round:
And there were gardens bright with sinuous rills,   20
Where blossom'd many an incense-bearing tree;
And here were forests ancient as the hills,
Enfolding sunny spots of greenery.

But oh! that deep romantic chasm which slanted
Down the green hill athwart a cedarn cover!   25
A savage place! as holy and enchanted
As e'er beneath a waning moon was haunted
By woman wailing for her demon-lover!
And from this chasm, with ceaseless turmoil seething,
As if this earth in fast thick pants were breathing,   30

A mighty fountain momently was forced:
Amid whose swift half-intermitted burst
Huge fragments vaulted like rebounding hail,
Or chaffy grain beneath the thresher's flail:
5   And 'mid these dancing rocks at once and ever
It flung up momently the sacred river.
Five miles meandering with a mazy motion
Through wood and dale the sacred river ran,
Then reach'd the caverns measureless to man,
10   And sank in tumult to a lifeless ocean:
And 'mid this tumult Kubla heard from far
Ancestral voices prophesying war!

The shadow of the dome of pleasure
Floated midway on the waves;
15   Where was heard the mingled measure
From the fountain and the caves.
It was a miracle of rare device,
A sunny pleasure-dome with caves of ice!

A damsel with a dulcimer[1]
20   In a vision once I saw:
It was an Abyssinian maid,
And on her dulcimer she play'd,
Singing of Mount Abora.
Could I revive within me
25   Her symphony[2] and song,
To such a deep delight 'twould win me,
That with music loud and long,
I would build that dome in air,
That sunny dome! those caves of ice!
30   And all who heard should see them there,—
And all should cry, Beware! Beware!—
His flashing eyes, his floating hair!

[1] a musical instrument with metallic wires and a sounding board.
[2] playing, an instrumental passage used as preface or refrain in a song.

Weave a circle round him thrice,
And close your eyes with holy dread,
For he on honey-dew hath fed,
And drunk the milk of Paradise.

LORD BYRON

CHILDE HAROLD'S PILGRIMAGE

[Extracts]

CANTO I. FAREWELL

Adieu, adieu! my native shore   5
   Fades o'er the waters blue;
The night-winds sigh, the breakers roar,
   And shrieks the wild sea-mew.
Yon sun that sets upon the sea
   We follow in his flight;   10
Farewell awhile to him and thee,
   My native land—Good night!

A few short hours and he will rise
   To give the morrow birth;
And I shall hail the main and skies,   15
   But not my mother earth.
Deserted is my own good hall,
   Its hearth is desolate;
Wild weeds are gathering on the wall,
   My dog howls at the gate.   20

. . . .

And now I'm in the world alone,
   Upon the wide, wide sea:
But why should I for others groan,
   When none will sigh for me?

Perchance my dog will whine in vain,
    Till fed by stranger hands;
But long ere I come back again
    He'd tear me where he stands.

5   With thee, my bark, I'll swiftly go
        Athwart the foaming brine;
    Nor care what land thou bear'st me to,
        So not again to mine.
    Welcome, welcome, ye dark blue waves!
10   And when you fail my sight,
    Welcome, ye deserts, and ye caves!
        My native land—Good night!

CANTO III. THE EVE BEFORE WATERLOO

There was a sound of revelry by night,
And Belgium's capital had gathered then
15 Her Beauty and her Chivalry, and bright
The lamps shone o'er fair women and brave men;
A thousand hearts beat happily; and when
Music arose with its voluptuous swell,
Soft eyes looked love to eyes which spake again,
20 And all went merry as a marriage bell;
But hush! hark! a deep sound strikes like a rising knell!

Did ye not hear it?—No; 'twas but the wind,
Or the car rattling o'er the stony street;
On with the dance! let joy be unconfined;
25 No sleep till morn, when Youth and Pleasure meet
To chase the glowing Hours with flying feet—
But hark! that heavy sound breaks in once more,
As if the clouds its echo would repeat;
And nearer, clearer, deadlier than before!
30 Arm! Arm! it is—it is—the cannon's opening roar!

Ah! then and there was hurrying to and fro,
And gathering tears, and tremblings of distress,
And cheeks all pale, which but an hour ago
Blushed at the praise of their own loveliness;
And there were sudden partings, such as press   5
The life from out young hearts, and choking sighs
Which ne'er might be repeated; who could guess
If ever more should meet those mutual eyes,
Since upon night so sweet such awful morn could rise!

And there was mounting in hot haste: the steed,   10
The mustering squadron, and the clattering car,
Went pouring forward with impetuous speed,
And swiftly forming in the ranks of war;
And the deep thunder peal on peal afar;
And near, the beat of the alarming drum   15
Roused up the soldier ere the morning star;
While thronged the citizens with terror dumb,
Or whispering, with white lips—"The foe! They come!
    they come!"

Canto IV. Rome

Oh, Rome! my country! city of the soul!
The orphans of the heart must turn to thee,   20
Lone mother of dead empires! and control
In their shut breasts their petty misery.
What are our woes and sufferance? Come and see
The cypress, hear the owl, and plod your way
O'er steps of broken thrones and temples,—Ye!   25
Whose agonies are evils of a day—
A world is at our feet as fragile as our clay.

The Niobe[1] of nations! there she stands,
Childless and crownless, in her voiceless woe;

[1] Niobe, in Greek mythology, for her impious pride in saying that her children were superior to the children of Leto (Apollo and Artemis) saw her children destroyed by the gods. She turned to stone, but wept eternally.

An empty urn within her withered hands,
Whose holy dust was scattered long ago;
The Scipios'[1] tomb contains no ashes now;
The very sepulchres lie tenantless
5   Of their heroic dwellers: dost thou flow,
Old Tiber! through a marble wilderness?
Rise, with thy yellow waves, and mantle her distress.

THE COLISEUM[2]; THE DYING GLADIATOR

Arches on arches! as it were that Rome,
Collecting the chief trophies of her line,
10   Would build up all her triumphs in one dome,[3]
Her Coliseum stands; the moonbeams shine
As 'twere its natural torches, for divine
Should be the light which streams here, to illume
This long-explored but still exhaustless mine
15   Of contemplation; and the azure gloom
Of an Italian night, where the deep skies assume

Hues which have words and speak to ye of heaven,
Floats o'er this vast and wondrous monument,
And shadows forth its glory. There is given
20   Unto the things of earth, which Time hath bent,
A spirit's feeling, and where he hath leant
His hand, but broke his scythe, there is a power
And magic in the ruined battlement,
For which the palace of the present hour
25   Must yield its pomp, and wait till ages are its dower.

[1] The family which contributed most to the greatness of ancient Rome. Their tomb was discovered in 1780. Byron may mean that modern Rome had lost even the memory of patriotism.

[2] Coliseum, Colosseum, the greatest ruin of ancient Rome, an amphitheater built about A.D. 80 by the emperors Vespasian and Titus, elliptical in shape, about 615 by 510 feet. The seats are supported by rings of arched galleries. It was used for gladiatorial combats and other spectacles.

[3] A stately edifice. The Coliseum had no roof.

And here the buzz of eager nations ran,
In murmured pity, or loud-roared applause,
As man was slaughtered by his fellow man.
And wherefore slaughtered? wherefore, but because
Such were the bloody Circus' genial laws,   5
And the imperial pleasure.—Wherefore not?
What matters where we fall to fill the maws
Of worms—on battle-plains or listed spot?
Both are but theatres—where the chief actors rot.

I see before me the Gladiator lie: 10
He leans upon his hand—his manly brow
Consents to death, but conquers agony,
And his drooped head sinks gradually low,
And through his side the last drops, ebbing slow
From the red gash, fall heavy, one by one,   15
Like the first of a thunder-shower; and now
The arena swims around him—he is gone,
Ere ceased the inhuman shout which hailed the wretch
    who won.

He heard it, but he heeded not—his eyes
Were with his heart, and that was far away: 20
He recked not of the life he lost nor prize,
But where his rude hut by the Danube lay—
There were his young barbarians all at play,
There was their Dacian[1] mother—he, their sire,
Butchered to make a Roman holiday—   25
All this rushed with his blood.—Shall he expire
And unavenged?—Arise! ye Goths,[2] and glut your ire!

But here, where Murder breathed her bloody steam;
And here, where buzzing nations choked the ways,

---

[1] Dacia, a district north of the Danube, furnished many gladiators to
Rome.
[2] The Goths, led by Alaric, sacked Rome, A.D. 410.

And roared or murmured like a mountain stream
Dashing or winding as its torrent strays;
Here, where the Roman millions' blame or praise
Was death or life—the playthings of a crowd—
5   My voice sounds much—and fall the stars' faint rays
On the arena void—seats crushed—walls bowed—
And galleries, where my steps seem echoes strangely loud.

A ruin—yet what ruin![1] from its mass
Walls, palaces, half-cities, have been reared;
10   Yet oft the enormous skeleton ye pass,
And marvel where the spoil could have appeared.
Hath it indeed been plundered, or but cleared?
Alas! developed, opens the decay,
When the colossal fabric's form is neared:
15   It will not bear the brightness of the day,
Which streams too much on all years, man, have reft away.

But when the rising moon begins to climb
Its topmost arch, and gently pauses there;
When the stars twinkle through the loops of time,
20   And the low night-breeze waves along the air
The garland forest, which the gray walls wear,
Like laurels on the bald first Cæsar's head
When the light shines serene but doth not glare—
Then in this magic circle raise the dead:
25   Heroes have trod this spot—'tis on their dust ye tread.

"While stands the Coliseum, Rome shall stand;
"When falls the Coliseum, Rome shall fall;
"And when Rome falls—the World." From our own
    land
Thus spake the pilgrims o'er this mighty wall

---

[1] For centuries material from the Coliseum, as from other buildings of
ancient Rome, was used to build the medieval and modern city.

In Saxon times, which we are wont to call
Ancient; and these three mortal things are still
On their foundations, and unaltered all—
Rome and her Ruin past Redemption's skill,
The World, the same wide den—of thieves, or what ye will. 5

SONNET ON CHILLON

Eternal Spirit of the chainless Mind!
    Brightest in dungeons, Liberty! thou art:
    For there thy habitation is the heart—
The heart which love of thee alone can bind;
And when thy sons to fetters are consigned—   10
    To fetters, and the damp vault's dayless gloom,
    Their country conquers with their martyrdom,
And Freedom's fame finds wings on every wind.
Chillon! thy prison is a holy place,
    And thy sad floor an altar—for 'twas trod,   15
Until his very steps have left a trace
    Worn, as if thy cold pavement were a sod,
By Bonnivard!—May none those marks efface!
    For they appeal from tyranny to God.

PERCY BYSSHE SHELLEY

THE CLOUD

I bring fresh showers for the thirsting flowers,   20
    From the seas and the streams;
I bear light shade for the leaves when laid
    In their noon-day dreams.
From my wings are shaken the dews that waken
    The sweet buds every one,   25
When rocked to rest on their mother's breast,
    As she dances about the sun.

I wield the flail of the lashing hail,
    And whiten the green plains under,
And then again I dissolve it in rain,
    And laugh as I pass in thunder.

5   I sift the snow on the mountains below,
    And their great pines groan aghast;
And all the night 'tis my pillow white,
    While I sleep in the arms of the blast.
Sublime on the towers of my skiey bowers,
10   Lightning my pilot sits;
In a cavern under is fettered the thunder,—
    It struggles and howls at fits;
Over earth and ocean, with gentle motion,
    This pilot is guiding me,
15   Lured by the love of the genii that move
    In the depths of the purple sea;
Over the rills, and the crags, and the hills,
    Over the lakes and the plains,
Wherever he dream, under mountain or stream,
20   The Spirit he loves remains;
And I all the while bask in heaven's blue smile,
    Whilst he is dissolving in rains.

The sanguine[1] sunrise, with his meteor eyes,
    And his burning plumes outspread,
25   Leaps on the back of my sailing rack,
    When the morning star shines dead,
As on the jag of a mountain crag,
    Which an earthquake rocks and swings,
An eagle alit one moment may sit
30   In the light of its golden wings.
And when sunset may breathe, from the lit sea beneath,
    Its ardours of rest and of love,

---

[1] red, the color of blood.

And the crimson pall of eve may fall
   From the depth of heaven above,
With wings folded I rest, on mine airy nest,
   As still as a brooding dove.

That orbèd maiden with white fire laden,   5
   Whom mortals call the moon,
Glides glimmering o'er my fleece-like floor,
   By the midnight breezes strewn;
And wherever the beat of her unseen feet,
   Which only the angels hear,   10
May have broken the woof of my tent's thin roof,
   The stars peep behind her and peer;
And I laugh to see them whirl and flee,
   Like a swarm of golden bees,
When I widen the rent in my wind-built tent,   15
   Till the calm rivers, lakes, and seas,
Like strips of the sky fallen through me on high,
   Are each paved with the moon and these.

I bind the sun's throne with a burning zone,
   And the moon's with a girdle of pearl;   20
The volcanoes are dim, and the stars reel and swim,
   When the whirlwinds my banner unfurl.
From cape to cape, with a bridge-like shape,
   Over a torrent sea,
Sunbeam-proof, I hang like a roof,   25
   The mountains its columns be.
The triumphal arch through which I march
   With hurricane, fire, and snow,
When the powers of the air are chained to my chair,
   Is the million-coloured bow;   30
The sphere-fire above its soft colours wove,
   While the moist earth was laughing below.

I am the daughter of earth and water,
   And the nursling of the sky;

I pass through the pores of the ocean and shores;
　　I change, but I cannot die.
For after the rain when, with never a stain,
　　The pavilion of heaven is bare,
5　And the winds and sunbeams with their convex gleams
　　Build up the blue dome of air.
I silently laugh at my own cenotaph,[1]
　　And out of the caverns of rain,
Like a child from the womb, like a ghost from the tomb,
10　I arise and unbuild it again.

TO A SKYLARK

Hail to thee, blithe spirit!
　　Bird thou never wert,
That from heaven, or near it,
　　Pourest thy full heart
15　In profuse strains of unpremeditated art.

Higher still and higher
　　From the earth thou springest
Like a cloud of fire;
　　The blue deep thou wingest,
20　And singing still dost soar, and soaring ever singest.

In the golden lightning
　　Of the sunken sun,
O'er which clouds are brightning,
　　Thou dost float and run;
25　Like an unbodied joy whose race is just begun.

The pale purple even
　　Melts around thy flight;
Like a star of heaven
　　In the broad day-light
30　Thou art unseen, but yet I hear thy shrill delight,

[1] a monument in honor of one who is buried elsewhere; here, the cloudless sky.

Keen as are the arrows
   Of that silver sphere,
Whose intense lamp narrows
   In the white dawn clear,
Until we hardly see, we feel that it is there.   5

All the earth and air
   With thy voice is loud,
As, when night is bare,
   From one lonely cloud
The moon rains out her beams, and heaven is overflowed.   10

What thou art we know not;
   What is most like thee?
From rainbow clouds there flow not
   Drops so bright to see
As from thy presence showers a rain of melody.   15

Like a poet hidden
   In the light of thought,
Singing hymns unbidden,
   Till the world is wrought
To sympathy with hopes and fears it heeded not: 20

Like a high-born maiden
   In a palace tower,
Soothing her love-laden
   Soul in secret hour
With music sweet as love, which overflows her bower: 25

Like a glow-worm golden
   In a dell of dew,
Scattering unbeholden
   Its aërial hue
Among the flowers and grass which screen it from the view: 30

Like a rose embowered
   In its own green leaves,
By warm winds deflowered,
   Till the scent it gives
5 Makes faint with too much sweet these heavy-wingèd thieves.

Sound of vernal showers
   On the twinkling grass,
Rain-awakened flowers,
   All that ever was
10 Joyous, and clear, and fresh, thy music doth surpass.

Teach us, sprite or bird,
   What sweet thoughts are thine;
I have never heard
   Praise of love or wine
15 That panted forth a flood of rapture so divine:

Chorus Hymenæal,[1]
   Or triumphal chaunt,
Matched with thine, would be all
   But an empty vaunt,
20 A thing wherein we feel there is some hidden want.

What objects are the fountains
   Of thy happy strain?
What fields, or waves, or mountains?
   What shapes of sky or plain?
25 What love of thine own kind? what ignorance of pain?

With thy clear keen joyance
   Languor cannot be—
Shadow of annoyance
   Never came near thee:
30 Thou lovest—but ne'er knew love's sad satiety.

---

[1] wedding chorus, from Hymen, god of marriage in classical mythology.

Waking or asleep,
    Thou of death must deem
Thing more true and deep
    Than we mortals dream,
Or how could thy notes flow in such a crystal stream?   5

We look before and after
    And pine for what is not:
Our sincerest laughter
    With some pain is fraught;
Our sweetest songs are those that tell of saddest thought.   10

Yet if we could scorn
    Hate, and pride, and fear;
If we were things born
    Not to shed a tear,
I know not how thy joy we ever should come near.   15

Better than all measures
    Of delightful sound—
Better than all treasures
    That in books are found—
Thy skill to poet were, thou scorner of the ground!   20

Teach me half the gladness
    That thy brain must know,
Such harmonious madness
    From my lips would flow,
The world should listen then—as I am listening now.   25

INDIAN SERENADE

I arise from dreams of thee
In the first sweet sleep of night,
When the winds are breathing low,
And the stars are shining bright:
I arise from dreams of thee,   30

And a spirit in my feet
Hath led me—who knows how?
To thy chamber window, Sweet!

The wandering airs they faint
On the dark, the silent stream—
The Champak[1] odours fail
Like sweet thoughts in a dream;
The nightingale's complaint,
It dies upon her heart;—
As I must on thine,
O! belovèd as thou art!

O lift me from the grass!
I die! I faint! I fail!
Let thy love in kisses rain
On my lips and eyelids pale.
My cheek is cold and white, alas!
My heart beats loud and fast;—
Oh! press it to thine own again,
Where it will break at last.

JOHN KEATS

ODE ON A GRECIAN URN

Thou still unravish'd bride of quietness,
    Thou foster-child of silence and slow time,
Sylvan historian, who canst thus express
    A flowery tale more sweetly than our rhyme:
What leaf-fring'd legend haunts about thy shape
    Of deities or mortals, or of both,
        In Tempe or the dales of Arcady?

[1] A tree of the magnolia family, having fragrant yellow flowers, much cultivated in India, where it is regarded as sacred.

What men or gods are these? What maidens loth?
  What mad pursuit? What struggle to escape?
    What pipes and timbrels? What wild ecstasy?

Heard melodies are sweet, but those unheard
  Are sweeter; therefore, ye soft pipes, play on;   5
Not to the sensual ear, but, more endear'd,
  Pipe to the spirit ditties of no tone:
Fair youth, beneath the trees, thou canst not leave
  Thy song, nor ever can those trees be bare;
    Bold Lover, never, never canst thou kiss,   10
Though winning near the goal—yet, do not grieve;
  She cannot fade, though thou hast not thy bliss,
    Forever wilt thou love, and she be fair!

Ah, happy, happy boughs! that cannot shed
  Your leaves, nor ever bid the Spring adieu: 15
And, happy melodist, unwearied,
  Forever piping songs forever new;
More happy love! more happy, happy love!
  Forever warm and still to be enjoy'd,
    Forever panting, and forever young;   20
All breathing human passion far above,
  That leaves a heart high-sorrowful and cloy'd,
    A burning forehead, and a parching tongue.

Who are these coming to the sacrifice?
  To what green altar, O mysterious priest,   25
Lead'st thou that heifer lowing at the skies,
  And all her silken flanks with garlands drest?
What little town by river or sea shore,
  Or mountain-built with peaceful citadel,
    Is emptied of this folk, this pious morn?   30
And, little town, thy streets for evermore
  Will silent be; and not a soul to tell
    Why thou art desolate, can e'er return.

O Attic[1] shape! Fair attitude! with brede[2]
Of marble men and maidens overwrought,
With forest branches and the trodden weed;
   Thou, silent form, dost tease us out of thought
5 As doth eternity: Cold Pastoral!
   When old age shall this generation waste,
     Thou shalt remain, in midst of other woe
Than ours, a friend to man, to whom thou say'st,
   "Beauty is truth, truth beauty,"—that is all
10   Ye know on earth, and all ye need to know.

TO AUTUMN

Season of mists and mellow fruitfulness,
   Close bosom-friend of the maturing sun;
Conspiring with him how to load and bless
   With fruit the vines that round the thatch-eaves run;
15 To bend with apples the moss'd cottage-trees,
   And fill all fruit with ripeness to the core;
     To swell the gourd, and plump the hazel shells
With a sweet kernel; to set budding more,
   And still more, later flowers for the bees,
20   Until they think warm days will never cease,
     For Summer has o'er-brimmed their clammy cells.

Who hath not seen thee oft amid thy store?
   Sometimes whoever seeks abroad may find
Thee sitting careless on a granary floor,
25   Thy hair soft-lifted by the winnowing wind;
Or on a half-reap'd furrow sound asleep,
   Drows'd with the fume of poppies, while thy hook
     Spares the next swath and all its twinèd flowers:
And sometimes like a gleaner thou dost keep
30   Steady thy laden head across a brook;
   Or by a cider-press, with patient look,
     Thou watchest the last oozings hours by hours.

[1] Athenian, Greek, from Attica; the territory of Athens.   [2] embroidery.

Where are the the songs of Spring? Ay, where are they?
   Think not of them, thou hast thy music too,—
While barrèd clouds bloom the soft-dying day,
   And touch the stubble-plains with rosy hue;
Then in a wailful choir the small gnats mourn   5
   Among the river sallows, borne aloft
     Or sinking as the light wind lives or dies;
And full-grown lambs loud bleat from hilly bourn;
   Hedge-crickets sing; and now with treble soft
   The red-breast whistles from a garden-croft[1];   10
   And gathering swallows twitter in the skies.

WHEN I HAVE FEARS

When I have fears that I may cease to be
   Before my pen has glean'd my teeming brain,
Before high pilèd books, in charact'ry,[2]
   Hold like rich garners the full-ripen'd grain;   15
When I behold, upon the night's starr'd face,
   Huge cloudy symbols of a high romance,
And think that I may never live to trace
   Their shadows, with the magic hand of chance;
And when I feel, fair creature of an hour!   20
   That I shall never look upon thee more,
Never have relish in the faery power
   Of unreflecting love!—then on the shore
Of the wide world I stand alone, and think
Till love and fame to nothingness do sink.   25

TO SLEEP

O soft embalmer of the still midnight!
   Shutting with careful fingers and benign
Our gloom-pleased eyes, embower'd from the light,
   Enshaded in forgetfulness divine;

---

[1] small, inclosed field, usually adjoining a house.   [2] characters, letters.

O soothest Sleep! if so it please thee, close,
    In midst of this thine hymn, my willing eyes,
Or wait the amen, ere thy poppy throws
    Around my bed its lulling charities;
5   Then save me, or the passèd day will shine
Upon my pillow, breeding many woes;
Save me from curious conscience, that still lords
    Its strength for darkness, burrowing like a mole;
Turn the key deftly in the oilèd wards,
10   And seal the hushèd casket of my soul.

ON THE SEA

It keeps eternal whisperings around
    Desolate shores, and with its mighty swell
    Gluts twice ten thousand caverns, till the spell
Of Hecate[1] leaves them their old shadowy sound.
15   Often 'tis in such gentle temper found
    That scarcely will the very smallest shell
    Be mov'd for days from whence it sometime fell,
When last the winds of heaven were unbound.
Oh, ye, who have your eye-balls vex'd and tir'd,
20   Feast them upon the wideness of the sea;
    Oh, ye, whose ears are dinn'd with uproar rude,
    Or fed too much with cloying melody,—
      Sit ye near some old cavern's mouth, and brood
Until ye start, as if the sea-nymphs quir'd!

THE GRASSHOPPER AND THE CRICKET

25   The poetry of earth is never dead:
    When all the birds are faint with the hot sun,
    And hide in cooling trees, a voice will run
From hedge to hedge about the new-mown mead;

[1] In classical mythology, the goddess of darkness and terror of night. She presided over enchantments.

That is the Grasshopper's—he takes the lead
  In summer luxury,—he has never done
    With his delights; for when tired out with fun
He rests at ease beneath some pleasant weed.
The poetry of earth is ceasing never: 5
  On a lone winter evening, when the frost
    Has wrought a silence, from the stove there shrills
The Cricket's song, in warmth increasing ever,
  And seems to one in drowsiness half lost,
    The Grasshopper's among some grassy hills.   10

ON FIRST LOOKING INTO CHAPMAN'S HOMER

Much have I travell'd in the realms of gold,
  And many goodly states and kingdoms seen;
  Round many western islands have I been
Which bards[1] in fealty to Apollo[2] hold.
Oft of one wide expanse had I been told   15
  That deep-brow'd Homer ruled as his demesne;
  Yet did I never breathe its pure serene
Till I heard Chapman speak out loud and bold:
Then felt I like some watcher of the skies
  When a new planet swims into his ken;   20
Or like stout Cortez when with eagle eyes
  He star'd at the Pacific—and all his men
Look'd at each other with a wild surmise—
  Silent, upon a peak in Darien.

LA BELLE DAME SANS MERCI[3]

O what can ail thee, knight-at-arms,   25
  Alone and palely loitering?
The sedge has wither'd from the lake,
  And no birds sing.

[1] poets.   [2] the god of poetry and music.   [3] the beautiful lady without mercy.

O what can ail thee, knight-at-arms,
    So haggard and so woe-begone?
The squirrel's granary is full,
    And the harvest's done.

5   I see a lily on thy brow
    With anguish moist and fever dew,
And on thy cheeks a fading rose
    Fast withereth too.

"I met a lady in the meads,
10   Full beautiful—a faery's child;
Her hair was long, her foot was light,
    And her eyes were wild.

"I made a garland for her head,
    And bracelets too, and fragrant zone;
15 She look'd at me as she did love,
    And made sweet moan.

"I set her on my pacing steed,
    And nothing else saw all day long,
For sideways would she lean, and sing
20   A faery's song.

"She found me roots of relish sweet,
    And honey wild, and manna-dew,
And sure in language strange she said—
    'I love thee true.'

25 "She took me to her elfin grot,[1]
    And there she wept and sigh'd full sore,
And there I shut her wild, wild eyes,
    With kisses four.

[1] grotto.

"And there she lullèd me asleep,
  And there I dream'd—ah! woe betide!—
The latest dream I ever dream'd
  On the cold hill's side.

"I saw pale kings and princes too,   5
  Pale warriors, death-pale were they all;
They cried—'La Belle Dame sans Merci
  Hath thee in thrall!'

"I saw their starved lips in the gloom,
  With horrid warning gapèd wide;   10
And I awoke, and found me here
  On the cold hill's side.

"And this is why I sojourn here,
  Alone and palely loitering,
Though the sedge is wither'd from the lake,   15
  And no birds sing."

SIR WALTER SCOTT

LOCHINVAR

O, young Lochinvar is come out of the west,
Through all the wide Border[1] his steed was the best;
And, save his good broadsword, he weapon had none,
He rode all unarmed, and he rode all alone.
So faithful in love, and so dauntless in war,   20
There never was knight like the young Lochinvar.

He stayed not for brake,[2] and he stopped not for stone,
He swam the Eske River where ford there was none;
But, ere he alighted at Netherby gate,   25

[1] between England and Scotland.   [2] thicket.

The bride had consented, the gallant came late;
For a laggard in love, and a dastard in war,
Was to wed the fair Ellen of brave Lochinvar.

So boldly he entered the Netherby Hall,
5 Among bridesmen, and kinsmen, and brothers, and all:
Then spoke the bride's father, his hand on his sword
(For the poor craven bridegroom said never a word),
"O come ye in peace here, or come ye in war,
Or to dance at our bridal, young Lord Lochinvar?"

10 "I long wooed your daughter, my suit you denied;—
Love swells like the Solway, but ebbs like its tide,—
And now am I come, with this lost love of mine,
To lead but one measure, drink one cup of wine.
There are maidens in Scotland more lovely by far,
15 That would gladly be bride to the young Lochinvar."

The bride kissed the goblet; the knight took it up,
He quaffed off the wine, and he threw down the cup.
She looked down to blush, and she looked up to sigh,
With a smile on her lips, and a tear in her eye.
20 He took her soft hand, ere her mother could bar,—
"Now tread we a measure!" said young Lochinvar.

So stately his form, and so lovely her face,
That never a hall such a galliard[1] did grace;
While her mother did fret, and her father did fume,
25 And the bridegroom stood dangling his bonnet and plume;
And the bride-maidens whispered, "'Twere better by far
To have matched our fair cousin with young Lochinvar."

One touch to her hand, and one word in her ear,
When they reached the hall-door, and the charger stood near;
30 So light to the croupe the fair lady he swung,

[1] a lively dance.

So light to the saddle before her he sprung;
   "She is won! we are gone over bank, bush, and scaur[1];
They'll have fleet steeds that follow," quoth young Lochinvar.

There was mounting 'mong Græmes of the Netherby clan;
Forsters, Fenwicks, and Musgraves, they rode and they ran: 5
There was racing and chasing on Cannobie Lee,[2]
But the lost bride of Netherby ne'er did they see.
So daring in love, and so dauntless in war,
Have ye e'er heard of gallant like young Lochinvar?

REDGAUNTLET

WANDERING WILLIE'S TALE

Ye maun[3] have heard of Sir Robert Redgauntlet of that 10
Ilk,[4] who lived in these parts before the dear years. The
country will lang mind him; and our fathers used to draw
breath thick if ever they heard him named. He was out wi'
the Hielandmen in Montrose's time; and again he was in the
hills wi' Glencairn in the saxteen hundred and fifty-twa; and 15
sae when King Charles the Second came in, wha was in sic
favour as the Laird of Redgauntlet? He was knighted at
Lonon court, wi' the King's ain sword; and being a redhot
prelatist,[5] he came down here, rampauging like a lion, with
commissions of lieutenancy, (and of lunacy, for what I ken,) 20
to put down a' the Whigs and Covenanters in the country.
Wild wark they made of it; for the Whigs were as dour[6] as
the Cavaliers were fierce, and it was which should first tire
the other. Redgauntlet was aye for the strong hand; and his
name is kend[7] as wide in the country as Claverhouse's or 25
Tam Dalyell's. Glen, nor dargle,[8] nor mountain, nor cave,

---

[1] precipice.   [2] the meadows near Netherby Castle.   [3] must.   [4] of
the same name or place; that is, Redgauntlet of Redgauntlet.   [5] high
churchman, a name given by Puritans and Presbyterians to those who
stood for episcopacy in church government.   [6] (door) obstinate.
[7] kenned, known.   [8] dell.

could hide the puir hill-folk[1] when Redgauntlet was out with
bugle and bloodhound after them, as if they had been sae
mony deer. And troth when they fand them, they didna mak
muckle mair[2] ceremony than a Hielandman wi' a roebuck—
5 It was just, "Will ye tak the test?"—if not, "Make ready—
present—fire!"—and there lay the recusant.[3]

Far and wide was Sir Robert hated and feared. Men
thought he had a direct compact with Satan—that he was
proof against steel—and that bullets happed[4] aff his buff-
10 coat[5] like hailstanes from a hearth—that he had a mear[6]
that would turn a hare on the side of Carrifra-gawns[7]—and
muckle to the same purpose, of whilk mair anon. The best
blessing they wared on him was, "Deil scowp wi'[8] Redgauntlet!" He wasna a bad maister to his ain folk though,
15 and was weel aneugh liked by his tenants; and as for the
lackies and troopers that raid out wi' him to the persecu-
tions, as the Whigs caa'd those killing times, they wad hae
drunken themsells blind to his health at ony time.

Now you are to ken that my gudesire lived on Redgaunt-
20 let's grund—they ca' the place Primrose-Knowe. We had
lived on the grund, and under the Redgauntlets, since the
riding days, and lang before. It was a pleasant bit; and I
think the air is callerer[9] and fresher there than ony where
else in the country. It's a' deserted now; and I sat on the
25 broken door-cheek three days since, and was glad I couldna
see the plight the place was in; but that's a' wide o' the mark.
There dwelt my gudesire,[10] Steenie Steenson, a rambling,
rattling chiel[11] he had been in his young days, and could play
weel on the pipes[12]; he was famous at "Hoopers and Gird-
30 ers"—a' Cumberland couldna touch him at "Jockie Lattin"
—and he had the finest finger for the backlilt between Berwick and Carlisle. The like o' Steenie wasna the sort that

---

[1] Covenanters.   [2] much more.   [3] dissenter, nonconformist.
[4] hopped.   [5] a coat of buff leather, worn for defense.   [6] mare.   [7] a
precipitous mountainside.   [8] run with, *or* quaff with.   [9] cooler.
[10] goodsire, grandsire.   [11] chield, young fellow.   [12] bagpipes.

they made Whigs o'. And so he became a Tory, as they ca'
it, which we now ca' Jacobites, just out of a kind of needces-
sity, that he might belang to some side or other. He had nae
ill-will to the Whig bodies, and liked little to see the blude
rin, though, being obliged to follow Sir Robert in hunting
and hosting,[1] watching and warding, he saw muckle mischief,
and maybe did some, that he couldna avoid.

Now Steenie was a kind of favourite with his master, and
kend a' the folks about the Castle, and was often sent for to
play the pipes when they were at their merriment. Auld
Dougal MacCallum, the butler, that had followed Sir Robert
through gude and ill, thick and thin, pool and stream, was
specially fond of the pipes, and aye gae my gudesire his gude
word wi' the Laird; for Dougal could turn his master round
his finger.

Weel, round came the Revolution, and it had like to have
broken the hearts baith of Dougal and his master. But the
change was not a'thegether sae great as they feared, and other
folk thought for. The Whigs made an unco crawing what
they wad do with their auld enemies, and in special wi' Sir
Robert Redgauntlet. But there were ower mony great folks
dipped in the same doings, to mak a spick and span new
warld. So Parliament passed it a' ower easy; and Sir Robert,
bating that he was held to hunting foxes instead of Covenanters, remained just the man he was. His revel was as
loud, and his hall as weel lighted, as ever it had been, though
maybe he lacked the fines of the nonconformists, that used
to come to stock his larder and cellar; for it is certain he
began to be keener about the rents than his tenants used to
find him before, and they behoved to be prompt to the rent-
day, or else the Laird wasna pleased. And he was sic an
awsome body, that naebody cared to anger him; for the
oaths he swore, and the rage that he used to get into, and
the looks that he put on, made men sometimes think him a
devil incarnate.

[1] mustering of armed men.

Weel, my gudesire was nae manager—no that he was a
very great misguider—but he hadna the saving gift, and he
got twa terms' rent in arrear. He got the first brash at
Whitsunday put ower wi' fair word and piping; but when
5 Martinmas came, there was a summons from the grund-
officer to come wi' the rent on a day preceese, or else Steenie
behoved to flit. Sair wark he had to get the siller; but
he was weel-freended, and at last he got the haill scraped
thegether—a thousand merks[1]—the maist of it was from a
10 neighbour they caa'd Laurie Lapraik—a sly tod.[2] Laurie had
walth o' gear—could hunt wi' the hound and rin wi' the hare
—and be Whig or Tory, saunt or sinner, as the wind stood.
He was a professor[3] in this Revolution warld, but he liked
an orra sough[4] of this warld, and a tune on the pipes weel
15 aneugh at a bytime, and abune a', he thought he had a gude
security for the siller he lent my gudesire ower the stocking
at Primrose-Knowe.

Away trots my gudesire to Redgauntlet Castle, wi' a heavy
purse and a light heart, glad to be out of the Laird's danger.
20 Weel, the first thing he learned at the Castle was, that Sir
Robert had fretted himsell into a fit of the gout, because
he did not appear before twelve o'clock. It wasna a'thegether
for sake of the money, Dougal thought; but because he
didna like to part wi' my gudesire aff the grund. Dougal was
25 glad to see Steenie, and brought him into the great oak parlour, and there sat the Laird his leesome lane,[5] excepting that
he had beside him a great, ill-favoured jackanape,[6] that was
a special pet of his; a cankered beast it was, and mony an
ill-natured trick it played—ill to please it was, and easily
30 angered—ran about the haill castle—chattering and yowling,
and pinching, and biting folk, especially before ill-weather,
or disturbances in the state. Sir Robert caa'd it Major Weir,
after the warlock[7] that was burnt; and few folk liked either

---

[1] marks, Scottish silver coins worth 13⅓ pence.   [2] fox.   [3] one who
professes great devotion to religion.   [4] extra chant.   [5] his dear self
alone.   [6] ape, monkey.   [7] wizard.

the name or the conditions of the creature—they thought
there was something in it by ordinar—and my gudesire was
not just easy in his mind when the door shut on him, and he
saw himself in the room wi' naebody but the Laird, Dougal
MacCallum, and the Major, a thing that hadna chanced to 5
him before.

Sir Robert sat, or, I should say, lay, in a great armed chair,
wi' his grand velvet gown, and his feet on a cradle; for he
had baith gout and gravel, and his face looked as gash and
ghastly as Satan's. Major Weir sat opposite to him, in a 10
red laced coat, and the Laird's wig on his head; and aye as
Sir Robert girned wi' pain, the jackanape girned too, like a
sheep's-head between a pair of tangs—an ill-faur'd,[1] fear-
some couple they were. The Laird's buff-coat was hung on a
pin behind him, and his broadsword and his pistols within 15
reach; for he keepit up the auld fashion of having the
weapons ready, and a horse saddled day and night, just as he
used to do when he was able to loup on horseback, and away
after ony of the hill-folk he could get speerings of. Some
said it was for fear of the Whigs taking vengeance, but I 20
judge it was just his auld custom—he wasna gien to fear ony
thing. The rental-book, wi' its black cover and brass clasps,
was lying beside him; and a book of sculduddry[2] sangs was
put betwixt the leaves, to keep it open at the place where it
bore evidence against the Goodman of Primrose-Knowe, as 25
behind the hand with his mails[3] and duties. Sir Robert gave
my gudesire a look, as if he would have withered his heart in
his bosom. Ye maun ken he had a way of bending his brows,
that men saw the visible mark of a horse-shoe in his forehead, deep-dinted, as if it had been stamped there.   30

"Are ye come light-handed, ye son of a toom[4] whistle?"
said Sir Robert. "Zounds! if you are——"

My gudesire, with as gude a countenance as he could put
on, made a leg, and placed the bag of money on the table wi'

[1] ill-favored, ugly.   [3] tribute, taxes.
[2] skulduddery, immoral, immorality.   [4] empty, empty-sounding.

a dash, like a man that does something clever. The Laird
drew it to him hastily—"Is it all here, Steenie, man?"

"Your honour will find it right," said my gudesire.

"Here, Dougal," said the Laird, "gie Steenie a tass[1] of
5 brandy down stairs, till I count the siller and write the
receipt."

But they werena weel out of the room, when Sir Robert
gied a yelloch that garr'd the Castle rock. Back ran Dougal
—in flew the livery-men—yell on yell gied the Laird, ilk ane
10 mair awfu' than the ither. My gudesire knew not whether to
stand or flee, but he ventured back into the parlour, where a'
was gaun hirdy-girdie—naebody to say "come in," and "gae
out." Terribly the Laird roared for cauld water to his feet, and
wine to cool his throat; and hell, hell, hell, and its flames,
15 was aye the word in his mouth. They brought him water,
and when they plunged his swoln feet into the tub, he cried
out it was burning; and folk say that it *did* bubble and
sparkle like a seething caldron. He flung the cup at Dougal's
head, and said he had given him blood instead of burgundy;
20 and, sure aneugh, the lass washed clotted blood aff the carpet
the neist day. The jackanape they caa'd Major Weir, it
jibbered and cried as if it was mocking its master; my
gudesire's head was like to turn—he forgot baith siller and receipt, and down stairs he banged; but as he ran, the shrieks
25 came faint and fainter; there was a deep-drawn shivering
groan, and word gaed through the Castle, that the Laird was
dead.

Weel, away came my gudesire, wi' his finger in his mouth,
and his best hope was, that Dougal had seen the money-
30 bag, and heard the Laird speak of writing the receipt. The
young Laird, now Sir John, came from Edinburgh, to see
things put to rights. Sir John and his father never gree'd
weel. Sir John had been bred an advocate,[2] and afterwards
sat in the last Scots Parliament and voted for the Union,[3]

---

[1] drinking-cup, glass.   [2] lawyer.   [3] with England, in 1707, in the
reign of Queen Anne.

having gotten, it was thought, a rug of the compensations[1]—
if his father could have come out of his grave, he would have
brained him for it on his awn hearthstane. Some thought it
was easier counting with the auld rough Knight than the fair-
spoken young ane—but mair of that anon.

Dougal MacCallum, poor body, neither grat nor graned,[2]
but gaed about the house looking like a corpse, but directing,
as was his duty, a' the order of the grand funeral. Now,
Dougal looked aye waur and waur[3] when night was coming,
and was aye the last to gang to his bed, whilk[4] was in a little
round just opposite the chamber of dais,[5] whilk his master
occupied while he was living, and where he now lay in state,
as they caa'd it, weel-a-day! The night before the funeral,
Dougal could keep his awn counsel nae langer; he cam doun
with his proud spirit, and fairly asked auld Hutcheon to sit
in his room with him for an hour. When they were in the
round, Dougal took ae tass of brandy to himsell, and gave
another to Hutcheon, and wished him all health and lang life,
and said that, for himsell, he wasna lang for this world; for
that, every night since Sir Robert's death, his silver call had
sounded from the state-chamber, just as it used to do at
nights in his lifetime, to call Dougal to help to turn him in
his bed. Dougal said, that being alone with the dead on that
floor of the tower, (for naebody cared to wake Sir Robert
Redgauntlet like another corpse,) he had never daured to
answer the call, but that now his conscience checked him for
neglecting his duty; for, "though death breaks service," said
MacCallum, "it shall never break my service to Sir Robert;
and I will answer his next whistle, so be you will stand by
me, Hutcheon."

Hutcheon had nae will to the wark, but he had stood by
Dougal in battle and broil, and he wad not fail him at this
pinch; so down the carles[6] sat ower a stoup of brandy, and

---

[1] a haul, a good bargain, in the adjustments made by the terms of the
Union.   [2] wept nor groaned.   [3] worse and worse.   [4] which.
[5] parlor, or best bedroom.   [6] fellows, boors.

Hutcheon, who was something of a clerk,[1] would have read a chapter of the Bible; but Dougal would hear naething but a blaud[2] of Davie Lindsay, whilk was the waur preparation.

When midnight came, and the house was quiet as the grave,
5 sure aneugh the silver whistle sounded as sharp and shrill as if Sir Robert was blowing it, and up gat the twa auld serving-men, and tottered into the room where the dead man lay. Hutcheon saw aneugh at the first glance; for there were torches in the room, which showed him the foul fiend, in his
10 ain shape, sitting on the Laird's coffin! Over he cowped[3] as if he had been dead. He could not tell how lang he lay in a trance at the door, but when he gathered himself, he cried on his neighbour, and getting nae answer, raised the house, when Dougal was found lying dead within twa steps of the
15 bed where his master's coffin was placed. As for the whistle, it was gaen anes and aye[4]; but mony a time was it heard at the top of the house on the bartizan,[5] and amang the auld chimneys and turrets, where the howlets have their nests. Sir John hushed the matter up, and the funeral passed over
20 without mair bogle[6]-wark.

But when a' was ower, and the Laird was beginning to settle his affairs, every tenant was called up for his arrears, and my gudesire for the full sum that stood against him in the rental-book. Weel, away he trots to the Castle, to tell his
25 story, and there he is introduced to Sir John, sitting in his father's chair, in deep mourning, with weepers[7] and hanging cravat, and a small walking rapier by his side, instead of the auld broadsword, that had a hundred-weight of steel about it, what with blade, chape,[8] and basket-hilt. I have heard their
30 communing so often tauld ower, that I almost think I was there mysell, though I couldna be born at the time. (In fact,

---

[1] scholar, one who can read and write.   [2] fragment.   [3] upset, capsized.   [4] gone once and forever.   [5] a small structure for observation or defense built over an angle of a wall or over an entrance gate. [6] specter, goblin.   [7] mourning bands.   [8] metal trimming of a scabbard, sometimes the whole scabbard.

Alan, my companion, mimicked, with a good deal of humour, the flattering, conciliating tone of the tenant's address, and the hypocritical melancholy of the Laird's reply. His grandfather, he said, had, while he spoke, his eye fixed on the rental-book, as if it were a mastiff-dog that he was afraid 5 would spring up and bite him.)

"I wuss[1] ye joy, sir, of the head seat, and the white loaf, and the braid lairdship. Your father was a kind man to friends and followers; muckle grace to you, Sir John, to fill his shoon—his boots, I suld say, for he seldom wore shoon, 10 unless it were muils when he had the gout."

"Ay, Steenie," quoth the Laird, sighing deeply and putting his napkin to his een, "his was a sudden call, and he will be missed in the country; no time to set his house in order— weel prepared Godward, no doubt, which is the root of the 15 matter—but left us behind a tangled hesp[2] to wind, Steenie. —Hem! hem! We maun go to business, Steenie; much to do, and little time to do it in."

Here he opened the fatal volume. I have heard of a thing they call Doomsday-book—I am clear it has been a rental 20 of back-ganging tenants.

"Stephen," said Sir John, still in the same soft, sleekit tone of voice—"Stephen Stevenson, or Steenson, ye are down here for a year's rent behind the hand—due at last term."

Stephen. "Please your honour, Sir John, I paid it to your 25 father."

Sir John. "Ye took a receipt then, doubtless, Stephen; and can produce it?"

Stephen. "Indeed I hadna time, an it like your honour; for nae sooner had I set doun the siller, and just as his 30 honour Sir Robert, that's gaen, drew it till him to count it, and write out the receipt, he was ta'en wi' the pains that removed him."

"That was unlucky," said Sir John, after a pause. "But ye maybe paid it in the presence of somebody. I want but 35

---

[1] wish.   [2] hasp, skein.

a *talis qualis*[1] evidence, Stephen. I would go ower strictly to work with no poor man."

Stephen. "Troth, Sir John, there was naebody in the room but Dougal MacCallum the butler. But, as your honour 5 kens, he has e'en followed his auld master."

"Very unlucky again, Stephen," said Sir John, without altering his voice a single note. "The man to whom ye paid the money is dead—and the man who witnessed the payment is dead too—and the siller, which should have been to the 10 fore, is neither seen nor heard tell of in the repositories. How am I to believe a' this?"

Stephen. "I dinna ken, your honour; but there is a bit memorandum note of the very coins; for, God help me! I had to borrow out of twenty purses; and I am sure that ilka 15 man there set down will take his grit oath for what purpose I borrowed the money."

Sir John. "I have little doubt ye *borrowed* the money, Steenie. It is the *payment* to my father that I want to have some proof of."

20 *Stephen.* "The siller maun be about the house, Sir John. And since your honour never got it, and his honour that was canna have ta'en it wi' him, maybe some of the family may have seen it."

Sir John. "We will examine the servants, Stephen; that 25 is but reasonable."

But lackey and lass, and page and groom, all denied stoutly that they had ever seen such a bag of money as my gudesire described. What was waur, he had unluckily not mentioned to any living soul of them his purpose of paying his rent. Ae 30 quean[2] had noticed something under his arm, but she took it for the pipes.

Sir John Redgauntlet ordered the servants out of the room, and then said to my gudesire, "Now, Steenie, ye see you have fair play; and, as I have little doubt ye ken better where to 35 find the siller than ony other body, I beg, in fair terms, and

---

[1] such as may be, reasonable.   [2] one young woman.

for your own sake, that you will end this fasherie[1]; for, Stephen, ye maun pay or flit."

"The Lord forgie your opinion," said Stephen, driven almost to his wit's end—"I am an honest man."

"So am I, Stephen," said his honour; "and so are all the 5 folks in the house, I hope. But if there be a knave amongst us, it must be he that tells the story he cannot prove." He paused, and then added, mair sternly, "If I understand your trick, sir, you want to take advantage of some malicious reports concerning things in this family, and particularly re- 10 specting my father's sudden death, thereby to cheat me out of the money, and perhaps take away my character, by insinuating that I have received the rent I am demanding.—Where do you suppose this money to be?—I insist upon knowing."

My gudesire saw every thing look sae muckle against him, 15 that he grew nearly desperate—however, he shifted from one foot to another, looked to every corner of the room and made no answer.

"Speak out, sirrah," said the Laird, assuming a look of his father's, a very particular ane, which he had when he was 20 angry—it seemed as if the wrinkles of his frown made that self-same fearful shape of a horse's shoe in the middle of his brow;—"Speak out, sir! I *will* know your thoughts;—do you suppose that I have this money?"

"Far be it frae me to say so," said Stephen.   25

"Do you charge any of my people with having taken it?"

"I wad be laith to charge them that may be innocent," said my gudesire; "and if there be any one that is guilty, I have nae proof."

"Somewhere the money must be, if there is a word of truth 30 in your story," said Sir John; "I ask where you think it is— and demand a correct answer?"

"In hell, if you *will* have my thoughts of it," said my gudesire, driven to extremity,—"in hell! with your father, his jackanape, and his silver whistle."   35

[1] annoyance, nonsense.

Down the stairs he ran, (for the parlour was nae place for him after such a word,) and he heard the Laird swearing blood and wounds behind him, as fast as ever did Sir Robert, and roaring for the bailie[1] and the baron-officer.

5   Away rode my gudesire to his chief creditor, (him they caa'd Laurie Lapraik,) to try if he could make ony thing out of him; but when he tauld his story, he got but the warst word in his wame—thief, beggar, and dyvour,[2] were the saftest terms; and to the boot of these hard terms, Laurie
10 brought up the auld story of his dipping his hand in the blood of God's saunts, just as if a tenant could have helped riding with the Laird, and that a laird like Sir Robert Redgauntlet. My gudesire was, by this time, far beyond the bounds of patience, and, while he and Laurie were at deil speed the
15 liars, he was wanchancie[3] aneugh to abuse Lapraik's doctrine as weel as the man, and said things that garr'd[4] folk's flesh grue[5] that heard them;—he wasna just himsell, and he had lived wi' a wild set in his day.

At last they parted, and my gudesire was to ride hame
20 through the wood of Pitmurkie, that is a' fou[6] of black firs, as they say.—I ken the wood, but the firs may be black or white for what I can tell.—At the entry of the wood there is a wild common, and on the edge of the common, a little lonely change-house,[7] that was keepit then by an ostler-wife,
25 they suld hae caa'd her Tibbie Faw, and there puir Steenie cried for a mutchkin[8] of brandy, for he had had no refreshment the haill day. Tibbie was earnest wi' him to take a bite of meat, but he couldna think o't, nor would he take his foot out of the stirrup, and took off the brandy wholely at twa
30 draughts, and named a toast at each:—the first was, the memory of Sir Robert Redgauntlet, and might he never lie quiet in his grave till he had righted his poor bond-tenant; and the second was, a health to Man's Enemy, if he would

---

[1] sheriff, magistrate.   [2] bankrupt.   [3] unlucky.   [4] made.
[5] creep.   [6] all full.   [7] alehouse, small inn, perhaps originally an inn where travelers changed horses.   [8] three quarters of an English pint.

but get him back the pock[1] of siller, or tell him what came o't, for he saw the haill world was like to regard him as a thief and a cheat, and he took that waur than even the ruin of his house and hauld.[2]

On he rode, little caring where. It was a dark night turned, and the trees made it yet darker, and he let the beast take its ain road through the wood; when, all of a sudden, from tired and wearied that it was before, the nag began to spring, and flee, and stend,[3] that my gudesire could hardly keep the saddle—Upon the whilk, a horseman, suddenly riding up beside him, said, "That's a mettle beast of yours, freend; will you sell him?"—So saying, he touched the horse's neck with his riding-wand, and it fell into its auld heigh-ho of a stumbling trot. "But his spunk's soon out of him, I think," continued the stranger, "and that is like mony a man's courage, that thinks he wad do great things till he come to the proof."

My gudesire scarce listened to this, but spurred his horse, with "Gude e'en to you, freend."

But it's like the stranger was ane that doesna lightly yield his point; for, ride as Steenie liked, he was aye beside him at the self-same pace. At last my gudesire, Steenie Steenson, grew half angry; and, to say the truth, half feared.

"What is it that ye want we me, freend?" he said. "If ye be a robber, I have nae money; if ye be a leal man, wanting company, I have nae heart to mirth or speaking; and if ye want to ken the road, I scarce ken it mysell."

"If you will tell me your grief," said the stranger, "I am one that, though I have been sair miscaa'd[4] in the world, am the only hand for helping my freends."

So my gudesire, to ease his ain heart, mair than from any hope of help, told him the story from beginning to end.

"It's a hard pinch," said the stranger; "but I think I can help you."

---

[1] poke, bag.
[2] hold, holding.
[3] twist, take long steps.
[4] sorely abused.

"If you could lend the money, sir, and take a lang day—
I ken nae other help on earth," said my gudesire.

"But there may be some under the earth," said the stranger.
"Come, I'll be frank wi' you; I could lend you the money
5 on bond, but you would maybe scruple my terms. Now, I
can tell you, that your auld Laird is disturbed in his grave
by your curses, and the wailing of your family, and if ye daur
venture to go to see him, he will give you the receipt."

My gudesire's hair stood on end at this proposal, but he
10 thought his companion might be some humoursome chield
that was trying to frighten him, and might end with lending
him the money. Besides, he was bauld wi' brandy, and
desperate wi' distress; and he said, he had courage to go
to the gate of hell, and a step farther, for that receipt.—The
15 stranger laughed.

Weel, they rode on through the thickest of the wood, when,
all of a sudden, the horse stopped at the door of a great
house; and, but that he knew the place was ten miles off,
my father would have thought he was at Redgauntlet Castle.
20 They rode into the outer court-yard, through the muckle
faulding yetts,[1] and aneath the auld portcullis; and the whole
front of the house was lighted, and there were pipes and
fiddles, and as much dancing and deray[2] within as used to
be in Sir Robert's house at Pace[3] and Yule,[4] and such high
25 seasons. They lap off, and my gudesire, as seemed to him,
fastened his horse to the very ring he had tied him to that
morning, when he gaed to wait on the young Sir John.

"God!" said my gudesire, "if Sir Robert's death be but a
dream!"

30 He knocked at the ha' door just as he was wont, and his
auld acquaintance, Dougal MacCallum,—just after his wont,
too,—came to open the door, and said, "Piper Steenie, are
ye there, lad? Sir Robert has been crying for you."

My gudesire was like a man in a dream—he looked for

---

[1] many folding gates.   [3] Easter.
[2] disturbance, disorderly merriment.   [4] Christmas.

the stranger, but he was gane for the time. At last he just tried to say, "Ha! Dougal Driveower, are ye living? I thought ye had been dead."

"Never fash[1] yoursell wi' me," said Dougal, "but look to yoursell; and see ye tak naething frae onybody here, neither meat, drink, or siller, except just the receipt that is your ain."

So saying, he led the way out through halls and trances[2] that were weel kend to my gudesire, and into the auld oak parlour; and there was as much singing of profane sangs, and birling[3] of red wine, and speaking blasphemy and sculduddry, as had ever been in Redgauntlet Castle when it was at the blithest.

But, Lord take us in keeping! what a set of ghastly revellers they were that sat round that table!—My gudesire kend mony that had long before gane to their place, for often had he piped to the most part in the hall of Redgauntlet. There was the fierce Middleton, and the dissolute Rothes, and the crafty Lauderdale; and Dalyell, with his bald head and a beard to his girdle; and Earlshall, with Cameron's blude on his hand; and wild Bonshaw, that tied blessed Mr. Cargill's limbs till the blude sprang; and Dunbarton Douglas, the twice-turned traitor baith to country and king. There was the Bluidy Advocate MacKenyie, who, for his worldly wit and wisdom, had been to the rest as a god. And there was Claverhouse, as beautiful as when he lived, with his long, dark, curled locks, streaming down over his laced buff-coat, and his left hand always on his right spule[4]-blade, to hide the wound that the silver bullet had made. He sat apart from them all, and looked at them with a melancholy, haughty countenance; while the rest hallooed, and sung, and laughed, that the room rang. But their smiles were fearfully contorted from time to time; and their laughter passed into such wild sounds, as made my gudesire's very nails grow blue, and chilled the marrow in his banes.

---

[1] trouble, bother.
[2] passageways.
[3] drinking, carousing.
[4] shoulder.

They that waited at the table were just the wicked serving-
men and troopers, that had done their work and cruel bidding
on earth. There was the Lang Lad of the Nethertown, that
helped to take Argyle; and the Bishop's summoner, that they
5 called the Deil's Rattle-bag; and the wicked guardsmen, in
their laced coats; and the savage Highland Amorites, that
shed blood like water; and many a proud serving-man,
haughty of heart and bloody of hand, cringing to the rich,
and making them wickeder than they would be; grinding the
10 poor to powder, when the rich had broken them to fragments.
And mony, mony mair were coming and ganging, a' as busy
in their vocation as if they had been alive.

Sir Robert Redgauntlet, in the midst of a' this fearful riot,
cried, wi' a voice like thunder, on Steenie Piper, to come to
15 the board-head where he was sitting; his legs stretched out
before him, and swathed up with flannel, with his holster
pistols aside him, while the great broadsword rested against
his chair, just as my gudesire had seen him the last time
upon earth—the very cushion for the jackanape was close to
20 him, but the creature itsell was not there—it wasna its hour,
it's likely; for he heard them say as he came forward, "Is not
the Major come yet?" And another answered, "The jackanape will be here betimes the morn." And when my gudesire
came forward, Sir Robert, or his ghaist, or the deevil in his
25 likeness, said, "Weel, piper, hae ye settled wi' my son for the
year's rent?"

With much ado my father gat breath to say, that Sir John
would not settle without his honour's receipt.

"Ye shall hae that for a tune of the pipes, Steenie," said
30 the appearance of Sir Robert—"Play us up 'Weel hoddled,[1]
Luckie.[2]'"

Now this was a tune my gudesire learned frae a warlock,
that heard it when they were worshipping Satan at their meetings; and my gudesire had sometimes played it at the ranting
35 suppers in Redgauntlet Castle, but never very willingly; and

---

[1] waddled.   [2] a title given to an elderly woman.

now he grew cauld at the very name of it, and said, for excuse, he hadna his pipes wi' him.

"MacCallum, ye limb of Beelzebub," said the fearfu' Sir Robert, "bring Steenie the pipes that I am keeping for him!"

MacCallum brought a pair of pipes might have served the piper of Donald of the Isles. But he gave my gudesire a nudge as he offered them; and looking secretly and closely, Steenie saw that the chanter was of steel, and heated to a white heat; so he had fair warning not to trust his fingers with it. So he excused himself again, and said, he was faint and frightened, and had not wind aneugh to fill the bag.

"Then ye maun eat and drink, Steenie," said the figure; "for we do little else here; and it's ill speaking between a fou man and a fasting."

Now these were the very words that the bloody Earl of Douglas said to keep the King's messenger in hand, while he cut the head off MacLellan of Bombie, at the Threave Castle; and that put Steenie mair and mair on his guard. So he spoke up like a man, and said he came neither to eat, or drink, or make minstrelsy; but simply for his ain—to ken what was come o' the money he had paid, and to get a discharge for it; and he was so stout-hearted by this time, that he charged Sir Robert for conscience-sake—(he had no power to say the holy name)—and as he hoped for peace and rest, to spread no snares for him, but just to give him his ain.

The appearance gnashed its teeth and laughed, but it took from a large pocket-book the receipt, and handed it to Steenie. "There is your receipt, ye pitiful cur; and for the money, my dog-whelp of a son may go look for it in the Cat's Cradle."

My gudesire uttered mony thanks, and was about to retire, when Sir Robert roared aloud, "Stop though, thou sack-doudling[1] son of a whore! I am not done with thee. HERE we do nothing for nothing; and you must return on this very day twelvemonth, to pay your master the homage that you owe me for my protection."

[1] bag-pipe playing.

My father's tongue was loosed of a suddenty, and he said aloud, "I refer mysell to God's pleasure, and not to yours."

He had no sooner uttered the word than all was dark around him; and he sunk on the earth with such a sudden shock, that he lost both breath and sense.

How lang Steenie lay there, he could not tell; but when he came to himsell, he was lying in the auld kirkyard[1] of Redgauntlet parochine[2] just at the door of the family aisle, and the scutcheon[3] of the auld knight, Sir Robert, hanging over his head. There was a deep morning fog on grass and gravestane around him, and his horse was feeding quietly beside the minister's twa cows. Steenie would have thought the whole was a dream, but he had the receipt in his hand, fairly written and signed by the auld Laird; only the last letters of his name were a little disorderly, written like one seized with sudden pain.

Sorely troubled in his mind, he left that dreary place, rode through the mist to Redgauntlet Castle, and with much ado he got speech of the Laird.

"Well, you dyvour bankrupt," was the first word, "have you brought me my rent?"

"No," answered my gudesire, "I have not; but I have brought your honour Sir Robert's receipt for it."

"How, sirrah?—Sir Robert's receipt!—You told me he had not given you one."

"Will your honour please to see if that bit line is right?"

Sir John looked at every line, and at every letter, with much attention; and at last, at the date, which my gudesire had not observed,—"*From my appointed place,*" he read, "*this twenty-fifth of November.*"—"What!—That is yesterday!—Villain, thou must have gone to hell for this!"

"I got it from your honour's father—whether he be in heaven or hell, I know not," said Steenie.

---

[1] churchyard, cemetery.   [2] parish.   [3] escutcheon, shield with armorial bearings.

"I will delate[1] you for a warlock to the Privy Council!"
said Sir John. "I will send you to your master, the devil,
with the help of a tar-barrel and a torch!"

"I intend to delate mysell to the Presbytery," said Steenie,
"and tell them all I have seen last night, whilk are things 5
fitter for them to judge of than a borrel[2] man like me."

Sir John paused, composed himsell, and desired to hear
the full history; and my gudesire told it him from point to
point, as I have told it you—word for word, neither more
nor less. 10

Sir John was silent again for a long time, and at last he
said, very composedly, "Steenie, this story of yours concerns
the honour of many a noble family besides mine; and if it
be a leasing-making,[3] to keep yourself out of my danger, the
least you can expect is to have a redhot iron driven through 15
your tongue, and that will be as bad as scauding your fingers
with a redhot chanter. But yet it may be true, Steenie; and
if the money cast up, I shall not know what to think of it.—
But where shall we find the Cat's Cradle? There are cats
enough about the old house, but I think they kitten without 20
the ceremony of bed or cradle."

"We were best ask Hutcheon," said my gudesire; "he
kens a' the odd corners about as weel as—another serving-
man that is now gane, and that I wad not like to name."

Aweel, Hutcheon, when he was asked, told them, that a 25
ruinous turret, lang disused, next to the clock-house, only
accessible by a ladder, for the opening was on the outside,
and far above the battlements, was called of old the Cat's
Cradle.

"There will I go immediately," said Sir John; and he took 30
(with what purpose, Heaven kens) one of his father's pistols
from the hall-table, where they had lain since the night he
died, and hastened to the battlements.

It was a dangerous place to climb, for the ladder was auld
and frail, and wanted ane or twa rounds. However, up got 35

[1] accuse. [2] rough, common. [3] slander.

Sir John, and entered at the turret door, where his body stopped the only little light that was in the bit turret. Something flees at him wi' a vengeance, maist dang him back ower —bang gaed the knight's pistol, and Hutcheon, that held the
5 ladder, and my gudesire that stood beside him, hears a loud skelloch.[1] A minute after, Sir John flings the body of the jackanape down to them, and cries that the siller is fund, and that they should come up and help him. And there was the bag of siller sure aneugh, and mony orra things besides, that
10 had been missing for mony a day. And Sir John, when he had riped[2] the turret weel, led my gudesire into the dining-parlour, and took him by the hand, and spoke kindly to him, and said he was sorry he should have doubted his word, and that he would hereafter be a good master to him, to make
15 amends.

"And now, Steenie," said Sir John, "although this vision of yours tends, on the whole, to my father's credit, as an honest man, that he should, even after his death, desire to see justice done to a poor man like you, yet you are sensible
20 that ill-dispositioned men might make bad constructions upon it, concerning his soul's health. So, I think, we had better lay the haill dirdum[3] on that ill-deedie[4] creature, Major Weir, and say naething about your dream in the wood of Pitmurkie. You had taken ower muckle brandy to be very
25 certain about onything; and, Steenie, this receipt," (his hand shook while he held it out,)—"it's but a queer kind of document, and we will do best, I think, to put it quietly in the fire."

"Od, but for as queer as it is, it's a' the voucher I have for
30 my rent," said my gudesire, who was afraid, it may be, of losing the benefit of Sir Robert's discharge.

"I will bear the contents to your credit in the rental-book, and give you a discharge under my own hand," said Sir John, "and that on the spot. And, Steenie, if you can hold your

---

[1] scream.   [3] whole disturbance.
[2] searched.   [4] mischievous.

tongue about this matter, you shall sit, from this term downward, at an easier rent."

"Mony thanks to your honour," said Steenie, who saw easily in what corner the wind was; "doubtless I will be comformable to all your honour's commands; only I would willingly speak wi' some powerful minister on the subject, for I do not like the sort of soumons of appointment whilk your honour's father—"

"Do not call the phantom my father!" said Sir John, interrupting him.

"Weel, then, the thing that was so like him,"—said my gudesire; "he spoke of my coming back to him this time twelvemonth, and it's a weight on my conscience."

"Aweel, then," said Sir John, "if you be so much distressed in mind, you may speak to our minister of the parish; he is a douce[1] man, regards the honour of our family, and the mair that he may look for some patronage from me."

Wi' that, my gudesire readily agreed that the receipt should be burnt, and the Laird threw it into the chimney with his ain hand. Burn it would not for them, though; but away it flew up the lum,[2] wi' a lang train of sparks at its tail, and a hissing noise like a squib.

My gudesire gaed down to the manse, and the minister, when he had heard the story, said, it was his real opinion, that though my gudesire had gaen very far in tampering with dangerous matters, yet, as he had refused the devil's arles,[3] (for such was the offer of meat and drink,) and had refused to do homage by piping at his bidding, he hoped, that if he held a circumspect walk hereafter, Satan could take little advantage by what was come and gane. And, indeed, my gudesire, of his ain accord, long forswore baith the pipes and the brandy—it was not even till the year was out, and the fatal day passed, that he would so much as take the fiddle, or drink usquebaugh[4] or tippenny.[5]

---

[1] sensible, quiet. [2] chimney. [3] earnest money. [4] whisky.
[5] two-penny ale.

Sir John made up his story about the jackanape as he liked
himself; and some believe till this day there was no more in
the matter than the filching nature of the brute. Indeed,
ye'll no hinder some to threap,[1] that it was nane o' the Auld
5 Enemy that Dougal and my gudesire saw in the Laird's room,
but only that wanchancy creature, the Major, capering on
the coffin; and that, as to the blawing on the Laird's whistle
that was heard after he was dead, the filthy brute could do
that as weel as the Laird himsell, if no better. But Heaven
10 kens the truth, whilk first came out by the minister's wife,
after Sir John and her ain gudeman were baith in the moulds.
And then my gudesire, wha was failed in his limbs, but not in
his judgment or memory—at least nothing to speak of—was
obliged to tell the real narrative to his freends, for the credit
15 of his good name. He might else have been charged for a
warlock.

JANE AUSTEN

THE WATSONS

Chapter VI[2]

The change in Emma's home society and style of life, in
consequence of the death of one friend and the imprudence
of another, had indeed been striking. From being the first
20 object of hope and solicitude to an uncle who had formed her
mind with the care of a parent, and of tenderness to an aunt
whose amiable temper had delighted to give her every indulgence; from being the life and spirit of a house where all had
been comfort and elegance, and the expected heiress of an
25 easy independence, she was become of importance to no one
—a burden on those whose affections she could not expect, an
addition in a house already overstocked, surrounded by in-

---

[1] aver, assert.
[2] Reprinted by permission of D. Appleton & Company, publishers.

ferior minds, with little chance of domestic comfort, and as little hope of future support. It was well for her that she was naturally cheerful, for the change had been such as might have plunged weak spirits in despondence.

She was very much pressed by Robert and Jane to return with them to Croydon, and had some difficulty in getting a refusal accepted, as they thought too highly of their own kindness and situation to suppose the offer could appear in less advantageous light to anybody else. Elizabeth gave them her interest, though evidently against her own, in privately urging Emma to go.

"You do not know what you refuse, Emma," said she, "nor what you have to bear at home. I would advise you by all means to accept the invitation; there is always something lively going on at Croydon. You will be in company almost every day, and Robert and Jane will be very kind to you. As for me, I shall be no worse off without you than I have been used to be; but poor Margaret's disagreeable ways are new to *you*, and they would vex you more than you think for, if you stay at home."

Emma was, of course, uninfluenced, except to greater esteem for Elizabeth by such representations; and the visitors departed without her.

On the following day, as Emma and Elizabeth were in the best parlour, setting the sofa before the fire for their father to lie on, for a little change, they heard a carriage stopping at the garden gate; and a minute or two later Nanny showed in Mrs. Blake and her little boy, closely followed by Mr. Howard.

Charles was carrying a beautiful bunch of greenhouse flowers and, on seeing Emma, he ran eagerly forward, saying—

"I have brought you these flowers, ma'am, because you were so good as to dance with me. Lord Osborne gave me anything I liked for you, and cut some for you himself."

Emma blushed as she smiled and curtsied, and blushed

again as she advanced to receive her other visitors and present her sister to them.

They had often observed Elizabeth at balls, and had considered her handsome, but they had never before spoken to her, and were at once favourably impressed by her unaffected good-humour and pleasant manner. Before long they were conversing with almost as little formality as though they had been old friends. On questioning Emma, Mrs. Blake easily drew from her some account of her former life and, on learning her aunt's name, recollected having heard it mentioned by friends in a manner entirely agreeable to Emma's feelings.

Presently Mr. Watson came into the room, and although he was a good deal surprised at finding himself in company, as Mr. Howard at once came forward with a show of friendliness, he had not time to lose his temper.

He was a man of considerable information, and finding the present society entirely congenial to him, contributed not a little to the pleasure of the visit, even going so far as to show Charles a volume of coloured prints; and before taking leave, Mr. Howard had persuaded him to join him, with his three daughters, at dinner, on the following Thursday, promising to send the carriage for them, and assuring him of his return at an early hour.

On Margaret's coming in from the village, where she had gone on an errand, she was all amazement on learning the arrangement; and displeased her father by enquiring if Mr. Musgrave and Lord Osborne were to be present.

"Mr. Howard expressly said they were to be by themselves," he replied, with the importance of an invalid. "He took particular care to assure me that I should suffer as little fatigue as possible."

He was therefore by no means too well pleased when, on the appointed evening, shortly after they had assembled in the drawing-room at Wickstead, Lord Osborne and Mr. Musgrave were ushered in; and before any explanation could be vouchsafed him, dinner was announced.

Turning to Lord Osborne, Mr. Howard said—

"As I cannot very well, my lord, ask Mr. Watson to hand in his daughter, I must ask him to conduct Mrs. Blake; and I will lead with Miss Watson if you will be good enough to give your arm to Miss Emma Watson; while Mr. Musgrave takes in Miss Margaret."

This arrangement was agreeable to all, except Mr. Musgrave, who, had he been of greater sensibility, would have been embarrassed by Margaret's manner towards him; and, as it was, felt not a little irritated by her determination to consider his escort as a *personal compliment*, rather than as *inevitable* on his part.

He had long since tired of his fancy for her, which indeed had always been of the slightest; and now in his determination to free himself from her, did not hesitate to go beyond the limits of propriety, openly disregarding her, and entering into conversation with everyone else in preference to her. Greatly mortified, she would have sunk under this neglect but for the kindness of Mrs. Blake, who addressed her as often as possible; and even Lord Osborne, vaguely aware that there was something wanting in ease, observed to her across the table that the roads were monstrous wet when it rained.

In the meantime, his lordship had not been enjoying himself either, to any great extent; for Emma, having perceived a volume on the drawing-room table with which she was familiar, on finding herself placed beside her host at the dinner table, fell to discussing it with him with much sense and spirit; and from this proceeded to contrast her favourite authors and the merits of their respective works. As Lord Osborne had as little knowledge of literature as well might be, he was compelled, despite the kindly efforts of his host, to sit more or less in silence, trying to look as if he had not less in his head than might reasonably be expected.

Elizabeth was only too glad to share her partner with her sister, as she did not very well know what to say to him; and she enjoyed listening to their conversation, the more so as they repeatedly explained to her the situation, or the point, in question. Moreover, she could not help hoping that another future, far different to what she had feared for her young sister, might possibly be in store for her.

5   With dessert, Charles arrived on the scene, which created a diversion in Lord Osborne's favour, as he came to place himself between the latter and his dear Miss Emma Watson, and both joined in the endeavour to entertain him.

On the ladies withdrawing, Lord Osborne turned to
10 Mr. Watson and said—

"You have a very beautiful daughter, sir," but he received in reply such a chilling bow that he could find nothing more to say; and Tom Musgrave nearly choked himself over his wine in the effort to control his merriment at his friend's
15 discomfiture. Mr. Howard then placed himself at the other side of Mr. Watson, and speedily restored him to good-humour by discussing the late visitation with him.

They were not long in returning to the drawing-room for tea; and shortly after, Mrs. Blake and Mr. Watson began to
20 play the new game of écarté,[1] proposing to one another with a pleasant air; whilst the others, seating themselves round the larger table, started vingt-un.[2]

They had scarcely commenced, however, when a carriage drove up to the door, and Miss Osborne and Miss Carr were
25 shown in.

"Oh, Mr. Howard! how could you have used us so?" cried Miss Osborne archly. "I protest we are vastly offended with you!—to give a party and leave us out!"

Miss Carr joined in, in the same strain. She had never
30 heard of anything so perfidious—it was really beyond everything she had ever known in all her life!

Mr. Howard received them with the quiet courtesy that was habitual to him; and when he deemed it possible to make

---

[1] (ā kär tā') a game of cards for two players.
[2] short for *vingt et un* (văn tā ûn'), twenty-one, a game which may be played by two or more.

his voice heard, expressed his sense of the honour they had
done him; but observed that one family was scarcely a party,
adding that Lord Osborne and Mr. Musgrave had been good
enough to invite themselves.

Lord Osborne remained silent, looking rather ashamed; 5
but Mr. Tom Musgrave protested vigorously that if Howard
were such a sly dog, plotting to cut them out like this, they
were bound to look after themselves!

The Miss Watsons and their father having been presented,
and tea declined, and Miss Carr having, further, declared 10
that there was nothing she so doted on as vingt-un, the game
was once more started.

Miss Osborne at once took possession of the chair at
Mr. Howard's right hand, which had previously been occu-
pied by Emma; and just as he was about to request the latter 15
to accept the one at his left, he found it already secured by
Miss Carr. Lord Osborne, therefore, shared Emma with
Charles; and Tom Musgrave devoted himself assiduously to
Miss Carr. Presently he was heard endeavouring to per-
suade her to accept him as her cavalier at the next meet. 20
Unfortunately this reminded Charles of the stuffed fox, and
again he implored Emma to come and see it, adding—

"Lord Osborne will now ask you himself, ma'am—will you
not, Lord Osborne?"

Before he could reply, Emma had hastily excused herself; 25
but Miss Carr, leaning forward, said impertinently—

"It is a pity you should not see the castle, Miss Watson;
it is thrown open to the public every Wednesday—all except
the private apartments."

Emma coloured and made no reply; but Lord Osborne 30
quite shocked his sister and her friend by saying—

"Lady Osborne will wait on Miss Watson."

Miss Osborne stared at her brother, but there was something in his face that compelled her to lower her eyes. Never
before had he so asserted himself, and she had not deemed 35
him capable of it.

At the conclusion of the game, Mr. Watson asked to return home—declining to wait for supper—and took leave with his daughters.

Mr. Howard conducted them to the carriage, and as
5 Emma curtsied in passing him, held out his hand to her, and retaining hers for a moment, thanked her in a low tone for the honour she had done him in coming.

CHARLES LAMB

ESSAYS OF ELIA

A Dissertation upon Roast Pig

Mankind, says a Chinese manuscript, which my friend M. was obliging enough to read and explain to me, for the first
10 seventy thousand ages ate their meat raw, clawing or biting it from the living animal, just as they do in Abyssinia to this day. This period is not obscurely hinted at by their great Confucius in the second chapter of his Mundane Mutations,[1] where he designates a kind of golden age by the term Cho-
15 fang, literally the Cook's holiday. The manuscript goes on to say, that the art of roasting, or rather broiling (which I take to be the elder brother), was accidentally discovered in the manner following. The swine-herd, Ho-ti, having gone out into the woods one morning, as his manner was, to collect
20 mast for his hogs, left his cottage in the care of his eldest son Bo-bo, a great lubberly boy, who being fond of playing with fire, as younkers of his age commonly are, let some sparks escape into a bundle of straw, which kindling quickly, spread the conflagration over every part of their poor mansion, till
25 it was reduced to ashes. Together with the cottage (a sorry antediluvian makeshift of a building, you may think it), what was of much more importance, a fine litter of new-farrowed pigs, no less than nine in number, perished. China

[1] earthly changes.

pigs have been esteemed a luxury all over the East from the
remotest periods that we read of. Bo-bo was in the utmost
consternation, as you may think, not so much for the sake
of the tenement, which his father and he could easily build
up again with a few dry branches, and the labour of an hour 5
or two, at any time, as for the loss of the pigs. While he was
thinking what he should say to his father, and wringing his
hands over the smoking remnants of one of those untimely
sufferers, an odour assailed his nostrils, unlike any scent
which he had before experienced. What could it proceed 10
from?—not from the burnt cottage—he had smelt that smell
before—indeed this was by no means the first accident of the
kind which had occurred through the negligence of this unlucky young firebrand. Much less did it resemble that of
any known herb, weed, or flower. A premonitory moistening 15
at the same time overflowed his nether lip. He knew not
what to think. He next stooped down to feel the pig, if there
were any signs of life in it. He burnt his fingers, and to cool
them he applied them in his booby fashion to his mouth.
Some of the crumbs of the scorched skin had come away with 20
his fingers, and for the first time in his life (in the world's
life indeed, for before him no man had known it) he tasted—
crackling! Again he felt and fumbled at the pig. It did not
burn him so much now, still he licked his fingers from a sort
of habit. The truth at length broke into his slow understand- 25
ing, that it was the pig that smelt so, and the pig that tasted
so delicious; and, surrendering himself up to the new-born
pleasure, he fell to tearing up whole handfuls of the scorched
skin with the flesh next it, and was cramming it down his
throat in his beastly fashion, when his sire entered amid the 30
smoking rafters, armed with retributory cudgel, and finding
how affairs stood, began to rain blows upon the young rogue's
shoulders, as thick as hail-stones, which Bo-bo heeded not
any more than if they had been flies. The tickling pleasure,
which he experienced in his lower regions, had rendered him 35
quite callous to any inconveniences he might feel in those

remote quarters. His father might lay on, but he could not beat him from his pig, till he had fairly made an end of it, when, becoming a little more sensible of his situation, something like the following dialogue ensued.

5 "You graceless whelp, what have you got there devouring? Is it not enough that you have burnt me down three houses with your dog's tricks, and be hanged to you, but you must be eating fire, and I know not what—what have you got there, I say?"

10 "O father, the pig, the pig, do come and taste how nice the burnt pig eats."

The ears of Ho-ti tingled with horror. He cursed his son, and he cursed himself that ever he should beget a son that should eat burnt pig.

15 Bo-bo, whose scent was wonderfully sharpened since morning, soon raked out another pig, and fairly rending it asunder, thrust the lesser half by main force into the fists of Ho-ti, still shouting out, "Eat, eat, eat the burnt pig, father, only taste,—O Lord,"—with such-like barbarous ejaculations,
20 cramming all the while as if he would choke.

Ho-ti trembled in every joint while he grasped the abominable thing, wavering whether he should not put his son to death for an unnatural young monster, when the crackling scorching his fingers, as it had done his son's, and applying
25 the same remedy to them, he in his turn tasted some of its flavour, which, make what sour mouths he would for a pretence, proved not altogether displeasing to him. In conclusion (for the manuscript here is a little tedious) both father and son fairly sat down to the mess, and never left off till
30 they had despatched all that remained of the litter.

Bo-bo was strictly enjoined not to let the secret escape, for the neighbours would certainly have stoned them for a couple of abominable wretches, who could think of improving upon the good meat which God had sent them. Never-
35 theless, strange stories got about. It was observed that Ho-ti's cottage was burnt down now more frequently than

ever. Nothing but fires from this time forward. Some would break out in broad day, others in the night-time. As often as the sow farrowed, so sure was the house of Ho-ti to be in a blaze; and Ho-ti himself, which was the more remarkable, instead of chastising his son, seemed to grow more indulgent 5 to him than ever. At length they were watched, the terrible mystery discovered, and father and son summoned to take their trial at Pekin, then an inconsiderable assize town.[1] Evidence was given, the obnoxious food itself produced in court, and verdict about to be pronounced, when the foreman of 10 the jury begged that some of the burnt pig, of which the culprits stood accused, might be handed into the box. He handled it, and they all handled it, and burning their fingers, as Bo-bo and his father had done before them, and nature prompting to each of them the same remedy, against the face 15 of all the facts, and the clearest charge which judge had ever given,—to the surprise of the whole court, townsfolk, strangers, reporters, and all present—without leaving the box, or any manner of consultation whatever, they brought in a simultaneous verdict of Not Guilty.   20

The judge, who was a shrewd fellow, winked at the manifest iniquity of the decision; and, when the court was dismissed, went privily, and bought up all the pigs that could be had for love or money. In a few days his Lordship's town house was observed to be on fire. The thing took wing, and 25 now there was nothing to be seen but fires in every direction. Fuel and pigs grew enormously dear all over the district. The insurance offices one and all shut up shop. People built slighter and slighter every day, until it was feared that the very science of architecture would in no long time be lost to 30 the world. Thus this custom of firing houses continued, till in process of time, says my manuscript, a sage arose, like our Locke, who made a discovery, that the flesh of swine, or indeed of any other animal, might be cooked (*burnt*, as they called it) without the necessity of consuming a whole house 35

[1] county seat, town where trials by jury are held.

to dress it. Then first began the rude form of a gridiron. Roasting by the string, or spit, came in a century or two later, I forget in whose dynasty. By such slow degrees, concludes the manuscript, do the most useful, and seemingly the
5 most obvious arts, make their way among mankind.——

Without placing too implicit faith in the account above given, it must be agreed, that if a worthy pretext for so dangerous an experiment as setting houses on fire (especially in these days) could be assigned in favour of any culinary
10 object, that pretext and excuse might be found in ROAST PIG.

Of all the delicacies in the whole *mundus edibilis*,[1] I will maintain it to be the most delicate—*princeps obsoniorum*.[2]

I speak not of your grown porkers—things between pig and pork—those hobbledehoys—but a young and tender suckling
15 —under a moon old—guiltless as yet of the sty—with no original speck of the *amor immunditiæ*,[3] the hereditary failing of the first parent, yet manifest—his voice as yet not broken, but something between a childish treble, and a grumble—the mild forerunner, or *præludium*,[4] of a grunt.

20 *He must be roasted.* I am not ignorant that our ancestors ate them seethed, or boiled—but what a sacrifice of the exterior tegument!

There is no flavour comparable, I will contend, to that of the crisp, tawny, well-watched, not over-roasted, *crackling*,
25 as it is well called—the very teeth are invited to their share of the pleasure at this banquet in overcoming the coy, brittle resistance—with the adhesive oleaginous—O call it not fat —but an indefinable sweetness growing up to it—the tender blossoming of fat—fat cropped in the bud—taken in the
30 shoot—in the first innocence—the cream and quintessence of the child-pig's yet pure food—the lean, no lean, but a kind of animal manna,—or, rather, fat and lean (if it must be so) so blended and running into each other, that both together make but one ambrosian result, or common substance.

---

[1] edible world.   [2] the chief of viands.   [3] love of uncleanness, the opposite of *munditia*; cf. p. 68.   [4] prelude.

Behold him, while he is "doing"—it seemeth rather a refreshing warmth, than a scorching heat, that he is so passive to. How equably he twirleth round the string!—Now he is just done. To see the extreme sensibility of that tender age, he hath wept out his pretty eyes—radiant jellies— 5 shooting stars—

See him in the dish, his second cradle, how meek he lieth! —wouldst thou have had this innocent grow up to the grossness and indocility which too often accompany maturer swinehood? Ten to one he would have proved a glutton, a 10 sloven, an obstinate, disagreeable animal—wallowing in all manner of filthy conversation—from these sins he is happily snatched away—

> Ere sin could blight, or sorrow fade,
> Death came with timely care—   15

his memory is odoriferous—no clown curseth, while his stomach half rejecteth, the rank bacon—no coalheaver bolteth him in reeking sausages—he hath a fair sepulchre in the grateful stomach of the judicious epicure—and for such a tomb might be content to die.   20

He is the best of sapors.[1] Pine-apple is great. She is indeed almost too transcendent—a delight, if not sinful, yet so like to sinning, that really a tender-conscienced person would do well to pause—too ravishing for mortal taste, she woundeth and excoriateth[2] the lips that approach her—like lovers' 25 kisses, she biteth—she is a pleasure bordering on pain from the fierceness and insanity of her relish—but she stoppeth at the palate—she meddleth not with the appetite—and the coarsest hunger might barter her consistently for a mutton chop.   30

Pig—let me speak his praise—is no less provocative of the appetite, than he is satisfactory to the criticalness of the censorious palate. The strong man may batten on him, and the weakling refuseth not his mild juices.

[1] savors, flavors.   [2] abrades, takes off the skin.

Unlike to mankind's mixed characters, a bundle of virtues and vices, inexplicably intertwisted, and not to be unravelled without hazard, he is—good throughout. No part of him is better or worse than another. He helpeth, as far as his little
5 means extend, all around. He is the least envious of banquets. He is all neighbours' fare.

I am one of those, who freely and ungrudgingly impart a share of the good things of this life which fall to their lot (few as mine are in this kind) to a friend. I protest I take as
10 great an interest in my friend's pleasures, his relishes, and proper satisfactions, as in mine own. "Presents," I often say, "endear Absents." Hares, pheasants, partridges, snipes, barn-door chickens (those "tame villatic[1] fowl"), capons, plovers, brawn,[2] barrels of oysters, I dispense as freely as I receive
15 them. I love to taste them, as it were, upon the tongue of my friend. But a stop must be put somewhere. One would not, like Lear, "give everything." I make my stand upon pig. Methinks it is an ingratitude to the Giver of all good flavours, to extradomiciliate, or send out of the house, slightingly (un-
20 der pretext of friendship, or I know not what), a blessing so particularly adapted, predestined, I may say, to my individual palate.—It argues an insensibility.

I remember a touch of conscience in this kind at school. My good old aunt, who never parted from me at the end of a
25 holiday without stuffing a sweetmeat, or some nice thing into my pocket, had dismissed me one evening with a smoking plumcake, fresh from the oven. In my way to school (it was over London Bridge) a grey-headed old beggar saluted me (I have no doubt at this time of day that he was a counter-
30 feit). I had no pence to console him with, and in the vanity of self-denial, and the very coxcombry of charity, schoolboy-like, I made him a present of—the whole cake! I walked on a little, buoyed up, as one is on such occasions, with a sweet soothing of self-satisfaction; but before I had got to the end
35 of the bridge, my better feelings returned, and I burst into

---

[1] farmyard. [2] the flesh of the boar.

tears, thinking how ungrateful I had been to my good aunt, to go and give her good gift away to a stranger, that I had never seen before, and who might be a bad man for aught I knew; and then I thought of the pleasure my aunt would be taking in thinking that I—I myself, and not another—would 5 eat her nice cake—and what should I say to her the next time I saw her—how naughty I was to part with her pretty present —and the odour of that spicy cake came back upon my recollection, and the pleasure and the curiosity I had taken in seeing her make it, and her joy when she sent it to the oven, 10 and how disappointed she would feel that I had never had a bit of it in my mouth at last—and I blamed my impertinent spirit of alms-giving, and out-of-place hypocrisy of goodness, and above all I wished never to see the face again of that insidious, good-for-nothing, old grey imposter.   15

Our ancestors were nice in their method of sacrificing these tender victims. We read of pigs whipt to death with something of a shock, as we hear of any other obsolete custom. The age of discipline is gone by, or it would be curious to inquire (in a philosophical light merely) what effect this 20 process might have towards intenerating[1] and dulcifying[2] a substance, naturally so mild and dulcet as the flesh of young pigs. It looks like refining a violet. Yet we should be cautious, while we condemn the inhumanity, how we censure the wisdom of the practice. It might impart a gusto—   25

I remember an hypothesis, argued upon by the young students, when I was at St. Omer's, and maintained with much learning and pleasantry on both sides, "Whether, supposing that the flavour of a pig who obtained his death by whipping (*per flagellationem extremam*) superadded a pleas- 30 ure upon the palate of a man more intense than any possible suffering we can conceive in the animal, is man justified in using that method of putting the animal to death?" I forget the decision.

His sauce should be considered. Decidedly, a few bread 35

[1] making tender.   [2] sweetening.

crumbs, done up with his liver and brains, and a dash of mild
sage. But, banish, dear Mrs. Cook, I beseech you, the whole
onion tribe. Barbecue your whole hogs to your palate, steep
them in shalots, stuff them out with plantations of the rank
5 and guilty garlic; you cannot poison them, or make them
stronger than they are—but consider, he is a weakling—a
flower.

DREAM–CHILDREN: A REVERIE

Children love to listen to stories about their elders, when
they were children: to stretch their imagination to the con-
10 ception of a traditionary great-uncle, or grandame, whom
they never saw. It was in this spirit that my little ones
crept about me the other evening to hear about their great-
grandmother Field, who lived in a great house in Norfolk
(a hundred times bigger than that in which they and papa
15 lived) which had been the scene—so at least it was generally
believed in that part of the country—of the tragic incidents
which they had lately become familiar with from the ballad
of the Children in the Wood. Certain it is that the whole
story of the children and their cruel uncle was to be seen
20 fairly carved out in wood upon the chimney-piece of the great
hall, the whole story down to the Robin Redbreasts, till a
foolish rich person pulled it down to set up a marble one of
modern invention in its stead, with no story upon it. Here
Alice put out one of her dear mother's looks, too tender to be
25 called upbraiding. Then I went on to say, how religious and
how good their great-grandmother Field was, how beloved
and respected by everybody, though she was not indeed the
mistress of this great house, but had only the charge of it
(and yet in some respects she might be said to be the mistress
30 of it too) committed to her by the owner, who preferred living in a newer and more fashionable mansion which he had
purchased somewhere in the adjoining county; but still she
lived in it in a manner as if it had been her own, and kept

up the dignity of the great house in a sort while she lived, which afterwards came to decay, and was nearly pulled down, and all its old ornaments stripped and carried away to the owner's other house, where they were set up, and looked as awkward as if some one were to carry away the old tombs 5 they had seen lately at the Abbey, and stick them up in Lady C.'s tawdry gilt drawing-room. Here John smiled, as much as to say, "that would be foolish, indeed." And then I told how, when she came to die, her funeral was attended by a concourse of all the poor, and some of the gentry too, of 10 the neighbourhood for many miles round, to show their respect for her memory, because she had been such a good and religious woman; so good indeed that she knew all the Psaltery by heart, ay, and a great part of the Testament besides. Here little Alice spread her hands. Then I told 15 what a tall, upright, graceful person their great-grandmother Field once was: and how in her youth she was esteemed the best dancer—here Alice's little right foot played an involuntary movement, till upon my looking grave, it desisted—the best dancer, I was saying, in the county, till a cruel disease, 20 called cancer, came, and bowed her down with pain; but it could never bend her good spirits, or make them stoop, but they were still upright, because she was so good and religious. Then I told how she used to sleep by herself in a lone chamber of the great lone house; and how she believed that an appari- 25 tion of two infants was to be seen at midnight gliding up and down the great staircase near where she slept, but she said "those innocents would do her no harm"; and how frightened I used to be, though in those days I had my maid to sleep with me, because I was never half so good or religious as she 30 —and yet I never saw the infants. Here John expanded all his eyebrows and tried to look courageous. Then I told how good she was to all her grandchildren, having us to the great house in the holidays, where I in particular used to spend many hours by myself, in gazing upon the old busts of the 35 twelve Cæsars, that had been Emperors of Rome, till the

old marble heads would seem to live again, or I to be turned
into marble with them; how I could never be tired with
roaming about that huge mansion, with its vast empty rooms,
with their worn-out hangings, fluttering tapestry, and carved
5 oaken panels, with the gilding almost rubbed out—sometimes in the spacious old-fashioned gardens, which I had almost to myself, unless when now and then a solitary garden-
ing man would cross me—and how the nectarines and peaches
hung upon the walls, without my ever offering to pluck them,
10 because they were forbidden fruit, unless now and then,—
and because I had more pleasure in strolling about among the
old melancholy-looking yew-trees, or the firs, and picking up
the red berries, and the fir apples, which were good for nothing but to look at—or in lying about upon the fresh grass,
15 with all the fine garden smells around me—or basking in the
orangery, till I could almost fancy myself ripening too along
with the oranges and the limes in that grateful warmth—or in
watching the dace that darted to and fro in the fish-pond, at
the bottom of the garden, with here and there a great sulky
20 pike hanging midway down the water in silent state, as if it
mocked at their impertinent friskings,—I had more pleasure
in these busy-idle diversions than in all the sweet flavours of
peaches, nectarines, oranges, and such like common baits of
children. Here John slyly deposited back upon the plate a
25 bunch of grapes which, not unobserved by Alice, he had meditated dividing with her, and both seemed willing to relinquish
them for the present as irrelevant. Then in somewhat a more
heightened tone, I told how, though their great-grandmother
Field loved all her grandchildren, yet in an especial manner
30 she might be said to love their uncle, John L——, because he
was so handsome and spirited a youth, and a king to the
rest of us; and, instead of moping about in solitary corners,
like some of us, he would mount the most mettlesome horse
he could get, when but an imp no bigger than themselves,
35 and make it carry him half over the county in a morning,
and join the hunters when there were any out—and yet he

loved the old great house and gardens too, but had too much
spirit to be always pent up within their boundaries—and how
their uncle grew up to man's estate as brave as he was handsome, to the admiration of everybody, but of their great-
grandmother Field most especially; and how he used to 5
carry me upon his back when I was a lame-footed boy—for
he was a good bit older than me—many a mile when I could
not walk for pain;—and how in after-life he became lame-
footed too, and I did not always (I fear) make allowance
enough for him when he was impatient, and in pain, nor 10
remember sufficiently how considerate he had been to me
when I was lame-footed; and how when he died, though he
had not been dead an hour, it seemed as if he had died a
great while ago, such a distance there is betwixt life and
death; and how I bore his death as I thought pretty well at 15
first, but afterwards it haunted and haunted me; and though
I did not cry or take it to heart as some do, and as I think he
would have done if I had died, yet I missed him all day long,
and knew not till then how much I had loved him. I missed
his kindness, and I missed his crossness, and wished him to 20
be alive again, to be quarrelling with him (for we quarrelled
sometimes), rather than not have him again, and was as
uneasy without him, as he, their poor uncle, must have been
when the doctor took off his limb. Here the children fell
a-crying, and asked if their little mourning which they had 25
on was not for uncle John, and they looked up, and prayed
me not to go on about their uncle, but to tell them some
stories about their pretty dead mother. Then I told how for
seven long years, in hope sometimes, sometimes in despair,
yet persisting ever, I courted the fair Alice W———n; and, as 30
much as children could understand, I explained to them what
coyness, and difficulty, and denial meant in maidens—when
suddenly, turning to Alice, the soul of the first Alice looked
out at her eyes with such a reality of re-presentment, that I
became in doubt which of them stood there before me, or 35
whose that bright hair was; and while I stood gazing, both

the children gradually grew fainter to my view, receding, and still receding till nothing at last but two mournful features were seen in the uttermost distance, which, without speech, strangely impressed upon me the effects of speech: "We are 5 not of Alice, nor of thee, nor are we children at all. The children of Alice call Bartrum father. We are nothing; less than nothing, and dreams. We are only what might have been, and must wait upon the tedious shores of Lethe millions of ages, before we have existence, and a name"—and immedi-10 ately awaking, I found myself quietly seated in my bachelor arm-chair, where I had fallen asleep, with the faithful Bridget unchanged by my side—but John L. (or James Elia) was gone forever.

THOMAS DE QUINCEY

JOAN OF ARC

[Extracts]

What is to be thought of *her*? What is to be thought of the 15 poor shepherd girl from the hills and forests of Lorraine, that —like the Hebrew shepherd boy[1] from the hills and forests of Judea—rose suddenly out of the quiet, out of the safety, out of the religious inspiration, rooted in deep pastoral solitudes, to a station in the van of armies, and to the more perilous 20 station at the right hand of kings? The Hebrew boy inaugurated his patriotic mission by an *act*, by a victorious *act*, such as no man could deny. But so did the girl of Lorraine, if we read her story as it was read by those who saw her nearest. Adverse armies bore witness to the boy as no pretender ; but so 25 they did to the gentle girl. Judged by the voices of all who saw them *from a station of good will*, both were found true and loyal to any promises involved in their first acts. Enemies it was that made the difference between their subsequent for-

[1] David, who killed Goliath, the giant commander of the Philistines.

tunes. The boy rose to a splendour and a noonday prosperity, both personal and public, that rang through the records
of his people, and became a byword among his posterity for a
thousand years, until the sceptre was departing from Judah.
The poor, forsaken girl, on the contrary, drank not herself 5
from that cup of rest which she had secured for France. She
never sang together with the songs that rose in her native
Domrémy as echoes to the departing steps of invaders. She
mingled not in the festal dances at Vaucouleurs which celebrated in rapture the redemption of France. No! for her 10
voice was then silent; no! for her feet were dust. Pure, innocent, noble-hearted girl! whom, from earliest youth, ever
I believed in as full of truth and self-sacrifice, this was
amongst the strongest pledges for *thy* truth, that never once—
no, not for a moment of weakness—didst thou revel in the 15
vision of coronets and honour from man. Coronets for thee!
Oh, no! Honours, if they come when all is over, are for those
that share thy blood. Daughter of Domrémy, when the gratitude of thy king shall awaken, thou wilt be sleeping the sleep
of the dead. Call her, King of France, but she will not hear 20
thee. Cite her by the apparitors[1] to come and receive a robe
of honour, but she will be found *en contumace*.[2] When the
thunders of universal France, as even yet may happen, shall
proclaim the grandeur of the poor shepherd girl that gave up
all for her country, thy ear, young shepherd girl, will have 25
been deaf for five centuries. To suffer and to do, that was thy
portion in this life; that was thy destiny; and not for a moment was it hidden from thyself. Life, thou saidst, is short;
and the sleep which is in the grave is long; let me use that
life, so transitory, for the glory of those heavenly dreams des- 30
tined to comfort the sleep which is so long! This pure
creature—pure from every suspicion of even a visionary self-
interest, even as she was pure in senses more obvious—never
once did this holy child, as regarded herself, relax from her

---

[1] officers who attended judges or magistrates.
[2] in contumacy, in contempt of court.

belief in the darkness that was travelling to meet her. She
might not prefigure the very manner of her death; she saw
not in vision, perhaps, the aërial altitude of the fiery scaffold,
the spectators without end, on every road, pouring into
5 Rouen as to a coronation, the surging smoke, the volleying
flames, the hostile faces all around, the pitying eye that
lurked but here and there, until nature and imperishable
truth broke loose from artificial restraints—these might not
be apparent through the mists of the hurrying future. But
10 the voice that called her to death, *that* she heard for ever.

Great was the throne of France even in those days, and
great was He that sat upon it; but well Joanna knew that
not the throne, nor he that sat upon it, was for *her*; but, on
the contrary, that she was for *them*; not she by them, but
15 they by her, should rise from the dust. Gorgeous were the
lilies of France, and for centuries had the privilege to spread
their beauty over land and sea, until, in another century, the
wrath of God and man combined to wither them; but well
Joanna knew, early at Domrémy she had read that bitter
20 truth, that the lilies of France would decorate no garland for
her. Flower nor bud, bell nor blossom, would ever bloom
for *her*!

.   .   .   .

Domrémy stood upon the frontiers, and, like other frontiers, produced a *mixed* race, representing the *cis*[1] and the
25 *trans*.[2] A river (it is true) formed the boundary line at this
point—the river Meuse; and *that*, in old days, might have
divided the populations; but in these days it did not; there
were bridges, there were ferries, and weddings crossed from
the right bank to the left. Here lay two great roads, not so
30 much for travellers that were few, as for armies that were too
many by half. These two roads, one of which was the great
highroad between France and Germany, *decussated* at this
very point; which is a learned way of saying that they
formed a St. Andrew's Cross, or letter X. I hope the com-

[1] on this side of.   [2] across, on the other side of.

positor will choose a good large X; in which case the point of intersection, the *locus* of conflux and intersection for these four diverging arms, will finish the reader's geographical education, by showing him to a hair's-breadth where it was that Domrémy stood. These roads, so grandly situated, as great trunk arteries between two mighty realms, and haunted for ever by wars or rumours of wars, decussated (for anything I know to the contrary) absolutely under Joanna's bedroom window; one rolling away to the right, past M. D'Arc's old barn, and the other unaccountably preferring to sweep round that odious man's pig-sty to the left.

On whichever side of the border chance had thrown Joanna, the same love to France would have been nurtured. For it is a strange fact, noticed by M. Michelet and others, that the Dukes of Bar and Lorraine had for generations pursued the policy of eternal warfare with France on their own account, yet also of eternal amity and league with France in case anybody else presumed to attack her. Let peace settle upon France, and before long you might rely upon seeing the little vixen Lorraine flying at the throat of France. Let France be assailed by a formidable enemy, and instantly you saw a Duke of Lorraine insisting on having his own throat cut in support of France; which favour accordingly was cheerfully granted to him in three great successive battles: twice by the English, viz., at Crécy and Agincourt, once by the Sultan at Nicopolis.

This sympathy with France during great eclipses, in those that during ordinary seasons were always teasing her with brawls and guerilla inroads, strengthened the natural piety to France of those that were confessedly the children of her own house. The outposts of France, as one may call the great frontier provinces, were of all localities the most devoted to the Fleurs de Lys. To witness, at any great crisis, the generous devotion to these lilies of the little fiery cousin that in gentler weather was for ever tilting at the breast of France, could not but fan the zeal of France's legitimate daughters;

while to occupy a post of honour on the frontiers against an
old hereditary enemy of France would naturally stimulate
this zeal by a sentiment of martial pride, by a sense of danger
always threatening, and of hatred always smouldering. That
5 great four-headed road was a perpetual memento to patriotic
ardour. To say "This way lies the road to Paris, and that
other way to Aix-la-Chapelle; this to Prague, that to Vienna,"
nourished the warfare of the heart by daily ministrations of
sense. The eye that watched for the gleams of lance or hel-
10 met from the hostile frontier, the ear that listened for the
groaning of wheels, made the highroad itself, with its relations to centres so remote, into a manual of patriotic duty.

The situation, therefore, *locally*, of Joanna was full of profound suggestions to a heart that listened for the stealthy
15 steps of change and fear that too surely were in motion. But,
if the place were grand, the time, the burden of the time, was
far more so. The air overhead in its upper chambers was
hurtling with the obscure sound; was dark with sullen fer-
menting of storms that had been gathering for a hundred and
20 thirty years. The battle of Agincourt in Joanna's childhood
had reopened the wounds of France. Crécy and Poictiers,
those withering overthrows for the chivalry of France, had,
before Agincourt occurred, been tranquilised by more than
half a century; but this resurrection of their trumpet wails
25 made the whole series of battles and endless skirmishes take
their stations as parts in one drama. The graves that had
closed sixty years ago seemed to fly open in sympathy with
a sorrow that echoed their own. The monarchy of France
laboured in extremity, rocked and reeled like a ship fighting
30 with the darkness of monsoons. The madness of the poor
king (Charles VI), falling in at such a crisis, like the case of
women labouring in child-birth during the storming of a city,
trebled the awfulness of the time. Even the wild story of
the incident which had immediately occasioned the explosion
35 of this madness—the case of a man unknown, gloomy, and
perhaps maniacal himself, coming out of a forest at noonday,

laying his hand upon the bridle of the king's horse, checking him for a moment to say, "Oh, king, thou art betrayed," and then vanishing, no man knew whither, as he had appeared for no man knew what—fell in with the universal prostration of mind that laid France on her knees, as before the slow un- 5 weaving of some ancient prophetic doom. The famines, the extraordinary diseases, the insurrections of the peasantry up and down Europe—these were chords struck from the same mysterious harp; but these were transitory chords. There had been others of deeper and more ominous sound. The 10 termination of the Crusades, the destruction of the Templars, the Papal interdicts, the tragedies caused or suffered by the house of Anjou, and by the Emperor—these were full of a more permanent significance. But, since then, the colossal figure of feudalism was seen standing, as it were on tiptoe, at 15 Crécy, for flight from earth: that was a revolution unparalleled; yet *that* was a trifle by comparison with the more fearful revolutions that were mining below the Church. By her own internal schisms, by the abominable spectacle of a double Pope—so that no man, except through political bias, 20 could even guess which was Heaven's vicegerent, and which the creature of Hell—the Church was rehearsing, as in still earlier forms she had already rehearsed, those vast rents in her foundations which no man should ever heal.

These were the loftiest peaks of the cloudland in the skies 25 that to the scientific gazer first caught the colors of the *new* morning in advance. But the whole vast range alike of sweeping glooms overhead dwelt upon all meditative minds, even upon those that could not distinguish the tendencies nor decipher the forms. It was, therefore, not her own age alone, 30 as affected by its immediate calamities, that lay with such weight upon Joanna's mind, but her own age as one section in a vast mysterious drama, unweaving through a century back, and drawing nearer continually to some dreadful crisis. Cataracts and rapids were heard roaring ahead; and signs 35 were seen far back, by help of old men's memories, which answered secretly to signs now coming forward on the eye, even as locks answer to keys. It was not wonderful that in such a haunted solitude, with such a haunted heart, Joanna should see angelic visions, and hear angelic voices. These voices whispered to her for ever the duty, self-imposed, of delivering France. Five years she listened to these monitory voices with internal struggles. At length she could resist no longer. Doubt gave way; and she left her home for ever in order to present herself at the dauphin's court.

THE VICTORIAN AGE

ALFRED TENNYSON

SIR GALAHAD

My good blade carves the casques[1] of men,
   . My tough lance thrusteth sure,
My strength is as the strength of ten,
   Because my heart is pure.
The shattering trumpet shrilleth high,   5
   The hard brands[2] shiver on the steel,
The splinter'd spear-shafts crack and fly,
   The horse and rider reel;
They reel, they roll in clanging lists,[3]
   And when the tide of combat stands,   10
Perfume and flowers fall in showers,
   That lightly rain from ladies' hands.

How sweet are looks that ladies bend
   On whom their favours fall!
For them I battle to the end,   15
   To save from shame and thrall[4];
But all my heart is drawn above,
   My knees are bow'd in crypt and shrine;
I never felt the kiss of love,
   Nor maiden's hand in mine.   20
More bounteous aspects on me beam,
   Me mightier transports move and thrill;
So keep I fair thro' faith and prayer
   A virgin heart in work and will.

[1] helmets.   [2] swords.   [3] fields of knightly combat or tournament.
[4] slavery.

When down the stormy crescent goes,
 A light before me swims,
Between dark stems the forest glows,
 I hear a noise of hymns.
Then by some secret shrine I ride;
 I hear a voice, but none are there;
The stalls are void,[1] the doors are wide,
 The tapers burning fair.
Fair gleams the snowy altar-cloth,
 The silver vessels sparkle clean,
The shrill bell rings, the censer swings,
 And solemn chaunts resound between.

Sometimes on lonely mountain-meres[2]
 I find a magic bark.
I leap on board; no helmsman steers;
 I float till all is dark.
A gentle sound, an awful light!
 Three angels bear the Holy Grail:
With folded feet, in stoles[3] of white,
 On sleeping wings they sail.
Ah, blessed vision! blood of God!
 My spirit beats her mortal bars,
As down dark tides the glory slides,
 And starlike mingles with the stars.

When on my goodly charger borne
 Thro' dreaming towns I go,
The cock crows ere the Christmas morn,
 The streets are dumb with snow.
The tempest crackles on the leads,
 And, ringing, springs from brand and mail;
But o'er the dark a glory spreads,
 And gilds the driving hail.

---

[1] the seats in the choir are empty. [2] mountain lakes. [3] long loose garments.

I leave the plain, I climb the height;
　　No branchy thicket shelter yields;
But blessed forms in whistling storms
　　Fly o'er waste fens[1] and windy fields.

A maiden knight—to me is given   5
　　Such hope, I know not fear;
I yearn to breathe the airs of heaven
　　That often meet me here.
I muse on joy that will not cease,
　　Pure spaces clothed in living beams,   10
Pure lilies of eternal peace,
　　Whose odors haunt my dreams;
And, stricken by an angel's hand,
　　This mortal armour that I wear,
This weight and size, this heart and eyes,   15
　　Are touch'd, are turn'd to finest air.

The clouds are broken in the sky,
　　And thro' the mountain walls
A rolling organ-harmony
　　Swells up, and shakes and falls.   20
Then move the trees, the copses nod,
　　Wings flutter, voices hover clear:
"O just and faithful knight of God!
　　Ride on! the prize is near."
So pass I hostel,[2] hall,[3] and grange[4];   25
　　By bridge and ford, by park and pale,[5]
All-arm'd I ride, whate'er betide,
　　Until I find the Holy Grail.

---

[1] marshes.　　[2] inn.　　[3] palace, manor house.　　[4] farmhouse.
[5] fence, paling.

ULYSSES

It little profits that an idle king,
By this still hearth, among these barren crags,
Match'd with an aged wife, I mete[1] and dole
Unequal laws unto a savage race,
5   That hoard, and sleep, and feed, and know not me.
I cannot rest from travel; I will drink
Life to the lees: all times I have enjoy'd
Greatly, have suffer'd greatly, both with those
That loved me, and alone; on shore, and when
10   Thro' scudding drifts the rainy Hyades[2]
Vext the dim sea: I am become a name;
For always roaming with a hungry heart
Much have I seen and known; cities of men
And manners, climates, councils, governments,
15   Myself not least, but honor'd of them all;
And drunk delight of battle with my peers,
Far on the ringing plains of windy Troy.
I am a part of all that I have met;
Yet all experience is an arch wherethro'
20   Gleams that untravell'd world, whose margin fades
For ever and for ever when I move.
How dull it is to pause, to make an end,
To rust unburnish'd, not to shine in use!
As tho' to breathe were life. Life piled on life
25   Were all too little, and of one to me
Little remains: but every hour is saved
From that eternal silence, something more,
A bringer of new things; and vile it were
For some three suns to store and hoard myself,
30   And this gray spirit yearning in desire

---

[1] measure, allot.

[2] (hī'à dēz) a cluster of stars in the constellation Taurus. The ancients thought that when they rose with the sun they brought rain.

To follow knowledge, like a sinking star,
Beyond the utmost bound of human thought.
   This is my son, mine own Telemachus,
To whom I leave the sceptre and the isle,—
Well-loved of me, discerning to fulfil   5
This labor, by slow prudence to make mild
A rugged people, and thro' soft degrees
Subdue them to the useful and the good.
Most blameless is he, centred in the sphere
Of common duties, decent not to fail   10
In offices of tenderness, and pay
Meet adoration to my household gods,
When I am gone. He works his work, I mine.
   There lies the port; the vessel puffs her sail;
There gloom the dark, broad seas. My mariners,   15
Souls that have toil'd, and wrought, and thought with
    me,—
That ever with a frolic welcome took
The thunder and the sunshine, and opposed
Free hearts, free foreheads—you and I are old;
Old age hath yet his honour and his toil;   20
Death closes all: but something ere the end,
Some work of noble note, may yet be done,
Not unbecoming men that strove with Gods.
The lights begin to twinkle from the rocks;
The long day wanes; the slow moon climbs; the deep 25
Moans round with many voices. Come, my friends,
'Tis not too late to seek a newer world.
Push off, and sitting well in order smite
The sounding furrows; for my purpose holds
To sail beyond the sunset, and the baths   30
Of all the western stars, until I die.
It may be that the gulfs will wash us down;
It may be we shall touch the Happy Isles,
And see the great Achilles, whom we knew.
Tho' much is taken, much abides; and tho'   35

We are not now that strength which in old days
Moved earth and heaven, that which we are, we are;
One equal temper of heroic hearts,
Made weak by time and fate, but strong in will
5   To strive, to seek, to find, and not to yield.

THE REVENGE

A Ballad of the Fleet, 1591

At Flores in the Azores Sir Richard Grenville lay,
And a pinnace, like a flutter'd bird, came flying from far away:
"Spanish ships of war at sea! we have sighted fifty-three!"
Then sware Lord Thomas Howard: "'Fore God I am no
    coward;
10 But I cannot meet them here, for my ships are out of gear,
And the half my men are sick. I must fly, but follow quick.
We are six ships of the line; can we fight with fifty-three?"

Then spake Sir Richard Grenville: "I know you are no
    coward;
You fly them for a moment to fight with them again.
15 But I've ninety men or more that are lying sick ashore
I should count myself the coward if I left them, my Lord
    Howard,
To these Inquisition dogs and the devildoms of Spain."

So Lord Howard past away with five ships of war that day,
Till he melted like a cloud in the silent summer heaven;
20 But Sir Richard bore in hand all his sick men from the land
Very carefully and slow,
Men of Bideford in Devon,
And we laid them on the ballast down below;
For we brought them all aboard,
25 And they blest him in their pain, that they were not left to
    Spain,
To the thumbscrew and the stake, for the glory of the Lord.

He had only a hundred seamen to work the ship and to fight,
And he sail'd away from Flores till the Spaniard came in
    sight,
With his huge sea-castles heaving upon the weather bow.
"Shall we fight or shall we fly?
Good Sir Richard, tell us now,   5
For to fight is but to die!
There'll be little of us left by the time this sun be set."
And Sir Richard said again: "We be all good English men.
Let us bang these dogs of Seville, the children of the devil,
For I never turn'd my back upon Don or devil yet."   10

Sir Richard spoke, and he laugh'd, and we roared a hurrah,
    and so
The little Revenge ran on sheer into the heart of the foe,
With her hundred fighters on deck, and her ninety sick
    below;
For half of their fleet to the right and half to the left were
    seen,
And the little Revenge ran on thro' the long sea-lane between. 15

Thousands of their soldiers look'd down from their decks and
    laugh'd,
Thousands of their seamen made mock at the mad little craft
Running on and on, till delay'd
By their mountain-like San Philip that, of fifteen hundred
    tons,
And up-shadowing high above us with her yawning tiers of
    guns,   20
Took the breath from our sails, and we stay'd.

And while now the great San Philip hung above us like a
    cloud
Whence the thunderbolt will fall
Long and loud,
Four galleons drew away   25

From the Spanish fleet that day,
And two upon the larboard and two upon the starboard lay,
And the battle-thunder broke from them all.

But anon the great San Philip, she bethought herself and went,
5 Having that within her womb that had left her ill content;
And the rest they came aboard us, and they fought us hand to
hand,
For a dozen times they came with their pikes and musque-
teers,
And a dozen times we shook 'em off as a dog that shakes his
ears
When he leaps from the water to the land.

10 And the sun went down, and the stars came out far over the
summer sea,
But never a moment ceased the fight of the one and the
fifty-three.
Ship after ship, the whole night long, their high-built galleons
came,
Ship after ship, the whole night long, with her battle-thunder
and flame;
Ship after ship, the whole night long, drew back with her
dead and her shame.
15 For some were sunk and many were shatter'd, and so could
fight us no more—
God of battles, was ever a battle like this in the world before?

For he said, "Fight on! fight on!"
Tho' his vessel was all but a wreck;
And it chanced that, when half of the summer night was gone,
20 With a grisly wound to be drest he had left the deck,
But a bullet struck him that was dressing it suddenly dead,
And himself he was wounded again in the side and the head,
And he said, "Fight on! fight on!"

And the night went down, and the sun smiled out far over the
    summer sea,
And the Spanish fleet with broken sides lay round us all in a
    ring;
But they dared not touch us again, for they fear'd that we
    still could sting,
So they watch'd what the end would be.
And we had not fought them in vain,   5
But in perilous plight were we,
Seeing forty of our poor hundred were slain,
And half of the rest of us maim'd for life
In the crash of the cannonades and the desperate strife;
And the sick men down in the hold were most of them stark
    and cold,   10
And the pikes were all broken or bent, and the powder was
    all of it spent;
And the masts and the rigging were lying over the side;
But Sir Richard cried in his English pride:
"We have fought such a fight for a day and a night
As may never be fought again!   15
We have won great glory, my men!
And a day less or more
At sea or ashore,
We die—does it matter when?
Sink me the ship, Master Gunner—sink her, split her in
    twain!   20
Fall into the hands of God, not into the hands of Spain!"

And the gunner said, "Ay, ay," but the seamen made reply:
"We have children, we have wives,
And the Lord hath spared our lives.
We will make the Spaniard promise, if we yield, to let
    us go;   25
We shall live to fight again and to strike another blow."
And the lion there lay dying, and they yielded to the foe.

And the stately Spanish men to their flagship bore him then,
Where they laid him by the mast, old Sir Richard caught at
    last,
And they praised him to his face with their courtly foreign
    grace;
But he rose upon their decks, and he cried:
5 "I have fought for Queen and Faith like a valiant man and
    true;
I have only done my duty as a man is bound to do.
With a joyful spirit I, Sir Richard Grenville, die!"—
And he fell upon their decks, and he died.

And they stared at the dead that had been so valiant and
    true,
10 And had holden the power and glory of Spain so cheap
That he dared her with one little ship and his English few;
Was he devil or man? He was devil for aught they knew,
But they sank his body with honour down into the deep,
And they mann'd the Revenge with a swarthier alien crew,
15 And away she sail'd with her loss and long'd for her own;
When a wind from the lands they had ruin'd awoke from
    sleep,
And the water began to heave and the weather to moan,
And or ever that evening ended a great gale blew,
And a wave like the wave that is raised by an earthquake
    grew,
20 Till it smote on their hulls and their sails and their masts and
    their flags,
And the whole sea plunged and fell on the shot-shatter'd navy
    of Spain,
And the little Revenge herself went down by the island crags
To be lost evermore in the main.

WAGES

Glory of warrior, glory of orator, glory of song,
  Paid with a voice flying by to be lost on an endless sea—
Glory of Virtue, to fight, to struggle, to right the wrong—
  Nay, but she aim'd not at glory, no lover of glory she;
Give her the glory of going on, and still to be.   5

The wages of sin is death: if the wages of Virtue be dust,
  Would she have heart to endure for the life of the worm
    and the fly?
She desires no isles of the blest, no quiet seats of the just,
  To rest in a golden grove, or to bask in a summer sky:
Give her the wages of going on, and not to die.   10

THE HIGHER PANTHEISM

The sun, the moon, the stars, the seas, the hills and the
    plains—
Are not these, O Soul, the Vision of Him who reigns?

Is not the Vision He? tho' He be not that which he seems?
Dreams are true while they last, and do we not live in
    dreams?

Earth, these solid stars, this weight of body and limb,   15
Are they not sign and symbol of thy division from Him?

Dark is the world to thee; thyself art the reason why,
For is He not all but thou, that hast power to feel "I am I"?

Glory about thee, without thee; and thou fulfillest thy
    doom,
Making Him broken gleams, and a stifled splendour and
    gloom.   20

Speak to Him, thou, for He hears, and Spirit with Spirit can
    meet—
Closer is He than breathing, and nearer than hands and feet.

God is law, say the wise; O Soul, and let us rejoice,
For if He thunder by law the thunder is yet His voice.

5 Law is God, say some; no God at all, says the fool,
For all we have power to see is a straight staff bent in a pool;

And the ear of man cannot hear, and the eye of man cannot
    see;
But if we could see and hear, this Vision—were it not He?

FLOWER IN THE CRANNIED WALL

Flower in the crannied wall,
10   I pluck you out of the crannies;
Hold you here, root and all, in my hand,
    Little flower—but if I could understand
What you are, root and all, and all in all,
    I should know what God and man is.

HANDS ALL ROUND

15   First pledge our Queen this solemn night,
       Then drink to England, every guest;
    That man's the best Cosmopolite
       Who loves his native country best.
    May freedom's oak for ever live
20   With stronger life from day to day;
    That man's the true Conservative
       Who lops the moulder'd branch away.
              Hands all round!
       God the traitor's hope confound!
25   To this great cause of Freedom drink, my friends,
       And the great name of England, round and round.

To all the loyal hearts who long
  To keep our English Empire whole!
To all our noble sons, the strong
  New England of the Southern Pole!
To England under Indian skies,   5
  To those dark millions of her realm!
To Canada whom we love and prize,
  Whatever statesman hold the helm.
         Hands all round!
  God the traitor's hope confound!   10
To this great name of England drink, my friends,
  And all her glorious empire, round and round.

To all our statesmen so they be
  True leaders of the land's desire!
To both our Houses, may they see   15
  Beyond the borough and the shire!
We sail'd wherever ship could sail,
  We founded many a mighty state;
Pray God our greatness may not fail
  Thro' craven fears of being great!   20
         Hands all round!
  God the traitor's hope confound!
To this great cause of Freedom drink, my friends,
  And the great name of England, round and round.

MORTE D'ARTHUR

So all day long the noise of battle roll'd   25
Among the mountains by the winter sea,
Until King Arthur's table, man by man,
Had fallen in Lyonness about their Lord,
King Arthur: then, because his wound was deep,
The bold Sir Bedivere uplifted him,   30
Sir Bedivere, the last of all his knights,
And bore him to a chapel nigh the field,

A broken chancel with a broken cross,
That stood on a dark strait of barren land.
On one side lay the Ocean, and on one
Lay a great water, and the moon was full.
5   Then spake King Arthur to Sir Bedivere:
"The sequel of to-day unsolders all
The goodliest fellowship of famous knights
Whereof this world holds record. Such a sleep
They sleep—the men I loved. I think that we
10   Shall never more, at any future time,
Delight our souls with talk of knightly deeds,
Walking about the gardens and the halls
Of Camelot, as in the days that were.
I perish by this people which I made,—
15   Tho' Merlin sware that I should come again
To rule once more—but let what will be, be,
I am so deeply smitten thro' the helm
That without help I cannot last till morn.
Thou therefore take my brand Excalibur,
20   Which was my pride: for thou rememberest how
In those old days, one summer noon, an arm
Rose up from out the bosom of the lake,
Clothed in white samite, mystic, wonderful,
Holding the sword—and how I row'd across
25   And took it, and have worn it like a king:
And, wheresoever I am sung or told
In aftertime, this also shall be known:
But now delay not: take Excalibur,
And fling him far into the middle mere:
30   Watch what thou seest, and lightly[1] bring me word."
To him replied the bold Sir Bedivere:
"It is not meet, Sir King, to leave thee thus,
Aidless, alone, and smitten thro' the helm.
A little thing may harm a wounded man.

[1] swiftly.

Yet I thy hest[1] will all perform at full,
Watch what I see, and lightly bring thee word."
   So saying, from the ruin'd shrine he stept
And in the moon athwart the place of tombs,
Where lay the mighty bones of ancient men,   5
Old knights, and over them the sea-wind sang
Shrill, chill, with flakes of foam. He, stepping down
By zig-zag paths, and juts of pointed rock,
Came on the shining levels of the lake.
   There drew he forth the brand Excalibur,   10
And o'er him, drawing it, the winter moon,
Brightening the skirts of a long cloud, ran forth
And sparkled keen with frost against the hilt:
For all the haft twinkled with diamond sparks,
Myriads of topaz-lights, and jacinth-work   15
Of subtlest jewellery. He gazed so long
That both his eyes were dazzled, as he stood,
This way and that dividing the swift mind,
In act to throw: but at the last it seem'd
Better to leave Excalibur conceal'd   20
There in the many-knotted water-flags,
That whistled stiff and dry about the marge.
So strode he back slow to the wounded King.
   Then spake King Arthur to Sir Bedivere:
"Hast thou perform'd my mission which I gave?   25
What is it thou hast seen? or what hast heard?"
   And answer made the bold Sir Bedivere:
"I heard the ripple washing in the reeds,
And the wild water lapping on the crag."
   To whom replied King Arthur, faint and pale: 30
"Thou hast betray'd thy nature and thy name,
Not rendering true answer, as beseem'd
Thy fealty, nor like a noble knight:
For surer sign had follow'd, either hand,
Or voice, or else a motion of the mere.   35

[1] behest, command.

This is a shameful thing for men to lie.
Yet now, I charge thee, quickly go again,
As thou art lief[1] and dear, and do the thing
I bade thee, watch, and lightly bring me word."
5   Then went Sir Bedivere the second time
Across the ridge, and paced beside the mere,
Counting the dewy pebbles, fix'd in thought;
But when he saw the wonder of the hilt,
How curiously and strangely chased, he smote
10   His palms together, and he cried aloud:
"And if indeed I cast the brand away,
Surely a precious thing, one worthy note,
Should thus be lost forever from the earth,
Which might have pleased the eyes of many men.
15   What good should follow this, if this were done?
What harm, undone? deep harm to disobey,
Seeing obedience is the bond of rule.
Were it well to obey then, if a king demand
An act unprofitable, against himself?
20   The King is sick, and knows not what he does.
What record, or what relic of my lord
Should be to aftertime, but empty breath
And rumours of a doubt? but were this kept,
Stored in some treasure-house of mighty kings,
25   Some one might show it at a joust of arms,
Saying, 'King Arthur's sword, Excalibur,
Wrought by the lonely maiden of the lake.
Nine years she wrought it, sitting in the deeps
Upon the hidden bases of the hills.'
30   So might some old man speak in the aftertime
To all the people, winning reverence.
But now much honour and much fame were lost."
So spake he, clouded with his own conceit,
And hid Excalibur the second time,
35   And so strode back slow to the wounded King.

[1] beloved.

Then spoke King Arthur, breathing heavily:
"What is it thou hast seen? or what hast heard?"
  And answer made the bold Sir Bedivere:
"I heard the water lapping on the crag,
And the long ripple washing in the reeds."   5
  To whom replied King Arthur, much in wrath:
"Ah, miserable and unkind, untrue,
Unknightly, traitor-hearted! Woe is me!
Authority forgets a dying king,
Laid widow'd of the power in his eye   10
That bow'd the will. I see thee what thou art,
For thou, the latest-left of all my knights,
In whom should meet the offices of all,
Thou wouldst betray me for the precious hilt;
Either from lust of gold, or like a girl   15
Valuing the giddy pleasure of the eyes.
Yet, for a man may fail in duty twice,
And the third time may prosper, get thee hence:
But, if thou spare to fling Excalibur,
I will arise and slay thee with my hands."   20
  Then quickly rose Sir Bedivere, and ran,
And, leaping down the ridges lightly, plunged
Among the bulrush-beds, and clutch'd the sword,
And strongly wheel'd and threw it. The great brand
Made lightnings in the splendour of the moon,   25
And flashing round and round, and whirl'd in an arch,
Shot like a streamer of the northern morn,[1]
Seen where the moving isles of winter[2] shock
By night, with noises of the northern sea.
So flash'd and fell the brand Excalibur: 30
But ere he[3] dipt the surface, rose an arm
Clothed in white samite, mystic, wonderful,
And caught him by the hilt, and brandish'd him
Three times, and drew him under in the mere.
And lightly went the other to the King.   35

[1] Aurora Borealis.   [2] icebergs.   [3] the sword, Excalibur.

Then spoke King Arthur, drawing thicker breath:
"Now see I by thine eyes that this is done.
Speak out: what is it thou hast heard, or seen?"
And answer made the bold Sir Bedivere:
5   "Sir King, I closed mine eyelids, lest the gems
Should blind my purpose, for I never saw,
Nor shall see, here or elsewhere, till I die,
Not tho' I live three lives of mortal men,
So great a miracle as yonder hilt.
10   Then with both hands I flung him, wheeling him;
But when I look'd again, behold an arm,
Clothed in white samite, mystic, wonderful,
That caught him by the hilt, and brandish'd him
Three times, and drew him under in the mere."
15   And answer made King Arthur, breathing hard:
"My end draws nigh; 'tis time that I were gone.
Make broad thy shoulders to receive my weight,
And bear me to the margin; yet I fear
My wound hath taken cold, and I shall die."
20   So saying, from the pavement he half rose,
Slowly, with pain, reclining on his arm,
And looking wistfully with wide blue eyes
As in a picture. Him Sir Bedivere
Remorsefully regarded thro' his tears,
25   And would have spoken, but he found not words,
Then took with care, and kneeling on one knee,
O'er both his shoulders drew the languid hands,
And rising bore him thro' the place of tombs.
But, as he walk'd, King Arthur panted hard,
30   Like one that feels a nightmare on his bed
When all the house is mute. So sigh'd the King,
Muttering and murmuring at his ear, "Quick, quick!
I fear it is too late, and I shall die."
But the other swiftly strode from ridge to ridge,
35   Clothed with his breath, and looking, as he walk'd,
Larger than human on the frozen hills.

He heard the deep behind him, and a cry
Before. His own thought drove him, like a goad.
Dry clash'd his harness in the icy caves
And barren chasms, and all to left and right
The bare black cliff clang'd round him, as he based   5
His feet on juts of slippery crag that rang
Sharp-smitten with the dint of armèd heels—
And on a sudden, lo! the level lake,
And the long glories of the winter moon.

Then saw they how there hove a dusky barge,   10
Dark as a funeral scarf from stem to stern,
Beneath them; and descending they were ware
That all the decks were dense with stately forms
Black-stoled, black-hooded, like a dream—by these
Three Queens with crowns of gold—and from them rose 15
A cry that shiver'd to the tingling stars,
And, as it were one voice, an agony
Of lamentation, like a wind, that shrills
All night in a waste land, where no one comes,
Or hath come, since the making of the world.   20
Then murmur'd Arthur, "Place me in the barge,"
And to the barge they came. There those three Queens
Put forth their hands, and took the King, and wept.
But she, that rose the tallest of them all
And fairest, laid his head upon her lap,   25
And loosed the shatter'd casque, and chafed his hands,
And call'd him by his name, complaining loud,
And dropping bitter tears against his brow
Striped with dark blood: for all his face was white
And colourless, and like the wither'd moon   30
Smote by the fresh beam of the springing east;
And all his greaves[1] and cuisses[1] dash'd with drops
Of onset; and the light and lustrous curls—
That made his forehead like a rising sun
High from the dais-throne—were parch'd with dust;   35

[1] armor for the legs, below and above the knee.

Or, clotted into points and hanging loose,
Mix'd with the knightly growth that fringed his lips.
So like a shatter'd column lay the King;
Not like that Arthur who, with lance in rest,
5   From spur to plume a star of tournament,
Shot thro' the lists at Camelot, and charged
Before the eyes of ladies and of kings.
   Then loudly cried the bold Sir Bedivere:
"Ah! my Lord Arthur, whither shall I go?
10   Where shall I hide my forehead and my eyes?
For now I see the true old times are dead,
When every morning brought a noble chance,
And every chance brought out a noble knight.
Such times have been not since the light that led
15   The holy Elders[1] with the gift of myrrh.
But now the whole Round Table is dissolved
Which was an image of the mighty world;
And I, the last, go forth companionless,
And the days darken round me, and the years,
20   Among new men, strange faces, other minds."
   And slowly answered Arthur from the barge:
"The old order changeth, yielding place to new,
And God fulfils Himself in many ways,
Lest one good custom should corrupt the world.
25   Comfort thyself: what comfort is in me?
I have lived my life, and that which I have done
May He within Himself make pure! but thou,
If thou shouldst never see my face again,
Pray for my soul. More things are wrought by prayer
30   Than this world dreams of. Wherefore, let thy voice
Rise like a fountain for me night and day.
For what are men better than sheep or goats
That nourish a blind life within the brain,
If, knowing God, they lift not hands of prayer
35   Both for themselves and those who call them friend?

[1] the Wise Men from the East.

For so the whole round earth is every way
Bound by gold chains about the feet of God.
But now farewell. I am going a long way
With these thou seest—if indeed I go—
(For all my mind is clouded with a doubt)   5
To the island-valley of Avilion[1];
Where falls not hail, or rain, or any snow,
Nor ever wind blows loudly; but it lies
Deep-meadow'd, happy, fair with orchard-lawns
And bowery hollows crown'd with summer sea,   10
Where I will heal me of my grievous wound."
    So said he, and the barge with oar and sail
Moved from the brink, like some full-breasted swan
That, fluting a wild carol ere her death,
Ruffles her pure cold plume, and takes the flood   15
With swarthy webs. Long stood Sir Bedivere
Revolving many memories, till the hull
Look'd one black dot against the verge of dawn,
And on the mere the wailing died away.

BUGLE SONG

From *The Princess*

The splendour falls on castle walls   20
    And snowy summits old in story;
The long light shakes across the lakes,
    And the wild cataract leaps in glory.
Blow, bugle, blow, set the wild echoes flying,
Blow, bugle; answer, echoes, dying, dying, dying.   25

    O hark, O hear! how thin and clear,
        And thinner, clearer, farther, farther going!
    O sweet and far from cliff and scar
        The horns of Elfland faintly blowing!

[1] variation from Avalon; cf. p. 22.

Blow, let us hear the purple glens replying:
Blow, bugle; answer, echoes, dying, dying, dying.

O love, they die in yon rich sky,
   They faint on hill or field or river:
5   Our echoes roll from soul to soul,
   And grow for ever and for ever.
Blow, bugle, blow, set the wild echoes flying,
And answer, echoes, answer, dying, dying, dying.

IN MEMORIAM

[Proem]

Strong Son of God, immortal Love,
10   Whom we, that have not seen thy face,
   By faith, and faith alone, embrace,
Believing where we cannot prove;

Thine are these orbs of light and shade;
   Thou madest Life in man and brute;
15   Thou madest Death; and lo, thy foot
Is on the skull which thou hast made.

Thou wilt not leave us in the dust:
   Thou madest man, he knows not why,
   He thinks he was not made to die;
20   And thou hast made him: thou art just.

Thou seemest human and divine,
   The highest, holiest manhood, thou.
   Our wills are ours, we know not how;
Our wills are ours, to make them thine.

Our little systems have their day;
   They have their day and cease to be:
   They are but broken lights of thee,
And thou, O Lord, art more than they.

We have but faith: we cannot know,   5
   For knowledge is of things we see;
   And yet we trust it comes from thee,
A beam in darkness: let it grow.

Let knowledge grow from more to more,
   But more of reverence in us dwell;   10
   That mind and soul, according well,
May make one music as before,

But vaster. We are fools and slight;
   We mock thee when we do not fear:
   But help thy foolish ones to bear;   15
Help thy vain worlds to bear thy light.

Forgive what seem'd my sin in me,
   What seem'd my worth since I began;
   For merit lives from man to man,
And not from man, O Lord, to thee.   20

Forgive my grief for one removed,
   Thy creature, whom I found so fair.
   I trust he lives in thee, and there
I find him worthier to be loved.

Forgive these wild and wandering cries,   25
   Confusions of a wasted youth;
   Forgive them where they fail in truth,
And in thy wisdom make me wise.

ROBERT BROWNING

MY STAR

All that I know
  Of a certain star
Is, it can throw
  (Like the angled spar)
5 Now a dart of red,
  Now a dart of blue;
Till my friends have said
  They would fain see, too,
My star that dartles the red and the blue!
10 Then it stops like a bird: like a flower, hangs furled:
  They must solace themselves with the Saturn above it.
What matter to me if their star is a world?
  Mine has opened its soul to me; therefore I love it.

"HOW THEY BROUGHT THE GOOD NEWS FROM GHENT TO AIX"

[16—]

I sprang to the stirrup, and Joris, and he;
15 I galloped, Dirck galloped, we galloped all three;
  "Good speed!" cried the watch, as the gate-bolts undrew;
  "Speed!" echoed the wall to us galloping through;
Behind shut the postern, the lights sank to rest,
And into the midnight we galloped abreast.

20 Not a word to each other; we kept the great pace
  Neck by neck, stride by stride, never changing our place;
I turned in my saddle and made its girths tight,
  Then shortened each stirrup, and set the pique right,
Rebuckled the cheek-strap, chained slacker the bit,
25 Nor galloped less steadily Roland a whit.

'Twas moonset at starting; but while we drew near
Lokeren, the cocks crew and twilight dawned clear;
At Boom, a great yellow star came out to see;
At Düffeld, 'twas morning as plain as could be;
And from Mecheln church-steeple we heard the half-chime, 5
So, Joris broke silence with, "Yet there is time!"

At Aershot, up leaped of a sudden the sun,
And against him the cattle stood black every one,
To stare thro' the mist at us galloping past,
And I saw my stout galloper Roland at last,   10
With resolute shoulders, each butting away
The haze, as some bluff river headland its spray:

And his low head and crest, just one sharp ear bent back
For my voice, and the other pricked out on his track;
And one eye's black intelligence,—ever that glance   15
O'er its white edge at me, his own master, askance!
And the thick heavy spume-flakes which aye and anon
His fierce lips shook upwards in galloping on.

By Hasselt, Dirck groaned; and cried Joris "Stay spur!
Your Roos galloped bravely, the fault's not in her,   20
We'll remember at Aix"—for one heard the quick wheeze
Of her chest, saw the stretched neck and staggering knees,
And sunk tail, and horrible heave of the flank,
As down on her haunches she shuddered and sank.

So, we were left galloping, Joris and I,   25
Past Looz and past Tongres, no cloud in the sky;
The broad sun above laughed a pitiless laugh,
'Neath our feet broke the brittle bright stubble like chaff;
Till over by Dalhem a dome-spire sprang white,
And "Gallop," gasped Joris, "for Aix is in sight!"   30

"How they'll greet us!"—and all in a moment his roan
Rolled neck and croup over, lay dead as a stone;

And there was my Roland to bear the whole weight
Of the news which alone could save Aix from her fate,
With his nostrils like pits full of blood to the brim,
And with circles of red for his eye-sockets' rim.

5 Then I cast loose my buff-coat, each holster let fall,
Shook off both my jack-boots, let go belt and all,
Stood up in the stirrup, leaned, patted his ear,
Called my Roland his pet-name, my horse without peer;
Clapped my hands, laughed and sang, any noise, bad or good,
10 Till at length into Aix Roland galloped and stood.

And all I remember is,—friends flocking round
As I sat with his head 'twixt my knees on the ground;
And no voice but was praising this Roland of mine,
As I poured down his throat our last measure of wine,
15 Which (the burgesses voted by common consent)
Was no more than his due who brought good news from
Ghent.

HERVÉ RIEL

On the sea and the Hogue, sixteen hundred ninety-two,
Did the English fight the French,—woe to France!
And, the thirty-first of May, helter-skelter thro' the blue,
20 Like a crowd of frightened porpoises a shoal of sharks pursue,
Came crowding ship on ship to St. Malo on the Rance,
With the English fleet in view.

'Twas the squadron that escaped, with the victor in full
chase;
First and foremost of the drove, in his great ship, Damfreville;
25 Close on him fled, great and small,
Twenty-two good ships in all;

And they signalled to the place
"Help the winners of a race!
   Get us guidance, give us harbour, take us quick—or,
      quicker still,
   Here's the English can and will!"

Then the pilots of the place put out brisk and leapt on board; 5
   "Why, what hope or chance have ships like these to pass?"
      laughed they:
"Rocks to starboard, rocks to port, all the passage scarred
   and scored,
Shall the Formidable here with her twelve and eighty guns
   Think to make the river-mouth by the single narrow way,
Trust to enter where 'tis ticklish for a craft of twenty tons, 10
   And with flow at full beside?
   Now 'tis slackest ebb of tide.
   Reach the mooring? Rather say,
While rock stands or water runs,
   Not a ship will leave the bay!"   15

Then was called a council straight.
Brief and bitter the debate:
"Here's the English at our heels; would you have them take
   in tow
All that's left us of the fleet, linked together stern and
   bow,
For a prize to Plymouth Sound?   20
Better run the ships aground!"
   (Ended Damfreville his speech.)
"Not a minute more to wait!
   Let the Captains all and each
   Shove ashore, then blow up, burn the vessels on the beach! 25
France must undergo her fate.

"Give the word!" But no such word
Was ever spoke or heard;

For up stood, for out stepped, for in struck amid all these
—A Captain? A Lieutenant? A Mate—first, second, third?
No such man of mark, and meet
With his betters to compete!
5   But a simple Breton sailor pressed by Tourville for
the fleet,
A poor coasting-pilot he, Hervé Riel the Croisickese.

And, "What mockery or malice have we here?" cries Hervé
Riel:
"Are you mad, you Malouins? Are you cowards, fools, or
rogues?
Talk to me of rocks and shoals, me who took the soundings,
tell
10 On my fingers every bank, every shallow, every swell
'Twixt the offing here and Grève where the river disem-
bogues?
Are you bought by English gold? Is it love the lying's for?
Morn and eve, night and day,
Have I piloted your bay,
15 Entered free and anchored fast at the foot of Solidor.
Burn the fleet and ruin France? That were worse than
fifty Hogues!
Sirs, they know I speak the truth! Sirs, believe me
there's a way!
Only let me lead the line,
Have the biggest ship to steer,
20   Get this Formidable clear,
Make the others follow mine,
And I lead them, most and least, by a passage I know well,
Right to Solidor past Grève,
And there lay them safe and sound;
25   And if one ship misbehave,
—Keel so much as grate the ground,
Why, I've nothing but my life,—here's my head!" cries
Hervé Riel.

Not a minute more to wait.
"Steer us in, then, small and great!
　Take the helm, lead the line, save the squadron!" cried its
　　chief.
Captains, give the sailor place!
　He is Admiral, in brief.　　　　　　　　　　　　　　　　5
Still the north-wind, by God's grace!
See the noble fellow's face
As the big ship, with a bound,
Clears the entry like a hound,
Keeps the passage as its inch of way were the wide sea's
　　profound!　　　　　　　　　　　　　　　　　　　10
　See, safe thro' shoal and rock,
　How they follow in a flock,
Not a ship that misbehaves, not a keel that grates the
　　ground,
　Not a spar that comes to grief!
The peril, see, is past,　　　　　　　　　　　　　　　15
All are harboured to the last,
And just as Hervé Riel hollas "Anchor!"—sure as fate
Up the English come, too late!

So, the storm subsides to calm:
　They see the green trees wave　　　　　　　　　　　20
　On the heights o'erlooking Grève.
Hearts that bled are stanched with balm.
"Just our rapture to enhance,
　Let the English rake the bay,
Gnash their teeth and glare askance　　　　　　　　　25
　As they cannonade away!
'Neath rampired Solidor pleasant riding on the Rance!"
How hope succeeds despair on each Captain's countenance!
Out burst all with one accord,
　"This is Paradise for Hell!　　　　　　　　　　　30
　Let France, let France's King
　Thank the man that did the thing!"

What a shout, and all one word,
  "Hervé Riel!"
As he stepped in front once more,
  Not a symptom of surprise
5   In the frank blue Breton eyes,
Just the same man as before.

Then said Damfreville, "My friend,
I must speak out at the end,
  Tho' I find the speaking hard.
10 Praise is deeper than the lips:
You have saved the King his ships,
  You must name your own reward.
'Faith our sun was near eclipse!
Demand whate'er you will,
15 France remains your debtor still.
Ask to heart's content and have! or my name's not Dam-
    freville."

Then a beam of fun outbroke
On the bearded mouth that spoke,
  As the honest heart laughed through
20 Those frank eyes of Breton blue:
"Since I needs must say my say,
  Since on board the duty's done,
  And from Malo Roads to Croisic Point, what is it but a
    run?—
Since 'tis ask and have, I may—
25 Since the others go ashore—
Come! A good whole holiday!
  Leave to go and see my wife, whom I call the Belle
    Aurore!"
That he asked and that he got,—nothing more.

Name and deed alike are lost:
30 Not a pillar nor a post
  In his Croisic keeps alive the feat as it befell;

Not a head in white and black
On single fishing-smack,
In memory of the man but for whom had gone to wrack
   All that France saved from the fight whence England bore
     the bell.
Go to Paris: rank on rank   5
  Search the heroes flung pell-mell
On the Louvre, face and flank!
   You shall look long enough ere you come to Hervé Riel.
So, for better and for worse,
Hervé Riel, accept my verse!   10
In my verse, Hervé Riel, do thou once more
Save the squadron, honour France, love thy wife the Belle
   Aurore!

UP AT A VILLA—DOWN IN THE CITY

(As Distinguished by an Italian Person of Quality)

Had I but plenty of money, money enough and to spare,
The house for me, no doubt, were a house in the city-square;
Ah, such a life, such a life, as one leads at the window there! 15

Something to see, by Bacchus, something to hear, at least!
There, the whole day long, one's life is a perfect feast;
While up at a villa one lives, I maintain it, no more than a
   beast.

Well now, look at our villa! stuck like the horn of a bull
Just on a mountain edge as bare as the creature's skull,   20
Save a mere shag of a bush with hardly a leaf to pull!
—I scratch my own, sometimes, to see if the hair's turned
   wool.

But the city, oh the city—the square with the houses! Why?
They are stone-faced, white as a curd, there's something to
   take the eye!

Houses in four straight lines, not a single front awry;
You watch who crosses and gossips, who saunters, who hur-
    ries by;
Green blinds, as a matter of course, to draw when the sun
    gets high;
And the shops with fanciful signs which are painted properly.

5 What of a villa? Tho' winter be over in March by rights,
    'Tis May perhaps ere the snow shall have withered well off
    the heights:
You've the brown ploughed land before, where the oxen
    steam and wheeze,
And the hills over-smoked behind by the faint gray olive-
    trees.

Is it better in May, I ask you? You've summer all at once;
10 In a day he leaps complete with a few strong April suns.
    'Mid the sharp short emerald wheat, scarce risen three fingers
    well,
The wild tulip, at end of its tube, blows out its great red bell
Like a thin clear bubble of blood, for the children to pick and
    sell.

Is it ever hot in the square? There's a fountain to spout and
    splash!
15 In the shade it sings and springs; in the shine such foam-
    bows flash
On the horses with curling fish-tails, that prance and paddle
    and pash
Round the lady atop in her conch—fifty gazers do not abash,
Tho' all that she wears is some weeds round her waist in a
    sort of sash.

All the year long at the villa, nothing to see though you
    linger,
20 Except yon cypress that points like death's lean lifted fore-
    finger.

Some think fireflies pretty, when they mix i' the corn and
    mingle,
Or thrid the stinking hemp till the stalks of it seem a-tingle.
Late August or early September, the stunning cicala[1] is shrill,
And the bees keep their tiresome whine round the resinous
    firs on the hill.
Enough of the seasons,—I spare you the months of the fever
    and chill.   5

Ere you open your eyes in the city, the blessed church-bells
    begin:
No sooner the bells leave off than the diligence[2] rattles in:
You get the pick of news, and it costs you never a pin.
By and by there's the traveling doctor gives pills, lets blood,
    draws teeth:
Or the Pulcinello[3]-trumpet breaks up the market beneath.   10
At the post-office such a scene-picture—the new play, piping
    hot!
And a notice how, only this morning, three liberal thieves[4]
    were shot.
Above it, behold the Archbishop's most fatherly of rebukes,
And beneath, with his crown and his lion, some little new law
    of the Duke's!
Or a sonnet with flowery marge, to the Reverend Don So-and-
    so,   15
Who is Dante, Boccaccio, Petrarca, St. Jerome, and Cicero,
"And moreover," (the sonnet goes rhyming,) "the skirts of
    St. Paul has reached,
Having preached us those six Lent-lectures more unctuous
    than ever he preached."
Noon strikes,—here sweeps the procession! our Lady borne
    smiling and smart,

---

[1] cicada, locust.   [2] stagecoach.   [3] (pōol chĕ nĕl'lō) Punchinello,
the clown of the traveling players, or Punch, the puppet in the Punch and
Judy show.   [4] patriots struggling for the unity and independence
of Italy.

With a pink gauze gown all spangles, and seven swords stuck
    in her heart!
Bang-whang-whang goes the drum, *tootle-te-tootle* the fife;
No keeping one's haunches still: it's the greatest pleasure in
    life.

But bless you, it's dear—it's dear! fowls, wine, at double
    the rate.
5 They have clapped a new tax upon salt, and what oil pays
    passing the gate
It's a horror to think of. And so, the villa for me, not the
    city!
Beggars can scarcely be choosers: but still—ah, the pity, the
    pity!
Look, two and two go the priests, then the monks with cowls
    and sandals,
And the penitents dressed in white shirts, a-holding the yel-
    low candles;
10 One, he carries a flag up straight, and another a cross with
    handles,
And the Duke's guard brings up the rear, for the better pre-
    vention of scandals:
Bang-whang-whang goes the drum, *tootle-te-tootle* the fife.
Oh, a day in the city-square, there is no such pleasure in life!

MY LAST DUCHESS

Ferrara

That's my last Duchess painted on the wall,
15 Looking as if she were alive. I call
That piece a wonder, now: Fra Pandolf's hands
Worked busily a day, and there she stands.
Will 't please you sit and look at her? I said
"Fra Pandolf" by design, for never read
20 Strangers like you that pictured countenance,
The depth and passion of its earnest glance,

But to myself they turned (since none puts by
The curtain I have drawn for you, but I)
And seemed as they would ask me, if they durst,
How such a glance came there; so, not the first
Are you to turn and ask thus. Sir, 'twas not   5
Her husband's presence only, called that spot
Of joy into the Duchess' cheek: perhaps
Fra Pandolf chanced to say, "Her mantle laps
Over my lady's wrist too much," or "Paint
Must never hope to reproduce the faint   10
Half-flush that dies along her throat": such stuff
Was courtesy, she thought, and cause enough
For calling up that spot of joy. She had
A heart—how shall I say?—too soon made glad,
Too easily impressed: she liked whate'er   15
She looked on, and her looks went everywhere.
Sir, 'twas all one! My favour at her breast,
The dropping of the daylight in the West,
The bough of cherries some officious fool
Broke in the orchard for her, the white mule   20
She rode with round the terrace—all and each
Would draw from her alike the approving speech,
Or blush, at least. She thanked men,—good! but thanked
Somehow—I know not how—as if she ranked
My gift of a nine-hundred-years-old name   25
With anybody's gift. Who'd stoop to blame
This sort of trifling? Even had you skill
In speech—(which I have not)—to make your will
Quite clear to such an one, and say, "Just this
Or that in you disgusts me; here you miss,   30
Or there exceed the mark"—and if she let
Herself be lessoned so, nor plainly set
Her wits to yours, forsooth, and made excuse,
—E'en then would be some stooping; and I choose
Never to stoop. Oh sir, she smiled, no doubt,   35
Whene'er I passed her; but who passed without

Much the same smile? This grew; I gave commands;
Then all smiles stopped together. There she stands
As if alive. Will't please you rise? We'll meet
The company below, then. I repeat,
5   The Count your master's known munificence
Is ample warrant that no just pretence
Of mine for dowry will be disallowed;
Though his fair daughter's self, as I avowed
At starting, is my object. Nay, we'll go
10 Together down, sir. Notice Neptune though,
Taming a sea-horse, thought a rarity,
Which Claus of Innsbruck cast in bronze for me!

HOME-THOUGHTS, FROM ABROAD

Oh, to be in England
Now that April's there,
15 And whoever wakes in England
Sees, some morning, unaware,
That the lowest boughs and the brush-wood sheaf
Round the elm-tree bole are in tiny leaf,
While the chaffinch sings on the orchard bough
20 In England—now!
And after April, when May follows,
And the whitethroat builds, and all the swallows!
Hark, where my blossomed pear-tree in the hedge
Leans to the field and scatters on the clover
25 Blossoms and dewdrops—at the bent spray's edge—
That's the wise thrush; he sings each song twice over,
Lest you should think he never could recapture
The first fine careless rapture!
And though the fields look rough with hoary dew,
30 All will be gay when noontide wakes anew
The buttercups, the little children's dower
—Far brighter than this gaudy melon-flower!

RABBI BEN EZRA

Grow old along with me!
The best is yet to be,
The last of life, for which the first was made:
Our times are in His hand
Who saith, "A whole I planned,   5
Youth shows but half; trust God: see all, nor be afraid!"

Not that, amassing flowers,
Youth sighed, "Which rose make ours,
Which lily leave and then as best recall?"
Not that, admiring stars,   10
It yearned, "Nor Jove, nor Mars;
Mine be some figured flame which blends, transcends them
    all!"

Not for such hopes and fears
Annulling youth's brief years,
Do I remonstrate: folly wide the mark!   15
Rather I prize the doubt
Low kinds exist without,
Finished and finite clods, untroubled by a spark.

Poor vaunt of life indeed,
Were man but formed to feed   20
On joy, to solely seek and find and feast:
Such feasting ended, then
As sure an end to men;
Irks care the crop-full bird? Frets doubt the maw-**crammed**
    beast?

Rejoice we are allied   25
To That which doth provide
And not partake, effect and not receive!

A spark disturbs our clod;
Nearer we hold of God
Who gives, than of His tribes that take, I must believe.

Then, welcome each rebuff
5 That turns earth's smoothness rough,
Each sting that bids nor sit nor stand but go!
Be our joys three-parts pain!
Strive, and hold cheap the strain;
Learn, nor account the pang; dare, never grudge the throe!

10 For thence,—a paradox
Which comforts while it mocks,—
Shall life succeed in that it seems to fail:
What I aspired to be,
And was not, comforts me:
15 A brute I might have been, but would not sink i' the scale.

What is he but a brute
Whose flesh has soul to suit,
Whose spirit works lest arms and legs want play?
To man, propose this test—
20 Thy body at its best,
How far can that project thy soul on its lone way?

Yet gifts should prove their use:
I own the Past profuse
Of power each side, perfection every turn:
25 Eyes, ears took in their dole,
Brain treasured up the whole;
Should not the heart beat once "How good to live and learn?"

Not once beat "Praise be Thine!
I see the whole design,
30 I, who saw power, see now love perfect too:

Perfect I call Thy plan:
Thanks that I was a man!
Maker, remake, complete,—I trust what Thou shalt do!"

For pleasant is this flesh;
Our soul, in its rose-mesh   5
Pulled over to the earth, still yearns for rest:
Would we some prize might hold
To match those manifold
Possessions of the brute,—gain most, as we did best!

Let us not always say   10
"Spite of this flesh to-day
I strove, made head, gained ground upon the whole!"
As the bird wings and sings,
Let us cry "All good things
Are ours, nor soul helps flesh more, now, than flesh helps
    soul!"   15

Therefore I summon age
To grant youth's heritage,
Life's struggle having so far reached its term:
Thence shall I pass, approved
A man, for aye removed   20
From the developed brute; a God tho' in the germ.

And I shall thereupon
Take rest, ere I be gone
Once more on my adventure brave and new:
Fearless and unperplexed,   25
When I wage battle next,
What weapons to select, what armour to indue.

Youth ended, I shall try
My gain or loss thereby;
Leave the fire ashes, what survives is gold: 30

And I shall weigh the same,
Give life its praise or blame:
Young, all lay in dispute; I shall know, being old.

For, note when evening shuts,
5 A certain moment cuts
The deed off, calls the glory from the gray:
A whisper from the west
Shoots—"Add this to the rest,
Take it and try its worth: here dies another day."

10 So, still within this life,
Tho' lifted o'er its strife,
Let me discern, compare, pronounce at last,
"This rage was right i' the main,
That acquiescence vain:
15 The Future I may face now I have proved the Past."

For more is not reserved
To man, with soul just nerved
To act to-morrow what he learns to-day:
Here, work enough to watch
20 The Master work, and catch
Hints of the proper craft, tricks of the tool's true play.

As it was better, youth
Should strive, thro' acts uncouth,
Toward making, than repose on aught found made:
25 So, better, age, exempt
From strife, should know, than tempt
Further. Thou waitedst age: wait death nor be afraid!

Enough now, if the Right
And Good and Infinite
30 Be named here, as thou callest thy hand thine own,

With knowledge absolute,
Subject to no dispute
From fools that crowded youth, nor let thee feel alone.

Be there, for once and all,
Severed great minds from small,   5
Announced to each his station in the Past!
Was I, the world arraigned,
Were they, my soul disdained,
Right? Let age speak the truth and give us peace at last!

Now, who shall arbitrate?   10
Ten men love what I hate,
Shun what I follow, slight what I receive;
Ten, who in ears and eyes
Match me: we all surmise,
They, this thing, and I, that: whom shall my soul believe?   15

Not on the vulgar mass
Called "work," must sentence pass,
Things done, that took the eye and had the price;
O'er which, from level stand,
The low world laid its hand,   20
Found straightway to its mind, could value in a trice:

But all, the world's coarse thumb
And finger failed to plumb,
So passed in making up the main account:
All instincts immature,   25
All purposes unsure,
That weighed not as his work, yet swelled the man's amount:

Thoughts hardly to be packed
Into a narrow act,
Fancies that broke thro' language and escaped: 30

All I could never be,
All, men ignored in me,
This, I was worth to God, whose wheel the pitcher shaped.

Ay, note that Potter's wheel,
5 That metaphor! and feel
Why time spins fast, why passive lies our clay,—
Thou to whom fools propound,
When the wine makes its round,
"Since life fleets, all is change; the Past gone, seize to-day!"

10 Fool! All that is, at all,
Lasts ever, past recall;
Earth changes, but thy soul and God stand sure:
What entered into thee,
That was, is, and shall be:
15 Time's wheel runs back or stops: Potter and clay endure.

He fixed thee mid this dance
Of plastic circumstance,
This Present, thou, forsooth, wouldst fain arrest:
Machinery just meant
20 To give thy soul its bent,
Try thee and turn thee forth, sufficiently impressed.

What tho' the earlier grooves
Which ran the laughing loves
Around thy base, no longer pause and press?
25 What tho' about thy rim,
Skull-things in order grim
Grow out, in graver mood, obey the sterner stress?

Look not thou down but up!
To uses of a cup,
30 The festal board, lamp's flash and trumpet's peal,

The new wine's foaming flow,
The Master's lips a-glow!
Thou, heaven's consummate cup, what needst thou with
    earth's wheel?

But I need, now as then,
Thee, God, who mouldest men!   5
And since, not even while the whirl was worst,
Did I,—to the wheel of life
With shapes and colours rife,
Bound dizzily,—mistake my end, to slake Thy thirst:

So, take and use Thy work,   10
Amend what flaws may lurk,
What strain o' the stuff, what warpings past the aim!
My times be in Thy hand!
Perfect the cup as planned!
Let age approve of youth, and death complete the same!   15

ELIZABETH BARRETT BROWNING

A MUSICAL INSTRUMENT

What was he doing, the great god Pan,
    Down in the reeds by the river?
Spreading ruin and scattering ban,
Splashing and paddling with hoofs of a goat,
And breaking the golden lilies afloat   20
    With the dragon-fly on the river?

He tore out a reed, the great god Pan,
    From the deep cool bed of the river,
The limpid water turbidly ran,
And the broken lilies a-dying lay,   25
And the dragon-fly had fled away,
    Ere he brought it out of the river.

High on the shore sat the great god Pan,
　　While turbidly flowed the river,
And hacked and hewed as a great god can
With his hard bleak steel at the patient reed,
5　　Till there was not a sign of the leaf indeed
　　To prove it fresh from the river.

He cut it short, did the great god Pan,
　　(How tall it stood in the river!),
Then drew the pith, like the heart of a man,
10　　Steadily from the outside ring,
And notched the poor dry empty thing
　　In holes as he sat by the river.

"This is the way," laughed the great god Pan,
　　(Laughed while he sat by the river)
15　"The only way since gods began
To make sweet music, they could succeed."
Then dropping his mouth to a hole in the reed,
　　He blew in power by the river.

Sweet, sweet, sweet, O Pan!
20　　Piercing sweet by the river!
Blinding sweet, O great god Pan!
The sun on the hill forgot to die,
And the lilies revived, and the dragon-fly
　　Came back to dream on the river.

25　Yet half a beast is the great god Pan
　　To laugh, as he sits by the river,
· Making a poet out of a man:
The true gods sigh for the cost and pain—
For the reed which grows never more again
30　　As the reed with the reeds of the river.

SONNETS FROM THE PORTUGUESE

I

I thought once how Theocritus had sung
Of the sweet years, the dear and wished-for years,
Who each one in a gracious hand appears
To bear a gift for mortals, old or young:
And, as I mused it in his antique tongue,   5
I saw in gradual vision through my tears,
The sweet, sad years, the melancholy years,
Those of my own life, who by turns had flung
A shadow across me. Straightway I was 'ware,
So weeping, how a mystic Shape did move   10
Behind me, and drew me backward by the hair;
And a voice said in mastery while I strove,
"Guess now who holds thee?"—"Death!" I said.
     But there,
The silver answer rang: "Not Death, but Love."

XLIII

How do I love thee? Let me count the ways.   15
I love thee to the depth and breadth and height
My soul can reach, when feeling out of sight
For the ends of Being and Ideal Grace.
I love thee to the level of everyday's
Most quiet need, by sun and candlelight.   20
I love thee freely, as men strive for Right;
I love thee purely, as they turn from Praise;
I love thee with the passion put to use
In my old griefs, and with my childhood's faith;
I love thee with a love I seemed to lose   25
With my lost saints,—I love thee with the breath,
Smiles, tears, of all my life!—and, if God choose,
I shall but love thee better after death.

MATTHEW ARNOLD

THE FORSAKEN MERMAN

Come, dear children, let us away;
Down and away below!
Now my brothers call from the bay,
Now the great winds shoreward blow,
5   Now the salt tides seaward flow;
Now the wild white horses play,
Champ and chafe and toss in the spray.
Children dear, let us away!
This way, this way!

10   Call her once before you go,—
Call once yet!
In a voice that she will know,—
"Margaret! Margaret!"
Children's voices should be dear
15   (Call once more) to a mother's ear;
Children's voices, wild with pain,—
Surely she will come again!
Call her once, and come away;
This way, this way!
20   "Mother dear, we cannot stay!
The wild white horses foam and fret."
Margaret! Margaret!

Come, dear children, come away down;
Call no more!
25   One last look at the white-walled town,
And the little gray church on the windy shore;
Then come down!
She will not come, though you call all day;
Come away, come away!

Children dear, was it yesterday
We heard the sweet bells over the bay?
In the caverns where we lay,
Through the surf and through the swell,
The far-off sound of a silver bell?   5
Sand-strewn caverns, cool and deep,
Where the winds are all asleep;
Where the spent lights quiver and gleam,
Where the salt weed sways in the stream,
Where the sea-beasts, ranged all round,   10
Feed in the ooze of their pasture-ground;
Where the sea-snakes coil and twine,
Dry their mail and bask in the brine;
Where great whales come sailing by,
Sail and sail, with unshut eye,   15
Round the world for ever and aye?
When did music come this way?
Children dear, was it yesterday?   Kelly

Children dear, was it yesterday
(Call yet once) that she went away?   20
Once she sate with you and me,
On a red gold throne in the heart of the sea,
And the youngest sate on her knee.
She combed its bright hair, and she tended it well,
When down swung the sound of a far-off bell.   25
She sighed, she looked up through the clear green
    sea;
She said, "I must go, for my kinsfolk pray
In the little gray church on the shore to-day.
'Twill be Easter-time in the world—ah me!
And I lose my poor soul, Merman! here with thee."   30
I said, "Go up, dear heart, through the waves;
Say thy prayer, and come back to the kind sea-caves!"
She smiled, she went up through the surf in the bay.

Children dear, was it yesterday?
Children dear, were we long alone?
"The sea grows stormy, the little ones moan;
Long prayers," I said, "in the world they say;
5   Come!" I said; and we rose through the surf in the bay
We went up the beach, by the sandy down
Where the sea-stocks bloom, to the white-walled town;
Through the narrow paved streets, where all was still,
To the little gray church on the windy hill.
10   From the church came a murmur of folk at their prayers,
But we stood without in the cold blowing airs.
We climbed on the graves, on the stones worn with rains,
And we gazed up the aisle through the small leaded panes.
She sate by the pillar; we saw her clear:
15   "Margaret, hist! come quick, we are here!
Dear heart," I said, "we are long alone;
The sea grows stormy, the little ones moan."
But, ah! she gave me never a look,
For her eyes were sealed to the holy book!
20   Loud prays the priest; shut stands the door.
Come away, children, call no more!
Come away, come down, call no more!

Down, down, down!
Down to the depths of the sea!
25   She sits at her wheel in the humming town,
Singing most joyfully.
Hark what she sings: "O joy, O joy,
For the humming street, and the child with its toy!
For the priest, and the bell, and the holy well;
30   For the wheel where I spun,
And the blessed light of the sun!"
And so she sings her fill,
Singing most joyfully,
Till the spindle drops from her hand,
35   And the whizzing wheel stands still.

She steals to the window, and looks at the sand,
And over the sand at the sea;
And her eyes are set in a stare;
And anon there breaks a sigh,
And anon there drops a tear, 5
From a sorrow-clouded eye,
And a heart sorrow-laden,
A long, long sigh,
For the cold strange eyes of a little Mermaiden,
And the gleam of her golden hair. 10

Come away, away, children;
Come, children, come down!
The hoarse wind blows colder;
Lights shine in the town.
She will start from her slumber 15
When gusts shake the door;
She will hear the winds howling,
Will hear the waves roar.
We shall see, while above us
The waves roar and whirl, 20
A ceiling of amber,
A pavement of pearl.
Singing, "Here came a mortal,
But faithless was she!
And alone dwell for ever 25
The kings of the sea."

But, children, at midnight,
When soft the winds blow,
When clear falls the moonlight,
When spring-tides are low; 30
When sweet airs come seaward
From heaths starred with broom,
And high rocks throw mildly
On the blanched sands a gloom;

Up the still, glistening beaches,
Up the creeks we will hie,
Over banks of bright seaweed
The ebb-tide leaves dry.
5   We will gaze, from the sand-hills,
At the white sleeping town;
At the church on the hill-side—
And then come back down,
Singing, "There dwells a loved one,
10   But cruel is she!
She left lonely for ever
The kings of the sea."

DOVER BEACH

The sea is calm to-night.
The tide is full, the moon lies fair
15   Upon the straits;—on the French coast, the light
Gleams and is gone; the cliffs of England stand,
Glimmering and vast, out in the tranquil bay.
Come to the window, sweet is the night-air!
Only, from the long line of spray
20   Where the sea meets the moon-blanched land,
Listen! you hear the grating roar
Of pebbles which the waves draw back, and fling,
At their return, up the high strand,
Begin and cease, and then again begin,
25   With tremulous cadence slow, and bring
The eternal note of sadness in.

Sophocles long ago
Heard it on the Ægean and it brought
Into his mind the turbid ebb and flow
30   Of human misery; we
Find also in the sound a thought,
Hearing it by this distant northern sea.

The Sea of Faith
Was once, too, at the full, and round earth's shore
Lay like the folds of a bright girdle furl'd.
But now I only hear
Its melancholy, long, withdrawing roar,   5
Retreating, to the breath
Of the night-wind, down the vast edges drear
And naked shingles of the world.

Ah, love, let us be true
To one another! for the world, which seems   10
To lie before us like a land of dreams,
So various, so beautiful, so new,
Hath really neither joy, nor love, nor light,
Nor certitude, nor peace, nor help for pain;
And we are here as on a darkling plain   15
Swept with confused alarms of struggle and flight,
Where ignorant armies clash by night.

MORALITY

We cannot kindle when we will
The fire which in the heart resides;
The spirit bloweth and is still,   20
In mystery our soul abides.
    But tasks in hours of insight willed
    Can be through hours of gloom fulfilled.

With aching hands and bleeding feet
We dig and heap, lay stone on stone;   25
We bear the burden and the heat
Of the long day, and wish 'twere done.
    Not till the hours of light return,
    All we have built do we discern.

Then, when the clouds are off the soul,   30
When thou dost bask in Nature's eye,

Ask how *she* viewed thy self-control,
Thy struggling, tasked morality,—
   Nature, whose free, light, cheerful air,
   Oft made thee, in thy gloom, despair.

5   And she, whose censure thou dost dread,
Whose eye thou wast afraid to seek,
See, on her face a glow is spread,
A strong emotion on her cheek!
   "Ah, child!" she cries, "that strife divine,
10   Whence was it, for it is not mine?

"There is no effort on *my* brow—
I do not strive, I do not weep;
I rush with the swift spheres, and glow
In joy, and when I will, I sleep.
15   Yet that severe, that earnest air,
   I saw, I felt it once—but where?

"I knew not yet the gauge of time,
Nor wore the manacles of space;
I felt it in some other clime,
20   I saw it in some other place.
   'Twas when the heavenly house I trod,
   And lay upon the breast of God."

THE LAST WORD

Creep into thy narrow bed,
Creep, and let no more be said!
25   Vain thy onset! all stands fast.
Thou thyself must break at last.

Let the long contention cease!
Geese are swans, and swans are geese.
Let them have it how they will!
30   Thou art tired; best be still.

They out-talk'd thee, hiss'd thee, tore thee?
Better men fared thus before thee;
Fired their ringing shot and pass'd,
Hotly charged—and sank at last.

Charge once more, then, and be dumb!   5
Let the victors, when they come,
When the forts of folly fall,
Find thy body by the wall!

CULTURE AND ANARCHY

CHAPTER I. SWEETNESS AND LIGHT

[Extracts]

The disparagers of culture make its motive curiosity;
sometimes, indeed, they make its motive mere exclusiveness   10
and vanity. The culture which is supposed to plume itself on
a smattering of Greek and Latin is a culture which is be-
gotten by nothing so intellectual as curiosity; it is valued
either out of sheer vanity and ignorance or else as an engine
of social and class distinction, separating its holder, like a   15
badge or title, from other people who have not got it. No
serious man would call this *culture*, or attach any value to it,
as culture, at all. To find the real ground for the very differing estimate which serious people will set upon culture, we
must find some motive for culture in the terms of which may   20
lie a real ambiguity; and such a motive the word *curiosity*
gives us.

I have before now pointed out that we English do not,
like the foreigners, use this word in a good sense as well as
in a bad sense. With us the word is always used in a some-   25
what disapproving sense. A liberal and intelligent eagerness
about the things of the mind may be meant by a foreigner
when he speaks of curiosity, but with us the word always

conveys a certain notion of frivolous and unedifying activity.
In the *Quarterly Review*, some little time ago, was an estimate of the celebrated French critic, Monsieur Sainte-Beuve,
and a very inadequate estimate it, in my judgment, was.
5 And its inadequacy consisted chiefly in this: that in our
English way it left out of sight the double sense really involved in the word *curiosity*, thinking enough was said to
stamp Monsieur Sainte-Beuve with blame if it was said that
he was impelled in his operations as a critic by curiosity, and
10 omitting either to perceive that Monsieur Sainte-Beuve himself, and many other people with him, would consider that
this was praiseworthy and not blameworthy, or to point out
why it ought really to be accounted worthy of blame and not
of praise. For as there is a curiosity about intellectual matters
15 which is futile, and merely a disease, so there is certainly a
curiosity,—a desire after the things of the mind simply for
their own sakes and for the pleasure of seeing them as they
are,—which is, in an intelligent being, natural and laudable.
Nay, and the very desire to see things as they are implies a
20 balance and regulation of mind which is not often attained
without fruitful effort, and which is the very opposite of the
blind and diseased impulse of mind which is what we mean
to blame when we blame curiosity. Montesquieu says:—
"The first motive which ought to impel us to study is the
25 desire to augment the excellence of our nature, and to render
an intelligent being yet more intelligent." This is the true
ground to assign for the genuine scientific passion, however
manifested, and for culture, viewed simply as a fruit of this
passion; and it is a worthy ground, even though we let the
30 term *curiosity* stand to describe it.

But there is of culture another view, in which not solely the
scientific passion, the sheer desire to see things as they are,
natural and proper in an intelligent being, appears as the
ground of it. There is a view in which all the love of our
35 neighbour, the impulses towards action, help, and beneficence, the desire for removing human error, clearing human

confusion, and diminishing human misery, the noble aspiration to leave the world better and happier than we found it,—motives eminently such as are called social,—come in as part of the grounds of culture, and the main and preeminent part. Culture is then properly described not as having its origin in curiosity, but as having its origin in the love of perfection; it is a *study of perfection*. It moves by the force, not merely or primarily of the scientific passion for pure knowledge, but also of the moral and social passion for doing good. As, in the first view of it, we took for its worthy motto Montesquieu's words: "To render an intelligent being yet more intelligent!" so, in the second view of it, there is no better motto which it can have than these words of Bishop Wilson: "To make reason and the will of God prevail!"

Only, whereas the passion for doing good is apt to be over-hasty in determining what reason and the will of God say, because its turn is for acting rather than thinking, and it wants to be beginning to act; and whereas it is apt to take its own conceptions, which proceed from its own state of development and share in all the imperfections and immaturities of this, for a basis of action; what distinguishes culture is, that it is possessed by the scientific passion as well as by the passion of doing good; that it demands worthy notions of reason and the will of God, and does not readily suffer its own crude conceptions to substitute themselves for them. And knowing that no action or institution can be salutary and stable which is not based on reason and the will of God, it is not so bent on acting and instituting, even with the great aim of diminishing human error and misery ever before its thoughts, but that it can remember that acting and instituting are of little use, unless we know how and what we ought to act and to institute.

This culture is more interesting and more far-reaching than that other, which is founded solely on the scientific passion for knowing. But it needs times of faith and ardour,

times when the intellectual horizon is opening and widening
all round us, to flourish in. And is not the close and bounded
intellectual horizon within which we have long lived and
moved now lifting up, and are not new lights finding free
5 passage to shine in upon us? For a long time there was no
passage for them to make their way in upon us, and then it
was of no use to think of adapting the world's action to them.
Where was the hope of making reason and the will of God
prevail among people who had a routine which they had
10 christened reason and the will of God, in which they were
inextricably bound, and beyond which they had no power of
looking? But now the iron force of adhesion to the old routine,
—social, political, religious,—has wonderfully yielded; the
iron force of exclusion of all which is new has wonderfully
15 yielded. The danger now is, not that people should obstinately
refuse to allow anything but their old routine to pass for reason and the will of God, but either that they should allow
some novelty or other to pass for these too easily, or else that
they should underrate the importance of them altogether, and
20 think it enough to follow action for its own sake, without
troubling themselves to make reason and the will of God
prevail therein. Now, then, is the moment for culture to be of
service, culture which believes in making reason and the will
of God prevail, believes in perfection, is the study and pur-
25 suit of perfection, and is no longer debarred, by a rigid invincible exclusion of whatever is new, from getting acceptance
for its ideas, simply because they are new.

.   .   .   .

The pursuit of perfection, then, is the pursuit of sweetness
and light. He who works for sweetness works in the end for
30 light also; he who works for light works in the end for sweetness also. But he who works for sweetness and light united,
works to make reason and the will of God prevail. He who
works for machinery, he who works for hatred, works only
for confusion. Culture looks beyond machinery, culture
35 hates hatred; culture has but one great passion, the passion

for sweetness and light. Yes, it has one yet greater!—the passion for making them *prevail*. It is not satisfied till we *all* come to a perfect man; it knows that the sweetness and light of the few must be imperfect until the raw and un-kindled masses of humanity are touched with sweetness and light. If I have not shrunk from saying that we must work for sweetness and light, so neither have I shrunk from saying that we must have a broad basis, must have sweetness and light for as many as possible. Again and again I have insisted how those are the happy moments of humanity, how those are the marking epochs of a people's life, how those are the flowering times for literature and art and all the creative power of genius, when there is a *national* glow of life and thought, when the whole of society is in the fullest measure permeated by thought, sensible to beauty, intelligent and alive. Only it must be *real* thought and *real* beauty; *real* sweetness and *real* light. Plenty of people will try to give the masses, as they call them, an intellectual food prepared and adapted in the way they think proper for the actual condition of the masses. The ordinary popular literature is an example of this way of working on the masses. Plenty of people will try to indoctrinate the masses with the set of ideas and judgments constituting the creed of their own pro-fession or party. Our religious and political organisations give an example of this way of working on the masses. I con-demn neither way; but culture works differently. It does not try to teach down to the level of inferior classes; it does not try to win them for this or that sect of its own, with ready-made judgments and watch-words. It seeks to do away with classes; to make all men live in an atmosphere of sweet-ness and light, and use ideas, as it uses them itself, freely,— to be nourished and not bound by them.

This is the *social idea*; and the men of culture are the true apostles of equality. The great men of culture are those who have had a passion for diffusing, for making prevail, for carrying from one end of society to the other, the best knowl-

edge, the best ideas of their time; who have laboured to
divest knowledge of all that was harsh, uncouth, difficult,
abstract, professional, exclusive; to humanise it, to make it
efficient outside the clique of the cultivated and learned, yet
5 still remaining the *best* knowledge and thought of the time,
and a true source, therefore, of sweetness and light. Such a
man was Abelard in the Middle Ages, in spite of all his imperfections; and thence the boundless emotion and enthusiasm
which Abelard excited. Such were Lessing and Herder in
10 Germany, at the end of the last century; and their services
to Germany were in this way inestimably precious. Generations will pass, and literary monuments will accumulate, and
works far more perfect than the works of Lessing and Herder
will be produced in Germany; and yet the names of these
15 two men will fill a German with a reverence and enthusiasm
such as the names of the most gifted masters will hardly
awaken. And why? Because they *humanised* knowledge;
because they broadened the basis of life and intelligence; because they worked powerfully to diffuse sweetness and light,
20 to make reason and the will of God prevail. With Saint
Augustine they said: "Let us not leave thee alone to make in
the secret of thy knowledge, as thou didst before the creation
of the firmament, the division of light from darkness; let the
children of thy spirit, placed in their firmament, make their
25 light shine upon the earth, mark the division of night and
day, and announce the revolution of the times; for the old
order is passed, and the new arises; the night is spent, the
day is come forth; and thou shalt crown the year with thy
blessing, when thou shalt send forth labourers into thy har-
30 vest sown by other hands than theirs; when thou shalt send
forth new labourers to new seed-times, whereof the harvest
shall be not yet."

WILLIAM MORRIS

THE LIFE AND DEATH OF JASON

To the Sea

O bitter sea, tumultuous sea,
Full many an ill is wrought by thee! —
Unto the wasters of the land
Thou holdest out thy wrinkled hand;
And when they leave the conquered town,   5
Whose black smoke makes thy surges brown,
Driven betwixt thee and the sun
As the long day of blood is done,
From many a league of glittering waves
Thou smilest on them and their slaves.   10
    The thin bright-eyed Phœnician
Thou drawest to thy waters wan,
With ruddy eve and golden morn
Thou temptest him, until, forlorn,
Unburied, under alien skies   15
Cast up ashore his body lies.
    Yea, whoso sees thee from his door,
Must ever long for more and more;
Nor will the beechen bowl suffice,
Or homespun robe of little price,   20
Or hood well-woven from the fleece
Undyed, or unspiced wine of Greece;
So sore his heart is set upon
Purple, and gold, and cinnamon;
For as thou cravest, so he craves,   25
Until he rolls beneath thy waves,
Nor in some landlocked, unknown bay
Can satiate thee for one day.

    Now, therefore, O thou bitter sea,
With no long words we pray to thee,   30

But ask thee, hast thou felt before
Such strokes of the long ashen oar?
And hast thou yet seen such a prow
Thy rich and niggard waters plough?
Nor yet, O sea, shalt thou be cursed,
If at thy hands we gain the worst,
And, wrapt in water, roll about
Blind-eyed, unheeding song or shout,
Within thine eddies far from shore,
Warmed by no sunlight any more.
Therefore, indeed, we joy in thee,
And praise thy greatness, and will we
Take at thy hands both good and ill,
Yea, what thou wilt, and praise thee still,
Enduring not to sit at home,
And wait until the last days come,
When we no more may care to hold
White bosoms under crowns of gold,
And our dulled hearts no longer are
Stirred by the clangorous noise of war,
And hope within our souls is dead,
And no joy is rememberèd.

So, if thou hast a mind to slay,
Fair prize thou hast of us to-day;
And if thou hast a mind to save,
Great praise and honour shalt thou have;
But whatso thou wilt do with us,
Our end shall not be piteous,
Because our memories shall live
When folk forget the way to drive
The black keel through the heaped-up sea,
And half dried up thy waters be.

ALGERNON CHARLES SWINBURNE

BY THE NORTH SEA[1]

[Extracts]

A land that is lonelier than ruin;
   A sea that is stranger than death:
Far fields that a rose never blew in,
   Wan waste where the winds lack breath;
Waste endless and boundless and flowerless   5
   But of marsh-blossoms fruitless as free:
Where earth lies exhausted, as powerless
      To strive with the sea.

Far flickers the flight of the swallows,
   Far flutters the weft of the grass   10
Spun dense over desolate hollows
   More pale than the clouds as they pass:
Thick woven as the weft of a witch is
   Round the heart of a thrall that hath sinned,
Whose youth and the wrecks of its riches   15
      Are waifs on the wind.

The pastures are herdless and sheepless,
   No pasture or shelter for herds:
The wind is relentless and sleepless,
   And restless and songless the birds;   20
Their cries from afar fall breathless,
   Their wings are as lightnings that flee;
For the land has two lords that are deathless:
      Death's self, and the sea.

   .   .   .   .

For the heart of the waters is cruel,   25
   And the kisses are dire of their lips,

[1] Reprinted from *Studies in Verse*, by permission of William Heinemann, Ltd.

And their waves are as fire is to fuel
  To the strength of the sea-faring ships,
Though the sea's eye gleam as a jewel
  To the sun's eye back as he dips.

5   Though the sun's eye flash to the sea's
  Live light of delight and of laughter,
And her lips breathe back to the breeze
  The kiss that the wind's lips waft her
From the sun that subsides, and sees
10   No gleam of the storm's dawn after.

And the wastes of the wild sea-marches
  Where the borderers are matched in their might—
Bleak fens that the sun's weight parches,
  Dense waves that reject his light—
15 Change under the change-coloured arches
  Of changeless morning and night.

The waves are as ranks enrolled
  Too close for the storm to sever:
The fens lie naked and cold,
20   But their heart fails utterly never:
The lists are set from of old,
  And the warfare endureth for ever.

CHARLES DICKENS

OUR MUTUAL FRIEND

CHAPTER V. BOFFIN'S BOWER

[Abridged]

Over against a London house, a corner house not far from
Cavendish Square, a man with a wooden leg had sat for some
25 years, with his remaining foot in a basket in cold weather,
picking up a living on this wise:—Every morning at eight

o'clock he stumped to the corner, carrying a chair, a clothes-horse, a pair of trestles, a board, a basket, and an umbrella, all strapped together. Separating these, the board and trestles became a counter, the basket supplied the few small lots of fruit and sweets that he offered for sale upon it and became 5 a foot-warmer, the unfolded clothes-horse displayed a choice collection of halfpenny ballads and became a screen, and the stool planted within it became his post for the rest of the day. All weathers saw the man at the post. This is to be accepted in a double sense, for he contrived a back to his wooden stool, 10 by placing it against the lamp-post. When the weather was wet, he put up his umbrella over his stock in trade, not over himself; when the weather was dry, he furled that faded article, tied it round with a piece of yarn, and laid it cross-wise under the trestles: where it looked like an unwhole- 15 somely forced lettuce that had lost in color and crispness what it had gained in size.

On the front of his sale-board hung a little placard, like a kettle-holder, bearing the inscription in his own small text:

> *Errands gone*
> *On with fi*
> *Delity By*
> *Ladies and Gentlemen*
> *I remain*
> *Your humble Servt:*
> *Silas Wegg.*

He had not only settled it with himself in course of time, that 20 he was errand-goer by appointment to the house at the corner (though he received such commissions not half a dozen times in a year, and then only as some servant's deputy), but also that he was one of the house's retainers and owed vassalage to it and was bound to leal and loyal interest in it. For this 25 reason he always spoke of it as "Our House," and, though his knowledge of its affairs was mostly speculative and all wrong, claimed to be in its confidence.

.   .   .   .

The only article in which Silas dealt, that was not hard, was gingerbread. On a certain day, some wretched infant
5 having purchased the damp gingerbread-horse (fearfully out of condition), and the adhesive bird cage, which had been exposed for the day's sale, he had taken a tin box from under his stool to produce a relay of those dreadful specimens, and was going to look in at the lid, when he said to himself,
10 pausing, "Oh! Here you are again!"

The words referred to a broad, round-shouldered, one-sided old fellow in mourning, coming comically ambling towards the corner, dressed in a pea overcoat, and carrying a large stick. He wore thick shoes, and thick leather gaiters,
15 and thick gloves like a hedger's. Both as to his dress and to himself, he was of an overlapping rhinoceros build, with folds in his cheeks, and his forehead, and his eyelids, and his lips, and his ears; but with bright, eager, childishly-inquiring gray eyes under his ragged eyebrows and broad-brimmed hat. A
20 very odd-looking old fellow altogether.

"Here you are again," repeated Mr. Wegg, musing. "And what are you now? Are you in the Funns, or where are you? Have you lately come to settle in this neighborhood, or do you own to another neighborhood? Are you in independent
25 circumstances, or is it wasting the motions of a bow on you? Come! I'll speculate! I'll invest a bow in you."

Which Mr. Wegg, having replaced his tin box, accordingly did, as he rose to bait his gingerbread-trap for some other devoted infant. The salute was acknowledged with—
30   "Morning, sir! Morning! Morning!"

("Calls me Sir!" said Mr. Wegg to himself. "*He* won't answer. A bow gone!")

"Morning, morning, morning!"

"Appears to be rather a 'arty old cock, too," said Mr. Wegg,
35 as before. "Good morning to *you*, sir."

"Do you remember me, then?" asked his new acquaintance, stopping in his amble, one-sided, before the stall, and speaking in a pouncing way, though with great good-humor.

"I have noticed you go past our house, sir, several times in the course of the last week or so." 5

"Our house," repeated the other. "Meaning"—

"Yes," said Mr. Wegg, nodding, as the other pointed the clumsy forefinger of his right glove at the corner house.

"Oh! Now, what," pursued the old fellow, in an inquisitive manner, carrying his knotted stick in his left arm as if 10 it were a baby, "what do they allow you now?"

"It's job-work that I do for our house," returned Silas, dryly, and with reticence; "it's not yet brought to an exact allowance."

.   .   .   .

"Now, Wegg," said Mr. Boffin, hugging his stick closer, 15 "I want to make a sort of offer to you. Do you remember when you first see me?"

The wooden Wegg looked at him with a meditative eye, and also with a softened air as descrying possibility of profit. "Let me think. I ain't quite sure, and yet I generally take a 20 powerful sight of notice, too. Was it on a Monday morning, when the butcher-boy had been to our house for orders, and bought a ballad of me, which being unacquainted with the tune, I run it over to him?"

"Right, Wegg, right! But he bought more than one." 25

"Yes, to be sure, sir; he bought several; and wishing to lay out his money to the best, he took my opinion to guide his choice, and we went over the collection together. To be sure we did. Here was him as it might be, and here was myself as it might be, and there was you, Mr. Boffin, as you 30 identically are, with your self-same stick under your very same arm, and your very same back towards us. To—be— sure!" added Mr. Wegg, looking a little round Mr. Boffin, to take him in the rear, and identify this last extraordinary coincidence, "your wery self-same back!" 35

"What do you think I was doing, Wegg?"

"I should judge, sir, that you might be glancing your eye down the street."

"No, Wegg. I was a-listening."

5   "Was you, indeed?" said Mr. Wegg, dubiously.

"Not in a dishonorable way, Wegg, because you was sing-ing to the butcher; and you wouldn't sing secrets to a butcher in the street, you know."

"It never happened that I did so yet, to the best of my
10 remembrance," said Mr. Wegg, cautiously. "But I might do it. A man can't say what he might wish to do some day or another." (This, not to release any little advantage he might derive from Mr. Boffin's avowal.)

"Well," repeated Boffin, "I was a-listening to you . . .
15 with hadmiration amounting to haw. I thought to myself, 'Here's a man with a wooden leg—a literary man with'"—

"N—not exactly so, sir," said Mr. Wegg.

"Why, you know every one of these songs by name and by tune, and if you want to read or to sing any one on 'em
20 off straight, you've only to whip on your spectacles and do it!" cried Mr. Boffin. "I see you at it!"

"Well, sir," returned Mr. Wegg, with a conscious inclina-tion of the head; "we'll say literary, then."

"'A literary man—*with* a wooden leg—and all Print is
25 open to him!' That's what I thought to myself, that morn-ing," pursued Mr. Boffin, leaning forward to describe, un-cramped by the clothes-horse, as large an arc as his right arm could make; "'all Print is open to him!' And it is, ain't it?"

30   "Why, truly, sir," Mr. Wegg admitted, with modesty; "I believe you couldn't show me the piece of English print, that I wouldn't be equal to collaring and throwing."

"On the spot?" said Mr. Boffin.

"On the spot."

35   "I know'd it! Then consider this. Here am I, a man without a wooden leg, and yet all print is shut to me."

"Indeed, sir?" Mr. Wegg returned with increasing self-complacency. "Education neglected?"

"Neg—lected!" repeated Boffin, with emphasis. "That ain't no word for it. I don't mean to say but what if you showed me a B, I could so far give you change for it as to answer Boffin."

"Come, come, sir," said Mr. Wegg, throwing in a little encouragement, "that's something, too."

"It's something," answered Mr. Boffin; "but I'll take my oath it ain't much."

"Perhaps it's not as much as could be wished by an inquiring mind, sir," Mr. Wegg admitted.

"Now, look here. I'm retired from business. Me and Mrs. Boffin—Henerietty Boffin—which her father's name was Henery, and her mother's name was Hetty, and so you get it—we live on a compittance under the will of a diseased governor."

"Gentleman dead, sir?"

"Man alive, don't I tell you? A diseased governor? Now, it's too late for me to begin shoveling and sifting at alpha-beds and grammar-books. I'm getting to be a old bird, and I want to take it easy. But I want some reading—some fine bold reading, some splendid book in a gorging Lord-Mayor's-Show of wollumes" (probably meaning gorgeous, but misled by association of ideas); "as'll reach right down your pint of view, and take time to go by you. How can I get that reading, Wegg? By," tapping him on the breast with the head of his thick stick, "paying a man truly qualified to do it, so much an hour (say twopence) to come and do it."

"Hem! Flattered, sir, I am sure," said Wegg, beginning to regard himself in quite a new light. "Hem! This is the offer you mentioned, sir?"

"Yes. Do you like it?"

"I am considering of it, Mr. Boffin."

"I don't," said Boffin, in a free-handed manner, "want to tie a literary man—*with* a wooden leg—down too tight. A

halfpenny an hour sha'n't part us. The hours are your own to choose, after you've done for the day with your house here. I live over Maiden-Lane way—out Holloway direction—and you've only got to go East-and-by-North when you've fin-
5 ished here, and you're there. Twopence halfpenny an hour," said Boffin, taking a piece of chalk from his pocket and getting off the stool to work the sum on the top of it in his own way; "two long'uns and a short'un—twopence halfpenny; two short'uns is a long'un and two two long'uns is four
10 long'uns—making five long'uns; six nights a week at five long'uns a night," scoring them all down separately, "and you mount up to thirty long'uns. A round'un! Half a crown!"

Pointing to this result as a large and satisfactory one, Mr. Boffin smeared it out with his moistened glove, and sat
15 down on the remains.

"Half a crown," said Wegg, meditating. "Yes. (It ain't much, sir.) Half a crown."

"Per week, you know."

"Per week. Yes. As to the amount of strain upon the
20 intellect now. Was you thinking at all of poetry?" Mr. Wegg inquired, musing.

"Would it come dearer?" Mr. Boffin asked.

"It would come dearer," Mr. Wegg returned. "For when a person comes to grind off poetry night after night, it is but
25 right he should expect to be paid for its weakening effect on his mind."

"To tell you the truth, Wegg," said Boffin, "I wasn't thinking of poetry, except in so fur as this:—If you was to happen now and then to feel yourself in the mind to tip me
30 and Mrs. Boffin one of your ballads, why then we should drop into poetry."

"I follow you, sir," said Wegg. "But not being a regular musical professional, I should be loath to engage myself for that; and therefore when I dropped into poetry, I should ask
35 to be considered so fur in the light of a friend "

At this, Mr. Boffin's eyes sparkled, and he shook Silas

earnestly by the hand; protesting that it was more than he could have asked, and that he took it very kindly indeed.

"What do you think of the terms, Wegg?" Mr. Boffin then demanded, with unconcealed anxiety.

Silas, who had stimulated this anxiety by his hard reserve 5 of manner, and who had begun to understand his man very well, replied with an air; as if he were saying something extraordinarily generous and great,—

"Mr. Boffin, I never bargain."

"So I should have thought of you!" said Mr. Boffin, 10 admiringly.

"No, sir. I never did 'aggle and I never will 'aggle. Consequently I meet you at once, free and fair, with—Done, for double the money!"

Mr. Boffin seemed a little unprepared for this conclusion, 15 but assented, with the remark, "You know better what it ought to be than I do, Wegg," and again shook hands with him upon it.

"Could you begin to-night, Wegg?" he then demanded.

"Yes, sir," said Mr. Wegg, careful to leave all the eager- 20 ness to him. "I see no difficulty if you wish it. You are provided with the needful implement—a book, sir?"

"Bought him at a sale," said Mr. Boffin. "Eight wollumes. Red and gold. Purple ribbon in every wollume, to keep the place where you leave off. Do you know him?" 25

"The book's name, sir?" inquired Silas.

"I thought you might have know'd him without it," said Mr. Boffin, slightly disappointed. "His name is Decline-And-Fall-Off The-Rooshan-Empire." (Mr. Boffin went over these stones slowly and with much caution.) 30

"Ay indeed!" said Mr. Wegg, nodding his head with an air of friendly recognition.

"You know him, Wegg?"

"I haven't been not to say right slap through him, very lately," Mr. Wegg made answer, "having been otherways 35 employed, Mr. Boffin. But know him? Old familiar declining and falling off the Rooshan? Rather, sir! Ever since I was not so high as your stick.". . .

"Where I live," said Mr. Boffin, "is called The Bower. Boffin's Bower is the name Mrs. Boffin christened it when we
5 come into it as a property. If you should meet with anybody that don't know it by that name (which hardly anybody does), when you've got nigh upon about a odd mile, or say and a quarter if you like, up Maiden Lane, Battle Bridge, ask for Harmony Jail, and you'll be put right. I shall expect
10 you, Wegg," said Mr. Boffin, clapping him on the shoulder with the greatest enthusiasm, "most jyfully. I shall have no peace or patience till you come. Print is now opening ahead of me. This night, a literary man—*with* a wooden leg"—he bestowed an admiring look upon that decoration,
15 as if it greatly enhanced the relish of Mr. Wegg's attainments —"will begin to lead me a new life! My fist again, Wegg. Morning, morning, morning!"

.   .   .   .

Pushing the gate, which stood ajar, Wegg looked into an enclosed space where certain tall, dark mounds rose high
20 against the sky, and where the pathway to the Bower was indicated, as the moonlight showed, between two lines of broken crockery set in ashes. A white figure advancing along this path, proved to be nothing more ghostly than Mr. Boffin, easily attired for the pursuit of knowledge, in an undress gar-
25 ment of short white smock-frock. Having received his lit- erary friend with great cordiality, he conducted him to the interior of the Bower, and there presented him to Mrs. Boffin, —a stout lady of a rubicund and cheerful aspect, dressed (to Mr. Wegg's consternation) in a low evening-dress of sable
30 satin, and a large black velvet hat and feathers.

"Mrs. Boffin, Wegg," said Boffin, "is a highflyer at Fashion. And her make is such that she does it credit. As to myself, I ain't yet as Fash'nable as I may come to be. Hen- erietty, old lady, this is the gentleman that's agoing to decline
35 and fall off the Rooshan Empire."

"And I am sure I hope it'll do you both good," said Mrs. Boffin.

It was the queerest of rooms, fitted and furnished more like a luxurious amateur tap-room than anything else within the ken of Silas Wegg. There were two wooden settles by the fire, one on either side of it, with a corresponding table before each. On one of these tables, the eight volumes were ranged flat, in a row, like a galvanic battery; on the other, certain squat case-bottles of inviting appearance seemed to stand on tiptoe to exchange glances with Mr. Wegg over a front row of tumblers and a basin of white sugar. On the hob, a kettle steamed; on the hearth, a cat reposed. Facing the fire between the settles, a sofa, a footstool, and a little table formed a centrepiece devoted to Mrs. Boffin. They were garish in taste and color, but were expensive articles of drawing-room furniture that had a very odd look beside the settles and the flaring gas-light pendent from the ceiling. There was a flowery carpet on the floor; but, instead of reaching to the fireside, its glowing vegetation stopped short at Mrs. Boffin's footstool, and gave place to a region of sand and sawdust. Mr. Wegg also noticed, with admiring eyes, that, while the flowery land displayed such hollow ornamentation as stuffed birds and waxen fruits under glass shades, there were, in the territory where vegetation ceased, compensatory shelves on which the best part of a large pie and likewise of a cold joint were plainly discernible among other solids. The room itself was large, though low; and the heavy frames of its old-fashioned windows, and the heavy beams in its crooked ceiling, seemed to indicate that it had once been a house of some mark, standing alone in the country.

"Do you like it, Wegg?" asked Mr. Boffin, in his pouncing manner.

"I admire it greatly, sir," said Wegg. "Peculiar comfort at this fireside, sir."

"Do you understand it, Wegg?"

"Why, in a general way, sir," Mr. Wegg was beginning

slowly and knowingly, with his head stuck on one side, as evasive people do begin, when the other cut him short,—

"You *don't* understand it, Wegg, and I'll explain it. These arrangements is made by mutual consent between Mrs. Boffin 5 and me. Mrs. Boffin, as I've mentioned, is a highflyer at Fashion; at present I'm not. I don't go higher than comfort, and comfort of the sort that I'm equal to the enjyment of. Well then. Where would be the good of Mrs. Boffin and me quarreling over it? We never did quarrel before we come 10 into Boffin's Bower as a property; why quarrel when we *have* come into Boffin's Bower as a property? So Mrs. Boffin, she keeps up her part of the room, in her way; I keep up my part of the room in mine. In consequence of which we have at once, Sociability (I should go melancholy mad without 15 Mrs. Boffin), Fashion, and Comfort. If I get by degrees to be a higher-flyer at Fashion, then Mrs. Boffin will by degrees come for'arder. If Mrs. Boffin should ever be less of a dab at Fashion than she is at the present time, then Mrs. Boffin's carpet would go back'arder. If we should both continny as 20 we are, why then *here* we are, and give us a kiss, old lady."

Mrs. Boffin who, perpetually smiling, had approached and drawn her plump arm through her lord's, most willingly complied. Fashion, in the form of her black velvet hat and feathers, tried to prevent it; but got deservedly crushed in 25 the endeavor.

"So now, Wegg," said Mr. Boffin, wiping his mouth with an air of much refreshment, "you begin to know us as we are. This is a charming spot, is the Bower; but you must get to apprechiate it by degrees. It's a spot to find out the 30 merits of, little by little, and a new'un every day. There's a serpentining walk up each of the mounds, that gives you the yard and neighborhood changing every moment. When you get to the top, there's a view of the neighboring premises, not to be surpassed. The premises of Mrs. Boffin's late father 35 (Canine Provision Trade), you look down into, as if they was your own. And the top of the High Mound is crowned with a lattice-work Arbor, in which, if you don't read out loud many a book in the summer, ay, and as a friend, drop many a time into poetry too, it sha'n't be my fault. Now, what'll you read on?"

"Thank you, sir," returned Wegg, as if there were nothing new in his reading at all. "I generally do it on gin and water."

"Keeps the organ moist, does it, Wegg?" asked Mr. Boffin, with innocent eagerness.

"N-no, sir," replied Wegg, coolly; "I should hardly describe it so, sir. I should say, mellers it. Mellers it, is the word I should employ, Mr. Boffin."

His wooden conceit and craft kept exact pace with the delighted expectation of his victim. The visions rising before his mercenary mind, of the many ways in which this connection was to be turned to account, never obscured the foremost idea natural to a dull over-reaching man, that he must not make himself too cheap.

Mrs. Boffin's Fashion, as a less inexorable deity than the idol usually worshipped under that name, did not forbid her mixing for her literary guest, or asking if he found the result to his liking. On his returning a gracious answer and taking his place at the literary settle, Mr. Boffin began to compose himself as a listener, at the opposite settle, with exultant eyes.

"Sorry to deprive you of a pipe, Wegg," he said, filling his own; "but you can't do both together. Oh, and another thing I forgot to name! When you come in here of an evening, and look round you, and notice anything on a shelf that happens to catch your fancy, mention it."

Wegg, who had been going to put on his spectacles, immediately laid them down, with the sprightly observation,—

"You read my thoughts, sir. *Do* my eyes deceive me, or is that object up there a—a pie? It can't be a pie."

"Yes, it's a pie, Wegg," replied Mr. Boffin, with a glance of some little discomfiture at the Decline and Fall.

"*Have* I lost my smell for fruits, or is it a apple-pie, sir?" asked Wegg.

"It's a veal and ham pie," said Mr. Boffin.

"Is it indeed, sir? And it would be hard, sir, to name the pie that is a better pie than a weal and hammer," said Mr. Wegg, nodding his head emotionally.

5   "Have some, Wegg?"

"Thank you, Mr. Boffin, I think I will, at your invitation. I wouldn't at any other party's, at the present juncture; but at yours, sir!—And meaty jelly too, especially when a little salt, which is the case where there's ham, is mellering to the 10 organ, is very mellering to the organ." Mr. Wegg did not say what organ, but spoke with a cheerful generality.

So, the pie was brought down, and the worthy Mr. Boffin exercised his patience until Wegg, in the exercise of his knife and fork, had finished the dish: only profiting by the oppor- 15 tunity to inform Wegg, that, although it was not strictly Fashionable to keep the contents of a larder thus exposed to view, he (Mr. Boffin) considered it hospitable; for the reason, that instead of saying, in a comparatively unmeaning manner, to a visitor, "There are such and such edibles downstairs; will 20 you have anything up?" you took the bold practical course of saying, "Cast your eye along the shelves, and, if you see anything you like there, have it down."

And now, Mr. Wegg at length pushed away his plate and put on his spectacles, and Mr. Boffin lighted his pipe and 25 looked with beaming eyes into the opening world before him, and Mrs. Boffin reclined in a fashionable manner on her sofa: as one who would be part of the audience if she found she could, and would go to sleep if she found she couldn't.

"Hem!" began Wegg, "this, Mr. Boffin and Lady, is the 30 first chapter of the first wollume of the Decline and Fall off" —here he looked hard at the book, and stopped.

"What's the matter, Wegg?"

"Why, it comes into my mind, do you know, sir," said Wegg with an air of insinuating frankness (having first again 35 looked hard at the book), "that you made a little mistake this morning, which I had meant to set you right in, only

something put it out of my head. I think you said Rooshan
Empire, sir?"

"It is Rooshan; ain't it, Wegg?"

"No, sir. Roman. Roman."

"What's the difference, Wegg?"   5

"The difference, sir?" Mr. Wegg was faltering and in
danger of breaking down, when a bright thought flashed upon
him. "The difference, sir? There you place me in a difficulty,
Mr. Boffin. Suffice it to observe that the difference is best
postponed to some other occasion when Mrs. Boffin does not 10
honor us with her company. In Mrs. Boffin's presence, sir,
we had better drop it."

Mr. Wegg thus came out of his disadvantage with quite a
chivalrous air; and not only that, but by dint of repeating
with a manly delicacy, "In Mrs. Boffin's presence, sir, we 15
had better drop it!" turned the disadvantage on Boffin, who
felt that he had committed himself in a very painful manner.

Then Mr. Wegg, in a dry, unflinching way, entered on his
task; going straight across country at everything that came
before him; taking all the hard words, biographical and 20
geographical; getting rather shaken by Hadrian, Trajan,
and the Antonines; stumbling at Polybius (pronounced
Polly Beeious, and supposed by Mr. Boffin to be a Roman
virgin, and by Mrs. Boffin to be responsible for that necessity
of dropping it); heavily unseated by Titus Antoninus Pius; 25
up again and galloping smoothly with Augustus; finally, getting over the ground well with Commodus,—who, under the
appellation of Commodious, was held by Mr. Boffin to have
been quite unworthy of his English origin, and "not to have
acted up to his name" in his government of the Roman 30
people. With the death of this personage, Mr. Wegg termi-
nated his first reading; long before which consummation several total eclipses of Mrs. Boffin's candle behind her black
velvet disc, would have been very alarming, but for being
regularly accompanied by a potent smell of burnt pens when 35
her feathers took fire, which acted as a restorative and woke

her. Mr. Wegg, having read on by rote and attached as few
ideas as possible to the text, came out of the encounter fresh;
but Mr. Boffin, who had soon laid down his unfinished pipe,
and had ever since sat intently staring with his eyes and mind
5 at the confounding enormities of the Romans, was so severely
punished that he could hardly wish his literary friend Good
night, and articulate "To-morrow."

"Commodious," gasped Mr. Boffin, staring at the moon,
after letting Wegg out at the gate and fastening it: "Com-
10 modious fights in that wild-beast-show, seven hundred and
thirty-five times, in one character only! As if that wasn't
stunning enough, a hundred lions is turned into the same
wild-beast-show all at once! As if that wasn't stunning
enough, Commodious, in another character, kills 'em all off
15 in a hundred goes! As if that wasn't stunning enough,
Vittle-us (and well named too) eats six millions' worth, English money, in seven months! Wegg takes it easy, but upon-
my-soul to a old bird like myself these are scarers. And
even now that Commodious is strangled, I don't see a way to
20 our bettering ourselves." Mr. Boffin added as he turned his
pensive steps towards the Bower and shook his head, "I
didn't think this morning there was half so many Scarers in
Print. But I'm in for it now!"

WILLIAM MAKEPEACE THACKERAY

THE VIRGINIANS

Volume II. Chapter I. Friends in Need

Quick, hackney-coach steeds, and bear George Warrington
25 through Strand and Fleet Street to his imprisoned brother's
rescue! Any one who remembers Hogarth's picture of a
London hackney-coach and a London street road at that
period, may fancy how weary the quick time was, and how
long seemed the journey;—scarce any lights, save those car-

ried by link-boys; badly hung coaches; bad pavements;
great holes in the road, and vast quagmires of winter mud.
That drive from Piccadilly to Fleet Street seemed almost as
long to our young man, as the journey from Marlborough to
London which he had performed in the morning.   5

He had written to Harry announcing his arrival at Bristol.
He had previously written to his brother, giving the great
news of his existence and his return from captivity. There
was war between England and France at that time; the
French privateers were for ever on the look-out for British   10
merchant-ships, and seized them often within sight of port.
The letter bearing the intelligence of George's restoration
must have been on board one of the many American ships
of which the French took possession. The letter telling of
George's arrival in England was never opened by poor Harry;   15
it was lying at the latter's apartments, which it reached on
the third morning after Harry's captivity, when the angry
Mr. Ruff had refused to give up any single item more of his
lodger's property.

To these apartments George first went on his arrival in   20
London, and asked for his brother. Scared at the likeness
between them, the maid-servant who opened the door
screamed, and ran back to her mistress. The mistress not
liking to tell the truth, or to own that poor Harry was actually a prisoner at her husband's suit, said Mr. Warrington   25
had left his lodgings; she did not know where Mr. Warrington was. George knew that Clarges Street was close to Bond
Street. Often and often had he looked over the London map.
Aunt Bernstein would tell him where Harry was. He might
be with her at that very moment. George had read in   30
Harry's letters to Virginia about Aunt Bernstein's kindness
to Harry. . . .

I suppose the Virginians' agent at Bristol had told George
fearful stories of his brother's doings. Gumbo, whom he met
at his aunt's door, as soon as the lad recovered from his   35
terror at the sudden re-appearance of the master whom he

supposed dead, had leisure to stammer out a word or two
respecting his young master's whereabouts, and present piti-
able condition; and hence Mr. George's sternness of demean-
our when he presented himself to the old lady. It seemed to
5 him a matter of course that his brother in difficulty should
be rescued by his relations. Oh, George, how little you know
about London and London ways! Whene'er you take your
walks abroad how many poor you meet:—if a philanthropist
were for rescuing all of them, not all the wealth of all the
10 provinces of America would suffice him!

But the feeling and agitation displayed by the old lady
touched her nephew's heart, when, jolting through the dark
streets towards the house of his brother's captivity, George
came to think of his aunt's behaviour. "She *does* feel my
15 poor Harry's misfortune," he thought to himself. "I have
been too hasty in judging her." Again and again, in the
course of his life, Mr. George had to rebuke himself with the
same crime of being too hasty. How many of us have not?
And, alas, the mischief done, there's no repentance will mend
20 it. Quick, coachman! We are almost as slow as you are in
getting from Clarges Street to the Temple. Poor Gumbo
knows the way to the bailiff's[1] house well enough. Again the
bell is set ringing. The first door is opened to George and his
negro; then that first door is locked warily upon them, and
25 they find themselves in a little passage with a little Jewish
janitor; then a second door is unlocked, and they enter into
the house. The Jewish janitor stares, as by his flaring tallow-
torch he sees a second Mr. Warrington before him. Come to
see that gentleman? Yes. But wait a moment. This is Mr.
30 Warrington's brother from America. Gumbo must go and
prepare his master first. Step into this room. There's a
gentleman already there about Mr. W.'s business (the porter
says), and another upstairs with him now. There's no end
of people have been about him.
35   The room into which George was introduced was a small

[1] deputy sheriff's.

apartment which went by the name of Mr. Amos's office, and where, by a guttering candle, and talking to the bailiff, sat a stout gentleman in a cloak and a laced hat. The young porter carried his candle too, preceding Mr. George, so there was a sufficiency of light in the apartment.   5

"We are not angry any more, Harry!" says the stout gentleman, in a cheery voice, getting up and advancing with an outstretched hand to the new comer. "Thank God, my boy! Mr. Amos here says, there will be no difficulty about James and me being your bail, and we will do your business   10 by breakfast-time in the morning. Why . . . Angels and ministers of grace! who are you?" And he started back as the other had hold of his hand.

But the stranger grasped it only the more strongly. "God bless you, sir!" he said. "I know who *you* are. You must   15 be Colonel Lambert of whose kindness to him my poor Harry wrote. And I am the brother whom you have heard of, sir; and who was left for dead in Mr. Braddock's action; and came to life again after eighteen months amongst the French; and live to thank God and thank you for your kindness to   20 my Harry," continued the lad with a faltering voice.

"James! James! here is news!" cries Mr. Lambert to a gentleman in red, who now entered the room. "Here are the dead come alive! Here is Harry Scapegrace's brother come back, and with his scalp on his head, too!" (George had   25 taken his hat off, and was standing by the light.) "This is my brother bail, Mr. Warrington! This is Lieutenant-Colonel James Wolfe, at your service. You must know there has been a little difference between Harry and me, Mr. George. He is pacified, is he, James?"   30

"He is full of gratitude," says Mr. Wolfe, after making his bow to Mr. Warrington.

"Harry wrote home about Mr. Wolfe, too, sir," said the young man, "and I hope my brother's friends will be so kind as to be mine."   35

"I wish he had none other but us, Mr. Warrington. Poor

Harry's fine folks have been too fine for him, and have ended by landing him here."

"Nay, your honours, I have done my best to make the young gentleman comfortable; and, knowing your honour before, when you came to bail Captain Watkins, and that your security is perfectly good,—if your honour wishes, the young gentleman can go out this very night, and I will make it all right with the lawyer in the morning," says Harry's landlord, who knew the rank and respectability of the two gentlemen who had come to offer bail for his young prisoner.

"The debt is five hundred and odd pounds, I think?" said Mr. Warrington. "With a hundred thanks to these gentlemen, I can pay the amount at this moment into the officer's hands, taking the usual acknowledgment and caution. But I can never forget, gentlemen, that you helped my brother at his need, and, for doing so, I say thank you, and God bless you, in my mother's name and mine."

Gumbo had, meanwhile, gone up stairs to his master's apartment, where Harry would probably have scolded the negro for returning that night, but that the young gentleman was very much soothed and touched by the conversation he had had with the friend who had just left him. He was sitting over his pipe of Virginia in a sad mood . . . when Mr. Wolfe's homely features and eager outstretched hand came to cheer the prisoner, and he heard how Mr. Lambert was below, and the errand upon which the two officers had come. In spite of himself, Lambert would be kind to him. In spite of Harry's ill temper, and needless suspicion and anger, the good gentleman was determined to help him if he might—to help him even against Mr. Wolfe's own advice, as the latter frankly told Harry. "For you were wrong, Mr. Warrington," said the Colonel, "and you wouldn't be set right; and you, a young man, used hard words and unkind behaviour to your senior, and what is more, one of the best gentlemen who walks God's earth. You see, sir, what his answer hath been to your wayward temper. You will bear with a friend who speaks frankly with you? Martin Lambert hath acted in this as he always doth, as the best Christian, the best friend, the most kind and generous of men. Nay, if you want another proof of his goodness, here it is: He has converted me, who, 5 as I don't care to disguise, was angry with you for your treatment of him, and has absolutely brought me down here to be your bail. Let us both cry Peccavimus[1]! Harry, and shake our friend by the hand! He is sitting in the room below. He would not come here till he knew how you would receive 10 him."

"I think he is a good man!" groaned out Harry. "I was very angry and wild at the time when he and I met last, Colonel Wolfe. Nay, perhaps he was right in sending back those trinkets, hurt as I was at his doing so. Go down to him, 15 will you be so kind, sir? and tell him I am sorry, and ask his pardon, and—and, God bless him for his generous behaviour." And here the young gentleman turned his head away, and rubbed his hand across his eyes.

"Tell him all this thyself, Harry!" cries the Colonel, tak- 20 ing the young fellow's hand. "No deputy will ever say it half so well. Come with me now."

"You go first, and I'll—I'll follow,—on my word I will. See! I am in my morning-gown! I will but put on a coat and come to him. Give him my message first. Just—just 25 prepare him for me!" says poor Harry, who knew he must do it, but yet did not much like that process of eating of humble-pie.

Wolfe went out smiling—understanding the lad's scruples well enough, perhaps. As he opened the door, Mr. Gumbo 30 entered it; almost forgetting to bow to the gentleman, profusely courteous as he was on ordinary occasions,—his eyes glaring round, his great mouth grinning—himself in a state of such high excitement and delight that his master remarked his condition.   35

[1] (pĕ kä′vĕ mo͞os) we have sinned.

"What, Gum? What has happened to thee? Hast thou got a new sweetheart?"

No, Gum had not got no new sweetheart, Master.

"Give me my coat. What has brought thee back?"

5 Gum grinned prodigiously. "I have seen a ghost, Mas'r!" he said.

"A ghost! and whose, and where?"

"Whar? Saw him at Madame Bernstein's house. Come with him here in the coach! He downstairs now with 10 Colonel Lambert!" Whilst Gumbo is speaking, as he is putting on his master's coat, his eyes are rolling, his head is wagging, his hands are trembling, his lips are grinning.

"Ghost—what ghost?" says Harry, in a strange agitation. "Is anybody—is—my mother come?"

15 "No, sir; no, Master Harry!" Gumbo's head rolls nearly off in its violent convolutions, and his master, looking oddly at him, flings the door open and goes rapidly down the stair.

He is at the foot of it, just as a voice within the little office, of which the door is open, is saying, "*and for doing so, I say* 20 *thank you, and God bless you in my mother's name and mine.*"

"Whose voice is that?" calls out Harry Warrington, with a strange cry in his own voice.

"It's the *ghost's*, Mas'r!" says Gumbo, from behind; and Harry runs forward to the room,—where, if you please, we 25 will pause a little minute before we enter. The two gentlemen who were there, turned their heads away. The lost was found again. The dead was alive. The prodigal was on his brother's heart,—his own full of love, gratitude, repentance.

"Come away, James! I think we are not wanted any more 30 here," says the Colonel. "Good-night, boys. Some ladies in Hill Street won't be able to sleep for this strange news. Or will you go home and sup with 'em, and tell them the story?"

No, with many thanks, the boys would not go and sup to-night. They had stories of their own to tell. "Quick, 35 Gumbo, with the trunks! Good-bye, Mr. Amos!" Harry felt almost unhappy when he went away.

GEORGE ELIOT

THE MILL ON THE FLOSS

[Extract from Book III. "The Downfall"]

CHAPTER III. THE FAMILY COUNCIL

It was at eleven o'clock the next morning that the aunts and uncles came to hold their consultation. The fire was lighted in the large parlor, and poor Mrs. Tulliver, with a confused impression that it was a great occasion, like a funeral, un-bagged the bell-rope tassels, and unpinned the curtains, adjust- 5 ing them in proper folds, looking round and shaking her head sadly at the polished tops and legs of the tables, which sister Pullet herself could not accuse of insufficient brightness.

Mr. Deane was not coming, he was away on business; but Mrs. Deane appeared punctually in that handsome new gig 10 with the head to it, and the livery-servant driving it, which had thrown so clear a light on several traits in her character to some of her female friends in St. Ogg's. Mr. Deane had been advancing in the world as rapidly as Mr. Tulliver had been going down in it. . . . 15

Mrs. Deane was the first to arrive; and when she had taken her seat in the large parlor, Mrs. Tulliver came down to her with her comely face a little distorted, nearly as it would have been if she had been crying. She was not a woman who could shed abundant tears, except in moments when the 20 prospect of losing her furniture became unusually vivid, but she felt how unfitting it was to be quite calm under present circumstances.

"Oh, sister, what a world this is!" she exclaimed as she entered; "what trouble, oh dear!" 25

Mrs. Deane was a thin-lipped woman, who made small well-considered speeches on peculiar occasions, repeating them afterward to her husband, and asking him if she had not spoken very properly.

"Yes, sister," she said deliberately, "this is a changing world, and we don't know to-day what may happen to-morrow. But it's right to be prepared for all things, and if trouble's sent, to remember as it isn't sent without a cause. I'm very sorry for you as a sister, and if the doctor orders jelly for Mr. Tulliver, I hope you'll let me know. I'll send it willingly; for it is but right he should have proper attendance while he's ill."

"Thank you, Susan," said Mrs. Tulliver, rather faintly, withdrawing her fat hand from her sister's thin one. "But there's been no talk o' jelly yet." Then after a moment's pause she added, "There's a dozen o' cut jelly-glasses up-stairs—I shall never put jelly into 'em no more."

Her voice was rather agitated as she uttered the last words, but the sound of wheels diverted her thoughts. Mr. and Mrs. Glegg were come, and were almost immediately followed by Mr. and Mrs. Pullet.

Mrs. Pullet entered crying, as a compendious mode, at all times, of expressing what were her views of life in general, and what, in brief, were the opinions she held concerning the particular case before her.

Mrs. Glegg had on her fuzziest front, and garments which appeared to have had a recent resurrection from rather a creasy form of burial; a costume selected with the high moral purpose of instilling perfect humility into Bessy and her children.

"Mrs. G., won't you come nearer the fire?" said her husband, unwilling to take the more comfortable seat without offering it to her.

"You see I've seated myself here, Mr. Glegg," returned this superior woman; "*you* can roast yourself, if you like."

"Well," said Mr. Glegg, seating himself good-humoredly, "and how's the poor man upstairs?"

"Dr. Turnbull thought him a deal better this morning," said Mrs. Tulliver; "he took more notice, and spoke to me; but he's never known Tom yet,—looks at the poor lad as if he was a stranger, though he said something once about Tom and the pony. The doctor says his memory's gone a long way back, and he doesn't know Tom because he's thinking of him when he was little. Eh dear, eh dear!". . .

"Sister Pullet," said Mrs. Glegg, severely, "if I understand right, we've come together this morning to advise and consult about what's to be done in this disgrace as has fallen upon the family. . . .

"If we aren't come together for one to hear what the other 'ull do to save a sister and her children from the parish, *I* shall go back. *One* can't act without the other, I suppose; it isn't to be expected as *I* should do everything."

"Well, Jane," said Mrs. Pullet, "I don't see as you've been so very forrard at doing. So far as I know, this is the first time as here you've been, since it's been known as the bailiff's in the house; and I was here yesterday, and looked at all Bessy's linen and things, and I told her I'd buy in the spotted tablecloths. I couldn't speak fairer; for as for the teapot as she doesn't want to go out o' the family, it stands to sense I can't do with two silver teapots, not if it *hadn't* a straight spout, but the spotted damask I was allays fond on."

"I wish it could be managed so as my teapot and chany[1] and the best castors needn't be put up for sale," said poor Mrs. Tulliver, beseechingly, "and the sugar-tongs the first things ever I bought."

"But that can't be helped, you know," said Mr. Glegg. "If one o' the family chooses to buy 'em in, they can, but one thing must be bid for as well as another."

"And it isn't to be looked for," said uncle Pullet, with unwonted independence of idea, "as your own family should pay more for things nor they'll fetch. They may go for an old song by auction."

"Oh dear, oh dear," said Mrs. Tulliver, "to think o' my chany being sold i' that way, and I bought it when I was

[1] china.

married, just as you did yours, Jane and Sophy; and I know you didn't like mine, because o' the sprig, but I was fond of it; and there's never been a bit broke, for I've washed it myself; and there's the tulips on the cups, and the roses, as
5 anybody might go and look at 'em for pleasure. You wouldn't like *your* chany to go for an old song and be broke to pieces, though yours has got no color in it, Jane,—it's all white and fluted, and didn't cost so much as mine. And there's the castors, sister Deane, I can't think but you'd like to have the
10 castors, for I've heard you say they're pretty."

"Well, I've no objection to buy some of the best things," said Mrs. Deane, rather loftily; "we can do with extra things in our house."

"Best things!" exclaimed Mrs. Glegg, with severity, which
15 had gathered intensity from her long silence. "It drives me past patience to hear you all talking o' best things, and buying in this, that, and the other, such as silver and chany. You must bring your mind to your circumstances, Bessy, and not be thinking o' silver and chany; but whether you shall get so
20 much as a flock-bed to lie on, and a blanket to cover you, and a stool to sit on. You must remember, if you get 'em, it'll be because your friends have bought 'em for you, for you're dependent upon *them* for everything; for your husband lies there helpless, and hasn't got a penny i' the world to call his
25 own. And it's for your own good I say this, for it's right you should feel what your state is, and what disgrace your husband's brought on your own family, as you've got to look to for everything, and be humble in your mind."

Mrs. Glegg paused, for speaking with much energy for the
30 good of others is naturally exhausting. Mrs. Tulliver, always borne down by the family predominance of sister Jane, who had made her wear the yoke of a younger sister in very tender years, said pleadingly:

"I'm sure, sister, I've never asked anybody to do anything,
35 only buy things as it 'ud be a pleasure to 'em to have, so as they mightn't go and be spoiled i' strange houses. I never

asked anybody to buy the things in for me and my children;
though there's the linen I spun, and I thought when Tom was
born,—I thought one o' the first things when he was lying i'
the cradle, as all the things I'd bought wi' my own money,
and been so careful of, 'ud go to him. But I've said nothing 5
as I wanted my sisters to pay their money for me. What my
husband has done for *his* sister's unknown, and we should ha'
been better off this day if it hadn't been as he's lent money
and never asked for it again."

"Come, come," said Mr. Glegg, kindly, "don't let us make 10
things too dark. What's done can't be undone. We shall
make a shift among us to buy what's sufficient for you;
though, as Mrs. G. says, they must be useful, plain things.
We mustn't be thinking o' what's unnecessary. A table, and
a chair or two, and kitchen things, and a good bed, and such- 15
like. Why, I've seen the day when I shouldn't ha' known
myself if I'd lain on sacking i'stead o' the floor. We get a
deal o' useless things about us, only because we've got the
money to spend."

"Mr. Glegg," said Mrs. G., "if you'll be kind enough to let 20
me speak, i'stead o' taking the words out o' my mouth,—I
was going to say, Bessy, as it's fine talking for you to say as
you've never asked us to buy anything for you; let me tell
you, you *ought* to have asked us. Pray, how are you to be
purvided for, if your own family don't help you? You must 25
go to the parish, if they didn't. And you ought to know that,
and keep it in mind, and ask us humble to do what we can for
you, i'stead o' saying, and making a boast, as you've never
asked us for anything."

"You talked o' the Mosses, and what Mr. Tulliver's done 30
for 'em," said uncle Pullet, who became unusually suggestive
where advances of money were concerned. "Haven't *they*
been anear you? They ought to do something as well as
other folks; and if he's lent 'em money, they ought to be
made to pay it back."   35

"Yes, to be sure," said Mrs. Deane; "I've been thinking

so. How is it Mr. and Mrs. Moss aren't here to meet us? It
is but right they should do their share."

"Oh, dear!" said Mrs. Tulliver, "I never sent 'em word
about Mr. Tulliver, and they live so back'ard among the lanes
5 at Basset, they niver hear anything only when Mr. Moss
comes to market. But I niver gave 'em a thought. I wonder
Maggie didn't, though, for she was allays so fond of her
aunt Moss."

"Why don't your children come in, Bessy?" said Mrs. Pul-
10 let, at the mention of Maggie. "They should hear what their
aunts and uncles have got to say; and Maggie,—when it's
me as have paid for half her schooling, she ought to think
more of her aunt Pullet than of aunt Mosses. I may go off
sudden when I get home to-day; there's no telling."

15 "If I'd had *my* way," said Mrs. Glegg, "the children 'ud
ha been in the room from the first. It's time they knew who
they've to look to, and it's right as *somebody* should talk to
'em, and let 'em know their condition i' life, and what they're
come down to, and make 'em feel as they've got to suffer for
20 their father's faults."

"Well, I'll go and fetch 'em, sister," said Mrs. Tulliver,
resignedly. She was quite crushed now, and thought of the
treasures in the storeroom with no other feeling than blank
despair.

25 She went upstairs to fetch Tom and Maggie, who were
both in their father's room, and was on her way down again,
when the sight of the storeroom door suggested a new thought
to her. She went toward it, and left the children to go down
by themselves.

30 The aunts and uncles appeared to have been in warm discussion when the brother and sister entered,—both with
shrinking reluctance; for though Tom, with a practical
sagacity which had been roused into activity by the strong
stimulus of the new emotions he had undergone since yester-
35 day, had been turning over in his mind a plan which he
meant to propose to one of his aunts or uncles, he felt by

no means amicably toward them, and dreaded meeting them all at once as he would have dreaded a large dose of concentrated physic, which was but just endurable in small draughts. As for Maggie, she was peculiarly depressed this morning; she had been called up, after brief rest, at three o'clock, and had that strange dreamy weariness which comes from watching in a sick-room through the chill hours of early twilight and breaking day,—in which the outside daylight life seems to have no importance, and to be a mere margin to the hours in the darkened chamber. Their entrance interrupted the conversation. The shaking of hands was a melancholy and silent ceremony, till uncle Pullet observed, as Tom approached him:

"Well, young sir, we've been talking as we should want your pen and ink; you can write rarely now, after all your schooling, I should think."

"Ay, ay," said Uncle Glegg, with admonition which he meant to be kind, "we must look to see the good of all this schooling, as your father's sunk so much money in, now,—

'When land is gone and money's spent,
   Then learning is most excellent.'

Now's the time, Tom, to let us see the good o' your learning. Let us see whether you can do better than I can, as have made my fortin without it. But I began wi' doing with little, you see; I could live on a basin o' porridge and a crust o' bread-and-cheese. But I doubt high living and high learning 'ull make it harder for you, young man, nor it was for me."

"But he must do it," interposed aunt Glegg, energetically, "whether it's hard or no. He hasn't got to consider what's hard; he must consider as he isn't to trusten to his friends to keep him in idleness and luxury; he's got to bear the fruits of his father's misconduct, and bring his mind to fare hard and to work hard. And he must be humble and grateful to his aunts and uncles for what they're doing for his mother and father, as must be turned out into the streets and go to

the workhouse if they didn't help 'em. And his sister, too," continued Mrs. Glegg, looking severely at Maggie, who had sat down on the sofa by her aunt Deane, drawn to her by the sense that she was Lucy's mother, "she must make up
5 her mind to be humble and work; for there'll be no servants to wait on her any more,—she must remember that. She must do the work o' the house, and she must respect and love her aunts as have done so much for her, and saved their money to leave to their nepheys and nieces."

10 Tom was still standing before the table in the center of the group. There was a heightened color in his face, and he was very far from looking humbled, but he was preparing to say, in a respectful tone, something he had previously meditated, when the door opened and his mother re-entered.

15 Poor Mrs. Tulliver had in her hands a small tray, on which she had placed her silver teapot, a specimen teacup and saucer, the castors, and sugar-tongs.

"See here, sister," she said, looking at Mrs. Deane, as she set the tray on the table, "I thought, perhaps, if you looked
20 at the teapot again,—it's a good while since you saw it,— you might like the pattern better; it makes beautiful tea, and there's a stand and everything; you might use it for every day, or else lay it by for Lucy when she goes to housekeeping. I should be so loath for 'em to buy it at the Golden Lion,"
25 said the poor woman, her heart swelling, and the tears coming,—"my teapot as I bought when I was married, and to think of its being scratched, and set before the travelers and folks, and my letters on it,—see here, E.D.,—and everybody to see 'em."

30 "Ah, dear, dear!" said aunt Pullet, shaking her head with deep sadness, "it's very bad,—to think o' the family initials going about everywhere,—it niver was so before; you're a very unlucky sister, Bessy. But what's the use o' buying the teapot, when there's the linen and spoons and everything to
35 go, and some of 'em with your full name,—and when it's got that straight spout, too."

"As to disgrace o' the family," said Mrs. Glegg, "that can't be helped wi' buying teapots. The disgrace is, for one o' the family to ha' married a man as has brought her to beggary. The disgrace is, as they're to be sold up. We can't hinder the country from knowing that." 5

Maggie had started up from the sofa at the allusion to her father, but Tom saw her action and flushed face in time to prevent her from speaking. "Be quiet, Maggie," he said authoritatively, pushing her aside. It was a remarkable manifestation of self-command and practical judgment in a 10 lad of fifteen, that when his aunt Glegg ceased, he began to speak in a quiet and respectful manner, though with a good deal of trembling in his voice; for his mother's words had cut him to the quick.

"Then, aunt," he said, looking straight at Mrs. Glegg, "if 15 you think it's a disgrace to the family that we should be sold up, wouldn't it be better to prevent it altogether? And if you and my aunt Pullet," he continued, looking at the latter, "think of leaving any money to me and Maggie, wouldn't it be better to give it now, and pay the debt we're going to be 20 sold up for, and save my mother from parting with her furniture?"

There was silence for a few moments, for every one, including Maggie, was astonished at Tom's sudden manliness of tone. Uncle Glegg was the first to speak. 25

"Ay, ay, young man, come now! You show some notion o' things. But there's the interest, you must remember; your aunts get five per cent on their money, and they'd lose that if they advanced it; you haven't thought o' that."

"I could work and pay that every year," said Tom, 30 promptly. "I'd do anything to save my mother from parting with her things."

"Well done!" said uncle Glegg, admiringly. He had been drawing Tom out, rather than reflecting on the practicability of his proposal. But he had produced the unfortunate result 35 of irritating his wife.

"Yes, Mr. Glegg!" said that lady, with angry sarcasm. "It's pleasant work for you to be giving my money away, as you've pretended to leave at my own disposal. And my money, as was my own father's gift, and not yours, Mr. Glegg;
5 and I've saved it, and added to it myself, and had more to put out almost every year, and it's to go and be sunk in other folks's furniture, and encourage 'em in luxury and extravagance as they've no means of supporting; and I'm to alter my will, or have a codicil made, and leave two or three hun-
10 dred less behind me when I die,—me as have allays done right and been careful, and the eldest o' the family; and my money's to go and be squandered on them as have had the same chance as me, only they've been wicked and wasteful. Sister Pullet, *you* may do as you like, and you may let your
15 husband rob you back again o' the money he's given you, but that isn't *my* sperrit."

"La, Jane, how fiery you are!" said Mrs. Pullet. "I'm sure you'll have the blood in your head, and have to be cupped. I'm sorry for Bessy and her children,—I'm sure I
20 think of 'em o' nights dreadful, for I sleep very bad wi' this new medicine,—but it's no use for me to think o' doing anything, if you won't meet me half-way."

"Why, there's this to be considered," said Mr. Glegg. "It's no use to pay off this debt and save the furniture, when
25 there's all the law debts behind, as 'ud take every shilling, and more than could be made out o' land and stock, for I've made that out from Lawyer Gore. We'd need save our money to keep the poor man with, instead o' spending it on furniture as he can neither eat nor drink. You *will* be so hasty,
30 Jane, as if I didn't know what was reasonable."

"Then speak accordingly, Mr. Glegg!" said his wife, with slow, loud emphasis, bending her head toward him significantly.

Tom's countenance had fallen during this conversation,
35 and his lip quivered; but he was determined not to give way. He would behave like a man. Maggie, on the contrary, after

her momentary delight in Tom's speech, had relapsed into her
state of trembling indignation. Her mother had been standing close by Tom's side, and had been clinging to his arm
ever since he had last spoken; Maggie suddenly started up
and stood in front of them, her eyes flashing like the eyes of
a young lioness.

"Why do you come, then," she burst out, "talking and in-
terfering with us and scolding us, if you don't mean to do
anything to help my poor mother,—your own sister,—if
you've no feeling for her when she's in trouble, and won't
part with anything, though you would never miss it, to save
her from pain? Keep away from us then, and don't come to
find fault with my father,—he was better than any of you;
he was kind,—he would have helped *you*, if you had been in
trouble. Tom and I don't ever want to have any of your
money, if you won't help my mother. We'd rather not have
it! We'll do without you."

Maggie, having hurled her defiance at aunts and uncles in
this way, stood still, with her large dark eyes glaring at them,
as if she were ready to await all consequences.

Mrs. Tulliver was frightened; there was something porten-
tous in this mad outbreak; she did not see how life could go
on after it. Tom was vexed; it was no *use* to talk so. The
aunts were silent with surprise for some moments. At length,
in a case of aberration such as this, comment presented itself
as more expedient than any answer.

"You haven't seen the end o' your trouble wi' that
child, Bessy," said Mrs. Pullet; "she's beyond everything
for boldness and unthankfulness. It's dreadful. I might
ha' let alone paying for her schooling, for she's worse nor
ever."

"It's no more than what I've allays said," followed
Mrs. Glegg. "Other folks may be surprised, but I'm not.
I've said over and over again,—years ago I've said,—'Mark
my words; that child 'ull come to no good; there isn't a bit
of our family in her.' And as for her having so much school-

ing, I never thought well o' that. I'd my reasons when I said *I* wouldn't pay anything toward it."

"Come, come," said Mr. Glegg, "let's waste no more time in talking,—let's go to business. Tom, now, get the pen and
5 ink—"

While Mr. Glegg was speaking, a tall dark figure was seen hurrying past the window.

"Why, there's Mrs. Moss," said Mrs. Tulliver. "The bad news must ha' reached her, then;" and she went out to open
10 the door, Maggie eagerly following her.

"That's fortunate," said Mrs. Glegg. "She can agree to the list o' things to be bought in. It's but right she should do her share when it's her own brother."

Mrs. Moss was in too much agitation to resist Mrs. Tul-
15 liver's movement, as she drew her into the parlor automati- cally, without reflecting that it was hardly kind to take her among so many persons in the first painful moment of arrival. The tall, worn, dark-haired woman was a strong contrast to the Dodson sisters as she entered in her shabby dress, with
20 her shawl and bonnet looking as if they had been hastily huddled on, and with that entire absence of self-consciousness which belongs to keenly felt trouble. Maggie was clinging to her arm; and Mrs. Moss seemed to notice no one else except Tom, whom she went straight up to and took by
25 the hand.

"Oh, my dear children," she burst out, "you've no call to think well o' me; I'm a poor aunt to you, for I'm one o' them as take all and give nothing. How's my poor brother?"

"Mr. Turnbull thinks he'll get better," said Maggie. "Sit
30 down, aunt Gritty. Don't fret."

"Oh, my sweet child, I feel torn i' two," said Mrs. Moss, al- lowing Maggie to lead her to the sofa, but still not seeming to notice the presence of the rest. "We've three hundred pounds o' my brother's money, and now he wants it, and you all
35 want it, poor things!—and yet we must be sold up to pay it, and there's my poor children,—eight of 'em, and the little

un of all can't speak plain. And I feel as if I was a robber.
But I'm sure I'd no thought as my brother—"

The poor woman was interrupted by a rising sob.

"Three hundred pounds! oh dear, dear," said Mrs. Tulliver, who, when she had said that her husband had done 5
"unknown" things for his sister, had not had any particular
sum in her mind, and felt a wife's irritation at having been
kept in the dark.

"What madness, to be sure!" said Mrs. Glegg. "A man
with a family! He'd no right to lend his money i' that way; 10
and without security, I'll be bound, if the truth was known."

Mrs. Glegg's voice had arrested Mrs. Moss's attention, and
looking up, she said:

"Yes, there *was* security; my husband gave a note for it.
We're not that sort o' people, neither of us, as 'ud rob my 15
brother's children; and we looked to paying back the money,
when the times got a bit better."

"Well, but now," said Mr. Glegg, gently, "hasn't your husband no way o' raising this money? Because it 'ud be a little
fortin, like, for these folks, if we can do without Tulliver's 20
being made a bankrupt. Your husband's got stock; it is but
right he should raise the money, as it seems to me,—not but
what I'm sorry for you, Mrs. Moss."

"Oh, sir, you don't know what bad luck my husband's had
with his stock. The farm's suffering so as never was for want 25
o' stock; and we've sold all the wheat, and we're behind with
our rent,—not but what we'd like to do what's right, and I'd
sit up and work half the night, if it 'ud be any good; but
there's them poor children,—four of 'em such little uns—"

"Don't cry so, aunt; don't fret," whispered Maggie, who 30
had kept hold of Mrs. Moss's hand.

"Did Mr. Tulliver let you have the money all at once?"
said Mrs. Tulliver, still lost in the conception of things which
had been "going on" without her knowledge.

"No; at twice," said Mrs. Moss, rubbing her eyes and 35
making an effort to restrain her tears. "The last was after

my bad illness four years ago, as everything went wrong,
and there was a new note made then. What with illness and
bad luck, I've been nothing but cumber all my life."

"Yes, Mrs. Moss," said Mrs. Glegg, with decision, "yours
5 is a very unlucky family; the more's the pity for *my* sister."

"I set off in the cart as soon as ever I heard o' what had
happened," said Mrs. Moss, looking at Mrs. Tulliver. "I
should never ha' stayed away all this while, if you'd thought
well to let me know. And it isn't as I'm thinking all about
10 ourselves, and nothing about my brother, only the money was
so on my mind, I couldn't help speaking about it. And my
husband and me desire to do the right thing, sir," she added,
looking at Mr. Glegg, "and we'll make shift and pay the
money, come what will, if that's all my brother's got to trust
15 to. We've been used to trouble, and don't look for much else.
It's only the thought o' my poor children pulls me i' two."

"Why, there's this to be thought on, Mrs. Moss," said
Mr. Glegg, "and it's right to warn you,—if Tulliver's made a
bankrupt, and he's got a note-of-hand of your husband's for
20 three hundred pounds, you'll be obliged to pay it; th' as-
signees 'ull come on you for it."

"Oh dear, oh dear!" said Mrs. Tulliver, thinking of the
bankruptcy, and not of Mrs. Moss's concern in it. Poor
Mrs. Moss herself listened in trembling submission, while
25 Maggie looked with bewildered distress at Tom to see if *he*
showed any signs of understanding this trouble, and caring
about poor aunt Moss. Tom was only looking thoughtful,
with his eyes on the tablecloth.

"And if he isn't made bankrupt," continued Mr. Glegg, "as
30 I said before, three hundred pounds 'ud be a little fortin for
him, poor man. We don't know but what he may be partly
helpless, if he ever gets up again. I'm very sorry if it goes
hard with you, Mrs. Moss, but my opinion is, looking at it
one way, it'll be right for you to raise the money; and looking
35 at it th' other way, you'll be obliged to pay it. You won't
think ill o' me for speaking the truth."

"Uncle," said Tom, looking up suddenly from his meditative view of the tablecloth, "I don't think it would be right for my aunt Moss to pay the money if it would be against my father's will for her to pay it; would it?"

Mr. Glegg looked surprised for a moment or two before he 5 said: "Why, no, perhaps not, Tom; but then he'd ha' destroyed the note, you know. We must look for the note. What makes you think it 'ud be against his will?"

"Why," said Tom, coloring, but trying to speak firmly, in spite of a boyish tremor, "I remember quite well, before I 10 went to school to Mr. Stelling, my father said to me one night, when we were sitting by the fire together, and no one else was in the room—"

Tom hesitated a little, and then went on.

"He said something to me about Maggie, and then he said: 15 'I've always been good to my sister, though she married against my will, and I've lent Moss money; but I shall never think of distressing him to pay it; I'd rather lose it. My children must not mind being the poorer for that.' And now my father's ill, and not able to speak for himself, I shouldn't 20 like anything to be done contrary to what he said to me."

"Well, but then, my boy," said uncle Glegg, whose good feeling led him to enter into Tom's wish, but who could not at once shake off his habitual abhorrence of such recklessness as destroying securities, or alienating[1] anything important 25 enough to make an appreciable difference in a man's property, "we should have to make away wi' the note, you know, if we're to guard against what may happen, supposing your father's made bankrupt—"

"Mr. Glegg," interrupted his wife, severely, "mind what 30 you're saying. You're putting yourself very forrard in other folks's business. If you speak rash, don't say it was my fault."

"That's such a thing as I never heard of before," said uncle Pullet, who had been making haste with his lozenge in order to express his amazement,—"making away with a 35

[1] transferring to another.

note! I should think anybody could set the constable on you for it."

"Well, but," said Mrs. Tulliver, "if the note's worth all that money, why can't we pay it away, and save my things from going away? We've no call to meddle with your uncle and aunt Moss, Tom, if you think your father 'ud be angry when he gets well."

Mrs. Tulliver had not studied the question of exchange, and was straining her mind after original ideas on the subject.

"Pooh, pooh, pooh! you women don't understand these things," said uncle Glegg. "There's no way o' making it safe for Mr. and Mrs. Moss but destroying the note."

"Then I hope you'll help me to do it, uncle," said Tom, earnestly. "If my father shouldn't get well, I should be very unhappy to think anything had been done against his will that I could hinder. And I'm sure he meant me to remember what he said that evening. I ought to obey my father's wish about his property."

Even Mrs. Glegg could not withhold her approval from Tom's words; she felt that the Dodson blood was certainly speaking in him, though, if his father had been a Dodson, there would never have been this wicked alienation of money. Maggie would hardly have restrained herself from leaping on Tom's neck, if her aunt Moss had not prevented her by herself rising and taking Tom's hand, while she said, with rather a choked voice:

"You'll never be the poorer for this, my dear boy, if there's a God above; and if the money's wanted for your father, Moss and me 'ull pay it, the same as if there was ever such security. We'll do as we'd be done by; for if my children have got no other luck, they've got an honest father and mother."

"Well," said Mr. Glegg, who had been meditating after Tom's words, "we shouldn't be doing any wrong by the creditors, supposing your father *was* bankrupt. I've been thinking o' that, for I've been a creditor myself, and seen no

end o' cheating. If he meant to give your aunt the money
before ever he got into this sad work o' lawing, it's the same
as if he'd made away with the note himself; for he'd made up
his mind to be that much poorer. But there's a deal o' things
to be considered, young man," Mr. Glegg added, looking ad- 5
monishingly at Tom, "when you come to money business,
and you may be taking one man's dinner away to make another man's breakfast. You don't understand that, I doubt?"

"Yes, I do," said Tom, decidedly. "I know if I owe money
to one man, I've no right to give it to another. But if my 10
father had made up his mind to give my aunt the money
before he was in debt, he had a right to do it."

"Well done, young man! I didn't think you'd be so sharp,"
said uncle Glegg, with much candor. "But perhaps your
father *did* make away with the note. Let us go and see if we 15
can find it in the chest."

THOMAS HARDY

THE RETURN OF THE NATIVE[1]

CHAPTER I. A FACE ON WHICH TIME MAKES BUT LITTLE
IMPRESSION

A Saturday afternoon in November was approaching the
time of twilight, and the vast tract of unenclosed wild known
as Egdon Heath embrowned itself moment by moment. Overhead the hollow stretch of whitish cloud shutting out the sky 20
was a tent which had the whole heath for its floor.

The heaven being spread with this pallid screen and the
earth with the darkest vegetation, their meeting-line at the
horizon was clearly marked. In such contrast the heath

[1] Reprinted by permission of Harper & Brothers and Macmillan & Co.,
Limited, publishers.

wore the appearance of an instalment of night which had
taken up its place before its astronomical hour was come:
darkness had to a great extent arrived hereon, while day
stood distinct in the sky. Looking upwards, a furze[1]-cutter
5 would have been inclined to continue work; looking down,
he would have decided to finish his faggot[2] and go home.
The distant rims of the world and of the firmament[3] seemed
to be a division in time no less than a division in matter.
The face of the heath by its mere complexion added half an
10 hour to evening; it could in like manner retard the dawn,
sadden noon, anticipate the frowning of storms scarcely gen-
erated, and intensify the opacity of a moonless midnight to a
cause of shaking and dread.

In fact, precisely at this transitional point of its nightly
15 roll into darkness the great and particular glory of the Egdon
waste began, and nobody could be said to understand the
heath who had not been there at such a time. It could best
be felt when it could not clearly be seen, its complete effect
and explanation lying in this and the succeeding hours before
20 the next dawn: then, and only then, did it tell its true tale.
The spot was, indeed, a near relation of night, and when night
showed itself an apparent tendency to gravitate together
could be perceived in its shades and the scene. The sombre
stretch of rounds and hollows seemed to rise and meet the
25 evening gloom in pure sympathy, the heath exhaling darkness
as rapidly as the heavens precipitated it. And so the obscurity in the air and the obscurity in the land closed together
in a black fraternization towards which each advanced
half-way.

30 The place became full of a watchful intentness now; for
when other things sank brooding to sleep the heath appeared
slowly to awake and listen. Every night its Titanic form
seemed to await something; but it had waited thus, unmoved,
during so many centuries, through the crises of so many

---

[1] a spiny, evergreen shrub, used for fuel.   [2] bundle of sticks or twigs.
[3] sky.

things, that it could only be imagined to await one last crisis
—the final overthrow.

It was a spot which returned upon the memory of those
who loved it with an aspect of peculiar and kindly congruity.
Smiling champaigns[1] of flowers and fruit hardly do this, for
they are permanently harmonious only with an existence of
better reputation as to its issues than the present. Twilight
combined with the scenery of Egdon Heath to evolve a thing
majestic without severity, impressive without showiness, em-
phatic in its admonitions, grand in its simplicity. The quali-
fications which frequently invest the façade of a prison with
far more dignity than is found in the façade of a palace
double its size lent to this heath a sublimity in which spots
renowned for beauty of the accepted kind are utterly wanting. Fair prospects wed happily with fair times; but alas,
if times be not fair! Men have oftener suffered from the
mockery of a place too smiling for their reason than from
the oppression of surroundings oversadly tinged. Haggard
Egdon appealed to a subtler and scarcer instinct, to a more
recently learnt emotion, than that which responds to the
sort of beauty called charming and fair.

Indeed, it is a question if the exclusive reign of this ortho-
dox beauty is not approaching its last quarter. The new
Vale of Tempe may be a gaunt waste in Thule: human souls
may find themselves in closer and closer harmony with external things wearing a sombreness distasteful to our race
when it was young. The time seems near, if it has not
actually arrived, when the chastened sublimity of a moor, a
sea, or a mountain will be all of nature that is absolutely in
keeping with the moods of the more thinking among mankind. And ultimately, to the commonest tourist, spots like
Iceland may become what the vineyards and myrtle-gardens
of South Europe are to him now; and Heidelberg and Baden
be passed unheeded as he hastens from the Alps to the sand-
dunes of Scheveningen.

[1] level fields.

The most thorough-going ascetic could feel that he had a
natural right to wander on Egdon: he was keeping within
the line of legitimate indulgence when he laid himself open
to influences such as these. Colours and beauties so far sub-
5 dued were, at least, the birthright of all. Only in summer
days of highest feather did its mood touch the level of gaiety.
Intensity was more usually reached by way of the solemn
than by way of the brilliant, and such a sort of intensity was
often arrived at during winter darkness, tempests, and mists.
10 Then Egdon was aroused to reciprocity; for the storm was its
lover, and the wind its friend. Then it became the home of
strange phantoms; and it was found to be the hitherto un-
recognized original of those wild regions of obscurity which
are vaguely felt to be compassing us about in midnight
15 dreams of flight and disaster, and are never thought of after
the dream till revived by scenes like this.

It was at present a place perfectly accordant with man's
nature—neither ghastly, hateful, nor ugly: neither commonplace, unmeaning, nor tame; but, like man, slighted and
20 enduring; and withal singularly colossal and mysterious in
its swarthy monotony. As with some persons who have
long lived apart, solitude seemed to look out of its countenance. It had a lonely face, suggesting tragical possibilities.

This obscure, obsolete, superseded country figures in
25 Domesday. Its condition is recorded therein as that of
heathy, furzy, briary wilderness—"Bruaria." Then follows
the length and breadth in leagues; and, though some uncer-
tainty exists as to the exact extent of this ancient lineal
measure, it appears from the figures that the area of Egdon
30 down to the present day has but little diminished. "Turbaria
Bruaria"—the right of cutting heath-turf—occurs in charters relating to the district. "Overgrown with heth and
mosse," says Leland of the same dark sweep of country.

Here at least were intelligible facts regarding landscape—
35 far-reaching proofs productive of genuine satisfaction. The
untameable, Ishmaelitish thing that Egdon now was it always

had been. Civilization was its enemy; and ever since the beginning of vegetation its soil had worn the same antique brown dress, the natural and invariable garment of the particular formation. In its venerable one coat lay a certain vein of satire on human vanity in clothes. A person on a 5 heath in raiment of modern cut and colours has more or less an anomalous look. We seem to want the oldest and simplest human clothing where the clothing of the earth is so primitive.

To recline on a stump of thorn in the central valley of Egdon, between afternoon and night, as now, where the eye 10 could reach nothing of the world outside the summits and shoulders of heathland which filled the whole circumference of its glance, and to know that everything around and underneath had been from prehistoric times as unaltered as the stars overhead, gave ballast to the mind adrift on change, 15 and harassed by the irrepressible New. The great inviolate place had an ancient permanence which the sea cannot claim. Who can say of a particular sea that it is old? Distilled by the sun, kneaded by the moon, it is renewed in a year, in a day, or in an hour. The sea changed, the fields changed, the 20 rivers, the villages, and the people changed, yet Egdon remained. Those surfaces were neither so steep as to be destructible by weather, nor so flat as to be the victims of floods and deposits. With the exception of an aged highway, and a still more aged barrow[1] presently to be referred to— 25 themselves almost crystallized to natural products by long continuance—even the trifling irregularities were not caused by pickaxe, plough, or spade, but remained as the very finger-touches of the last geological change.

The above-mentioned highway traversed the lower levels 30 of the heath, from one horizon to another. In many portions of its course it overlaid an old vicinal way, which branched from the great Western road of the Romans, the Via Iceniana,

---

[1] A hill or mound, often one built over the remains of the dead. Cf. the barrow, called howe or burg, which Beowulf's followers built in his honor, p. 5.

or Ikenild Street, hard by. On the evening under consideration it would have been noticed that, though the gloom had
increased sufficiently to confuse the minor features of the
heath, the white surface of the road remained almost as
5 clear as ever.

THE ROMAN ROAD[1]

The Roman Road runs straight and bare
As the pale parting-line in hair
Across the heath. And thoughtful men
Contrast its days of Now and Then,
10   And delve, and measure, and compare;

Visioning on the vacant air
Helmed legionaries, who proudly rear
The Eagle, as they pace again
                    The Roman Road.

15   But no tall brass-helmed legionnaire
Haunts it for me. Uprises there
A mother's form upon my ken,
Guiding my infant steps, as when
We walked that ancient thoroughfare,
20   The Roman Road.

ROBERT LOUIS STEVENSON

EL DORADO[2]

It seems as if a great deal were attainable in a world where
there are so many marriages and decisive battles, and where
we all, at certain hours of the day, and with great gusto and
despatch, stow a portion of victuals finally and irretrievably

[1] From *Time's Laughingstocks*, reprinted by permission of Macmillan &
Co., Limited, and Harper & Brothers, publishers.
[2] From *Virginibus Puerisque*, Charles Scribner's Sons, authorized publishers.

into the bag which contains us. And it would seem also, on
a hasty view, that the attainment of as much as possible was
the one goal of man's contentious life. And yet, as regards
the spirit, this is but a semblance. We live in an ascending
scale when we live happily, one thing leading to another in an
endless series. There is always a new horizon for onward-
looking men, and although we dwell on a small planet, im-
mersed in petty business and not enduring beyond a brief
period of years, we are so constituted that our hopes are
inaccessible, like stars, and the term of hoping is prolonged
until the term of life. To be truly happy is a question of
how we begin and not of how we end, of what we want and
not of what we have. An aspiration is a joy for ever, a possession as solid as a landed estate, a fortune which we can
never exhaust and which gives us year by year a revenue of
pleasurable activity. To have many of these is to be spirit-
ually rich. Life is only a very dull and ill-directed theatre
unless we have some interests in the piece; and to those who
have neither art nor science, the world is a mere arrangement
of colours, or a rough footway where they may very well
break their shins. It is in virtue of his own desires and curi-
osities that any man continues to exist with even patience,
that he is charmed by the look of things and people, and that
he wakens every morning with a renewed appetite for work
and pleasure. Desire and curiosity are the two eyes through
which he sees the world in the most enchanted colours: it is
they that make women beautiful or fossils interesting: and
the man may squander his estate and come to beggary, but if
he keeps these two amulets he is still rich in the possibilities
of pleasure. Suppose he could take one meal so compact
and comprehensive that he should never hunger any more;
suppose him, at a glance, to take in all the features of the
world and allay the desire for knowledge; suppose him to do
the like in any province of experience—would not that man
be in a poor way for amusement ever after?

One who goes touring on foot with a single volume in his

knapsack reads with circumspection, pausing often to reflect, and often laying the book down to contemplate the landscape or the prints in the inn parlour; for he fears to come to an end of his entertainment, and be left companionless on the
5 last stages of his journey. A young fellow recently finished the works of Thomas Carlyle, winding up, if we remember aright, with the ten note-books upon Frederick the Great. "What!" cried the young fellow, in consternation, "is there no more Carlyle? Am I left to the daily papers?" A more
10 celebrated instance is that of Alexander, who wept bitterly because he had no more worlds to subdue. And when Gibbon had finished the *Decline and Fall*, he had only a few moments of joy; and it was with a "sober melancholy" that he parted from his labours.

15   Happily we all shoot at the moon with ineffectual arrows; our hopes are set on inaccessible El Dorado; we come to an end of nothing here below. Interests are only plucked up to sow themselves again, like mustard. You would think, when the child was born, there would be an end to trouble; and
20 yet it is only the beginning of fresh anxieties; and when you have seen it through its teething and its education, and at last its marriage, alas! it is only to have new fears, new quivering sensibilities, with every day; and the health of your children's children grows as touching a concern as that
25 of your own. Again, when you have married your wife, you would think you were got upon a hilltop, and might begin to go downward by an easy slope. But you have only ended courting to begin marriage. Falling in love and winning love are often difficult tasks to overbearing and rebellious
30 spirits; but to keep in love is also a business of some importance, to which both man and wife must bring kindness and goodwill. The true love story commences at the altar, when there lies before the married pair a most beautiful contest of wisdom and generosity, and a life-long struggle
35 towards an unattainable ideal. Unattainable? Ay, surely

unattainable, from the very fact that they are two instead
of one.

"Of making books there is no end," complained the
Preacher; and did not perceive how highly he was praising
letters as an occupation. There is no end, indeed, to making 5
books or experiments, or to travel, or to gathering wealth.
Problem gives rise to problem. We may study for ever, and
we are never as learned as we would. We have never made
a statue worthy of our dreams. And when we have discovered
a continent, or crossed a chain of mountains, it is only to find 10
another ocean or another plain upon the further side. In the
infinite universe there is room for our swiftest diligence and
to spare. It is not like the works of Carlyle, which can be
read to an end. Even in a corner of it, in a private park, or
in the neighbourhood of a single hamlet, the weather and the 15
seasons keep so deftly changing that although we walk there
for a lifetime there will be always something new to startle
and delight us.

There is only one wish realisable on the earth; only one
thing that can be perfectly attained: Death. And from a 20
variety of circumstances we have no one to tell us whether it
be worth attaining.

A strange picture we make on our way to our chimæras,
ceaselessly marching, grudging ourselves the time for rest;
indefatigable, adventurous pioneers. It is true that we shall 25
never reach the goal; it is even more than probable that
there is no such place; and if we lived for centuries and were
endowed with the powers of a god, we should find ourselves
not much nearer what we wanted at the end. O toiling hands
of mortals! O unwearied feet, travelling ye know not 30
whither! Soon, soon, it seems to you, you must come forth
on some conspicuous hilltop, and but a little way further,
against the setting sun, descry the spires of El Dorado. Little
do ye know your own blessedness; for to travel hopefully is a
better thing than to arrive, and the true success is to labour. 35

THOMAS BABINGTON MACAULAY

THE HISTORY OF ENGLAND

CONCLUSION OF CHAPTER III

Of the blessings which civilisation and philosophy bring
with them a large proportion is common to all ranks, and
would, if withdrawn, be missed as painfully by the labourer
as by the peer.[1] The market-place which the rustic can now
5 reach with his cart in an hour was, a hundred and sixty years
ago, a day's journey from him. The street which now affords
to the artisan, during the whole night, a secure, a convenient,
and a brilliantly lighted walk was, a hundred and sixty years
ago, so dark after sunset that he would not have been able
10 to see his hand, so ill paved that he would have run constant
risk of breaking his neck, and so ill watched that he would
have been in imminent danger of being knocked down and
plundered of his small earnings. Every bricklayer who falls
from a scaffold, every sweeper of a crossing who is run over
15 by a carriage, may now have his wounds dressed and his
limbs set with a skill such as, a hundred and sixty years ago,
all the wealth of a great lord like Ormond, or of a merchant
prince like Clayton, could not have purchased. Some frightful diseases have been extirpated by science; and some have
20 been banished by police. The term of human life has been
lengthened over the whole kingdom, and especially in the
towns. The year 1685 was not accounted sickly; yet in the
year 1685 more than one in twenty-three of the inhabitants of
the capital died. At present only one inhabitant of the capi-
25 tal in forty dies annually. The difference in salubrity[2] between the London of the nineteenth century and the London
of the seventeenth century is very far greater than the difference between London in an ordinary year and London in
a year of cholera.

[1] a nobleman, a member of the House of Lords.   [2] healthfulness.

Still more important is the benefit which all orders of society, and especially the lower orders, have derived from the mollifying[1] influence of civilisation on the national character. The groundwork of that character has indeed been the same through many generations, in the sense in which the groundwork of the character of an individual may be said to be the same when he is a rude and thoughtless schoolboy and when he is a refined and accomplished man. It is pleasing to reflect that the public mind of England has softened while it has ripened, and that we have, in the course of ages, become, not only a wiser, but also a kinder people. There is scarcely a page of the history or lighter literature of the seventeenth century which does not contain some proof that our ancestors were less humane than their posterity. The discipline of workshops, of schools, of private families, though not more efficient than at present, was infinitely harsher. Masters, well born and bred, were in the habit of beating their servants. Pedagogues knew no way of imparting knowledge but by beating their pupils. Husbands, of decent station, were not ashamed to beat their wives. The implacability of hostile factions was such as we can scarcely conceive. Whigs were disposed to murmur because Stafford was suffered to die without seeing his bowels burned before his face. Tories reviled and insulted Russell as his coach passed from the Tower to the scaffold in Lincoln's Inn Fields. As little mercy was shown by the populace to sufferers of a humbler rank. If an offender was put into the pillory, it was well if he escaped with life from the shower of brickbats and paving-stones. If he was tied to the cart's tail, the crowd pressed round him, imploring the hangman to give it the fellow well, and make him howl. Gentlemen arranged parties of pleasure to Bridewell on court days for the purpose of seeing the wretched women who beat hemp there whipped. A man pressed to death for refusing to plead, a woman burned for coining,[2] excited less sympathy than is now felt for a galled

---

[1] softening, making less harsh.   [2] making counterfeit coins.

horse or an overdriven ox. Fights compared with which a boxing-match is a refined and humane spectacle were among the favourite diversions of a large part of the town. Multitudes assembled to see gladiators hack each other to pieces
5 with deadly weapons, and shouted with delight when one of the combatants lost a finger or an eye. The prisons were hells on earth, seminaries of every crime and of every disease. At the assizes[1] the lean and yellow culprits brought with them from their cells to the dock[2] an atmosphere of stench and
10 pestilence which sometimes avenged them signally on bench,[3] bar,[4] and jury. But on all this misery society looked with profound indifference. Nowhere could be found that sensitive and restless compassion which has, in our time, extended a powerful protection to the factory child, to the Hindoo
15 widow, to the negro slave, which pries into the stores and water-casks of every emigrant ship, which winces at every lash laid on the back of a drunken soldier, which will not suffer the thief in the hulks[5] to be ill fed or overworked, and which has repeatedly endeavoured to save the life even of the
20 murderer. It is true that compassion ought, like all other feelings, to be under the government of reason, and has, for want of such government, produced some ridiculous and some deplorable effects. But the more we study the annals of the past, the more shall we rejoice that we live in a merci-
25 ful age, in an age in which cruelty is abhorred, and in which pain, even when deserved, is inflicted reluctantly and from a sense of duty. Every class doubtless has gained largely by this great moral change: but the class which has gained most is the poorest, the most dependent, and the most defenceless.
30   The general effect of the evidence which has been submitted to the reader seems hardly to admit of doubt. Yet, in spite of evidence, many will still image to themselves the England of the Stuarts as a more pleasant country than the England in which we live. It may at first sight seem strange

---

[1] sessions of the superior courts.   [2] the prisoner's place in a court room.   [3] judges.   [4] lawyers.   [5] prison ships.

that society, while constantly moving forward with eager
speed, should be constantly looking backward with tender
regret. But these two propensities, inconsistent as they may
appear, can easily be resolved into the same principle. Both
spring from our impatience of the state in which we actually 5
are. That impatience, while it stimulates us to surpass preceding generations, disposes us to overrate their happiness.
It is, in some sense, unreasonable and ungrateful in us to be
constantly discontented with a condition which is constantly
improving. But, in truth, there is constant improvement 10
precisely because there is constant discontent. If we were
perfectly satisfied with the present, we should cease to con-
trive, to labour, and to save with a view to the future. And
it is natural that, being dissatisfied with the present, we
should form a too favourable estimate of the past.   15

In truth we are under a deception similar to that which
misleads the traveller in the Arabian desert. Beneath the
caravan all is dry and bare; but far in advance, and far in
the rear, is the semblance of refreshing waters. The pilgrims
hasten forward and find nothing but sand where an hour be- 20
fore they had seen a lake. They turn their eyes and see a
lake where an hour before they were toiling through sand.
A similar illusion seems to haunt nations through every stage
of the long progress from poverty and barbarism to the
highest degrees of opulence and civilisation. But, if we reso- 25
lutely chase the mirage backward, we shall find it recede
before us into the regions of fabulous antiquity. It is now
the fashion to place the golden age of England in times when
noblemen were destitute of comforts the want of which would
be intolerable to a modern footman, when farmers and shop- 30
keepers breakfasted on loaves the very sight of which would
raise a riot in a modern workhouse, when to have a clean
shirt once a week was a privilege reserved for the higher class
of gentry, when men died faster in the purest country air
than they now die in the most pestilential lanes of our towns, 35
and when men died faster in the lanes of our towns than they

now die on the coast of Guiana. We too shall, in our turn, be outstripped, and in our turn be envied. It may well be, in the twentieth century, that the peasant of Dorsetshire may think himself miserably paid with twenty shillings a
5 week; that the carpenter at Greenwich may receive ten shillings a day; that labouring men may be as little used to dine without meat as they now are to eat rye bread; that sanitary police and medical discoveries may have added several more years to the average length of human life; that numerous
10 comforts and luxuries which are now unknown, or confined to a few, may be within the reach of every diligent and thrifty workingman. And yet it may then be the mode to assert that the increase of wealth and the progress of science have benefited the few at the expense of the many, and to talk of
15 the reign of Queen Victoria as the time when England was truly merry England, when all classes were bound together by brotherly sympathy, when the rich did not grind the faces of the poor, and when the poor did not envy the splendour of the rich.

THOMAS CARLYLE

SARTOR RESARTUS

The Everlasting Yea

[Extracts]

20   'Beautiful it was to sit there, as in my skyey Tent, musing
'and meditating; on the high table-land, in front of the
'Mountains; over me, as roof, the azure Dome, and around
'me, for walls, four azure-flowing curtains,—namely, of the
'Four azure Winds, on whose bottom-fringes also I have seen
25 'gilding. And then to fancy the fair Castles, that stood shel-
'tered in these Mountain hollows; with their green flower-
'lawns, and white dames and damosels, lovely enough: or
'better still, the straw-roofed Cottages, wherein stood many

'a Mother baking bread, with her children round her:—all
'hidden and protectingly folded-up in the valley-folds; yet
'there and alive, as sure as if I beheld them. Or to see, as
'well as fancy, the nine Towns and Villages, that lay round
'my mountain-seat, which, in still weather, were wont to 5
'speak to me (by their steeple-bells) with metal tongue; and,
'in almost all weather, proclaimed their vitality by repeated
'Smoke-clouds; whereon, as on a culinary horologue, I might
'read the hour of the day. For it was the smoke of cookery,
'as kind housewives at morning, midday, eventide, were boil- 10
'ing their husbands' kettles; and ever a blue pillar rose up
'into the air, successively or simultaneously, from each of the
'nine, saying, as plainly as smoke could say: Such and such
'a meal is getting ready here. Not uninteresting! For you
'have the whole Borough, with all its love-makings and 15
'scandal-mongeries, contentions and contentments, as in
'miniature, and could cover it all with your hat.—If, in my
'wide Wayfarings, I had learned to look into the business of
'the World in its details, here perhaps was the place for
'combining it into general propositions, and deducing infer- 20
'ences therefrom.

  'Often also could I see the black Tempest marching in
'anger through the distance: round some Schreckhorn, as
'yet grim-blue, would the eddying vapour gather, and there
'tumultuously eddy, and flow down like a mad witch's hair; 25
'till, after a space, it vanished, and, in the clear sunbeam,
'your Schreckhorn stood smiling grim-white, for the vapour
'had held snow. How thou fermentest and elaboratest in
'thy great fermenting-vat and laboratory of an Atmosphere,
'of a World, O Nature!—Or what is Nature? Ha! why do 30
'I not name thee God? Art thou not the "Living Garment of
'God"? O Heavens, is it, in very deed, HE, then, that ever
'speaks through thee; that lives and loves in thee, that lives
'and loves in me?

  'Fore-shadows, call them rather fore-splendours, of that 35
'Truth, and Beginning of Truths, fell mysteriously over my

'soul. Sweeter than Dayspring to the Shipwrecked in Nova
'Zembla; ah, like the mother's voice to her little child that
'strays bewildered, weeping, in unknown tumults; like soft
'streamings of celestial music to my too-exasperated heart,
5 'came that Evangel. The Universe is not dead and demoniacal,
'a charnel-house with spectres; but godlike, and my Father's!

'With other eyes, too, could I now look upon my fellow
'man: with an infinite Love, an infinite Pity. Poor, wander-
'ing, wayward man! Art thou not tried, and beaten with
10 'stripes, even as I am? Ever, whether thou bear the royal
'mantle or the beggar's gabardine, art thou not so weary, so
'heavy-laden; and thy Bed of Rest is but a Grave. O my
'Brother, my Brother, why cannot I shelter thee in my
'bosom, and wipe away all tears from thy eyes!—Truly, the
15 'din of many-voiced Life, which, in this solitude, with
'the mind's organ, I could hear, was no longer a maddening
'discord, but a melting one; like inarticulate cries, and sob-
'bings of a dumb creature, which in the ear of Heaven are
'prayers. The poor Earth, with her poor joys, was now my
20 'needy Mother, not my cruel Stepdame; Man, with his so
'mad Wants and so mean Endeavours, had become the dearer
'to me; and even for his sufferings and his sins, I now first
'named him Brother. Thus was I standing in the porch of
'that "*Sanctuary of Sorrow*"; by strange, steep ways, had I
25 'too been guided thither; and ere long its sacred gates would
'open, and the "*Divine Depth of Sorrow*" lie disclosed to me.'

'. . . Man's Unhappiness, as I construe, comes of his Great-
'ness; it is because there is an Infinite in him, which with all
'his cunning he cannot quite bury under the Finite. Will
30 'the whole Finance Ministers and Upholsterers and Con-
'fectioners of modern Europe undertake, in joint-stock
'company, to make one Shoeblack HAPPY? They cannot ac-
'complish it, above an hour or two: for the Shoeblack also has
'a Soul quite other than his Stomach; and would require, if
35 'you consider it, for his permanent satisfaction and satura-
'tion, simply this allotment, no more, and no less: *God's in-*

'*finite Universe altogether to himself*, therein to enjoy infi-
'nitely, and fill every wish as fast as it rose. Oceans of
'Hochheimer, a Throat like that of Ophiuchus: speak not of
'them; to the infinite Shoeblack they are as nothing. No
'sooner is your ocean filled, than he grumbles that it might 5
'have been of better vintage. Try him with half of a Uni-
'verse, of an Omnipotence, he sets to quarrelling with the
'proprietor of the other half, and declares himself the most
'maltreated of men.—Always there is a black spot in our
'sunshine: it is even, as I said, the *Shadow of Ourselves*. 10

'But the whim we have of Happiness is somewhat thus.
'By certain valuations, and averages, of our own striking, we
'come upon some sort of average terrestrial lot; this we
'fancy belongs to us by nature, and of indefeasible right. It is
'simple payment of our wages, of our deserts; requires neither 15
'thanks nor complaint; only such *overplus* as there may
'be do we account Happiness; any *deficit* again is Misery.
'Now consider that we have the valuation of our own deserts
'ourselves, and what a fund of Self-conceit there is in each
'of us,—do you wonder that the balance should so often dip 20
'the wrong way, and many a Blockhead cry: See there, what
'a payment; was ever worthy gentleman so used!—I tell
'thee, Blockhead, it all comes of thy Vanity; of what thou
'*fanciest* those same deserts of thine to be. Fancy that thou
'deservest to be hanged (as is most likely), thou wilt feel it 25
'happiness to be only shot: fancy that thou deservest to be
'hanged in a hair-halter, it will be a luxury to die in hemp.

'So true it is, what I then said, that *the Fraction of Life*
'*can be increased in value not so much by increasing your*
'*Numerator as by lessening your Denominator*. Nay, unless 30
'my Algebra deceive me, *Unity* itself divided by *Zero* will
'give *Infinity*. Make thy claim of wages a zero, then; thou
'hast the world under thy feet. Well did the Wisest of our
'time write: "It is only with Renunciation (*Entsagen*) that
'Life, properly speaking, can be said to begin." 35

'I asked myself: What is this that, ever since earliest

'years, thou hast been fretting and fuming, and lamenting
'and self-tormenting, on account of? Say it in a word: is it
'not because thou art not HAPPY? Because the THOU (sweet
'gentleman) is not sufficiently honoured, nourished, soft-
5 'bedded, and lovingly cared-for? Foolish soul! What Act
'of Legislature was there that *thou* shouldst be Happy? A
'little while ago thou hadst no right to *be* at all. What if
'thou wert born and predestined not to be Happy, but to be
'Unhappy! Art thou nothing other than a Vulture, then,
10 'that fliest through the Universe seeking after somewhat to
'*eat*; and shrieking dolefully because carrion enough is not
'given thee? Close thy *Byron*; open thy *Goethe*.'

'*Es leuchtet mir ein*, I see a glimpse of it!' cries he elsewhere: 'there is in man a HIGHER than Love of Happiness: he
15 'can do without Happiness, and instead thereof find Blessed-
'ness! Was it not to preach-forth this same HIGHER that sages
'and martyrs, the Poet and the Priest, in all times, have spoken
'and suffered; bearing testimony, through life and through
'death, of the Godlike that is in Man, and how in the Godlike
20 'only has he Strength and Freedom? Which God-inspired
'Doctrine art thou also honoured to be taught; O Heavens!
'and broken with manifold merciful Afflictions, even till thou
'become contrite, and learn it! O thank thy Destiny for
'these; thankfully bear what yet remain: thou hadst need
25 'of them; the Self in thee needed to be annihilated. By be-
'nignant fever-paroxysms is Life rooting out the deep-seated
'chronic Disease, and triumphs over Death. On the roaring
'billows of Time, thou art not engulfed, but borne aloft into
'the azure of Eternity. Love not Pleasure; love God. This
30 'is the EVERLASTING YEA, wherein all contradiction is solved:
'wherein whoso walks and works, it is well with him.'

And again: 'Small is it that thou canst trample the Earth
'with its injuries under thy feet, as old Greek Zeno trained
'thee: thou canst love the Earth while it injures thee, and
35 'even because it injures thee; for this a Greater than Zeno
'was needed, and he too was sent. . . .'

HEROES AND HERO-WORSHIP

The Hero as a Man of Letters

[Johnson]

As for Johnson, I have always considered him to be, by nature, one of our great English souls. A strong and noble man; so much left undeveloped in him to the last: in a kindlier element what might he not have been,—Poet, Priest, sovereign Ruler! On the whole, a man must not complain of his 'element,' of his 'time,' or the like; it is thriftless work doing so. His time is bad: well then, he is there to make it better!—Johnson's youth was poor, isolated, hopeless, very miserable. Indeed, it does not seem possible that, in any the favourablest outward circumstances, Johnson's life could have been other than a painful one. The world might have had more of profitable *work* out of him, or less; but his *effort* against the world's work could never have been a light one. Nature, in return for his nobleness, had said to him, Live in an element of diseased sorrow. Nay, perhaps the sorrow and the nobleness were intimately and even inseparably connected with each other. At all events, poor Johnson had to go about girt with continual hypochondria, physical and spiritual pain. Like a Hercules with the burning Nessus'-shirt on him, which shoots-in on him dull incurable misery: the Nessus'-shirt not to be stript-off, which is his own natural skin! In this manner *he* had to live. Figure him there, with his scrofulous diseases, with his great greedy heart, and unspeakable chaos of thoughts; stalking mournful as a stranger in this Earth; eagerly devouring what spiritual thing he could come at: school-languages and other merely grammatical stuff, if there were nothing better! The largest soul that was in all England; and provision made for it of 'fourpence-halfpenny a day.' Yet a giant invincible soul; a true man's. One remembers always that story of the shoes at Oxford: the rough, seamy-faced, rawboned College Servi-

tor stalking about, in winter-season, with his shoes worn-out;
how the charitable Gentleman Commoner secretly places a
new pair at his door; and the rawboned Servitor, lifting
them, looking at them near, with dim eyes, with what
5 thoughts,—pitches them out of window! Wet feet, mud,
frost, hunger or what you will; but not beggary: we cannot
stand beggary! Rude stubborn self-help here; a whole world
of squalor, rudeness, confused misery and want, yet of nobleness and manfulness withal. It is a type of the man's life,
10 this pitching-away of the shoes. An original man;—not a
secondhand, borrowing or begging man. Let us stand on our
own basis, at any rate! On such shoes as we ourselves can
get. On frost and mud, if you will, but honestly on that;—
on the reality and substance which Nature gives *us*, not on
15 the semblance, on the thing she has given another than us!—
And yet with all this rugged pride of manhood and self-
help, was there ever soul more tenderly affectionate, loyally
submissive to what was really higher than he? Great souls
are always loyally submissive, reverent to what is over them;
20 only small mean souls are otherwise. I could not find a better proof of what I said the other day, That the sincere man
was by nature the obedient man; that only in a World of
Heroes was there loyal Obedience to the Heroic. The essence
of *originality* is not that it be *new*: Johnson believed alto-
25 gether in the old; he found the old opinions credible for him,
fit for him; and in a right heroic manner lived under them.
He is well worth study in regard to that. For we are to say
that Johnson was far other than a mere man of words and
formulas; he was a man of truths and facts. He stood by
30 the old formulas; the happier was it for him that he could so
stand: but in all formulas that *he* could stand by, there
needed to be a most genuine substance. Very curious how,
in that poor Paper-age, so barren, artificial, thick-quilted
with Pedantries, Hearsays, the great Fact of this Universe
35 glared in, forever wonderful, indubitable, unspeakable, divine-
infernal, upon this man too! How he harmonised his

Formulas with it, how he managed at all under such circumstances: that is a thing worth seeing. A thing 'to be looked
at with reverence, with pity, with awe.' That Church of
St. Clement Danes, where Johnson still *worshipped* in the era
of Voltaire, is to me a venerable place.   5

It was in virtue of his *sincerity*, of his speaking still in
some sort from the heart of Nature, though in the current
artificial dialect, that Johnson was a Prophet. Are not all
dialects 'artificial'? Artificial things are not all false;—nay
every true Product of Nature will infallibly *shape* itself; we 10
may say all artificial things are, at the starting of them, *true*.
What we call 'Formulas' are not in their origin bad; they
are indispensably good. Formula is *method*, habitude; found
wherever man is found. Formulas fashion themselves as
Paths do, as beaten Highways, leading towards some sacred 15
or high object, whither many men are bent. Consider it.
One man, full of heartfelt earnest impulse, finds-out a way
of doing somewhat,—were it of uttering his soul's reverence
for the Highest, were it but of fitly saluting his fellow-man.
An inventor was needed to do that, a *poet*; he has articulated 20
the dim-struggling thought that dwelt in his own and many
hearts. This is his way of doing that; these are his footsteps,
the beginning of a 'Path.' And now see: the second man
travels naturally in the footsteps of his foregoer, it is the
easiest method. In the footsteps of his foregoer; yet with 25
improvements, with changes where such seem good; at all
events with enlargements, the Path ever *widening* itself as
more travel it;—till at last there is a broad Highway whereon
the whole world may travel and drive. While there remains
a City or Shrine, or any Reality to drive to, at the farther 30
end, the Highway shall be right welcome! When the City is
gone, we will forsake the Highway. In this manner all Institutions, Practices, Regulated Things in the world have
come into existence, and gone out of existence. Formulas all
begin by being *full* of substance; you may call them the *skin*, 35
the articulation into shape, into limbs and skin, of a sub-

stance that is already there: *they* had not been there otherwise. Idols . . . are not idolatrous till they become doubtful, empty for the worshipper's heart. Much as we talk
against Formulas, I hope no one of us is ignorant withal of
5 the high significance of *true* Formulas; that they were, and
will ever be, the indispensablest furniture of our habitation
in this world.——

Mark, too, how little Johnson boasts of his 'sincerity.'
He has no suspicion of his being particularly sincere,—of
10 his being particularly anything! A hard-struggling, weary-
hearted man, or 'scholar' as he calls himself, trying hard to
get some honest livelihood in the world, not to starve, but to
live—without stealing! A noble unconsciousness is in him.
He does not 'engrave *Truth* on his watch-seal'; no, but he
15 stands by truth, speaks by it, works and lives by it. Thus it
ever is. Think of it once more. The man whom Nature has
appointed to do great things is, first of all, furnished with that
openness to Nature which renders him incapable of being
*in*sincere! To his large, open, deep-feeling heart Nature is
20 a Fact: all hearsay is hearsay; the unspeakable greatness of
this Mystery of Life, let him acknowledge it or not, nay even
though he seem to forget it or deny it, is ever present to *him*,
—fearful and wonderful, on this hand and on that. He has a
basis of sincerity; unrecognised, because never questioned or
25 capable of question. Mirabeau, Mahomet, Cromwell, Napoleon: all the Great Men I ever heard-of have this as the
primary material of them. Innumerable commonplace men
are debating, are talking everywhere their commonplace doctrines, which they have learned by logic, by rote, at second-
30 hand: to that kind of man all this is still nothing. He
must have truth; truth which *he* feels to be true. How shall
he stand otherwise? His whole soul, at all moments, in all
ways, tells him that there is no standing. He is under the
noble necessity of being true. Johnson's way of thinking
35 about this world is not mine, any more than Mahomet's was:
but I recognise the everlasting element of heart-*sincerity* in

both; and see with pleasure how neither of them remains ineffectual. Neither of them is as *chaff* sown; in both of them is something which the seed-field will *grow*.

Johnson was a Prophet to his people; preached a Gospel to them,—as all like him always do. The highest Gospel he preached we may describe as a kind of Moral Prudence: 'in a world where much is to be done, and little is to be known,' see how you will *do* it! A thing well worth preaching. 'A world where much is to be done, and little is to be known:' do not sink yourselves in boundless bottomless abysses of Doubt, of wretched god-forgetting Unbelief;—you were miserable then, powerless, mad: how could you *do* or work at all? Such Gospel Johnson preached and taught;—coupled, theoretically and practically, with this other great Gospel, 'Clear your mind of Cant!' Have no trade with Cant: stand on the cold mud in the frosty weather, but let it be in your own *real* torn shoes: 'that will be better for you,' as Mahomet says! I call this, I call these two things *joined together*, a great Gospel, the greatest perhaps that was possible at that time.

Johnson's Writings, which once had such currency and celebrity, are now, as it were, disowned by the young generation. It is not wonderful; Johnson's opinions are fast becoming obsolete: but his style of thinking and of living, we may hope, will never become obsolete. I find in Johnson's Books the indisputablest traces of a great intellect and a great heart;—ever welcome, under what obstructions and perversions soever. They are *sincere* words, those of his; he means things by them. A wondrous buckram style,—the best he could get to then; a measured grandiloquence, stepping or rather stalking along in a very solemn way, grown obsolete now; sometimes a tumid *size* of phraseology not in proportion to the contents of it: all this you will put-up with. For the phraseology, tumid or not, has always *something within it*. So many beautiful styles and books, with *nothing* in them;—a man is a *male*factor to the world who writes

such! *They* are the avoidable kind!—Had Johnson left
nothing but his *Dictionary*, one might have traced there a
great intellect, a genuine man. Looking to its clearness of
definition, its general solidity, honesty, insight and success-
5 ful method, it may be called the best of all Dictionaries.
There is in it a kind of architectural nobleness; it stands
there like a great solid square-built edifice, finished, sym-
metrically complete: you judge that a true Builder did it.

JOHN RUSKIN

THE STONES OF VENICE

VOLUME II. CHAPTER IV. ST. MARK'S

§ X. And now I wish that the reader, before I bring him
10 into St. Mark's Place, would imagine himself for a little time
in a quiet English cathedral town, and walk with me to the
west front of its cathedral. Let us go together up the more
retired street, at the end of which we can see the pinnacles of
one of the towers, and then through the low gray gateway,
15 with its battlemented top and small latticed window in the
centre, into the inner private-looking road or close, where
nothing goes in but the carts of the tradesmen who supply
the bishop and the chapter, and where there are little shaven
grass-plots, fenced in by neat rails, before old-fashioned
20 groups of somewhat diminutive and excessively trim houses,
with little oriel and bay windows jutting out here and there,
and deep wooden cornices and eaves painted cream colour
and white, and small porches to their doors in the shape of
cockle-shells, or little, crooked, thick, indescribable wooden
25 gables warped a little on one side; and so forward till we
come to larger houses, also old-fashioned, but of red brick,
and with gardens behind them, and fruit walls, which show
here and there, among the nectarines, the vestiges of an old
cloister arch or shaft, and looking in front on the cathedral

square itself, laid out in rigid divisions of smooth grass and
gravel walk, yet not uncheerful, especially on the sunny
side where the canons' children are walking with their
nurserymaids. And so, taking care not to tread on the grass,
we will go along the straight walk to the west front, and 5
there stand for a time, looking up at its deep-pointed porches
and the dark places between their pillars where there were
statues once, and where the fragments, here and there, of a
stately figure are still left, which has in it the likeness of a
king, perhaps indeed a king on earth, perhaps a saintly king 10
long ago in heaven; and so, higher and higher up to the great
mouldering wall of rugged sculpture and confused arcades,
shattered, and gray, and grisly with heads of dragons and
mocking fiends, worn by the rain and swirling winds into yet
unseemlier shape, and coloured on their stony scales by the 15
deep russet-orange lichen, melancholy gold; and so, higher
still, to the bleak towers, so far above that the eye loses itself
among the bosses of their traceries, though they are rude and
strong, and only sees, like a drift of eddying black points,
now closing, now scattering, and now settling suddenly into 20
invisible places among the bosses and flowers, the crowd of
restless birds that fill the whole square with that strange
clangour of theirs, so harsh and yet so soothing, like the cries
of birds on a solitary coast between the cliffs and sea.

§ XI. Think for a little while of that scene, and the mean- 25
ing of all its small formalisms, mixed with its serene sublimity. Estimate its secluded, continuous, drowsy felicities,
and its evidence of the sense and steady performance of such
kind of duties as can be regulated by the cathedral clock;
and weigh the influence of those dark towers on all who have 30
passed through the lonely square at their feet for centuries,
and on all who have seen them rising far away over the
wooded plain, or catching on their square masses the last rays
of the sunset, when the city at their feet was indicated only
by the mist at the bend of the river. And then let us quickly 35
recollect that we are in Venice, and land at the extremity of

the Calle Lunga San Moisè, which may be considered as
there answering to the secluded street that led us to our
English cathedral gateway.

§ XII. We find ourselves in a paved alley, some seven feet
5 wide where it is widest, full of people, and resonant with cries
of itinerant salesmen—a shriek in their beginning, and dying
away into a kind of brazen ringing, all the worse for its con-
finement between the high houses of the passage along which
we have to make our way. Over-head an inextricable con-
10 fusion of rugged shutters, and iron balconies and chimney
flues pushed out on brackets to save room, and arched windows with projecting sills of Istrian stone, and gleams of
green leaves here and there where a fig-tree branch escapes
over a lower wall from some inner cortile, leading the eye up
15 to the narrow stream of blue sky high over all. On each
side, a row of shops, as densely set as may be, occupying, in
fact, intervals between the square stone shafts, about eight
feet high, which carry the first floors: intervals of which one
is narrow and serves as a door; the other is, in the more
20 respectable shops, wainscotted to the height of the counter
and glazed above, but in those of the poorer tradesmen
left open to the ground, and the wares laid on benches and
tables in the open air, the light in all cases entering at the
front only, and fading away in a few feet from the threshold
25 into a gloom which the eye from without cannot penetrate,
but which is generally broken by a ray or two from a feeble
lamp at the back of the shop, suspended before a print of the
Virgin. The less pious shopkeeper sometimes leaves his
lamp unlighted, and is contented with a penny print; the
30 more religious one has his print coloured and set in a little
shrine with a gilded or figured fringe, with perhaps a faded
flower or two on each side, and his lamp burning brilliantly.
Here at the fruiterer's, where the dark-green water-melons
are heaped upon the counter like cannon balls, the Madonna
35 has a tabernacle of fresh laurel leaves; but the pewterer
next door has let his lamp out, and there is nothing to be

seen in his shop but the dull gleam of the studded patterns
on the copper pans, hanging from his roof in the darkness.
Next comes a "Vendita Frittole e Liquori," where the Virgin,
enthroned in a very humble manner beside a tallow candle on
a back shelf, presides over certain ambrosial morsels of a 5
nature too ambiguous to be defined or enumerated. But a
few steps farther on, at the regular wine-shop of the calle,
where we are offered "Vino Nostrani a Soldi 28.32," the
Madonna is in great glory, enthroned above ten or a dozen
large red casks of three-year-old vintage, and flanked by 10
goodly ranks of bottles of Maraschino, and two crimson
lamps; and for the evening, when the gondoliers will come
to drink out, under her auspices, the money they have gained
during the day, she will have a whole chandelier.

§ XIII. A yard or two farther, we pass the hostelry of the 15
Black Eagle, and, glancing as we pass through the square
door of marble, deeply moulded, in the outer wall, we see the
shadows of its pergola of vines resting on an ancient well,
with a pointed shield carved on its side; and so presently
emerge on the bridge and Campo San Moisè, whence to the 20
entrance into St. Mark's Place, called the Bocca di Piazza
(mouth of the square), the Venetian character is nearly destroyed, first by the frightful façade of San Moisè, which we
will pause at another time to examine, and then by the mod-
ernising of the shops as they near the piazza, and the min- 25
gling with the lower Venetian populace of lounging groups of
English and Austrians. We will push fast through them into
the shadow of the pillars at the end of the "Bocca di Piazza,"
and then we forget them all; for between those pillars there
opens a great light, and, in the midst of it, as we advance 30
slowly, the vast tower of St. Mark seems to lift itself visibly
forth from the level field of chequered stones; and, on each
side, the countless arches prolong themselves into ranged
symmetry, as if the rugged and irregular houses that pressed
together above us in the dark alley had been struck back into 35
sudden obedience and lovely order, and all their rude case-

ments and broken walls had been transformed into arches charged with goodly sculpture, and fluted shafts of delicate stone.

§ XIV. And well may they fall back, for beyond those
5 troops of ordered arches there rises a vision out of the earth, and all the great square seems to have opened from it in a kind of awe, that we may see it far away—a multitude of pillars and white domes, clustered into a long low pyramid of coloured light; a treasure-heap, it seems, partly of gold,
10 and partly of opal and mother-of-pearl, hollowed beneath into five great vaulted porches, ceiled with fair mosaic, and beset with sculpture of alabaster, clear as amber and delicate as ivory—sculpture fantastic and involved, of palm leaves and lilies, and grapes and pomegranates, and birds clinging
15 and fluttering among the branches, all twined together into an endless network of buds and plumes; and, in the midst of it, the solemn forms of angels, sceptred, and robed to the feet, and leaning to each other across the gates, their figures indistinct among the gleaming of the golden ground through
20 the leaves beside them, interrupted and dim, like the morning light as it faded back among the branches of Eden, when first its gates were angel-guarded long ago. And round the walls of the porches there are set pillars of variegated stones, jasper and porphyry, and deep-green serpentine spotted with
25 flakes of snow, and marbles, that half refuse and half yield to the sunshine, Cleopatra-like, "their bluest veins to kiss" —the shadow, as it steals back from them, revealing line after line of azure undulation, as a receding tide leaves the waved sand; their capitals rich with interwoven tracery,
30 rooted knots of herbage, and drifting leaves of acanthus and vine, and mystical signs, all beginning and ending in the Cross; and above them, in the broad archivolts, a continuous chain of language and of life—angels, and the signs of heaven, and the labours of men, each in its appointed season
35 upon the earth; and above these, another range of glittering pinnacles, mixed with white arches edged with scarlet flowers

—a confusion of delight, amidst which the breasts of the Greek horses are seen blazing in their breadth of golden strength, and the St. Mark's Lion, lifted on a blue field covered with stars, until at last, as if in ecstasy, the crests of the arches break into a marble foam, and toss themselves far into the blue sky in flashes and wreaths of sculptured spray, as if the breakers on the Lido shore had been frost-bound before they fell, and the sea-nymphs had inlaid them with coral and amethyst.

Between that grim cathedral of England and this, what an interval! There is a type of it in the very birds that haunt them; for, instead of the restless crowd, hoarse-voiced and sable-winged, drifting on the bleak upper air, the St. Mark's porches are full of doves, that nestle among the marble foliage, and mingle the soft iridescence of their living plumes, changing at every motion, with the tints, hardly less lovely, that have stood unchanged for seven hundred years.

§ XV. And what effect has this splendour on those who pass beneath it? You may walk from sunrise to sunset, to and fro, before the gateway of St. Mark's, and you will not see an eye lifted to it, nor a countenance brightened by it. Priest and layman, soldier and civilian, rich and poor, pass by it alike regardlessly. Up to the very recesses of the porches, the meanest tradesmen of the city push their counters; nay, the foundations of its pillars are themselves the seats—not "of them that sell doves" for sacrifice, but of the vendors of toys and caricatures. Round the whole square in front of the church there is almost a continuous line of cafés, where the idle Venetians of the middle classes lounge, and read empty journals; in its centre the Austrian bands play during the time of vespers, their martial music jarring with the organ notes—the march drowning the miserere, and the sullen crowd thickening round them—a crowd, which, if it had its will, would stiletto every soldier that pipes to it. And in the recesses of the porches, all day long, knots of men of the lowest classes, unemployed and listless, lie basking in

the sun like lizards; and unregarded children—every heavy
glance of their young eyes full of desperation and stony de-
pravity, and their throats hoarse with cursing—gamble, and
fight, and snarl, and sleep, hour after hour, clashing their
5 bruised centesimi upon the marble ledges of the church porch.
And the images of Christ and His angels look down upon it
continually.

THE QUEEN OF THE AIR

THE HERCULES OF CAMARINA

Address to the Students of the Art School of South Lambeth
March 15th, 1869

[Extract]

Among the photographs of Greek coins which present so
many admirable subjects for your study, I must speak for
10 the present of one only: the Hercules of Camarina. You
have, represented by a Greek workman, in that coin, the face
of a man, and the skin of a lion's head. And the man's face
is like a man's face, but the lion's skin is not like a lion's skin.

Now there are some people who will tell you that Greek
15 art is fine, because it is true; and because it carves men's
faces as like men's faces as it can.

And there are other people who will tell you that Greek art
is fine because it is not true; and carves a lion's skin so as to
look not at all like a lion's skin.

20   And you fancy that one or other of these sets of people
must be wrong, and are perhaps much puzzled to find out
which you should believe.

But neither of them are wrong, and you will have eventually to believe, or rather to understand and know, in recon-
25 ciliation, the truths taught by each;—but for the present,
the teachers of the first group are those you must follow.

It is they who tell you the deepest and usefullest truth,
which involves all others in time. *Greek art, and all other*

*art, is fine when it makes a man's face as like a man's face
as it can.* Hold to that. All kinds of nonsense are talked to
you, now-a-days, ingeniously and irrelevantly about art.
Therefore, for the most part of the day, shut your ears, and
keep your eyes open: and understand primarily, what you 5
may, I fancy, understand easily, that the greatest masters of
all greatest schools—Phidias, Donatello, Titian, Velasquez,
or Sir Joshua Reynolds—all tried to make human creatures
as like human creatures as they could; and that anything
less like humanity than their work, is not so good as theirs. 10

Get that well driven into your heads; and don't let it out
again, at your peril.

Having got it well in, you may then farther understand,
safely, that there is a great deal of secondary work in pots,
and pans, and floors, and carpets, and shawls, and archi- 15
tectural ornament, which ought, essentially, to be *unlike*
reality, and to depend for its charm on quite other qualities
than imitative ones . . .

Granted, however, that these tresses may be finely placed,
still they are not like a lion's mane. So we come back to the 20
question,—if the face is to be like a man's face, why is not
the lion's mane to be like a lion's mane? Well, because it
can't be like a lion's mane without too much trouble;—and
inconvenience after that, and poor success, after all. Too
much trouble, in cutting the die into fine fringes and jags; in- 25
convenience after that,—because fringes and jags would spoil
the surface of a coin; poor success after all,—because, though
you can easily stamp cheeks and foreheads smooth at a blow,
you can't stamp projecting tresses fine at a blow, whatever
pains you take with your die. 30

So your Greek uses his common sense, wastes no time,
loses no skill, and says to you, "Here are beautifully set
tresses, which I have carefully designed and easily stamped.
Enjoy them; and if you cannot understand that they mean
lion's mane, heaven mend your wits." 35

See then, you have in this work, well-founded knowledge,

simple and right aims, thorough mastery of handicraft,
splendid invention in arrangement, unerring common sense
in treatment,—merits, these, I think, exemplary enough to
justify our tormenting you a little with Greek Art. But it
5 has one merit more than these, the greatest of all. It always
means something worth saying. Not merely worth saying
for that time only, but for all time. What do you think this
helmet of lion's hide is always given to Hercules for? You
can't suppose it means only that he once killed a lion, and
10 always carried the skin afterwards to show that he had, as
Indian sportsmen send home stuffed rugs, with claws at
the corners, and a lump in the middle which one tumbles
over every time one stirs the fire. What *was* this Nemean
Lion, whose spoils were evermore to cover Hercules from
15 the cold? Not merely a large specimen of Felis Leo, ranging
the fields of Nemea, be sure of that. This Nemean cub was
one of a bad litter. Born of Typhon and Echidna,—of the
whirlwind and the snake,—Cerberus his brother, the Hydra
of Lerna his sister,—it must have been difficult to get his
20 hide off him. He had to be found in darkness too, and dealt
upon without weapons, by grip at the throat—arrows and
club of no avail against him. What does all that mean?

It means that the Nemean Lion is the first great adversary
of life, whatever that may be—to Hercules, or to any of us,
25 then or now. The first monster we have to strangle, or be
destroyed by, fighting in the dark, and with none to help us,
only Athena standing by to encourage with her smile. Every
man's Nemean Lion lies in wait for him somewhere. The
slothful man says, there is a lion in the path. He says well.
30 The quiet *un*slothful man says the same, and knows it too.
But they differ in their farther reading of the text. The
slothful man says, I shall be slain, and the unslothful, IT
shall be. It is the first ugly and strong enemy that rises
against us, all future victory depending on victory over that.
35 Kill it; and through all the rest of life, what was once dreadful is your armour and you are clothed with that conquest

for every other, and helmed with its crest of fortitude for evermore.

Alas, we have most of us to walk bare-headed; but that is the meaning of the story of Nemea,—worth laying to heart and thinking of, sometimes, when you see a dish garnished 5 with parsley, which was the crown at the Nemean games.

WALTER PATER

THE CHILD IN THE HOUSE[1]

[Extract]

As Florian Deleal walked, one hot afternoon, he overtook by the wayside a poor aged man, and, as he seemed weary with the road, helped him on with the burden which he carried, a certain distance. And as the man told his story, it 10 chanced that he named the place, a little place in the neighbourhood of a great city, where Florian had passed his earliest years, but which he had never since seen, and, the story told, went forward on his journey comforted. And that night, like a reward for his pity, a dream of that place came 15 to Florian, a dream which did for him the office of the finer sort of memory, bringing its object to mind with a great clearness, yet, as sometimes happens in dreams, raised a little above itself, and above ordinary retrospect. The true aspect of the place, especially of the house there in which he had 20 lived as a child, the fashion of its doors, its hearths, its windows, the very scent upon the air of it, was with him in sleep for a season; only, with tints more musically blent on wall and floor, and some finer light and shadow running in and out along its curves and angles, and with all its little carv- 25 ings daintier. He awoke with a sigh at the thought of almost thirty years which lay between him and that place, yet with

[1] Reprinted by permission of Macmillan & Co., Limited, and Dodd, Mead & Company, publishers.

a flutter of pleasure still within him at the fair light, as if it were a smile, upon it. And it happened that this accident of his dream was just the thing needed for the beginning of a certain design he then had in view, the noting, namely, of
5 some things in the story of his spirit—in that process of brain-building by which we are, each one of us, what we are. With the image of the place so clear and favourable upon him, he fell to thinking of himself therein, and how his thoughts had grown up to him. In that half-spiritualised house he
10 could watch the better, over again, the gradual expansion of the soul which had come to be there—of which indeed, through the law which makes the material objects about them so large an element in children's lives, it had actually become a part; inward and outward being woven through
15 and through each other into one inextricable texture—half, tint and trace and accident of homely colour and form, from the wood and the bricks; half, mere soul-stuff, floated thither from who knows how far. In the house and garden of his dream he saw a child moving, and could divide the main
20 streams at least of the winds that had played on him, and study so the first stage in that mental journey.

The *old house*, as when Florian talked of it afterwards he always called it (as all children do, who can recollect a change of home, soon enough but not too soon to mark a
25 period in their lives), really was an old house; and an element of French descent in its inmates—descent from Watteau, the old court-painter, one of whose gallant pieces still hung in one of the rooms—might explain, together with some other things, a noticeable trimness and comely whiteness about
30 everything there—the curtains, the couches, the paint on the walls with which the light and shadow played so delicately; might explain also the tolerance of the great poplar in the garden, a tree most often despised by English people, but which French people love, having observed a certain fresh
35 way its leaves have of dealing with the wind, making it sound, in never so slight a stirring of the air, like running water.

The old-fashioned, low wainscoting went round the rooms, and up the staircase with carved balusters and shadowy angles, landing half-way up at a broad window, with a swallow's nest below the sill, and the blossom of an old pear-tree showing across it in late April, against the blue, below which the perfumed juice of the find of fallen fruit in autumn was so fresh. At the next turning came the closet which held on its deep shelves the best china. Little angel faces and reedy flutings stood out round the fireplace of the children's room. And on the top of the house, above the large attic, where the white mice ran in the twilight—an infinite, unexplored wonderland of childish treasures, glass beads, empty scent-bottles still sweet, thrums of coloured silks, among its lumber—a flat space of roof, railed round, gave a view of the neighbouring steeples; for the house, as I said, stood near a great city, which sent up heavenwards, over the twisting weather-vanes, not seldom, its beds of rolling cloud and smoke, touched with storm or sunshine. But the child of whom I am writing did not hate the fog because of the crimson lights which fell from it sometimes upon the chimneys, and the whites which gleamed through its openings, on summer mornings, on turret or pavement. For it is false to suppose that a child's sense of beauty is dependent on any choiceness or special fineness, in the objects which present themselves to it, though this indeed comes to be the rule with most of us in later life; earlier, in some degree, we see inwardly; and the child finds for itself, and with unstinted delight, a difference for the sense, in those whites and reds through the smoke on very homely buildings, and in the gold of the dandelions at the roadside, just beyond the houses, where not a handful of earth is virgin and untouched, in the lack of better ministries to its desire of beauty.

This house then stood not far beyond the gloom and rumours of the town, among high garden-walls, bright all summer-time with Golden-rod, and brown-and-golden Wall-flower—*Flos Parietis*, as the children's Latin-reading father taught them to call it, while he was with them. Tracing back the threads of his complex spiritual habit, as he was used in after years to do, Florian found that he owed to the place many tones of sentiment afterwards customary with 5 him, certain inward lights under which things most naturally presented themselves to him. The coming and going of travellers to the town along the way, the shadow of the streets, the sudden breath of the neighbouring gardens, the singular brightness of bright weather there, its singular 10 darknesses which linked themselves in his mind to certain engraved illustrations in the old big Bible at home, the coolness of the dark, cavernous shops round the great church, with its giddy winding stair up to the pigeons and the bells— a citadel of peace in the heart of the trouble—all this acted 15 on his childish fancy, so that ever afterwards the like aspects and incidents never failed to throw him into a well-recognised imaginative mood, seeming actually to have become a part of the texture of his mind. Also, Florian could trace home to this point a pervading preference in himself for a kind of 20 comeliness and dignity, an *urbanity* literally, in modes of life, which he connected with the pale people of towns, and which made him susceptible to a kind of exquisite satisfaction in the trimness and well-considered grace of certain things and persons he afterwards met with, here and there, 25 in his way through the world.

AN ESSAY OF RECENT LITERATURE

RUDYARD KIPLING

THE FEET OF THE YOUNG MEN[1]

Now the Four-way Lodge is opened, now the Hunting Winds
  are loose—
  Now the Smokes of Spring go up to clear the brain;
Now the Young Men's hearts are troubled for the whisper
  of the Trues,
  Now the Red Gods make their medicine again!
Who hath seen the beaver busied? Who hath watched the
  black-tail mating?   5
  Who hath lain alone to hear the wild-goose cry?
Who hath worked the chosen water where the ouananiche is
  waiting,
  Or the sea-trout's jumping-crazy for the fly?

> *He must go—go—go away from here!*
> *On the other side the world he's overdue.*   10
> *'Send your road is clear before you when the old Spring-*
> *fret comes o'er you,*
> *And the Red Gods call for you!*

So for one the wet sail arching through the rainbow round
  the bow,
  And for one the creak of snow-shoes on the crust;
And for one the lakeside lilies where the bull-moose waits
  the cow,   15
  And for one the mule-train coughing in the dust.

[1] Reprinted from *Collected Verse of Rudyard Kipling*, by permission of
the author and of Doubleday, Page & Company and Methuen & Company, Ltd., publishers.

Who hath smelt wood-smoke at twilight? Who hath heard
    the birch-log burning?
  Who is quick to read the noises of the night?
Let him follow with the others, for the Young Men's feet are
    turning
  To the camps of proved desire and known delight!

5   *Let him go—go,* etc.

Do you know the blackened timber—do you know that
    racing stream
  With the raw, right-angled log-jam at the end;
And the bar of sun-warmed shingle where a man may bask
    and dream
  To the click of shod canoe-poles round the bend?
10 It is there that we are going with our rods and reels and
    traces,
  To a silent, smoky Indian that we know—
To a couch of new-pulled hemlock, with the starlight on our
    faces,
  For the Red Gods call us out and we must go!

     They must go—go, etc.

15 Do you know the shallow Baltic where the seas are steep and
    short,
  Where the bluff, lee-boarded fishing-luggers ride?
Do you know the joy of threshing leagues to leeward of your
    port
  On a coast you've lost the chart of overside?
It is there that I am going, with an extra hand to bale her—
20   Just one able 'long-shore loafer that I know.
He can take his chance of drowning, while I sail and sail and
    sail her,
  For the Red Gods call me out and I must go!

     He must go—go, etc.

Do you know the pile-built village where the sago-dealers
      trade—
   Do you know the reek of fish and wet bamboo?
Do you know the steaming stillness of the orchid-scented
      glade
   When the blazoned, bird-winged butterflies flap through?
It is there that I am going with my camphor, net, and boxes, 5
   To a gentle, yellow pirate that I know—
To my little wailing lemurs, to my palms and flying-foxes,
   For the Red Gods call me out and I must go!

    He must go—go, etc.

Do you know the world's white roof-tree—do you know that
      windy rift   10
   Where the baffling mountain-eddies chop and change?
Do you know the long day's patience, belly-down on frozen
      drift,
   While the head of heads is feeding out of range?
It is there that I am going, where the boulders and the snow
      lie,
   With a trusty, nimble tracker that I know.   15
I have sworn an oath, to keep it on the Horns of Ovis Poli,
   And the Red Gods call me out and I must go!

    He must go—go, etc.

Now the Four-way Lodge is opened—now the Smokes of
      Council rise—
   Pleasant smokes, ere yet 'twixt trail and trail they choose— 20
Now the girths and ropes are tested: now they pack their
      last supplies:
   Now our Young Men go to dance before the Trues!
Who shall meet them at those altars—who shall light them
      to that shrine?
   Velvet-footed, who shall guide them to their goal?

Unto each the voice and vision: unto each his spoor and
    sign—
Lonely mountain in the Northland, misty sweat-bath 'neath
    the Line—
    And to each a man that knows his naked soul!
White or yellow, black or copper, he is waiting, as a lover,
5   Smoke of funnel, dust of hooves, or beat of train—
Where the high grass hides the horseman or the glaring flats
    discover—
Where the steamer hails the landing, or the surf-boat brings
    the rover—
Where the rails run out in sand-drift . . . Quick! ah, heave
    the camp-kit over!
    For the Red Gods make their medicine again!

10   *And we go—go—go away from here!*
      On the other side the world we're overdue!
      'Send the road is clear before you when the old Spring-
        fret comes o'er you,
      And the Red Gods call for you!

THE BELL BUOY[1]

    They christened my brother of old—
15   And a saintly name he bears—
    They gave him his place to hold
      At the head of the belfry-stairs,
      Where the minster-towers stand
    And the breeding kestrels cry.
20   Would I change with my brother a league inland?
      (*Shoal! 'Ware shoal!*) Not I!

[1] Reprinted from *Collected Verse of Rudyard Kipling*, by permission of
the author and of Doubleday, Page & Company and Methuen & Company,
Ltd., publishers.

In the flush of the hot June prime,
   O'er smooth flood-tides afire,
I hear him hurry the chime
   To the bidding of checked Desire;
     Till the sweated ringers tire   5
And the wild bob-majors die.
     Could I wait for my turn in the godly choir?
(*Shoal! 'Ware shoal!*) Not I!

When the smoking scud is blown,
   When the greasy wind-rack lowers,   10
Apart and at peace and alone,
   He counts the changeless hours.
   He wars with darkling Powers
(I war with a darkling sea);
     Would he stoop to my work in the gusty mirk?   15
(*Shoal! 'Ware shoal!*) Not he!

There was never a priest to pray,
   There was never a hand to toll,
When they made me guard of the bay,
   And moored me over the shoal.   20
   I rock, I reel, and I roll—
My four great hammers ply—
     Could I speak or be still at the Church's will?
(*Shoal! 'Ware shoal!*) Not I!

The landward marks have failed,   25
   The fog-bank glides unguessed,
The seaward lights are veiled,
   The spent deep feigns her rest:
   But my ear is laid to her breast,
I lift to the swell—I cry!   30
     Could I wait in sloth on the Church's oath?
(*Shoal! 'Ware shoal!*) Not I!

At the careless end of night
    I thrill to the nearing screw;
I turn in the clearing light
    And I call to the drowsy crew;
5   And the mud boils foul and blue
As the blind bow backs away.
    Will they give me their thanks if they clear the banks?
(*Shoal! 'Ware shoal!*) Not they!

The beach-pools cake and skim,
10   The bursting spray-heads freeze,
I gather on crown and rim
    The grey, grained ice of the seas,
    Where, sheathed from bitt to trees,
The plunging colliers lie.
15   Would I barter my place for the Church's grace?
(*Shoal! 'Ware shoal!*) Not I!

Through the blur of the whirling snow,
    Or the black of the inky sleet,
The lanterns gather and grow,
20   And I look for the homeward fleet.
    Rattle of block and sheet—
"Ready about—stand by!"
    Shall I ask them a fee ere they fetch the quay?
(*Shoal! 'Ware shoal!*) Not I!

25 I dip and I surge and I swing
    In the rip of the racing tide,
By the gates of doom I sing,
    On the horns of death I ride.
    A ship-length overside,
30 Between the course and the sand,
    Fretted and bound I bide
        Peril whereof I cry.
    Would I change with my brother a league inland?
(*Shoal! 'Ware shoal!*) Not I!

'FOR ALL WE HAVE AND ARE'[1]

(1914)

For all we have and are,
For all our children's fate,
Stand up and take the war,
The Hun is at the gate!
Our world has passed away,   5
In wantonness o'erthrown.
There is nothing left to-day
But steel and fire and stone!
   Though all we knew depart,
   The old Commandments stand:—   10
   'In courage keep your heart,
   In strength lift up your hand.'

Once more we hear the word
That sickened earth of old:—
'No law except the Sword   15
Unsheathed and uncontrolled.'
Once more it knits mankind,
Once more the nations go
To meet and break and bind
A crazed and driven foe.   20

Comfort, content, delight,
The ages' slow-bought gain,
They shrivelled in a night.
Only ourselves remain
To face the naked days   25
In silent fortitude,

[1] Reprinted from *The Years Between*, by permission of the author and of Doubleday, Page & Company and Methuen & Company, Ltd., publishers.

Through perils and dismays
Renewed and re-renewed.
Though all we made depart,
The old Commandments stand:—
5 'In patience keep your heart,
In strength lift up your hand.'

No easy hope or lies
Shall bring us to our goal,
But iron sacrifice
10 Of body, will, and soul.
There is but one task for all—
One life for each to give.
Who stands if Freedom fall?
Who dies if England live?

JOSEPH CONRAD

TYPHOON [1]

Chapter XVI

15 As soon as his mate had gone, Captain MacWhirr sidled
and staggered as far as the wheel-house. Its door being
hinged forward, he had to fight the gale for admittance, and
when at last he managed to enter, it was as if he had been
fired through the wood. He stood within, holding the handle.
20 The steering gear leaked steam and in the confined space
the glass of the binnacle made a shiny oval in a thin white
fog. The wind howled, hummed, whistled, with sudden
booming gusts that rattled the doors and the shutters in the
vicious patter of sprays. Two coils of lead-line and a small
25 canvas bag hung on a long lanyard swung wide off and came
back, clinging to the bulkheads. The gratings under foot
were nearly afloat, with every sweeping blow of a sea water
squirted violently through the cracks all round the door, and

[1] Reprinted by permission of Doubleday, Page & Company, publishers.

the man at the helm had flung down his cap, his coat, and
stood propped against the gear-casing in a striped cotton
shirt open on his breast. The little brass wheel in his hands
seemed a bright and fragile toy. The cords of his neck stood
hard and lean, a dark patch lay in the hollow of his throat, 5
and his face was still and sunken as in death.

Captain MacWhirr wiped his eyes. The sea that had
nearly taken him overboard had to his great annoyance
washed his sou-wester hat off his bald head. The fluffy, fair
hair, soaked and darkened, resembled a mean skein of cotton 10
threads festooned round his bare skull. He breathed heavily
and his face, glistening with sea water, was of a hot crimson
with the wind, with the sting of sprays. He looked as though
he had come off sweating from before a furnace.

"You here?" he muttered heavily. 15

The second mate had also found his way into the wheel-
house. He had fixed himself in a corner with his knees up,
a fist pressed against each temple, and this attitude suggested
rage, sorrow, resignation, surrender, with a sort of concentrated unforgiveness. He said mournfully and defiantly: 20

"My watch below now. Ain't it?"

The steam-gear clattered, stopped, clattered again; and
the helmsman's eyeballs seemed to project out of a hungry
face, as if the compass card behind the binnacle glass had
been meat. God knows how long he had been there steering, 25
as if forgotten by all his shipmates. The bells had not been
struck, there had been no reliefs, the ship's routine had gone
down wind, but he was trying to keep her head north-
northeast. The rudder might have been gone for all he knew,
the fires out, the engines broken down, the ship ready to roll 30
over like a corpse. He was anxious not to get muddled and
lose control of her head, because the compass card swung far
both ways, wriggling on the pivot, and sometimes seemed to
whirl right around. It was hard to make out the course she
was making. He suffered from mental stress. He was horri- 35
bly afraid also of the wheel-house going. Mountains of

water kept on falling on it. When the ship took one of her desperate dives the corners of his lips twitched.

Captain MacWhirr looked up at the wheel-house clock. Screwed to the bulkhead, it had a white face, on which the
5 black hands appeared to stand quite still. It was half-past one in the morning.

"Another day," he muttered to himself. The second mate heard him and, lifting his head as one grieving amongst ruins:

10 "You won't see it break," he exclaimed. His wrists and his knees could be seen to shake violently. "No, by God, you won't! . . ." He took his head again between his fists.

The body of the helmsman had moved slightly, but his head didn't budge on his neck,—like a stone head fixed to
15 look one way from a column. During a roll that all but took his booted legs from under him, and in the very stagger to save himself, Captain MacWhirr said austerely:

"Don't you pay any attention to that man."

And then, with an indefinable change of tone, very grave,
20 he added:

"He isn't on duty."

The sailor said nothing. The hurricane boomed, shaking the little place, which seemed air-tight; and the light of the binnacle flickered all the time.

25 "You haven't been relieved," Captain MacWhirr went on, looking down. "I want you to stick on, though, as long as you can. You've got the hang of her. Another man coming here might make a mess of it. Wouldn't do. No child's play. And the hands are probably busy with a job down below
30 . . . Think you can?"

The steering-gear leaped into an abrupt short clatter, stopped smouldering like an ember, and the still man, with a motionless gaze, burst out as if all the passion in him had gone into his lips:

35 "By heavens, sir, I can steer for ever if you don't talk to me."

"Oh! Aye! All right . . ." The Captain lifted his eyes
for the first time to the man. . . . "Hackett."

And he seemed to dismiss this matter from his mind. He
stooped to the engine-room speaking-tube, blew in, and bent
his head. Mr. Rout, below, answered, and at once Captain 5
MacWhirr put his lips to the mouthpiece.

Chapter XVII

With the uproar of the gale around him he applied alternately his lips and his ear, and the engineer's voice mounted
to him, harsh and as if out of the heat of an engagement.
One of the stokers was disabled, the others had given up, the 10
second engineer and the donkey-man were firing up. The
third was standing by the steam valve. The engines were
being tended by hand. How was it above?

"Bad enough. It rests with you," said Captain MacWhirr.
Was the mate down there yet? No? He would be presently. 15
Would Mr. Rout let him talk through the speaking-tube.
Through the deck speaking-tube. Because he—the Captain
—was going out again on the bridge directly. There was some
trouble with the Chinamen. They were fighting amongst
themselves. Couldn't allow fighting, anyhow.   20

Mr. Rout had gone away, and Captain MacWhirr could
feel against his ear the pulsation of the engines like the beat
of the ship's heart. Mr. Rout's voice down there cried
something, distantly. The ship pitched headlong, the pulsation leaped with a hissing tumult and stopped dead. Cap- 25
tain MacWhirr's face was impassive and his eyes were fixed
aimlessly at the crouching shape of the second mate. Again
Mr. Rout's voice cried out in the depths, and the pulsating
beat recommenced, with slow strokes—growing swift.

Mr. Rout came back to the tube.   30

"It don't matter much what they do," he said hastily;
and then, with irritation, "She takes these dives as if she
never meant to come up again."

"Awful sea," said the Captain's voice from above.

"Don't let me drive her under," barked Solomon Rout up the pipe.

"Dark and rain. Can't see what's coming," uttered the
5 voice. "Must—keep—her—moving—enough to steer—and chance it," it went on to state distinctly.

"I am doing as much as I dare."

"We are—getting—smashed up—a good deal up here," proceeded the voice mildly. "Doing—fairly well—though.
10 Of course, if the wheel-house should go . . ."

Mr. Rout, bending an attentive ear, muttered peevishly something under his breath.

But the deliberate voice up there became animated to ask:
"Jukes turned up yet?" Then, after a short wait: "I wish
15 he would bear a hand. I want him to be done and come up here in case of anything—look after the ship. I am all alone. The second mate lost . . ."

"What?" shouted Mr. Rout into the engine-room, taking his head away. Then up the tube he cried, "Gone over-
20 board?" and clapped his ear to.

"Lost his nerve," the voice from above was proceeding in a matter-of-fact tone. "Damn awkward, this."

Mr. Rout, listening with bowed neck, opened his eyes wide.
However, he heard something like the sounds of a scuffle and
25 broken exclamations coming down to him. He strained his hearing, and all the time Beale, the third engineer, with his arms upraised, held between the palms of his hands the rim of a little black wheel projecting at the side of a big copper pipe. He seemed to be poising it above his head, as though
30 it were a correct attitude in some sort of game.

To steady himself he pressed his shoulder against the white bulkhead, with one knee bent and a sweat-rag tucked in the belt hung upon his hip. His smooth cheek was begrimed and flushed, and the coal-dust on his eyelids, like the black
35 pencilling of a make-up, enhanced the liquid brilliance of the whites, giving to his youthful face something of a feminine,

exotic, and fascinating aspect. When the ship pitched he would with hasty movements of his hands screw hard at the little wheel.

"Gone crazy," began the Captain's voice suddenly. "Rushed at me—just now. Had to knock him down—this minute. You heard, Mr. Rout?"

"The devil!" muttered Mr. Rout. "Look out, Beale."

His voice rang out like the blast of a warning trumpet between the iron walls of the engine-room. Painted white, they rose high into the dusk of the skylight, sloping like a roof; and the whole lofty space resembled a chamber in a monument, divided by floors of iron grating with lights flickering at different levels, and the still gloom within the columnar stir of machinery under the motionless swelling of the cylinders. A loud and wild resonance, made up of all the noises of the hurricane, dwelt in the still warmth of the air. There was in it the smell of hot metal, of oil, and a slight mist of steam. The blows of the sea seemed to traverse it, in an unringing, stunning shock, from side to side.

Gleams, like pale, long flames, trembled upon the polish of metal, from the flooring below the enormous crank-heads emerged in their turns with a flash of brass and steel—going over; while the connecting rods, big-jointed, like skeleton limbs, seemed to thrust them down and pull them up again with an irresistible precision. And deep in the half-light other rods dodged to and fro, crossheads nodded quickly, disks of metal rubbed against each other, swift and gentle in a commingling of shadows and gleams.

ALFRED NOYES

TALES OF THE MERMAID TAVERN[1]

[Introduction]

Under that foggy sunset London glowed,
Like one huge cob-webbed flagon of old wine.
And, as I walked down Fleet Street, the soft sky
Flowed thro' the roaring thoroughfares, transfused
5 Their hard sharp outlines, blurred the throngs of black
On either pavement, blurred the rolling stream
Of red and yellow busses, till the town
Turned to a golden suburb of the clouds.
And, round that mighty bubble of St. Paul's,
10 Over the up-turned faces of the street,
An air-ship slowly sailed, with whirring fans,
A voyager in the new-found realms of gold,
A shadowy silken chrysalis whence should break
What radiant wings in centuries to be.

15 So, wandering on, while all the shores of Time
Softened into Eternity, it seemed
A dead man touched me with his living hand,
A flaming legend passed me in the streets
Of London—laugh who will—that City of Clouds,
20 Where what a dreamer yet, in spite of all,
Is man, that splendid visionary child
Who sent his fairy beacon through the dusk,
On a blue bus before the moon was risen,—
This Night, at eight, The Tempest!

Dreaming thus,
25 (Small wonder that my footsteps went astray!)
I found myself within a narrow street,
Alone. There was no rumour, near or far,

[1] Reprinted by permission of the author and of William Blackwood &
Sons and Frederick A. Stokes Company, publishers.

Of the long tides of traffic. In my doubt
I turned and knocked upon an old inn-door,
Hard by, an ancient inn of mullioned panes,
And crazy beams and over-hanging eaves:
And, as I knocked, the slowly changing west   5
Seemed to change all the world with it and leave
Only that old inn steadfast and unchanged,
A rock in the rich-coloured tides of time.

And, suddenly, as a song that wholly escapes
Remembrance, at one note, wholly returns,   10
There, as I knocked, memory returned to me.
I knew it all—the little twisted street,
The rough wet cobbles gleaming, far away,
Like opals, where it ended on the sky;
And, overhead, the darkly smiling face   15
Of that old wizard inn; I knew by rote
The smooth sun-bubbles in the worn green paint
Upon the doors and shutters.

                              There was one
Myself had idly scratched away one dawn,
One mad May-dawn, three hundred years ago,   20
When out of the woods we came with hawthorn boughs
And found the doors locked, as they seemed to-night.
Three hundred years ago—nay, Time was dead!
No need to scan the sign-board any more
Where that white-breasted siren of the sea   25
Curled her moon-silvered tail among such rocks
As never in the merriest seaman's tale
Broke the blue-bliss of fabulous lagoons
Beyond the Spanish Main.

                        And, through the dream,
Even as I stood and listened, came a sound   30
Of clashing wine-cups: then a deep-voiced song

Made the old timbers of the Mermaid Inn
Shake as a galleon shakes in a gale of wind
When she rolls glorying through the Ocean-sea.

SONG

Marchaunt Adventurers, chanting at the windlass,
5   Early in the morning, we slipped from Plymouth Sound,
All for Adventure in the great New Regions,
   All for Eldorado and to sail the world around!
Sing! the red of sun-rise ripples round the bows again.
   Marchaunt Adventurers, O sing, we're outward bound,
10 All to stuff the sunset in our old black galleon,
   All to seek the merchandise that no man ever found.

Chorus: Marchaunt Adventurers!
                  Marchaunt Adventurers!

Marchaunt Adventurers, O, whither are ye bound?—
15 All for Eldorado and the great new Sky-line,
   All to seek the merchandise that no man ever found.

Marchaunt Adventurers, O, what'ull ye bring home again?—
   Wonders and works and the thunder of the sea!
Whom will ye traffic with?—The King of the Sunset!
20   What shall be your pilot then?—A wind from Galilee.
   Nay, but ye be marchaunts, will ye come back empty-
      handed?—
   Ay, we be marchaunts, though our gain we ne'er shall see.
Cast we now our bread upon the waste wild waters.
   After many days, it shall return with usury.

25 *Chorus*:   Marchaunt Adventurers!
                  Marchaunt Adventurers!

What shall be your profit in the mighty days to be?—
Englande!—Englande!—Englande!—Englande!—
   Glory everlasting and the lordship of the sea!

And there, framed in the lilac patch of sky
That ended the steep street, dark on its light,
And standing on those glistering cobblestones
Just where they took the sunset's kiss, I saw
A figure like foot-feathered Mercury,   5
Tall, straight and splendid as a sunset-cloud.
Clad in a crimson doublet and trunk-hose,
A rapier at his side; and, as he paused,
His long fantastic shadow swayed and swept
Against my feet.
        A moment he looked back,   10
Then swaggered down as if he owned a world
Which had forgotten—did I wake or dream?—
Even his gracious ghost!
        Over his arm
He swung a gorgeous murrey-coloured cloak
Of Ciprus velvet, caked and smeared with mud   15
As on the day when—did I dream or wake?
And had not all this happened once before?—
When he had laid that cloak before the feet
Of Gloriana! By that mud-stained cloak,
'Twas he! Our Ocean-Shepherd! Walter Raleigh!   20
He brushed me passing, and with one vigorous thrust
Opened the door and entered. At his heels
I followed—into the Mermaid!—through three yards
Of pitch-black gloom, then into an old inn-parlour
Swimming with faces in a mist of smoke   25
That up-curled, blue, from long Winchester pipes,
While—like some rare old picture, in a dream
Recalled—quietly listening, laughing, watching,
Pale on that old black oaken wainscot floated
One bearded oval face, young, with deep eyes,   30
Whom Raleigh hailed as "Will!"
        But as I stared
A sudden buffet from a brawny hand
Made all my senses swim, and the room rang

With laughter as upon the rush-strewn floor
My feet slipped and I fell. Then a gruff voice
Growled over me—"Get up now, John-a-dreams,
Or else mine host must find another drawer!
5   Hast thou not heard us calling all this while?"
And, as I scrambled up, the rafters rang
With cries of "Sack! Bring me a cup of sack!
Canary! Sack! Malmsey! and Muscadel!"
I understood and flew. I was awake,
10   A leather-jerkined pot-boy to these gods,
A prentice Ganymede to the Mermaid Inn!

PRINCETON[1]

(1917)

The first four lines of this poem were written for inscription on the first joint memorial to the American and British soldiers who fell in the Revolutionary War. This memorial was recently dedicated at Princeton.

Here Freedom stood, by slaughtered friend and foe,
    And, ere the wrath paled or that sunset died,
Looked through the ages: then, with eyes aglow,
15   *Laid them, to wait that future, side by side.*

Now lamp-lit gardens in the blue dusk shine
    Through dog-wood red and white,
And round the gray quadrangles, line by line,
    The windows fill with light,
20   Where Princeton calls to Magdalen, tower to tower,
    Twin lanthorns of the law,
And those cream-white magnolia boughs embower
    The halls of old Nassau.

The dark bronze tigers crouch on either side
25   Where red-coats used to pass,

[1] Reprinted, by permission, from *The New Morning*, by Alfred Noyes. Copyright, 1918, by Alfred Noyes.

And round the bird-loved house where Mercer died
   And violets dusk the grass,
By Stony Brook that ran so red of old,
   But sings of friendship now,
To feed the old enemy's harvest fifty-fold   5
   The green earth takes the plough.

Through this May night if one great ghost should stray
   With deep remembering eyes,
Where that old meadow of battle smiles away
   Its blood-stained memories,   10
If Washington should walk, where friend and foe
   Sleep and forget the past,
Be sure his unquenched heart would leap to know
   Their hosts are joined at last.

Be sure he walks, in shadowy buff and blue,   15
   Where those dim lilacs wave,
He bends his head to bless, as dreams come true,
   The promise of that grave,
Then with a vaster hope than thought can scan,
   . Touching his ancient sword,   20
Prays for that mightier realm of God in man,
   "Hasten Thy Kingdom, Lord.

"Land of new hope, land of the singing stars,
   Type of the world to be,
The vision of a world set free from wars   25
   Takes life, takes form, from thee,
Where all the jarring nations of this earth,
   Beneath the all-blessing sun,
Bring the new music of mankind to birth,
   And make the whole world one."   30

And those old comrades rise around him there,
   Old foemen, side by side,

With eyes like stars upon the brave night-air,
    And young as when they died,
To hear your bells, O beautiful Princeton towers,
    Ring for the world's release.   ·
5   They see you, piercing like gray swords through flowers,
    And smile from hearts at peace.

SONG FROM *DRAKE*[1]

Ye that follow the vision
    Of the world's weal afar,
Have ye met with derision
10   And the red laugh of war;
Yet the thunder shall not hurt you,
    Nor the battle-storms dismay;
Tho' the sun in heaven desert you,
    "Love will find out the way."

15   When the pulse of hope falters,
    When the fire flickers low
On your faith's crumbling altars,
    And the faithless gods go;
When the fond hope ye cherished
20   Cometh, kissing, to betray;
When the last star hath perished,
    "Love will find out the way."

When the last dream bereaveth you,
    And the heart turns to stone,
25   When the last comrade leaveth you
    In the desert, alone;
With the whole world before you
    Clad in battle-array,
And the starless night o'er you,
30   "Love will find out the way."

[1] Reprinted by permission of the author and of William Blackwood & Sons and Frederick A. Stokes Company, publishers.

Your dreamers may dream it
  The shadow of a dream,
Your sages may deem it
  A bubble on the stream;
Yet our kingdom draweth nigher   5
  With each dawn and every day,
Through the earthquake and the fire
  "Love will find out the way."

Love will find it, tho' the nations
  Rise up blind, as of old,   10
And the new generations
  Wage their warfares of gold;
Tho' they trample child and mother
  As red clay into the clay,
Where brother wars with brother,   15
  "Love will find out the way."

WILLIAM BUTLER YEATS

THE LAKE ISLE OF INNISFREE[1]

I will arise and go now, and go to Innisfree,
  And a small cabin build there, of clay and wattles made;
Nine bean rows will I have there, a hive for the honey bee,
  And live alone in the bee-loud glade.   20

And I shall have some peace there, for peace comes dropping
    slow,
  Dropping from the veils of the morning to where the
    cricket sings;
There midnight's all a glimmer, and noon a purple glow,
  And evening full of the linnet's wings.

[1] From *Poems*, by W. B. Yeats. Reprinted by special arrangement
with The Macmillan Company, publishers.

I will arise and go now, for always night and day
   I hear lake water lapping with low sounds by the shore;
While I stand on the roadway, or on the pavements gray,
   I hear it in the deep heart's core.

WHEN YOU ARE OLD[1]

5   When you are old and gray and full of sleep,
      And nodding by the fire, take down this book,
      And slowly read, and dream of the soft look
   Your eyes had once, and of their shadows deep;

How many loved your moments of glad grace,
10   And loved your beauty with love false or true;
      But one man loved the pilgrim soul in you,
   And loved the sorrows of your changing face.

And bending down beside the glowing bars
      Murmur, a little sad, *From us fled Love*;
15   *He paced upon the mountains far above,*
   And hid his face amid a crowd of stars.

JAMES MATTHEW BARRIE

A WINDOW IN THRUMS[2]

CHAPTER II. ON THE TRACK OF THE MINISTER

On the afternoon of the Saturday that carted me and my
two boxes to Thrums, I was ben in the room playing Hendry
at the dambrod. I had one of the room chairs, but Leeby
20 brought a chair from the kitchen for her father. Our door
stood open, and as Hendry often pondered for two minutes
with his hand on a "man," I could have joined in the gossip
that was going on but the house.

[1] From *Poems*, by W. B. Yeats. Reprinted by special arrangement with
The Macmillan Company, publishers.

[2] From *A Window in Thrums*; copyright, 1896. Reprinted by permission
of Charles Scribner's Sons and Hodder and Stoughton, Ltd.

"Ay, weel, then, Leeby," said Jess, suddenly, "I'll warrant the minister'll no be preachin' the morn."

This took Leeby to the window.

"Yea, yea," she said (and I knew she was nodding her head sagaciously) ; I looked out at the room window, but all I could see was a man wheeling an empty barrow down the brae.

"That's Robbie Tosh," continued Leeby ; "an' there's nae doot 'at he's makkin' for the minister's, for he has on his black coat. He'll be to row the minister's luggage to the post-cart. Ay, an' that's Davit Lunan's barrow. I ken it by the shaft's bein' spliced wi' yarn. Davit broke the shaft at the saw-mill."

"He'll be gaen awa for a curran (number of) days," said Jess, "or he would juist hae taen his bag. Ay, he'll be awa to Edinbory, to see the lass."

"I wonder wha'll be to preach the morn—tod, it'll likely be Mr. Skinner, frae Dundee ; him an' the minister's chief, ye ken."

"Ye micht gang up to the attic, Leeby, an' see if the spare bedroom vent (chimney) at the manse is gaen. We're sure, if it's Mr. Skinner, he'll come wi' the post frae Tilliedrum the nicht, an' sleep at the manse."

"Weel, I assure ye," said Leeby, descending from the attic, "it'll no be Mr. Skinner, for no only is the spare bedroom vent no gaen, but the blind's drawn doon frae tap to fut, so they're no even airin' the room. Na, it canna be him ; an' what's mair, it'll be naebody 'at's to bide a'nicht at the manse."

"I wouldna say that ; na, na. It may only be a student ; an' Marget Dundas (the minister's mother and housekeeper) michtna think it necessary to put on a fire for him."

"Tod, I'll tell ye wha it'll be. I wonder I didna think o' 'im sooner. It'll be the lad Wilkie ; him 'ats' mither mairit on Sam'l Duthie's wife's brither. They bide in Cupar, an' I mind 'at when the son was here twa or three year syne he was juist gaen to begin the diveenity classes in Glesca."

"If that's so, Leeby, he would be sure to bide wi' Sam'l. Hendry, hae ye heard 'at Sam'l Duthie's expeckin' a stranger the nicht?"

"Haud yer tongue," replied Hendry, who was having the worst of the game.

"Ay, but I ken he is," said Leeby triumphantly to her mother, "for ye mind when I was in at Johnny Watt's (the draper's) Chirsty (Sam'l's wife) was buyin' twa yards o' chintz, an' I couldna think what she would be wantin' 't for!"

"I thocht Johnny said to ye 'at it was for a present to Chirsty's auntie?"

"Ay, but he juist guessed that; for, though he tried to get oot o' Chirsty what she wanted the chintz for, she wouldna tell 'im. But I see noo what she was after. The lad Wilkie'll be to bide wi' them, and Chirsty had bocht the chintz to cover the airm-chair wi'. It's ane o' thae hair-bottomed chairs, but terrible torn, so she'll hae covered it for 'im to sit on."

"I wouldna wonder but ye're richt, Leeby; for Chirsty would be in an oncommon fluster if she thocht the lad's mither was likely to hear 'at her best chair was torn. Ay, ay, bein' a man, he wouldna think to tak aff the chintz an' hae a look at the chair withoot it."

Here Hendry, who had paid no attention to the conversa-tion, broke in:

"Was ye speirin' had I seen Sam'l Duthie? I saw 'im yesterday buyin' a fender at Will'um Crook's roup."

"A fender! Ay, ay, that settles the queistion," said Leeby; "I'll warrant the fender was for Chirsty's parlor. It's preyed on Chirsty's mind, they say, this fower-and-thirty year 'at she doesna hae a richt parlor fender."

"Leeby, look! That's Robbie Tosh wi' the barrow. He has a michty load o' luggage. Am thinkin' the minister's bound for Tilliedrum."

"Na, he's no, he's gaen to Edinbory, as ye micht ken by the bandbox. That'll be his mither's bonnet he's takkin'

back to get altered. Ye'll mind she was never pleased wi'
the set o' the flowers."

"Weel, weel, here comes the minister himsel, an' very
snod he is. Ay, Marget's been puttin' new braid on his coat,
an' he's carryin' the sma' black bag he bocht in Dundee last 5
year: he'll hae's nicht-shirt an' a comb in't, I dinna doot.
Ye micht rin to the corner, Leeby, an' see if he cries in at
Jess McTaggart's in passin'."

"It's my opeenion," said Leeby, returning excitedly from
the corner, "'at the lad Wilkie's no to be preachin' the morn, 10
after a'. When I gangs to the corner, at ony rate, what
think ye's the first thing I see but the minister an' Sam'l
Duthie meetin' face to face? Ay, weel, it's gospel am tellin'
ye when I say as Sam'l flung back his head an' walkit richt
by the minister!"   15

"Losh keep's a', Leeby; ye say that? They maun hae
haen a quarrel."

"I'm thinkin' we'll hae Mr. Skinner i' the poopit the morn
after a'."

"It may be, it may be. Ay, ay, look, Leeby, whatna bit 20
kimmer's that wi' the twa jugs in her hand?"

"Eh! Ou, it'll be Lawyer Ogilvy's servant lassieky gaen
to the farm o' T'nowhead for the milk. She gangs ilka
Saturday nicht. But what did ye say—twa jugs? Tod, let's
see! Ay, she has so, a big jug an' a little ane. The little 25
ane'll be for cream; an', sal, the big ane's bigger na usual."

"There maun be something gaen on at the lawyer's if
they're buyin' cream, Leeby. Their reg'lar thing's twopence
worth o' milk."

"Ay, but I assure ye that sma' jug's for cream, an' I dinna 30
doot mysel but 'at there's to be fower pence worth o' milk
this nicht."

"There's to be a puddin' made the morn, Leeby. Ou, ay,
a' thing points to that; an' we're very sure there's nae
puddins at the lawyer's on the Sabbath onless they hae 35
company."

"I dinna ken wha they can hae, if it be na that brither o' the wife's 'at bides oot by Aberdeen."

"Na, it's no him, Leeby; na, na. He's no weel to do, an' they wouldna be buyin' cream for 'im."

5 "I'll run up to the attic again, an' see if there's ony stir at the lawyer's hoose."

By-and-bye Leeby returned in triumph.

"Ou, ay," she said, "they're expectin' veesitors at the lawyer's, for I could see twa o' the bairns dressed up to the 10 nines, an' Mistress Ogilvy doesna dress at them in that way for naething."

"It far beats me though, Leeby, to guess wha's comin' to them. Ay, but stop a meenute, I wouldna wonder, no, really I would not wonder but what it'll be—"

15 "The very thing 'at was passin' through my head, mother."

"Ye mean 'at the lad Wilkie'll be to bide wi' the lawyer i'stead o' wi' Sam'l Duthie? Sal, am thinkin' that's it. Ye ken Sam'l an' the lawyer married on cousins; but Mistress Ogilvy ay lookit on Chirsty as dirt aneath her feet. She 20 would be glad to get a minister, though, to the hoose, an' so I warrant the lad Wilkie'll be to bide a'nicht at the lawyer's."

"But what would Chirsty be doin' gettin' the chintz an' the fender in that case?"

25 "Ou, she'd been expectin' the lad, of course. Sal, she'll be in a michty tantrum aboot this. I wouldna wonder though she gets Sam'l to gang ower to the U. P.'s."

Leeby went once more to the attic.

"Ye're wrang, mother," she cried out. "Whaever's to 30 preach the morn is to bide at the manse, for the minister's servant's been at Baker Duff's buyin' short-bread—half a lippy, nae doot."

"Are ye sure o' that, Leeby?"

"Oh, am certain. The servant gaed in to Duff's the noo, 35 an' as ye ken fine, the manse fowk doesna deal wi' him, except they're wantin' short-bread. He's Auld Kirk."

Leeby returned to the kitchen, and Jess sat for a time ruminating.

"The lad Wilkie," she said at last, triumphantly, "'ll be to bide at Lawyer Ogilvy's; but he'll be gaen to the manse the morn for a tea-dinner." 5

"But what," asked Leeby, "aboot the milk an' the cream for the lawyer's?"

"Ou, they'll be hae'n a puddin' for the supper the nicht. That's a michty genteel thing, I've heard."

It turned out that Jess was right in every particular. 10

GEORGE W. RUSSELL

DUST[1]

I heard them in their sadness say,
"The earth rebukes the thought of God;
We are but embers wrapped in clay
A little nobler than the sod."

But I have touched the lips of clay, 15
Mother, thy rudest sod to me
Is thrilled with fire of hidden day,
And haunted by all mystery.

GILBERT KEITH CHESTERTON

A DEFENCE OF UGLY THINGS[2]

There are some people who state that the exterior, sex, or physique of another person is indifferent to them, that 20 they care only for the communion of mind with mind; but these people need not detain us. There are some statements

[1] From *Collected Poems by A. E.* Reprinted by special arrangement with The Macmillan Company.

[2] Reprinted from *The Defendant* by permission of the author and of Dodd, Mead and Company and J. M. Dent & Sons, Ltd., publishers.

that no one ever thinks of believing, however often they
are made.

But while nothing in this world would persuade us that a
great friend of Mr. Forbes Robertson, let us say, would experience no surprise or discomfort at seeing him enter the
room in the bodily form of Mr. Chaplin, there is a confusion
constantly made between being attracted by exterior, which
is natural and universal, and being attracted by what is called
physical beauty, which is not entirely natural and not in the
least universal. Or rather, to speak more strictly, the conception of physical beauty has been narrowed to mean a certain kind of physical beauty which no more exhausts the
possibilities of external attractiveness than the respectability
of a Clapham builder exhausts the possibilities of moral
attractiveness.

The tyrants and deceivers of mankind in this matter have
been the Greeks. All their splendid work for civilization
ought not to have wholly blinded us to the fact of their great
and terrible sin against the variety of life. It is a remarkable fact that while the Jews have long ago been rebelled
against and accused of blighting the world with a stringent
and one-sided ethical standard, nobody has noticed that the
Greeks have committed us to an infinitely more horrible
asceticism—an asceticism of the fancy, a worship of one
æsthetic type alone. Jewish severity had at least common-
sense as its basis; it recognized that men lived in a world of
fact, and that if a man married within the degrees of blood
certain consequences might follow. But they did not starve
their instinct for contrasts and combinations; their prophets
gave two wings to the ox and any number of eyes to the
cherubim with all the riotous ingenuity of Lewis Carroll.
But the Greeks carried their police regulation into elfland;
they vetoed not the actual adulteries of the earth but the
wild weddings of ideas, and forbade the banns of thought.

It is extraordinary to watch the gradual emasculation of
the monsters of Greek myth under the pestilent influence of

the Apollo Belvedere. The chimæra was a creature of whom any healthy-minded people would have been proud; but when we see it in Greek pictures we feel inclined to tie a ribbon round its neck and give it a saucer of milk. Who ever feels that the giants in Greek art and poetry were really big—big 5 as some folk-lore giants have been? In some Scandinavian story a hero walks for miles along a mountain ridge, which eventually turns out to be the bridge of the giant's nose. That is what we should call, with a calm conscience, a large giant. But this earthquake fancy terrified the Greeks, and 10 their terror has terrified all mankind out of their natural love of size, vitality, variety, energy, ugliness. Nature intended every human face, so long as it was forcible, individual, and expressive, to be regarded as distinct from all others, as a poplar is distinct from an oak, and an apple-tree from a 15 willow. But what the Dutch gardeners did for trees the Greeks did for the human form; they lopped away its living and sprawling features to give it a certain academic shape; they hacked off noses and pared down chins with a ghastly horticultural calm. And they have really succeeded so far 20 as to make us call some of the most powerful and endearing faces ugly, and some of the most silly and repulsive faces beautiful. This disgraceful *via media*, this pitiful sense of dignity, has bitten far deeper into the soul of modern civilization than the external and practical Puritanism of Israel. The 25 Jew at the worst told a man to dance in fetters; the Greek put an exquisite vase upon his head and told him not to move.

Scripture says that one star differeth from another in glory, and the same conception applies to noses. To insist that one type of face is ugly because it differs from that of the Venus 30 of Milo is to look at it entirely in a misleading light. It is strange that we should resent people differing from ourselves; we should resent much more violently their resembling ourselves. This principle has made a sufficient hash of literary criticism, in which it is always the custom to complain of the 35 lack of sound logic in a fairy tale, and the entire absence of

true oratorical power in a three-act farce. But to call another man's face ugly because it powerfully expresses another man's soul is like complaining that a cabbage has not two legs. If we did so, the only course for the cabbage would be
5 to point out with severity, but with some show of truth, that we were not a beautiful green all over.

But this frigid theory of the beautiful has not succeeded in conquering the art of the world, except in name. In some quarters, indeed, it has never held sway. A glance at Chinese
10 dragons or Japanese gods will show how independent are Orientals of the conventional idea of facial and bodily regularity, and how keen and fiery is their enjoyment of real beauty, of goggle eyes, of sprawling claws, of gaping mouths and writing coils. In the Middle Ages men broke away
15 from the Greek standard of beauty, and lifted up in adoration to heaven great towers, which seemed alive with dancing apes and devils. In the full summer of technical artistic perfection the revolt was carried to its real consummation in the study of the faces of men. Rembrandt declared the sane
20 and manly gospel that a man was dignified, not when he was like a Greek god, but when he had a strong, square nose like a cudgel, a boldly-blocked head like a helmet, and a jaw like a steel trap.

This branch of art is commonly dismissed as the grotesque.
25 We have never been able to understand why it should be humiliating to be laughable, since it is giving an elevated artistic pleasure to others. If a gentleman who saw us in the street were suddenly to burst into tears at the mere thought of our existence, it might be considered disquieting and un-
30 complimentary; but laughter is not uncomplimentary. In truth, however, the phrase 'grotesque' is a misleading description of ugliness in art. It does not follow that either the Chinese dragons or the Gothic gargoyles or the goblinish old women of Rembrandt were in the least intended to be comic.
35 Their extravagance was not the extravagance of satire, but simply the extravagance of vitality; and here lies the whole

key of the place of ugliness in æsthetics. We like to see a
crag jut out in shameless decision from the cliff, we like to
see the red pines stand up hardily upon a high cliff, we like
to see a chasm cloven from end to end of a mountain. With
equally noble enthusiasm, we like to see the red hair of a 5
friend stand up hardily in bristles upon his head, we like to
see his mouth broad and clean cut like the mountain crevasse.
At least some of us like all this; it is not a question of humour.
We do not burst with amusement at the first sight of the
pines or the chasm; but we like them because they are ex- 10
pressive of the dramatic stillness of Nature, her bold experiments, her definite departures, her fearlessness and savage
pride in her children. The moment we have snapped the
spell of conventional beauty, there are a million beautiful
faces waiting for us everywhere, just as there are a million 15
beautiful spirits.

JOHN MASEFIELD

THE WIDOW IN THE BYE STREET[1]

[Introduction to Part I]

Down Bye Street, in a little Shropshire town,
There lived a widow with her only son:
She had no wealth nor title to renown,
Nor any joyous hours, never one.   20
She rose from ragged mattress before sun
And stitched all day until her eyes were red,
And had to stitch, because her man was dead.

Sometimes she fell asleep, she stitched so hard,
Letting the linen fall upon the floor;   25
And hungry cats would steal in from the yard,

[1] From *Collected Poems of John Masefield*. Reprinted by special arrangement with The Macmillan Company and Sidgwick and Jackson,
publishers.

And mangy chickens pecked about the door,
Craning their necks so ragged and so sore
To search the room for bread-crumbs, or for mouse,
But they got nothing in the widow's house.

5   Mostly she made her bread by hemming shrouds
For one rich undertaker in the High Street,
Who used to pray that folks might die in crowds
And that their friends might pay to let them lie sweet;
And when one died the widow in the Bye Street
10   Stitched night and day to give the worm his dole.
The dead were better dressed than that poor soul.

Her little son was all her life's delight,
For in his little features she could find
A glimpse of that dead husband out of sight,
15   Where out of sight is never out of mind.
And so she stitched till she was nearly blind,
Or till the tallow candle end was done,
To get a living for her little son.

Her love for him being such she would not rest,
20   It was a want which ate her out and in,
Another hunger in her withered breast
Pressing her woman's bones against the skin.
To make him plump she starved her body thin.
And he, he ate the food, and never knew,
25   He laughed and played as little children do.

When there was little sickness in the place
She took what God would send, and what God sent
Never brought any colour to her face
Nor life into her footsteps when she went.
30   Going, she trembled always withered and bent,
For all went to her son, always the same,
He was the first served whatever blessing came.

Sometimes she wandered out to gather sticks,
For it was bitter cold there when it snowed.
And she stole hay out of the farmer's ricks
For bands to wrap her feet in while she sewed,
And when her feet were warm and the grate glowed   5
She hugged her little son, her heart's desire,
With "Jimmy, ain't it snug beside the fire?"

So years went on till Jimmy was a lad
And went to work as poor lads have to do,
And then the widow's loving heart was glad   10
To know that all the pains she had gone through,
And all the years of putting on the screw,
Down to the sharpest turn a mortal can,
Had borne their fruit, and made her child a man.

THE OLD FRONT LINE[1]

[Extracts]

This description of the old front line, as it was when the 15
Battle of the Somme began, may some day be of use. All
wars end; even this war will some day end, and the ruins
will be rebuilt and the field full of death will grow food, and
all this frontier of trouble will be forgotten. When the
trenches are filled in, and the plough has gone over them, the 20
ground will not long keep the look of war. One summer
with its flowers will cover most of the ruin that man can
make, and then these places, from which the driving back of
the enemy began, will be hard indeed to trace, even with
maps. It is said that even now in some places the wire has 25
been removed, the explosive salved, the trenches filled, and
the ground ploughed with tractors. In a few years' time,
when this war is a romance in memory, the soldier looking

---

[1] From *The Old Front Line*, by John Masefield. Reprinted by special
arrangement with The Macmillan Company, publishers.

for his battlefield will find his marks gone. Centre Way, Peel Trench, Munster Alley, and these other paths to glory will be deep under the corn, and gleaners will sing at Dead Mule Corner.

. . . .

5   If the description of this old line be dull to read, it should be remembered that it was dull to hold. The enemy had the lookout posts, with the fine views over France, and the sense of domination. Our men were down below with no view of anything but of stronghold after stronghold, just up above, 10 being made stronger daily. And if the enemy had strength of position he had also strength of equipment, of men, of guns, and explosives of all kinds. He had all the advantages for nearly two years of war, and in all that time our old front line, whether held by the French or by ourselves, was 15 nothing but a post to be endured, day in day out, in all weathers and under all fires, in doubt, difficulty, and danger, with bluff and makeshift and improvisation, till the tide could be turned. If it be dull to read about and to see, it was, at least, the old line which kept back the tide and stood 20 the siege. It was the line from which, after all those months of war, the tide turned and the besieged became the attackers.

. . . .

Much of the relief and munitioning of the fighting lines was done at night. Men going into the lines saw little of where they were going. They entered the gash of the com- 25 munication trench, following the load on the back of the man in front, but seeing perhaps nothing but the shape in front, the black walls of the trench, and now and then some gleam of a star in the water under foot. Sometimes as they marched they would see the starshells, going up and bursting like 30 rockets, and coming down with a wavering slow settling mo- tion, as white and bright as burning magnesium wire, shed- ding a kind of dust of light upon the trench and making the blackness intense when they went out. . . .

In the fire trench they saw little more than the parapet.

If work were being done in the No Man's Land, they still saw little save by these lights that floated and fell from the enemy and from ourselves. They could see only an array of stakes tangled with wire, and something distant and dark which might be similar stakes, or bushes, or men, in front of what could only be the enemy line. When the night passed, and those working outside the trench had to take shelter, they could see nothing, even at a loophole or periscope, but the greenish strip of ground, pitted with shell-holes and fenced with wire, running up to the enemy line. There was little else for them to see, looking to the front, for miles and miles, up hill and down dale.

The soldiers who held this old front line of ours saw this grass and wire day after day, perhaps, for many months. It was the limit of their world, the horizon of their landscape, the boundary. What interest there was in their life was the speculation, what lay beyond that wire, and what the enemy was doing there. They seldom saw an enemy. They heard his songs and they were stricken by his missiles, but seldom saw more than, perhaps, a swiftly moving cap at a gap in the broken parapet, or a grey figure flitting from the light of a starshell. Aëroplanes brought back photographs of those unseen lines. Sometimes, in raids in the night, our men visited them and brought back prisoners; but they remained mysteries and unknown.

. . . .

The tumult of these days and nights cannot be described nor imagined. The air was without wind yet it seemed in a hurry with the passing of death. Men knew not which they heard, a roaring that was behind and in front, like a presence, or a screaming that never ceased to shriek in the air. No thunder was ever so terrible as that tumult. It broke the drums of the ears when it came singly, but when it rose up along the front and gave tongue together in full cry it humbled the soul.

. . . .

In our trenches after seven o'clock on that morning, our men waited under a heavy fire for the signal to attack. Just before half-past seven, the mines at half a dozen points went up with a roar that shook the earth and brought down the
5 parapets in our lines. Before the blackness of their burst had thinned or fallen the hand of Time rested on the half-hour mark, and along all that old front line of the English there came a whistling and a crying. The men of the first wave climbed up the parapets, in tumult, darkness, and the
10 presence of death, and having done with all pleasant things, advanced across the No Man's Land to begin the Battle of the Somme.

HERBERT ASQUITH

THE VOLUNTEER[1]

Here lies a clerk who half his life had spent
Toiling at ledgers in a city grey,
15 Thinking that so his days would drift away
With no lance broken in life's tournament:
Yet ever 'twixt the books and his bright eyes
The gleaming eagles of the legions came,
And horsemen, charging under phantom skies,
20 Went thundering past beneath the oriflamme.

And now those waiting dreams are satisfied
From twilight to the halls of dawn he went;
His lance is broken; but he lies content
With that high hour, in which he lived and died.
25 And falling thus, he wants no recompense,
Who found his battle in the last resort;
Nor needs he any hearse to bear him hence,
Who goes to join the men of Agincourt.

[1] Reprinted by permission of Sidgwick and Jackson, Ltd., publishers.

NOTES

Heavy-faced figures refer to pages, and regular figures refer to lines. For diacritical marks see Key to Pronunciation preceding the Index

2 13 **Wedergeats:** Weather Geats, a tribe of the southern part of the Scandinavian peninsula.

3 15 **kinsman of Ecgtheow:** Beowulf was Ecgtheow's son.—31 **The yellow wood:** The shields of the Geats were regularly of wood. In preparation for his battle with the dragon Beowulf had made an iron shield.

12 21 **monks . . . after the rule of St. Benedict:** St. Benedict of Nursia (480–544) reformed abuses in the monastic life of his time. Members of the order of monks which he founded, named from him Benedictines, are sometimes called Black Monks from their dress.—24 **Pentecost:** Whitsunday, a church festival celebrating the descent of the Holy Spirit on the apostles, the seventh Sunday after Easter.

13 8 **hide:** a measure of land, variously defined, as the amount necessary to support one free household, the amount one ox can plow in a year; in Domesday Book it was 120 acres, Domesday Book being the register mentioned here.—13 **mark:** a weight for gold or silver, formerly in common use in various parts of Europe, usually about eight ounces.—17 **hart . . . hind:** the male and female of the red deer.

15 17 **canvass our compact:** restate our agreement. The Green Knight, who had entered Arthur's banqueting-hall without armor, had proposed, as a Christmas game, to give his gisarme, or battle-ax, to one of the assembled knights who should agree to strike him a blow with it and a year and a day later receive from the Green Knight a blow in return.

19 13 **Cornwall:** in the southwest of England, now a county.—15 **Modred** (mō'drĕd): Arthur's nephew and a Knight of the Round Table, who rebelled against the king.—21 **Camelford:** today a town in Cornwall, which claims to be the ancient Camelot, King Arthur's capital. (See page 248.) It is not, however, "by the river Tamar," which forms the boundary between Cornwall and Devonshire. Tradition has associated Camelot with other places in Wales, in Somersetshire, and near Winchester.

22 2 **Uther:** king of Britain, father of Arthur.—26 **Merlin:** the magician, poet, and prophet. (See Tennyson's poem "Merlin" and the "Idylls of the King.") Old Welsh poems, attributed to Merlin, have come down to the present day.

24 9 **Alisaundre:** Alexandria in Egypt, taken in 1365, by the King of Cyprus, Pierre de Lusignan, who, however, immediately abandoned it.— 15 **Algezir:** Algeciras, a seaport of southern Spain, near Gibraltar, held

399

by the Moors 713–1344, when Alphonso XI of Castile, after besieging it for twenty months with the help of crusaders from all over Europe, captured and destroyed it. In 1704 Spanish colonists from Granada began to resettle the place.—16 **Lyeys, Satalye:** now Ayas and Adalia, in Armenia and Asia Minor respectively. They were taken from the Turks by Pierre de Lusignan.

26 26 **Cristofre:** St. Christopher was the patron saint of forests. Brooches of this sort were valued as charms against accidents.

27 2 **outridere:** the officer of the monastery whose duty it was to ride out to look after the estates belonging to the monastery.—23 **Austyn:** Augustine. St. Augustine, Bishop of Hippo (354–430), wrote a long letter to some nuns, advising them about the regulation of their life. In the eleventh century, on the basis of this letter and other writings by St. Augustine, there was formulated the Rule of St. Augustine, followed by the Augustinian monks and nuns. St. Augustine, the missionary to England and first archbishop of Canterbury, was a Benedictine monk. He died about 613.

28 21 **Middelburgh . . . Orewelle:** an island port off the Dutch coast . . . the English port of Orwell, now Harwich. From 1384 to 1388 Middelburg was the wholesale wool market. Today it is the capital of the province of Zeeland.

29 1 **Clerk:** During the Dark Ages only the clergy could read and write. —13 **philosophre . . . gold in cofre:** In the Middle Ages "philosophy" meant all the liberal arts and sciences, including the search for the philosophers' stone, which was supposed to have the power of turning baser metals into gold and silver. Chaucer is poking fun at a popular superstition.

30 12 **sooty:** Until the time of Queen Elizabeth chimneys were rare in England. Probably the smoke from the widow's fire had no outlet except a hole in the roof and cracks in the walls.—**bour:** bower, sleeping-place, private apartments. Chaucer humorously applies to the two rooms of the hut (which the family doubtless shared with the animals) the names of the principal apartments of a castle, hall and bower, as we in a similar case might speak of the drawing-room and boudoir.

31 5 **Malvern hillside:** a chain of hills ten miles long, forming the watershed between the Severn and Wye rivers, in the west of England.

32 12 **What Paul preacheth:** in the fifth chapter of the Epistle to the Ephesians: "Because of these things cometh the wrath of God upon the children of disobedience."—21 **St. James's:** the shrine of St. James of Compostella in the province of Galicia, northwestern Spain. It was a popular resort of pilgrims.—25 **pestilence season:** 1349. The black death (bubonic plague) carried off about half the population of England at this time.

33 8 **King's Bench:** the highest court of common law, consisting of the chief justice (originally the king himself) and four junior judges.

34 3 **Merlin:** see note on **22** 26.—4 **Canterbury:** a city in the southeast of England. It was the capital of Ethelbert, fourth Saxon king of Kent, in 597, when Augustine and his monks entered there on the conversion of the Anglo-Saxons to Christianity. The Archbishop of Canterbury, known as the Primate of all England, still officiates at the coronation of an English sovereign.

37 16 **seneschal, constable, chamberlain, warden:** high officials under the crown. These titles show something of the various origins of the English language. Seneschal (from the Teutonic by way of the French) originally meant old servant; constable (from the Low Latin *comes stabuli*), count of the stable, master of the horse; the chamberlain (similar words are found in both German and French) originally had charge of the king's private apartments, then he became steward of the royal household and the court, then receiver of the public funds; a warden (found in Middle English and Old French) was a watchman or guard. Cf. the warder of the cliffs in Beowulf and the Warden of the Cinque Ports.

38 11 **domination of the moon:** faith in astrology was still lively in Caxton's day.

44 *Agincourt* (ăj'ĭn kōrt, French á'zhăN'koor'): a village in northern France where on St. Crispin's Day, October 25, 1415, Henry V of England was victor over the French. The French outnumbered the English more than four to one, but were unable, because of the nature of the ground with woods on each side, to extend their front, and they were hampered by their heavy armor in miry ground. The English lost 13 men at arms and 100 foot; the French lost 5000 of the nobility killed and 1000 more taken prisoner. Sir Thomas Erpingham commanded the archers. See also page 225.

45 17 **Poitiers** (pwä tyā'): a town of western France, 61 miles from Tours. The battle here between King John of France and Edward the Black Prince on September 19, 1356, was the second of three great English victories in the Hundred Years' War, the others being Crécy and Agincourt.
—**Cressy:** Crécy, a town of northern France, where on August 26, 1346, the English under Edward III, great grandfather of Henry V, won a decisive victory over the French under King Philip of Valois. King Edward himself took no active part in the battle, and held his division in reserve, wishing to give the honor of the victory to his young son, called the Black Prince from the color of his armor. When word was brought him that the prince was in serious danger, he sent only a few knights as reinforcement, saying, "Let the boy win his spurs." At Crécy the English archers with their long bows not only defeated the French cross-bowmen but withstood successive attacks by the French knights and kept most of them from even reaching the English line. Feudal warfare placed its main reliance on the mounted, mail-clad knight. Because the common footsoldiers were the decisive element in the English victory, Crécy sometimes is spoken of as marking, on the military side, the beginning of the decay of feudalism.

50 25 **Tithon:** favorite of Aurora, goddess of the dawn. He obtained from the gods the gift of immortality, but not of immortal youth, and grew old and gray. The line means that the gray of dawn has turned to the rose of dawn.

52 *Astrophel and Stella:* star-lover and star. Stella was Lady Penelope Devereux, sister to the Earl of Essex.

55 *Song of the Cyclops:* from "Londons Tempe." The Cyclopes were one-eyed giants who worked in the shops of Vulcan, the god of metalworking, under Mount Etna. Vulcan, when cast out of heaven, fell to the island of Lemnos.

56 2 **dame's coach . . . sparrows:** Venus, consort of Vulcan, was represented sometimes with sparrows, sometimes with doves.—7 **Gorgon:** in Greek mythology, a monster represented as a young woman with snaky hair, so frightful that every living thing on looking at her was turned to stone. Her head, cut off by Perseus, was given to Athena, who placed it on her shield. It is represented on the ægis of Zeus (Jove) also. See Gayley, *Classic Myths*, pp. 208–210.—17 **Pan:** the god of wild life, protector of flocks and shepherds, inventor of the shepherd's pipe, or flute, represented with the body of a man and the horns and hoofs of a goat. See Gayley, *Classic Myths*, p. 45.

58 *Tamburlaine:* Mongol conqueror (1333?–1405), born near Samarkand.

63 *Harfleur:* French seaport, near Havre, captured by Henry V in 1415, before the battle of Agincourt. See note on **44**.

64 18 **Saint George:** patron saint of England from the time of Edward III.

65 6 **Mermaid Wine:** wine of the Mermaid Tavern in London, frequented by Jonson. In the days when few could read, street signs were pictures or models of persons, animals, or things. A mermaid is a mythical inhabitant of the sea represented as a woman with the tail of a fish.

66 21 **Sherwood:** a royal forest in Nottinghamshire, England, famous as the refuge of Robin Hood.

67 1 **Trent:** a river which flows through Nottinghamshire.

70 *The Noble Nature:* from A Pindaric Ode.

75 5 **my semblance might deceive:** Milton looked younger than his years, as a portrait of him at this period shows.

77 13 **ethereal and fifth essence:** Aristotle taught that every natural substance is made up of matter (which he divided into earth, air, fire, and water) and its essence, or immaterial part.

90 7 **Darius:** Darius III, king of Persia, defeated by Alexander in the battle of Arbela. As a matter of fact, he was not killed until the year following Alexander's destruction of the royal palaces of Persepolis.

91 18 **Revenge:** for the destruction of Greek temples by the Persians. Alexander fired the Persian palaces as a symbol of his conquest, and then ordered the flames put out. See Breasted, *Ancient Times*, p. 437.

93 6 Tabard: the inn from which Chaucer's pilgrims set out for Canterbury. A tabard was a herald's coat (see note on **65** 6). The Tabard Inn was burned in the great fire of Southwark and rebuilt in 1676. That inn was torn down in 1875 and replaced by a modern tavern.—7 **Southwark:** a suburb of London, now a metropolitan borough, on the south side of the Thames. Here stood the Globe Theatre, where many of Shakespeare's plays were produced for the first time.

94 11 Arcite: The story of Palamon and Arcite appears first in the works of Boccaccio (bŏk kä'chō), an Italian author (1313–1375). Dryden worked the story over in his play, "The Two Noble Kinsmen."

95 4 One of our late great poets: Abraham Cowley (1618–1667).— 19 *auribus istius temporis accommodata:* Investigations made since Dryden's time show that Chaucer's versification was more accurate than Dryden thought; pronunciation had changed a good deal, and many errors had been made in copying Chaucer's work.

99 5 dole: to give in charity. Since charity is not always given cheerfully, the word in modern usage has come to mean to give in small portions, grudgingly.

100 *Althea:* Lucy Sacheverell. She is also the Lucasta of the preceding poem. The grates at which she whispered were those of the prison to which the Long Parliament sent Lovelace because of his petition in behalf of King Charles I.

103 20 broke: correct as the past participle when Walton wrote.

105 4 milky way: where, according to some of the ancients, the souls of the just went after death.

106 4 three realms: Scotland had been united with England only five years before Pope wrote this poem.—14 **Snuff:** The taking of snuff had just come into fashion.—19 **dine:** In Queen Anne's time dinner ordinarily was at three o'clock. Among fashionable people it was at four or later.

109 16 The berries crackle, and the mill . . . : Apparently the entire preparation of coffee, including roasting and grinding, was carried on in the drawing-room at this period.—20 **China's earth:** "China" really came from China, or at least from the Orient, in Pope's day, the first successful attempts at imitation in Europe being made about 1740.—27 **Coffee . . . makes the politician wise:** In the seventeenth and eighteenth centuries coffee-houses were very popular, filling the place which newspapers, magazines, and clubs fill today. Politics naturally formed the subject of discussion at many of them, and to such an extent that Charles II tried to suppress coffee-houses as centers of political agitation. All sorts of groups, however, made coffee-houses their headquarters: bankers gathered at one, doctors at another; at one the talk would be of books or plays, at another of religion.

111 16 small pillow: It was customary for a fashionable lady to receive morning calls propped up in bed with a small, richly ornamented pillow.—17 **solemn days:** Formal calls were paid on days of marriage or mourning.

113 1 **ladies . . . in their chairs:** Sedan chairs were much used in cities until about the beginning of the nineteenth century. Franklin, when he was old and gouty, was carried about Philadelphia in a sedan chair.

115 31 **Otway:** Thomas Otway (1652–1685), English dramatic poet.

122 1 **Churchill's poetry:** Charles Churchill (1731–1764) was an English poet and satirist. He had attacked Johnson in "The Ghost."— 19 **Downing-street, Westminster:** where now the government offices are located.—26 **the Mitre:** a tavern near Fleet Street and the Temple. See notes on **65** 6 and **93** 6.

123 5 **Sir John Fielding's office:** Sir John Fielding was successor to his half brother, Henry Fielding, the novelist, as principal justice of the peace for Middlesex and Westminster. He entered office in 1754, after Henry Fielding had undermined his health in an effort to subdue a specially turbulent "gang of villains and cutthroats." This post of justice of the peace carried with it, besides a salary, a house in Bow Street. Bow Street Police Court is now the most important of the police courts in metropolitan London.

126 1 **Curfew:** "cover fire," a bell rung at a certain hour in the evening, warning citizens to cover or extinguish their fires.

128 1 **village-Hampden:** John Hampden (1594–1643) stood for the rights of the people and the power of Parliament against the king by refusing to pay the twenty shillings of ship money levied on his property by Charles I. He was killed in the civil war which led to the execution of the king.

137 19 **"springs exulting on triumphant wing":** quoted from Pope's "Windsor Forest."

138 9 **"An honest man's the noblest work of God":** quoted from Pope's "Essay on Man."

143 *Bannockburn:* where the Scots defeated the English in 1314. After the death of Wallace, Robert Bruce declared himself king of Scotland and roused the Scots against the English under Edward II. From the hostility of this period grew the long border warfare, celebrated in song and story, during which life and property were never safe from raiders from across the frontier.

145 1 **without Aldgate:** outside the old walled City of London toward the east. The City, containing 673 acres, is now one of the smallest of the twenty-nine divisions of metropolitan London. Through Aldgate one of the two main highways from the east enters London. The City gates were closed regularly at sunset until 1760, when they were pulled down. The walls of the City, however, never were formally pulled down; they disappeared gradually as buildings encroached upon them.—2 **Whitechapel:** still one of the poorer districts of London, while the fashionable residence quarters are still in the "west part of the city."

146 29 **John Hayward's care:** John Hayward was a grave-digger in the parish of St. Stephen, Coleman Street, a "large parish." Coleman Street runs from a point near the Bank of England to London Wall.

148 32 **Leadenhall Street:** leads from Aldgate High Street to Cornhill, passing the head of Bishopsgate Street. At the head of Cornhill are the Royal Exchange and the Bank of England, the financial center of London.

151 *Rydal Mount:* in the Lake District, Wordsworth's home for more than thirty years.

153 17 **Will no one tell me what she sings?** The Highland Lass sang in Gaelic.

154 *She was a Phantom of Delight:* Mrs. Wordsworth was the subject of this poem, written about two years after marriage.

155 6 **Furness-fells:** hills west of Windermere.— *Upon Westminster Bridge:* Wordsworth obtained this view of London at six o'clock in the morning from the top of the Dover coach, as he was setting out with his sister Dorothy for France. He composed the poem on the journey.

156 *The Extinction of the Venetian Republic:* Venice, at the head of the Adriatic, enjoyed great commercial advantages during the Middle Ages, when great numbers of crusaders sought the Holy Land and when all western Europe was eager to buy the silks, spices, and other products of the East. The victory of the Venetians (A.D. 1000) over the Dalmatian pirates gave Venice control of the Adriatic. Every year on Ascension Day this victory was celebrated by a magnificent ceremony in which the doge, the chief magistrate, flung a ring into the sea, saying, "We wed thee, O sea, in token of perpetual dominion." The supremacy of Venice in Oriental trade lasted until the voyages of Columbus, Magellan, and other explorers opened new trade routes and transferred the advantage of position to the cities of western Europe. For two hundred years after the fall of Constantinople, Venice held the first important line of defense against the Turks. In 1797 Napoleon divided the territory of the Venetian Republic and handed part of it, with the city itself, over to Austria.

159 *Kubla Khan:* Coleridge said he composed this poem in his sleep after reading a passage from "Purchas his Pilgrimage" in which are found some of the names and ideas in the poem. When he wakened, he had a clear recollection of the poem and began to write it down, but was called away on business, and when he returned most of the remainder of the poem had escaped his memory. Kublai Khan (1216?-1294) was a grandson of Jenghis Khan, founder of the Mongol dynasty. "Khan" is Tatar for "sovereign." Kublai reigned over an extensive empire in central Asia, China, and Russia.

161 *Childe:* a medieval title for a youth of noble birth. Its exact significance has been lost. Childe Harold, the hero of this poem, is a young man who has been bored by pleasures and seeks novelty in travel.

162 *The Eve before Waterloo:* June 15, 1815. The British army was encamped near Brussels. To avoid a panic among the citizens of Brussels, Wellington ordered his officers to attend a ball given by the Duchess of Richmond. The battle of the next day was that of Quatre Bras; Waterloo came two days later.

165 10 **Gladiator:** Some gladiators were voluntary; others were barbarian captives forced to fight for the amusement of Rome. The statue of The Dying Gladiator, now called The Dying Gaul, is in the Capitoline Museum in Rome.

166 22 **laurels . . . Cæsar's head:** A decree of the Senate permitted Julius Cæsar to wear a laurel wreath on all occasions. He was especially pleased at the decree because it enabled him to conceal his baldness.— 26 **"While stands the Coliseum . . . the World":** a superstition which has come down to us through the Venerable Bede.

167 *Chillon:* a castle on the shore of Lake Geneva. In the dungeons beneath it were confined early reformers and prisoners of state. The pillars in these dungeons still show the rings to which prisoners were fettered.— 18 **Bonnivard:** François de Bonivard (1493–1570), a Swiss patriot, was imprisoned in Chillon for six years by the Duke of Savoy and was set free only when his native city of Geneva had established its independence.

174 *Grecian Urn:* It is said that this urn was one still kept at Holland House in London, but Keats's descriptions of the carvings do not fit this vase exactly.—26 **Tempe:** a beautiful valley in Greece, between the mountains Olympus and Ossa.— **Arcady:** Arcadia, a picturesque mountainous district in Greece, noted for the contentment and happiness of its people. In Arcadia Apollo served as a herdsman and Hercules performed some of his labors.

177 *When I Have Fears:* written in January, 1818.

179 18 **Chapman:** George Chapman (1559?–1634), English poet, translated Homer into English verse.—21 **Cortez:** It was Balboa who first crossed the Isthmus of Panama (Darien) to the Pacific.— *La Belle Dame Sans Merci:* Keats took the title from a French poem which he had read in a poor translation.

181 *Lochinvar:* known also as Lady Heron's Song, from *Marmion.*— 24 **Eske River:** on the border between England and Scotland.—25 **Netherby gate:** Netherby Castle was on the eastern, or English, bank.

182 11 **Love swells like the Solway . . . tide:** Solway Firth, into which the Eske empties, is very shallow and subject to extreme and rapid ebb and flow of the tide.

183 14 **Montrose's time:** James Graham, Marquess of Montrose (1612–1650), commanded the forces of Charles I in Scotland during the Civil War. Except Cromwell, he was the greatest soldier in that war.—15 **Glencairn:** William, ninth earl of Glencairn, was deprived of his peerage by the Scots parliament for taking the part of Charles I in the Civil War. In 1653 Charles II gave him command of the royalist forces in Scotland. His rising was unsuccessful, and he was imprisoned; but after the Restoration he was made lord chancellor.—21 **Whigs:** the "country" party which grew up in England and Scotland during the reigns of Charles I and Charles II. They stood for the power of parliament against the Tories, who upheld the power of the king and court. Both names were first used, in 1680, in derision by the opposite sides: "Whigs" was short for "Whigamores," Scots dissenters; "Tories" were originally Irish highwaymen or outlaws. Tories came to be called "Conservatives" and Whigs "Liberals."—**Covenanters:** signers of the National Covenant of Scotland, 1638, in protest against the restoration of episcopacy and the prayer book.—23 **Cavaliers:** the royalist party, Tories. Originally a cavalier was a horseman, a knight.—25 **Claverhouse:** John Graham of Claverhouse (about 1649–1689). Both as an officer in the army and as a civil official, he was active in the efforts to suppress the Covenanters. He was known to one side as a relentless persecutor, to the other as a gallant soldier and loyal statesman. He died in battle in behalf of the deposed James II, who had created him Viscount Dundee in 1688. He is celebrated in Scott's song, "Bonny Dundee."— 26 **Tam Dalyell:** (died 1685) was made in 1666 commander-in-chief in Scotland to subdue the Covenanters. His severity made his name a terror to the peasants.

184 5 **tak the test:** There were various Test Acts, intended to secure conformity to the established order. That of 1681 was so self-contradictory that no one could logically and honestly subscribe to its requirements.—17 **killing times:** 1685 was known especially as the killing time.—30 **Cumberland:** a county in northwest England, including part of the Lake District. Carlisle, its capital, is near the border, not far from the old Roman Wall, while Berwick-on-Tweed is on the east coast. For centuries Berwick was fought over by the English and Scots, though the Tweed became the boundary between England and Scotland in the twelfth century.

185 2 **Jacobites:** from *Jacobus*, the Latin form of James; the extreme royalists who refused to accept the deposition of James II.—16 **the Revolution:** that of 1688, which deposed James II and brought in William and Mary.

186 4 **Whitsunday . . . Martinmas:** May 15 and November 11, respectively, when, according to Scottish law, rents and interest were due.

191 1 **Alan:** Alan Fairford, one of the characters in *Redgauntlet*, to whom Darsie Latimer, another character, is writing an account of his adventures with the blind fiddler, Wandering Willie, to whom he refers here as "my companion."—20 **Doomsday-book:** Domesday Book, the book in which was recorded the inventory or survey of the lands of England ordered by William the Conqueror in 1086. See **13** 8.

197 17 **Middleton . . . Rothes:** These men and the others named were active in the persecution of the Covenanters.—20 **Mr. Cargill:** the Covenanting minister who excommunicated the king. He was beheaded.

198 6 **Amorites:** a heathen tribe in Palestine, with whom the Israelites were long at war. The name is applied to the wild Highland clans who sided with the Jacobites.

204 17 **The change in Emma's** . . . **style of life:** Emma Watson, the youngest daughter of an invalid clergyman, had been brought up by a childless aunt and her husband. Shortly after the death of the uncle, who had taken a father's place toward Emma, the aunt married an army officer, who did not wish Emma as a member of his family. Consequently, just before the story opens, Emma had been returned unexpectedly to her own family, whom she had not seen since she was a very little girl. At least from the point of view of Emma and her family, the aunt's second marriage had been an "imprudence."

205 5 **Robert and Jane:** Emma's brother and his wife, who had just brought home another sister, Margaret, from a visit she had been making them at Croydon, near London, where the aërodrome is now.—9 **Elizabeth:** the oldest sister, who managed the household.—28 **Mrs. Blake and** . . . **Mr. Howard:** sister and brother living in the neighboring village of Wickstead, where Mr. Howard was rector, close to Osborne Castle. Emma had attracted their attention by her kindness in dancing with little Charles Blake at the first party she had attended after returning to her father's house.

206 27 **Mr. Musgrave and Lord Osborne:** the most conspicuous, if not the only "eligible" bachelors in the neighborhood. Mr. Musgrave had paid some attention to Margaret Watson before her visit to Croydon.

208 17 **the late visitation:** a church meeting which Mr. Watson had exerted himself to attend.—24 **Miss Osborne and Miss Carr:** Lord Osborne's sister and a friend who was visiting her at Osborne Castle.

210 8 **my friend M.:** Thomas Manning, Lamb's lifelong friend. He knew fifteen languages, and was considered the greatest Chinese scholar in England; but this particular Chinese manuscript was a merry invention of Lamb's.—13 **Confucius** (551–478 b.c.): Chinese philosopher.

215 14 **Ere sin could blight:** quoted from Coleridge's "Epitaph on an Infant."

216 28 **over London Bridge:** indicates that Lamb was making up the incident. His school was not across the river.

217 27 **St. Omer's:** a Catholic college for English boys in the city of St. Omer, France. Lamb never studied there.

218 17 **ballad of the Children in the Wood:** in Percy's *Reliques of Ancient English Poetry.*

219 6 **the Abbey:** Westminster.

220 30 **their uncle, John L——:** This essay was written a short time after the death of Lamb's brother John.

221 30 **Alice W——n:** Alice Winterton (in real life Ann Simmons), the sweetheart of Lamb's boyhood. She married a wealthy pawnbroker named Bartrum.

222 8 **Lethe** (lē'thē): in classical mythology, the river whose waters caused forgetfulness, in the land of the dead.—11 **the faithful Bridget:** Lamb's sister Mary.—*Joan of Arc:* born some time between 1410 and 1412 at Domrémy, a little village on the border of Champagne and Lorraine, near the town of Vaucouleurs (vō kōō lûr'), in what is now the Department of the Vosges, France. She roused the French against the conquering English and led them to victory, making possible the coronation of Charles VII at Reims. She was burned at the stake in Rouen (rwäɴ) in 1431. Cf. George Bernard Shaw's play, "Saint Joan."

224 16 **the lilies of France:** the fleurs-de-lys, the symbol of the royal power in France until the destruction of the monarchy by the Revolution of 1789.

225 14 **Michelet** (mēsh lĕ'): Jules Michelet (1798–1874). His monumental *History of France* in nineteen volumes was not completed until 1867; but Volumes IV and V, covering the period 1380–1461, were published in 1840–1841. In this essay on Joan of Arc, published in *Tait's Magazine* in March and August, 1847, De Quincey criticizes Michelet's treatment of Joan of Arc.—25 **Crécy . . . Agincourt:** see note on **45** 17 and **44.**—26 **Nicopolis:** In 1396 John the Fearless, Duke of Burgundy, led a band of crusaders, mostly French knights, against the Ottoman Turks, then advancing into Europe. These crusaders went down the Danube into the Balkans, and met a decisive defeat at Nicopolis, now Nikopol in Bulgaria.

226 21 **Poictiers:** Poitiers. See note on **45** 17.—31 **Charles VI:** "Charles the Mad," King of France (1380–1422). He declared as his heir his son-in-law, King Henry V of England, the victor at Agincourt, thus disinheriting his son, the dauphin, who was crowned at Reims as Charles VII.

227 6 **famines:** There were three severe famines in England and France in the fourteenth century.—7 **extraordinary diseases:** In 1348–1349 all Europe suffered a terrible epidemic of bubonic plague, known as the black death. In some parts of France it was said that only a tenth to a sixteenth of the population survived. See note on **32** 25.—**insurrections of the peasantry:** In France the rising known as the Jacquerie (zhäk rē') from the name Jacques Bonhomme (zhäk bŏ nŏm'), given in contempt by the nobles to the peasants, occurred in 1358. In England the peasants' revolt led by Wat Tyler came in 1381. The discontent of the peasantry was caused partly by the shortage of laborers after the black death, partly by the breaking down of the feudal system, partly by the burdens of the Hundred Years' War.—11 **Crusades:** wars undertaken to deliver the Holy Land from the Mohammedans. Begun in 1096, they are commonly regarded as coming to an end about 1271. However, the name long continued to be used in diplomacy and in launching military enterprises, especially against Mohammedans. Henry V of England was planning a new crusade when he died in 1422.—**Templars:** a religious and military order, known as the Knights of the Temple or Knights Templars from its quarters at Jerusalem in the palace known as Solomon's Temple; organized about 1118 for the protection of the Holy Sepulcher and of pilgrims. The Templars spread throughout Europe; they grew rich, powerful, haughty, roused the hatred and jealousy of rulers in both church and state, and finally were suppressed in 1312. Scott makes Sir Brian de Bois Guilbert in *Ivanhoe* a Templar.—12 **Papal interdicts:** decrees by the Pope prohibiting the offices of the church. When a city or country was placed under an interdict the churches were closed and all the functions of the church, including marriage, baptism, and burial, were suspended. In 1200 Pope Innocent III pronounced an interdict against France, and a few years later one against England.—13 **Emperor:** emperor of the Holy Roman Empire. The last of the Hohenstaufen emperors, Conradin, grandson of Frederick II, was beheaded in 1268 by Charles of Anjou, brother of St. Louis, to whom the Pope had given the southern possessions of the Hohenstaufens. The oppression and cruelty of Charles roused the popular revolt of 1282, known as the Sicilian Vespers, in which the people of Sicily tried to exterminate the French and did kill thousands of them.—15 **feudalism:** For a simple exposition of this complex form of social organization, see *Medieval and Modern Times*, by James Harvey Robinson, pp. 103–109.— 20 **a double Pope:** The Great Schism, in which rival popes struggled for supremacy, lasted from 1378 to 1417.

229 *Sir Galahad :* in the legends of Arthur and the Round Table, the son of Sir Lancelot and the fair Elaine, of whom it was prophesied that she should be the mother of the noblest knight ever born. Sir Galahad was the only knight who could sit in the Siege Perilous. He succeeded in the quest of the Holy Grail, the cup or platter used by Christ at the Last Supper, which was visible to none but the pure in heart.

232 *Ulysses :* king of Ithaca, one of the Ionian Isles. He is the chief hero of Homer's *Odyssey* and one of the heroes of the *Iliad*. When he returned to Ithaca after twenty years' absence only his dog knew him.— 3 **aged wife:** Penelope. During her husband's long absence she had put off importunate suitors by saying that even if Ulysses were dead she could not marry again till she had finished a shroud for her old father-in-law. Then every night she took out the work she had done during the day, so that the shroud was never finished.—17 **Troy:** a city of Asia Minor, south of the Dardanelles. Because Helen, wife of Menelaus, king of Sparta, had eloped with Paris, a prince of Troy, the allied armies of Greece besieged Troy for ten years, finally capturing it and burning it to the ground. Ulysses did not want to go on the expedition against Troy, and pretended madness in the hope of exemption; but having embarked on the enterprise, he passed through many other adventures before returning to Ithaca.

233 33 **Happy Isles:** the Islands of the Blessed, supposed by the ancients to lie west of Gibraltar, in the Western Ocean. Cf. "Avalon" in Celtic mythology (p. 22), Keats's "western islands" (p. 179), and the modern phrase "going west," for dying.—34 **Achilles (à kǐl'ēz):** Greek hero in the siege of Troy and king of the fierce tribe of the Myrmidons (mûr'mǐ dǒnz).

234 *The Revenge:* A contemporary account of this battle by Sir Walter Raleigh, who was cousin to Sir Richard Grenville, has come down to us, and was followed by Tennyson in this poem. Sir Walter Raleigh said, "If Lord Howard had stood to his guns, the Spanish fleet would have been annihilated."—6 **Sir Richard Grenville:** commanded the fleet of seven ships which carried Sir Walter Raleigh's colonists to Roanoke Island in North Carolina in 1585. On the way home he captured a Spanish ship. The next year he went again to America with provisions for the colonists, who had disappeared. He did much for the commercial development of Bideford (bǐd'ê fērd) in Devonshire, in the southwest of England, a sea-coast town which was a possession of the Grenville family from the time of the Norman Conquest until the eighteenth century. For a long time it had a considerable trade with Mediterranean ports, Spain, and America, its importation of tobacco from Maryland and Virginia being especially important. At the time of this battle, Sir Richard Grenville was second in command to Lord Thomas Howard, who had been sent out to intercept Spanish treasure ships. He was in command of the Revenge, a ship of five hundred tons which Drake had commanded against the Spanish Armada in 1588. Cf. Kingsley's picture of Sir Richard Grenville in *Westward Ho!* and Stevenson's in the essay on "English Admirals" in *Virginibus Puerisque.*—7 **pinnace:** a light sailing vessel, often used as a tender for a large vessel.—17 **Inquisition:** an ecclesiastical court concerned with the detection and punishment of heretics. In Spain during the sixteenth century it was under state control and was notoriously cruel.

235 9 **Seville (sěv'ĭl):** an important commercial and industrial city of Spain, at times its capital.—10 **Don:** Spanish equivalent to "Mr." Formerly given only to noblemen and gentlemen.—25 **galleons (gǎl'ê ǔnz):** large sailing vessels, sometimes with three or four decks, used for both war and commerce. Galleons were used especially by the Spanish as treasure ships in their trade with America.

236 2 **larboard . . . starboard:** the left-hand and right-hand sides respectively of a ship to one on board who faces the bow. Larboard is now port.

238 5 **Queen and Faith:** under Elizabeth England became Protestant.

239 *Pantheism :* the doctrine that the universe, as a whole, is God. The doctrine varies from that which regards the material world as the only reality to that which regards the material world as the expression of a divine personality. See Carlyle's phrase, "Living Garment of God," p. 341.

240 *Hands All Round :* shows Tennyson as the nation's laureate, the writer of "occasional" poetry.

241 28 **Lyonness:** a legendary place, supposed to adjoin Cornwall but to have disappeared long ago forty fathoms deep in the sea.

242 13 **Camelot:** see note on **19** 21.—15 **Merlin:** see note on **22** 26.

—19 my brand Excalibur (ĕks kăl'ĭ bûr): Arthur's magical sword. There were two legends about this sword, or two swords. One is told in Malory's *Morte Darthur* (see page 34). The other (told by Tennyson) is that the sword was held up from the middle of a lake by an arm "clothed in white samite," which disappeared under the water when Arthur took the sword. Samite was a fabric of heavy silk, sometimes interwoven with gold threads.

249 13 swan . . . ere her death: The swan was believed to sing just before dying.

252 *"How They Brought the Good News from Ghent to Aix":* The distance from Ghent to Aix-la-Chapelle, by the route which the names of the towns indicate, is over ninety miles. Browning wrote the poem while he was at sea and longing for a ride on his horse York. Though the incident is imaginary, the date, 16—, shows that Browning had in mind the troubled times of the Thirty Years' War and of the struggles of the Netherlands against the tyranny of Spain. Possibly he had in mind the temporary union of the various parts of the Netherlands against the Duke of Alva, but if so he forgot that this union was accomplished at Ghent in 1576.— 18 postern: a back door or gate, planned for escape. The use of this word and the indirect route suggest a city besieged or in danger and a countryside partly occupied by the enemy.—23 pique: pommel.

253 5 Mecheln: Mechelin. The Flemish form is Mechelen.

254 5 buff-coat: see page 184, note 5. The buff-coat and the long jack-boots, worn partly as armor in the seventeenth century, would add appreciably to the weight carried.—*Hervé Riel:* Browning published this poem in the *Cornhill Magazine* in 1871, and gave the proceeds, a hundred pounds, to aid sufferers from the siege of Paris. The story of Hervé Riel is a true one from the war, between England and the Netherlands on one side and France on the other, in which France aided the exiled English king, James II.—17 the Hogue: La Hogue (là ŏg'): cape and adjacent roadstead on the coast of Normandy. Exiled Jacobites and French troops were encamped here, waiting for the French fleet under the Count of Tourville to clear a passage for them to cross into England. There was a series of naval engagements, extending over four days, partly in foggy weather. The name was given from the final blow, when the English burned thirteen French ships under the eyes of James II and the French generals.— 21 St. Malo (săN mà lŏ'): a seaport town in Brittany, at the mouth of the Rance, on the left bank. The tides here are so violent that the appearance of the coast changes constantly.—23 the squadron that escaped: About half the French fleet under Damfreville escaped to the shelter of the harbor fortifications.

256 5 pressed: forced into the naval service.—6 Croisickese: a native of Croisic in Brittany.—8 Malouins (mà loo ăN'): inhabitants of St. Malo.—11 Grève: La Grève (là grĕv'), the sands between St. Malo and Mont St. Michel.—disembogues: empties.—15 Solidor: a fort at the mouth of the Rance.

257 27 **rampired:** fortified, inclosed with a rampart.

259 7 **the Louvre** (loo'vr'): the great palace in Paris, now used as a museum of art.

261 2 **thrid:** archaic for thread.—16 **Dante:** Dante Alighieri (dän'tä ä'lĕ gyâ'rē) (1265–1321), the chief poet of Italy.—**Boccaccio** (bŏk kä'chō) (1313–1375): Italian poet and story-writer.—**Petrarca:** Francesco Petrarch (1304–1374), Italian poet, famous especially for his sonnets.—**St. Jerome** (340–420): one of the Latin fathers of the church, author of the translation of the Bible known as the Vulgate.—19 **the procession! our Lady:** On Holy Thursday the image of the Virgin was carried in procession through the streets.

262 5 **oil pays passing the gate:** In some countries of Europe cities still tax all provisions brought into them. All vehicles, including streetcars, are halted at the city limits for customs examination.—*Ferrara:* capital of the province of Ferrara in northern Italy, the seat of the Este (ĕs'tä) family, famous from the tenth century. In the fifteenth and sixteenth centuries the Estes were dukes of Ferrara. Like the tyrants of other Italian city-states, of whom the Medicis in Florence are the most famous example, they combined liberality toward art and science with absolute despotism in government. In this poem the Duke of Ferrara is represented as just ending a conference with the representative of an unnamed count concerning his marriage with the count's daughter. Casually the duke lifts a curtain and shows the count's ambassador the picture of his last duchess, intending that his next duchess shall have a hint of what to expect if she fails to show adequate appreciation of the honor of being his wife.— 19 **"Fra Pandolf":** like "Claus of Innsbruck" (see page 264, line 12), an artist of Browning's imagination.

264 10 **Neptune:** in Roman mythology, god of the sea.

265 *Rabbi Ben Ezra* (about 1092–1167): born in Toledo, Spain. He traveled widely in northern Africa and western Europe, carrying to the Jews of Italy, France, and England the treasures of Moorish knowledge. Distinguished as a poet and as a writer on mathematics and astronomy, he is known especially for his sensible and lively commentaries on the Hebrew Bible. It is characteristic of Browning's scholarly knowledge that this poem represents the real rabbi's view of life as well as Browning's. Here old age is not to be dreaded as a time of weakness and weariness but is to be the climax and fruition of all the joys and hopes and struggles that have gone before, a time of understanding and of joyful anticipation of life after death as an "adventure brave and new" (see page 267, line 24). The figure which represents life as the potter's wheel, and the soul as a cup or pitcher which God, the master potter, makes for his own use, is taken from the Bible. "But now, O Lord, thou art our father; we are the clay, and thou our potter; and we all are the work of thy hand" (Isaiah lxiv, 8. See also Jeremiah xviii, 3–6, and Fitzgerald's *Rubaiyat*, stanzas 83–90).—11 **Jove:** the planet Jupiter.

267 27 **indue:** put on.

268 3 **Young:** when I was young.

269 7 **Was I . . . Right?** Was I, whom the world accused, right, or were they, whom my soul scorned, right?

271 16 **Pan:** see note on **56** 17.—18 **ban:** bane, destruction.

273 1 **Theocritus** (thē ŏk'rĭ tŭs): Greek poet of the third century before Christ. The lines referred to are from the fifteenth idyl, "Tardiest of the Immortals are the beloved Hours, but dear and desired they come, for always, to all mortals, they bring some gift with them." Cf. Emerson's poem "Days."

275 21 **sate** (săt or sāt): archaic form of "sat."

276 6 **down:** dune, hill.

277 32 **heaths:** waste land, open and level, with vegetation consisting largely of heath plants, or heather.—**broom:** a shrub with slender branches, small leaves, and showy yellow flowers.

278 *Dover Beach :* on the southeast coast of England, the point nearest France, the Channel (straits) here being only about twenty miles wide.
—27 **Sophocles** (sŏf'ŏ klēz) (496–406 B.C.): Greek tragic poet.

280 17 **gauge** (gāj): measure.—18 **manacles:** handcuffs, fetters.

282 3 **Sainte-Beuve** (sănt bûv'): Charles Augustin Sainte-Beuve (1804–1869). For many years a literary essay by him appeared every Monday in a Paris newspaper.—23 **Montesquieu** (môn tĕs kē û'): Charles de Secondat de Montesquieu (1689–1755), French philosopher and jurist.

284 28 **sweetness and light:** Though Matthew Arnold is often called the apostle of sweetness and light, this phrase was used originally by Swift in *The Battle of the Books* : "The two noblest things, which are sweetness and light."

286 7 **Abelard** (á bā lär'): French scholastic philosopher (1079–1142). One of the greatest of medieval teachers, he was interested especially in giving rational expression to the teachings of the church. He is remembered in modern times chiefly in connection with the beautiful and learned Héloïse.—9 **Lessing:** Gotthold Ephraim Lessing (1729–1781), German dramatist, scholar, and critic. He is known for his explanation of the laws of art, especially the drama, poetry, and sculpture.—**Herder:** Johann Gottfried Herder (1744–1803), German writer on literature and art. In contrast with Lessing, who directed artists to the study of Greek models, Herder urged German writers to be true to themselves and to develop their national qualities and national traditions.—20 **St. Augustine** (ô gŭs'tĭn) (354–430): Bishop of Hippo. See note on **27** 23.

287 **Jason:** commander of the Argonauts on the voyage in search of the golden fleece. See Gayley, *Classic Myths*, pp. 230–236.—11 **Phœnician** (fē nĭsh'ăn): one of the early inhabitants of the coast of Syria. They were the earliest sailors and merchants. Tyre and Sidon were their principal cities at home, and Carthage was their most important colony.—24 **Purple:** Tyrian purple was the dye most sought for luxury and splendor. It was not the color we call purple, but a vivid red.

289 13 **weft:** web, something woven.—14 **thrall:** bondman, slave.

290 13 **fens:** marshes.—24 **Cavendish** (căv'ĕn dĭsh) **Square:** in the West End, just off Oxford Street, near the fashionable shopping district of Bond and Regent streets.

291 24 **vassalage:** the service which a vassal or dependent owed his lord. This word, like "retainer," one who owes service (often military) to a household, comes down from the feudalism of the Middle Ages. See note on **227** 15.

292 13 **pea overcoat:** an overcoat of thick, coarse woolen.—22 **Funns:** funds. Wegg means, "I wonder if you have an income from government bonds."

295 16 **compittance:** Boffin seems to have confused "pittance," an inadequate allowance, with "com'petence," a comfortable income.—**diseased:** Boffin means "deceased."—23 **Lord-Mayor's-Show:** the gorgeous procession in which the newly elected Mayor of London goes from the City to Westminster Hall to take the oath of office. A dinner is part of the celebration.

296 3 **Maiden-Lane:** then a suburban lane. It has been replaced by York Road, which passes the Great Northern and Midland railway stations.

298 8 **Battle Bridge:** near King's Cross; took its name from the great battle between the Romans under Paulinus and the Britons under Queen Boadicea, which for many years was supposed to have been fought here. It is now thought that this battle was fought outside London, somewhere on Watling Street between London and Chester.

299 4 **tap-room:** barroom.

303 21 **Hadrian, Trajan, the Antonines, Augustus, Commodus:** Roman emperors.—22 **Polybius** (pŏ lĭb'ĭ ŭs) (205–123 B.C.): Greek historian.—35 **burnt pens:** quills. The word "pen" originally meant a quill, or feather. Metal pens did not come into common use until the middle of the nineteenth century.

304 16 **Vittle-us:** Vitellius (vĭ tĕl'ĭ ŭs) (A.D. 15–69), Roman emperor. —*The Virginians:* The Virginians were twin brothers, George and Harry Warrington. George, serving under Colonel George Washington in Braddock's campaign, was wounded in the disastrous defeat and taken as a prisoner to Canada, where he was kept for over a year, his family mourning him as dead. In grief over the loss of his brother, Harry, at the age of seventeen, went to England and was received as the heir to a great colonial estate. Society at this period was absorbed in gambling. At first Harry made such large sums at cards and the races and by various bets that he was called the Fortunate Youth. Then his luck changed; he lost everything, and was imprisoned for debt. George, having escaped from Canada, came to London in search of his brother.—25 **Strand and Fleet Street:** The main thoroughfare running east from the center of London. The Strand begins at Trafalgar Square, whence the Haymarket runs to the head of Piccadilly. Originally the Strand was the bank of the Thames, while Fleet Street took its name from Fleet Brook.

305 3 **Piccadilly:** a famous street in the West End of London, about a mile long. Bond and Regent streets connect it with Oxford Street (see note on **304** 25). Harry Warrington in his time of prosperity had taken lodgings at the house of a Mr. Ruff in Bond Street.—4 **Marlborough:** a town about seventy miles from London on the way from Bristol, where George had landed.—27 **Clarges Street . . . Bond Street:** Harry's Aunt Bernstein, a pleasure-loving old lady, had a house in Clarges Street, six blocks down Piccadilly from Bond Street.—34 **Gumbo:** the negro servant Harry had brought with him from Virginia.

306 21 **the Temple:** the London house of the Knights Templars (see note on **227** 11). From the fourteenth century the property has been occupied by schools of law, the Inner Temple (within the City limits) and the Middle Temple. In 1670 a gateway, known as Temple Bar, was built by Sir Christopher Wren between Fleet Street and the Strand. For a long time it was customary to expose the heads of criminals on spikes on the top of Temple Bar. At this point George turned from the Strand into Chancery Lane and thence into Cursitor Street, where Harry was locked up in the house of the bailiff, or deputy sheriff.

307 28 **James Wolfe:** later General Wolfe, killed in 1759, in his victory over Montcalm at Quebec.

308 31 **you were wrong, Mr. Warrington:** Colonel Lambert had returned, as being altogether too expensive, gifts which Harry, at the height of his success in gaming, had sent to the Lambert girls, and Harry had resented angrily this implied criticism of his conduct.

310 30 **ladies in Hill Street:** Mrs. Lambert and the Lambert daughters.

311 *The Downfall :* Mr. Tulliver, on receiving news of the unfavorable decision of a lawsuit, as a result of which he will probably be forced into bankruptcy, has suffered an apoplectic stroke and lies helpless as this chapter opens.—7, 10 **sister Pullet, Mrs. Deane:** Mrs. Tulliver's sisters. Their maiden name was Dodson.—13 **St. Ogg's:** the neighboring town.

312 15 **Mrs. Glegg:** another sister of Mrs. Tulliver.

313 16 **bailiff:** deputy sheriff.

314 20 **flock-bed:** a bed filled with locks (flocks) of coarse wool or with rags.

320 9 **codicil:** a document adding to or modifying a will.—18 **to be cupped:** to have blood drawn in order to relieve congestion.

327 19 **Egdon Heath:** under this name Hardy has grouped a number of tracts of waste land interspersed with woodland and tillage.

329 11 **façade** (fà säd′): the front of a building.—24 **Vale of Tempe** (tĕm′pē): a valley in Greece between Mount Olympus and Mount Ossa, celebrated by the poets as the symbol of all that is loveliest in woodland beauty.—**Thule** (thū′lē): the "farthest north" of the Greeks and Romans, perhaps Norway was meant, perhaps Iceland, or the Faroe or Shetland Islands.—35 **Scheveningen** (sкā'věn ïng'ĕn): a seaside resort near The Hague.

330 1 **ascetic:** one who practices extreme self-denial.—25 **Domesday:** see note on **191** 20.—33 **Leland:** John Leland (about 1506–1552), a student of English antiquities, who, at the time when Henry VIII dissolved the monasteries, tried to preserve the manuscripts of the monastic libraries. —36 **Ishmaelitish** (ĭsh'mȧ ĕl ĭt ĭsh): outcast, wild; from Ishmael, the outcast son of Abraham and Hagar, of whom it was foretold: "He will be a wild man; his hand will be against every man, and every man's hand against him" (Genesis xvi, 12).

331 32 **vicinal way** (vĭs'ĭ năl): the road which served the neighborhood, in distinction from the great highway, which carried the traffic through the whole region; from *vicinalis*, Latin for "neighboring."—33 **Via Iceniana** (wē'ȧ ē'kĕn ĭ ä'nà): The Romans were wonderfully skillful roadbuilders, and in spite of centuries of neglect through barbarous and medieval times, many of their roads can be traced still.

332 1 **Ikenild Street:** in its general course, believed to be older than the Roman occupation, a prehistoric ridgeway across the Chiltern and Berkshire hills, which the Romans improved and used through part of its course.—*El Dorado* (ĕl dṓ rä'dō): the golden; a city or country rich in gold, which the Spanish adventurers of the sixteenth century thought existed in the interior of South America; hence a place of fabulous wealth.

333 29 **amulet:** a charm worn to ward off evil.

335 23 **chimæra** (kī mē'rȧ): in Greek mythology a she monster breathing fire, having the head of a lion, the body of a goat, and the tail of a dragon (see Gayley, *Classic Myths*, pp. 214–215); hence a frightful or foolish creature of the imagination.

336 17 **Ormond:** James Butler, first Duke of Ormonde (1610–1688), Irish soldier and statesman.

337 21 **Whigs ... Tories:** see note on **183** 21.—22 **Stafford:** William Howard, Viscount Stafford (1614–1680), accused by Titus Oates of taking part in the popish plots, and beheaded.—24 **Russell:** Lord William Russell (1639–1683), a leader of the Whig, or country, party, accused of plotting insurrection and the death of the king, declared guilty, and executed. When the passions of the time had died down it was realized that both Russell and Stafford had suffered unjustly, and the sentences against them were reversed so as to permit their descendants to enjoy their titles.—25 **Tower:** the Tower of London, fortress and state-prison, on the Thames, just outside the old city wall on the east, on the site of an old Roman fortress; built by William the Conqueror to overawe the citizens of London.— **Lincoln's Inn Fields:** now a public garden. Lincoln's Inn, one of the four great law schools in London, took its name from the property of the Earl of Lincoln which it acquired early in the fourteenth century. Its gatehouse, opening on Chancery Lane (see note on **306** 21), was built in the time of King Henry VIII. Ben Jonson is said to have worked as a brick-layer on the adjacent wall.—29 **tied to the cart's tail**: Criminals were often tied to the rear of a cart and whipped as they were dragged through the streets.—32 **Bridewell**: a prison, pulled down in 1864. Before the prison there was a Bridewell Palace on this spot, which took its name from a "miraculous" well of St. Bride or St. Bridget. Bridewell Palace is the scene of the third act of Shakespeare's *Henry VIII*.—34 **pressed to death**: If a person were accused of a crime and refused to answer either "guilty" or "not guilty" to the indictment, he might be pressed to death. Though this form of punishment gradually fell into disuse, it was not formally abolished until 1772.

338 33 **of the Stuarts**: during the Stuart monarchy, 1603–1689, includ-ing the period of the Great Rebellion and Cromwell's Protectorate.

341 8 **horologue** (hŏr'ṓ lŏg): horologe (hŏr'ṓ lŏj) ; timepiece, clock.—23 **Schreckhorn**: Peak of Terror.

342 1 **Dayspring to the Shipwrecked in Nova Zembla**: Barents, whose expedition was wrecked on Nova Zembla in 1596, wrote of the first glimpse of the sun in the northern winter: "On January 27, we saw it mounting in all its roundness on the horizon, which rendered us very happy. We thank God for the mercy he vouchsafed to us by restoring the light."—5 **Evangel**: gospel, good news.—6 **charnel-house**: place where the bodies or bones of the dead are placed.—11 **gabardine**: gaberdine (găb'ẽr dēn') ; a coarse, loose coat or smock.—27 **Man's Unhappiness**: see Browning's "Rabbi Ben Ezra," p. 265.

343 3 **Hochheimer** (hŏĸ'hīm er): a kind of wine, from Hochheim, near Mainz in Germany.—**Ophiuchus** (ŏf ĭ ū'kŭs): a constellation, represented on charts as a man holding the Serpent in his hands.—33 **the Wisest of our time**: Johann Wolfgang von Goethe (fōn gû'tẽ) (1749–1832), the greatest of German writers and one of the great men of the world. He taught that the greatest happiness is to be found in unselfish, useful work.—34 *Entsagen:* ĕnt sä'gĕn.

344 12 **Close thy** *Byron* ; **open thy** *Goethe* : stop trying, like Byron, to make yourself happy; try instead, like Goethe, to be of use to others.—13 *Es leuchtet mir ein:* ĕs loiĸ'tĕt mẽr īn.—33 **Zeno** (zē'nō) (about 336–264 B.C.): Greek philosopher, founder of the school of Stoics.—34 **thou canst love the Earth . . . for this a Greater than Zeno was needed**: an allusion to the words of Christ, "Love your enemies . . . do good to them that hate you" (Matthew v, 44).

345 1 **Johnson**: Dr. Samuel Johnson.—18 **hypochondria**: imaginary illness or illness caused by an unhealthy condition of the nervous system.—19 **Hercules . . . Nessus'-shirt**: Hercules (hûr'cŭ lēz) was poisoned by putting on a shirt dipped in the blood of the treacherous Nessus. See Gayley, *Classic Myths*, pp. 225–226. Johnson suffered from scrofula, which disfigured his face and impaired his sight.—29 **Fourpence-halfpenny a day**: When Johnson first went to London and was struggling to earn a

NOTES 419

living by his pen he thought that he dined well on six pennyworth of meat and a pennyworth of bread at an alehouse.—31 **College Servitor** . . . **Gentleman Commoner**: at Oxford students formerly were divided into six groups. Gentleman Commoners held next to the highest social rank, while College Servitors had the lowest place and helped pay their way by performing certain menial duties.

346 34 **Pedantry**: overemphasis of unimportant details.

347 3 **Church of St. Clement Danes**: built in 1688, from plans by Sir Christopher Wren, in the middle of the Strand (see note on **304** 25).— 5 **Voltaire**: François Marie Arouet de Voltaire (1694–1778), French philosopher and man of letters, noted for his mocking skepticism.

348 25 **Mirabeau** (mē rà bō'): Honoré Gabriel Victor Riquetti, Comte de Mirabeau (1749–1791), French statesman of the earlier part of the Revolution.— **Mahomet** (mà hŏm'ĕt): Mohammed (about 570–632), Arabian prophet, founder of Islam or Mohammedanism.— **Cromwell**: Oliver Cromwell (1599–1658), English general and statesman who ruled as Lord Protector of England after the execution of Charles I.— **Napoleon**: Napoleon Bonaparte (1769–1821), Corsican, who made himself Emperor of France and tried to conquer all Europe.

349 29 **buckram**: stiff, precise.—32 **tumid**: swollen, pompous.

350 10 **St. Mark's Place**: the great central square of Venice, in front of St. Mark's Cathedral.—27 **fruit walls**: In England, where the summers are cool, the choicer fruits, such as pears, peaches, and nectarines, often are grown against walls for the sake of the additional warmth for ripening them.

351 3 **canons**: clergymen connected with the cathedral.

352 1 **Calle Lunga San Moisè** (càl'lā lo͞on'gà sàn mō ē'zā): long street of St. Moses.—12 **Istrian stone**: fine limestone, much like marble, from Istria (ĭs'trĭ à), the peninsula at the head of the Adriatic.—14 **cortile** (kôr tē'lā): courtyard.

353 3 **"Vendita Frittole e Liquori"** (vān dē'ta frēt tō'lā ā lē kō'rē): fried food and drinks for sale.—5 **ambrosial** (ăm brō'zhĭ àl): delicious, from "ambrosia," in classical mythology the food of the gods.—8 **"Vino Nostrani a Soldi . . ."** (vē'nō nōs trä'nē ä sōl'dē): local (home-grown) wine at . . . cents.—11 **Maraschino** (măr à skē'nō): a liqueur made from the marasca cherry, a wild, black cherry.—12 **gondoliers** (gŏn dŏ lērs'): men who row gondolas, the long, slender boats which served Venice as cabs.—20 **Campo**: square.

354 26 **Cleopatra-like**: See Shakespeare's *Antony and Cleopatra*, Act II, Scene v.—32 **archivolts** (är'kĭ vōlts): stone-work composing arched or "vaulting" construction.

355 2 **Greek horses**: four horses of gilded bronze over the principal entrance to St. Mark's Cathedral. They are believed to have adorned the triumphal arches of Nero and Trajan. Constantine sent them to Constantinople, whence the Doge Enrico Dandolo carried them to Venice as spoils of war in 1204.—3 **St. Mark's Lion:** the winged lion, symbol of St. Mark, the patron saint of Venice.—7 **Lido** (lē′dō): the long bar across the lagoon from Venice, famous for its bathing beach.—30 **Austrian bands:** bands of the Austrian garrison. In 1797 Napoleon destroyed the independence of Venice and gave the city to Austria. It was made part of United Italy in 1866.—32 **miserere** (mĭz ĕ rē′rĕ or mĕ zâ rā′rā): "have mercy"; the first word, in Latin, of the fifty-first Psalm: "Have mercy upon me, O God."—34 **stiletto:** stab. A stiletto is a slender, pointed dagger.

356 5 **centesimi** (sĕn tĕs′ĭ mē): Italian copper coins worth a fifth of a cent each.— *Camarina* (cä mä rē′nä): a city on the southern coast of Sicily, founded in 599 B.C., destroyed and rebuilt several times. It was finally and completely destroyed in A.D. 853.—*South Lambeth:* a district in London, south of the Thames.—10 **Hercules:** The slaying of the Nemean (nē̆ mē′ăn) lion was the first labor of Hercules. See Gayley, *Classic Myths*, pp. 216–217. The city of Nemea (nē′mē̆ ȧ) gave its name to the Nemean games, similar to the Olympic games, held every two years beginning in 573 B.C. The prize awarded the victor in these games was a wreath of parsley.

357 7 **Phidias** (fĭd′ĭ ȧs) (about 500–432 B.C.): the greatest of Greek sculptors, contemporary and associate of Pericles.— **Donatello** (dŏn ä tĕl′lō) (1386–1466): Italian sculptor.—**Titian** (tĭsh′ăn) (1477–1576): Venetian painter.—**Velasquez** (vä läs′kȧth) (1599–1660): Spanish painter.—8 **Sir Joshua Reynolds** (1723–1792): English portrait painter.

358 18 **Cerberus** (sûr′bêr ŭs): the three-headed dog with the tail of a serpent which guarded the entrance to the infernal regions.— **Hydra of Lerna:** the nine-headed water serpent which laid waste the country of Argos. The destruction of this monster was the second labor of Hercules. —27 **Athena** (à thē′nä): goddess of wisdom, of law and civic virtue, and of the arts both of peace and of war.

360 26 **Watteau** (vȧ tō′) (1684–1721): Jean Antoine, French painter.

361 13 **thrums:** bits, scraps.

362 20 *urbanity:* from the Latin *urbanitas*, the quality of the city man, hence refinement. Cf. Matthew Arnold's definition: "Urbanity, the tone of the city, of the center, the tone which always aims at a spiritual and intellectual effect, and, not excluding the use of banter, never disjoins banter itself from politeness, from felicity."

363 5 **black-tail:** black-tailed deer.—7 **ouananiche** (wȧ nȧ nēsh′): a small, very active, landlocked salmon, found in and near Lake St. John, Canada.—11 **'Send:** God send, God grant.

364 10 **traces:** used in fishing. A trace is a short line between the main line and the bait, in a spinning tackle.—16 **fishing-luggers:** A lugger is a vessel carrying one or more lugsails, a lugsail being a four-sided sail hung more or less obliquely on the mast by means of a yard (spar) which is raised and lowered with the sail.

365 7 **lemurs:** animals in some respects like monkeys and in some re-

spects like foxes, found chiefly in Madagascar and neighboring islands.—
16 **Ovis Poli:** the wild sheep of the Pamir plateau on the edge of Turkestan, named for the Venetian Marco Polo, who saw it on his travels to the East in the thirteenth century. The rams have very large, wide-sweeping horns.

366 1 **spoor:** track, trail.—18 **minster-towers:** towers of the church of a monastery. Because the church has remained often after the monastery has disappeared, "minster" has come to be used of any large church.—
19 **kestrels:** small European falcons, somewhat resembling the sparrow hawk of North America.

367 6 **bob-majors:** Bob-major is the name given to a system of change ringing on eight bells.

368 13 **bitt:** a heavy timber or iron fastened to the deck of a ship for securing ropes, cables, etc.—**trees:** crosstrees, pieces of timber or metal placed horizontally at the top of a mast. To the trees are fastened the ropes (shrouds) which support the mast.—21 **sheet:** rope which regulates the angle of a sail to the wind.—22 **"Ready about—stand by!":** notice to the crew to tack; that is, to shift the sails so that the wind will strike them at the same angle but on the other side of the ship.

369 4 **The Hun:** here meaning "the German," reminiscent of the time in the fifth century when the Huns under Attila, "the Scourge of God," invaded Gaul (France) and threatened western Europe.

370 21 **binnacle:** a case containing the ship's compass with a lamp for use at night.

371 21 **My watch below:** my time off duty. A watch on shipboard is usually four hours.

372 29 **job down below:** Captain MacWhirr had sent the first mate, Jukes, to quell a panic and riot among the coolie passengers whom the ship was taking back to China.

376 *Mermaid Tavern:* see page 65 and note on **65** 6.—3 **Fleet Street:** see note on **304** 25.—9 **mighty bubble of St. Paul's:** the dome of St. Paul's Cathedral, designed by Sir Christopher Wren. This great church, built on a slight eminence, dominates the City. One going through Fleet Street from the Strand (westward) looks toward St. Paul's.—24 *The Tempest:* Shakespeare's play.

377 3 **mullioned panes:** panes set between slender, upright bars.—
29 **Spanish Main:** the mainland of Spanish America.

378 2 **galleon:** see note on **235** 25.—4 **Marchaunt Adventurers:** the Merchant Adventurers of England, incorporated in 1551 for the discovery of unknown lands, with Sebastian Cabot as governor for life. It was one of the early companies chartered for foreign trade, and attained great wealth and influence. At one time it employed in the Netherlands alone as many as 50,000 persons and was influential enough to keep the Spanish Inquisition out of Antwerp in the time of Charles V.—7 **Eldorado:** see note on **332**.

379 5 **foot-feathered Mercury:** In classical mythology Mercury, the messenger of the gods, had winged feet.—7 **doublet**: a close-fitting garment worn in western Europe from the fifteenth to the seventeenth century. It reached from the neck to the waist or a little below, and was made with or without sleeves.—**trunk-hose**: short, puffed and slashed breeches.—8 **rapier**: a straight, narrow, two-edged sword.—14 **murrey-coloured**: mulberry-colored, dark crimson.—19 **Gloriana**: Queen Elizabeth.—31 **Whom Raleigh hailed as "Will!"**: Shakespeare.

380 7 **Sack**: white wine from southern Europe.—8 **Canary**: wine from the Canary Islands, similar to Madeira.—**Malmsey** (mäm′zĭ): a rich, sweet wine, originally made in Greece.—**Muscadel** (mŭs kả dĕl′): muscatel, a rich, sweet wine, made from muscat grapes, produced in Italy and France. The names of these imported wines suggest the growing commerce of Elizabethan England.—11 **Ganymede**: in classical mythology, cup-bearer to the gods.—20 **Magdalen** (môd′lĭn): Magdalen College, perhaps the most beautiful of the colleges of Oxford University, founded in 1458. In 1687 James II interfered unconstitutionally in the election of a president of Magdalen, in spite of the brave and determined resistance made by the Fellows of the College. This incident roused the feeling of educated Englishmen against James and helped to bring about the Revolution of the following year.—21 **lanthorns** (lănt′hôrns): archaic form of "lanterns."—23 **Nassau**: Nassau Hall at Princeton, built in 1756 and named in honor of King William, originally housed the whole college. In 1783, when the State House in Philadelphia was threatened by mutinous soldiers, Congress sat for a time in Nassau Hall.

381 1 **Mercer**: Hugh Mercer, born in Aberdeen, Scotland, about 1720. After the Battle of Culloden, in which he served as surgeon's assistant in the army of the Young Pretender, he emigrated to Virginia and practiced medicine there. He served as a volunteer in Braddock's expedition against Fort Duquesne. At the outbreak of the Revolution he joined the Continental Army, and was made brigadier general. He was mortally wounded at the Battle of Princeton in 1777.

382 14 **"Love will find out the way"**: see page 52.

383 *Innisfree:* Heather Island.—24 **linnet's wings**: The linnet, a common songbird, is named from its fondness for the seeds of flax (*linum*) and hemp.

384 *Thrums:* Barrie gives this name to a little village of weavers. Thrums are the ends of a weaver's warp threads. See also note on **361 13.**—18 **ben in the room**: in the parlor. See page 136, note 4.—**Hendry**: a weaver, head of the household. Jess, his wife, was a cripple, who had not been out of the kitchen for many years but kept eyes and hands busy beside the kitchen window. Leeby was their only daughter.—19 **dambrod** (dảm′brŏd): checkerboard.

385 7 **brae** (brā): hillside.—18 **chief**: friendly, intimate.—23 **manse**: the minister's house.—36 **Glesca**: Glasgow.

NOTES

386 8 **the draper's:** a shop where cloth is sold.—26 **speirin'** (spēr'ĭn): asking.—27 **roup** (roup): auction.

387 4 **snod** (snŏd): trim, neat.—20 **whatna bit kimmer:** what little girl.

388 27 **U. P.'s:** United Presbyterians.—32 **lippy:** a fourth of a peck. —36 **Auld Kirk:** old church.

390 4 **Mr. Forbes Robertson:** Sir Johnston Forbes-Robertson, English actor, noted for his interpretation of Shakespeare's *Hamlet.*—6 **Mr. Chaplin:** Charles Chaplin, motion-picture actor.—14 **Clapham:** a district in London south of the Thames, in the neighborhood of the school where Ruskin talked about the Hercules of Camarina (see page 356).

391 1 **Apollo Belvedere** (bĕl vē̆ dēr' or bĕl vȧ̆ dā'rā) : a statue in the Vatican, long regarded as the ideally perfect figure of a man.—**chimæra:** see note on **335** 23.—23 *via media* (wē'ȧ mā'dĭ ȧ): middle way.—30 **Venus of Milo** (mē'lō): a statue found on the island of Melos (Italian *Milo*) and now in the museum of the Louvre in Paris, by many considered the most beautiful example we have of Greek sculpture.

392 24 **grotesque** (grō̆ tĕsk'): ludicrous, whimsical, extravagant.—33 **gargoyles** (gär'goilz): waterspouts, often fantastically carved, projecting from the roof of a building, usually ending in the misshapen head of an animal or a man.

393 17 **Shropshire:** a county in the west of England, adjoining Wales; the inhabitants are occupied largely in mining and grazing.

395 16 **Somme** (sŭm): river in France, 147 miles long, from Saint-Quentin to the English Channel. The Battle of the Somme, east and northeast of Amiens, lasted four months, from July to November, 1916. The Germans were driven back a few miles, at a cost of six or seven hundred thousand killed and wounded on each side.—26 **salved** (sălvd): saved, rescued.

396 2 **paths to glory:** see page 127, line 10.

398 16 **tournament:** see page 35, note 5.—20 **oriflamme** (ŏr'ĭ flăm): the sacred banner of St. Denis, carried in battle by the early kings of France; hence, a battle flag.—28 **Agincourt:** see note on **44.**

INDEX AND PRONOUNCING VOCABULARY

KEY TO PRONUNCIATION

ā, as in fate; ȧ, as in senate; ă, as in fat; ä, as in arm; à, as in ask; a̤, as in all;
   a, as in what; â, as in care; ȧ, as in sofa
ē, as in mete; ė, as in event; ĕ, as in met; ê, as in there; ē, as in maker
ī, as in ice; ĭ, as in it
ō, as in old; ȯ, as in obey; ŏ, as in not; ọ, as in move; ô, as in horse; ōō, as in
   food; ŏŏ, as in foot
ū, as in use; ů, as in unite; ŭ, as in up; ŭ, as in circus; û, as in fur; ṳ, as in
   rule; ü, French sound of u, as in vue
ou, as in out
к, like ch in German ich or ach
ŋ, like n in ink
n, indicating nasalization of preceding vowel, as in bon
th, as in thin; th, as in then

INDEX AND PRONOUNCING
VOCABULARY

SAd "

S1D

Br

JACOB VARATH